I0096433

PREHISTORIC PRECEDENCE

HOW THE HUMAN SPECIES INVENTED THE BIBLE

PETER BYCROFT

Prehistoric Precedence: How the human species invented the Bible
© Peter Bycroft 2024

All rights reserved. No part of this publication may be reproduced, stored in a retrieval system, or transmitted in any form or by any means, electronic, mechanical, photocopying, recording or otherwise, without the prior written permission of the author.

ISBN: 978-1-923289-15-4 (Paperback)
ISBN: 978-1-923289-25-3 (eBook)

A catalogue record for this work is available from the National Library of Australia

Printed in Australia by Clark & Mackay
Published by Clark & Mackay
clark-mackay.com.au
7 Colebard Street East, Acacia Ridge, Qld, 4110, Australia

All reasonable attempts to contact copyright holders have been conducted and all copyright holders have been listed, where appropriate. If there is any concern regarding copyright, please contact the publisher.

About Peter Bycroft

Peter Bycroft is a polymath, environmental psychologist, and secular humanist. He holds an honours degree in Architecture, a Master of Science in Environmental Psychology and has held Head of Department and Professorial positions in four of Australia's leading Universities.

Peter spent more than twenty-five years as an independent research and business management consultant to the Australian Federal, State and Local Government Sectors, during which time he won multiple awards for his research work, organisational modelling, and evaluation strategies.

In the late 1970s whilst working with Australia's First Nations Indigenous communities on Mornington Island in the Gulf of Carpentaria, he was made an invited member of the Australian Indigenous Barramundi Dreaming clan of the Ganggalida Nation. The Ganggalida Nation's country covers the north-west of Queensland; this stretches from the Northern Territory border in the west to the eastern town of Burketown in the Southern Gulf of Carpentaria.

Peter has extensive experience in scientific research and writing. He has published as an academic in the fields of Indigenous Australians, Government policy and practice, Art and Culture, Suicide Prevention, Organisational and Environmental Psychology, Regional Economic Development, Performance Management and Evaluation.

Peter retired in 2018 and has been applying his research skills to his hobby—a passionate interest in mythology and religion. He is specifically interested in the prehistoric origin and influences on the Hebrew Bible and the Christian Old Testament.

Table of Contents

List of Figures

Introduction

This book is a broad-based cross-disciplinary investigation into the origin of the stories in one of the most influential books in the world: the Hebrew Bible, which is also the main component of the Christian Old Testament. Together, the Hebrew Bible/Christian Old Testament (HB/OT) and the Christian New Testament have been collectively referred to for many centuries as 'the Bible'.

The Bible began with the writing and rewriting of ancient belief systems by hundreds of Hebrew scribes in the Middle East over a period of approximately six hundred years from around 900 BCE to 300 BCE. These Hebrew scribes continued an ancient Middle Eastern tradition started by Sumerian scribes who preceded them by some two thousand years (3500 BCE onwards). Middle Eastern scribes were often highly educated, literate members of the cultural elite. They worked in temples and palaces and were involved in writing economic, administrative, and contractual documents, letters, literary works, heroic tales, mythological stories, codes of behaviour, and laws.[1]

Along with the Islamic religion, followers of the Bible (Judaism and Christianity) are referred to as the *Abrahamic religions*, because all three religions claim to descend from the Hebrew patriarch Abraham as described in the HB/OT.

The Pew Research Centre estimates that the combined Abrahamic religions account for around four billion followers globally. Around 32% of all religious people are Christian, around 24% are Muslim and 0.2% follow Judaism. The Pew Research Centre anticipates that, by 2050, the Abrahamic religions will have more than six billion followers globally, comprising around 32% Christian, 30% Muslim, and 0.2% following Judaism.[2]

In its several guises, the belief in the Abrahamic God has had a significant impact on the modern world. The word *god* pervades everyday language—'god only knows', 'thank

---

[1]   Kramer (1971), pp. 165-228.
[2]   SOURCE: https://www.pewresearch.org/religion/2015/04/02/religious-projections-2010-2050/ retrieved on 5 July 2022.

god', 'for god's sake', 'god willing', 'godforsaken', 'god help us', 'so help me god', 'in god's name'. And the Christian story has provided the baseline for how the world defines each year from the biblically defined date of the birth of Jesus Christ—even though it is now widely accepted that the date originally chosen as the birth year of Jesus is probably out by some four, and possibly six, years.

The Hebrew Bible, and its manifestation as the Christian Old Testament, is referred to as the Judeo-Christian Bible. It has had a significant influence on human society since it was first written around two and a half to three thousand years ago. It was written in a time prior to the emergence of science, chemistry, physics, medicine, astronomy, and global communication. It was written when the collective belief was that the Earth was a flat disk floating in the ocean with a hemispherical sky-dome above it and that the planets were gods, and most societies were transitioning from hunter-gatherer lifestyles to agricultural, pastoral, and sedentary communities. Along with this transition came a convergence and consolidation of prehistoric beliefs, their written expression, the emergence of collective religious practices and temples, and a new concept of anthropomorphic gods. But even then, many prehistoric beliefs and mythological stories were adapted, re-badged, and maintained as the foundation of today's three most influential religions.

The approach adopted in this research

This book and the associated research started by exploring the origin of the human species and the circumstances that facilitated its long-term survival and development. The investigation explores the many locations, cultures, innovations, and mythologies that predate the HB/OT. The prehistoric foundations of the biblical stories are examined, as is the available evidence of the emergence of the Israelites—where they came from and how and why they wrote the HB/OT. This is explored largely from an external (non-biblical) evidence-based perspective but with regular reference back to the related biblical stories and text.

The geographic, cultural, economic, and social changes from a hunter-gatherer's conception of gods and the universe to what is now called the Hebrew Bible, or the Christian Old Testament, commenced around 4000 BCE. This is a period that researchers refer to as the Bronze Age. The Bronze Age delivered many cultural, technological, and societal innovations that are now largely taken for granted. Amongst these was the invention of the alphabet and writing. Together, these innovations facilitated the emergence of Hebrew scribes and the Hebrew Bible, which occurred in many iterations across several hundred years commencing in written form from around 900 BCE.[3]

This book follows the course of human innovation over time until this influential religious text was written. Along the way, it explores the HB/OT's foundations, primary influences, precedents, and mythological origins.

About the author

I was brought up in a family of Catholics who, over time, began to collectively question their faith. Over time, my family, including both of my parents, eventually left organised religion and became what I can now, in retrospect, describe as secular humanists—enquiring, ethical, rational, evidence-based, believers in the value of history, science, evidence, evolution, and human nature. But more importantly, we believed in—and lived lives that supported—the innate fairness, generosity, empathy, and natural sense of wonder of the human species.

An emerging interest in religion

Despite being a secular humanist, I had always retained an interest in religion. I spent several years working with Indigenous/First Australians in collaboration with my friend and academic colleague Professor Paul Memmott, AO. Paul and I were attempting to document and better understand the complex culture of Indigenous Australians.[4] In the early 1970s, during our field work in Northern Australia, I was welcomed into the Barramundi Dreaming clan of the Ganggalida nation. Their traditional country covers the north-west of Queensland, Australia, stretching from the Northern Territory border in the west to the eastern town of Burketown in the southern Gulf of Carpentaria. This was an honour that I continue to respect by not eating barramundi. This is despite my knowledge that, like all religions, this is essentially a cultural phenomenon. Over time, I became even more fascinated by the role of religion, the many religions of the world and, specifically, the two interrelated religions Judaism and Christianity. I began to read very widely across biblical, atheist, historical, scientific, religious and non-religious books, and articles.

In November 1979, whilst undertaking an academic sabbatical in North America, I met the late Professor Lynn White Jr, a professor of economic history at UCLA.

---

[3]   Issa (2017).
[4]   SOURCE: Memmott (2007), p. xi.

Professor White published a journal article in 1967 in which he developed a theory about the Christian origins of the ecological crisis. Amongst other claims, he stated that it is the Christian God's will (as expressed in the HB/OT) 'that man exploit nature for his proper ends … and that by destroying pagan animism, Christianity made it possible to exploit nature in a mood of indifference to the feelings of natural objects'.[5] The journal article caused a major furore from Christians and historians alike. For the past fifty years, scholars have continued to re-analyse and debate White's theories and arguments.[6]

My meeting with Professor White in 1979 influenced my thinking in many ways. He had just published his book on medieval religion and technology.[7] White's collection of essays in this book, and less so his journal article, stimulated my thinking about how society, culture, technology, and religion have been integrally linked in different ways throughout the ages.

Two of the more recent critics of White's original journal article have expressed his impact in words that reflect my own thinking:

> *Even if many of White's assumptions and conclusions have been called into question …his larger point … that we need to examine the underlying values and philosophical worldviews that motivate human activity in nature as revealed …. in our cultural and environmental history remains as significant now as it was in 1967.*[8]

The principle of examining the historical, economic, technological, and cultural background of religion was one of the main inspirations for undertaking the research that has led to this book.

The shaping of this book

In the early 1970s, as I was completing my postgraduate degree at the University of Surrey in England, one of my statistics professors taught me a valuable lesson. At that time, the national media were headlining a research study that apparently had found that around 60% of married men have had an extramarital affair. The research came from a survey of readers of the American sex magazine *Forum*. My statistics professor immediately fired off a letter to the editor of one of London's major newspapers wherein he claimed that 100% of

---

[5] White (1967), p. 1205.
[6] See for example Callicott (1990); Minteer and Manning (2005).
[7] White (1978).
[8] Minteer and Manning (2005), p. 172.

British men were employed in the construction industry. He claimed that this information came from a survey he had undertaken of subscribers to the *Construction Industry Journal*!

The lesson I learnt was this: if you use just one source for your information, then you run a significant risk of holding beliefs that may well be a fabrication based on your reliance on information from that single source.

As modern science evolves, it becomes increasingly indefensible to base knowledge about human evolution and related beliefs on just one source—in this case, the Hebrew Bible. The science and understanding of the past (what happened, who was there, when and what they were doing and believing) can now be informed by a wide range of independently verifiable evidence. The search for an accurate chronology and an accurate understanding of the lifestyles of ancient times can now draw upon evidence from multiple converging sources. This includes astronomical (past lunar-solar events), ice-core analysis, seismological records, radiocarbon dating, paleoclimatic research, paleobotany, dendrochronology (ancient tree ring analysis), archaeological findings, geopolitical events, ancient texts and historical documents, ancient king lists, linguistics, genomics, genealogical data, knowledge of ancient battles, trade and cultural exchange networks and shared /common patterns of mythological beliefs.[9]

The use of multiple and convergent methods

The use of many sources is referred to as using *multiple and convergent methods*—what scientific literature refers to as *triangulation* or *consilience*.[10, 11] It involves using more than one discipline or method, research direction, and data/information source to focus on the same topic. Adopting multiple lines of inquiry, as opposed to undue reliance on a single source of information, significantly increases the credibility and historical accuracy of any conclusions.

Adam Izdebski and his colleagues, in discussing the need for examining archaeological evidence from the Middle East from multiple perspectives, have stated:

> *One can still observe the persistent tendency in several contributions to oversimplify the social or natural processes, to focus on one-sided explanations, or to be based on observations of authors representing just one or two fields. This is not least the case when it comes to the Mediterranean region.[12]*

---

[9]   See for instance: Wiener (2007).
[10] SOURCE: definition in Bycroft and Judd, 1989, pp.30-31.
[11] Izdebski et al (2016).
[12] Izdebski et al (2016), p. 6.

The following discussion uses evidence from multiple sources to build an understanding of the prehistoric, geographic, societal, cultural, mythological, and linguistic influences that led to the content, structure, and beliefs in the Judeo-Christian Bible (the Hebrew Bible and the Christian Old Testament).

An evidence-based journey

The journey starts by examining the formation of the continents by the tectonic plates and identifying the geomorphic opportunities that emerged (fertile plains with free-flowing rivers at the base of ore-carrying mountain ranges). This occurred in several locations globally, where there were small groups of hunter-gatherers and the potential for agricultural (native edible crops) and pastoral (native edible animals) development. Several comparatively similar geomorphological locations witnessed the emergence of what historians and archaeologists refer to as 'the cradles of civilisation'. The historically most important one for the emergence of civilisation and the HB/OT occurred in the Middle East. It is referred to as the *Fertile Crescent*, and it began as the foundation for what is now called 'civilisation' from around 4000 BCE to 3500 BCE. The Fertile Crescent includes the Levant, where the Egyptian textual evidence indicates the Israelites most likely first emerged.

Time perspective

It can be easy to distort the perception of time when looking back in history. When it is stated that the Bible was probably commenced in or around 900 BCE and that it reports on events from 4000 BCE (biblical creation of the universe) or 1400 BCE (biblical birth of Moses), this needs to be placed in a realistic and believable time perspective. The Hebrew scribes were writing about events that occurred at least one thousand years before writing itself existed. The Bible was written many more years (often thousands of years) after the events that were being described. The biblical text then went through many iterations by many authors over hundreds of years. It was probably compiled from oral histories that had been repeated over hundreds of years prior to the invention of the alphabet, writing, and the development of a scribal culture.

It requires a significant suspension of judgement in the search for authenticity in a document with this complex history. This is why the search for biblical authenticity and historical accuracy has preoccupied biblical scholars for centuries.

Most scholars accept that the Hebrew Bible was written over a period of some five to six hundred years (roughly 900 BCE to 300 BCE) by teams of Hebrew scribes. Life expectancy around that time was 35 years for women and 45 years for men.[13] A conservative estimate is that a period of 3,000 years is the equivalent of 100 to 125 generations.[14] This suggests that there were many scribes involved in the gradual unfolding and finalisation of the biblical narratives.

If the Bible is a genuine historical account, prior to being written, it could only have been passed down orally, through memorisation, religious ceremony, and symbolism across generations for most of those thousands of years. In the process, the stories have gone through more than one hundred generations and through several versions, interpretations, enhancements, successive revisions, redactions, and embellishments.

The Hebrew scribes were ancient people, and their perspectives on life and myth were very different from today. Their mental outlook, their horizons, their ways of seeing, their way of being, believing, understanding, and explaining things were very different from the modern scientific world. The Hebrew scribes were pre-scientific, and they had a job to do—position themselves and differentiate their culture and their mythologies from everything else around them.

Use of biblical references and reference dates

The Judeo-Christian Bible is the Holy Book of the largest number of believers and two of the most influential religions of all world religions. Where biblical text is directly referenced or quoted, the source is the English Standard Version.[15]

Where dates and specific eras or years are referenced, the culturally neutral terms of BCE (before the current/common era) instead of the traditional BC (before Christ) and CE (current/common era) instead of the archaic AD (*Anno Domini*; 'in the year of the Lord') will be used. This practice is religiously neutral and reflects the common notations used by Jewish writers for more than a century.

---

[13] SOURCE: https://www.scientificamerican.com/article/life-and-death-in-nabada/ retrieved on 21 June 2021; see also Eshed and Gopher (2013), pp. 99-101.

[14] Goring-Morris and Belfer-Cohen (2011), p. S198.

[15] Holy Bible: English Standard Version published by HarperCollins Publishers © 2001 by Crossway Bibles, a division of Good News Publishers. Used by permission. All rights reserved.

Chapter 1

Understanding History

The research and the evidence covered in this book focuses largely on the influence of prehistoric mythologies on the emerging Hebrew Bible. *Prehistory* is a term used traditionally to describe the period prior to the invention of writing. Writing was developed by the Sumerians and Egyptians in rudimentary forms from around 4000 BCE (cuneiform and hieroglyphics respectively). The Sumerian cuneiform scribal culture spread fairly rapidly across the Middle East. However, prehistoric research is largely based on a retrospective, often speculative, reconstruction of the past from non-textual, often archaeological/artefactual, evidence. It is interpretative by nature and relies on a convergence of evidence and scientific consensus about its applicability and meaning.

After the invention of the alphabet and writing, a wide range of information was recorded and has become available to assist historical research. Textual, reliable, repetitive, and evidentiary documents, artefacts, and records increased exponentially once a communicable alphabet (originally of Canaanite and Phoenician origin) was in relatively wide circulation from around 1500 BCE.

The availability of writing and the spread of literacy had a major impact on religions. Concepts that had, up until then, been conveyed in ritual, poetry, oral stories, dance, and ceremony could now be written down and more widely distributed. Nicholas Wade has proposed that the availability of writing saw the emphasis within religions shift from an oral culture of rituals and emotional engagement to a scribal culture of creeds and intellectual belief. He described it in this way:

> *With the advent of literacy, religious narratives could now be written down and studied. The sacred text became an increasingly prominent part of religious practice, matching the shift in emphasis from ritual to belief.*[16]

---

[16]   Wade (2010), p. 87 and p. 142.

The main approaches to understanding history

History involves the retrospective and systematic study of change over time. It usually involves bringing together a range of available and often diverse evidence about aspects of human development covering social, cultural, political, religious, economic, genomic, technological, and lifestyle issues.

There are three broad traditions in the study of history. There are those who see history as a narrative, a documentation of the progressive power and influence of a supreme deity over human existence. The Greek father of history, Herodotus of Halicarnassus (around 400 BCE), was himself criticised by his youthful contemporary philosopher Thucydides for focusing too much on deities. Thucydides was the first to focus historical attention on strict standards of impartiality and dependence on facts without mention of any assumed intervention of deities.[17] Biblical advocates represent a modern version of those who see history as largely the evidence of a deity. In this version, history is seen as a series of acts of god, divine interventions, or divine revelations.[18]

Secondarily, there are those who see history as a reliable memory of significant events of the past independent of deities. These memories represent a small, usually symbolic or symptomatic, part of what happened in the past. The memories are an aide-mémoire. History is seen as a factual narrative that has accumulated over time from a variety of trusted sources. This approach to history sees selected events as a reminder of the past. In this approach, history is a noun. It is a collection of things—memories, artefacts, stories, photos, events, people, objects, and buildings. This history narrative is about remembering.

History and the past are not the same thing. A third approach sees history as multidimensional, continuously challengeable and changing. This view accepts that history is a science—the 'science of the past'. The past is continuously rediscovered and reshaped as new evidence emerges. In this approach, history is a systematic investigative process—a process of ongoing forensic investigation into a series of yet-to-be-discovered actively and continuously unearthed lessons from the past. A search that never tires. History is an evidentiary science from which lessons and understandings are continuously discovered, adapted, and improved. In this approach, perspectives on history are forever changing.

---

[17] See: Banner (2022).
[18] See: Eusebius (2011).

An example of a one-dimensional historical narrative

When I was in primary/elementary school in Australia in the mid-1950s, for most of my nine young years there, I was told both verbally and in teaching material that the British navigator and explorer James Cook *discovered* Australia in 1770.[19] At school, we often celebrated this great achievement and, in some parts of Australia, it is still believed and celebrated. Across Australia, there are multiple plaques claiming that James Cook 'discovered' Australia. For example, in a Christian church in the parish of Cook's River, Sydney (named after the navigator) the plaque on the church's external wall reads *Parish of Cook's River, named—April 12, 1838, after Captain James Cook, Discoverer of Australia.*

The belief that Captain Cook discovered Australia persists in some quarters today despite considerable evidence to the contrary:

Indigenous occupation prior to Cook

The journals of Captain Cook and his crew mention the Indigenous Australians who they encountered on their journey up the east coast of Australia. These were Australia's Indigenous First Nations Peoples, who had been in Australia for around 60,000 years prior to Cook's arrival.

Portuguese explorers prior to Cook

In the early 1500s, there were Portuguese colonies in Timor, which is around 650 kilometres north of Australia. There is some (largely circumstantial) evidence that the Portuguese seafarer Cristóvão de Mendonça, who explored South-East Asia in the early 1500s, led a fleet of four ships into Botany Bay south of Sydney in 1522—around 250 years before Captain James Cook.[20]

In 1595, Portuguese-born Spanish explorers Álvaro de Mendaña de Neira and Pedro Fernandez de Quiros sailed across the Pacific Ocean to the Solomon Islands in search of a great southern land. Many people believe that Pedro Fernandez De Quiros came ashore in 1606, where the Queensland city of Gladstone is now located. De Quiros referred to the land where he landed as 'La Austrialia del Espiritu Santo' (southern land of the Holy Spirit), employing a term derived from the Latin word *australis*, which means 'southern'.

---

[19] See: https://theconversation.com/captain-cook-discovered-australia-and-other-myths-from-old-school-text-books-128926.
[20] See: Trickett (2007).

Pedro Fernandez De Quiros' first mate was Luis Váez de Torres who, some months later (late 1606), sailed along the southern coast of New Guinea through what is now called Torres Strait (after this explorer).

Dutch explorers prior to Cook

On 26 February 1606, Dutch East Indies navigator and governor, Willem Janszoon, landed on the west coast of Cape York Peninsula in North Queensland in his ship, the *Duyfken*. He is the first recorded European to land in Australia. He made landfall near what is now the town of Weipa. Janszoon produced a map of the coastline of what is now called the Gulf of Carpentaria.

Dutch merchant captain Dirk Hartog (Dirck Hatichs) and his crew in the ship *Eendracht* landed on the west coast of Australia on 25 October 1616. Whilst there, Hartog nailed a Dutch pewter dish to a timber post on a remote island (which is now called Dirk Hartog Island) in Shark Bay (named later by Englishman William Dampier in 1699; see below). Hartog's pewter dish is regarded as Australia's oldest European maritime relic.

In 1619, Dutch navigator and early astronomer Frederick de Houtman sailed northwards up the west Australian coast. He observed what is now Rottnest Island off the coast of Perth. He discovered a group of 122 small coral reefs and shoals, which are named after him as the Houtman Abrolhos (a sailing term for danger).

In 1623, Dutch explorer Jan Carstensz was commissioned by the Dutch East India Company to follow the journey of Willem Janszoon (above) to find out more about this southern land. Carstensz's journal mentions his meeting with an Aboriginal person on the west coast of Cape York Peninsula in North Queensland. The Aboriginal person had a piece of metal that Carstensz assumed came from Willem Janszoon's ship the *Duyfken*. Carstensz mapped the Gulf of Carpentaria and named the Gulf after Pieter Carpentier (1586 to 1659), administrator of the Dutch East India Company and then-governor-general in Batavia (Indonesia).

In 1629, the Dutch East India ship the *Batavia* was shipwrecked on a small group of islands off the west coast of Australia just north of what is now the township of Broome. There was a mutiny and at least two of the ship's mutineers made it to the west coast of Australia. These two are regarded as the first Europeans to permanently live on the Australian mainland. Six of the mutineers were eventually hanged on 2 October 1629 on Long Island in the Houtman Abrolhos archipelago. They are recorded as the first Europeans to be legally executed in Australia.

Dutch East Indies navigator and explorer Abel Tasman, in his search for the great southern continent, stumbled onto Australia's southern Island of Tasmania in 1642. Tasman named it *Van Diemen's Land* after his boss, Anthony van Diemen, governor-general of the Dutch East Indies. It was renamed Tasmania after the explorer himself in 1855.

In 1656, the Dutch ship *Vergulde Draeck*, on its way to the Dutch East Indies colony (now Indonesia), was wrecked on a coral reef, some one hundred kilometres north of what is now the town of Perth in Western Australia. In 1658, a Dutch search party on the ship *Waeckende Boey* landed on the west Australian coast just south of the wreck site but failed to find survivors.

In 1696, Dutch Captain Willem Hesselsz de Vlamingh spent six days on Rottnest Island (which he mistakenly named 'rats' nest island' after the small marsupial quokkas that inhabit the island). He sailed into the Swan River and named it Zwaanenrivier ('swan river' in Dutch) after the large number of swans he observed there.

Appearance on maps prior to Cook

The existence of the west coast of what is now called Australia was sufficiently well-known in Europe that it had started to appear on maps of the world. In 1658, Amsterdam-based art and map dealer Nicholas Visscher produced a map of the world with an accurate outline of most of the west coastline of Australia.[21] In 1663, Parisian cartographer Melchisé-dech Thévenot produced world maps that contained surprisingly accurate details of a large part of the Australian coastline.[22]

In 1684, AM Angelique DV, likely the daughter of Pierre Duval, geographer to then-king of France, Louis XIV, published a map that shows the western half of the Australian continent. This map was published eighty-six years before Cook's 'discovery' of Australia.

English explorer prior to Cook

Some seventy years before Cook's arrival, English explorer, pirate, privateer, navigator, and naturalist William Dampier sailed between Dirk Hartog Island and the western Australian mainland into Shark Bay on 6 August 1699. He named Shark Bay—a name that remains today. Dampier landed ashore on the Australian mainland and was the first known European to start documenting Australian flora and fauna.

---

[21]   SOURCE: National Library of Australia (2013), p. 151.
[22]   SOURCE: State Library of New South Wales (2006), p. 17.

With the frequency of visits to the west coast of Australia by Dutch navigators, the early maps reflected this by identifying the Australian continent as 'New Holland' ('Hollandia Nova'). In Cook's own journals, he frequently referred to parts of the East Coast of Australia as 'New Holland'.[23] How, based on this evidence, the island continent was able to be claimed as having been 'discovered' more than one hundred years later by the British will remain a mystery. The longevity and ubiquity of the 'Captain Cook discovered Australia' myth, despite the overwhelming evidence to the contrary, highlights a major difficulty for people studying the past. There is an oft-repeated cliché that 'history is written by the victors and framed according to the prejudices and bias existing on their side'.[24]

Even in the light of contradictory information, a continuously repeated, taught, and memorised one-sided view of history can survive. The taken-for-granted stories become fact and difficult to challenge, no matter how much evidence exists to the contrary. This approach to history is about memorising and glorifying the past. The mythological, historical narrative gives comfort, continuity, and confidence in an uncomplicated, unquestioned, unambiguous, self-fulfilling, repetitive, and easily understood, albeit erroneous, view of the past.

The science of the past

An alternative approach is to see history as not being about deities or 'people, dates, and things' but as a dynamic process of objectively understanding the human species, human enterprise, and human achievement. It is evidence-based, scientific, empirical, and iterative. The word 'history' itself emerged from a Greek word meaning 'enquiry', 'to know', or 'the seeking of knowledge'.

History as a science involves the continuous, investigative exploration of the human condition. It is subject to critical scrutiny. It is an organic process, a continuous search for meaning and knowledge. In the words of Adjei Adjepong, who has completed a wide-ranging review of the different definitions and approaches to history:

History is an activity idea: history as a search or an inquiry for accurate information about people, things, or events, the collection and interpretation of sources and the production of a body of knowledge.[25]

---

23 SOURCE: https://www.nma.gov.au/exhibitions/endeavour-voyage/cooks-journal/august-1770 retrieved on 9 December 2022.
24 SOURCE: https://slate.com/culture/2019/11/history-is-written-by-the-victors-quote-origin.html Retrieved on 8 August 2021.
25 Adjepong (2020), p. 19.

There is a profound link between how humanity has emerged over time and the lessons to be learnt by a better integration of knowledge of the past with an improved understanding of emerging human-environment systems. This requires an integrated understanding of history across multiple dimensions.[26] Boivin and Crowther propose that the 'privileged antiquarian origins of archaeology' need to be substantially revised to better assess past solutions, practices, and sustainability'. This involves engagement with multidisciplinary teams that can include archaeologists, urban researchers, ecologists, agronomists, geneticists, anthropologists, paleoanthropologists, and sociologists.[27]

This approach to history and archaeology is not about memorising the past. It is about understanding and leveraging the lessons from the past. In modern archaeology, what is found in excavations is no longer about a cultural artefact to be recorded, classified, and displayed in a museum. Each archaeological discovery had a context; it was in use in a cultural process, dynamic, understandable, interpretable, and embedded in a socio-political and ideological human past. And it is open to enquiry.[28]

The multi-dimensional view of history

The conventional view of history involved a narrative that recorded stories about famous people (explorers, prophets, leaders), their exploits (discoveries, announcements, prophecies, conquests, achievements), places (where they came from, where they were, where they went) and dates. The Captain Cook example cited above, and to some extent, the Hebrew Bible/Christian Old Testament reflect this tradition. This approach tends to omit the investigative, analytical, and contextual study of how and why these people, events, and dates occurred and how they might provide insights, generalisations, and learnings for a better understanding of humanity.

Historians now distinguish four different categorisations for historical research:

- **Prehistory.** Prehistory has been traditionally defined as the times prior to the development of writing, written records, agriculture, pastoralism, and sedentary living (villages, towns, and city-states). The concept was developed by Scottish-born Canadian archaeologist and ethnologist Daniel Wilson (1816–1892) who

---

26 See: Costanza et al (2012); Cornell et al (2010).
27 Boivin and Crowther (2021), p. 279.
28 Adapted from Grayling (2021), p. 247.

saw it closely linked to the science of archaeological investigations.[29] It was a concept that was popularised by Sir John Lubbock, who was President of the Anthropological Institute of Great Britain and Ireland in 1871.[30] These advocates emphasised that the focus of prehistorical research and prehistory was essentially informed by and about archaeology, anthropology, and ethnography.

- **Conventional history.** Conventionally, 'history' began with the development of writing, agriculture, domestication of animals, and sedentary living (around 1500 BCE). Conventional history has involved documentary and archaeological evidence of past events and how they relate to or reflect the human condition. Conventional history has tended to report on a series of events in time and place. This approach to history has often delivered a one-dimensional, parochial view of the past (see *An example of a one-dimensional historical narrative* above).

- **Big history** involves writing about the past from a significantly wider perspective. Advocates of big history believe that understanding and learning about the human condition needs to involve a much broader scale of historical enquiry. It needs to be multi-dimensional, focusing on the overall human implications of the past.[31] Big history advocates believe that the conventional approach to history (above) limits study to the past 10,000 years and neglects the common themes from the much longer time when humans existed on Earth. Big history begins with the big bang, the formation of the universe and events that have led to the present.[32] It bridges the humanity–science divide by including potential evidence from a range of disciplines (cosmology, geology, geography, biology, archaeology, anthropology, history, culture, and religion). This approach facilitates a better understanding of the universe and of the emergence of humanity.[33]

- **Deep history** draws on multiple fields and a broader scale of enquiry. It aims to better understand the propensities and desires of the human species. Deep historians believe that history did not begin with the invention of writing but with the evolution of anatomically modern humans. Deep history is not limited by definitions of specific eras or chronologies (Stone Age, Bronze Age, Iron Age). Deep historical understanding transcends regional specificity and simplistic assumptions

---

[29] Kehoe (1991).
[30] Cited in Gamble (2015), pp. 150-151.
[31] Christian (1991).
[32] Brown (2012).
[33] Hesketh (2014).

(such as 'agriculture began in the Fertile Crescent'). It searches for deeper cross-cultural understandings of the human condition. Much of conventional history (above) is Eurocentric, culturally myopic, gender-biased (hunter = males, gatherer = females), patriarchal, socially, and culturally simplistic and superficial.[34] The works of Professor Paul Memmott at the University of Queensland, Australia, to understand and communicate the detailed cultural, domiciliary, kinship, mythological, seasonal, architectural, and settlement pattern complexity of Indigenous Australians is an excellent example of deep historical research. Memmott has presented a detailed exposé of the complexity, integrity, and meaningfulness of the life of Australia's First Nation's people to a depth that has been rarely if ever understood or explained before.[35]

History as a deeper understanding of the dimensions of human imagination

The United Kingdom's foremost archaeologist, anthropologist, and advocate for 'deep history', Clive Gamble, has questioned the assumption about the point in time when prehistory transitioned to conventional history. In line with similar opinions of authors such as Jaques Cauvin (2003), Kit Wesler (2014) and Yuval Noah Harari (2015), Gamble sees the transition from prehistory to conventional history as a reflection of changes in the intellectual/cognitive capacity of the human species. The most common term for the human species is *homo sapiens*—this is Latin for 'wise human'.

Gamble believes that the 'modern world/civilisation' did not start with writing, farming, and settled life. It commenced when artefacts transitioned from being functional, utilitarian objects for family or kinship groups to collective imaginative, symbolic structures that strengthened socioecology and social complexity and reflected new levels of imagination, social significance, and cultural capital.[36] Gamble uses the astronomically aligned Göbekli Tepe in Türkiye (9000 BCE), built by hunter-gatherers and not by a sedentary community, as a focal point for his argument (see *Significant communal structures in the Northern Levant,* page 158).[37]

---

[34] Maynes and Waltner (2012).
[35] Memmott (2022).
[36] Gamble (2016).
[37] SOURCE: https://www.smithsonianmag.com/history/Göbekli-tepe-the-worlds-first-temple-83613665/ retrieved on 8 March 2021.

The intellectual ability to abstract from utilitarian to imaginative symbolic systems ultimately led to an alphabet and writing. It is a key focus for better understanding human development and the transition from prehistoric to conventional history thousands of years before the emergence of agriculture and writing systems. The human capacity, propensity, and desire to imagine and invent abstract systems is a common theme across the many alternative socio-cultural and religious systems of the past. It is the foundation of the religious systems that currently exist across the modern world.[38]

---

[38] See Harari (2015).

Chapter 2

The World's Religions and Their Adherents

The human species has developed many different religions, most of which have tens of thousands of adherents. Dictionary.com defines a religion in the following way:

A set of beliefs concerning the cause, nature, and purpose of the universe, especially when considered as the creation of a superhuman agency or agencies, usually involving devotional and ritual observances, and often containing a moral code governing the conduct of human affairs.[39]

There are currently (2023) around 4,200 different religions in the world.[40] The twenty-one largest religions and their approximate number of adherents are:

1. Christianity (2.4 billion)
2. Islam (1.9 billion)
3. Hinduism (1.2 billion)
4. Nonreligious (Secular/Agnostic/Atheist) (1.1 billion)
5. Buddhism (500 million)
6. Folk religion (400 million)
7. Chinese traditional religion (394 million)
8. Primal-indigenous (300 million)
9. African traditional and Diasporic (100 million)
10. Shinto (100 million)
11. Sikhism (23 million)

---

[39] SOURCE: https://www.dictionary.com/browse/religion retrieved on 7 October 2020.
[40] Data sourced from multiple sources.

12. Juche (19 million)
13. Spiritism (15 million)
14. Judaism (15 million)
15. Bahai (7 million)
16. Jainism (4.2 million)
17. Cao Dai (4 million)
18. Zoroastrianism (2.6 million)
19. Tenrikyo (2 million)
20. Neo-Paganism (1 million)
21. Unitarian-Universalism (800,000).[41]

Nearly 75 per cent of the world's population practices one of the five most influential organised religions in the world: Buddhism, Christianity, Hinduism, Islam, and Judaism. Even though most religions claim their teachings have existed since the beginning of the world or the dawn of human civilisation, reasonably accurate commencement dates have been established for most contemporary religions.

Currently, the oldest (still practised) religions in the world are:[42]

1.	Zoroastrianism[43] and Hinduism	2300 BCE
2.	Buddhism	563 BCE
3.	Confucianism	551 BCE
4.	Jainism	527 BCE
5.	Judaism	300 BCE[44]
6.	Shinto	300 BCE
7.	Christianity	1 CE
8.	Taoism	42 CE
9.	Islam	570 CE.

---

[41] SOURCE: https://www.theregister.co.uk/2006/10/06/the_odd_body_religion/ retrieved on 7 October 2020.

[42] SOURCE: adapted and reedited from https://www.worldatlas.com/articles/oldest-religions-in-the-world.html retrieved on 7 October 2020.

[43] There is some debate about when the founder of Zoroastrianism lived. Some researchers have suggested Zoroaster lived in 6000 BCE; others suggest 2300 BCE; some believe that it was sometime between 1700 BCE and 1000 BCE; many believe he was around in 700 BCE to 600 BCE. In line with the emergence of writing, Zoroastrianism did not emerge as written text until around 600 BCE. However, because of the very close similarities between Zoroastrianism and Hinduism it is most likely the foundations of both go back to at least the second millennium BCE.

[44] Adler (2022).

Based on the Dictionary.com definition of religion cited above, and as discussed later, there were many religions, now defunct, that predate these examples and from which some or many of the contemporary religious stories and beliefs have been adapted.

The various holy books

There is an interesting pattern in the practices of most of the world's major religions—they all tend to have a holy book that articulates their beliefs and practices.[45]

- The Persian/Zoroastrians (circa 2500 BCE to 1400 BCE) have the Avesta, which includes, as central to their beliefs, the writings of their spiritual leader Zoroaster, known as the Gathas.
- The Hindus (circa 2300 BCE to 1500 BCE) do not have one sacred book but have many books contained within four 'Vedas'—the Rig Veda (the oldest and most important), the Sama Veda (song knowledge), the Yajur Veda (worship/ritual knowledge and observances) and the Atharva Veda (marriage, funerals, chants, spells, prayers, hymns, and lifestyle issues), which together provide the Vedas scriptures.
- The Jainists (circa 700 BCE to 500 BCE) have the Tiloya Panatti, a document that contains a total of 5,677 verses divided into nine chapters.
- Buddhism (circa 600 BCE to 500 BCE) has the Sutras: the words and teachings of the Buddha. There are several noncanonical Buddhist texts that provide supplementary teachings, rules of conduct and commentary on transitional states after death.
- Confucian (circa 600 BCE to 500 BCE) texts consist of the 'Five Classics and Four Books'. The Five Classics are the Book of Odes, Book of Documents, Book of Changes, Book of Rites, and the Spring and Autumn Annals. The Four Books are Great Learning, Doctrine of the Mean, Analects and Mencius.
- Judaism (circa 500 BCE to 300 BCE) has the Hebrew Bible (a version of which is the Christian Old Testament).

---

[45] NOTE: dates shown for the emergence of each religion are approximate. More detail, more discussion and more specific dates of the religions that predate and influenced the Hebrew Bible are discussed later in this book.

- The Taoist's (circa 140 CE) book is called the Tao Te Ching (or Dao De Jing or Daode Jing)—'the way and its power'—and is also known as the Lao-tzu, from the name of the traditionally ascribed author.
- The Bible, Old and New Testament (circa 200 CE to 500 CE) is the Christian holy book.
- The Muslims (circa 600 CE) have the Quran, which they regard as containing the final revelations of God.
- Shinto (circa 600 CE) practitioners have the Kojiki or 'records of ancient matters' and the Nihon-gi or 'chronicles of Japan'.
- The Sikh (circa 1400 CE to 1500 CE) sacred scripture is the Adi Granth, which is a collection of nearly 6,000 hymns of the Sikh gurus (religious leaders) and various early and medieval saints of different religions and castes.
- The Bahá'í (circa 1800 CE) have the Kitáb-i-Aqdas or Aqdas as the central book of their faith.
- The North Korean Juche (circa 1965 CE) followers have Kim Jong-Il's treatise *On the Juche Idea*.

Almost all institutionalised myths, legends, and beliefs have sacred texts or books outlining their spiritual, supernatural, and religious assumptions. There is another common belief that they all share. They all regard their specific book as a divinely inspired set of instructions. Their book is, therefore, the singular 'textbook for life'. Followers of each sacred text memorise, meditate, pray, chant, and sing these texts or selected quotations, as essential parts of the primary master plan for their sense of being and their spiritual lives.

From prehistory to the Hebrew Bible and Christian Old Testament

This book begins with what is known about the world and how it has shaped humanity and delivered opportunities for cultural development across the millennia prior to the first historical mention of Israelites in around 1205 BCE. It was largely in the Northern Hemisphere that geological, geomorphological, technological, cultural, agricultural, pastoral, and mythological concepts emerged. They were shared across geographic and cultural boundaries and together they laid the platform for the Eastern Mediterranean to become a major birthplace of civilisation. It was here, in the Levant and the Fertile Crescent, that a group identified as Israelites emerged in the late Bronze Age. From there, the writing of the Hebrew Bible began.

On this journey, a great deal is owed to the emergence of the scientific discipline of archaeology. Archaeology began in the late seventeenth century but did not really mature as a reliable discipline and a reliable source of prehistoric artefacts, cultures, and beliefs until around the 1920s and 1930s. The historical veracity of the biblical stories could not be checked against any other evidence until major excavations in and around Mesopotamia (largely contemporary Iraq), the Levant, and Egypt unearthed massive amounts of artefactual material from that period. This partly explains how the Bible maintained its dominance as a sole source of information for many people throughout the past two thousand years. The current research draws on much of the relatively recent archaeological, linguistic, textual (cuneiform, hieroglyphics, text), and paleoclimatic research—and genomic evidence—to better understand the context and the emergence of the Hebrew scribes and the writing of the Hebrew Bible.

By far the most significant advance in the better understanding of where the human species came from and how they got there has been the relatively recent advances in genomics (the scientific study of the structure, function, evolution, mapping, and editing of ancient genomes). This is a powerful, objective scientific field of research that complements archaeology and linguistics. Genomics originated in 1953 but has only become an extremely powerful historical tool since around 2010.[46] The combination of biblical stories, archaeology, linguistics, and genomics is fundamental to the current investigation.

The Hebrew Bible, the Israelites, and the Levant

There is some dispute over when the twenty-four books of the Hebrew Bible were finally and formally decided (canonised). It is generally accepted that the major components of the final version of the Hebrew Bible were drafted and rewritten over some six hundred years by multiple Hebrew scribes (from around 900 BCE to 300 BCE). It is likely that this occurred gradually, through many iterations and variations, with the final content being decided incrementally between 200 BCE and 200 CE.[47] Israeli academic and archaeologist Yonatan Adler believes that it was not until around 100 BCE that the Hebrew Bible, Judaism, and the broadly accepted laws of the Torah (the Pentateuch or first five books of the Hebrew Bible) could be identified as a fully functioning religion.[48]

---

[46]   Reich (2019), pp. xxii to xxvi.
[47]   SOURCE: https://www.historyofinformation.com/detail.php?id=139 retrieved on 10 November 2022.
[48]   Adler (2022).

For many hundreds of years since then, the HB/OT has been seen as the definitive history of the Israelites. Historically, the Israelites originated in the eastern Mediterranean/Levant. The term *Levant* has been used for many years as a generic term to collectively describe a range of locations in the eastern Mediterranean—the word *levant* being derived from the Italian *levante*, meaning 'rising'—reflecting the fact of the sun rising in the east (of the Mediterranean). *Levant* is the present participle of the French word to rise 'lever'. The geographic term means the countries of the eastern Mediterranean—where the sun rises.

Since the emergence of archaeology in the late 1800s, an increasing amount of extra-biblical evidence has been emerging about the prehistoric cultures and the communities in the Levant. There is now a wealth of evidence about what was happening in and around the Levant prior to and after the emergence of the Israelites. Most of this evidence is not mentioned in the Bible. The emergence of the Bible is now informed by an extensive amount of evidence independent of biblical accounts. This has two main advantages: it provides a cross reference for the biblical stories and, it gives a greater understanding of the rich cultural heritage of ancient Eurasia, the Middle East, Egypt, the Levant, and north-west India. It was within this rich cultural milieu that the Hebrew scribes began to write the Bible. The evidence shows that they were significantly influenced by the diverse sources around them as they wrote.

The influence of the Middle East mythological traditions on the Old Testament

The HB/OT emerged in the ancient Middle East. It is a classic example of many of the mythological traditions that had spread across Middle East communities including Egypt, Iran and the Indus Valley in North-west India. Swiss historian of religion Othmar Keel has explained the link between the ancient Middle East and the HB/OT in the following way:

> *We now see the Bible imbedded in a broad stream of traditions of the most diverse kind and provenance. Only when this rich environment has been systematically included in the study of the OT do OT conventionalities and originalities clearly emerge. It then becomes evident where the biblical texts are carried by the powerful current of traditions in force for centuries, and where they give an intimation of a new energy inherently their own.*[49]

---

[49]   Keel (1997), p. 7.

The Hebrew Bible and the Christian Old Testament

Apart from the Dead Sea Scrolls[50], there is no ancient copy of the Hebrew Bible (apart from various fragments) written in the original Hebrew by the ancient Hebrew scribes. The oldest available full version of the Hebrew Bible/the Christian Old Testament is the Septuagint, which is in the Greek language. It was probably translated from Ancient Hebrew during Alexander the Great's occupation of the Middle East and Egypt (from around 300 BCE onwards).

These two slightly different versions of the Hebrew Bible are in use today. The first is referred to as the Hebrew (Masoretic) Bible. Tradition has it that it was handed down by word of mouth, ritual, and via many available fragments, codices, and manuscripts brought together across many generations by Jewish elders. The second is the Septuagint, which is the oldest Greek translation of the Hebrew Bible. The two versions have different adherents across the Jewish and Christian faiths, with the Septuagint having more influence on the Roman Catholic and Eastern Orthodox 'Old Testament' versions of the Bible.

One of the major differences between the Hebrew Bible and the Septuagint relates to the calculation of when the biblical God created the universe. In accordance with the Hebrew Bible and subsequent determination by biblical scholar Rabbi Yossi ben Halafta in the second century CE, humanity and the Jewish calendar commenced with God's creation of the universe and Adam and Eve in or around 3761 BCE.[51] Followers of the Septuagint version of the Bible tend to locate the date of God's creation of the universe and Adam and Eve as sometime in early to mid-5000 BCE. The Anglican Archbishop James Ussher in around 1600 CE used the Bible to calculate God's creation of the universe at around 4004 BCE.[52]

---

[50] Vermes (1965).
[51] SOURCE: https://www.jewishvirtuallibrary.org/timeline-for-the-history-of-judaism; Greenburg (2017), p. 18.
[52] Stanford Encyclopedia of Philosophy (2017), pp. 13-14.

Chapter 3

Mythology, Religion, and Spirituality

T he Bible does not stand alone. Myth and religion are two of the all-pervading complex systems that human beings have invented and in which they have been embedded for millennia. For centuries, authors have attempted to unambiguously define and better understand *myth* and *religion*, with limited consensus.

Defining Mythology

Jaan Puhvel, a comparative linguist and mythologist, explored the possible origin of the word *myth* and ended up suggesting that:

> *In myth are expressed the thought patterns by which a group formulates self-cognition and self-realisation, attains self-knowledge and self-confidence, explains its own source and being and that of its surroundings, and sometimes tries to chart its destinies.*[53]

Joseph Campbell, probably the world's leading authority on myth, describes myth in a variety of ways:

- Clues to the spiritual potentialities of human life
- The experience of meaning
- The experience of life—it puts your mind in touch with the experience of being alive.[54]

Encyclopedia Britannica describes a myth as:

> *[A symbolic narrative] usually of unknown origin and at least partly traditional, that ostensibly relates actual events and that is especially associated with religious belief. … As with all religious symbolism, there is no attempt to justify mythic narratives or even render*

---

[53] Puhvel (1989), p. 2.
[54] Campbell (1991), p. 5.

them plausible. Every myth presents itself as an authoritative, factual account, no matter how much the narrated events are at variance with natural law or ordinary experience.[55]

Most authorities agree, as do most online dictionaries, that the word *myth* may or may not imply falsehood.[56] Mythologist Campbell claims that myth is not a lie:

> *… it is an organisation of symbolic images and narratives, metaphorical of the possibilities of human experience and the fulfillment of a given culture at a given time. Mythology is a system of images that endows the mind and the sentiments with a sense of participation in a field of meaning.*[57]

Myth plays a significant cosmological, cultural, and sociological function. Cosmologically, it provides a mechanism for humans to picture themselves in relation to nature—what Campbell sees as locating themselves in a relationship between Father Sky and Mother Earth. Culturally and sociologically, myth works to create, support, and validate a specific set of culturally appropriate social, moral, and ethical beliefs.[58]

Probably the most highly regarded author on the beliefs of contemporary Judaism, and a winner of a Jewish Book Council National Jewish Book Award, is Howard Schwartz. Howard Schwartz's book *Tree of Souls* (2007) is regarded as the first comprehensive anthology of Jewish mythology. Schwartz discusses the two possible definitions of the word *myth* and accepts that the term can contain truths and non-truths.

The use of the word myth throughout the current book is as defined by Schwartz without an assumption about its veracity:

> *Myth refers to a people's sacred stories about origins, deities, ancestors, and heroes. Within a culture, myths serve as the divine charter, and myth and ritual are inextricably bound.*[59]

From mythology to religion

Encyclopedia Britannica has analysed the stages in the evolution of Mesopotamian mythology towards organised religion between the fourth and first millennia BCE. They suggest that the unfolding of myth towards organised religion in Mesopotamia involved identifiable stages:

---

[55]   See: https://www.britannica.com/topic/myth retrieved on 19 October 2022.
[56]   See for example: https://www.dictionary.com/browse/myth.
[57]   Campbell (2001), pp. 1-2 and p. 8.
[58]   Campbell (2001), p. 103.
[59]   Schwartz (2007), p. xliv.

- worship of the forces of nature, often in non-human forms
- a gradual characterisation of gods of the planets in human form, each with a specific function (sun, moon, planets, fertility)
- by the second and first millennium BCE, a growing emphasis on personal religion, including concepts of sin and forgiveness
- with the emergence of an alphabet and a literary tradition (1500 BCE onwards)—religious texts proliferated, including 'god lists', myths, magic, epic stories, hymns, laments, prayers, psalms, rituals, omen texts, and incantations
- socio-cultural and religious organisation, each entered into a monarchical structure dominated by a single sovereign leader (god and king) of an imagined or real 'nation state'.[60]

Defining Religion

The word *religion* has avoided an agreed and unambiguous definition. Priest, linguist, and ethnologist Wilhelm Schmidt defined religion as:

- Subjectively, it is the knowledge and consciousness of dependence upon one or more transcendental personal powers, to which man stands in reciprocal relation.
- Objectively, it is the sum of the outward actions in which it is expressed and made manifest as prayer, sacrifice, sacraments, liturgy, ascetic practices, ethical prescriptions, and so on.[61]

Archaeology Professor Kit Wesler has attempted to explain how religion has been defined in theory, anthropology, evolutionary psychology, archaeology, and in terms of symbols, scale, complexity, and organisational frameworks, without really determining a concise and unambiguous definition.[62]

Biblical scholar Ziony Zevit defined religion in the following way:

- acknowledgment of a reality of supernatural beings, forces, powers, and cosmic existence
- reverence for objects, places, times, and actions considered sacred, that is, separated from ordinary/profane objects, places, times, and actions

---

60   See: https://www.britannica.com/topic/Mesopotamian-religion/Stages-of-religious-development retrieved on 15 November 2022.
61   Schmidt (2014), p. 2.
62   Wesler (2014) pp. 1-29.

- regularly repeated ritual activities for a variety of purposes, including ritual magic
- conformance to stipulated codes and accepted norms alleged to have been revealed by the supernatural beings, forces, or powers
- communication with the supernatural through prayer, singing, drumming, or dancing
- experience of feelings described by participants as awe, fear, bliss, mystery, guilt, adoration, or obligation
- espousing and maintaining a holistic, though not necessarily systematic, unified whole or worldview of the universe
- association with, and conformity of one's own life priorities to, a group of like-minded people bound by this worldview.[63]

Robert Bellah (after Lindbeck) believes that religion can be best understood by moving conceptually backward and forwards between three concepts:

- religion as a series of propositional truth claims that are stated conceptually
- religion reflecting a general human capacity for religious experience that is actu-alised differently in different religious traditions
- a basic human preference for symbolic forms that, amongst other things, shape religious experience and religious emotions.[64]

Webb Keane believes that 'in the history of social and cultural anthropology, the category of "religion" has long stood for the general problem of apparently strange beliefs'.[65]

As early as 1913, leading American sociologist Charles A. Ellwood proposed that, despite religion being largely about certain metaphysical beliefs, such as a belief in God, and in the soul and in personal responsibility, it was primarily a socio-cultural phenome-non that has played a critical part in cultural evolution. This is essentially independent of any attempt to examine the worthiness or scientific basis for the various religious claims, beliefs, rituals, or practices. Religion, and in particular organised religion, plays a key role in conservative emotional, social, cultural, and moral control.[66]

An online search produces many possible definitions, but *religion* can most probably and most succinctly be defined as:

---

[63] Zevit (2001), pp. 11-13.
[64] Bellah (2011), pp. 11-12.
[65] Keane (2008), p. S110.
[66] Ellwood (1913), pp. 292-300.

A set of beliefs concerning the cause, nature, and purpose of the universe, especially when considered as the creation of a superhuman agency or agencies, usually involving devotional and ritual observances, and often containing a moral code governing the conduct of human affairs.[67]

Myth and *religion* differ in scope but have overlapping aspects. Generally, mythology can be considered a key component of religion, but religion also includes aspects of ritual, morality, theology, prayer, sacrifice, sacraments, liturgy, and mystical experience.

Defining Spirituality

Spirituality is clearly different from religion and can be associated with experiences that have neither a transcendent reference point nor, necessarily, an implication of non-material forces, persons, or gods.

The word *spirit* has a very long history. It began in the Western Eurasian Steppe in the formative years of the Proto Indo-European language (see *Indo-European language group*, page 64). It most likely originated in the language of the Kurgan cultural group located in the Pontic Steppe north of the Black Sea some five thousand or more years ago. The Kurgan word was *spies* which meant *breath* or *to breathe*. The Latin form is *spiritus* which also had the original meaning of *breath* or *breathing*. Over time the word developed a wider range of polysemic meanings. French linguist Alexandre François has documented the evolution of the very many meanings of the word *breathe* (and by association, *spirit*) to include [68]:

- breath of life
- vital force
- living
- soul
- divine breath – supernatural power
- supernatural being (good/bad) spirit

American neuroscientist and philosopher, Sam Harris believes that *spirituality* is an achievable experience of the human mind independent of religion. He sees self-transcending love, ecstasy, feelings of bliss, and inner light as achievable inner spiritual experiences available through Buddhist practices, meditation, experiences of conscious peace and self-reflection.[69]

Elkins has proposed that human spirituality has six qualities:

- it is universal

---

[67] SOURCE: https://www.dictionary.com/browse/religion retrieved on 11 February 2021.
[68] Francois, (2008), p. 202.
[69] Harris, (2015).

- it is a uniquely human phenomenon
- its common core is a phenomenological longing for the sacred (based on things and experience rather than a sense of being)
- it reflects a human capacity to respond to the unknown, the mysterious, the awe-inspiring or the supernatural
- it is characterised by a 'mysterious energy', aligned with a search for the 'sacred' in its broadest definition (being experienced or felt in the achievement of goals, roles, responsibilities, experiences, or relationships)
- its ultimate aim is compassion and loving action towards others.[70]

Controversial neuropsychologist and cosmologist[71], Rhawn Joseph, believes that spiritual consciousness and related symbolism are specifically linked to the evolution of the temporal and frontal lobes in early hominins. He believes that the ability to imagine the existence of a soul, spirits, ghosts, and the related creation of rituals to better understand and control these goes back some 30,000 years. Joseph believes that these beliefs can be directly linked to the growth and evolution of the temporal and frontal lobes in the human brain over thousands of years. He claims that this neurophysiological capability is directly linked to the emergence of love, fear, mystical awe, spiritual consciousness, religious symbolism, and ritual.[72]

Institutionalised spirituality has traditionally been the prerogative of organised religions. However, in more recent times, it has been defined as beliefs about an individual human's inner search and innate yearning for the 'sacred' or the 'sacred experience' detached from myth and religion. Louise Delagran at the University of Minnesota's Earl E Bakken Center for Spirituality & Healing has proposed that whilst spirituality might incorporate some elements of religion, they are not the same. They are two overlapping concepts. Delagran defines spirituality in the following way:

Spirituality is a broad concept with room for many perspectives. In general, it includes a sense of connection to something bigger than ourselves, and it typically involves a search for meaning in life. As such, it is a universal human experience—something that touches us all.

---

[70] Elkins (1998), pp. 32-33.
[71] For example—Rhawn Joseph has controversial views on the interplanetary origin of life and disagrees with the Darwinian version of human evolution.
[72] Joseph (2011).

People may describe a spiritual experience as sacred or transcendent or simply a deep sense of aliveness and interconnectedness.[73]

Myth and metaphor in the search for transcendence

A common concept across the many definitions of religion, mythology, spirituality, the sacred, personal journeys, and meditation is 'transcendence'. Transcendence implies an experience that goes over and above normal experience or beyond the limits of the known. The word combines the Latin prefix for 'beyond' with the word *scandare*, which means 'to climb'. Transcendence is literally *to climb beyond*.

Joseph Campbell believes that in common use, transcendence can have two distinct meanings—to go past, outside, or beyond something or something that is beyond all conceptualisation/beyond the concepts of the human mind.[74] It implies moving beyond or exceeding physical needs/limits and escaping reality to a more peaceful place (emotionally and/or spiritually). Campbell sees the transcendent as unknowable and unknown.[75] He draws extensively on Eastern/Oriental cults (Zen Buddhism, Hinduism, Chinese yin-yang) to emphasise that the search for the unknown is an inner spiritual search for meaning and experience.

German-Swiss psychologist and philosopher Karl Jaspers hypothesised that there was an historical period (around the first millennium BCE) when, at approximately the same time, most mythologies moved away from immediate and local concerns and towards transcendence. This included Persian Zoroastrianism, Confucianism, Daoism, Indian metaphysicians (Hinduism, Buddhism, Jainism), and Greek and Hebrew philosophers. Jaspers referred to this as the 'Axial Age' because it involved a shift or turnaround in mythological, philosophical, and religious thinking and focus. Pre-axial thinking was 'what' and 'how' thinking about the materialistic world, which focused on explaining the world in a narrative and analogical style. Axial thinking witnessed a transition to 'why' thinking, which was more analytical and reflective, with a long-term spiritual focus.[76]

In the Axial Age, scribes across most of the prehistoric religions, at approximately the same time, created myths, metaphors, historical characterisations, symbols, and stories around this entirely human inner search for meaning. The metaphors they interweaved

---

[73] See: https://www.takingcharge.csh.umn.edu/what-spirituality retrieved on 20 May 2022.
[74] Campbell (2001), p. 92.
[75] Campbell with Bill Moyers (1991), p. 56.
[76] See: https://www.britannica.com/list/the-axial-age-5-fast-facts retrieved on 25 January 2023.

into their religious texts allowed their followers to realise the transcendent, infinite, and abundant nature of being.[77]

To Joseph Campbell, the role of myth and religion is largely this pursuit of transcendence—an escape, an awakening to the experience of awe, wonder, humility, and respect for the mystery of life. Since the first millennium BCE, religious scribes across all religions have been writing about transcendence using a mix of metaphor, poetry, imagination, mysticism, and creativity to unfold stories that embody beliefs about life, the universe, the unknown, the sacred, and the divine.[78] These are not factual or true stories. They are mechanisms, metaphorical representations of spiritual realities, that reflect lessons of life and the exclusively human search for meaning and experience of the unknown. Their persistence can be largely attributed to the unique human variant of the NF1 "knowledge gene" which gave the ability to remember, learn and store complex knowledge system (oral, spatial, musical, mytholigical).[79]

The transition from the sacred to the divine

In prehistoric times, through totemists, animists, and shamanists, the early hunter-gatherers tended to see the sacred as inherent in all things. It was the responsibility of humans to respect, support, and represent the animate and inanimate to ensure wellbeing, survival, and order in life and the universe around them. The sacred could be found in places (mountains, rivers, caves) that required special respect and through certain rituals. The sacred could be in imagined beings—ghosts, ancestors, spirits, and demons that were regarded as purveyors or protectors of both good and evil. The sacred was often identified through deification (for example, of the planets), but these gods and goddesses were not capable of conscious responses to human behaviour. They personified, or were responsible for, specific aspects of creation, life, and human survival or were the purveyors/embodiment of divine principles or qualities.[80]

The transition from this notion of the sacred to one involving gods and goddesses that could actively observe, judge, respond, and intervene in human behaviour emerged initially from the Sumerians and the Zoroastrians (from around 4000 BCE onwards). This came in parallel with the emergence of abstraction, symbolism, and a belief in anthropomorphic gods and goddesses who had superior human-like characteristics and talents and were hierarchically organised like the human organisations of the time.

---

[77] Campbell (2001), p. 6.
[78] Campbell (2001), pp. 37-42.
[79] Kelly, (2024), pp.9-31.
[80] Holland (2010), p. xxvi.

In general, across all prehistoric locations, divine messages or responses were mediated by an intermediatory specialist who was the recognised conduit and interpreter who could implore the gods for a message or a response.[81] The notion of the 'sacred' began to transition to a notion of the 'divine'—the sacred gods as predetermined symbols that were incapable of judging or responding uniquely to human behaviours transitioned into anthropomorphic gods and goddesses who could actively intervene as and when required or as was their whim.

Ancient mythologies gradually transitioned into a belief that life was a continuous conversation and negotiation with gods and goddesses who had superior human-like motivations and abilities to respond. This concept was eventually hybridised and embedded into most of the leading contemporary mythologies, including Judaism and Christianity. The notion of a divine mediator began with shamans and transitioned through a belief in god-kings to priests, pastors, and holy men.

The cognitive and imaginative invention of religion

Geologist and geochemist Marc Defant has explained how the emergence of hominins was largely the result of rare, statistically improbable events in galactic time.[82] The unique evolution of life on Earth was the result of an unusual coincidence of favourable events and circumstances. One outcome was the development over time of the unique size of the human species' brain relative to body mass. This unique brain, plus the comparatively longer human species growth, development, maturation, and reproductive rates (longer gestation periods, slower post-natal maturation rates, older age of reproductive maturity and longer life spans) was largely responsible for the abilities that differentiated humans from all other species and previous hominins.[83] The evolutionary biological advantages and the human brain-to-body mass ratio created extraordinary abilities to imagine, invent, make tools, share information, cooperate, communicate, and organise collectively.

Charles Ellwood saw religion as emerging from these abilities for human self-consciousness and powers of abstract thought and reasoning.[84] In a similar vein, Yuval Noah Harari describes the critical role played in human evolution by the unique ability

---

[81] Brown, D. (2006), p. 73.
[82] See: Why We are Alone in the Galaxy | Marc Defant | TEDxUSF—YouTube retrieved on 2 February 2023
[83] See: https://www.mpg.de/617475/pressRelease20101111 retrieved on 18 February 2023.
[84] Ellwood (1913), p. 295.

to create explanations of the world through the interaction of imagination, ideas, images, and fantasies.[85]

These unique cognitive abilities were instrumental in the evolution of the human species across tens of thousands of years. They were instrumental in the development of religions. They are responsible for the many different attempts to explain the unknown and share this information. It has resulted in the more than four thousand different religious explanations of life and the universe currently promoted across the globe.

Yuval Noah Harari believes that what differentiates the human species from other species is the human imagination's ability to create believable fictional stories. It is not so much the capabilities of individual humans that differentiate the species from others, but rather the ability to develop flexible, collective, collaborative, large-scale fictional stories and systems. Religion is but one of these fictional realities, along with culture, economics, legal systems, nationhood, statehood, human rights, business entities, corporations, kinship and family systems, and sophisticated networks of cooperation. To Harari, the human species has two realities—one related to objective entities (rocks, trees, climate) and the other based on the ability to imagine and implement non-objective fictional realities and shared fictional systems.[86]

Harari's belief in the uniquely human ability to imagine through the creative power of the human brain has some affinity with Rhawn Joseph's theory that the growth and evolution of the temporal and frontal lobes correlate with the emergence of love, fear, mystical awe, spiritual consciousness, religious symbolism, and ritual.[87] Modern science has identified the temporal lobe as a key player in the processing of emotions, affectation, language, and aspects of visual perception. Modern science has identified the frontal lobe as a key player in expressive language, and the ability to plan, organise, and control emotions and behaviour. Joseph Campbell, the world's leading mythologist, claims that the images and energy of the metaphorical language of myth and religion flow from the common source of human imagination.[88]

Almost all commentators, whether religious or not, see religion and language as imaginative tools that are culturally unifying and culturally differentiating forces. Harari believes that these systems imagined and implemented by the human species are not like

---

[85] Harari (2015), p. 42.
[86] Adapted from https://www.ted.com/talks/yuval_noah_harari_what_explains_the_rise_of_humans?language=en retrieved on 2 June 2022.
[87] Joseph (2011).
[88] Campbell (2001), p. xii.

DNA and are not transmitted genetically. He asserts that the human brain is not large enough to contain all the externally imagined systems that have evolved over time. They are imagined systems of social order that are propagated and defended by a variety of institutionalised systems (family structures, mores, laws, governments, economics, and religion).[89]

The wide variety of organised religious experiences fulfil a complex range of human personal, intellectual, social, and cultural needs. To construct mythologies, imagine other worlds, and invent religions are ubiquitous human characteristics, and there are many theories about why this is occurring and what unique role religion fulfils, including:

- A manifestation of the unique human species' ability to imagine and invent arbitrary systems of belief and to collectively believe in them as if real and meaningful[90]
  - religion is an imagined and fabricated/fictional reality, as are, for example, democracy, money, ideologies, politics, and capitalism
  - a manifestation of the human species' intellectual shift from material thinking to abstract and symbolic metaphorical thinking
  - a result of the transition from hunter-gatherers focusing on the essential or essence of self and things to a collective urban and ideological focus on an existential, transcendental, and meaningful existence.[91]
- A material expression of a universally held human search for meaning[92]
  - a natural cross-cultural neurological need for a wider spectrum of complex human consciousness including altered states of consciousness/trance-like experiences
  - a universal human condition seeking emotional closure through imagining the existence of an unseen supernatural realm
  - creating a blissful mental state that will lift people collectively above the turmoil of daily life.
- Building confidence about the unknown
  - giving meaning and purpose to life beyond the utilitarian
  - making the world less frightening and reducing feelings of hopelessness

---

[89] Harari (2015), pp. 134-137.
[90] after Harari (2015).
[91] Bierlein (1994), p. 93.
[92] Lewis-Williams (2010), pp. 136-148 and Kneale (2013), pp. 7-8.

- fulfilling a human desire for continuity, certainty, comfort, security, and pre-dictability
- projecting and personifying human cultural, social, ethical, and personal values into the unknown powers of the universe
- creating an explanatory framework for supernatural, transcendental, and spiritual experiences, or things that are beyond understanding or human control.
- Reinforcing cultural/ethnic proprietary
  - differentiating beliefs, rituals, and practices from others
  - cultural unification, strengthening nationalism—claiming unique historical origins, pre-eminence, and unique spiritual knowledge
  - subjugating individual interests, impulses, and waywardness to a moral and ethical loyalty, devotion, self-restraint, and self-sacrifice for the greater good or for the sake of a larger group (community, cult, religion, country, culture, nation and/or society)
  - providing cultural legitimacy and membership.
- Creating a sense of belonging
  - reinforcing a sense of community and belonging
  - collectively and collaboratively belonging to or believing in something bigger than the known and the currently explicable.
- Replacing risk and responsibility with reassurance
  - creating another entity to which a person can turn when faced with the unknown, a crisis, loss of confidence, fear, pain, 'evilness', or powerlessness
  - imagining a higher being that is omnipresent and omnipotent and that can offer shelter, comfort, and succour in difficult emotional times
  - giving social values, morality, and ethical practices a religious sanction overseen by an invisible personal god/spiritual being
  - energising life through these sanctioned and outsourced hopes and fears.
- Social and behavioural control
  - confirming and validating traditional ideals, beliefs, morals, and values
  - systemic endorsement of what is 'right' and 'wrong' and how this is rewarded/punished
  - creating a customary reality by universalising values and making them absolute

- an organised system of defining and demarcating beliefs and values as part of the machinery of social control and organisational cohesion—alongside other agencies such as language, social stratification, and government.

This is a complex package of hypothesised needs and expectations that, when achieved and believed, can and have led historically to happiness and fulfilment. But they have led to fundamentalism (strict, unwavering attachment), fanaticism, self-righteousness, cultism, and/or ruthlessly-enforced conformity for members and the suppression, invasion, or conversion of non-believers.[93]

Understanding the collective religious experience

The emergence of group-mindedness

Psychologist and linguist Michael Tomasello and his colleagues have undertaken a comprehensive analysis of the evolution of group-mindedness in humans.[94] They have identified the emergence of multiple forms of group-mindedness and cooperation over time with the transition from hunter-gatherers to contemporary civilised societies. Tomasello and his colleagues hypothesise that hunter-gatherer collaborative foraging required a set of skills that clearly differentiated the human species from other related mammalian primate species. The levels of communication, collaboration, and commitment to a shared goal provided the basis for the gradual emergence of prosocial behaviour, interdependence, and altruism.

As the human species groups got larger, sedentary, more structured, interdependent, and complex, concepts of convention, conformity, coherence, uniformity, the enforcement of social norms, group-mindedness and institutionalisation became key mechanisms for collective certainty and control. This package of attributes established the notion of culture, group identification, and the unique way each group thinks about the world and relates to one another as social and moral agents.

Religious practices are one of these group-minded cultural mechanisms. As Yuval Noah Harari has highlighted, it is a mistake to look for differences at the level of individuals and families. Significant, even astounding, differences begin to appear when thousands of human species co-locate. The systemic differences are largely driven by attempts

---

93   See for example: Rowland (2008); Roy (2015).
94   Tomasello et al (2012); Tomasello (2014).

to define and explain the world through the interaction of imagination, ideas, images, and fantasies.[95]

Person-independent standing patterns of behaviour

Psychologists William James,[96] and Kurt Lewin,[97] gestalt psychologist, Kurt Koffka,[98] and ecological psychologists, Roger Barker, Harold Wright, and Paul Gump[99] introduced the notion of *holism* or 'the totality of the situation' to understanding collective human behaviour. They see human species' behaviour as a complex integration of the person through thought/cognition, memories, emotion, perception, attitudes, expectations, physical reactions, and action (James and Koffka); sensation, instincts, and habits (James); the context of the environmental milieu/behaviour setting (Barker, Wright, and Gump); or the 'life space' (Lewin) in which they find themselves. In their day, these psychologists were promoting radical ideas for a psychological profession that had largely focused on reducing thought, motivation, and behaviour into infinitesimally small parts of individual behaviour for analysis.

The ecological psychologists (Barker, Gump, and Wright) specialised in observing humans in their usual day-to-day habitats. They observed that humans experience (passing in and out of) many different 'behaviour settings'.[100] They observed that these behaviour settings tend to contain person-independent 'standing patterns of behaviour'—the same behaviour repertoire and behaviour patterns occur within these settings independent of which individuals are participating. Cultures and communities have stable patterns of interaction and behaviours based on historical, physical, symbolic, and environmental cues. These cues dictate (a) the degree of involvement and (b) the acceptable range of behaviours in a specific setting.[101]

The work of these revolutionary psychologists confirms that humans do not live in isolation but are essentially social animals. They are embedded in an historical, social, and cultural milieu that has created acceptable and repetitive patterns of collective behaviour. Following on from William James, Emile Durkheim described a concept of 'collective

---

[95]   Harari (2015), p. 42.
[96]   See: James (1948).
[97]   See: Lewin (1951).
[98]   See: Koffka (1935).
[99]   See: Barker and Wright (1955); Barker and Gump (1964).
[100]   See: Barker and Wright (1949).
[101]   See: Gump (1971).

effervescence' as the key driver of social alliances and solidarity. He saw this as overriding of individual interests and fundamental to religious beliefs and a shared notion of the "sacred".[102] Following Durkheim, sociologist Randall Collins believes that the interaction rituals/situations humans find themselves in provide the agency for understanding social life well beyond any focus on individual skills or talents.[103] Psychologist Albert Bandura has explained that *cultures evolve over generations and shape the ways people need to live to survive in the particular cultural milieu in which they are immersed.*[104] Human groups differentiate themselves through this ability to imagine and implement shared collectively believed systems (social, familial, economic, technological, religious). Each cultural group is comprised of a mix—often unique—of these shared behavioural and belief systems, which include religious practices.

Religion—a mechanism for cultural unification

In the early 1960s, Welsh socialist writer, political commentator and cultural theoriser Raymond Williams suggested that there are three definitions of (and ways to study) culture:

- as an ideal search for perfection through the discovery, description, and living of a certain agreed set of absolute and universal values. Here cultures develop and come to rely on established traditions
- a social artefact reflecting a particular way of life and a particular set of meanings and values
- a living, dynamic documentary in which culture is the gradual unfolding and recording of a body of intellectual and imaginative work, human thought, and experience over time.[105]

Contemporary cultures are a complex mix of all three of Raymond Williams' definitions. John B Thompson has reviewed many definitions of culture and specifically how culture relates to the promotion of specific ideologies. He sees the multi-dimensionality of culture. He emphasises the importance of distinguishing the concept of culture from the concept of civilisation. Culture is the unique package of practical, symbolic, and structural rituals that unite wholistically a specific group of humans.[106] In Yuval Noah Harari's

---

[102] See: Ono (1996); Draper (2014); Throop and Laughlin (2002).
[103] Collins (2004).
[104] Bandura (2006), p. 172.
[105] Williams (1961), p. 57.
[106] Thompson (1990), pp. 124-145.

words, culture is the 'network of artificial instincts that enable millions of strangers to cooperate effectively'.[107]

American anthropologist Donald Brown has proposed a concept of 'human universals' (also referred to as 'cultural universals'). These are 'those features of culture, society, language, behaviour, and mind that, so far as the record has been examined are found among all peoples known to ethnography and history.' Myths, legends, and beliefs are one example of what Brown refers to as absolute universals. Myths, legends, and beliefs have been found in one form or another amongst all peoples yet known.[108] Their commonality across cultures suggests that they could well have provided an evolutionary advantage.

Religious belief systems as cultural universals promote consciously and subconsciously the accumulated values, priorities, and expectations of each culture and society. This occurs in a way that transcends the simple distribution, promotion, and practice of beliefs, rituals, and prayers. Religions are actively shaping and reflecting cultural, social and community beliefs, values, ethics, rituals, practices, and anticipated outcomes. Like language, religion is a codification of a particular culture.

In Albert Bandura's words, 'People do not operate as autonomous agents. Nor is their behaviour wholly determined by situational influences. Rather, human functioning is a product of a reciprocal interplay of intrapersonal, behavioural, and environmental determinants.[109] People are mutually embedded in a reciprocal relationship with their communities, their cultural systems, and their beliefs.

Some theoreticians see the evolution of religion from hunter-gatherers to centralised institutional religions as a move from the more intuitive, episodic, sensory, experiential events (undifferentiated, participatory, mythic, chanting, dancing, drum beating, trancing) to a more rational, propositional, analytical, centralised doctrinal system of control (differentiated, symbolic, abstract, descriptive, linguistic, systematised, integrative, ritualised). It is claimed that these two conceptions (right-brain fiction versus left-brain fact) reflect quite different cognitive and mental functions.[110]

It is more likely that modern-day religions contain different levels of emphasis on both forms of religious experience. The growing evangelical Christian movement contains a greater emphasis on the right-brain functions while the traditional Catholic Mass emphasises more of the left-brain functions.

---

[107]   Harari (2015), p. 181.
[108]   Brown, D.E. (2004), pp. 47-48.
[109]   Bandura (2006), p. 165.
[110]   Watts (2020), pp. 90-91.

A significant gap in the science and religion literature

There are currently (as of 2023) more than four thousand different religions across the world. There have been many more religions throughout history. There is often a debate about the similarities or differences between religion as a concept and the concept of science.

The *Stanford Encyclopedia of Philosophy* contains a major summary of the emerging field of studying 'science and religion'. It proposes that:

> *['Science and religion'] is a recognized field of study with dedicated journals, academic chairs, scholarly societies, and recurring conferences. Most of its authors are theologians, philosophers with an interest in science or (former) scientists with long-standing interests in religion, some of whom are also ordained clergy.*[111]

A common cliché is that science is just another religion. Archaeologist David Lewis-Williams has explained the significant and obvious difference between religion and science in the following way:

> *Although there are many diverse cultures in the world, there is today only one kind of science. We know it works because it makes verifiable discoveries and produces technologies that function no matter what the beliefs of the people using them may be. The moon is not a divine dwelling place; it is a large lump of dry rock. We know this statement is true because scientific theories of physics and the complex technologies derived from them have enabled people to go there and check. We also know that belief systems founded on the unpredictable interventions of supernatural beings and forces could never lead to the success of science.*[112]

Stephen Jay Gould, American palaeontologist, evolutionary biologist, and historian of science, has proposed that science and religion vary substantially in their domains of expertise—domains that do not overlap:

> *Science is the empirical constitution of the universe, and religion is the search for proper ethical values and the spiritual meaning of our lives. The attainment of wisdom in a full life requires extensive attention to both domains.*[113]

---

[111]   Stanford Encyclopedia of Philosophy (2017), https://plato.stanford.edu/entries/religion-science/#Brie-HistFielScieReli retrieved on 19 July 2022.

[112]   Lewis-Williams (2010), pp. 23-24.

[113]   SOURCE: http://www.blc.arizona.edu/courses/schaffer/449/Gould%20Nonoverlapping%20Magisteria.htm retrieved on 25 February 2022.

This differentiation is supported by mythologist J F Bierlein, who explains that:

> *Science and myth are two different things directed towards two very different questions. Science tells us how things happen; myth (and religion) tells us why things happen. Science relies on objective observation to show us the causes of things. Myth and religion rely on things beyond our senses, our faculty of feeling in order to show us a purpose.*[114]

The 'why' approach of religion and the 'how' approach of science helps to differentiate the two approaches to understanding the universe and humanity. Religion and science are both attempting to develop an explanation for three concepts about life and the universe—causation, purpose, and agency.

Religion is based on a 'top-down' approach to explaining causation—where the universe and humanity originated. Based on the belief that the complexity of the universe could not have happened by chance, they propose the existence of an all-knowing 'intelligent designer'.[115] This is an imagined whole-of-universe, superior-being 'downward causation'. The intelligent designer is an anthropomorphic male god whose purpose for humanity is to be worshipped with a promise of eternal providence and life immortal in paradise. Lessons are learnt through 'divine agency'—messages from God through miracles or mysterious happenings and/or through God's endorsed mediators/agents (shamans, biblical prophets, Hindu monastic or holy men, clergy, clerics, popes, priests, pastors, rabbis, imams, and gurus). Religion lives in the natural world but it has a certain future that is largely controlled by supernatural forces.

Science is based on a 'bottom-up' approach based on the principles of physics, chemistry, evolution, and knowable natural laws. The purpose here is in some ways emergent, circumstantial, accidental, and opportunistic. Over time, the right mix of environmental conditions, elements, and opportunities has caused the gradual creation, growth, and evolution of life. Understanding this, and these basic principles, can give the human species some control over the direction and purpose of humanity. However, external circumstances can and will change, so the likely future remains uncertain. The agency (knowledge, direction, and learning) lies entirely within science and its application. Science lives in the natural world, which is subject to scientific study and understanding.

---

[114]   Bierlein (1994), pp. 314-315.
[115]   See: https://www.britannica.com/topic/intelligent-design retrieved on 19 July 2022.

This is an upwards understanding based primarily on applying the principles of physics, chemistry, and knowable natural laws.

Science writers and religious writers continue to argue the relative merits of each other's approach. This has led to a significant silo problem in studies of the history of religion and specifically the Hebrew and Christian Bibles. In 1918, American sociologist Professor Charles Ellwood bemoaned the fact that the rationalists and the religious tended to form two mutually exclusive philosophical camps in the study of religion. He stated:

> *Self-styled 'rationalists' have repeatedly asserted that science can find nothing in religious beliefs except superstition, error, or 'the will-to-power' on the part of the privileged class. On the other hand, representatives of religion have not infrequently proclaimed it to be outside of the field of science, and have sometimes resented its scientific study almost as if it were a species of 'sacrilege'. Both attitudes have made difficult a truly rational, scientific, and objective understanding of religion as a social phenomenon.[116]*

The separate research silos of 'reason' and 'religion' have a similar problem in their research about the Bible. These fields have expanded exponentially since 1918. A difficulty with each of these silos is that they are essentially self-reinforcing intellectual echo chambers. Adherents/practitioners tend to talk most often to people within their own jurisdiction/discipline. They rarely and insufficiently talk to or collaborate openly, honestly, and objectively with researchers outside their area. Each silo runs a very high risk of what psychologists refer to as *motivated confirmation bias*—a desire to research and interpret information in a way that supports pre-existing beliefs and values that they wish to maintain.[117]

Richard Delisle has described this dilemma in paleoanthropological research in the following way: 'Theories give meaning to facts and not the other way around, and … collecting observations is not a passive activity since it is always being done with a hypothesis in mind.'[118]

---

[116] Ellwood (1918), p. 335.
[117] Nickerson, R. (1998).
[118] Delisle (2012), p. 288.

Chapter 4

The Human Journey Prior to the Emergence of Israel

The emergence of the human species

It is now generally accepted that the human species is the sole survivor of several more archaic human/hominin species (*Australopithecus*, *Homo erectus*, *Homo rudolfensis*, *Homo neanderthalensis*, *Homo heidelbergensis*, *Homo floresiensis*, *Homo antecessor*, *Homo habilis*, *Homo naledi*, *Denisovans*). Several of these earlier hominids departed Africa in different waves hundreds of thousands of years prior to the human species.[119] These human ancestors, perhaps in three different waves containing three different but related hominins, travelled out of Africa commencing as far back as 1.8 million years ago.[120, 121]

The archaeological and the DNA evidence, taken together,

> [indicate] that humans did not evolve in a simple linear fashion, but that human evolution resembles an intricate branching tree with many dead ends, in line with the evolution of other species.[122]

The Eastern Mediterranean and, specifically, the Levant, represent a land bridge connecting Africa, Asia, and Europe. Early hominins had only one land route to travel out of Africa.

---

[119] Stewart and Stringer (2012); O'Connell et al. (2018); Reich (2019) pp. 39-45.
[120] SOURCE: https://australian.museum/learn/science/human-evolution/hominid-and-hominin-whats-the-difference/ retrieved on 13 October 2020.
[121] SOURCE: Baumer (2012), pp. 20-21; https://humanorigins.si.edu/evidence/human-fossils/species/homo-erectus retrieved on 13 October 2020; and https://www.nhm.ac.uk/discover/homo-erectus-our-ancient-ancestor.html retrieved on 13 October 2020.
[122] Stanford Encyclopedia of Philosophy (2017), p. 17.

There is extensive archaeological evidence of early hominins being in the Levant for hundreds of thousands of years and, specifically, in the location now identified as Israel. There is a high density of archaeological sites in Israel that are providing valuable information about the lifestyles and technologies of Palaeolithic (Old Stone Age) foragers, hunters, and fishers. A key and influential site is Tabun Cave at Mount Carmel, which is providing extensive information on the range and evolution of flint tools and other raw materials by human ancestors in Israel hundreds of thousands of years before the writing of the Bible.[123]

Anatomically modern humans (AMH), who are the ancestors of modern humans, followed the same route as these early hominins. They ventured slowly and sporadically out of Africa by foot and in family/tribal groups around 100,000 years ago. The human species most likely originated in East Africa (Sudan, Tanzania, Kenya, and/or Ethiopia).[124] They would have gradually travelled up the eastern side of the Nile River valley, across the only land bridge connecting Africa with Eurasia (where the Suez Canal is now located) to the Sinai Peninsula and up the east Mediterranean Coast. By tectonic plate, geographic, and geological circumstance, once they had crossed the land bridge to the Sinai Peninsula, the human species' ancestors' primary route out of Africa involved settling in or crossing through the Levant, the Middle East, the Fertile Crescent, the Caucuses, and the Eurasian Steppe—referred to as the Middle East, South-West and Central Asia.

From the ancient geographic crossroad of the Middle East, the human species opportunistically scattered over hundreds of thousands of years to the south, north, and east into the lands now called Saudi Arabia (south); the Near or Middle East, Central Asia, the Caucuses, and the Eurasian Steppes (north); and the Iranian Plateau and along the Indian Ocean coast to the Indus Valley (east). The Mediterranean and the Red Sea and the absence of seacraft and/or navigational abilities gave early humans little alternative. They were essentially wandering kin-based tribal foragers and hunter-gatherers with rudimentary stone tools and basic, family-oriented social structures. In the Levant and, specifically, in what is now Israel, there is evidence dating back some two to three hundred thousand years of human-like ancestors found in Mugharet el-Zuttiyeh ('the cave of the robbers') in Upper Galilee, Israel.[125]

---

[123]   See: Shimelmitz, Kuhn and Weinstein-Evron (2020).
[124]   Shreeve (2005).
[125]   Zuttiyeh | The Smithsonian Institution's Human Origins Program (si.edu) retrieved on 14 June 2021.

The journey to 'civilisation' and ethnic differentiation

The out-of-Africa journey eventually and largely opportunistically led to what is now called 'civilisation'. The transition from family-based, foraging hunter-gatherers living by hunting, collecting, fishing, scavenging, and forest gardening to herding, pastoralism, and agriculture through to towns and cities and a semblance of civilisation happened gradually for the human species over tens of thousands of years (Figure 1).

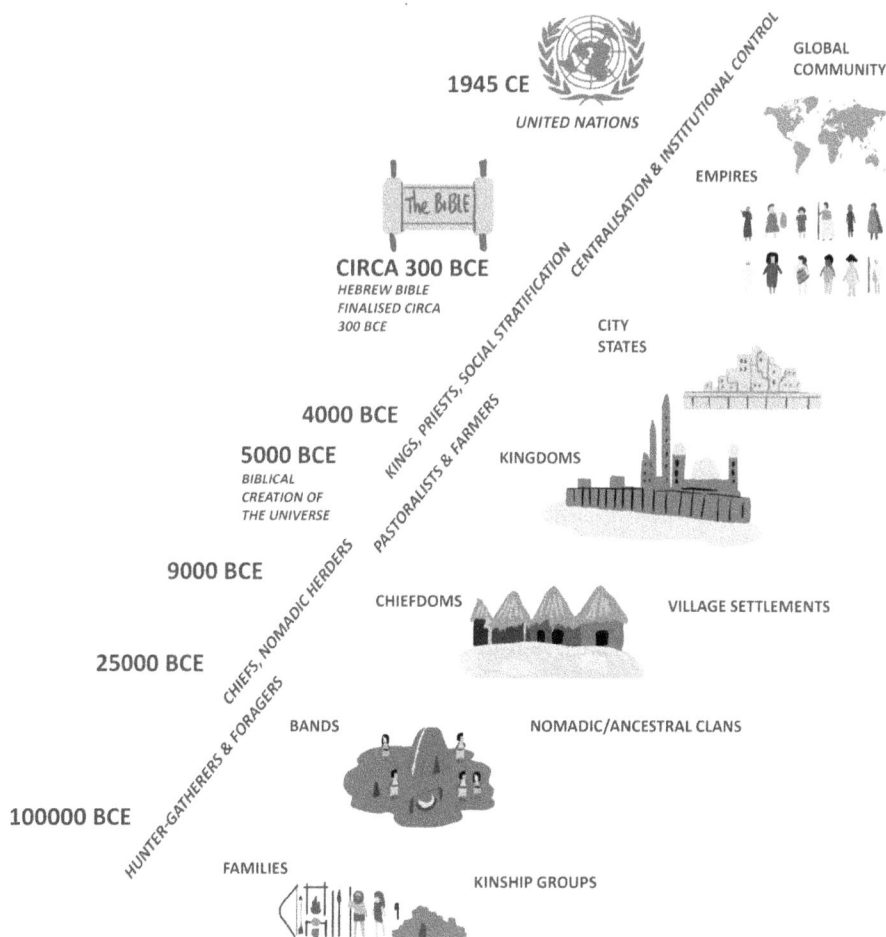

Figure 1: *Notional historical journey of the human species from hunter-gatherer to civilisation[a]*

---

[a] Based on information in Flannery (1972).

The earliest of the human species were family groups surviving as hunter-gatherers. The transition from family groups through nomadic bands to tribes, chiefdoms, kingdoms, cities, and empires reflected complex cognitive, intellectual, communication, symbolic, and mythological transformations over these thousands of years. The simplest step from family-based hunter-gatherers to cooperative nomadic bands has been described in the following way by world-renowned Higgs boson particle physicist Guido Tonelli in his book, *Genesis: The Story of How Everything began*, which outlines human history from the origin of the universe to modern civilisation:

> *In order to organise a large hunting party, you must have a strategy, a plan of attack devised with other members of the group, using sophisticated forms of communication and well-defined hierarchies. You need groups that are willing to shout and make a noise to beat and herd wild animals to a prearranged place, or towards a trap where the strongest and bravest can pounce.*[126]

Israeli historian Yuval Noah Harari claims that the human species' evolutionary journey towards group identification and differentiation was largely driven by cognitive and cooperative evolution:

> *How is it that we now have intercontinental missiles with nuclear warheads, whereas 30,000 years ago we had only sticks with flint spearheads? Physiologically, there has been no significant improvement in our tool-making capacity over the last 30,000 years … However, our capacity to cooperate with large numbers of strangers has improved dramatically.*[127]

Norwegian anthropologist Fredrik Barth has studied the social organisation of cultural differences and ethnic identity.[128] Barth has proposed that there is a range of characteristics of ethnic group identification. Barth's focus is on the ethnic boundaries that groups define themselves with rather than the cultural issues within the group. According to Barth's writings, the key characteristics of ethnic identity are:

- it is largely biologically self-perpetuating
- it is not defined by culture but by social organisation

---

[126]   Tonelli (2021), p. 205.
[127]   Harari (2015), p. 43.
[128]   Barth (2007).

- the roots of this social organisation are not cultural content but dichotomisation, such that the ethnic boundary is a social boundary formed through interaction with and differentiation from others
- it is based on ascription and self-identification. It is situationally dependent and can change
- it contains shared fundamental cultural values (e.g., class, ideology, political structures, social mores, language, locality, sexuality, gender, and religion)
- it has a made-up field of communication and interaction
- it contains a membership that identifies itself, and is identified by others, as constituting a category distinguishable from other categories of the same order.[129]

---

[129] Adapted from Potts (2004), p. 45; Barth (2007); Hummell (2014), p. 49.

Chapter 5

Geomorphological Opportunities for the Emergence of 'Civilisation'

The world is a complex place geodynamically and geomorphologically. Planet Earth evolved over millions of years. The geodynamics and geomorphological shaping of the planet created significant opportunities for the emergence and survival of the human species, civilisations, cultures, societies, and a variety of lifestyles and economies. Communities, cultures, mythologies, technologies, and lifestyles emerged incrementally and varied widely across time, depending largely in part on the geographic location and the initial opportunities provided by the dynamics of the tectonic plates.

The creation of the continents

Tectonic plate theory seems obvious now. The east coast of the South American continent looks like it could fit nicely into the profile of the west coast of Africa and the northern profile of Australia might even squeeze into the Indian/Bangladesh and Myanmar coastal profiles in the Bay of Bengal.

Sea-travelling explorers, as early as Magellan in the 1500s, had noticed this possibility on their maps. Palaeontologists found fossils of similar species on continents that are now separated by great geographic or oceanic distance. It was Alfred Wegener who proposed his theory of 'continental drift' in 1915, which really began a broader understanding of the world's tectonic plates and their movement over time.[130] Alfred Wegener's 'continental drift' theory was later disproved, but it laid the groundwork for the development of modern plate tectonics.

---

[130]   SOURCE: http://scecinfo.usc.edu/education/k12/learn/plate2.htm.

It is now accepted that the progressive movement of the world's tectonic plates eventually created the continents of the world as they are now known.

Earthquakes, volcanoes, and other active geologic features around the world contribute to this process and tend to align along distinct belts that correspond to the edges of the eight major tectonic plates. The eight major tectonic plates cover the bulk of the continents and the Pacific Ocean and there are many smaller plates (defined by scientists as *minor plates* and *microplates*).

Scientists estimate that the tectonic processes began on Earth some 3.3 to 3.5 billion years ago. The plates tend to jostle about in fits and starts punctuated by occasional earthquakes and volcanic eruptions. This movement of the tectonic plates occurs at an exceedingly slow time scale compared to the lifespan of a human or an animal. So behavioural and cultural adaptation to the ultimately significant geological and geomorphological changes can be easily accommodated within any human lifespan, historical period, societal or cultural epoch, age, or era.[131]

The emerging cradles of civilisation

From early beginnings and notionally through the stages and timing shown in Figure 1, the Middle East and the Central Asian regions were the first to see the emergence of uniquely different prehistoric human species communities and lifestyles. It was significantly influenced in these locations by the different geomorphology and the edible endemic wild animal and plant species available in each region.

Professor of Science Communication at the University of Westminster, Lewis Dartnell has outlined how the geomorphology (the juxtaposition of mountains, valleys, and rivers) created by the movement of the tectonic plates significantly impacted the emergence of the world's six best-known major ancient *cradles of civilisations* (Figure 2).

Dartnell has shown how tectonic plate movements and the resulting geomorphology facilitated the emergence of modern humanity and the gradual development of civilisation in these early locations—where floodplains contain rich soil and rivers provide irrigation for crops and a means of transportation—that were highly favourable for human life.

In the first instance, the gradual crushing together of tectonic plates produced depressed basins at the feet of mountain ranges from which flow rivers onto rich arable plains. The result is rift valleys that deliver a 'mosaic environment of different habitats'—delivering a variety of different locales in close proximity: woods and grasslands, ridges,

---

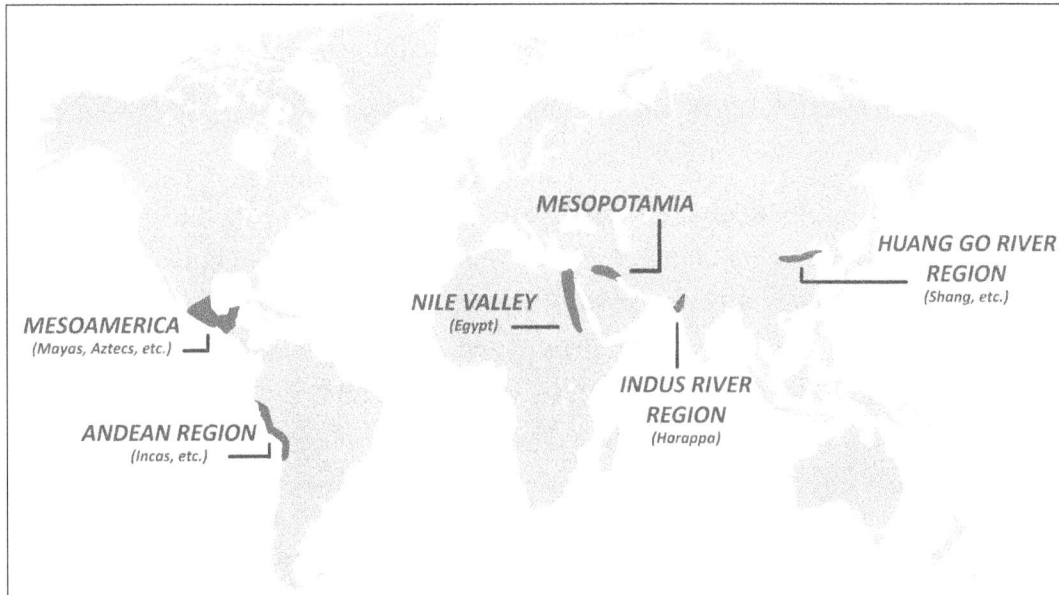

Figure 2: *The six locations afforded development opportunities by the impact of the tectonic plates*[a]

[a]   SOURCE: modified from https://evolutionistx.files.wordpress.com/2016/05/picture-41.png retrieved on 9 May 2023.

steep escarpments, hills, plateaus and plains, depressed basins, valleys, rivers and deep freshwater lakes on the floor of the rift.[132]

In the second instance, it is not just the depressed basins at the feet of mountain ranges that hold rich arable land. Volcanoes also produce fertile agricultural soil.[133] These geological, tectonic plate dynamics have produced a situation where most of the major ancient civilisations emerged in locations close to and exploiting the opportunities provided at tectonic plate margins.

The tectonic plate activity occurred in these several locations but at distinctly different times. In these locations, comparatively complex cultures, mythologies, and agricultural practices emerged between 4000 BCE and 1700 BCE. The tectonic plates and the resultant geomorphology created opportunities for the emergence of the following six possible 'cradles of civilisation':

- Mesopotamia (the Fertile Crescent including the Levant)
- Egypt (the Nile Valley)

---

[132]   Dartnell (2018), p. 12 and p. 28.
[133]   Dartnell (2018), p. 28.

- Indus Valley (north-western region of India)
- Huang Ho/Yellow River region (China)
- Norte Chico (on Peru's north-central Pacific coast)
- Mesoamerica (present-day Mexico, Guatemala, and Belize).

These six global opportunities all emerged where rivers, river plains and mountain ranges created a fertile environment for sedentary living and the emergence of agriculture and the domestication of animals. The emergence of early sedentary, agriculturally based communities occurred in several different locations in and around the Middle East and Central Asia but at approximately the same time. In Mesopotamia, north-western India, China, and Egypt this occurred, in part, because these locations had an interesting combination of qualities—a warm climate that encouraged rapid crop growth and an annual cycle of flooding that naturally regenerated the fertility of the soil.[134]

The opportunities, lifestyles, and emerging economies in the Middle East (Mesopotamia/ Fertile Crescent/Levant) and Central Asian (the Eurasian Steppe) regions were quite different, but, from around 12000 BCE, these two regions were to play a foundation role in the emergence of modern humans, modern languages, modern civilisations, and contemporary mythologies.

Barry Cunliffe has commented on the emergence from around 6000 BCE onwards of precocious economic, social, and fully fledged complex farming communities in two of these six locations—the Middle East (Fertile Crescent) and much further east in northern China (Yellow River and Yangtze valleys). He has stated (Figure 3):

Why the communities in these two regions should have become increasingly complex, moving rapidly along a trajectory that took them from simple foraging to organised food production and urban living, is, in large part, the result of geography.[135]

There was an additional geomorphological advantage created by the tectonic plates. Eastern Europe was connected to western China by a common latitudinal extensive grassland steppe. The geographical advantage of what is referred to as the Eurasian Steppe provided a natural west–east pathway/highway for innovation, cultural, linguistic, genetic, and mythological exchanges across Central Asia (Figure 4).

---

[134] https://www.britannica.com/technology/history-of-technology/Technology-in-the-ancient-world retrieved on 10 July 2021.

[135] Cunliffe (2017), p. 25 and p. 35.

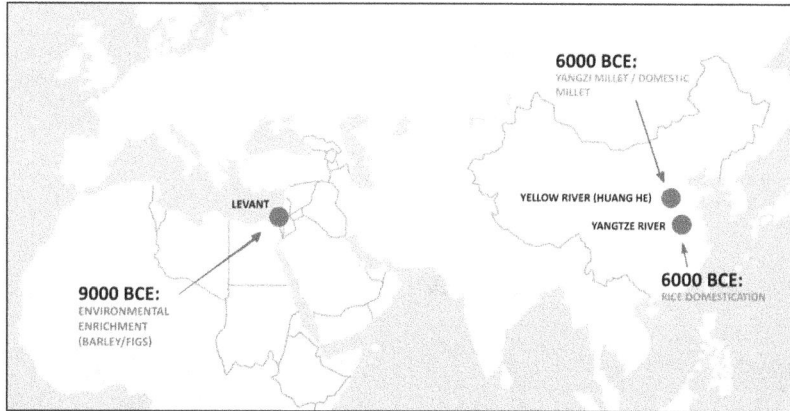

Figure 3: *The first fully-fledged complex farming communities in the Middle East and China showing their initial crops[b]*

---

[b] Map sourced from: https://sdaworldhistory.edublogs.org/u1/afro-eurasia-1kmfh96/ retrieved on 9 May 2023.

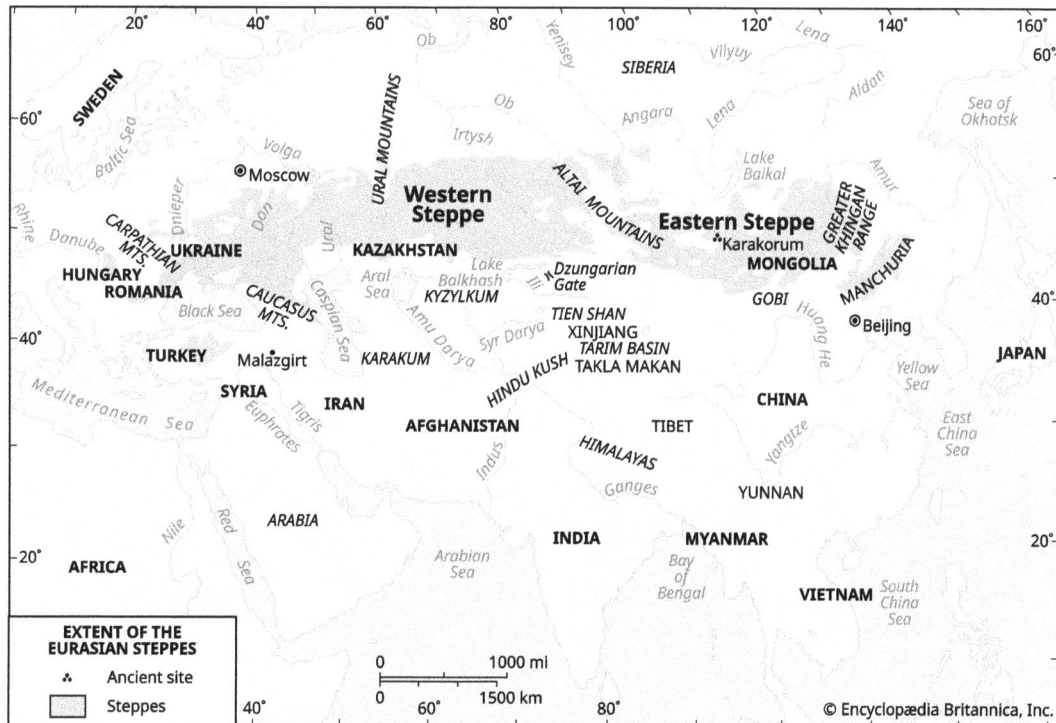

Figure 4: *The Eurasian Steppe[c]*

---

[c] SOURCE: https://www.britannica.com/place/the-Steppe retrieved on 9 May 2023.
Reprinted with permission from *Encyclopaedia Britannica*, © 2014 by Encyclopædia Britannica, Inc.

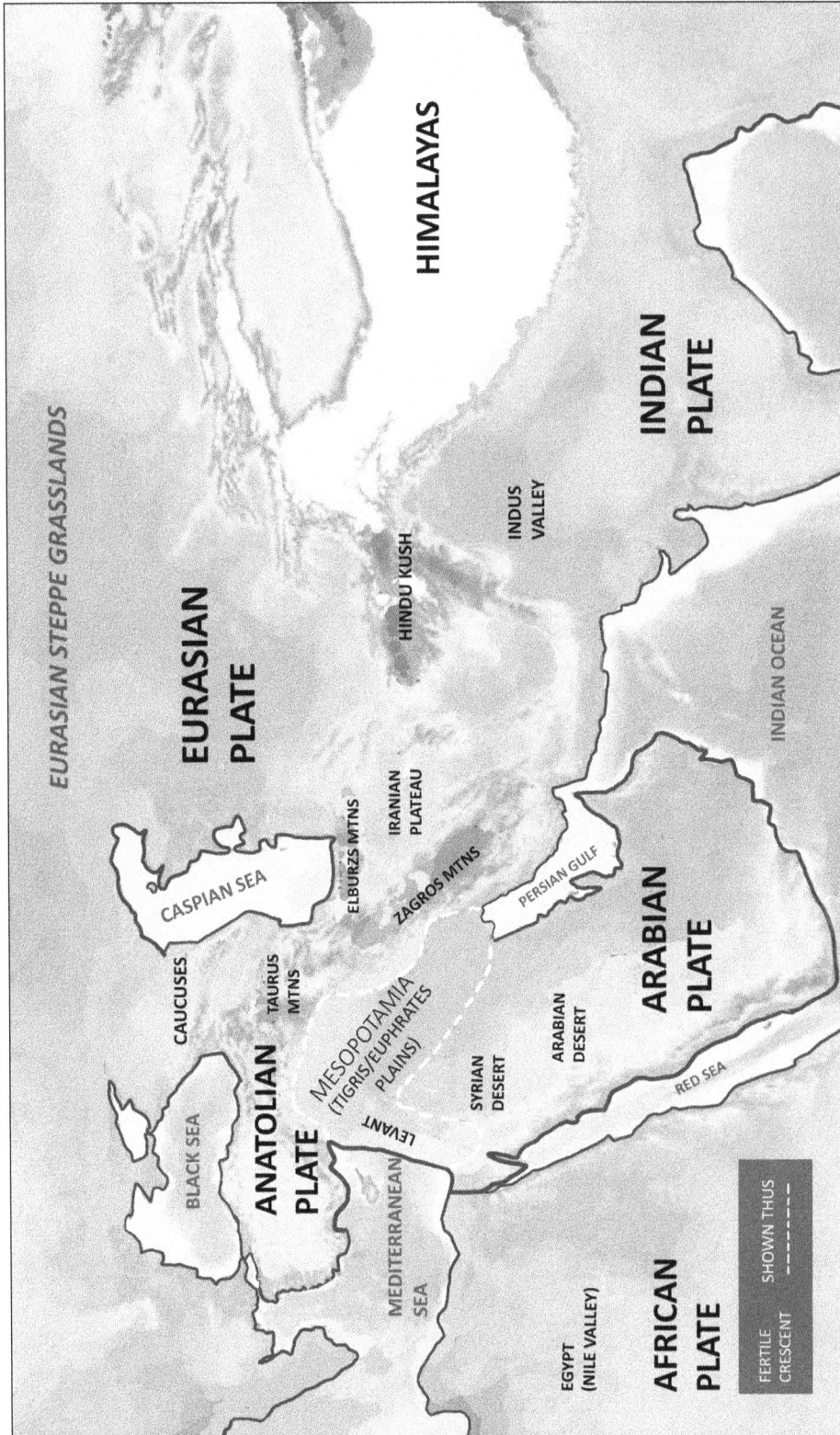

Figure 5: The main locations discussed in this book that were facilitated by the tectonic plates

To the south of the Eurasian Steppe, the Fertile Crescent, the Levant, Egypt, and Northern India were separated from the Steppe by a mixed combination of west-to-east geological and geomorphological barriers. This 'bridging', 'intermediate zone' of potential natural barriers included the Caspian, Black, and Aral Seas; the Caucus, Taurus, Zagros, Elburz, Pamir, and Altai Mountains; the Hindu Kush and Himalaya mountain ranges; and the great desert and semidesert regions of Central Asia (Figure 5).

Genomic research by the Max Planck Institute for the Science of Human History and the Eurasia Department of the German Archaeological Institute has found that geographic boundaries (the mountains and the steppe) tend also to be genetic boundaries. Over the centuries and across prehistory, an interaction zone formed where the traditions of the Mesopotamian civilisation interacted with the cultures of the Caucasus and the Great/Eurasian Steppe. Genetic research shows that the Maykop culture in the Caucuses (3700 BCE to 3000 BCE) is genetically far more related to civilisations to their south than to those in the adjacent steppes to their north.[136]

The Fertile Crescent emerges

Figure 5 illustrates the mountain ranges (along the fault line from north-west towards south-east) created by the crashing together at the intersection of the Arabian, Eurasian, and Indian tectonic plates. The crescent shape of the Fertile Crescent is a geomorphic opportunity—the arc of the Taurus and Zagros Mountains to the north and the southern incursion of the Syrian and Arabian Deserts formed this crescent shape. The opportunity developed here was enhanced by the availability of the two mighty rivers—the Tigris and the Euphrates—flowing south from the Zagros Mountains into the Persian Gulf and the availability of the Mediterranean Sea to the west (Figure 5). This was the main location that would deliver the first 'cradle of civilisation' and eventually the emergence of the Israelites and the Hebrew scribes.

The Central Asian mountain corridor emerges

The Ancient Middle East, especially the Levant and Mesopotamia, was geographically and opportunistically the first viable location for the human species to begin their journey out of Africa and to relocate their hunter-gatherer lifestyles. Their predecessors

---

[136] SOURCE: https://www.sciencedaily.com/releases/2019/02/190204085933.htm retrieved on 9 May 2023.

the Neanderthals, and the Denisovans many years before them, moved gradually along the shoreline of the Persian Gulf and the Arabian Sea to the north-west of India and the Indus Valley. From there, in pursuit of mammoth and bison, they moved into and settled in Siberia/Mongolia. There is a fortunate geomorphological opportunity provided for travel between the Middle East, Siberia, Mongolia, and western China. In addition to the movement of early species and early hominins from Africa up through the Middle East and into Siberia and Mongolia, this pathway provided opportunities for influences from Siberia and Mongolia to travel west into the Middle East and Europe.

The pathway referred to as the Central Asian Mountain Corridor travels in and around the mountain ranges from Siberia and through Mongolia skirting the Hindu Kush and the Elburz and Zagros Mountains (Figure 5). Like the Eurasian Steppe, this mountain corridor provided an alternative westward pathway for innovation. There is archaeological (material culture) and genomic evidence that, more than thirty thousand years ago, mass migration of North Asian hunter-gatherers from Siberia occurred along this corridor and had a major influence on technology and beliefs systems in the Middle East, Anatolia, and eventually Europe.[137]

The opportunities/advantages created by a common latitude

In addition to the opportunities created by the movement of the tectonic plates, the Northern Hemisphere provides two other major geographic opportunities that facilitated the early emergence of civilisation in that hemisphere and eventually in the Fertile Crescent.[138]

The first is the fact of the shared latitude and resultant similar climatic conditions on the east–west axis of the Eurasian Steppe. Localities distributed along the same latitude share the same day length, seasonal variations, and development ideas. Innovations can travel rapidly along this horizontal geographic axis. Animals, plants, and humans respond similarly to latitude-related features of climate, and these commonalities travel rapidly across communities living in the same and contiguous latitudes.

The second (and related) geographic advantage provided to prehistoric communities in the Northern Hemisphere is the existence of the west-to-east belt of grassland of the Great or Eurasian Steppe. This extends for some 9,000 kilometres from the Middle Danube

---

[137] See: https://arkeonews.net/the-migration-movement-that-started-from-siberia-30000-years-ago-may -have-shaped-Göbeklitepe/ retrieved on 1 July 2022.

[138] Diamond (2005).

region in what is now known as Hungary in the west through Ukraine and Central Asia to Manchuria in the east. The word *steppe* means 'wasteland' or 'trampled place; flat, bare' in old Russian. It reflects the fact that steppes are essentially vast, monotonous, treeless seas of grassland stretching out into the distance. They thrive in temperate climates in between the tropics and the polar regions and provided an excellent opportunity for prehistoric horseman cultures to travel and graze mainly sheep and cattle.

Although mountain ranges interrupt the Eurasian Steppe, dividing it into distinct segments; in prehistoric times, the prehistoric horsemen would cross these barriers easily. As a result, steppe peoples have interacted and shared innovation across the entire breadth of the Eurasian grassland for millennia.

Closely linked to these geographic advantages, and clearly a product of them, was the emergence of the ancient network of trade routes that would eventually become the Silk Road. The Middle East component parts of this trade route emerged in the Bronze Age (around 3000 BCE). The Silk Road, as it is now known, was not formally consolidated until the Han Dynasty of China in around 130 BCE. It then linked the regions of the ancient world in commerce between the ancient Greek city of Antioch to the Huang Ho/ Yellow River Region in China—largely along or adjoining the Eurasian Steppe.[139]

---

[139]   SOURCE: https://geography.name/silk-road/.

New Scientific Approaches to Understanding Prehistoric Communities' Origins and Influences

How innovation grows

In prehistoric times, ideas and innovations spread in one of two ways—by population movement and subsequent intermixing of genes (migration or invasion) or by trans-cultural learning (e.g., the prehistoric trade networks exposed different communities to different ideas). Scientists now accept that there is a strong correlation between geography, genetics, and linguistics in situations where populations have intermingled by geographic co-location or proximity. Prehistoric data from genomics, geography, and language tend to largely correlate.[140] There are some exceptions. Some religious groups have a prohibition on marriages with partners in the same location but not in the same religion. This can impact the influence of geographical proximity or cohabitation of a region on the other investigative factors.

The evolution of archaeological evidence

It is estimated that over 90% of human development occurred in prehistoric times prior to the emergence of a common alphabet and the written expressions of culture. The interest in past cultures and the desire to dig up evidence of their beliefs, their artefacts, and their lifestyles goes back thousands of years. As early as 550 BCE, the last king of Babylon,

---

[140]   See for example: Jeong et al. (2019).

Nabonidus, was involved in digging up the foundations of an older building. In around 230 CE, the Roman Emperor Alessandro Severo undertook failed attempts to excavate the ruins of Pompeii. In the seventeenth and eighteenth centuries CE, the antiquarian movement began, wherein elite persons began to demonstrate their interest in the past by collecting historical artefacts.[141]

Andrew Lawler, in *National Geographic*'s online magazine, described the emergence of an interest in archaeology in this way:

> *At least as far back as the last king of Babylon, more than 2,500 years ago, rulers and the rich have collected antiquities to bask in the reflected beauty and glory of previous times. Roman emperors transported at least eight Egyptian obelisks across the Mediterranean to embellish their capital. During the Renaissance, one of these pagan monuments was raised in the heart of St. Peter's Square.*
>
> *In 1710, a French aristocrat paid workers to tunnel through Herculaneum, a town near Pompeii that had lain largely undisturbed since the deadly explosion of Vesuvius in AD 79. The unearthed marble statues sparked a craze that spread across Europe for digging up ancient sites.[142]*

Prior to the emergence of writing, evidence of prior human activity hinged around the availability of sites/excavations in which one or all of four types of archaeological evidence of human habitation could be found:

- **Artefacts**—portable materials, including stone and other tools, grinding stones, clothing, plates, pottery, jewellery, weapons, figurines, carved objects
- **Structures**—megaliths, buildings, foundations of houses and other structures, post holes, walls, village layouts, remnants of ceremonial, ritual, or mythological buildings/structures
- **Organic and/or inorganic remains**—including fauna and flora remains, grain, seeds, animal bones, charcoal, minerals, shells/seashells
- **Evidence of other human activity**—fire/cooking pits, burial sites, burial structures and burial paraphernalia, human remains, cave paintings, rock carvings.

In the early days of archaeology, the primary motivation was either a religious crusade (to validate the Bible) or treasure hunting. Early amateur archaeologists were often engaged

---

141   Jewkes (2013).
142   Lawler (2021).

in a search for museum pieces (primarily artefacts). These could then be sent back to the explorer's home-country museums or for individuals to display evidence of their plunder of ancient artefacts in their display cabinets. Whether a religious crusade or a treasure hunt, early archaeology was rarely an effort to understand or try to place artefacts in a meaningful historical, locational, or cultural context. There are not many things more fascinating than a tangible ancient artefact unearthed mysteriously, visually interesting, suggesting something about cultural heritage, history, or justifying a specific ideology. Those heady early days of archaeology have successfully entertained the Hollywood movie industry for many years.

The first modern archaeologist was arguably John Aubrey, who investigated Stonehenge and other stone circles in Avebury, England, from around 1649 CE. It was not until the discovery of the Rosetta stone (dating from around 196 BCE) in 1801 CE in Memphis, Egypt, that the first decipherment of Egyptian hieroglyphics was made in the 1820s CE. This discovery opened the door to major advances in Middle Eastern and Egyptian archaeology. Anatolian/Turkish and Mesopotamian archaeology commenced in the early to mid-1800s. Detailed Egyptian and Levantine archaeology did not commence until the late 1800s.

Archaeologists are reluctant to identify fixed dates for the beginning and end of specific stages in human development. The stages that have been identified are based largely on archaeological evidence of developments in the use of stone, copper, bronze and iron tools and the skills and technology associated with the development of these tools. Conventionally, it has been referred to as the 'Three-Age System'—Stone Age, Bronze Age, and Iron Age.[143] Different parts of the globe transitioned through these stages at different times, so the following is a broad generalisation:

- The Palaeolithic Era (or Old Stone Age)—from the earliest evidence of hominins (around 2.6 million years ago) to around 50,000 years ago
- The Upper Palaeolithic Era (or Late Stone Age)—from around 50,000 years ago to 10,000 years ago
- The Neolithic Era (or New Stone Age)—beginning around 10000 BCE and ending between 4500 BCE and 2000 BCE in various parts of the world
- The Copper/Chalcolithic Age—from around 5000 BCE to 3000 BCE
- Bronze Age—from around 3300 BCE to 1200 BCE
- Iron Age—around 1200 BCE to 500 BCE.

---

[143]   Kuhrt (2009A), p. 9.

Archaeologists have given names to separately identifiable cultures within these different eras. Initially, in the absence of written records, most of the names chosen by archaeologists for identifying different historico-cultural groups used terms that reflected archaeological locations, common artefacts (mainly pottery), and burial and/or other cultural practices discovered in their excavations. Some examples include:

- Natufian Culture (13000 BCE to 9000 BCE)—a sedentary or semi-sedentary group of hunter-gatherers who had several permanent and temporary settlement sites in the Levant (modern-day Palestine, Israel, Jordan, Lebanon, and Southern Syria). Natufians are likely to be the first hunter-gatherers to start intermittent farming. They are named after a Shuqba cave (Wadi an-Natuf) near the town of Shuqba in the western Judean Mountains

- The Khiamian culture (9700 BCE to 8700 BCE)—named after the excavation site of El Khiam, situated on the banks of the Dead Sea, where researchers have found the oldest known chert (crystalline quartz) stone arrows heads with lateral notches. Evidence of the Khiamian culture has been found in Jordan (Azraq), Sinai (Abu Madi), and as far north as the Middle Euphrates (Mureybet)

- Halaf Culture (6500 BCE to 5500 BCE)—an early Mesopotamian farming society that emerged in northern Mesopotamia and Syria. They shared a common culture and produced pottery that is among the finest ever made in the Middle East. This culture is known as Halaf, after the site of Tell Halaf in north-eastern Syria where it was first identified

- The Kurgan culture (the Russian/nomadic Turkish word *kurgan* means 'embankment', 'artificial mound', or 'high grave')—Copper Age to Early Bronze Age (5000 BCE to 3000 BCE) Eurasian Steppe peoples who buried their dead in deep shafts within artificial burial mounds

- Shell Mound People, or Kitchen-Middeners—Stone Age hunter-gatherers who got their name from the distinctive mounds (middens) of shells and other kitchen debris they left behind. There is archaeological evidence of these peoples in North and South Europe, Iberia, North Africa, and North and South America around 4000 BCE to 2000 BCE

- The Maykop culture (3700 BCE to 3000 BCE). Named after a royal burial site found in Maykop in the Kuban River valley in the North-West Caucasus region

- Pit Grave, Ochre Grave, or Yamnaya culture (from the Russian word *yama*—'related to pits') (3300 BCE to 2600 BCE), a West Eurasian Steppe culture whose dead were interred in 'pit graves' rather than in communal structures

- The Canaanites, who livied in the Levant (3500 BCE to 1150 BCE). Their name most probably comes from an old Semitic/Hurrian word *kinaḫḫu* denoting 'reddish-purple,' referring to the rich purple or crimson dye produced in the area and the wool fabrics coloured with this dye

- Corded Ware culture—early European culture (3100 BCE to 2350 BCE) named after the cord-like impressions or ornamentation characteristic of their pottery

- Sintashta culture (2400 BCE to 1800 BCE), named after the Sintashta archaeological site. Probably the home of the earliest known chariots and the people who played a major role in the development of ancient mobile warfare

- Bell Beaker culture (2800 BCE to 1800 BCE)—named after the inverted-bell beaker drinking vessel used by these groups at the very beginning of the European Bronze Age

- Catacomb Culture (2800 BCE to 1700 BCE)—named after their burials, which were based on the shaft grave of the Pit Grave/Yamnaya culture with a burial niche added at its base that often contained ornaments such as silver rings and weapons (stone and metal axes, arrows, daggers, and maces)

- Timber Grave or Srubnaya (from the Russian word *srub*—'timber frame') culture (1800 BCE to 1200 BCE)—named after their use of timber constructions within their burial pits, which were grouped together in cemeteries consisting of five to ten kurgans

- The Urnfield culture (1300 BCE) from around the Danube. They are widely believed to be the forebears of the European Celts. Their name derives from their common burial practice of interring the cremated remains of their deceased in urns and burying the urns

- Israelites (1205 BCE onwards)—first mentioned in the Merneptah Stele by a name that identifies their belief in the Canaanite god El. The name 'Israel' in the Semitic languages means 'to contend, fight or wrestle [*isra* from *sarah*] with the Canaanite god (El)'. The first mention of the name Israel appears to reflect a specific mythological cult within the prehistoric indigenous Canaanite peoples.

There is a close link between specific types of archaeological evidence and the understanding of prehistoric lifestyles. Portable materials/artefacts in abundance and across many global locations have provided insights into the lifestyles of the human species' prehistoric hunter-gatherer ancestors. Once these ancestors settled down, evidence of new 'sedentary lifestyle artefacts' emerged in archaeological excavations. These included pottery, new composite tools, burial practices, centralised communal buildings, structured village layouts, common ritual objects, and stable fauna and flora remains. This evidence reflected the changing nature of these communities, their economies, and their cultural and religious practices.

In the modern scientific world, whilst archaeology provided the foundation for knowledge of prehistory, it has become just one piece in the jigsaw puzzle of how prehistoric humans, communities, and mythological beliefs evolved. Archaeology can be structured into three main categories—prehistoric archaeology (prior to the emergence of writing), historic archaeology (concerned primarily with the alphabet and written communications) and modern archaeology (multi-disciplinary and technologically advanced).

Modern approaches to archaeology now see archaeological evidence supplemented by a combination of geography, genomics, linguistics, written evidence, and sophisticated technology (radiocarbon dating, paleoclimatic methods, satellite imagery, and ground penetrating radar, for example). This combination of evidence delivers a much better and more comprehensive understanding of how populations, languages, genes, and ideas have spread throughout prehistory (prior to the availability of written evidence).

This multifaceted approach is what scientific researchers call *triangulation*—collaboratively using more than one science, method, or source, and coming from more than one research direction to focus on a specific topic. It significantly increases the likely factual nature or historical accuracy of the work and gives more likelihood of defensible confirmation of the findings.[144]

The impact of writing on archaeological evidence

As rudimentary forms of writing and evidence of symbolic communication began to emerge in archaeological excavations, more expansive and more reliable evidence about prehistoric cultures became available. Artefactual evidence, combined with written communications, demonstrates how different groups in geographic proximity, and with similar artefacts, technology, economies, burial practices, and built forms (houses and settlement patterns) began to evolve into identifiably differentiated cultures. This occurred as archaeology moved from artefact or location names to naming these cultures with the names they called themselves in their symbolic and available written communications.

With the emergence of rudimentary writing on archaeological artefacts, cultures were now able to be identified by the names they (or their neighbours) called them. This did not

---

144 See definition in Bycroft and Judd (1989).

happen until written evidence was found containing the names of the Eurasian Steppe warrior nomads the Scythians (900 BCE to 200 CE) and the Cimmerians/Kimmerians (800 BCE to 700 BCE). Archaeology moved towards defining geographic areas and eras by the names of the then-ruling empires (e.g., Assyrian, Babylonian, Persian, Greek/Hellenistic, Roman). This new nomenclature replaced the dependence on a generic name related to either a cultural practice, specific artefacts, or the location of specific archaeological sites.

Linguistic and genomic analysis supplementing archaeological evidence

Archaeology has been significantly enhanced by the growth of linguistics and genomics. Whilst language and genetic evidence are far less tangible than physical artefacts, they have both become major contributors to understanding and investigation into prehistory.

Philology is the systematic study of the development and history of languages while *linguistics* involves the study of the structure and development of a language and its relationship to other languages. Philology, linguistics, genomics, and archaeological analysis of material culture and artefactual evidence are seen as complementary tools in the scientific attempts to accurately reconstruct life as it was before the availability of an alphabet and written records.

Philology and linguistics have been used to accurately date works, construct the history of peoples, and determine the likely cultural, historical, and linguistic heritage of different peoples.

The role of linguistic analysis

The origin of different languages

The biblical explanation of the origin of the world's many languages is articulated in Genesis 11:1–9. Essentially, it claims that up until a certain time (estimated by biblical scholars to be around 3500 BCE—3000 BCE), there was only one language in the world. Apparently, this was the case until the people of Babylon decided to build a tower that went all the way up to bring them closer to heaven. This was the Tower of Babel. In retaliation, the Hebrew God inflicted them with multiple languages and scattered them across the globe. Biblical scholars interpret this allegory as evidence that their God created the world's profusion and diversity of cultures in around 3000 BCE as evidenced through this language metaphor.[145]

---

[145]   Hiebert (2007), p. 57.

The science of archaeology, archeoacoustics[146], and linguistics tells quite a different story. It is highly likely that different languages developed across a period from two million to 50,000 years ago. Many researchers believe that gestural communication in the development of prehistoric stone tool-making was the prelude to spoken language.[147]

Miyagawa, Lesure, and Nobrega hypothesise that the development of symbolic thinking and language owes a great deal to the cave art of early humans. Prehistoric cave art is ubiquitous across ancient cultures around the world. Ancient cave art exists on every major continent occupied by modern humans. Miyagawa and his colleagues believe that there is a link between cave acoustics and those art forms (largely and most often hooved animals). The authors see a strong correlation between the echoing of the sound of hooved animals (in a cave), the subject matter of the art, the beginnings of the (unique to the human species) cognitive ability to think symbolically, and the gradual emergence of language—art and language are external symbolic forms of internal mental states. To them, diversity in languages existed at least 70,000 to 100,000 years ago.[148]

The diverse prehistoric languages in the Middle East

Mesopotamia and the Eurasian Steppe differed significantly in their geomorphology and in the opportunities for economic development. The largely sedentary farmers of Mesopotamia had quite different lifestyles from the nomadic tribes of the Steppe grasslands to their north. These two geomorphologically different locations are the origin of two of the most widely used and distinctly different language groups common across the modern world.

The Middle East during and leading up to the Bronze Age was not a unified entity but an overlapping and often interchangeable and varying mix of cultural, political, linguistic, economic, and trading systems. There was an incredibly large and geographically dense range of nations, kingdoms, empires, principalities, city-states, tribes, communities, ethnicities, cultures, and influences occurring in and around Mesopotamia, the Levant, and Egypt during the early Bronze Age (from around 3000 BCE onwards).

This was the time when many of these linguistically differentiated communities were transitioning from largely nomadic hunter-gatherers to sedentary agricultural and pastoral communities. Initially, there were multiple languages across these prehistoric communities.

---

[146] The study of acoustics at archaeological sites.

[147] SOURCE: https://www.sciencemag.org/news/2015/01/human-language-may-have-evolved-help-our-ancestors-make-tools retrieved on 11 August 2021.

[148] Miyagawa et al (2018).

The now-extinct Bronze Age Mesopotamian/Fertile Crescent languages include Sumerian, multiple variants of the Semitic language, Akkadian (which had Assyrian and Babylonian variations), Ugaritic, Eblaite, Amorite, Phoenician, Ammonite, Moabite, Edomite, Ancient North Arabic, Nabatean, Punic, and Philistine.

This level of linguistic diversity is not uncommon in geographically contiguous hunter-gatherer communities. At the time of the European invasion of Australia, the local Indigenous First Nations peoples, who were primarily hunter-gatherers, had around 290 to 363 languages belonging to an estimated 28 language families and language isolates that were spoken by Indigenous Australians of mainland Australia and a few nearby islands. By the late eighteenth century, there were still more than 250 distinct Indigenous social groupings and a similar number of Indigenous languages or varietals across the Australian continent.[149]

It is estimated that the cultural diversity in the ancient Middle East was similarly reflected in the existence of a wide variety of up to fifteen languages spoken within and across the region and around seven different writing systems in existence in the early Bronze Age.[150]

The three most important language families at the time

Most species have rudimentary ways of communicating, but the human species is the only one that has developed a complex language system. It may well have started as simple gestures: body language, sign language, drawings to illustrate objectives or intent or mouthing of sounds or vocalisations, such as found in African click languages.[151] Eventually a communicable language became an evolutionarily advantageous ability (with fully articulated language systems emerging around 50,000 years ago). There are multiple theories about how language evolved including:[152]

- As groups got larger (than family clans) there was a need for a better communication system.
- Advantageous sexual selection results from a better communication system.
- As environments got more complex (larger social groups, plants, animals, tools, art, weapons) there was a need for a more complex information and encoding system.

---

[149] SOURCE: https://en.wikipedia.org/wiki/Australian_Aboriginal_languages retrieved on 4 February 2021.

[150] Kuhrt (2009A), p. 4.

[151] See: https://www.britannica.com/topic/click-languages retrieved on 26 August 2023.

[152] Adapted in part from Wade (2007), pp. 40-49.

- There are unique regions in the human cortex that facilitate language namely Broca's area in the inferior frontal gyrus (IFG), Wernicke's area in the superior temporal gyrus (STG), as well as parts of the middle temporal gyrus (MTG) and the inferior parietal and angular gyrus in the parietal lobe.[153]
- There is a specific group of human genes (FOXP2) which facilitated the development of language.

It is highly likely that language systems developed in geographically different locations as a result of the advantageous occurrence of all or most of these factors.

Seven main contemporary language families (Niger-Congo, Austronesian, Trans-New Guinea, Sino-Tibetan, Indo-European, Afro-Asiatic and Turkic) emerged across tens of thousands of years through this process. Three of these contemporary language families are important to understanding the prehistoric Levant and the emergence of the Hebrew language, the Hebrew scribes, and the Hebrew Bible:

- Indo-European (originating in the Anatolia/Western Eurasian Steppe/Caucuses or north of the Black Sea)
- Turkic (originating in East Asia/Eastern Eurasian Steppe/Western China)
- Afro-Asiatic (originating in the Levant, Mesopotamia, and North Africa).

The Indo-European language group

Indo-European languages have evolved into what is currently the most widespread language group in today's world—having originated between 9500 BCE to 8000 BCE and spread with migration and agricultural practices from the western Eurasian Steppes.[154]

The steppes to the north of the Black Sea are the most likely original homeland of the speakers of the Proto-Indo-European language (PIE), the progenitor of the Indo-European language family.[155] It probably emerged in the Kurgan Culture from around 4500 BCE. However, some researchers suggest it originated further east towards the Caspian Sea, and yet others suggest Anatolia.[156]

Detailed analysis by leading genomic researcher David Reich and his colleagues provides significant evidence for the spread of this language. They suggest that this language

---

[153] Friederici (2011), pp. 1358-1359.
[154] Gray et al (2011).
[155] Manco (2015), p. 122.
[156] SOURCE: https://en.wikipedia.org/wiki/Black_Sea#History retrieved on 3 February 2021.

family expanded across the Eurasian Steppe due to the increased mobility (horses, wagons, chariots) from west to east and, to some extent, to the south.

Originating north of the Black Sea or in Anatolia, the Caucuses and/or Armenia, the Indo-European language travelled with the Eurasian Steppe nomads. From around 3000 BCE, it spread westward into Eastern Europe and eastward into Western Asia and the Indus Valley. This occurred largely via the Yamnaya cultural group (see later discussion, page 211). Genomic analysis confirms strong West Eurasian ancestry in the genes of prehistoric cultures across the Eurasian Steppe as far east as the Indus Valley and Northern India.[157] Sanskrit, which is the classical language of India and the liturgical language of the Hindu, Buddhist, and Jainism religions, evolved from this genetic and linguistic pathway.

The Turkic Language Group

The homeland of the Turkic peoples and their language was probably somewhere between the Transcaspian steppe (east of the Caspian Sea in Central Asia) and north-eastern Asia (Manchuria), with genetic evidence pointing to its origin closer to Bactria, Southern Siberia, and Mongolia.[158]

The Afro-Asiatic Semitic language

What is known from the earliest writing (cuneiform) systems is that the Semitic language was commonly spoken by the Sumerians in Mesopotamia (from around 3000 BCE). This was even though the Sumerians had their own language isolate (apparently unrelated to any other known language). The Middle East during the Bronze Age had many language groups. Several of these were spoken by communities in and around the Levant, including Lulubi, Gutian, Kassite, Sumerian, Elamite and Marhasi all of which are now extinct and of obscure origin.

There are conflicting theories on the origin of the Semitic language. Hebrew is a Semitic language that is part of the broader Afro-Asiatic language family related to Egyptian Coptic (Figure 6). Semitic may have emerged in Mesopotamia, the Levant, the East Mediterranean, the Arabian Peninsula, or North Africa, all of which spoke versions of Semitic. It has been estimated that the earliest forms of the Semitic language

---

[157]   Reich (2019) pp. 117-122 and pp. 133-140.
[158]   Tantuǧ et al. (2018).

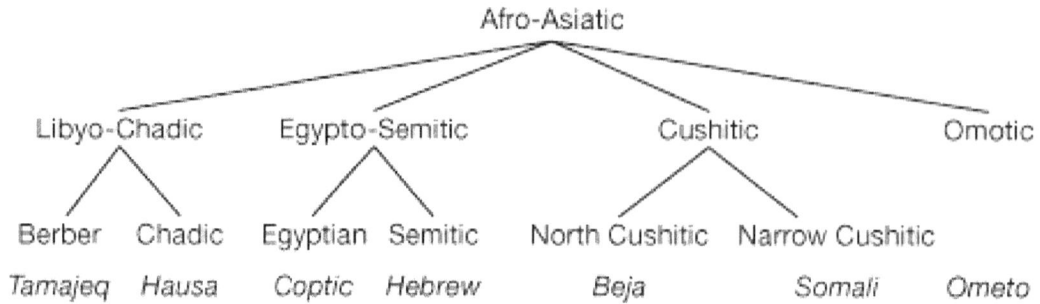

```
                            Afro-Asiatic

     Libyo-Chadic      Egypto-Semitic        Cushitic              Omotic

   Berber   Chadic   Egyptian  Semitic   North Cushitic   Narrow Cushitic

  Tamajeq   Hausa    Coptic   Hebrew         Beja            Somali      Ometo
```

Figure 6: *The Afro-Asiatic language family*[b]

---

[b]   SOURCE: https://www.britannica.com/topic/Afro-Asiatic-languages retrieved on 9 May 2023. Reprinted with permission from *Encyclopaedia Britannica*, © 2008 by Encyclopædia Britannica, Inc.

probably diverged from Afro-Asiatic in around 5000 BCE.[159] The most recent and most widely held view is that Semitic became widespread in the Levant from around 3800 BCE from where various related dialects (including Akkadian, Aramaic, Canaanite, Carthaginian, Phoenician, Punic, Ugaritic, Classical Arabic, and Mishnaic Hebrew) spread to the Middle East, the Horn of Africa, the southern Arabian peninsula, and North Africa.

In addition to their own language isolates, the Semitic language was spoken by other communities in Mesopotamian and in the Northern Levant (from around 2500 BCE).[160] It is closely related to Arabic and Aramaic as well as to Hebrew (Figure 6 and Figure 7). The word 'Israel' is an early Semitic/Eblaite language word. In fact, as shown in Figure 7 (centre-right), the language used in the Hebrew scriptures and religious writing is a derivative of the ancient Canaanite version of the Semitic language, which included Hebrew, Moabite, Phoenician, and Punic and was primarily spoken in ancient times in Palestine and by tribal groups on the Mediterranean coast of Syria.[161]

The Afro-Asiatic Middle East Semitic family of languages has the distinction of being the first historically attested group of languages to use an alphabet, derived from the Proto-Canaanite alphabet, to record their writings. The Proto-

---

[159]   Kitchen et al. (2009).
[160]   Manco (2015), p. 83.
[161]   See also: https://www.britannica.com/topic/Semitic-languages retrieved on 6 April 2021.

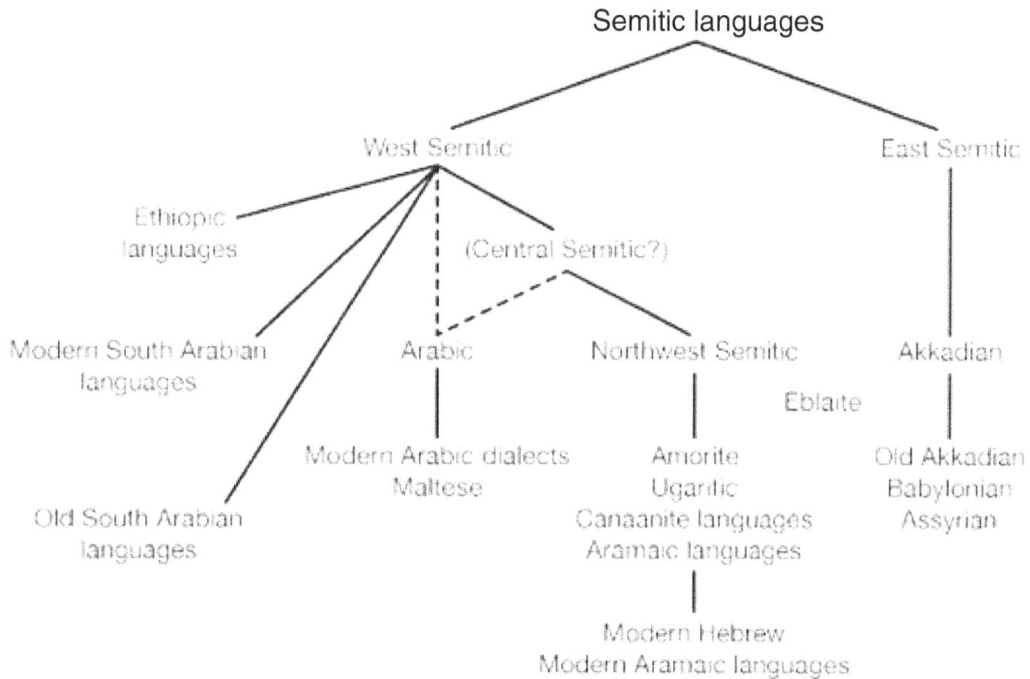

Figure 7: *Interrelationships between the ancient and modern Semitic languages[c]*

---

[c]   SOURCE: https://www.britannica.com/topic/Semitic-languages retrieved on 3 February 2021. Reprinted with permission from *Encyclopaedia Britannica*, © 2008 by Encyclopædia Britannica, Inc

Canaanite alphabet itself originated from the far earlier Sumerian Cuneiform logographic/syllabic writing in the region. Figure 8 is a notional distribution of these three language groupings from around the early Bronze Age. They tend to reflect the major zones of regular interaction of the communities (trading, linguistic, migration, genomic, culturally) in those regions.

In today's world, Semitic-based languages are spoken by more than 330 million people across much of West Asia, North Africa, the Horn of Africa, Malta, and in small pockets in the Caucasus. It includes Hebrew, Arabic, Aramaic, and Ethiopian (the Amharas) language groups. The Afro-Asiatic/Semitic language distribution pattern tends to reflect the genomic, economic, and trading pathways evident in the Middle East, Mesopotamia, and Egypt throughout prehistory.

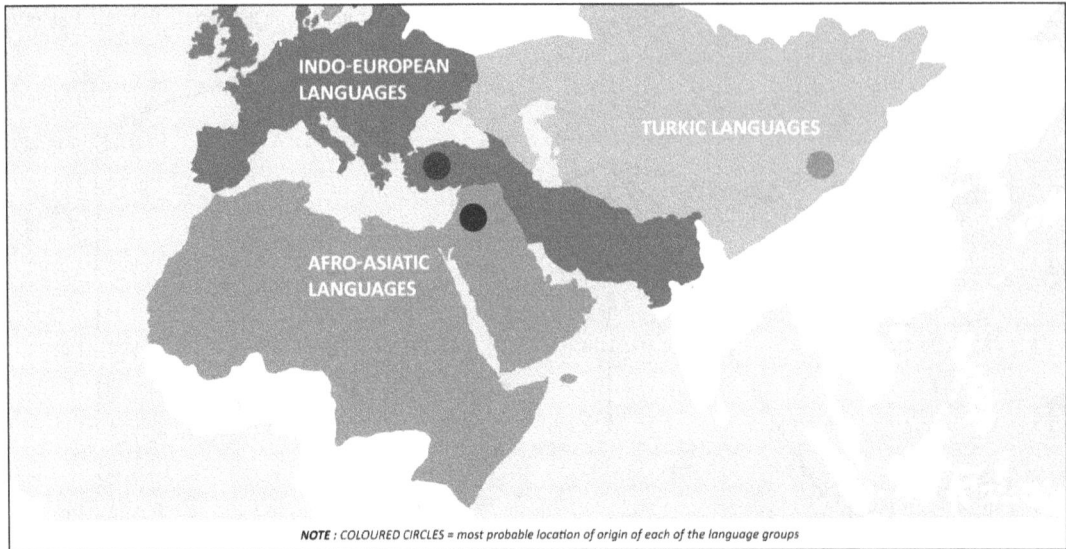

Figure 8: *Notional distribution of three language groupings during the Bronze Age*[d]

---

[d]   Map adapted from https://sdaworldhistory.edublogs.org/u1/afro-eurasia-1kmfh96/ retrieved on 3 February 2021.

The impact of genomic analysis

In 1953, American molecular biologist, geneticist, and zoologist James Dewey Watson and his colleague, British molecular biologist, biophysicist, and neuroscientist Francis Crick, delivered an academic paper proposing the double-helix structure of the DNA (deoxyribonucleic acid) molecule.[162] DNA is a long molecule that contains hereditary material—a unique genetic code. It is the chemical compound that contains the instructions needed to develop and direct the activities of nearly all living organisms.[163]

Watson and Crick's discovery started a new and rapidly growing global research effort mapping the human genome, studying the genes and other information encoded in an individual's genome—the complete set of instructions in their DNA. Scientists could now extract ancient DNA (aDNA) from skeletons found at archaeological sites. The science

---

[162]   Watson and Crick (1953).
[163]   Watson (2006), pp. 63-85.

behind aDNA is relatively new. The first fully sequenced ancient human genome—from a man who lived about 4,000 years ago in Greenland—was published only in 2010.[164] Prehistoric research had, up until the mid-1950s, relied largely on assumptions and interpretations based on things people and cultures had left behind through language, art, pottery, burial sites, cuneiform, and hieroglyphic texts. The genomics avenue of research is not, like archaeology, focused on things people left behind, but rather on the people themselves and their genetic origins.

Archaeogenetics—the study of ancient DNA using various molecular genetic methods and DNA resources—has changed prehistoric research. This form of genetic analysis can be applied to human, animal, and plant specimens. Ancient DNA can be extracted from various fossilised specimens including old bones, teeth, eggshells, soil samples, and artificially preserved tissues in human and animal specimens.[165]

Andrew Lawler has described the impact of genomics on knowledge of the past in this way:

> *The single most revolutionary development of recent decades is our ability to extract genetic material from old bones. Ancient DNA has given us an intimate glimpse into how our ancestors interacted with Neanderthals. It has also led to the discovery of our long-lost cousins the Denisovans, as well as the extraordinarily small people of the Indonesian island of Flores.*[166]

Platt et al., have undertaken genomic analysis of prehistoric populations in three locations in South-West Asia to better understand what specific groupings emerged in these locations after anatomically modern humans (AMH) had left Africa and had survived the Earth's Last Glacial Period (12,000 years ago).[167]

The Platt team were particularly interested in how these three originating populations who were isolated during the Last Glacial Period emerged and then dispersed over time into other regions—primarily throughout South-West Asia and into Europe and Africa. The three foundation populations, and the regions that had distinctive

---

[164] SOURCE: https://www.wired.com/2010/02/inuk-genome/ accessed on 1 August 2020.
[165] Krause and Trappe (2021), pp. 8-10.
[166] Lawler (2021).
[167] The subregion of Asia, bounded on the west by the Mediterranean Sea, the Sinai Peninsula, and the Red Sea and on the south and southeast by the Indian Ocean and the Persian Gulf and extending northwards to the Caspian and the Black Seas.

genetic signatures—where populations had survived unfavourable conditions of global glaciation—were identified as being:

- A northern group based around the east coast of the Black Sea, Georgia, and Eastern Türkiye
- A Levantine group
- A third group in the Southern Arabian Peninsula.[168]

The genomic research was based on samples from nine South-West Asian populations (from Georgia, Armenia, Türkiye, Lebanon, Syria, Palestine, Jordan, Saudia Arabia, and Yemen). The analysis confirmed that, following the last glacial period, these three regions were the main source of the descendants who occupied South-West Asia during the Stone Age (10000 BCE to 4000 BCE). They eventually became the primary gene pools for the various Bronze Age populations in the broad Middle East, Central Asian region, and along the Eurasian Steppe.

Genomic research has found that much of the world's current population is at least partially descended from the prehistoric Eurasian Steppe nomads—the ones who are genetically linked to Platt's post-glacial northern group based around the east coast of the Black Sea/Georgia /Eastern Türkiye. Approximately two-thirds of European men have been confirmed by ancient DNA tests to have arrived in Europe with the Indo-European migrations from the Pontic Steppe during the Bronze Age.[169]

The Eurasian Steppe has been a significant contributor to the world's gene pool. Genomic researchers Jeong et al. (2019) describe the Eurasian Steppe gene flow thusly:

Inner Eurasia has functioned as a conduit for human migration and cultural transfer since the first appearance of modern humans in this region. As a result, we observe deep sharing of genes between Western and Eastern Eurasian populations in multiple layers.[170]

The Germany-based Max Planck Institute for Evolutionary Anthropology in Leipzig and the Max Planck Institute for the Science of Human History in Jena are leaders globally in archaeogenetics. Their work on prehistorical genomic evidence from the Eurasian Steppe demonstrates that, from around 4000 BCE, there was a multi-directional sharing of

---

[168] Platt et al. (2017).
[169] SOURCE: https://www.eupedia.com/history/5000_years_of_steppe_migrations_into_europe.shtml retrieved on 19 October 2020.
[170] Jeong et al. (2019), p. 973.

know-how, innovation, and genes culminating in far-reaching genetic associations between the prehistoric peoples of the Caucuses, Siberia, Northeast Asia, and the Americas.[171]

Genomic scientists have confirmed how this Eurasian Steppe genetic pathway travelled much further eastwards than China. There are close links between the genetics of prehistoric Siberians (the Eastern Eurasian Steppe) and Native Americans:

Four mitochondrial clans dominate the genetics of Native Americans. All four have easily reconstructed and obvious genetic links with people living in Siberia or north-Central Asia today.[172]

Jeong et al.'s genomic research identified three main genetic pathways along the Eurasian Steppe that tend to mirror the three distinct west-to-east and east-to-west geographic, latitudinal regions and associated travel opportunities along the Steppe:

A northern band (genetic pathway) runs through the Arctic tundra and boreal forests. This population has the clearest genetic affinity with early hunter-gatherers known as Ancient North Eurasians (ANE) and is also strongly linked to Native Americans.

A middle band (genetic pathway) runs through the southern forests and steppe. This population shows Late Bronze Age steppe ancestries linked to both western herders and people from the Amur River basin on the border of modern Russia and China.

Finally, a southern band (genetic pathway) corresponds to the lower steppe and shrubland region. This population shows a strong West and South Asian influence, linking it to Mesolithic Caucasus hunter-gatherers and Neolithic Iranians.[173]

These sporadic but dynamic genetic, geographic, migratory, and cultural pathways have been responsible for the spread and interchange of innovations, including the spread of universal languages and mythologies across the Eurasian Steppe and down into the Middle East.

Genomic research by the Max Planck Institute for the Science of Human History and the Eurasia Department of the German Archaeological Institute has found that, whilst geographic boundaries (the mountains, the rivers, and the Steppe) tended to be genetic boundaries, over the centuries and across prehistory an interaction zone formed to the

---

[171] SOURCE: https://www.sciencedaily.com/releases/2019/02/190204085933.htm retrieved on 4 February 2021.
[172] Sykes (2002), p. 279.
[173] SOURCE: https://cosmosmagazine.com/biology/eurasian-migration-advanced-Steppe-by-Steppe/ retrieved on 19 October 2020.

south, where the traditions of the Mesopotamian civilisation interacted with the cultures of the Levant, the Iranian Plateau, Indus Valley, the Caucasus, and the Eurasian Steppe.

Genetic evidence confirms that the prehistoric sedentary Maykop culture in the Western Caucuses between the Black and the Caspian seas (3700 BCE to 3000 BCE) is more genetically related to civilisations to their south and east than to those nomadic (mainly the Yamnaya culture) in the adjacent steppes to their north.[174]

This and other related genomic research suggest that there was a 'sharp genetic boundary' to the north of the Caucus Mountains that acted as a barrier to prehistoric gene flow.[175] Artefactual evidence from the Maykop culture suggests that the Maykop may have come initially from Iran and Central Asia via Mesopotamia and Syro-Anatolia to the Caucuses in around 4000 BCE.[176]

Genomic research by Wang et al. at the Max Planck Institute for the Science of Human History found genetic links of ancient Maykop peoples to southern Anatolian and Northern Syria farmers, Caucasian hunter-gatherers, and Eastern Steppe peoples— and to North Asians, Siberians, and North Americans.[177]

Genomic research tends to consistently confirm the archaeological evidence of extensive mobility and interchange between prehistoric and Bronze Age peoples in the Eurasian Steppe, the Iranian plateau, the Indus Valley, Mesopotamia, the Fertile Crescent, the Levant, and Egypt:

- DNA from Ancient Egyptians shows they are most closely related to ancient populations in the Levant and to Neolithic populations from the Anatolian Peninsula and Europe[178]
- DNA from Ancient Iranians shows a strong link to the Ancient South Caucuses, Anatolia, and to a lesser extent, Mesopotamian populations
- Genetic studies of Bronze Age Canaanite remains (from the Northern Levant) have identified a close link to the peoples of the Zagros Mountains, the Caucuses and the Southern Levant

---

[174] SOURCE: https://www.sciencedaily.com/releases/2019/02/190204085933.htm retrieved on 9 May 2023.

[175] SOURCE: https://www.sciencedaily.com/releases/2019/02/190204085933.htm retrieved on 4 February 2021.

[176] SOURCE: https://en.wikipedia.org/wiki/Maykop_culture retrieved on 4 February 2021.

[177] Wang et al. (2019).

[178] SOURCE: https://www.mpg.de/11317890/genome-ancient-egyptian-mummies retrieved on 23 March 2021.

- Genomic analysis of examples from nine sites across a wide geographic expanse including Lebanon, Israel, and Jordan has found that the archaeological and historical 'Canaanites' shared a uniform material culture and a coherent and homogenous prehistoric origin, where they are genetically more closely related to each other than to any neighbouring populations.[179]

The impact of historical analysis

As outlined earlier, historical research has undergone a multi-dimensional change in the past one hundred years. The conventional approach of listing memorable events, learnings, dates, times, and the names of key players has faded almost into insignificance if not irrelevance. Historical research is now a valuable source of information that poses questions about the origin of humanity and the often taken-for-granted collectively held views of the past.

The word 'history' emerged from a Greek word meaning 'enquiry', 'to know' or 'the seeking of knowledge'. The Australian Curriculum Assessment and Reporting Authority defines history in the following way:

> History identifies the concepts of evidence, continuity and change, cause and effect, significance, perspectives, empathy, and contestability as integral to the development of historical understanding.[180]

History is now seen as a dynamic and ever-changing perspective on previous life, geographic locations, societies, cultures, and times. It is continuously open to question. In the eyes of the American Historical Association, historical research now requires a recognition of the need for core competencies, including an awareness of 'the provisional nature of knowledge, the disciplinary preference for complexity, and the comfort with ambiguity that history requires'.[181]

This dynamic and continuous re-assessment of historical information comes from two main directions. Firstly, the acceptance that, for too long, historical research has been dominated by the Western world and the emergence of 'civilisation' from the Middle East,

---

[179] Agranat-Tamir et al. (2020), p. 1154.
[180] https://www.australiancurriculum.edu.au/f-10-curriculum/humanities-and-social-sciences/history/structure/ retrieved on 6 March 2023.
[181] https://www.historians.org/teaching-and-learning/why-study-history/careers-for-history-majors/history-discipline-core retrieved on 6 March 2023.

Eurasia, the Mediterranean, and Europe. This has occurred at the expense of the wealth of information available from other geographic and cultural entities. Secondly, historical research now no longer needs to rely almost exclusively on the interpretation of ancient artefacts and texts. Linguistics, genomics, seismology, paleoclimatic data and the continuing emergence of new archaeological data have significantly increased the breadth and depth of evidence of the past.

These two trends have seen, for example, the rapid growth of hardcopy and online access to a wealth of alternative perspectives and evidence on the history of humanity, cultures, and mythologies. Key sources include, for example, the *World History Encyclopedia*, *National Geographic*, *Encyclopedia Britannica*, Oxford University's *New Oxford World History* and Academia History (<academia.edu/Documents/in/History>). There is now a very wide range of published books and articles about the history of humanity. The majority of these do not use the HB/OT as an historical source (see Bibliography). This does not mean that there are no historians who continue to accept the HB/OT as an historical document.

Susan Wise Bauer, educator, author, and evangelical Christian, interweaves defensible historical facts with biblical and other religious stories (Sumerian, Egyptian, Indian, Chinese) in an otherwise excellent summary of the history of the ancient world.[182] Bauer's work is fascinating and typical of this genre as she interweaves religious myth into genuine history making it difficult to differentiate fact from myth. For instance, Bauer repeats in detail the biblical story of Abraham and his father Terah as descendants of biblical Shem as if it is an historical fact. She continues with lengthy sections about the life of Abraham and repeats the biblical claim that Shem, Terah's father, was a son of Noah. According to the Hebrew scribes, after the flood wiped out everyone except those on the ark, Shem became the father of all the Western Semites. Most objective researchers now agree that the Noah story is demonstrably a fictional allegorical story. It does not belong in an historical textbook.

Defensibly alternative historical sources are now so accessible and voluminous that they provide a great opportunity for a multi-dimensional and factual re-assessment of the historical foundations of contemporary religious beliefs.

The impact of seismological evidence

Although not used extensively, seismic evidence linked to archaeologic evidence has provided a broader understanding of what has happened in the past. This is particularly the case for the examination of events in the prehistoric Middle East.

---

[182] Bauer (2007), pp. 127-137.

The Southern Levant is a seismic region. It is located at the intersection of the African, Arabian, and Anatolian tectonic plates. The Dead Sea Transform Fault Line/Dead Sea Rift is at the intersection of the African and Arabian plates and runs north-south through the Levant. There are three related tectonic rifts splaying across the Levant—the Levant Rift (an elongated series of structural basins that extends for more than 1,000 kilometres from the northern Red Sea to southern Anatolia), the Jordan Rift (running the entire length of the Jordan River valley), and the El Gharb Rift (running across north-western Syria). Rifts can be imagined as deep cracks in the Earth's surface that move during localised earthquakes.

There is strong evidence that the East Mediterranean and the Aegean experienced earthquakes (an 'earthquake storm' lasting some fifty years) that decimated Canaanite towns at around the same time as the Bronze Age collapse, the invasion of the Sea Peoples, and the emergence of the Israelites.[183] The oldest recorded earthquake in the Middle East was around 1274 BCE to 1234 BCE in Nineveh, the oldest and most-populous city of the ancient Assyrian empire situated in the northern Fertile Crescent on the east bank of the Tigris River.[184] There is strong supporting evidence of earthquake damage causing the destruction and evacuation of an Egyptian Canaanite town in the Levant at around the same time.[185]

The town of Jericho sits on the Dead Sea Transform Fault Line. The archaeological evidence shows that the walls of Jericho have been rebuilt many times following their destruction by a series of earthquakes (from around 1573 BCE) and that Jericho was largely unoccupied from the fifteenth century to around the tenth century BCE.[186]

According to the Hebrew scribes in the book of Joshua (written around 700 BCE), under the leadership of Joshua, on the seventh day, seven priests carrying seven *shofars* (the Jewish religious horn made from rams' horns), encircled Jericho seven times and then blew their horns. The sound of the horns caused the walls to collapse, and the Israelites entered and conquered Jericho. They 'destroyed all that was in the city, both man and woman, both young and old, and ox, and sheep, and ass … and they burnt the city with fire, and all that was therein'.[187]

---

[183]   Nur and Cline (2000); Fiaccavento (2014), pp. 219-222.
[184]   Barnikel and Vetter (2012), p. 3.
[185]   Barako (2007), p. 511.
[186]   Ramos (2016).
[187]   Adapted from the Book of Joshua 6: 13-24.

The biblical description of the collapsed walls and the damage to the city of Jericho matches the archaeological evidence of the impact of an earthquake. In the words of Jewish scholar Jonathan L Friedmann:

Most likely is that the fall of Jericho began as a recollection of an ancient earthquake, accumulated folkloric details in the oral transmission, and was eventually incorporated into the conquest narrative.[188]

The biblical story of Joshua attacking and destroying Jericho and causing the walls to fall is the Hebrew scribes' use of a mythological story to explain the remnants of these seismic events.

There are multiple other references in the HB/OT to seismic events that the Hebrew scribes have attributed to the actions of their God or conveyors of supernatural messages, including:

- Genesis 19:24-25—'Then the Lord rained down burning sulfur on Sodom and Gomorrah—from the Lord out of the heavens. Thus, he overthrew those cities and the entire plain, destroying all those living in the cities—and also the vegetation in the land.'
- 2 Samuel 22: 8-10—'The earth trembled and quaked, the foundations of the heavens shook; they trembled because he was angry. Smoke rose from his nostrils; consuming fire came from his mouth, burning coals blazed out of it. He parted the heavens and came down; dark clouds were under his feet.'
- 1 Kings 19:11-12—'The Lord said, "Go out and stand on the mountain in the presence of the Lord, for the Lord is about to pass by." Then a great and powerful wind tore the mountains apart and shattered the rocks before the Lord, but the Lord was not in the wind. After the wind there was an earthquake, but the Lord was not in the earthquake. After the earthquake came a fire, but the Lord was not in the fire. And after the fire came a gentle whisper.'
- Isaiah 29:6—'The Lord Almighty will come with thunder and earthquake and great noise, with windstorm and tempest and flames of a devouring fire.'
- Jeremiah 10:10—'But the Lord is the true God, he is the living God, and an everlasting king: at his wrath the earth shall tremble, and the nations shall not be able to abide his indignation.'

---

[188] Friedmann (2020), p. 173.

- Ezekiel 38:19—'In my zeal and fiery wrath I declare that at that time there shall be a great earthquake in the land of Israel.'
- Amos 1:1—'The words of Amos, one of the shepherds of Tekoa—the vision he saw concerning Israel two years before the earthquake, when Uzziah was king of Judah and Jeroboam son of Jehoash was king of Israel.'
- Zechariah 14:4-5—'On that day his feet will stand on the Mount of Olives, east of Jerusalem, and the Mount of Olives will be split in two from east to west, forming a great valley, with half of the mountain moving north and half moving south. You will flee by my mountain valley, for it will extend to Azel. You will flee as you fled from the earthquake in the days of Uzziah King of Judah. Then the Lord my God will come, and all the holy ones with him.'

The impact of paleoclimatic research

Paleoclimatology involves the study of past climatic events and their probable impact on the environment and subsequently on human-environment interaction. It is usual to integrate paleoclimatic evidence with historical, archaeological, linguistic, and genomic evidence to construct a better understanding and a more accurate reconstruction of different societal and religious trends in prehistoric times.[189]

The scientific reconstruction of ancient climatic events is a relatively recent science.[190] The emergence of the science of paleoclimatology has been stimulated in some ways by evidence of the major glaciation events of the past and evidence of the impact of climate change on the prehistoric Middle East. Paleoclimatology has enabled the identification of the most notable climate events in the history of the planet. It provides insights into why certain lifestyle, cultural, societal, technological, economic, and religious changes may have occurred in ancient civilisations.

Paleoclimatology has shown how, between around twenty thousand and twelve thousand years ago, the average global temperature (averaged in one-thousand-year increments) increased from around minus ten degrees Celsius to zero degrees Celsius. This significant increase in global warming had a dramatic impact on the lifestyles of the human species in and around the Middle East.

---

[189] Izdebski et al. (2016).
[190] Fairbridge (2009).

In the much colder environments, hunter-gatherer groups were small—usually family and kin. They were seasonally highly mobile in pursuit of game and edible seasonal vegetation. Campsites were generally short-term and located along routine hunting pathways. During the coldest times, ancient humans found shelter, usually in deep caves where their knowledge of fire provided added warmth and comfort. These caves were where early hunter-gatherers shaped rudimentary stone tools and where they began to illustrate aspects of their life in realistic, symbolic, and abstract drawings on the cave walls.

The human, animal, and vegetation advantages of a warming climate created several circumstantial opportunities for the transition of hunter-gatherers towards agriculture, pastoralism, and more permanent, sedentary lifestyles. This was particularly the case for hunter-gatherer groups in the Middle East, including ancient Anatolia, the Fertile Crescent, Mesopotamia, and the Levant.

Climatic evidence of past river floods or major droughts in ancient Egypt (Nile Valley), Mesopotamia, the Indus Valley, and China added a new dimension to the search to better understand the past. Evidence of the impact of climate change on the Bronze Age Dark Ages collapse, as well as biblical stories of similar events (primarily in Genesis), have stimulated the growth of prehistoric paleoclimatic research in recent years.

Haldon et al. have expressed it in this way:

> *Interactions within socio-environmental systems are hardly simple. Many societies, for example, have evolved precisely in locations where the environment was difficult to control: complex sedentary groups first arose in flood-prone river basins rather than more stable environmental contexts, suggesting that solving environmental problems contributed to the development of these societies.[191]*

There is a complex link between seismic activity, climatic consequences, and social impact. Yale University historian Joseph Manning and his colleagues have studied social vulnerability and socio-cultural responses to abrupt hydroclimatic shocks in Egypt in the third century BCE.[192] They tested how past climatic changes and, specifically, volcanically induced Nile River failures have influenced human societies. They measured the extent to which the complex relationship between volcanic and climatic disruptions had delivered either a top-down response (state, elite, priestly decree, or religious dictate) or a bottom-up response (domestic unrest, citizen revolts, or uprisings).

---

[191] Haldon et al. (2018), p. 1.
[192] Manning et al (2017).

Manning and his colleagues found that, despite an extensive history of invasions, war, and territorial disputes in the region, following seismic-climatic events, these tended to cease as the focus of rulers switched to managing internal domestic unrest and revolts. They state that:

> … *eruptions are associated with revolt onset against elite rule, and the cessation of Ptolemaic state warfare with their great rival, the Seleukid Empire. Eruptions are also followed by socioeconomic stress with increased hereditary land sales, and the issuance of priestly decrees to reinforce elite authority.*

This data relates to Egypt and the Nile Valley during the Ptolemaic period (305 BCE to 030 BCE)—the very period during which most researchers believe the HB/OT was being finalised. There is no doubt that these regular seismic-climatic-environmental disruptions occurring across the Levant and Egypt influenced Hebrew scribe storytelling. The HB/OT is replete with accounts of disruptive volcanic, environmental, and socio-cultural events. These can now be confidently described as recurring natural phenomena that the Hebrew scribes have attributed to their God, most specifically in the stories told in the biblical Books of Amos, Zechariah, and Ezekiel.

Chapter 7

The Geographic Region Where the Hebrew Bible Emerged

The geographic areas where the HB/OT emerged include the Levant, but significant influences came from the Fertile Crescent, the Ancient Near East, the Iranian Plateau, the Indus Valley, Egypt, the Caucuses (the region between the Black and the Caspian Seas), Central Asia, the Great/Eurasian Steppe, the Mediterranean, and even indirect influences from prehistoric Mongolia and Siberia.

The Ancient Near East

The Ancient Near East is a term that usually refers to the broader geographic region roughly equivalent to and containing Mesopotamia (modern Iraq, southeast Türkiye, southwest Iran, north-eastern Syria, and Kuwait), ancient Egypt, ancient Iran (Elam, Media, Parthia, and Persia), Anatolia/Asia Minor and Armenian Highlands (Türkiye's Eastern Anatolia Region, Armenia, north-western Iran, southern Georgia, and western Azerbaijan), the Levant (modern Syria, Lebanon, Palestine, Israel, and Jordan), Cyprus, and the Arabian Peninsula.

The Ancient Near East is a difficult and complex region to investigate. Jaan Puhvel has described it in these words:

Unlike Egypt, which constituted a specific remarkably self-contained, almost monolithic, ethnically and linguistically uniform tradition, the ancient Near East at large was not one civilisation but many, more or less contiguous by geography and stretched out along a time span of several millennia. We must pick and choose among Sumerians, East Semites (Akkadians = Babylonians + Assyrians), Hurrians, and Proto-Indians in Mesopotamia, West Semites in the area of Syria, Lebanon, and Palestine (from Ebla in the third millennium to Ugarit in the second, to Phoenicians, Canaanites, and Hebrews in the first), Indo-European speaking Hittites and

81

Luwians in Anatolia (= Asia Minor), and likewise Indo-European Iranians in the whole vast territory between Asia Minor, Mesopotamia, and India. And it is not always easy to say where ancient Greece ends and Near East begins, owing to extensive cultural interpenetration.[193]

The term 'Near East' has largely fallen into disuse in contemporary academic and political circles and has been replaced by the term *Middle East*. This includes modern-day Egypt, the Arabian Peninsula, Cyprus, Iraq, Iran, Israel, Jordan, Lebanon, Palestinian territories, Syria, Türkiye, and the South Caucasus.

The Levant

Traditionally, the Levant describes the Eastern Mediterranean at large, but the term has also been used to denote a large area in Western Asia formed on the west by the lands bordering the eastern shores of the Mediterranean, roughly bounded on the north by the Taurus Mountains, on the south by the Arabian Desert and on the east, extending towards the Zagros Mountains and the Iranian Plateau (Figure 9).

Figure 9: Modern-day Levant[a]

[a]   SOURCE: Adapted from https://freeradiopeace.com/levant.html retrieved on 25 March 2021.

[193]   Puhvel (1989), p. 22.

The Fertile Crescent

The Levant is a region within the larger geographic area, historically referred to as the *Fertile Crescent* (Figure 10). The Crescent shape itself owes much to the geomorphology created by the impact of the tectonic plates. The arc of the Zagros Mountains to the north and east, the incursion of the Syrian and Negev Deserts from the south, and the north-west–to–south-east flow of the Tigris and Euphrates Rivers, created a natural crescent. This natural arc became the major prehistoric travel route for early human species and set the scene for the emergence of modern civilisations and of the HB/OT. For millennia, travel north and south followed either the Mediterranean coast line or the paths of the two rivers and their many tributaries. The major route from Mesopotamia to the Levant was north and west along the foothills of the Zagros Mountains. Within this travel path, various communities emerged taking advantage of the rivers, fertile plains, and the Mediterranean shoreline.[194]

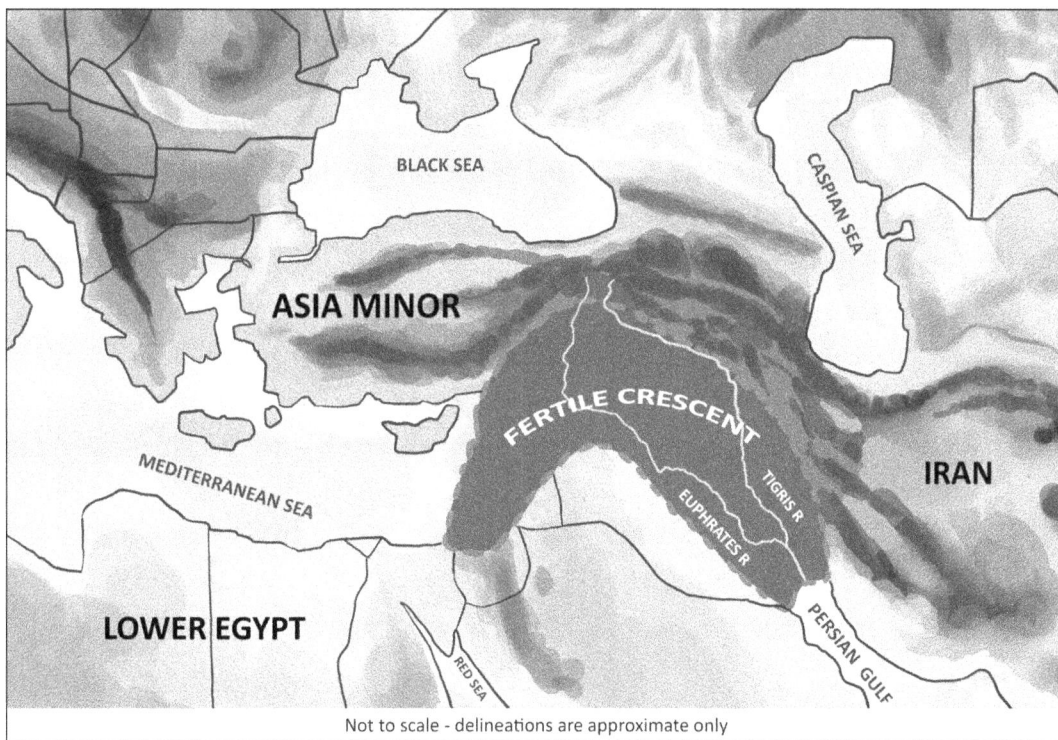

Figure 10: *Tectonic geomorphology created the Fertile Crescent*[b]

---

[b] Map sourced from https://owlcation.com/humanities/Ancient-Mesopotamian retrieved on 5 February 2021.

---

[194] Clarke et al. (2016), pp. 98-99.

The Levant's unique archaeological evidence[195]

The Levant was historically the main route out of Africa for early human ancestors. The Mediterranean to the west and the Sinai, Negev, and Arabian Deserts to the east and south channelled early hominids north along the Eastern Mediterranean coast. Research by the Max Planck Institute for the Science of Human History has confirmed that the Middle East and, in particular, the Levant, Anatolia, and the Western Eurasian Steppe were, across millennia, the main genetic pathways and thus the main migration pathways for the earliest human ancestors out of Africa and into Europe and Asia.[196]

As a result, Israel, the Levant, and Saudi Arabia contain some of the earliest archaeological evidence of modern humans' closest ancestors, *Homo erectus*, their settlement, and their activities outside of Africa. One of the oldest archaeological sites containing evidence of *Homo erectus* (from 1.5 million years ago), containing hand axes and mammalian and human bones, has been found in the Jordan Valley just south of the Sea of Galilee.[197] To date (as of 2024), this is the oldest evidence of ancient hominins in the Middle East.

Evidence of the human species' footprints dating from around 100,000 years ago has been found in the Nefud/Arabian Desert in Saudi Arabia.[198] One of the oldest skulls of the human species found outside of Africa (from around 100,000 years ago) has been found in the Qafzeh and Es Skhul Caves in Israel.[199] There is substantial evidence of early human ancestors being in Boker Tachtit, a significant archaeological site in the Wadi Zin basin/Ein Ovdat canyon in the Negev Desert in Southern Israel. This site is regarded as the earliest known migration point for the human species out of Africa into the Levant. It appears that some of the rudimentary stone tools found here may well have either come from or been influenced by similar tools found in excavations in the Nile Valley and

---

[195] NOTE: The terms Levant, Fertile Crescent and Ancient Middle East are used throughout this book in a generic way and, depending on the context, may include historic, prehistoric and current locations known as Egypt, Iraq, Iran, Afghanistan, the Indus Valley, Israel, Jordan, Lebanon, Palestine, Syria, Türkiye, Anatolia, parts of Georgia and Azerbaijan.

[196] See: Genetic testing reveals that Europe is a melting pot, made of immigrants (nationalgeographic.com) retrieved on 12 May 2022.

[197] Bar-Yosef and Goren-Inbar (1993).

[198] Gibbons (2020).

[199] Trinkaus (1995).

Yemen.[200] There is evidence here of early human species interacting with Neanderthals during the Middle Palaeolithic period (50,000 to 250,000 years ago).[201]

It is interesting, but largely circumstantial, that the Levant is also the location of the origin of one of the most influential religious texts, the HB/OT. As a result, some of the earliest and most interesting archaeological studies of early human species tend to coincide with the most interesting historical investigations into the origins of the HB/OT. The Levant is one of the most fascinating locations for studies of the emergence of the human species, the emergence of the scientific discipline of archaeology, and the gradual development and writing of the HB/OT.

Israel in the Levant

The very first evidence of the existence of the Israelites emerged in the Canaanite hills in around 1205 BCE. Over time, the ancient Northern Israeli Kingdom occupied the region known as Samaria. Samaria was a Canaanite region in central ancient Palestine. It was bordered by the Judaean desert to the south, Galilee to the north, the Jordan River to the east, and the Mediterranean Sea to the west.[202]

The cross-cultural and innovation opportunities in the Levant and the Fertile Crescent

In contemporary terms, the Fertile Crescent can include Israel, Palestine, Iraq, Syria, Lebanon, Egypt, and Jordan, as well as the surrounding portions of Türkiye and Iran. In addition to the Tigris and Euphrates rivers, other water sources include the Jordan River. The inner boundary of the Fertile Crescent is usually delimited by the dry climate of the Syrian and Negev Deserts to the south. Around the outer boundary are the Anatolian and Armenian highlands to the north, the Sahara Desert to the west, Sudan to the south, and the Iranian Plateau to the east.

Historically, the geographic location of the Fertile Crescent, and thereby the Levant, provided an enormous opportunity to share and absorb innovations from eclectic nomadic and trading communities and cultures. This interchange and adoption of ideas was wide-

---

[200]   Boaretto et al (2021), p. 8.
[201]   Zonshine (2021).
[202]   SOURCE: https://www.britannica.com/place/Samaria-historical-region-Palestine retrieved on 13 March 2023.

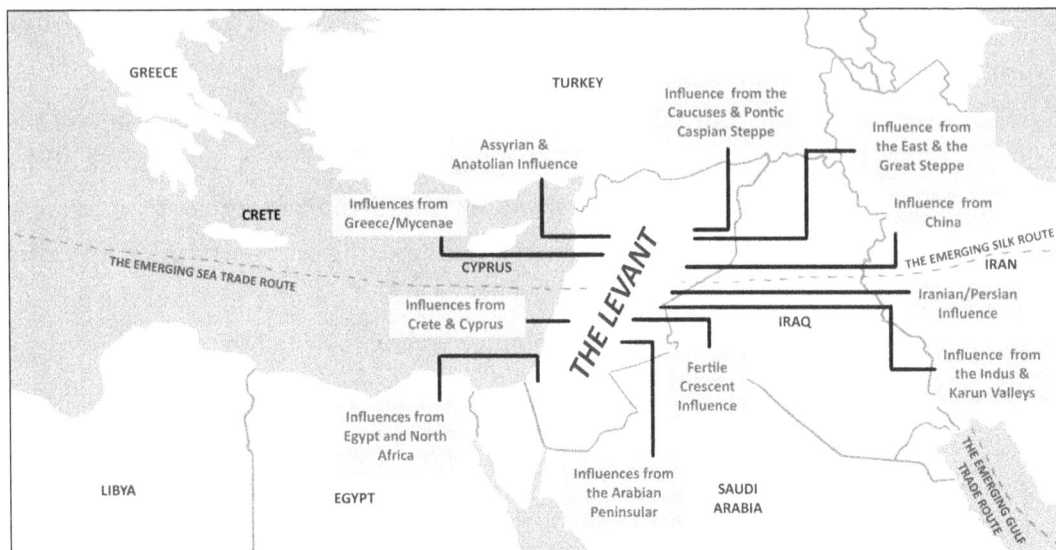

Figure 11: *360° of cross-cultural influences in the development of culture, agriculture and religion in the Levant*[d]

---

[d] Base map sourced from: https://www.google.com/maps/place/Levant/@35.6005455,35.514 7073,5z/data=!4m5!3m4!1s0x151618afe5727d5b:0xfac4620cf032a4a0!8m2!3d34.0757336!4d3 7.9784585!5m1!1e4 retrieved on 9 September 2023.

ranging and included sharing of agricultural practices, warfare strategies and weapons, animal husbandry, technology, art, culture, religious and administrative processes, and eventually writing systems (Figure 11).

Frederico Zangani (2018) described the Levant in the following way:

The complexity and diversity of the Levant may be easily explained in light of its geographical characteristics, geopolitical location and sociolinguistic composition: a region characterised by a diversity of environments, serving as an interface between Egyptian, Mesopotamian, Anatolian and Mediterranean worlds, inhabited by various ethnic groups speaking and writing several Semitic and non-Semitic languages.[203]

---

[203] Zangani (2018), p. 407.

This was the complex and regularly interacting environment within which the HB/OT was conceived and largely written in the first millennium (BCE).

The rich sources of influence in and around the emergence of Israel in the Levant were not limited to the simple geographic flow of ideas and innovations. Israel was first mentioned in around 1205 BCE. This was after the emergence and consolidation of many of the rich and diverse cultures in the East Mediterranean region since the Stone Age. The region was awash with various cultures and influences, all of which played a part in the emergence of Israel and the ideas contained in the HB/OT.

Across prehistory, the key influences on the Levant and ultimately on the Hebrew scribes came from Egypt, Central Asia, the Iranian Plateau, Siberia, the Eurasian Steppe, the Mediterranean, and the Middle East over thousands of years of development. These influences included literally hundreds of different languages, multiple cultures and religious mythologies waxing and waning, and invading, influencing, or peacefully infiltrating each other across differing geographical realms, trade routes, and conquests.

Across the Middle East and the Eurasian Steppes and throughout prehistory, many notional 'kingdoms' have been identified by archaeologists and historians. In most cases, these kingdoms were not universally aligned and governed common peoples, but, most often a convenient, loose-knit confederation of culturally similar, tribal federations, local powers, city-states, and smaller communities. The large, ever-changing and continuously inventing and influencing groups may well have been geographically scattered at times, but they were regularly interacting, overtaking, influencing, aligning, and re-aligning with each other's emerging cultures and beliefs.

In 1904, Hebrew scholar Grey Hubert Skipwith explained that 'the common civilisation of antiquity was correlated with a common religion. Similar elements of thought and worship recur continually in different connexions' and that

> *many, and perhaps all, the analogies which the (religious) traditions (of the island of Crete and Israel) present may prove to consist in, or be derived from, elements common to all of the ancient world.*[204]

Dead Sea Scrolls scholar Russell E. Gmirikin has recently shown the very high correlation between the Hebrew laws as expressed in the Pentateuch (also known as the Law/Torah) and early Greek, specifically Plato's laws (around 428 BCE to 348 BCE). Gmirikin claims that the biblical laws were essentially adapted by seventy Jewish scholars and that

---

[204]   Skipwith (1904), pp. 57-59.

later tradition credits these scholars with the translation of the Pentateuch into Greek around 273–269 BCE. They developed the biblical laws from the Mesopotamian/Babylonian Hammurabi Law Code (1810 BCE to 1750 BCE) and the Greek laws of the time. Gmirikin states that 'the Pentateuch was written around 270 BCE using Greek sources found at the Great Library of Alexandria'.[205]

In 1918, Assyriologist Daniel Luckenbill described the Hebrew scribes as:

> … *warblers of poetic prose (who) were enunciating their expanding faith in an eternal, almighty, and ubiquitous god [and] calmly availed themselves of the inexhaustible store of myths and legends which were afloat in the land, and, thus supplied, easily filled in the gaps.*[206]

The main influences on the Hebrew scribes

Throughout prehistory, the identifiably different groups in Egypt, Central Asia, Siberia, the Eurasian Steppe, the Indus Valley, and the Middle East included hunters and gatherers, horsemen, forest farmers, vegetative propagators, nomadic cattle breeders, pastoral nomads, crop and domesticated animal farmers, artisans, fishermen, trading and exchanging networks and, emerging sedentary, non-nomadic societies.[207]

There were four unique opportunities that facilitated the emergence of Israel and the writing and distribution of the HB/OT:

1. The Levant's advantageous geographic location drew influence from and influenced Africa, the Middle East, Central Asia, the Eurasian Steppe, Northern India, and eventually Europe.

2. A catastrophic collapse of the large empires in the region in around 1200 BCE facilitated the emergence of Israel.

3. Subsequently, as new empires conquered and controlled most of the Middle East, the upper echelon of the Israelites, including the Hebrew scribes, were deported to different locations where they experienced and were able to document and learn from other cultures and other mythologies.

4. One thousand years after the Bronze Age collapse, in around 340 BCE, Alexander the Great took control of Anatolia, Levant, Mesopotamia, the Fertile Crescent, the Iranian Plateau, and Egypt, bringing the Greek influence and language to an emerging Israelite nation and to the translation of the Bible into Greek.

---

[205] Gmirkin (2019), pp. 1-4.
[206] Luckenbill (1918), pp. 25-26.
[207] Baumer (2016) page 1.

The advantageous location of the Levant

One thousand years before the emergence of Israel, the Northern Hemisphere, including the Middle East, the Eurasian Steppe, West Asia, North India, North Africa, and Europe, was pulsating with a variety of different cultures, lifestyles, and livelihoods. There was a rich diversity of hunter-gatherer, nomadic, farming, and state-based systems (Figure 12).

In the thousands of years prior to that date, there is significant factual evidence of the existence of multiple cultures and communities dating back as far as 5000 BCE. Figure 13 illustrates the main locations that had a major influence on the emergence of Israel and on the content, structure and writing of the HB/OT. The Hebrew scribes were not working in a vacuum. Figure 13 highlights the incredibly large and geographically dense range of nations, kingdoms, empires, principalities, city-states, tribes, tribal confederations, communities, ethnicities, cultures, and influences occurring in and around Mesopotamia, the Levant, and Egypt in the thousands of years prior the emergence of Israel. The mythologies and beliefs of many of these groups formed the palette from which the Hebrew scribes created the stories that became the HB/OT.

As can be seen in Figure 13, many groups waxed and waned over time—sometimes through conquests and sometimes through migration, peaceful infiltration, technological or climatic change, or economic opportunities. Paul Collins described the situation some four hundred years before the emergence of the Israelites thus:

> *By the beginning of the sixteenth century BC the influence of a number of kingdoms that had once dominated extensive territories within the region stretching from the Aegean and northwest Africa to the mountains of western Iran had greatly diminished. Moving across these lands around 1600, a traveller would have passed through a kaleidoscope of states and settled and mobile communities forming networks of close relationships or heated rivalries.*[208]

Whilst these many cultural entities in and around the Levant were in constant contact with each other, the Levant itself became a focal point for the transference and hybridisation of regional ideas and innovations. For example, Jeffrey Emanuel has outlined the critical role of the Levant in the development, sharing and rapid spread of improvements in the design of ships and maritime technology in and around 1500 BCE to 1300 BCE. He singles out the Levant as a territory where geography, topography, and its location in the

---

[208] Collins, P. (2008), p. 14.

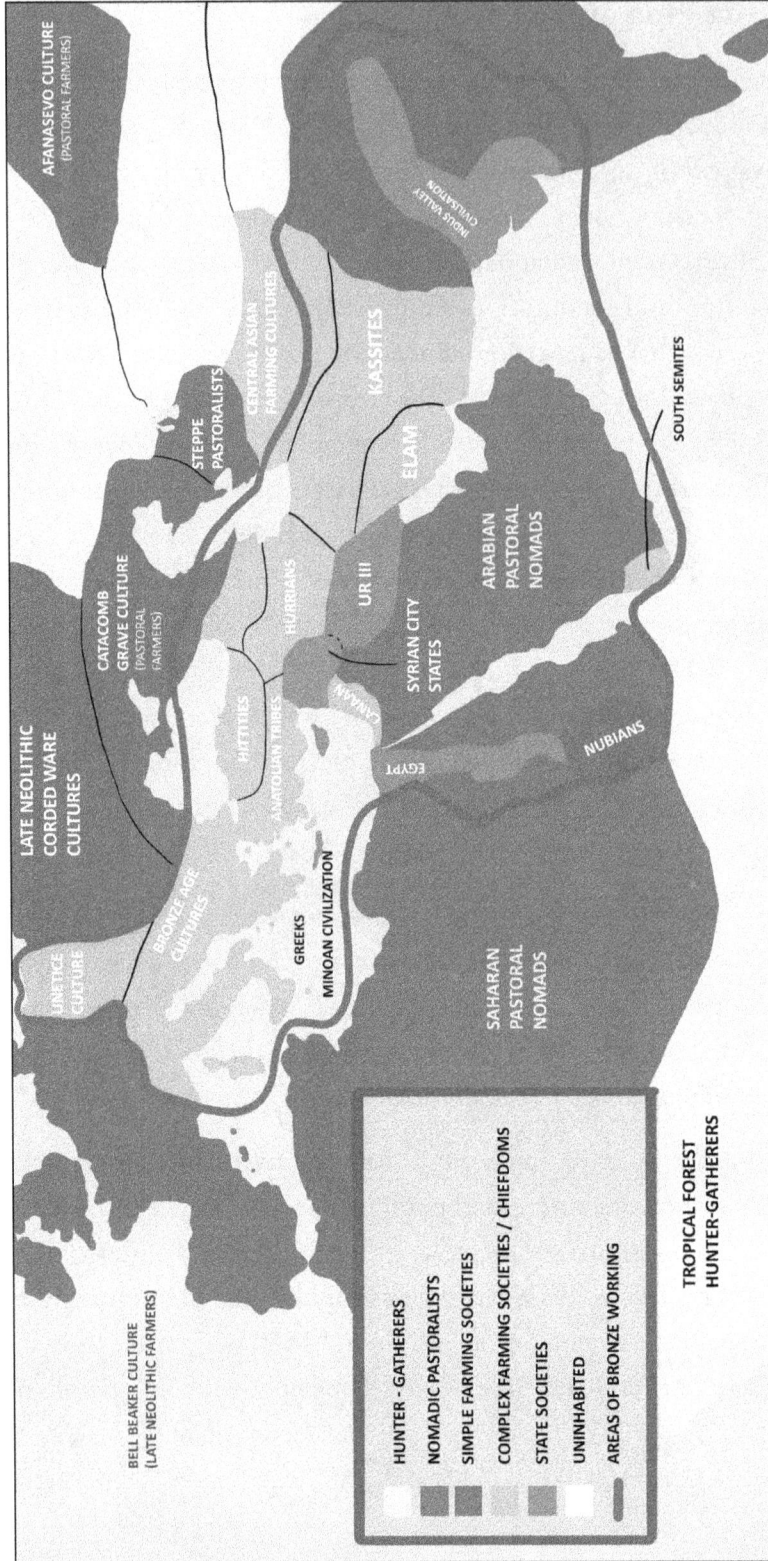

Figure 12: *The key Northern Hemisphere communities in 2000 BCE[e]*

---

[e] SOURCE: adapted from User: Mr.absurd Image:World_2000_BCE.png adapted from User:Briangotts, Public Domain, https://com-mons.wikimedia.org/w/index.php?curid=2959565 retrieved on 14 May 2022.

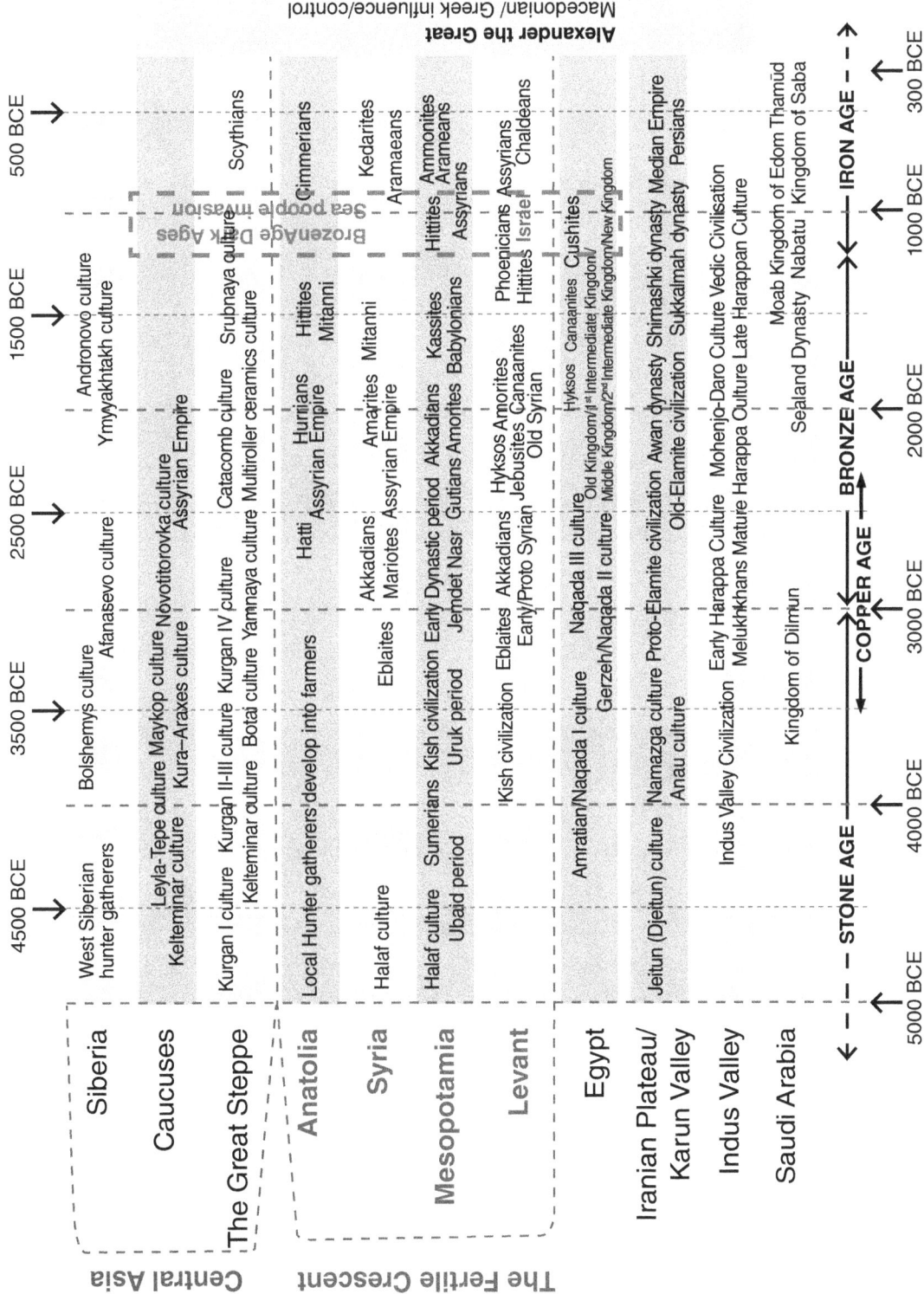

Figure 13: *The rich cultural diversity and overlapping influences prior to and around the emergence of Israel*[f]

NOTE: dates and cultural groupings in Figure 13 are approximate and for illustrative purposes only

Information in Figure 13 is drawn from a wide range of sources – see Bibliography.

middle of heavily trafficked crossroads of people and polities laid the groundwork for multidirectional, multi-layered diffusion of technologies and cultural influence.[209]

The Bronze Age collapse/Dark Ages and emerging Iron Age

The second major influence that provided a great opportunity for the emergence of Israel and other culturally differentiated entities was the catastrophic collapse of many of the Middle Eastern kingdoms and communities. The Middle East region suffered a major collapse around 1200 BCE. The collapse was total in the Middle East, and it occurred at around the same time as the emergence of the Iron Age. The date of the full Iron Age, when iron, for the most part, replaced bronze in implements and weapons, varied geographically. It began in the Middle East and south-eastern Europe about 1200 BCE but in other locations much later.[210] The predominant use of iron was in tools and weapons, with iron swords being one of the first manifestations of this new metal.

There was a related collapse of the Middle East-to-Mediterranean trade networks. This collapse has been variously attributed to a major invasion of the Middle East by the 'sea peoples', and/or a climatic change(largely prolonged drought), a famine across Anatolia, economic, volcanic, and/or a comprehensive social and political collapse that gave rise to this period being referred to as 'the Bronze Age Dark Ages' or the 'Bronze Age collapse' (Figure 13). The growth, development, exchange and trade dynamism, and the potential of the Bronze Age ended comprehensively, unceremoniously, and somewhat mysteriously with this Late Bronze Age collapse.

The fascinating fact about the Bronze Age collapse and the emergence of the Iron Age is that they occurred almost simultaneously with the development and spread of the alphabet and written language. Almost all currently preserved ancient manuscripts come from the Iron Age.[211] The Iron Age marked a significant technological (stronger tools, weaponry, more permanent cities) and intellectual change (manuscript culture and the Age of Literacy), which was fortuitous for the emerging Israelites.[212]

---

[209] Emanuel (2016), p. 269.
[210] SOURCE: https://www.britannica.com/event/Iron-Age.
[211] SOURCE: https://newsroom.posco.com/en/the-iron-age-of-civilization/.
[212] SOURCE: https://www.coursehero.com/file/p5qvrhr/McLuhan-divided-human-history-into-4-periods
       -or-epochs-1-The-Tribal-Age-An/.

Opportunities to harvest surrounding mythological stories

The third major opportunity that facilitated the development of the HB/OT was the exiling of the Israeli elite including the Hebrew Scribes to several important locations across the Middle East. In these locations, the Scribes were exposed to several other mythologies, religious practices and laws which were progressively blended into the emerging HB/OT.

The arrival of Alexander the Great

The fourth major influence—which probably had its greatest impact on the production and distribution of the HB/OT and, in particular, the emergence of the two different versions of the Hebrew Bible—was the invasion and success of Alexander the Great. This occurred from around 340 BCE around one thousand years after the Bronze Age collapse (see right side of Figure 13). Alexander managed to unify a large portion of the Levant and the Fertile Crescent. It was during this time that Greek versions of the HB/OT, including the version that had the most influence on the emergence of Christianity—the Septuagint—began to be circulated. This is when the Hebrew Bible (in Hebrew) and the Septuagint (a Greek version of the Hebrew Bible) first diverged.

Chapter 8

The Underlying Lunisolar Origin of Contemporary Mythologies

The ancient storylines

Ancient mythologies across Europe, Eurasia, and the Middle East tended to follow two storylines or combinations of both:

- Ancient European prehistoric cultures tended to build their mythologies around or concerned exclusively with women, taking a female (or specifically a feminist) point of view. This hinged around early agricultural practices and fertility beliefs. The female (goddess, shaman, or both) was a birth-giver, mother, root-gatherer, and seed-planter. The mythologies elaborated on feminine cycles, lunar phases, animals, and seasonal changes. The sky, planets, and stars prominent in Eurasia and Middle East mythologies figured marginally in ancient European symbolism.[213]

- Most Eurasian and Middle East cultures identified celestial objects (sun, moon, planets, and stars) with gods and spirits. They related these objects and their annual movement to understanding and predicting rain, drought, seasons, agricultural phenomena, fertility, and the motivation of their associated mythological gods and goddesses.

- By the time of the emergence of the Israelites, mythologies in Mesopotamia, the Fertile Crescent, and the Levant were largely an amalgamation of these two approaches—celestial gods and planetary, solar, and lunar cycles blended with seasonal agricultural cropping cycles and female fertility.

---

[213] https://www.encyclopedia.com/environment/encyclopedias-almanacs-transcripts-and-maps/prehistoric-religions-old-europe retrieved on 6 December 2021.

The astronomical influence on ancient mythologies

Some of the world's oldest cave paintings reveal how ancient people appear to have had relatively advanced knowledge and an apparent fascination with astronomy and linking it to mythological stories. Ancient prehistoric artworks at sites across Europe designate animals symbolising star constellations in the night sky. In some cases, ancient artworks were used to represent dates or mark events such as comet strikes. The archaeological evidence suggests that perhaps even 40,000 years ago, humans were keeping track of time using knowledge of how the position of the stars slowly changed over thousands of years.[214]

There is evidence dating back some 30,000 years of what appears to be early prehistoric communities having carved/engraved bone plates of mobiliary art (small transportable art carried from place to place) used as notional calendars recording the monthly motion of the moon and/or the yearly solar path.[215]

Evidence of prehistoric temple-like astronomical structures date from around 9000 BCE in the Levant/Southern Türkiye (Boncuklu Tarla, Göbekli Tepe, and Karahan/ Keçili Tepe) and from 5000 BCE in the Egyptian/Nubian desert (Nabta Playa). However, from around 4000 BCE onwards, greater astronomical advances were made by the Sumerians, Mesopotamians, Chaldeans, Babylonians, and Indus Valley cultures. These prehistoric cultures began to systematically observe the heavens and to make observations about the link between changing configurations of the sun, moon, planets, and stars and the seasons and weather.[216] They deified much of what they observed and wove these into complex mythologies. The recognition of cosmic order was instrumental in the development of an orderly mythology. From around 3200 BCE, the awareness of a cosmic order came with the parallel notion that society should participate in this cosmic order *because it is, in fact, the basic order of one's life.*[217]

This was occurring universally across prehistoric communities in the Middle East, Eurasia, and Central Asia thousands of years before the emergence of the Israelites and the Hebrew scribes. The mythologies that evolved in these cultures focused on the importance

---

214   SOURCE: https://www.sciencedaily.com/releases/2018/11/181127111025.htm retrieved on 10 May 2021.

215   Pasztor (2011).

216   See: Macquire (2022), The History of Astronomy in the Ancient World—World History Encyclopedia retrieved on 26 May 2022.

217   Campbell (2001), p. 3.

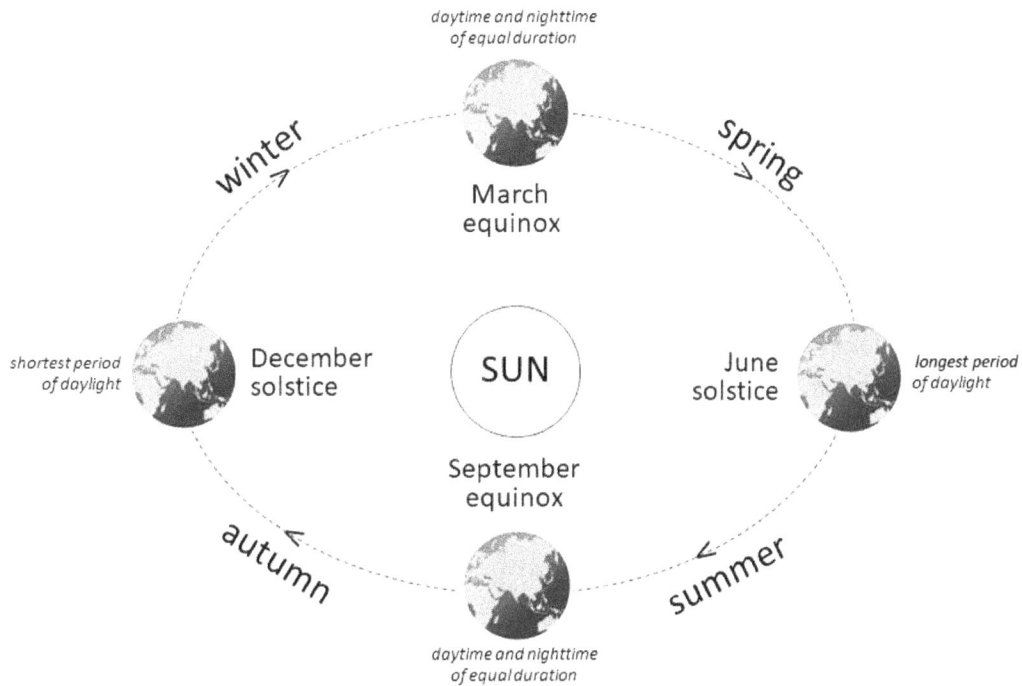

Figure 14: Northern Hemisphere solar journey[a]

---

[a] Based on: https://www.timeanddate.com/calendar/spring-equinox.htmlretrieved on 9 September 2023.

of changing configurations over time of the moon, the sun, and five 'sacred' (the then-known/observable) planets. The five sacred planets of prehistory were Jupiter, Venus, Saturn, Mercury, and Mars. These became embedded into different mythologies.

The embedding of the moon and sun into mythological stories hinged on four inter-related and recurring astronomical phenomena—the moon (and its phases), the sun (the solstice and equinox), the seasons (which vary from hemisphere to hemisphere according to the Earth's axis of rotation) (see Figure 14), the related agricultural and animal husbandry advantages, and the acquired knowledge of how and when these four—the sun, the moon, the seasons, the agricultural harvest and lamb-breeding—interacted over time.

Across most prehistoric cultures, the twice-yearly occurrences of each of the major lunisolar events—the equinox and the solstice—were the foundations for celebrations about the balance of nature, fertility, renewal, seasonal cropping, and pastoral advantages linked to mythological stories and beliefs.

The importance of the sun

The word solstice comes from the Latin *sol* ('sun') and *sistere* ('to stand still'). It refers to the times when the sun appears to reach its most southerly or northerly point—it appears to stop and then turn around. Solstices mark the brightest (longest) and darkest (shortest) days of the year. The equinox, from *aequus* ('equal') and *nox* ('night') refers to the moment at which the plane of Earth's equator passes through the centre of the sun's disk, or the moment that the sun passes over the celestial equator. On these dates, there are approximately equal hours of daylight and darkness.

The ancient Sumerians (4000 BCE to 2004 BCE) believed that the sun god was responsible for creating the distinction between day and night. They believed that this divine action was only done on two days within the year—on the spring and autumnal equinox—because these were the two times when day and night were of equal length. These are the days on which the sun god is visible and invisible for an equal number of hours.[218] Three thousand years later, the Hebrew scribes adapted this concept into their own creation story (Genesis 1:3-5):

> And god said 'let there be light; and there was light. And god separated the light from the darkness. God called the light Day, and the darkness he called Night. And there was evening and there was morning, the first day.

Across many ancient cultures, the sun was regarded as the chief god, the supreme being, with the other heavenly bodies being lesser gods in a celestial hierarchy. The Greek god Helios was the personification of the sun. This concept was most likely adopted by the Greeks from widely held beliefs across prehistoric Eurasian and Middle Eastern cultures, which saw the sun as the supreme god in the heavens. Martin Goodman has suggested that the Roman sun god Sol Invictus was most likely an adaptation of the Jewish Rabbis (around 300 CE) conceiving god 'in terms both anthropomorphic and fiery, noting that, because god is fire, it is impossible to go up to the heavens to join him'.[219]

The modern belief that there is a supreme being/god in heaven is a legacy of the prehistoric belief that the sun, up in heaven, was a god. However, not all religions believe in the existence of a god. Buddhism (from 563 BCE) and Confucianism (from 551 BCE), for instance, believe in spirits but not in a supreme deity. Buddhists believe that there are supernatural figures that can help or hinder them on their path to enlightenment. Buddhists also believe in rebirth, where a person's soul can be born again into a different

---

[218] Radau (1902), p. 106.
[219] Goodman (2008), p. 572.n

body depending on how well they have lived in their current life. Confucians believe that living a life of good moral character will lead to cosmic harmony. They believe in the spirits of their ancestors and of Confucius himself.

The origin of the 'son of god'

Over time, the concept of gods transitioned from being ambiguous spiritual entities (hunter-gatherer beliefs) through being lunisolar deities to human-like superior beings (Sumerians) to one supreme male sun god (Zoroastrians, ancient Egyptians). Inevitably, if the deity is a supreme male god with an anthropomorphic personality, then it seemed logical that this god would produce a son as the literal anthropomorphic embodiment of this god.[220]

This metaphor exists in the mythology of the Zoroastrians in their belief in the sun god and how humans were first created and the Christian adaptation of this into their stories of Jesus and of Adam. Two thousand years before Christianity, the Zoroastrians believed that their god (Āhurā Mazdā) had a son, Yima. Yima was sent down to Earth by the sun god (cf. Jesus) with two options—to either establish the Zoroastrian religion (cf. Jesus) or to establish the human race (cf. Adam).[221] Yima chose the latter and became the first man to be king on Earth and the first man to die.[222] The Zoroastrian legend is that Yima eventually sinned and, as punishment, the sun god removed immortality from humans (cf. Adam). Yima eventually became the Zoroastrian god of the underworld and death.

Hinduism (from 2300 BCE), closely related to Zoroastrianism, also tells of a sun god and creator of the universe (Surya) who had a son Yama who is also regarded as the first mortal to die. Yama also transitions into becoming the Hindu god of death.[223]

A more common and widely held myth related to the divine association of god-kings as rulers. Many of the prehistoric Middle Eastern and Egyptian cultures believed in a divine link between their king and their supreme deity. In some cases, there was a belief that the king was the result of a divine birth—the son of god. For example, in the coronation of the Egyptian King Haremhab (1500 BCE to 1295 BCE), Egyptian inscriptions declare that the supreme leader of the Egyptian deities, Amun, declared of Haremhab that 'you are my son, the heir who came from my flesh'.[224]

---

[220] Adapted from Stephen A. Geller as cited in Smith (2010), p. 179.
[221] https://www.britannica.com/topic/Yima retrieved on 17 February 2022.
[222] Boyce (2001), pp. 12-13.
[223] Schomp (2005), p. 14.
[224] See a good discussion of this issue in Collins, J.J. (2011), pp. 293-305.

The Pharoah Akhenaten who introduced monotheism into ancient Egyptian religion referred to himself as the son of god.[225] He adopted the persona of the god Shu who along with the goddess Tefnut were the first couple created by the Egyptian primordial god Atum. According to ancient Egyptian beliefs Atum created everything. Both concepts, a supreme god who created everything who has a son who is a divine leader morphed over time into key concepts woven into Christianity.

The phrase 'sons of god' was a common phrase across the mythologies of the Middle East.[226] The kingdom of the ancient Mediterranean Canaanite port of Ugarit used the phrase regularly in poetic cuneiform texts. It has a long history. It is a ubiquitous Zoroastrian, Middle Eastern, and Egyptian phrase with many meanings. The Hebrew Bible also uses the phrase with many different meanings. Genesis 6: 1-2 states:

When human beings began to increase in number on the earth and daughters were born to them, the sons of God saw that the daughters of humans were beautiful, and they married any of them they chose.

There is some debate about the meaning of this biblical use of the phrase. As early as 1894, Baptist clergyman and academic William Rainey Harper attempted to explain the many possible meanings of the phrase in the following way:

- It simply refers to men—because they are created in the image of God
- Sons of biblical Cain were called this because of their commercial enterprise
- Sons of biblical Seth who were easily snared by women
- It referred to high-ranking holy men
- It referred to idolaters—polytheists
- It refers to angels.[227]

The concept that a king or a god-king was a son of god, that a holy person was a son of god, that two gods had given birth to a son, that angels are sons of god, or that a son of a god had been sent to Earth were widely held beliefs in the Middle East and Egypt for centuries prior to the biblical story of Jesus.

All four Christian gospels refer to Jesus as 'the son of God'. Mark's gospel, which is regarded as the first gospel to be written, was written around 70 CE. This is at least two

---

[225] Jack (2016), pp. 23-24.
[226] See: https://www.encyclopedia.com/religion/encyclopedias-almanacs-transcripts-and-maps/sons-god retrieved on 8 February 2023.
[227] Harper (1894), pp. 441-442.

thousand years after Hinduism and Zoroastrianism promoted the mythological notion of the 'son of god'. Mark's gospel contains two references to Jesus being the son of God:

- 'And there came a voice from heaven, saying, Thou art my beloved Son, in whom I am well pleased.' (Mark 1:11)
- 'And there was a cloud that overshadowed them: and a voice came out of the cloud, saying, This is my beloved Son: hear him.' (Mark 9:7).

Luke's gospel (Luke 1:35) tells of the angel advising Mary of her child as being 'the Son of God'. The HB/OT and the Christian New Testament have simply continued the long-held tradition of using this apparently colloquial phrase to describe specific persons of divine or allegorical interest.

The influence of prehistoric sun worshipping

In prehistoric times, annual celebrations were held at the times of the two equinoxes (September and March) and at the times of the two solstices (June and December).

- The September equinox marked the start of autumn and many myths, religious festivals, and customs occur on this date. Because this is autumn and the time when leaves turn yellow and fruit, crops, and vegetables ripen, most celebrations focused on the harvest.
- The March equinox was by far the most important ancient festival time (see *Reverence for the Northern Hemisphere spring equinox*, page 103).
- The Northern Hemisphere June solstice is the longest day of the year and occurs around 21 June and is called the summer solstice or midsummer. This is when most prehistoric cultures planned their planting and harvesting calendars. Cultures prehistorically and currently from all around the globe celebrated Mother Earth and fertility at this time with feasts, picnics, dance, and music.

However, the most significant sun worshipping event that was common across prehistoric communities in the Northern Hemisphere related to the December (winter) solstice, which occurs typically on or about 21 December and is the shortest day of the year. This is the day with the shortest period of daylight and the longest night-time of the year.

This is when the sun appears to stop, turn around, and 'rise again'. Northern hemisphere mythological festivals included farming-related rituals of midwinter and the winter solstice, especially the practice of offering gifts or sacrifices to the gods and usually the sun god during the winter sowing season.[228] For many cultures, this recurring astronomical event was seen as a turning point (a rising or re-birth) of the 'light'.

The Syrian sun god Sol was adopted by the Romans (from 625 BCE) as Sol Invictus (the 'unconquerable sun'). Roman Emperor Constantine the Great (306 CE to 337 CE), who converted to Catholicism and was responsible for Christianity being recognised as the Roman religion, was originally a member of the Roman Sol Invictus cult.[229] The ancient Romans would celebrate the December (winter) solstice annually as their Saturnalia festival, which primarily honoured their agricultural god Saturn. It celebrated the time when the sun enters Capricorn, the astrological house of Saturn. The Saturnalia celebration was a time for feasting, goodwill, generosity to the poor, the exchange of gifts, and the decoration of trees.

In the words of mythologist and author Barbara G. Walker:

> *At the end of each winter solstice period, when the light began to grow, all the ancient world celebrated the birth of the solar god from his virgin mother; the god was called Light of the World, Sun of Righteousness, Saviour, Son of God, Good Shepherd, He who rises with healing in his wings and many similar epithets.*[230]

The prehistoric celebrations of this Northern Hemisphere winter solstice solar event are recognised as the original source of many of the traditions now associated with the Christian celebration of Christmas and the Jewish celebration of Hanukkah.

Reverence for the rising sun god

Goodman has shown how the Jewish cult of the Essenes (from around 200 BCE) offered prayers to the sun before it rose as though they were entreating the sun god to rise.[231]

As far back as there are reliable records, there is evidence of ancient religious structures being oriented east–west to catch the sunrise. This reflected the ancient belief in the sun being a heavenly deity. The first ceremonial communal ritual structure to be discovered, Göbekli Tepe in northern Levant/South-Eastern Türkiye (from around 9000 BCE), had stone pillars that are believed to be celestial markers that were erected in astronomical alignment with a key important star. Ancient Maltese temples (dating from around 5000 BCE to 2000 BCE) had a strong astronomical alignment to the sunrise, sunset, moonrise, and moonset during the Northern Hemisphere winter solstice.

---

[228] SOURCE: https://www.history.com/topics/ancient-rome/saturnalia retrieved on 11 May 2021.
[229] Denova (2021C).
[230] Walker (2010), p. 130.
[231] Goodman (2008), p. 572.n

Ancient Stonehenge has large stone structures that align with the solstice's axes.[232] Interestingly, DNA evidence from England's ancient henges, mounds, and stone circles, including Stonehenge, suggests that the builders of these monuments have strong ancestral links to the mass migration into the UK across Europe from Anatolia (Türkiye) in around 4000 BCE.[233] The Persian King Darius (550 BCE to 486 BCE) had his palace in the Persian Achaemenian kingdom capital city of Persepolis built so it was oriented to capture the sunrise at the spring equinox.[234]

This ancient mythological tradition of orienting religious structures east–west to take advantage of the rising sun (the prehistoric supreme being) and specifically to align the structures with the rising sun god has continued in the design of most contemporary Christian churches.[235] By canonical decree, modern-day Christian churches are solar-aligned—designed to have their altar at the eastern end, the façade and main entrance at the western end, and the aisle aligning with the east–west axis.

Reverence for the Northern Hemisphere spring equinox

There are remnants of the prehistoric link to female goddesses and fertility in the continuation of Jewish and Christian religious celebrations, symbolism, and rituals linked to the lunisolar (Northern Hemisphere) March/April equinox and the commencement of spring. In prehistory, this was when Middle Eastern communities celebrated female fertility, renewal/rebirth, and the commencement of spring (celebrating goddesses, eggs, regeneration, rebirth, resurrection, lambing, and crop seeding). This is during the 'vernal equinox'—from the Latin word *ver*, which means spring and the Latin words for 'equal night'. This is when the sun crosses the celestial equator and equalises night and day.

To the ancient Mesopotamians, the year commenced at the first new moon following the vernal equinox. There were twelve lunar months in the Mesopotamian year. Each lunar month began on the evening of the new moon or, if the new moon was not observed, the new month started thirty days after the previous month.[236]

---

[232] https://www.theguardian.com/culture/2013/sep/08/stonehenge-ice-age-solstice-axis retrieved on 8 December 2021.

[233] Smith, R. (2022).

[234] Boyce (2001), p. 57.

[235] Sparavigna and Dastru (2018).

[236] Smith, G. (1875), p. 18.

The vernal equinox (March/April) was almost universally the time/date/month for the prehistoric celebration of female fertility, female goddesses, the end of winter, ancestor worship, the commencement of the new year and of spring, lamb-breeding, and the crop-planting season across Central Asia, the Middle East, and Northern India. According to the Sumerians, prosperity came to Mesopotamia when the gods made the ewe give birth to the lamb and made the grain increase in the furrows.[237]

The Sumerians, Babylonians, and Assyrians celebrated their fertility and the commencement of spring festivals at this time. This was also the time the Babylonians (Akitu festival) and Persians and ancient Iranians (Nowruz new year festival) celebrated rebirth, new beginnings, prosperity, and the triumph of the divine order over chaos in the gods' act of creation. Like the Jewish Passover and the Christian Easter, the Persian Nowruz owes a great deal to the earlier Mithraism (Norouz Festival) and Zoroastrianism (Farvardegan/ Hamsapathmidee-e Festival). The Greco-Egyptian celebration of the cult god Serapis (circa 320 BCE onwards), who was regarded as the lord of all, the deity of the sun, and lord of healing and fertility, was also celebrated at this lunisolar calendrical time.

Well prior to the arrival of Christianity, Neolithic (Stone Age) Irish celebrated this same lunisolar event as their Ēostre or Ostara festival to celebrate their goddess of the dawn, commencement of spring, and fertility. Prehistoric Dutch and Germans also held similar festivals to celebrate spring and their spring goddesses—called Ooster (Dutch) and Ostern (German). These linguistically related terms for spring and fertility goddesses are believed by many to be the origin of the word Easter. Ēostre the spring fertility goddess is believed to have mated with the solar god during the spring equinox and, nine months later (at the winter solstice), a man/god was born. This ancient myth has been carried forward in the Christian story of Jesus (see *Lunar-solar events and the life and death of god-kings including Jesus*, see page 112).

Contemporary reverential practices of the Hindu Holi festival (Festival of Love/Festival of Spring); the East European (Slovakian, Hungarian, Polish, and Czech Republic) celebrations of spring, female beauty, fertility and the chasing away of bad spirits; the Chinese Qingming, or Tomb-Sweeping Festival; the Japanese Shunbun no Hi spring equinox festival; the Jewish Passover; the Theravada Buddhist's New Year; and the Christian Easter (death and resurrection of Jesus) are all held at or around the same lunisolar event. This is reflective of the prehistoric celebrations of female fertility, the Northern Hemisphere vernal equinox, full moon, end of winter, first day of astronomical spring, and

---

[237] Kramer (1968), p. 42.

commencement of the lamb-breeding and cereal cycles (winter barley harvesting/spring barley planting). Both the Jewish Passover Seder celebrations and the Last Supper story in the Christian Old Testament occur on the same significant vernal equinox day, and both involve sharing a meal of roast lamb.

The Islamic religion's most significantly sacred month, Ramadan, is a lunisolar-based celebration beginning with the sighting of the new moon in April. It involves a meal of lamb meat. Ramadan is significant because the Islamists believe that it was in this month that the angel Gabriel appeared to the Prophet Muhammad and revealed to him the Quran, the Islamic holy book.[238]

The dates for most of these various lunisolar fertility and spring harvest festivals can vary from any time between late February to late April because of the subtle variations in how each culture has historically remembered and celebrated the Northern Hemisphere transition from winter and autumn to spring and the related moon phases. For instance, the Hindu Holi Festival commences in the Hindu month of Phalguna (February to March) on the last full moon day or the first new moon day at the end of winter; the Chinese Qingming (Tomb-Sweeping) Festival commences on the fifteenth day after the spring equinox; the Persian Nowruz festival usually commences between 19 and 22 March (the first day of the spring equinox), the Jewish Passover is celebrated on the fourteenth day of the full moon of spring (full moon of the month of Aries, the ram) and lasts for seven or eight days; the Christian Easter celebration was originally held on the same date as the Passover but, by canonical decree, must be on the first Sunday following the first full moon of spring.[239] This means that the Christian Easter celebration can occur on any Sunday between 21 March and 25 April depending on the year and its lunisolar cycle.

Biblical repackaging of the Northern Hemisphere vernal equinox

The Hebrew calendar is an adaptation of the Babylonian calendar, including the adaptation of the monthly Babylonian names (see Figure 15). The first month of the Hebrew calendar is Nissan, which usually falls in March–April on the modern-day Gregorian calendar. This is based on the ancient celebration of the vernal equinox when, in the Northern Hemisphere, barley is planted and lambing begins; it is the first month of spring. The fifteenth day of Nissan is when the Israelites celebrate the biblical 'exodus story' from Egypt.

---

238 See: Why Ramadan is the most sacred month in Islamic culture (nationalgeographic.com) retrieved on 29 March 2022.
239 Eusebius (2011), p. 155.

Babylonian month	Hebrew Name
• Nisanu	Nisan / Nissan
• Ayaru	Iyar
• Simanu	Sivan
• Du`uzu	Tammuz
• Abu	Av
• Ululu	Elul
• Tashritu	Tishrei
• Arakhsamna	Cheshvan
• Kislimu	Kislev
• Tebetu	Tevet
• Shabatu	Shevat
• Adaru	Adar I
• Adaru	Adar/Adar II

Figure 15: *Origin of Hebrew names for months*

The same dates were adopted by Christians for Easter and the death and resurrection of Jesus.

The Hebrew word for the month of Nissan is based on the Babylonian word *nisanu*, which was an adaptation of the Sumerian word *nisag*, which meant 'first fruits'. The Hebrew first fruits celebration, called Shavuot, was an adaptation of the Sumerian practice carried across into a celebration of the Israelite wheat harvest, which is celebrated in around May and June. Agriculturally, the Jewish Passover celebration aligns with the new moon and barley ripening in March-April and the Jewish first fruits celebration aligns with the wheat harvest in May-June. The Passover signified the beginning of the barley festival and Shavuot signified the end of the wheat harvest.

The Passover celebration was originally adapted by the Hebrew scribes from the agricultural and pastoral celebrations of the Mesopotamians and Canaanites. Early Israelites continued these rituals by undertaking two different rituals that were eventually merged into the Passover. These ritual celebrations were Pesach (a semi-nomadic pastoral/herders' ritual to ward off evil spirits, which included a sacrificial lamb) and Hag Hamatzot (a spring harvest ritual celebrated by farmers).[240] These were merged into and rebranded as the Passover or Paschal celebration (from the Greek *pascha* and Hebrew *pesah*, words that mean 'to jump' or 'to pass over').

Christian mythology continued the associations with prehistoric agricultural practices—the Passover became the Christian Easter celebration and Shavuot was rebranded by Christians as the Holy Day of Pentecost or Whitsun.[241] The liberation of the Jews and the resurrection of Jesus during the vernal equinox are metaphors for the ancient agricultural belief that the vegetation god dies in autumn and is resurrected in spring and appropriate rituals are developed around these dates.[242]

It is not a coincidence that the Jewish celebration of the Passover/Exodus from Egypt and the Christian celebration of the death and resurrection of Christ occur at the time of the Northern Hemisphere vernal equinox. Beneath them lies the same key principle—although packaged differently mythologically. In the words of Joseph Campbell, a renowned authority on mythologies, the Jewish and Christian writers have chosen this time of year and this metaphor for followers to reflect on a release from bondage in a transcendent spiritual sense—born again, released (from Egypt in the Jewish metaphor and released from original sin in the Christian metaphor). Both metaphors reflect the original transition from winter to spring—the bursting forth of nature, the moon throwing off its shadow and the return of the sun, the fertility of crops, and the beginning of the lambing season. The Jewish and Christian stories are metaphoric symbols in a personal liberation and a transcendental spiritual sense.[243]

The authors of both the HB/OT and the Christian New Testament have simply continued the long-held tradition of religious celebrations, renewal/rebirth symbolism, and rituals linked to the lunisolar (Northern Hemisphere) March/April equinox, the commencement of spring and the commencement of winter barley harvesting/spring barley

---

[240] Gilad (2021).

[241] Wade (2010), p. 132 and p. 168.

[242] Holland (2010) p. 174.

[243] Campbell (2001), pp. 103-104; Kennedy (1979).

planting and the lambing season. The Christian story of the Last Supper is based on the Jewish celebrations of the Passover. The Last Supper story involves Jesus and the apostles sharing a meal of roast lamb on the eve of the fifteenth day of Nisan in the Hebrew calendar, as part of the Jewish Passover Seder celebration. The Passover Seder meal is a ritual, continuing today, that involves the retelling of the Hebrew biblical story of the liberation of the Israelites from slavery in ancient Egypt.

The Episcopal Church of St Augustine in Oklahoma City, USA, describes these contemporaneous mythological stories in the following way:

> *In the Old Testament, God's Passover resulted in the gift of freedom to the Hebrew people from their Egyptian masters. In the New Testament, the Paschal Mystery is the central tenet of Christianity that resulted in the salvation of Christ's followers.*[244]

No matter how much it has been repackaged, re-branded, or appropriated by different mythologies, the Northern Hemisphere vernal equinox lunisolar full moon event is the underlying reason for most contemporary religious celebrations held at this time. The commencement of the lambing and planting season and the prehistoric celebration of female fertility ironically remains the original reason for religious scribes linking the March/April lunar solar event of spring to the contemporary religious mythological stories, beliefs, rituals, and practices of today.

The lunisolar origin of the 'lamb of god' concept

Sheep were the first livestock species to be domesticated (from around 9000 BCE). They held a particularly high position in the rituals and mythologies of the ancient Middle East and Egypt. The Northern Hemisphere vernal equinox is the time when the astrological sign for fish (Pisces—19 February to 20 March) transitions to the astrological sign for sheep (Aries, the ram—21 March to 19 April).

At this time, the ancient Egyptians worshipped the supreme god Khnum, who they believed had created humankind from clay. Khnum was a ram-headed god of fertility who was celebrated with the transition to the astrological month of Aries (spring equinox) on the fifteenth of Nissan. The Egyptian name of the month and the celebration were adopted by the Egyptians and the Hebrew scribes from the Sumerian (*nisag*) and

---

244 https://www.sac-okc.org/canterbury-canticle/where-does-the-word-paschal-come-from retrieved on 25 April 2022.

Akkadian (*nisanu*) celebrations. The Hebrew scribes adopted the same date as the Egyptian, Sumerian, and Akkadian spring celebrations for their Passover story, including the metaphoric significance of the ram, lamb, and sheep.

The importance of this metaphor, and in particular the significance of a sacrificial male lamb, was carried across mythologies for several thousands of years commencing with the Mesopotamians. It reflects the critical symbolism of the killing of a male lamb to placate the gods—a practice that was common in ancient communities and the embedding of this into contemporary religious mythologies. The choice of a male lamb over a female as the most appropriate sacrificial offering has been widely debated. In ancient times, a lamb was considered a highly prized sacrificial offering to the divine. The meat of a male lamb was the preferred meat for the elite across Mesopotamia. The lower class would only eat other types, ages, and gender of sheep or goat meat.[245] It is most likely that the sacrificial male lamb reflects these beliefs. The male lamb was regarded as the most appropriate symbol of the patriarchal and hierarchical society.[246] Evidence of the significance of a sacrificial male lamb historically includes:

- Archaeological evidence of an ancient ceremonial double burial—a human with a young lamb—as far back as Neolithic times (7100 BCE to 5700 BCE) in ancient Anatolia (Türkiye)[247]

- The ancient Mesopotamians' most popular deity was the goddess Inanna/Ishtar (from around 3000 BCE).[248] Inanna/Ishtar was associated with the moon, fertility, love, beauty, sex, material abundance, war, justice, and political power. She was specifically celebrated by the Mesopotamians as the goddess of fertility each year in the Northern Hemisphere vernal equinox lunisolar full moon event. The slaughtering of male lambs was the primary sacrificial offering to placate Inanna/Ishtar[249]

- The Mesopotamians' belief in omens from the gods meant that they had established several methods by which to access these divine messages. One of the most popular methods was hepatoscopy—the reading of gods' omens from a sheep's liver[250]

---

[245] Kozuth (2010), p. 533.
[246] See also: https://theopolisinstitute.com/a-male-without-defect/ retrieved on 11 May 2023.
[247] Russell and During (2006).
[248] Pryke (2017), p. 27.
[249] Kozuh (2010), p. 535.
[250] Hooke (1955), p. 333.

- The metaphor of the slaughtering of a lamb as a gesture to God is repeated several times in the HB/OT—for example, in Isaiah 53:7 and Jeremiah 11:19 (both most likely written during the Babylonian Exile around 550 BCE)
- The HB/OT's story of Abraham (written during the Babylonian Exile) replaced the killing of his son Isaac with the killing of a ram—referred to ever since as 'the lamb of God' (Genesis 22: 6-13)
- In the biblical story of the Exodus (Exodus 12–most likely written during the Babylonian Exile), the Israelites are instructed to take and kill a year-old male lamb without defect ('the Passover lamb'). They are instructed to take the lamb on the tenth day of the month and slaughter it on the fourteenth day. This sacrifice occurs in March-April—it is essentially based on the vernal equinox lunisolar full moon event of the Mesopotamians sacrificing a lamb to the fertility goddess Inanna/Ishtar (above)
- The Christian New Testament states that when John the Baptist sees Jesus, he exclaims, 'Behold the Lamb of God' (John 1:29). This is a poetic, retrospective reference by the pseudepigraphic author/s of John's gospel to link Jesus to the notion of the sacrificial lamb of prehistory.[251]

The link to the Northern Hemisphere vernal equinox and the associated lambing season has been carried across into many Jewish and Christian mythological metaphors. The HB/OT (Psalm 78:52) introduced this metaphor celebrating the Passover (linked to the vernal equinox) in the following way, explaining how God led his people out of Egypt: 'He brought his people out like a flock … he led them like sheep through the wilderness.'

In the East Semitic language of Akkadian, the word for Aries is *agru*, which translates as 'the farm worker'. The shepherd metaphor originated with the Sumerian kings and was continued by the Babylonians. Sumerian kings wore stylised versions of a shepherd's hat. The importance of the metaphor was not lost on the Egyptian pharaoh Akhenaten, who was one of the first leaders in prehistory to introduce monotheism. There is archaeological evidence of Akhenaten holding a shepherd's crook, the logic being that:

… there is a symbiotic relationship between a shepherd and his flock. A shepherd is a herder of sheep, leading them to greener pastures. He tends to the flock; he makes sure the sheep are well

---

[251] It is generally accepted that the four gospels were not written by Mathew, Mark, Luke and John – see Walker (2010), p. 153; and (599) Dr. Bart Ehrman Destroys The Crucifixion and The Resurrection History—YouTube retrieved on 18 January 2023.

fed and he protects them from predators. That is why the sheep willingly obey him. A king is a herder of men. He tends to their many needs, makes sure they have plenty of food, and he protects them from hostile foreign powers. In return they willingly give him their allegiance and their obedience.[252]

The prehistoric shepherd and lamb metaphor has been transmitted through biblical scripture. It continues in the language of many contemporary Christian pastors (a word derived from the Babylonians and pastoralism) who see themselves as 'shepherds' undertaking a 'pastoral ministry' and guiding and caring for their 'flock' (followers). This metaphor is simply a reflection of the ancient world linking vernal equinox celebrations, the importance of sheep, the sacrificial lamb, and the lambing season. The Hebrew scribes, when they were constructing the HB/OT, adopted this metaphor because it had relevance to the surrounding mythologies, activities, and lifestyles of the people of those times.

The popular Christian phrase 'Agnus Dei'—which is used across the Catholic Mass, in the liturgy, and in a specific hymn—comes from the Latin words for 'lamb of God'.[253] The hymn itself contains the lines 'Holy are You, Lord God Almighty / Worthy is the Lamb / Worthy is the Lamb.'

The Mesopotamian god Tammuz/Dumuzi was referred to as 'the shepherd king' of the Mesopotamian city of Uruk.[254] The Hebrew scribes continued the metaphor of their God being a shepherd when they wrote Psalm 23, which states:

The Lord is my shepherd; I shall not want. He maketh me to lie down in green pastures: he leadeth me beside the still waters. He restoreth my soul: he leadeth me in the paths of righteousness for his name's sake. (Psalm 23:1-3).

The Sumerians traditionally depicted their priest/god-king as a bearded man wearing a long robe and a shepherd's cap.[255] Many Christian depictions of God in art are a continuation of the lamb metaphor and are largely based on prehistoric Middle Eastern precedents. This tradition is reflected primarily in the multiple images that are available showing Jesus as a shepherd with lambs.[256]

---

[252] See: https://sumerianshakespeare.com/70701/507901.html retrieved on 9 June 2022.

[253] See: https://www.britannica.com/topic/Agnus-Dei-liturgical-chant retrieved on 17 January 2023

[254] Kramer (1956), p. 359.

[255] https://www.ancientworldmagazine.com/articles/evolution-sumerian-kingship/ retrieved on 1 July 2022.

[256] See for instance: https://www.dreamstime.com/illustration/jesus-christ-good-shepherd.html retrieved on 12 October 2022.

Lunar-solar events and the life and death of 'god-kings' including Jesus

The Mesopotamians (Sumerians, Akkadians, Babylonians) had a complex mythology built around the interaction of the solar and lunar cycles with fertility and nature. As shown above, the Easter, Passover, and Christ's death and resurrection stories align with the dates and much of the symbolism of the ancient Middle East mythological festivals around the commencement of spring, the planting of seeds, the lambing season, and fertility.

It is lesser known that the Mesopotamians believed that a god and a god-king's fate was determined at their birth and that they would eventually die on the same date they were conceived.[257] The Mesopotamian fertility celebrations were held each year according to the lunisolar calendar. The festivities and rituals were linked to the moon phase and the Northern Hemisphere spring/vernal equinox.

The most well-known Mesopotamian mythological story relates to the god Dumuzi, also called Tammuz.[258] The Mesopotamians would write the letter 'T' on their left chest near their hearts in honour of Tammuz. The Hebrews adopted this symbol, which is referred to as the *tau* cross (*tau* is the last letter of the Hebrew alphabet). According to the Hebrew Book of Ezekiel, the *tau* cross sign was to be placed on the forehead of the poor to save them from extermination (Ezekiel 9:4). This Zoroastrian and Hebrew ancient mythological practice may have contributed to the practice of believers in the Christian faith making a similar sign of the cross in memory of Jesus. In fact, historically the Romans in the time of Christ preferred to crucify convicts on the *tau* cross, which is shaped identically to the Sumerian Tammuz symbol. Despite this, most Christians believe that Jesus was crucified on the Latin cross (see Figure 16).

There is a more fundamental lunisolar link between Tammuz, Mesopotamian and Zoroastrian beliefs, and the biblical life and death of Jesus. The Mesopotamian myth about the birth of god-kings has been carried on in the Christian story of Jesus. The phrase 'newborn king' has been widely associated with the biblical birth of Jesus (adapted from Mathew, 2:2). Mathew's gospel was written in Greek around 70 CE. It is widely accepted that it was not written by the apostle Mathew but by someone or by persons very familiar with Judaism and the Old Testament. Mathew's gospel is significantly focused on showing how Jesus is the Messiah, as promised in the HB/OT and in Jewish tradition and

---

257   Van Oudheusden (2019), p. 12.
258   Van Oudheusden (2019), pp. 68-72; Frazer (1998), pp. 302-304; https://en.wikipedia.org/wiki/Dumuzid retrieved on 7 September 2020.

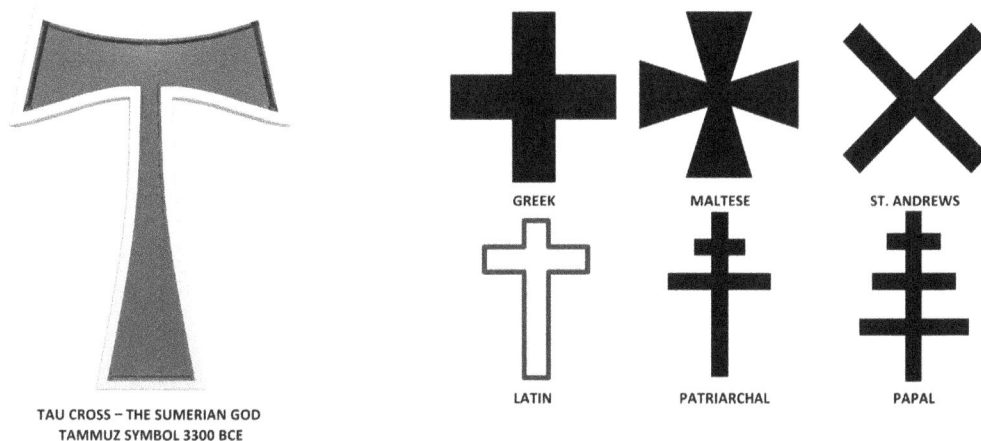

TAU CROSS – THE SUMERIAN GOD
TAMMUZ SYMBOL 3300 BCE

GREEK   MALTESE   ST. ANDREWS

LATIN   PATRIARCHAL   PAPAL

Figure 16: Tammuz cross symbol compared to Christian variants[c]

---

[c] Adapted from https://study.com/academy/lesson/christian-religious-symbols-origin-history-examples.html and https://www.ancient-symbols.com/symbols-directory/cross-of-tau.html retrieved on 10 August 2023.

that his life is the fulfilment of Old Testament prophecies. The author is most likely to have been familiar with the Mesopotamian influence on the Hebrew scribes.

There are several versions of when Jesus may have been born. The most popular is that he was born on 25 December (at the time of December solstice celebrations). If this is the case then, in accordance with the Mesopotamian lunisolar mythology, Jesus the god-king would have been conceived nine months earlier on or around the March equinox (around 25 March). Many Christians actually celebrate this day (25 March) as the day of the Feast of the Annunciation, as the New Testament declares that it was on this day that the angel Gabriel announced to the virgin Mary that she was carrying the child of God (Luke 1: 26-31).

The twenty-fifth of March aligns with the Northern Hemisphere vernal equinox and is nine full months before Christmas. It continues the Mesopotamian and later mythological beliefs that a god-king is conceived on the same date of his later death and resurrection (Easter, or the same date of Tammuz's death and resurrection) and the same lunisolar date of the ancient Middle East fertility festivals.[259] This accords with the same concepts

---

[259] SOURCE: https://www.biblicalarchaeology.org/daily/people-cultures-in-the-bible/jesus-historical-jesus/how-december-25-became-christmas/ retrieved on 7 September 2020.

later adopted into Judaism linking the time of the deaths of prophets to their conception or birth.[260]

The impact of the annual solstice and equinox cycles on the writing of Christian mythological stories was not only reflected in Jesus' conception, birth, and death story. The birth of John the Baptist, and the subsequent Saint John the Baptist saint's day, is Midsummer's Day. Midsummer's Day is the Northern Hemisphere date of the June solstice (24 June). So, according to the writers of the Christian New Testament, Jesus was conceived and died on the Northern Hemisphere spring equinox and was born on the date of the winter solstice, and John the Baptist was born on the date of the Northern Hemisphere June solstice. This pattern is either coincidental or a reflection of the impact of the annual lunisolar cycles on ancient mythological writing and practices at the time.

The long history of virgin birth and resurrection myths

Prehistoric mythological beliefs from ancient Türkiye, Iran, Mesopotamia, and the Levant (from at least 8000 BCE) reveal a common ancient fascination with miraculous or mystical notions of conception, pregnancy, reproduction, sexuality, and birth. Early statuettes of female spiritual beings found in the Levant were often dual-gendered (containing representations of both female and male anatomical parts) and/or without genitalia, a navel, or breasts.[261] In some cases, the associated mythological story involved the belief that women were the procreators of the cosmos, the Earth, its creatures, and its natural features. In these myths, the beginning of the universe was believed to be a result of divine procreation, which occurred with or without a male partner. Hence, the many ancient Middle Eastern fertility festivals and female spiritual beings were celebrated around the commencement of the Northern Hemisphere spring season.

In other prehistoric mythologies, the fascination with conception, pregnancy, reproduction, sexuality, and birth was used to demonstrate the mysterious god-like origin of a specific ruler, god, prophet or god-king. The Mesopotamians and later mythologies believed that a god-king is conceived on the same date of his later death and resurrection. The great Egyptian god, Atum mated with his own shadow and gave birth to two children. The Egyptian sun god Ra was believed to have circumcised himself and, from the

---

[260]   SOURCE: https://www.historytoday.com/archive/did-romans-invent-christmas retrieved on 25 September 2020.
[261]   Schmandt-Besserat (1998), p. 113.

spilt blood, two other gods came into being.[262] The ancient Vedic (Zoroastrian, Hindu, and Buddhist) action and storm god Indra (around 1500 BCE) was conceived by a virgin who was impregnated by Spenta Mainyu (the Zoroastrian Holy Ghost).[263] According to Tibetan Buddhist tradition, Indra ascended into heaven when he died.

The Zoroastrians (around 1000 BCE) believed that Zoroaster would have a son, born of a virgin bathing in a lake. The son would become the saviour of the world.[264] The Persian apocalyptic myth (from around 500 BCE) claims that over thousands of years, three different saviours will be sent to Earth by the wise lord and that each of these will be born of a virgin miraculously impregnated by the prophet Zoroaster whilst swimming in a sacred lake.[265, 266]

The Eurasian Steppe Scythians had two creation stories, both of which involved a god impregnating a female goddess who belonged to the Earth.[267] The Egyptian god Amun impregnates the Egyptian Queen Ahmose to produce the divine child Hatshepsut, who became the longest-reigning female pharaoh in ancient Egypt's history (1473 BCE to 1458 BCE). The virgin Egyptian Queen Mutemwiya is impregnated by the god Kneph and gives birth to the Pharaoh Amenhotep III (around 1400 BCE to 1380 BCE). During the Egyptian Eighteenth Dynasty (1550 BCE to 1292 BCE), most Egyptian rulers believed that they were the progeny of a divine union between their mothers and the sun god Amun-Re.[268]

The Greek-related Phrygian (West Anatolia/Türkiye) vegetation deity Attis was born of a virgin Nana. The Attis mythological story includes the fact that Attis died by self-mutilation and was resurrected (around 1200 BCE).[269]

The Old and New Testaments contain several examples of mysterious, miraculous, or different procreational births. The HB/OT tells us that Lot's two daughters had sex with their father and bore his two children (Moab and Ammon, who the Hebrew scribes named after two Levantine kingdoms of the same names). In addition to the Jesus virgin birth story in the New Testament, John the Baptist's mother, Elizabeth, is described as

---

[262] Cox and Morris (2012), p. 249.
[263] Boyce (2001), p. 21.
[264] Boyce (1984), p. 57.
[265] Boyce (1984), p. 67.
[266] Bierlein (1994), pp. 240-241.
[267] Cunliffe (2019), p. 267.
[268] See: Ramses II ruled for 70 years and had 100 children. Egypt paid the price. (nationalgeographic.com) retrieved on 21 February 2023.
[269] See: https://www.britannica.com/topic/Attis retrieved on 12 May 2022.

infertile until the angel Gabriel appeared to his father, Zechariah, to declare that she was pregnant.

The fascination with the virgin birth of or by a god on 25 December was a commonly shared myth across many of the cultures pre-dating Judaism and Christianity:

- **Horus**—the Egyptian sky god, born on 25 December to a virgin in a papyrus thicket in the Egyptian delta marshes around 3,000 years before Jesus[270]
- **Attis**—the ancient Anatolian god was born of the virgin Nana on 25 December, died and was resurrected three days after his death some 1,200 years before Jesus[271]
- **Krishna**—A Hindu god, born on 25 December to a virgin around 900 years before Jesus. Krishna's mother was the inspiration for the Christian Virgin Mary story. After Krishna was born, an angel appeared to his mother warning her to escape with her son, which she did to live with shepherds at the foot of the sacred Hindu Mountain[272]
- **Hercules**—A Greek god, born on 25 December to a virgin around 800 years before Jesus
- **Mithra**—A Persian god, born on 25 December to a virgin 600 years before Jesus. Mithra's birth was witnessed by shepherds and three wise men and his death and resurrection occurred at the vernal equinox[273]
- **Dionysus**—A Greek god, born on 25 December to a virgin around 500 years before Jesus
- **Tammuz**—The Mesopotamian/Babylonian god, born on 25 December to a virgin, around 400 years before Jesus
- **Hermes**—A Greek god, born on 25 December to a virgin around 200 years before Jesus
- **Adonis**—A Phoenician god, born on 25 December to a virgin around 200 years before Jesus.[274]

---

[270] Shaw (2014), pp. 84-85.
[271] https://stellarhousepublishing.com/attis/ retrieved on 22 August 2022.
[272] Black (2007), p. 147.
[273] Walker (2010), p. 131.
[274] SOURCE: https://www.nairaland.com/4251378/list-gods-born-virgin-25th retrieved on 25 September 2020.

The resurrection myth is a common myth prior to the emergence of the Jesus story. The Greek cults of Dionysus, the Anatolian cult of Attis, and the Anatolian/Greek cult of Cybele each contained a story of a god who dies and is then resurrected. Nicholas Wade believes that this common myth reflects:

> *… a common idea, presumably inherited from the dawn of agriculture … [where] a vegetation god …. dies in autumn and must be resurrected in the spring with appropriate rituals.*[275]

Jonathan Black has detailed how the New Testament's outline of the life of Jesus appears to be a patchwork of ideas appropriated from previous mythologies:

> *Born to a carpenter and a virgin, like Krishna; born on December 25, like Mithras; heralded by a star in the East, like Horus; walking on water and feeding the five thousand from a small basket, like Buddha; performing healing miracles, like Pythagoras; raising from the dead, like Elisha; executed on a tree, like Adonis; ascending into heaven, like Hercules, Enoch and Elijah.*[276]

The importance of the moon

The phases of the moon are linked to the relative positions of the sun, the moon, and the Earth in the moon's 29-day monthly orbit of the Earth. There are four main phases of the moon—the new moon, the first quarter, the full moon, and the last or third quarter (Figure 17).

A significant mythological benchmark for many prehistoric communities in the Northern Hemisphere was the first full moon that occurred after the March/April equinox. This annual astronomical event always marked the beginning of spring, the barley and wheat harvest, and the consistently predictable commencement of the birthing season for (in particular) lambs. This commencement of crop-planting and birthing of a valued domesticated animal is why, in many prehistoric communities, the mythology at this time of year revolves around fertility and a fertility goddess.[277]

Moon worship was particularly strong in Canaan and Mesopotamia prior to the emergence of the Israelites. The Mesopotamian cities of Ur and Harran and the Canaanite

---

275   Wade (2010), p. 168.
276   Black (2007), p. 210.
277   Pryke (2017), pp. 8-9.

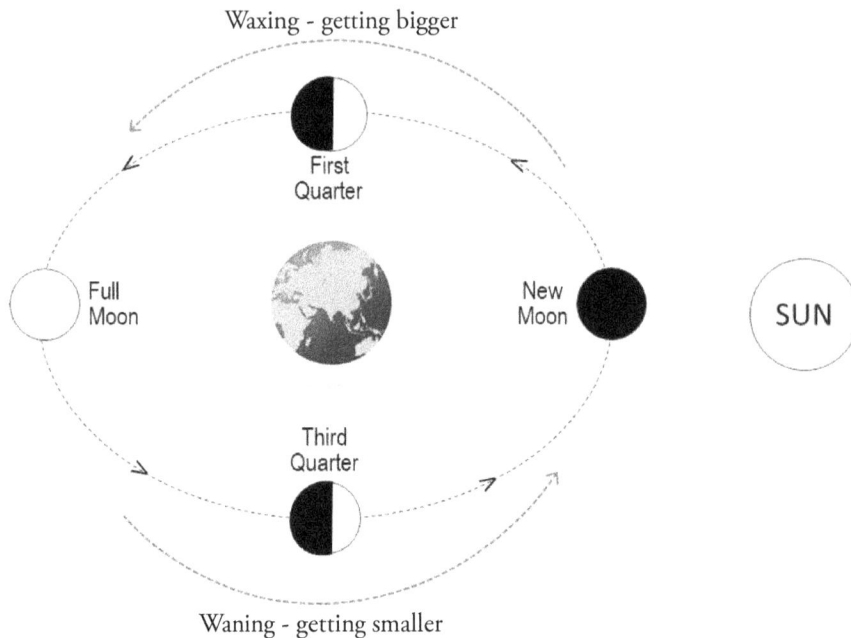

Figure 17: *The four main phases of the moon*[d]

---

[d] CREDIT: NASA/JPL-Caltech: https://spaceplace.nasa.gov/oreo-moon/en/ retrieved on 11 May 2021.

city of Jericho (named after the Canaanite lunar deity Yarikh) were all major centres of moon worship.

The moon, universally identified as female, and the moon's annual relationship with the sun were the foundation of Middle Eastern mythologies involving virgin birth. The full moon, when it is brightened by the sun in the spring equinox, is seen as a symbol of virgin birth—the sun god impregnating and giving new life/new brightness to the female moon. This is most likely the origin of the many virgin birth mythologies associated with the prehistoric Northern Hemisphere spring equinox and the associated full moon, and likely why the Christian Annunciation and the Easter celebrations, on the first Sunday following the full moon on or after the spring equinox, are celebrated at this annual lunisolar event.

Abraham, the Bible, and the moon

The importance of the moon to Judaism is reflected in the fact that the Jewish calendar is a lunisolar calendar. It is based on the link between moon phases and the position of the sun. It was originally adapted from the Babylonian lunisolar calendar and linked to the Babylonian moon-worshipping mythology.

The biblical story of Abraham the patriarch of Judaism has very strong links to the earlier Sumerian/Akkadian/Babylonian/Israeli moon worship. The Bible places Abraham's origin in Ur. From there, he journeys towards Canaan via selected locations that have close links to the Sumerian moon god, Sin. Abraham's first stop is the city of Harran. The Sumerian myth had the moon god Sin/Nanna (Sin=Akkadian; Nanna=Sumerian) leaving Ur and travelling north to Nippur, a city dedicated to Enil, the supreme god of the Sumerian deities. Sin/Nanna travelled to Nippur to seek a blessing from Enil (the Sumerian ruler of the cosmos) that would secure prosperity and abundance for the city of Ur.[278] By around 2200 BCE, the King of the Akkadian Empire who was based in Nippur was Naram-Sin, whose name translates as 'beloved of the moon god Sin'. The biblical journey of Abraham reflects the Sumerian moon god's journey.

There are even stronger links to the Sumerian/Akkadian moon-worshipping tradition when the names of Abraham's family are translated. Susan Wise Bauer has identified a link between the names the Hebrew scribes have given to Abraham's father, Terah's family and the Sumerian/Akkadian moon god, who had a temple at Ur and also in Harran.

To the Mesopotamians, the moon god (Sin/Nanna) was one of the most senior astral deities—along with the sun god (Utu/Shamash). The mysterious moon god controlled time (lunar months) and knew the destinies of all.[279] All Sumerian cities had a temple to the god of that city—in the case of the god of Ur and Harran, this god was the moon god. The ancient Israelites had a moon-worshipping cult. Andrew F Keys believes that the Abraham family story and their journey via key Mesopotamian moon-worshipping centres reflected respect for this ancient Israeli cult.[280] Abraham's family's biblical links to the moon god included:

- His father Terah's name means 'worshipper of the moon god Sin/Nanna'
- The name of Abraham's wife and half-sister, Sarai, is the Akkadian version of Ningal, the goddess and female partner of the moon god Sin
- Terah's granddaughter Milcah is named after Sin's daughter, Malkatu
- Abraham's brother's name is Haran—the name of a Sumerian/Akkadian moon-worshipping city

---

278 Kramer (2007), pp. 69-71.
279 Roux (1992), pp. 87-88.
280 Key (1965), p. 21.

- Abraham's (Abram) own name, whilst the meaning is ambiguous, relates to moon worship.[281]

These references to the Sumerian and Akkadian moon god by the biblical scribes are strengthened when the scribes go on to tell that Terah and Abraham's journey to Canaan under God's direction makes its first stopover in the small town of Harran, a recognised centre of Mesopotamian moon worship.[282] Paul Kriwaczek claims that the Hebrew scribes' story of Terah's family relocation from Ur to Harran was most probably based on the move of the Mesopotamian moon cult from Ur to Harran following the invasion of Ur by the Elamites in around 1750 BCE.[283]

There is additional support for linking Abraham to moon worship in accepted Rabbinic elaborations on the Biblical Abraham story. Howard Schwartz produced an award-winning compilation of the mythology of Judaism. He brought together biblical stories, Jewish oral lore, Midrashic, Talmudic, Kabbalistic and Hasidic texts to create a fully integrated explanation of Jewish mythology. In referring to the myth of Abraham and his relationship to the moon, Schwartz quotes from Jewish Midrashic texts:

When Abraham was still a boy, he saw the sun shining upon the earth, and he thought that surely the sun must be God, and therefore he would serve it......but when evening came and the sunset, Abraham said to himself, surely this cannot be God. And Abraham wondered who made the heavens and the earth. That night, when Abraham lifted his eyes to the sky, he saw the stars and the moon before him, and he thought that the moon must have created the world, and the stars were its servants. And Abraham served the moon and prayed to it all night.[284]

Other biblical references to the moon god

The name of Mount Sinai, mentioned in the biblical Moses story as the location where Moses received the Ten Commandments, is a reference to the ancient Mesopotamian and Israeli moon god Sin/Nanna.[285] Prior to its incorporation into the Moses story by the

---

281   Bauer (2007), p. 128.
282   Bauer,(2007), pp. 128-129.
283   Kriwaczek (2010), p. 163.
284   Schwartz (2007), pp. 328–329.
285   Key (1965), pp. 22-23

Hebrew scribes, Mount Sinai was referred to as Mount Ishtar. Ishtar was the mythological daughter of the moon god Sin and the mountain's new name, Sinai, is a Hebrew scribe's reference to Sin, the moon god.[286]

Jericho, a city that receives a major focus in the writings of the Hebrew scribes, is associated with moon worship. Jericho's name in Hebrew, Yerih̬o, is generally thought to derive from the Canaanite word *reah̬* ('fragrant'), but other theories hold that it originates in the Canaanite word for 'moon' (*yareah̬*) or the name of the lunar deity Yarikh, for whom the city was an early centre of worship.

Astral Religion and Astral/Celestial Divination

It is generally agreed that the first astronomers were most likely priests who determined that celestial objects and events were manifestations of the divine, hence early astronomy's connection to what is now called astrology.

Astral religion involves the veneration of the stars and planets as specific deities. Celestial divination can be associated with astral religion, but it is a much broader concept. Celestial divination involves any event in the sky that a specific culture believes is a message from god/the gods. The gods could send messages to humans (good, bad, or prophecies about the future) through various signs, which were mediated by a third-party religious shaman/priest/diviner.[287]

To ancient astrologers, the planets represented the will of the gods and their direct influence on human affairs. Arthur Koestler described it in these terms:

The most fascinating objects in the sky were the planets, or vagabond stars. Only seven of these existed among thousands of lights suspended from the firmament. … All other stars remained stationary, fixed in the pattern of the firmament revolving once a day round the earth-mountain, but never changing their places in the pattern. The seven vagabond stars revolved with them, but at the same time they had a motion of their own, like flies wandering over the surface of a spinning globe. Yet they did not wander all across the sky: their movements were confined to a narrow lane, or belt … the Zodiac … [which] was divided into twelve sections…..each of which was named after a constellation of fixed stars in the neighbourhood.[288]

---

[286] Hall (1980), p. 29.
[287] Brown, D. (2006), p. 73.
[288] Koestler (1959), p. 21

The placing of mythological meaning on celestial events originated as an important aspect of scholarly activity in Mesopotamia. Several hundred cuneiform tablets attest to its practice and provide details of the different types of omens that were drawn from observations of the sky. This tradition included the naming of the planets (the vagabond stars) after associated gods—a practice that originated with the Sumerians, who are regarded as laying the foundations for modern astronomy, astrology, and contemporary religious observances.

The Sumerians and the Babylonians regarded their divinities and their related planets as responsible for all matters pertaining to the natural and social order. Selected gods were individually linked to the seven classical planets—those that can be easily seen with the naked eye—the sun, the moon, and the five sacred planets—Mercury, Venus, Mars, Jupiter, and Saturn. It helped that the Sumerian priests regarded the number seven as the ideal, special, and all-potent number.[289] The planets were, therefore, originally named after seven Sumerian (Akkadian and Babylonian) gods (Figure 18).

The modern-day names for the planets come from the astral religious beliefs of either the ancient Greeks or Romans, namely:

- Mars is the Roman god of war.
- Mercury is the god of commerce, travel, and thievery in Roman mythology.
- Jupiter was the king of the gods in Roman mythology.
- Venus is the Roman goddess of love and beauty.
- Saturn is the Roman god of agriculture.
- Uranus is the ancient Greek deity of the heavens, the earliest supreme god.
- Neptune was the Roman god of the sea.
- Pluto is the Roman god of the underworld in Roman mythology.

Although the stars and planets were not considered divinities, they were regarded as physical manifestations of divine powers that existed beyond the heavens. Each god had a designated astral aspect and the seven planets that could be observed in the heavens were each associated with their specific god (Figure 18). The Sumerians and subsequent Mesopotamians dedicated each city to a specific god and erected temples to this specific god. There was a temple to the moon god Sin/Nanna in Harran and in Ur—two towns that the Hebrew scribes associated with Abraham and his family.

---

[289] Muroi (2014).

Planet	Sumerian gods	Akkadian gods	Babylonian gods	Mythological Association
Sun	bisebi	samas	utu/shamash	patron god of the sun/illuminator of all, the whole of heaven/truth, justice & right/ destroyer of evil
Moon	aku	sin	nanna/sin	moon god/lord of heaven/lord of the moon/chief of the gods
Mars	simutu	mustabarru	nergal	pastoral god/underworld/forest fires/fevers & plagues
Mercury	bibbu	lubat-gud	enki/nabu/nebo	god of astronomy/god of subterranean freshwater ocean/creator god/determiner of destinies/god & patron of writing/irrigation & agriculture
Jupiter	dapinu	umun-sig-ea	marduk	king of all gods/magic/wisdom/ water & vegetation
Venus	zib/zig	dele-bat	inanna/ishtar	lady of heaven/ godess of sexual love/war godess/queen of all the inhabited world/ governer of the people/feminine form of the divine
Saturn	lu-lim	lu-bat-sag-us	ninurta/ninib	warrior god/farmer god/lord of arable land/god of agriculture

Figure 18: *The Mesopotamian gods linked to the seven classical planets*[e]

---

[e] Compiled from multiple sources – see Bibliography.

The beliefs of the Ancient Israelites were influenced by these more powerful and populous neighbours (Egyptians, Canaanites, Sumerians, Assyrians, and Babylonians). There were astral religious and celestial divination cults in the early mythological practices of Ancient Israel when the Hebrew scribes were gradually adapting, and in some cases demonising, these regional practices and beliefs in their early drafts of the HB/OT.[290]

Elon Gilad, an editor and writer at the popular contemporary Israelite newspaper *Haaretz*, has written about his fascination with the extent to which the Israelites, after they had conquered Canaan (according to the Bible), continued to call their cities by the names of Canaanite ancient astral deities. Despite the intention that they should not be tempted to worship foreign gods, the Bronze Age Israelites retained the names of (amongst many others):

---

[290] Cooley (2011), pp. 281-285.

- Jerusalem—named by the Canaanites after their god of the evening star, Shalem
- Jericho—named after the Canaanite moon god Yareakh
- Several cities/towns that referred to the head of the Canaanite pantheon, El
- Several that referred to the Canaanite sun god Shemesh
- Several others that referred to the Canaanite storm god Baal.[291]

The emergence of the zodiac

The Sumerians (3000 BCE) and Babylonians (1800 BCE) were systematic observers of the stars. They were aware that the planets moved against a background of fixed stars. They grouped these into constellations, which were then given mythological importance and divine, animate, inanimate, and individual names. This was the beginning of the zodiac—a word that, in Greek, means 'a cycle or circle of little animals'.

- The Babylonians maintained star catalogues. They observed that the sun 'moved' through twelve of the star constellations each year—a discovery that led them to divide the year into twelve months (Figure 19). They believed that celestial events controlled earthly events and that these constellations had powers over life on Earth.

The first four Babylonian zodiac constellations were linked to the four significant lunisolar annual events:

- Taurus, the bull linked to the vernal equinox
- Leo, the lion marking the summer solstice
- Scorpius, the scorpion signifying the autumn equinox
- Capricornus, the goat identifying the winter solstice.

The astral origins of monotheism and the heavenly father

Even some animist religions believed in a supreme deity. The ancient Mongols, who believed in many spirits across the natural world, believed in a supreme sky god called Mongke Tengri who was the creator of humanity and the world and protected humans from malevolent demons. Eurasian Steppe nomadic and semi-nomadic cultures, including the Khvalynsk culture (from around 4900 BCE), the Yamnaya (from around 3300 BCE), the Aryans/Indo-Iranians (descendants from the Sintashta and Andronovo Steppe

---

[291]   Gilad (2020).

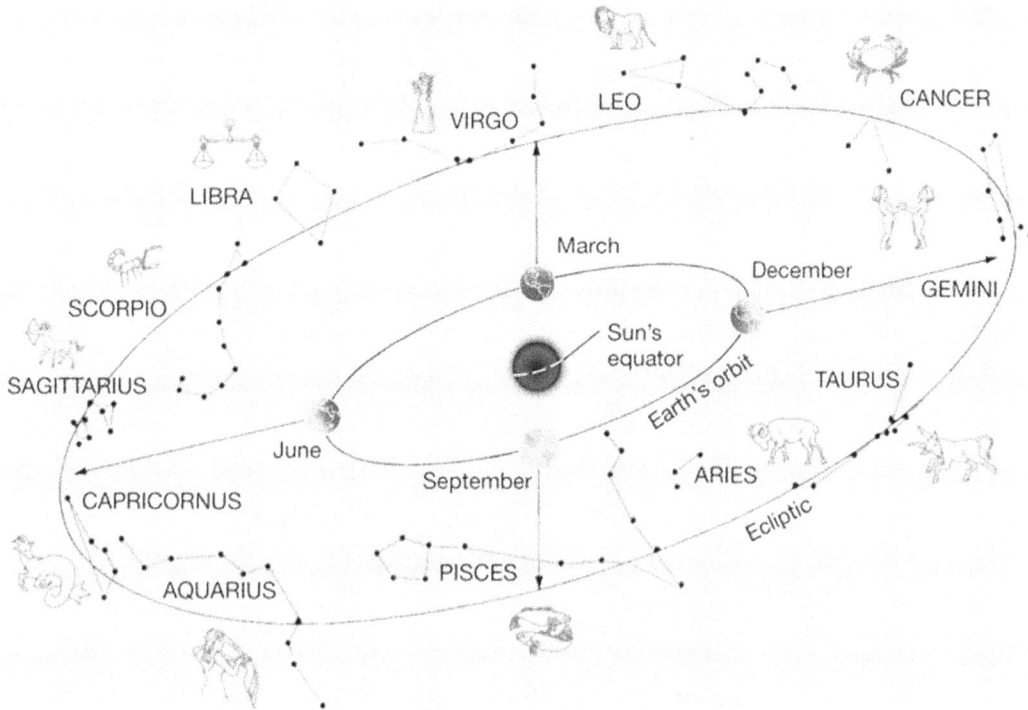

Figure 19: *The zodiac provided the mythological backdrop to the (apparent) sun's path[f]*

---

[f] SOURCE: Chaisson, Eric; McMillan, Steve; Astronomy Today; 9th edition; (c) 2018. Reprinted by permission of Pearson Education, Inc.

cultures from around 2000 BCE), and the Vedic/Hindu religion (from around 1500 BCE) believed in the daylight-sky-god, Dyeus/Dyaus who was the father sky and divine personification of the daylight's bright sky.[292] The Zoroastrians believed in a supernatural entity called, in the ancient Iranian Avestan language, Daeva or Daiva.[293] It is highly likely that the word *deity*, which is most often claimed to have originated from the Latin language (*deus* meaning 'god'), originated here thousands of years before its use in Latin.

From around 3000 BCE, many of the Middle Eastern cultures (Mesopotamians, Sumerians, Akkadians, Babylonians, Assyrians, and Hurrians) began to worship an East Semitic supreme deity who controlled wind, air, Earth, and storms. This supreme god had a variety of often interchangeable names, but when written in Assyrian and Sumerian cuneiform, it translated as 'the god of the whole heaven'. This 'high god' was seen

---

[292] Wilkinson (2009), p. 162 and pp. 188-189.
[293] Boyce (2001), p. 11.

as being utterly transcendent, removed from the world that he created[294] and is often addressed as the 'sky or heavenly father' or lord of heaven (ancient Egyptian creation god Ptah) and was often either a reigning or former king of the gods. The sky father is most often a deity conceived as reigning over the others, or at least is the most powerful god. When the main sky deity was believed to be feminine, she often held the title of the 'Queen of Heaven'.[295]

Some prehistoric religions recognised a complementary polarity between Earth and the sky, which culminated in gender-based deities as the supreme mated pair.[296] This could take the form of a sky father and an Earth mother while, in other religions, the mated couple is a sky goddess (female) and an Earth god (male).[297] The Ancient Egyptians' first sky goddess was the very beautiful and kind Nut, who ruled over the sky while her brothers Geb, the god of the Earth, and Thoth, the god of the moon, wisdom, magic, equilibrium, and divine words, ruled over other aspects of the Egyptian world.[298]

The Canaanites' religion, from which the Israelites emerged, was monolatrist (worshipping one god while acknowledging the existence of others).[299] As mentioned earlier, the Vedic religion of the ancient Indo-European-speaking peoples who entered India about 1500 BCE from the Middle East (present-day Iran) followed the Middle Eastern trend of one supreme sky god, Dyáuṣ Pitṛ́. This was the Vedic sky father and chief father deity of the Vedic pantheon and Prithvi Mata is the mother Earth.[300]

Schmidt, citing the work of English anthropologist and founder of cultural anthropology Edward Burnett Tylor (1832-1917), explains that monotheism emerged in three ways:

- raising up to primacy one of the existing polytheistic gods (e.g., the sky/sun god—the ancient Sumerians)
- modelling the notion of god around a human model where there is a primary god similar to a king (e.g., the pharoah—the ancient Egyptians)

---

[294] See: https://www.britannica.com/topic/High-God retrieved on 10 May 2021.
[295] See: https://religion.wikia.org/wiki/List_of_sky_deities#Ancient_Near_East retrieved on 10 May 2021.
[296] This gender-based polarity is most likely one of the influences that led to the Hebrew scribes developing the Adam and Eve story (see later discussion).
[297] See: https://religion.wikia.org/wiki/List_of_sky_deities#Ancient_Near_East retrieved on 10 May 2021.
[298] See: https://study.com/academy/lesson/sky-god-names-mythology-quiz.html retrieved on 10 May 2021.
[299] See: https://religion.wikia.org/wiki/Canaanite_religion retrieved on 10 May 2021.
[300] See: https://en.wikipedia.org/wiki/Dyaus retrieved on 11 May 2021.

- a fusing of the range of polytheistic powers into one all-pervading deity (e.g., Zoroastrianism and Hebrew scribes).[301]

Some claim that the proximity of the Roman Saturnalia festival to the winter solstice was a celebration of solar monotheism—the belief that the sun god/sky father/high god ultimately encompasses all divinities as one.

Prior to the emergence of the Israelites and the Hebrew scribes, the Persian prophet Zoroaster in around 1500 BCE declared that he had received a vision from their supreme god, Āhurā Mazdā, declaring that only one god existed and it was himself, Āhurā Mazdā. Zoroastrianism is now regarded as the first monotheistic religion in the world.[302] The Egyptian Pharaoh Akhenaten (1351 BCE to 1334 BCE) also introduced a new system that made the Egyptian sun god Aten the highest deity and the one supreme god in the land. The pharaoh changed his own name from Amunhotep to Akhenaten, which meant 'Servant of Aten'.

In many ways, the Persian Prophet Zoroastrians and the Egyptian Pharaoh Akhenaten set the scene for the Jewish and Christian concept of monotheism. Renowned Egyptologist Erik Hornung describes the Egyptian Pharaoh Akhenaten's influence in the following way:

We have before our eyes the first world religion in history, since the Aten is not a national, but a universal god; he could be accepted by all humanity, caring for all the nations of the world and for all living creatures, giving breath even to the chick in the egg.[303]

Paul Kriwaczek has explained the emergence of the concept of one superior divinity as coming from several different influences. The Assyrian god Ashur was not just treated as the supreme god above all other gods but, as and when required, the Assyrians would merge all gods into one entity—local divinities were merged into being different manifestations of the same god Ashur (ca 2500 BCE).[304]

New York Professor of Bible and Ancient Middle Eastern Studies Baruch Levine believes that the Assyrian control over the Middle East over hundreds of years, including the time of the emergence of the Israelites, was instrumental in the development of Israelite biblical monotheism. The widely held god-king concept fitted neatly into the

---

[301]   Schmidt (2014), p. 76.
[302]   (358) Ancient Persia and the Achaemenid Persian Empire—YouTube retrieved on 24 August 2022.
[303]   Hornung (1992), p. 49.
[304]   Kriwaczek (2010), p. 231.

ideological explanation of the success of major empires and the defeat of smaller vassal states such as the emerging Israelites.

The transition towards monotheism followed a pattern from celestial city-states governed by a divine council or king through a kingdom of hierarchical deities to a world empire ruled over by an imperial king and god. Levine believes that the Israelite prophets (through Isaiah Chapters 1–39) needed to explain how the Assyrians, led by their supreme god Ashur, could defeat the Israelites, led by their supreme god Yahweh. The biblical explanation was that Yahweh was controlling the Assyrian god Ashur and the defeat of the Israelites was Yahweh's divine abandonment of the Israelites because of their moral intransigence, culpability, and idolatry. There was a need for a politico-ideological 'god-idea' big enough to measure up to and explain the control of the entire world—the successes and the defeats. It was a specific response to Assyrian imperialism so that it could be shown that the Israelites had an ideologically supreme god who controlled whatever the gods of all other cultures achieved—whether good or bad for the Israelites.[305]

This explanation of the one supreme universal god largely responsible for the many successes and failures of an ethnic group is a recurring metaphor throughout the Hebrew Bible. Jonathan Lipnick of the Israel Institute of Biblical Studies sees the Israelites' emerging religion as being defined by an 'active relationship of struggle, confrontation, and dialogue' with this supreme being.[306]

Eventually, over time, a doctrine emerged across the prehistoric Middle East that the world and the heavens were controlled by one omnipotent all-pervading deity who had neither a wife nor family.[307] These trends had developed well before the emergence of the Hebrew scribes and the Hebrew Bible/Old Testament.[308] They were the primary influences and the origin of the Jewish and Christian belief in one singular, supreme heavenly father, essentially originating in the sun god. This is why, to this day, there remains a widely held religious belief that the supreme god and heavenly paradise are located 'up there' somewhere in the sky.

Paul Kriwaczek has described the Hebrew scribes' promotion of a single omnipotent and omnipresent god in the following way:

---

[305] Levine (2005), pp. 411-419.
[306] SOURCE: https://www.youtube.com/watch?v=VxxhgzDOd58 retrieved on 18 February 2021.
[307] Schmidt (2014), p. 64.
[308] Irwin (1946), p. 225.

The new theology was far from an utterly revolutionary and unprecedented religious movement. The Judeo-Christian-Islamic tradition that began in the Holy Land was not a total break with the past, but grew out of religious ideas that had already taken hold of Late Bronze and Early Iron Age northern Mesopotamia, the world view of the Assyrian kingdom, which would spread its faith as well as its power right across western Asia over the course of the following centuries.[309]

---

[309] Kriwaczek (2010), p. 231.

Chapter 9

Mythologies Evolving into Organised Religion

Prehistoric mythologies and the journey to a monotheistic god

A mythological order is a system of images that gives consciousness a sense of meaning in existence, which, my dear friend, has no meaning—it simply is. But the mind goes asking for meanings; it can't play unless it knows (or makes up) some system of rules.[310]

—Joseph Campbell

There is no doubt that shared mythological beliefs were a major contributor to the cultural, technological, and economic evolution of the human species. Joseph Henrich believes that the evolution of supernatural beliefs and rituals resulted from three unique human characteristics:

- our species willingness to learn from others, often in contrast to our own experience
- our cognitive ability to explore alternative concepts of reality
- the impact of intergroup competition on cultural evolution.[311]

Joseph Campbell suggests that mythologies have a fourfold function within human society:

- the mystical/metaphysical function—awakening and maintaining in the individual a sense of awe and gratitude before the 'mystery of being' and his or her participation in it

---

[310] Campbell (2004), p. 7.
[311] Henrich (2021), pp. 128-133.

- the cosmological function—explaining the shape of the universe
- the sociological function—validating and supporting the existing social order
- the pedagogical/psychological function—guiding the individual through the stages of life.[312]

It is a worthwhile endeavour to explore the manifestations of mythologising up to and during the times of the Israelites to better understand and begin to explain the context, emergence, and content of the HB/OT. The transition from foragers through farmers to kingdoms correlated with and influenced the transition of communities from tribal through sedentary farming villages to city-states. Religious beliefs transitioned in parallel from beliefs in largely inanimate, natural, or planetary deities through the personification of deities, to divine goddesses to divine kings and eventually to anthropomorphic male gods.

Campbell has suggested that mythologies have evolved over time and across the Ages through four main stages:

- *The Way of the Animal Powers*—the myths of Palaeolithic (Stone Age) hunter-gatherers, which focus on shamanism and animal totems.
- *The Way of the Seeded Earth*—the myths of Neolithic, agrarian cultures (Stone Age transitioning into the Copper and early Bronze Ages), which focus upon a mother goddess and associated fertility rites.
- *The Way of the Celestial Lights*—the myths of Bronze Age city-states with pantheons of gods ruling from the heavens and the planets, led by a masculine god-king.
- *The Way of Man*—religion and philosophy as it developed after the Axial Age (c. sixth century BCE), in which the mythic imagery of previous eras was made consciously metaphorical, reinterpreted as referring to psycho-spiritual, not literal-historical, matters. This transition is evident in the East in Buddhism, Vedanta, and philosophical Taoism; and in the West in the mystery cults, Platonism, Judaism, Christianity, and Gnosticism.[313]

In preliterate, prehistoric hunter-gatherer times, as in some contemporary examples, the structural and core foundation for religion has most commonly been a set of myths depicting supernatural powers relating to, explaining, or controlling everyday events.

---

[312] SOURCE: https://en.wikipedia.org/wiki/Joseph_Campbell#Functions_of_myth retrieved on 18 November 2020.

[313] SOURCE: https://en.wikipedia.org/wiki/Joseph_Campbell#Functions_of_myth retrieved on 18 November 2020.

Matthew Kneale has documented evidence of a surprisingly common set of structural and mythological practices in contemporary hunter-gatherer societies:

> *All across the world, from the Artic to Australia, from Patagonia to southern Africa, these [hunter-gatherer] peoples, despite having had no contact with one another for many thousands of years, had a great deal in common. They all lived in tribes of the same size, of around 150 people. They all moved from place to place with the seasons, and in search of animals to hunt. And they were all very interested in the curious business of going into a trance. Entering a trance, in fact, lay at the centre of all their beliefs.[314]*

In addition to trance-like phenomena, prehistoric (and prescientific) mythology tended to deify what each culture did not understand and what was most important to their survival. Historical researchers are largely in agreement that praxis (community practice, lifestyle, and custom) influences cognition (beliefs) and cultural concepts (explanations about everything). Hunter-gatherers tended to deify natural/geomorphological phenomena, animals or human-animal deities, women, and fertility, whilst early prehistoric sedentary agricultural communities were more likely to have deities related to the planets, the solar or lunar cycles, and planting or animal breeding cycles.

In the words of Regan Gearhart:

> *While it cannot be conclusively known how … prehistoric people interacted with nature religiously, there is compelling evidence that their spirituality and beliefs were influenced by the world around them.[315]*

In this context, it is not surprising that early hunter-gatherer societies were so dependent on the natural environment that animism, totemism, and shamanism were the major early forms of mythologies or religious beliefs. Hunter-gatherers had a significant working knowledge and dependency on knowing the seasons by understanding the patterns of climatic variations (changes in temperature, winds, rain, angle of the sun) and the life-cycle patterns of the vegetation and animals on which they depended—when and where they were available and plentiful. Traditionally, therefore, hunter-gatherers tended not to wantonly exploit their environment. They tended to maintain a dialogue with their environment in a more spiritual and symbolic way.[316]

---

[314] Kneale (2013), pp. 7-8.
[315] Gearhart, 2015, p. 4.
[316] Verhoeven (2011), p. 80.

Prehistoric totemism and shamanism were the first manifestations of a belief in the existence of a 'soul' or 'spirit' in humans, in nature, and in animals. These mythological explanations of human relationships with the world around them and the spiritual world are what Campbell referred to as 'The Way of the Animal Powers'. Prehistoric mythologies and the imagining of gods were often also linked to women and fertility (the divine goddess), animals (totemism), the planets, a natural or geomorphic feature (mountains, a river), the planets/a constellation (the seven observable planets, Orion's belt, the Milky Way), a dead ancestor (ancestor cults), an imagined giant, or an ambiguous combination of some or all of these.

From Animism to monotheism

Social anthropologists believe that religion evolved through stages from animism to totemism to shamanism to polytheism to monotheism.[317] This did not happen in isolation nor linearly nor always in this sequence. It was integrally related to the ethnographic context, worldview, cognitive and symbolic abilities, economy, and survival strategies of the human species at different places and different times in their own evolution.

Animism

Hunter-gatherers began as small family or clan groups who foraged to survive. Because their worldview and their survival depended on their symbiotic relationship with everything around them, they believed that they were part of a complex multi and interspecies community. They worshipped nature. Their mythology is referred to as animism wherein all things—humans, animate, inanimate, and natural phenomena—can act towards each other intentionally. This was the beginning of the notion that everything had an essence, a spirit-being or a 'soul'. As family and clan groups united to form tribal groups, animism transitioned into totemism. This reflected new cognitive, symbolic, and organisational capabilities and necessities. A spiritual division of labour emerged, where specific families, clans or individuals were believed to have a kinship or mystical relationship with the spirit-being of animals or natural objects.

Totemism

Totemism is a word that came from the North American Indian tribal language of the Ojibwa people. It means 'one's brother-sister kin' and reflects the nature of the spiritual

---

317 Lewis-Williams (2010), pp. 134-135.

beliefs in the then-known world.[318] Totemism is the belief system where humans are believed to have kinship or a mystical relationship with a spirit being such as an animal or plant. A totem is a multifaceted set of ideas and ways of behaviour built on a world-view about nature. There are ideological, mystical, emotional, reverential, and genealogical relationships of social groups or specific persons with animals or natural objects: their totem.[319] The world's oldest continuous culture, the Indigenous Australians, prior to the arrival of Europeans, was a hunter-gatherer civilisation with a fully developed totemic system of beliefs.[320, 321] My own experience of being welcomed into the Barramundi Dreaming clan of the Australian Ganggalida Nation in the early 1970s entrusted me with a shared responsibility for ensuring the survival and propagation of the barramundi fish species in alignment with and respect for the beliefs of my adopted Indigenous Australian tribal family.

Shamanism

The word *shaman* comes from the Mongolian/Siberian Manchu-Tungus language word *šaman*, which is the noun form of the verb *ša*, 'to know'; thus, a shaman is literally 'one who knows.'[322] It is highly likely that the first shamans emerged in the Mongolia/Siberia geographic area in prehistory as spiritual mediators.[323] Different variations of this concept of a spiritual leader spread along the Eurasian Steppe to the west, southwards into Mesopotamia and Northern India, and eastward through Asia and across the Bering Land Bridge into North America.[324] A shaman was a central person believed to have direct intercourse, access, and influence with the transcendent/'other world', permitting them to act as healers, diviners, and communicators with gods or the spirit world. It is possible that the first shamans were female and had originally emerged to manage crises within the complex network of the animate and inanimate, life, illness, seasons, climate, natural

---

[318] SOURCE: https://www.britannica.com/topic/totemism-religion retrieved on 28 February 2022.
[319] SOURCE:https://www.auessays.com/essays/sociology/the-reality-of-totemism-sociology-essay.phpretrieved on 8 January 2021.
[320] Klein (2018).
[321] Several Indigenous Australia hunter-gatherer communities also had shamanic healers. See: Ventegodt and Kordova (2017).
[322] SOURCE: https://www.britannica.com/topic/shamanism retrieved on 8 January 2021
[323] Ashe (2018), pp. 40-43.
[324] SOURCE: https://ericwedwards.wordpress.com/2014/05/04/shamanism-archaeology-and-prehistory / retrieved on 8 January 2021.

environment, and the forces of nature.[325,326] As hunter-gatherers began to slowly transition into pastoralism, early domestication of endemic crops and sedentary village/town life mythologies changed alongside them. The concept of a complex, symbiotic network of mutually supportive spiritual relationships became more complex. Three new mythological concepts emerged with shamanism—apart from the known physical world, there is another reality/another invisible world; the belief that there was some more powerful external control/controller of these spiritual relationships; and the need for a mediator who was or could be connected with the control of these relationships and the other world.

Polytheism

Settlements grew as agriculture and pastoralism consolidated. The new economies created surpluses and new organisational systems, and a new social stratification emerged. In addition, seasonal variations became critical drivers of social and economic survival and success. New larger towns, city-states, and eventually empires turned their mythological attention skywards. The complex network of souls in the natural environment of the hunter-gatherers and shamans now expanded to include the sun, the moon, the planets, and the seasons. Multiple mythological changes occurred—deification of the observable planets, the sun, the moon, the stars, and the seasons. Shamans transformed into institutionalised priests. Sun-kings and god-kings (the embryonic form of today's monarchs and popes) were invented and many of the gods and goddesses became human-like—reflecting the new human organisational systems and the social organisational structures on Earth.

Monotheism

Technological developments (the wheel, plough, bow, wagon, chariot) saw a significant increase in the size of settlements, productivity, trade, and economic opportunity for sedentary communities. With it came nations, empires territorial ambition and warfare. The male warrior and the male god-king emerged. Social organisation and control evolved into theopolitical hagiarchies—government and the people controlled by deities or a city deity and priests/holy men. Initially, most Middle Eastern mythologies believed in many gods, with one supreme being ruling over the others. This gradually transitioned into a

---

[325]   Hall (1980), p. 168.
[326]   See also Tedlock (2005).

general belief in a singular supreme male god. Monotheism commenced in the Iranian Plateau with Zoroastrianism (around 1500 BCE) and in Egypt with Pharaoh Akhenaten (1353 BCE to 1334 BCE) and was eventually adopted by the Hebrew scribes (around 500 BCE).

Former Roman Catholic nun biblical and religious scholar Karen Armstrong has proposed that the hunter-gatherer beliefs were holistic. The divine was in everything and could be experienced in humanity as well as in animate and inanimate nature.[327] This stems from an apparent fascination with life in everything, a sense of being, and survival. Seeing in everything a soul/spirit/the sacred/the divine that was making their lives possible and livable. Robert Bellah (after Karl Luckert) has described it as a time:

> *… when all things were interchangeable: not only powerful beings, humans, and animals, but insects, plants, and features of the natural environment such as mountains were all 'alive', and could take the form of one another.*[328]

Over time, this holistic and integrated view of the then-known world shifted from a respect for the divine (soul/spirit/the sacred) in everything to a belief that there were anthropomorphic gods, saints, angels, and demons everywhere.[329] Across millennia, animism morphed into a belief in a group of anthropomorphic super-human beings and, from there, a belief in one singular anthropomorphic male god.

The transition from a hunter-gatherer belief in a spiritual world all around them to a mediated belief in an active and benevolent human-like god has occupied theologians for centuries. Believers/theists see this as a debate between natural religion (everything in nature is divine) and believers in an ever-present, active, and benevolent God who reveals his/her messages through a variety of mechanisms (revelations, signs, miracles, or through mediators such as shamans, priests, and pastors). The modern version integrating both beliefs is the intelligent design movement;[330] the modern version of the latter is organised religion—specifically, the evangelical movement.[331] Fundamentally, however, both belief systems link back to three obvious and rather simple ideas—a sense of wonder about life/a

---

[327]   Armstrong (1993), p. 15.
[328]   Bellah (2011), p. 163.
[329]   White (1978), p. 237.
[330]   Sheldrake (2020), p. 38.
[331]   For discussions of this debate see, for example: Torrance (1970); Sherry (2003); Swinburne (2007).

sense of being, a search for explanations of the unknown, and the creation of imaginary belief systems to unify groups of people.

Biblical adaptation of concepts from Shamanism in the Levant

Shamanism was common across prehistoric Northern Mesopotamia some 12,000 years ago in the Natufian culture, which occupied much of the Levant (contemporary Israel, Jordan, Lebanon, and parts of Syria) at that time.[332] In fact, the oldest shamanic grave yet to be found is of a female shaman buried twelve thousand years ago, covered in blackened/roasted shells of tortoises (the flesh of which was considered by the Natufians as a delicacy). The female shaman's grave was found by Israeli archaeologists in a small sunlit cave in northern Israel.[333]

There is also substantial evidence that shamanism was commonly practised across early Israel during the mid to late Bronze Age (1500 BCE).

Archaeological excavations in Israel and the text of the HB/OT contain a wealth of evidence that many of the biblical stories have been adaptations of Levantine and Mesopotamian shamanic beliefs. This extends from biblical references to animism and the power of animals to heal or help humans to the deification of ancestors, the calling on the spirits of these ancestors, natural objects having anthropomorphic characteristics, the use of masks, special chants or psalms, the spiritual power of music, incense burning, references to the Hebrew God having various theriomorphic (animal) forms or characteristics, key prophets (e.g., Jacob, Elijah and Elisha) having obvious shamanic abilities, magic rituals, and the use of special garments. These are all biblical adaptations of prehistoric Levantine shamanic practices.[334]

The ubiquity of shamanism

Female shamanic spiritual leaders were widespread across prehistoric Europe and Eurasia. A grave of a female shaman has been found in southern Sweden dating to at least seven thousand years ago. The Swedish female shaman was buried upright, seated cross-legged on a bed of antlers with a belt fashioned from more than 100 animal teeth (from deer,

---

[332] Benz and Bauer (2015).
[333] Pringle (2010).
[334] See: Miller II (2011).

wild boar, and moose) and in a short cape fashioned of feathers from crows, magpies, gulls, jays, geese, and ducks.[335]

Benz and Bauer believe that the common ideological concepts of shamanism could be found across northern Mesopotamia from 9600 BCE onwards—some eight thousand years before the emergence of the Israelites and some four thousand years before the biblical God created the world and the universe. Benz and Bauer quote the work of Strathern and Stewart (2008) in describing the role of the shaman in the following way:

> *The shaman has been considered a 'manager of crisis' between nature and society and between people and spirits. His position depends on his skills at controlling evil spirits, on his success in healing, and above all on the confidence of the community in those skills. The healing sessions are often acted out as 'social drama, reinforce(ing) the need for community solidarity'.[336]*

It is fascinating that in prehistoric times, hunter-gatherers were obviously sharing and interchanging the fundamentals of their mythological beliefs reflected in the common occurrence of particularly female figurines and shamanism.

Under totemic and shamanic systems of beliefs, it is not surprising that the early prehistoric mythologies were polytheistic—there were so many things around that the hunter-gatherers depended upon which they did not understand. To them, it was axiomatic that there must be a whole range of spiritual beings controlling and providing these assets. Most prehistoric cultures believed that there was meaning in everything and that this was reflected in supernatural forces existing in animate and inanimate objects. In the absence of writing and of a closed system of beliefs or a doctrinal establishment (as has emerged in contemporary mythologies/religions), the more open prehistoric cultures tended to believe in the existence of innumerable spiritual beings and independent spirits concerned with human affairs and capable of helping or harming human interests.

There is extensive evidence (statues, drawings, feminine iconography, burial artefacts) that during the Stone Age (Palaeolithic Age) and up until the Bronze Age, the pre-eminence and influence of women, female shamans, matriarchal societies, and beliefs in a supreme divine goddess were common.[337] Some two hundred portable Stone Age female figurines constructed from clay, limestone, chalk, bone, Mammoth

---

[335] See: https://www.nationalgeographic.com/history/article/7000-year-old-woman-reconstruction-sweden -hunter-gatherer November 12, 2019, retrieved on 17 June 2021.

[336] Benz and Bauer (2015), pp. 12-13.

[337] See: Graves (1961); Hall (1980); Patai (1990); Husain (1997); Cauvin (2003); Wilkinson (2009); Wesler (2014).

tusks, or stone have been found across Europe and Asia.[338] These finds highlight the ubiquity of reverence for the female over the male some 30,000 years ago.[339] There were several possible reasons for this. The fertility of humans and reproduction in nature were well-known but little understood. Goddesses were associated with a variety of other equally misunderstood phenomena—snakes, bulls, lions, panthers, the moon, and trees.

In prehistory, the veneration of the sun had translated into it being a sky god—the 'father in heaven'. The link between creation myths, a sun god, the Earth, fertility, and the need for a female partner and a son translated into the emergence of a mother goddess. Karen Armstrong elaborates:

> *In Syria, she was identified as Asherah, consort of El, the High God, or as Anat, El's daughter; in Sumer in Mesopotamia, she was called Inanna; in Egypt, Isis; and in Greece she became Hera, Demeter and Aphrodite.*[340]

In a well-known Middle Eastern late Stone Age archaeological site just east of Jericho and close to the Jordanian capital of Amman, female figurines have been found (dating from around 8000 BCE). They most probably symbolise the creation myth. According to French-American Middle Eastern archaeologist Denise Schmandt-Besserat, the stone female-influenced statuettes came from a culture where female effigies represented deities; they were housed in temples and shrines. They were a metaphor for the divine creation of the universe and were the subject of cultic ceremonies, offerings, and prayers.[341]

Archaeology Professor Kit Wesler has proposed that organised symbolic and ceremonial mythological practices emerged over time through the following stages:

- patterned symbolic or ceremonial activity did not appear until the emergence of cognitively modern human species around 70,000 years ago
- shamanism appeared as almost universal among the prehistoric non-agricultural human species

---

[338] SOURCE: https://www.world-archaeology.com/features/object-lesson-venus-of-renancourt/ retrieved on 26 January 2022, See also: https://indianculture.gov.in/artefacts-museums/mother-goddess-2 retrieved on 16 May 2022.

[339] Who were these 'Queens of the Stone Age'? (nationalgeographic.com), retrieved on 26 January 2022.

[340] Armstrong (2005), p. 46.

[341] Schmandt-Besserat (1998), pp. 115-116.

- agriculture introduced a stable settlement, appreciation of seasonal and climatic influences and the introduction of formal, traditional, invariant, and rule-governed practices. Mythology began to revolve around the seasons, the planets, goddesses, fertility, and connection to ancestors and regional cults

- the consolidation of states and kingdoms introduced more formalised rituals, service to authority, and the emergence of anthropomorphic gods and god-kings. Thus began the dominant ideology of religion, or at least an ascendant ideology that was deeply informed by a unified mythological explanation of the known world and the universe

- as civilisation emerged, the foundation for contemporary world religions was laid—sovereign kings, controlling elites, identifiable deities, shamanic priests, obedience to the cosmic order, institutionalisation, formalised places of worship/ temples, gods, cemeteries, retainer burials, and coercive power.[342]

There are interesting parallels between the techniques and skills claimed by shamans and those claimed by many members of modern-day religions. David Lewis-Williams described these shamanic techniques in the following way:

> *The 'therapeutic needs' that they are said to heal are largely of their own making. Like other religious systems, shamanism fills the world with potentially harmful spirits that cause great anxiety in believers. Shamans then use a variety of techniques to banish these spirits and apparently to cure their patients.*[343]

In modern Christianity, the Pentecostals and the broader evangelicals are the religious movements that have brought shamanic practices back into their routine contemporary rituals and beliefs. Moojan Momen has described their processes thusly:

> *The religious professional among these groups is usually a skilled orator who can raise the emotions of his audience. In the course of an evangelical religious event, it may be claimed that miracles, ecstatic trances, speaking in tongues, exorcism, healing and other extraordinary events have occurred. In traditional religions, the shaman performs a similar function, healing, discerning evil spirits and driving them out, and inducing trances.*[344]

---

[342] Wesler (2014), pp. 272-274.
[343] Lewis-Williams (2010), p. 125.
[344] Momen (1999), pp. 123-124.

Consolidation of religious ideas and symbols

French archaeologist Jaques Cauvin specialised in the prehistory of the Levant and Middle East. Cauvin's research suggests that archaeological excavations in and around the Levant demonstrate that it was most likely a restructuring of human mentality that accelerated the transition of belief systems towards anthropomorphic monotheism between the thirteenth and tenth millennium BCE. Cauvin sees this as a transformation in world views evolving into new religious ideas and symbols.[345]

Cauvin proposes that the decisive step that saw the transition of hunter-gatherers to farmers involved the emergence of symbolic systems, which created the foundation for and necessary abstraction for the emergence of anthropomorphic religion, writing systems and eventually the alphabet. When farming first appeared in Anatolia, the Levant and Mesopotamia around 10000 BCE, it correlated with a collective cognitive change, a restructuring of human mentality and the emergence of symbol-making. This was reflected in the emergence of rectilinear rather than circular housing, more structured social systems, the building of the first centralised cult structures, the gradual development of writing systems (abstract cuneiform or hieroglyphic symbols) and, eventually, the first anthropomorphic masculine and feminine divinities.

Cauvin claims that the psycho-cultural, symbolic change brought on by 'the transformation of the mind' was more responsible for the transition from forager to farmer than climatic change, material resources, or economic factors.[346] The abstraction from nature-based gods to human/female gods to abstract symbolic thinking drove intentional cultivation and commenced the process of human dominion over nature. In Cauvin's view, this intellectual shift created the agency necessary for agriculture—a psycho-cultural change that reached its zenith in the HB/OT's claim that God said:

> *Let us make man in our image, according to our likeness; and let them have dominion over the fish of the sea, and over the birds of the air, and over all the wild animals of the earth, and over every creeping thing that creeps upon the earth (Genesis 1:26).*

Over thousands of years, religious beliefs had moved from deifying and being subservient to and dependent on nature, planets, and animals to dominion over them. The hunter-gatherer perception of nature and location was not as a detached 'place' but as

---

[345] Cauvin (2003), p. 29.
[346] Cauvin et al (2001).

integral to them, their worldview and mythology. Over time, this transitioned away from the sanctification of nature and place to the abstraction of humans and mythologies from, and over and above, nature. In parallel with this, there was a gradual emergence of anthropomorphic monotheism, sanctified dogma, and the institutionalisation of religious hierarchies in parallel with the centralisation of government and politico-religious power.

The contextual evolution of mythological beliefs

Mythologies/religious beliefs are as integral to cultures as are economies, technologies, language, social structures, worldviews, family, and community relationships. Mythologies did not evolve in a logical linear fashion, and they did not occur uniformly or universally over time. Nor did they emerge in the same way across different geographic regions. The emergence of the Abrahamic religions followed a circumstantial, contextual, and chaotic stop-and-start process from the mythologies that emerged during the transition from hunter-gatherers to farmers to modern Western civilisation. The diversity of mythologies historically and contemporarily is a manifestation of the diversity of cultures historically and contemporaneously. This is because the variations and the changes over time in mythologies correlate with and are integrated with the growth of symbolic and abstract thinking, cultural, economic, and technological change, emerging social and cultural systems, surrounding plant and animal opportunities, and emerging cultural beliefs.

Nicholas Wade has summarised the journey from hunter-gatherer conceptions of a diverse presence of supernatural agents to monotheism in the following way:

- the hunter-gatherer's concept of the supernatural world involved sustained and socially cohesive egalitarian communal dances and trances as a means of communicating with the spirits
- early agricultural societies focused their religious beliefs on the cycle of seasons and the demands of planting, harvesting, and pastoralism. This was manifested in celebrations becoming essentially lunisolar agricultural and fertility festivals exemplified by the Canaanite predecessors to the Jewish Passover and the Christian Easter celebrations
- as sedentary agricultural and pastoral communities became more common, social hierarchies emerged and priests began to centralise and monopolise access to the sacred and the supernatural

- with the invention of writing, the emergence of sacred texts became more centralised and a didactic means emerged for accessing the supernatural and binding and unifying a community around a belief system
- from around 700 BCE, the Hebrew scribes took advantage of the new alphabet and their access to a wide range of past texts and inscriptions to amalgamate existing agricultural rituals, history, and past mythologies—a replacement of a miscellany of deities into one andromorphic god and a claimed divine right to certain territories as tools for creating a new nation.[347]

Summarising the conceptual journey to an anthropomorphic male god

It happened over hundreds of thousands of years, yet the progression of the Abrahamic religions from the hunter-gatherer notions of a world of natural (animate and inanimate) spirits to a belief in a singular anthropomorphic male god can now be fully understood.

In the words of Barbara Walker, 'Religion is a cultural artefact. … It is in the human mind rather than from alleged divine utterances'.[348] The evolution of the mythological beliefs of the Abrahamic religions largely followed and reflected the socio-cultural and economic evolution of the human species as it occurred specifically in the prehistoric Eurasian Steppe and the Middle East.

- When life and survival depended on hunting and gathering, the gods and the spirits were found in animate and inanimate nature.
- When the Eurasian Steppe hunter-gatherers domesticated and trained the horse and became nomads moving from camp to camp, their gods transitioned into personifications of the elements with which they were familiar—Earth, sky, sun, fire, and the animals on which they depended. Their nomadic dependency on their women (fertility, child rearing, skilled horseriding), was reflected in the Scythian female warriors (most likely the origin of the Greek Amazonian myth) and an increasing number of female goddesses.[349, 350]

---

[347] Wade (2010), pp. 189-190.

[348] Walker (2010), pp. 6-7.

[349] See: The Real Amazons: Separating Fact from Fiction (nationalgeographic.com) retrieved on 4 August 2022.

[350] Smith, S. (2021).

- When the Middle Eastern hunter-gatherers became sedentary and dependent on the seasons for their agriculture and pastoralism, their gods and their belief system transitioned to deification of the sun, the moon, the planets, and the associated seasonal cycles.
- When these sedentary settlements merged and expanded into increasingly larger cities with complex hierarchical human organisational models of governance, the gods were shaped into similar organisational structures (multiple deities with different responsibilities organised hierarchically under one supreme leader/god).
- As the control of larger empires and cultures consolidated around a sole male leader, king, god-king, or pharaoh, multiple deities transitioned into a singular autocratic male god who had most of the male human features and characteristics (e.g., a kingdom, a body, a head, arms and legs and a tendency to set the rules, to control, be worshipped, give love and show anger, fury and wrath).

This was where and when the Hebrew scribes stepped in to gradually transition the multiple Israeli cults worshipping many gods into a belief in a monotheistic human-like god.

Emerging anthropomorphism and patriarchy

The Sumerians were the first to claim that the sole purpose of humanity's existence was to serve the gods and, in the mind and the mythology of the Sumerians, the gods must have human-like characteristics. Acclaimed French Assyriologist Jean Bottero explained how the Sumerians invented anthropomorphic gods in the following way:

> *To make sense of both the world and their own existence, they had therefore postulated a supernatural society of 'gods', conceived in their own image but to a superlative degree, infinitely stronger, wiser and endowed with endless life. … To explain 'suffering', another set of beings had been concocted, inferior, it is true, to their creators and sovereigns of the Universe, but superior to their victims and freely able to provoke the misfortunes likely to poison the latter's existence.[351]*

---

[351]   Bottero (2001), pp. 166-167.

Sumerian authority Samuel Kramer explained emerging anthropomorphism in Sumerian mythology in this way:

> *Operating, directing and supervising this universe, the Sumerian theologian assumed was a pantheon consisting of a group of living beings, manlike in form but superhuman and immortal, who, though invisible to the mortal eye, guided and controlled the cosmos in accordance with well-laid plans and duly prescribed laws. The great realms of heaven, earth, sea, and air; the major astral bodies, sun, moon and planets; such atmospheric forces as wind, storm and tempest; and finally, on earth, such natural entities as river, mountain and plain, such cultural entities as city and state, dike and ditch, field and farm, and even such implements as the pickaxe, brick mould and plow—each was deemed to be under the charge of one or another anthropomorphic, but superhuman being who guided its activities in accordance with established rules and regulations.[352]*

The Sumerians developed their concept of human-like gods based on their observations of their own society. They could see that all their institutions and enterprises were managed and supervised and controlled by living human beings. There must, therefore, be a similar arrangement managing the cosmos.[353]

The emerging mythologies in the prehistoric Indus Valley reflected a similar pattern of beliefs. The Rig Veda, one of the four sacred Hindu canonical texts that were first written down in north-western India at the same time as the HB/OT, contains various hymns for praying to Vedic Gods such as Agni (the fire god), Indra (lord of heavens), Mitra, Varuna (water god) and Surya (sun god).[354]

The Sumerian deities were modelled on themselves, but the gods were much more powerful and intelligent; they resembled earthly sovereigns and lived for eternity. The Sumerians extended the shamanic notion that everything had a soul to the notion that the spiritual and physical realms were not mutually exclusive—a concept that gradually spread throughout the mythologies of the Fertile Crescent, the Levant, and Egypt under the Sumerian influence.

Natural forces and natural phenomena were now personified. Mythologist JF Bierlein has classified this transition as a transition from the essential or essence to the exis-

---

[352] Kramer (1963), pp. 113-114.
[353] Kramer (1956), p. 77.
[354] https://en.wikipedia.org/wiki/Rigveda accessed on 24 August 2020.

tential and meaningful existence.[355] This occurred when the hunter-gatherer's spiritual relationship with the natural environment and survival evolved into the city-dweller's personification of natural phenomena and the invention of a notion of eternal paradise after death.

It was through the Sumerian mythology that religion moved from deifying planets, constellations, animals, animal parts, plants, and nature (mountains, fires, etc.) to anthropomorphism and the move from feminine to masculine gods.

From around 2000 BCE, the ancient Mesopotamians (Sumerians, Babylonians, Akkadians) and the Canaanites believed that the whole of creation was the unfolding of a divine scripture in the hands of a group of anthropomorphic deities. Indeed, as Hebrew scholar Grey Hubert Skipwith has shown, the civilisations of antiquity in and around the Middle East shared a common mythology to such an extent that the mythologies on the island of Crete (some 1,000 kilometres away from the Levant by sea) were very similar to those of the Israelites in the Levant from around 1205 BCE.[356]

The Sumerian gods were originally male or female, engaged in intercourse, and reacted to stimuli with both reason and emotion. Like humans, the Sumerian gods and the Hebrew singular God could be unpredictable and, oftentimes, capricious.[357] The Hebrew Bible's concept of a human-like male god who projected human characteristics such as love, understanding, anger, and punishment while wearing human clothes (generally shepherd's clothing) was adapted from the ancient Sumerian mythology.

Goddesses, fertility, matriarchy, and the emergence of male leaders

The transition from totemism and animism to anthropomorphic gods was initially manifested in the emergence of female goddesses integrated with and worshipped by female shamans and matriarchal communities. In several cultures (Greeks, Minoans, Anatolians, Elamites, Sumerians, Scythians, Egyptians, Canaanites, early Hebrews, and Indus Valley Harappans), archaeologists have confirmed the pre-eminence of women through female figurines, fertility symbols, and women's burials that were more elaborate than men's burials. Mesopotamian authority Jean Bottero believes that shamanistic females were the

---

[355]   Bierlein (1994), p. 93.
[356]   Skipwith (1904), p. 57 and p. 59.
[357]   See: https://www.metmuseum.org/toah/hd/deit/hd_deit.htm retrieved on 31 October 2022.

Mesopotamians' preferred source of communication—'inspired divination'—with the supernatural.[358]

There is some debate about the reasons behind the evidence from the graves of females, but most scholars believe that burial artefacts are key indicators of a regional predominance of matriarchy and goddess worship cultures leading into the Bronze Age. There is substantial evidence that the Eurasian Steppe Scythians worshipped goddesses and included women as warriors, warrior queens, and representatives in high positions in society.[359]

Across most of the prehistoric mythologies, the images of the female goddesses were rarely accompanied by a male god but instead by an animal representative of male virility (bull, lion, snake, panther). Except for the Indus Valley and Iranian cultures, in the Middle East, the masculine force that was initially symbolised by these images of bulls, lions, snakes, and panthers was gradually replaced by a male warrior, male god-king, and all-powerful male gods. There are multiple theories about how this happened, although it is accepted that it owes much to the mobile Eurasian Steppe warrior culture. It happened gradually, over a period of several centuries and at different times in different locations.

The evidence is scant and still developing, but what does exist suggests that during the ice age (up until around 10000 BCE) there was most likely a gender imbalance, with women significantly outnumbering men. There are several hypotheses to explain this possibility, including a belief that there was a higher death rate of male babies; that cultural change affects reproductive success among males; that males are more susceptible to major climatic changes, temperature extremes, and/or major crises; that males are more likely to be killed in warfare; that culturally, male babies were more likely to be the subject of infanticide; and that there is a subsequent correlation between female goddesses, female origin myths, and the high status of women. These hypotheses include a belief that a warming climate will eventually benefit male survival. It is believed that from around twelve thousand years ago, the warming climate in the Middle East returned it to a more balanced adult sex ratio (ASR).[360] In addition, the domestication of the horse, the increased dominance of males in warfare, and the move towards a sedentary culture

---

[358] Bottero (2004), pp. 170-172.

[359] SOURCE: World History Encyclopedia (2021), History of the Scythians: an Ancient Nomadic Culture—YouTube retrieved on 3 November 2021.

[360] See: Helle et al. (2007); Catalano and Bruckner (2008); Chen (2014); Rettner (2014); Karmin et al (2015); O'Grady (2015); Kramer (2017); Scutti (2019); and https://www.youtube.com/watch?v=X-TeAQkOavjA&ab_channel=AncientArchitects retrieved on 12 August 2022.

saw the emphasis move away from female leaders and female goddesses to predominantly males, male gods, and male god-kings/leaders.

In the Eastern Steppe region, parts of the Iranian plateau and in Bactria, this pattern was reflected in archaeological evidence of a major decline in small agriculturally based settlements, the presence of the invading Steppe warriors, and a significant decline in the production of female terracotta figurines.[361]

As settlements grew and groups of family clans got larger in the Eastern Steppe and they created agricultural and livestock surpluses, new divisions of labour began to emerge. Here, the systems of organisation were gradually transitioning from kin-based to organisational systems that were more hierarchically and inequitably based on power, social division, wealth, and social prestige.[362]

Resource and economic surpluses provided the opportunity for the emergence of specialist potters, craftspeople, blacksmiths, administrators, priests, and labourers. Religious leaders in Bactria were initially elected from the community. Religious leadership began to gradually transfer from generation to generation. Control over temples and tributes by the priestly elite gradually transitioned into the private ownership of emerging priest-kings who gained increasing religious, economic, demographic, and geographic power.

The early Eastern Steppe Bactrian social structure evolved over time from clan-based goddess-worshipping families to a more complex six-tiered social structure united around a male god-king and a shared ideology. Like many locations in the Middle East, these new communities were now ruled by theocratic male priests and religious officials. For instance, the six-tiered Bactrian social structure consisted of:

1. Male city rulers/leaders (palace people, priest-kings, god-kings)
2. Religious ideology servants (temple people)
3. Military people (the original Steppe warrior culture)
4. Handicraftsmen (potters, blacksmiths, weavers, jewellers)
5. The general population (peasants, stock-breeders, farmers, merchants)
6. Poor people with no rights (labourers, slaves).[363]

---

[361]   Masson (1996), pp. 326–329.
[362]   Bellah (2011) p. 211.
[363]   Togaev (2020), pp. 1580-1581.

Recent evidence suggests that women did hold power and rulership for much longer in some parts of prehistoric Mesopotamia and in prehistoric Europe. The oldest and most lavish tomb yet to be found from ancient Mesopotamia is of a female queen who died around 2400 BCE.[364] In Ancient Spain, there is archaeological evidence of a female surviving as a powerful ruler until at least 1700 BCE.[365] There are major remnants of celebrations of the divine goddess and female fertility in today's annual religious practices (see below).

Eventually, most of the Middle East matriarchal societies were overtaken and subsumed by more socially structured patriarchal warrior cultures leading up to and throughout the Bronze Age. This was accompanied by the downplaying of goddesses and female shamans and the emergence of male-dominated monotheism originating in Zoroastrianism and in Egypt. This was eventually appropriated and written into the Hebrew Bible (around 500 BCE) and thereafter into the Christian Old and New Testaments (from around 70 CE onwards).

However, the worship of the female as a goddess or spirit has continued down to today through Zoroastrianism, Hinduism, and Buddhism. Along with Judaism, these are the four oldest religions in the world, and there is substantial overlap in the origin of their mythological beliefs.

Judaism is the only one of these four religions that has abandoned the veneration of a female goddess. The Zoroastrians worship Anahita, the goddess of the waters ('heavenly river'), fertility, healing, and wisdom, who is believed to be the inspiration for the cult of the ancient Mesopotamian goddess Inanna-Ishtar.[366] Tara is a female spirit revered in both Hinduism and Buddhism. Tara personifies compassion and offers salvation from the suffering of rebirth and death.[367]

With emerging male-dominated concepts of gods and the gradual replacement of females by male intermediaries (male shamans and priests), female shamans were gradually transformed and ostracised as *witches*. The Code of (Babylonian King) Hammurabi (1810 BCE to 1750 BCE), a set of 282 laws inscribed in stone, was a

---

[364] SOURCE: The Most Lavish Mesopotamian Tomb Ever Found Belongs to a Woman—Atlas Obscura retrieved on 24 February 2022.

[365] SOURCE: Ancient woman may have been powerful European leader, 4,000-year-old treasure suggests (nationalgeographic.com) retrieved on 25 March 2021.

[366] Malandra (1983), p. 119.

[367] Mark (2021B).

major influence on the development of the biblical Ten Commandments. Prior to the Hammurabi Code, the Mesopotamians believed that illness and evil came from witches and/or warlocks (male witches). However, the Mesopotamian focus was on the victim and not the perpetrator. Small substitute figurines were used ceremonially as a cure. The Mesopotamian healing rituals involved the abuse, disfigurement, burial, and burning of these figurines as there was no focus on, or attempts to identify, the alleged perpetrators.[368]

The Code of Hammurabi referred to witches as 'sisters of god' and specified that 'If a "sister of a god" open [*sic*] a tavern, or enter [*sic*]a tavern to drink, then shall this woman be burned to death'.[369] Witches are briefly mentioned in the Bible, where they are largely derided:

- Thou shall not suffer a witch to live (Exodus 22:18).
- A man also or woman that hath a familiar spirit, or that is a wizard, shall surely be put to death: they shall stone them with stones: their blood shall be upon them (Leviticus 20:27).

Unfortunately, the historical rituals of stoning (HB/OT) or burning (Babylonians) female figurines or targeted females translated over time into motivation for actions by subsequent male-dominated religions, and specifically the Christian popes in the Middle Ages. The Middle Ages burning of witches was most frequently done under the auspice of the erroneously named fifteenth-century Pope Innocent VIII (1480 CE to 1492 CE). Pope Innocent oversaw the burning to death of any female who was identified as a witch. From around 1400 CE to around 1880 CE, when the burning of female witches stopped, it is unclear exactly how many thousands of women were unfairly, unreasonably, erroneously and, most often, publicly burnt to death at the stake across those almost five hundred years.[370]

---

[368] See: https://www.asor.org/anetoday/2014/09/witchcraft-in-ancient-mesopotamia/ retrieved on 13 May 2022.

[369] See: https://avalon.law.yale.edu/ancient/hamframe.asp retrieved on 13 May 2022.

[370] See: Witch panics killed thousands throughout history (nationalgeographic.com) retrieved on 13 May 2022.

Transitioning to monotheistic male gods

The shift from the deification of animals, planets, geographic features, females, and fertility and ancestors towards a belief in anthropomorphic superhuman male deities evolved over a long period of time (shown notionally in Figure 20).

Cauvin (2003), Wesler (2014), and Harari (2015) believe that there is a significant correlation between the rise in the human species' mental capacity, the importance of agriculture and a sedentary way of life, emerging statehood, developing chiefdoms, belief in an afterlife, the ascent of a favoured ancestor to godhood, belief in a range of human-like gods (male and female), the deification of living leaders, and the building of temples—all of which began collectively with the Sumerians in the early Bronze Age. This complex and interrelated package of human, cultural, administrative, and mythological developments was manifested in a trend towards institutionalisation and the codification of gods as supernatural personalities at the same time as the desire for unified statehood emerged.[371]

The longevity of the 'god-king' concept

The unification of statehood around a god-king or god-queen was an invention of the Sumerians. It was one of the devices used to unify and control an increasingly complex city state or emerging kingdom. As the transition from nomadic hunter-gatherers to sedentary agriculturalists and pastoralists evolved, settlements became much larger, and new divisions of labour and more hierarchically social structures followed. A shared mythology/belief system and leadership by a god-king or god-queen were instrumental in maintaining order. The god-king or god-queen was not only the monarch or sovereign of the kingdom or empire, but they also had a direct link to god. This link has been sustained in some contemporary cultures—most notably the British monarchy where the king or queen is also the leader of the Churches of England and Scotland. This dual function of the god-king is also the key principle underlying the role of Jesus and of the pope in the Christian belief system—a combination of secular leadership but with a clear pipeline, representation and responsiveness to God.

---

[371] Wesler (2014), pp. 152-158 and pp. 272-274.

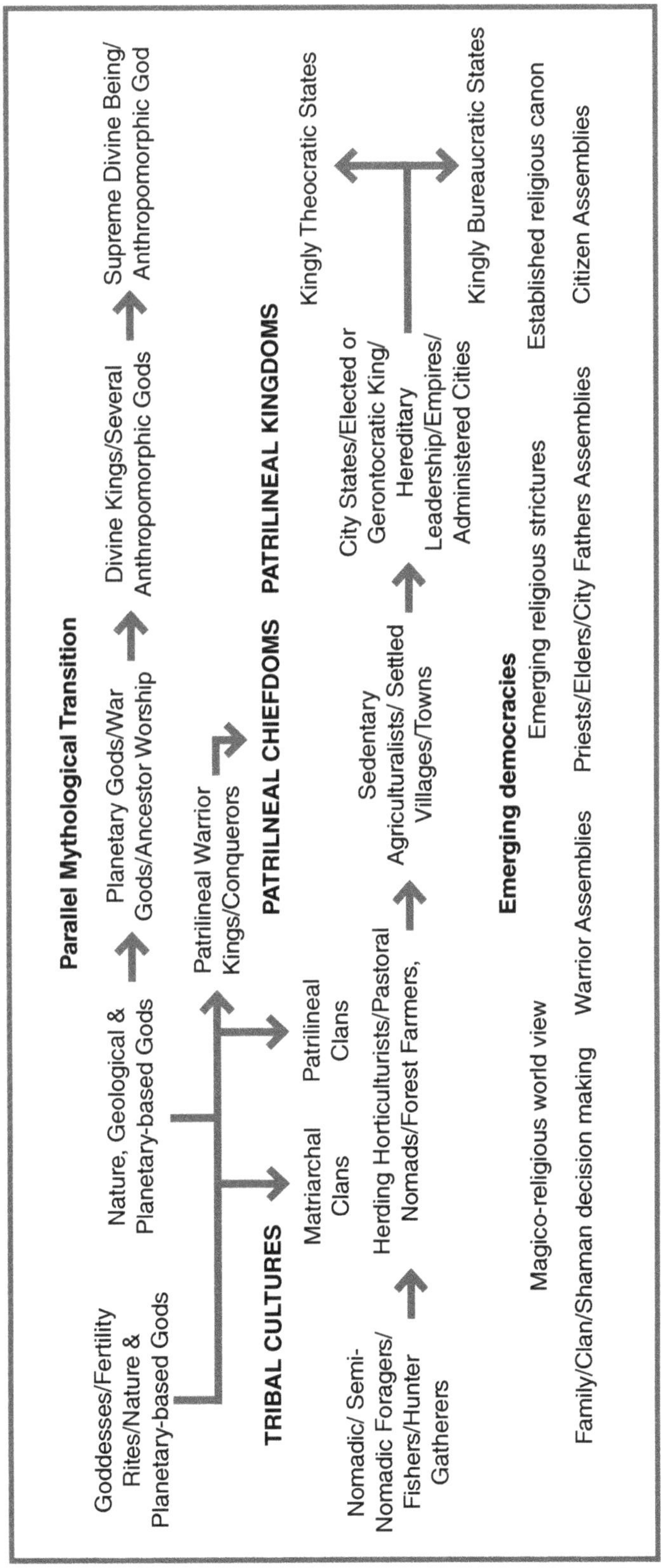

Figure 20: Notional diagrammatic of prehistoric Ancient Middle East time-based transition of mythologies with socio-cultural and political changes

Built form to symbolise and reflect mythological beliefs

Apart from artefacts such as pottery and tools and evidence relating to housing design and settlement patterns, there are two structures that have most informed archaeologists in their attempts to reconstruct the gradual evolution of religious beliefs prior to and influencing the Hebrew scribes. The two structures that archaeologists believe most likely reflect emerging religious beliefs and/or collective mythological practices are the symbolism of tombs/burial practices and the emergence of centralised religious structures.

Tombs and Burial Practices

The foraging and largely nomadic human species' biological and cultural evolution saw cognitive abilities develop that allowed the differentiation of themselves from nature. One manifestation of this was the emergence of a variety of practices for the deliberate disposal and visible marking of locations of the dead.

Archaeological evidence of burials and mortuary practices in terms of their location, density, gender, proximity, and style is used by researchers as an indicator of the emergence over time of social, cultural, organisational, and mythological structures and stability. The emergence of intentional burial practices and mass gravesites (the earliest versions of what are now called cemeteries) and the ritual preparation of the dead for/ and belief in an afterlife were initial stages of the emergence of more complex religious beliefs and practices.

In general, early nomadic hunter-gatherers tended to bury their dead where they lay or in shallow pits, often at wide locations across the landscape or right next to or close to their regular/routine places of settlement.[372] A move from ad hoc disposal to formal, intentional burial practices in an excavated identifiable grave reflected a major change in the treatment of bodies and in attitude to nature, life, and death. Rhawn Joseph believes that there is archaeological evidence of complex mortuary practices and beliefs that imply an early hominin belief in an afterlife dating back some tens of thousands of years.[373]

---

[372] See: Littleton and Allen (2007) for a discussion of the burial practices of Australia's First Nations hunter-gatherers.

[373] Joseph (2011).

Archaeological evidence of intentional, purposeful burials of individuals has been found in Africa from around eighty thousand years ago.[374]

Most archaeologists believe that the intentional treatment of the deceased implies a level of cultural complexity only found in the human species. British Museum authority on Ancient Mesopotamia, Irving Finkel believes that the emergence of intentional mass gravesites and the ritual preparation of the dead in graves with associated grave goods has been occurring for at least 50,000 years. This signifies an early and emerging belief in and preparation for a presumed afterlife.

Finkel believes that burial with grave goods implies three prehistoric beliefs about death:

- something survives of a human being after death
- something escapes the grasp of the corpse and goes somewhere
- something, if it goes somewhere, can quite reasonably be expected to be capable of coming back.[375]

There is evidence of the earliest sedentary agricultural settlers in ancient Anatolia (Türkiye) burying their dead underneath their rudimentary homes from around 7100 BCE to 5700 BCE. Emerging burial rituals from other prehistoric cultures included the Kurgan culture (5000 BCE to 3000 BCE) burying their dead in deep shafts within artificial burial mounds; the Maykop culture (3700 BCE to 3000 BCE) having differentiated burial practices for royalty from those of the general population; and the Pit Grave, Ochre Grave, or Yamnaya culture (3300 BCE to 2600 BCE) interring their dead in 'pit graves' rather than in communal structures.

In several cultures (Greeks, Minoans, Anatolians, Elamites, Sumerians, Egyptians, Canaanites, early Hebrews, and Indus Valley Harappans), archaeologists have confirmed the eminence of women leader-goddesses-shamans as their burials were more elaborate than men's burials. The ancient Egyptian burial practices were, by far the most elaborate—reflecting their complex beliefs in an afterlife and in immortality. This saw the building of elaborate pharaonic royal burial chambers (the pyramids) and including in them large quantities of resources for the afterlife.

---

[374] See: Martinon-Torres et al. (2021).
[375] Finkel (2021), pp. 3-5.

The Canaanite and Israeli rock-cut tombs

When they first emerged historically (in 1205 BCE), the ancient Israelites carried over many of the burial practices they inherited from the Canaanites, Egyptians, Phoenicians, and the Palestinians with whom they shared the Levant. Cave habitation and the use of caves for tombs in the Levant dates to at least 50000 BCE.[376] It was in the Neolithic Era in communities in the Levant that caves became the locus of intense ritual behaviour with a mortuary/funerary emphasis.[377]

The Bronze Age Canaanite and Phoenician communities continued this practice in developing rock-cut bench tombs—a practice that was continued by the Israelites.[378] These more elaborate Canaanite/Ancient Israelite tombs involved the use of rock-cut tombs for the burial of the elite (high-ranking officials, middle and upper class) as distinct from the general populous, who were mainly buried in simple pit graves.

The Israelite rock-cut tombs could become quite complex, varying from single chambers to multi-chambered or complex designs and usually cut into rock or located in a cave and usually belonging to a single or nuclear family.[379] The HB/OT makes many references to key biblical figures being buried in a 'cave' (Abraham, Sarah, Isaac, Rebekah, Jacob, and Leah). Rock-cut tombs are mentioned in the Book of Judges (Judges 8:32), the Second Book of Samuel (2 Samuel 2:32), and the Second Book of Kings (2 Kings 9:28, 21:26, 23:16, 23:30).

The rock-cut tomb was the type of tomb that the writers of the Christian New Testament believe was owned by Joseph of Arimathea (a town and a person that, to this day, has not been definitively identified/confirmed) and was the type of tomb in which they claim that the body of Jesus was placed (e.g., Mark 15:42–47).[380]

Kit Wesler has explained how religious beliefs most probably evolved to a belief in an afterlife with the advent of sedentary communities, 'retainer burials', and associated tomb offerings. Wesler describes a retainer burial as when a chosen (focus) person:

---

[376]   Rowan and Ilan (2012), p. 87.
[377]   Rowan and Ilan (2012), p. 101.
[378]   See: Fantalkin (2008).
[379]   See: https://en.wikipedia.org/wiki/Rock-cut_tombs_in_ancient_Israel retrieved on 6 May 2021.
[380]   Scholars generally accept that the New Testament gospels were written by persons other than the Apostles Mathew, Mark, Luke and John. See Walker (2010), p. 153.

> *… is placed in an elaborate tomb often wearing sumptuous or symbolic regalia, accompanied by the finest crafts and manufactures that his or her society can provide plus one or more other persons who are evidently of lesser status.[381]*

These burial processes, amid funerary paraphernalia and private possessions, initially signified ancestor worship, a belief in and preparedness for an afterlife and the emerging deification of a chosen person. There is some evidence that the link between ancestor worship, the worshipping of natural forces and of local spirits, funerary and burial practices, the growth of sedentary agricultural practices, and the socio-political unifying of communities became the catalyst for the construction of early temple-like burial structures—embryonic forms of what are now called mausoleums or crypts.[382]

Symbolic burials, involving some form of ritual or burial structure, are regarded by archaeologists as being symptomatic of the continued emergence of abstract thinking in the human species. Symbolic burials indicate an ability to imagine and communicate ideas about things that are not immediate, such as primitive communications about nearby food or approaching danger.

Centralised religious structures

Initially, the key components of contemporary religious church-based practices found their embryonic form in the early hunter-gatherer cave-based rituals thirty millennia ago. Matthew Kneale has summarised these in the following way (after David Lewis-Williams, 2004):

> *People would have crept into the depth of caves, far beyond the reach of any natural light, using simple lamps made from animal fat on flat pieces of stone, with strands of juniper as wicks. These would have flickered feebly, illuminating only tiny patches of the (cave) paintings. Deep into the caves, perhaps with a small congregation gathered round them, shamans would have entered a trance and tried to contact the spirits. There could well have been music. A number of bone flutes have been found in early caves, while people may also have sung or chanted, and used stalagmites as natural bells, striking them to produce deep booming sounds.[383]*

---

[381] Wesler (2014), p. 90.
[382] Kornienko (2009), p. 97.
[383] Kneale (2013), pp. 9-10.

As nomadic hunter-gatherers began to build social and cultural unification, the cave rituals were relocated to ideological architectural structures. This involved the construction of the first centralised human-made communal structures symptomatic of the increasing ability of the human species to think collectively in symbolic and abstract terms. There is strong evidence that nomads and some early hunter-gatherer communities in Northern Mesopotamia (currently South-Eastern Türkiye) worshipped and offered sacrifices to nature and planetary-based gods in significant and meaningful landscape locations.[384] This occurred when worship practices moved from nature generally to specifically identified symbolic sites.

It was during the Bronze Age that the practice of worshipping specific anthropomorphic deities and the construction of centralised cult structures began to merge together. Specific structures/temples built to represent, symbolise, or reflect collectively held beliefs began in around 9000 BCE in the Fertile Crescent/Northern Levant/South-Eastern Türkiye. This is some four thousand years before the biblical God created the universe and some eight thousand years prior to the emergence of the Hebrew scribes. These public cult structures—around or through which ancestors were worshipped, communities unified, astronomical events ritualised and mythological ceremonies and sacrifices held—were most often built to reflect, symbolise, or placate one or more specific deities.

Centralised religious structures were the physical manifestation of commonly shared stories explaining the unknown world and unifying otherwise disparate communities. The oral practice of telling and repeating mythological stories and oral histories became more convincing once there was a visible, physical structure around which various rituals and practices could be constructed. The building of centralised cult structures symbolised the gradual emergence of the human species' cognitive abilities to imagine other worlds.

These prehistoric centralised cult structures were the precedents for modern-day centralised religious places of worship such as temples, churches, synagogues, mosques, and Buddhist monasteries.

Significant communal structures in the Northern Levant

The first ceremonial communal ritual structure to be discovered, Göbekli Tepe, was built on the highest point of an elongated mountain ridge in northern Levant/South-Eastern Türkiye in around 9000 BCE. Here are the world's oldest known megaliths—huge

---

[384] Kornienko (2009); Tobolczyk (2016), p. 1399.

T-shaped stone pillars which predate the Great Pyramid of Egypt by some seven thousand years, Stonehenge in England by six thousand years, and the Sumerian ziggurats by five thousand years. The Göbekli Tepe structures were most probably built by hunter-gatherers and not by a sedentary community.[385] In fact, there are similar sites of a similar age east of Göbekli Tepe (Boncuklu Tarla and Karahan/ Keçili Tepe). This suggests that there was most probably a lost civilisation of semi-sedentary hunter-gatherers engaged in collective religious practices well before the emergence of agriculture and sedentary communities.[386]

There is some dispute over the astronomical function of the Göbekli Tepe. The key researchers excavating the site are sceptical that it was a prehistoric astronomical observatory. However, they do not exclude the possible astronomic link or orientation of the Göbekli Tepe monuments. They feel that convincing evidence is still lacking.[387]

Others, however, have shown how the builders of Göbekli Tepe had a good working knowledge of the cosmic geography of their time. The stone pillars are believed to be celestial markers that were erected in astronomical alignment with a key important star (Deneb in the constellation Cygnus) and with the Milky Way's Great Rift, which was regarded throughout prehistory as the entry point into the sky world.[388]

Deneb is one of the brightest stars in the sky. Deneb and the constellation Cygnus are part of the 'Summer Triangle' of stars, which appear overhead around solar midnight during summer in the Northern Hemisphere. The Summer Triangle is visible in the eastern sky in early morning during spring and in autumn and winter evenings. The Summer Triangle is visible in the western sky in the Northern Hemisphere until January.

The large T-shaped columns in Göbekli Tepe hint at the emergence of a belief in anthropomorphic gods. As well as containing animal representations, the columns are believed to be abstract anthropomorphic images: 'Some of the pillars have arms and hands sculptured on wider sides, as well as other features, which make resemblance to statues of human-like beings.'[389]

Göbekli Tepe sits in the core of the Fertile Crescent at its northern edge and would have most probably been a pilgrimage destination for hunter-gatherers from Africa,

---

[385] SOURCE: https://www.smithsonianmag.com/history/Göbekli-tepe-the-worlds-first-temple-83613665/ retrieved on 8 March 2021.

[386] See: https://sailingstonetravel.com/karahan-tepe-kecili-tepe/ and https://arkeonews.net/a-12-000-year -old-temple-was-found-during-excavations-in-boncuklu-tarla-in-southeastern-turkey/ retrieved on 3 August 2022.

[387] Notroff et al (2017), p. 59. See also the response by Sweatman and Tsikritsis (2017).

[388] Collins (2014), pp. 88-93.

[389] Tobolczyk (2016), p. 1400.

Anatolia, Mesopotamia, and the Levant. It is close to the prehistoric north-west Mesopotamian city of Harran, which was dedicated by the prehistoric Mesopotamians to the Akkadian/Sumerian moon god Sin/Nanna. Several thousand years later, Harran (biblical spelling is 'Haran') was appropriated by the Hebrew scribes as the home of Abraham's father, Terah. According to the Bible, Harran was visited by Abraham (a name also associated with moon worship) and his family on their rather indirect journey from the city of Ur (a city also dedicated to the moon god) on their way to Canaan.

Archaeologists have found evidence of a settlement contemporary with and just northeast of Göbekli Tepe. The site of Gre Fılla Höyük ('Gre Fılla Mound') in the province of Diyarbakir in eastern Türkiye contains temple-like structures ten metres in diameter with upright stone columns (stele) around which rituals appear to have been performed.[390]

Some sixty kilometres north-west of Göbekli Tepe, and in the north of the Fertile Crescent, is Nevalı Çori (8400 BCE to 8000 BCE), where there is convincing archaeological evidence of grand buildings with huge T-shaped stone pillars that functioned in some way as cultish ceremonial religious structures.[391]

Evidence of communal ritual structures dating from around 9000 BCE has been found at other sites in the Fertile Crescent/Mesopotamia (Figure 21). These include Jerf el-Ahmar near the Euphrates River in Northern Syria and Tell Ain el-Kerkh in North-West Syria/Northern Levant (between the Euphrates and the Mediterranean) from around 7000 BCE.[392] There are multiple other locations in northern Mesopotamia from around 9000 BCE that contain structures that had a specific communal cult function and were protected by symbols of divine power (Figure 21).[393]

There is recent evidence of monumental communal prehistoric stone structures from 6000 BCE in the oasis of Dûmat al-Jandal (northern Saudi Arabia) that were most likely left by nomadic pastoralists and dedicated to practices such as funerary and commemorative rituals.[394]

Prior to the discovery of Göbekli Tepe, the megalithic temples of Ggantija on the Mediterranean Island of Malta (dating from around 5000 BCE to 2000 BCE and older than the Egyptian pyramids) were thought to be the oldest example of prehistoric temples.

---

[390] https://www.thearchaeologist.org/blog/a-special-structure-contemporary-to-gbeklitepe-found-at-gre-flla-hyk-in-eastern-turkey retrieved on 22 September 2022.
[391] Collins (2014), pp. 21-28.
[392] Finlayson et al., (2011).
[393] Kornienko (2009).
[394] Munoz et al (2020).

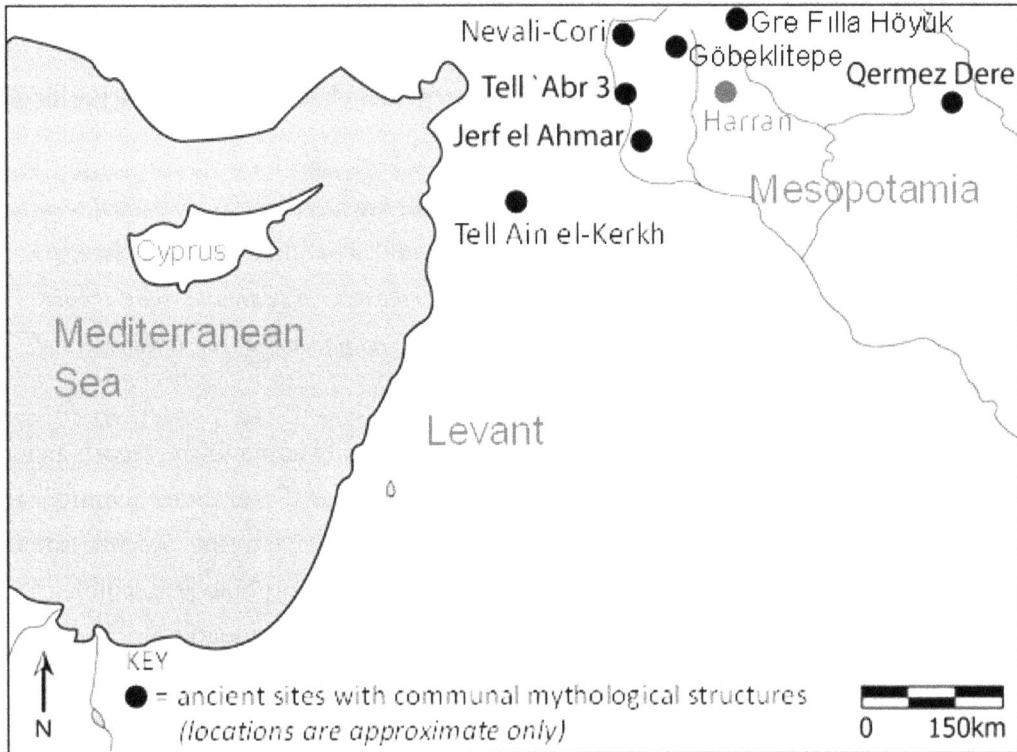

Figure 21: *Locations of early communal buildings that have a mythological function in northern Mesopotamia (9000 BCE to 7000 BCE)*[b]

---

[b] Map adapted from Finlayson et al. (2011). Base map reprinted with permission from Professor Bill Finlayson.

Maltese folklore states that they were built in one day and one night by a female giant.[395] Archaeologists have determined that they were, in fact, a ceremonial site dedicated to the 'great Earth mother', a goddess of fertility and to fertility rites.[396]

The Maltese temples have a strong astronomical alignment to the sunrise, sunset, moonrise, and moonset during the Northern Hemisphere winter solstice.[397] This is an early and interesting example of the astronomical lunisolar origins of the choice of dates and symbolism which correspond with the ancient celebration of the Roman Saturnalia

---

[395] SOURCE: https://en.wikipedia.org/wiki/Megalithic_Temples_of_Malta retrieved on 7 March 2021.
[396] SOURCE: https://en.wikipedia.org/wiki/%C4%A0gantija retrieved on 7 March 2021.
[397] Sparavigna (2016).

festival (commencing around 300 BCE onwards). These dates were contemporarily rebranded as the Christian celebration of Christmas (from around 336 CE onwards).

Andrew Curry has summarised the view of German archaeologist Klaus Schmidt and world authority on Göbekli Tepe in the following way:

> *Scholars have long believed that only after people learned to farm and live in settled communities did they have the time, organization and resources to construct temples and support complicated social structures. But Schmidt argues it was the other way around: the extensive, coordinated effort to build the monoliths literally laid the groundwork for the development of complex societies.*[398]

Schmidt's hypothesis sits comfortably with the view of Yuval Harari and the French archaeologist Jaques Cauvin (discussed above, page 9 and page 152).[399] Cauvin, Schmidt, and Harari seem to agree that the transition from hunter-gatherers to farming, sedentarism and 'civilisation' was not primarily nor simply determined by geomorphological, edible crops, pastoral animals, and the availability of arable land. They see the foundations of civilisation as being more a consequence of the emergence of abstract thinking and symbolic systems including religion, codification of gods, centralised ritualised mythological architecture, and evolving communication systems (from pictorial to cuneiform and hieroglyphics to abstract writing systems and eventually to consonants, vowels, and the alphabet).

The religious origin of temples, ziggurats and pyramids

The notion of a god sitting on top of a mountain was the key belief that influenced the emergence of centralised religious structures such as ziggurats, step pyramids, and pyramids. The Egyptian pyramids, whilst having several other important functions and meanings, are essentially a metaphor for the primeval hill.[400] It is highly likely that ziggurats emerged from ancient mythological beliefs in Mongolia/Siberia where the creator was believed to be sitting on top of a golden mountain in the middle of the sky prior to creating the cosmos. From here, they travelled as a focus of religious and social life down through the Iranian Plateau cultures, through Mesopotamia and Sumer into Egypt and eastwards into Mesoamerica.[401]

---

[398]   Curry (2008), https://www.smithsonianmag.com/history/Göbekli-tepe-the-worlds-first-temple-83613665/ retrieved on 7 March 2021.
[399]   Harari (2015).
[400]   Keel (1997), p. 113.
[401]   Kurtkaya (2020), pp. 33-37.

The word ziggurat can mean 'height or pinnacle' (Assyrian), 'rising building' (Akkadian) or 'temple-tower' (modern usage). Unlike the much later Egyptian pyramids, the Mesopotamian ziggurats had a flat top, on which a temple or shrine was usually constructed in reverence to the city's ruling god. The oldest known precursors of the ziggurats were flat-topped raised platforms that date from the Mesopotamian prehistoric Ubaid period during the sixth millennium BCE. One of the oldest ziggurats currently known is Sialk ziggurat, which was built in central Iran in around 3000 BC where the oldest human settlements date back to around 6000 BCE. There is archaeological evidence of the ruins of a much older Sumerian ziggurat in the ancient city of Uruk that included a temple dedicated to the Sumerian sun god and supreme deity An/Anu (An was the Sumerian word for heaven). The Anu ziggurat was most likely built in the late fourth millennium BCE.[402]

Over hundreds of years, ziggurats as religious centres were built by ancient Sumerians, Akkadians, Elamites, Eblaites, and Babylonians as part of their temple complexes. These early forms of ziggurats emerged originally from the Eastern Steppes/South-West Asia and travelled south-west to eventually end up in the forms and slightly different functions of the Egyptian pyramids. The very first Egyptian pyramid, the Pyramid of Djoser (2670 BCE–2650 BCE) was a step pyramid, a shape which reflects its most likely influence being the stepped ziggurats in Mesopotamia.

The ziggurat had multiple symbolic and mythological meanings to the Mesopotamians— the ziggurat was usually centrally located; they signified the mountain on which the creator sat prior to the act of creation; they symbolised the primeval mound from which the universe was created; they linked the heaven, the Earth, and the underworld; they created a holy place on top of which the gods or symbols of the gods could meet or dwell.

Many of these metaphors continue in the present day, in which religious buildings are located on the highest geographic points, towering up to the heavens, and full of religious meaning and metaphors. There is an obvious link between the internal layout of the ancient Sumerian temples and modern religious buildings. British Historian Paul Kriwaczek described this in the following way:

In the middle of the fourth millennium BCE a huge building, larger than the Parthenon in Athens, partly or wholly constructed of imported limestone, stood on a central platform in the

---

[402] SOURCE: https://www.khanacademy.org/humanities/ap-art-history/ancient-mediterranean-ap/ancient-near-east-a/a/white-temple-and-ziggurat-uruk retrieved on 24 March 2022.

Eanna quarter (of the ancient Sumerian city of Uruk). The shrine was even more remarkable for the fact that its ground plan almost exactly anticipated, by 3,000 years, the layout of Christian churches. There was a central nave, a crossways transept, a narthex or lobby, and an apse at one end flanked by the two rooms that in a Christian sanctuary would be called the diaconicon and the prothesis.[403]

The economic theory for the emergence of religion

There is a strongly held economic theory behind the emergence of religion and, specifically, centralised communal structures, particularly in Southern Mesopotamia, where both emerged for apparently the first time in an integrated way. All Sumerian cities were dedicated to a specific deity for whom temples were constructed and around which rites and rituals, including tithing, were regularly performed. These temples were places of astrological, spiritual, religious, and ceremonial importance.

It is suggested by economists that once larger-scale sedentary agricultural and animal husbandry settlements grew, they created agricultural and livestock surpluses. These surpluses then became the basis for a division of labour and a *redistribution economy*. Some folks produced the surplus and others decide what to do with the surplus—why and how it is to be redistributed.

But this division of labour cannot be sustained if implemented by force—there needs to be some unifying ideological reason for the providers and the distributors to unite. This would include the development and management of *economic means*, such as the prehistoric mass production of standardised bowls, storage containers, and transport systems (of which there is significant archaeological evidence). But it would require a unifying ideology or common belief system. Economists believe that religion and the collaborative building of centralised monumental structures around which developed communal rites and rituals, initially in Southern Mesopotamia, were key *noneconomic means* of regulating production and distribution.[404]

Middle Eastern historian Massimo Maiocchi describes the economic pressure for religion in early Mesopotamia in this way:

---

[403] Kriwaczek (2010), p. 40.
[404] Foster and Foster (2009), pp. 27-28.

The joint efforts of the workforce under the supervision of a central authority, combined with technological innovations and favourable environmental conditions, produced a large surplus. However, the producers were required to deliver such surplus to organizations embedded in a system primarily devoted to accumulation and distribution—a painful process for producers, which requires an ideological explanation ultimately residing in religious thought via divine legitimisation of the elite.[405]

In some ways, the search for a definitive answer to the question of which came first—new mental capacities, abstraction, agriculture, surplus production, or religion—is flawed. Most likely, the prehistoric/Bronze Age process of human development was a consequence of all these factors—an intellectual shift towards abstraction, the development of agricultural and livestock surpluses, the emergence of a shared ideology as an organising system, and unifying energy, the geomorphological and locational opportunities, and the cultural characteristic of each and unifying energy group, the most significant exemplar being the Sumerians who arrived in Southern Mesopotamia around 4000 BCE.

---

[405] Maiocchi (2019), p. 414.

Chapter 10

What Humanity Achieved Prior to the Emergence of Israel and the Writing of the Hebrew Bible

The different historical periods

Historians tend to classify history into different historical periods based on what archaeological, historical, pottery, and DNA evidence indicates emerged in that era. The three most common categorisations of historical periods in the gradual development of humanity and the emergence of civilisations are Stone Age (from around 3.3 million years ago until around 3300 BCE), Bronze Age (from around 3300 BCE to 1300 BCE), and Iron Age (from around 1300 BCE to around 100 BCE). The term Copper Age (Chalcolithic—derived from the Greek word for copper) is used to describe a period that overlaps the Stone and the Bronze Ages. The Copper Age lasted from around 3500 BCE to 2300 BCE.

The intellectual revolutions behind human development

There is a growing body of evidence and an increasingly large number of scientists and researchers that link human development across these periods to significant brain development and improved intellectual capacities. Israeli historian Yuval Noah Harari believes that human intellectual capacities journeyed over millennia through:

- A cognitive revolution (between 70,000 and 30,000 years ago). This is the period from which archaeological excavation started to regularly find handmade tools and rudimentary art in ancient human species sites

- An agricultural revolution (some 12,000 years ago) when the human species started to manipulate and manage the lives of plants and animals[406]
- A scientific revolution (some 500 years ago) when the religious search for God's messages gradually evolved into discoveries contrary to religious belief, and initiated objective scientific research.[407]

Like Harari, evolutionary psychologist Richard G Coss believes that there was a significant technological transition from the Middle Stone Age to the late Stone Age some seventy thousand years ago. He proposes that more advanced cognitive abilities due to evolutionary changes in brain organisation saw a transition from simple stone tools and small prey hunting to hand-thrown spears and large prey hunting. The commensurate and significantly enhanced perceptual-motor coordination with this technological change (from chipping at stones to making and throwing projectiles) was largely responsible for the emergence of cave art representations. So cognitive development impacted improvements in technology together with artistic communication—a cognitive and perceptual relationship between spear throwing and external visualisation and representation (drawing).[408]

Subsequently, and over a very long period, there was a restructuring of human mentality and mental capacities reflected in art and communication moving from working with pictorial concepts, imagery, and myths (cave paintings, female figurines) through the symbolic (nature and planetary gods, pictograms, ideographic and syllabic cuneiform images, hieroglyphics) to the abstract (alphabets, writing, unifying ideologies, social stratification, organised government, and religion).

The human species is 'wired for story-telling'. The human species does not only tend to see and invent stories as explanations for the patterns around them. They invent stories to unify otherwise disparate groups.[409] Harari lists religion as one of the fictional systems developed by the human species. He suggests that once humans congregated in large groups, cooperation was enhanced by—in fact, reliant on—an imagined sense of order. This most likely began not with agriculture and city formation, but when hunter-gatherer:

> … *stories about ancestral spirits and tribal totems were strong enough to enable 500 people to trade seashells, celebrate the odd festival, and join forces to wipe out a Neanderthal band.*[410]

---

[406] See also Cauvin (2003), p. 29.
[407] Harari (2015), p. 3.
[408] See: Coss (2017).
[409] https://www.wired.com/2011/03/why-do-we-tell-stories/ retrieved on 17 August 2022.
[410] Harari (2015), p. 115.

While imagined explanations, technical skills, and discoveries are not applicable universally, and all dates are approximate and can vary widely depending on geographic location, the following summary outlines some of the major cultural steps made by human ancestors over time. This initially occurred largely in Africa, the Eurasian Steppe, Central Asia, and the Middle East, but in other less well-known locations, as intellectual capacities evolved, unifying imagined stories emerged and 'civilisations' formed.

Major technological and material-cultural achievements during the Stone Age

From between three million years ago until around six thousand years ago, early humans (hominins) tended to be largely hunter-gatherers living by hunting and collecting seafood, eggs, nuts, and fruits, as well as scavenging and forest gardening, shaping, and using stone tools (hammer stones, scrappers, sharpeners, choppers, cleavers, cereal harvesting tools, arrow, and spearheads).

This period has been termed 'the Stone Age'. The phrase 'stone age' conceals some very important innovations that occurred during this period and reflects the emergence of civilised society across a range of continents and often independently of each other. For example:

Up to 50,000 years ago

- The oldest, simple stone tools made by human ancestors, found in the savannahs of East Africa (called Oldowan tools after the Olduvai Gorge in Tanzania), are dated at around 2.6 million years ago. Oldowan tools have been found in many excavation sites including in Ethiopia, Tanzania, Kenya, Chad, Algeria, Egypt, and Georgia.[411]
- a significant archaeological find of evidence of an ancient material culture including flint axes and evidence of settlement by the ancestors of modern humans—*Homo erectus*—on the banks of an ancient stream in Central Israel (estimated as dating to 500,000 years ago).[412]

---

[411] See: Susman (1991).
[412] SOURCE: https://www.bbc.com/news/world-middle-east-42598519 and https://mfa.gov.il/MFA/IsraelExperience/History/Pages/Important-and-rare-prehistoric-site-uncovered-in-central-Israel-7-January-2017.aspx.

- the creation by early humans, in a variety of global locations, of specialised tools such as fishing nets, hooks, and bone harpoons (around 80,000 years ago)[413]
- the world's earliest known cave paintings were produced in Spain more than 65,000 years ago by Neanderthals.[414]
- sea levels were so low between Australia and New Guinea that they formed a single continent. There is evidence that groups of humans moved from Southeast Asia onto this landmass, some settling in what is now New Guinea, and others travelling farther south into Australia (around 60,000 to 50,000 years ago).[415]
- the emergence across several different geographic locations of modern cultural behaviour, including the creation by different human communities of art and non-functional/symbolic cultural objects e.g., cave/rock painting, narrative art-works, notched decorative bones (around 50,000 years ago).

From 40,000 years ago to around 12,000 years ago

- Evidence of elaborate Indigenous Australian fish traps near Brewarrina in NSW, Australia—consisting of a network of rock weirs and pools stretching for around half a kilometre along the riverbed to catch fish as they swam upstream (from more than 40,000 years ago)[416]
- first evidence of modern humans in Britain is a jawbone found in Kent's Cavern in Devon (dated to around 40,000 years ago)[417]
- the emergence of simple handmade pottery and ceramics using pit firing methods in Central Asia and the Middle East (around 40,000 years ago)
- the oldest example found so far of artistic representation by hominin ancestors, dating from around 33,000 years ago is a lion-headed figurine carved from a mammoth tusk and found in a cave in the Hohlenstein cliffs in south-west Germany[418]

---

[413] SOURCE: https://www2.palomar.edu/anthro/homo2/mod_homo_5.htm.
[414] The astonishing—and accidental—Ice Age discovery made by Spanish spelunkers (nationalgeographic.com) retrieved on 24 September 2022.
[415] SOURCE: https://www.nytimes.com/2017/03/08/science/aboriginal-australians-dna-origins-australia.html.
[416] SOURCE: https://www.environment.nsw.gov.au/heritageapp/ViewHeritageItemDetails.aspx?ID=5051305
[417] See: Pettitt and White (2010).
[418] Kneale (2013), p. 5.

- paintings of horses and other animals in Chauvet Cave in France (dated at around 30,000 years ago)[419]

- evidence of plant cropping in the Solomon Islands (around 28,000 years ago)[420]

- remnants of dwellings made of mammoth tusks and a ceramic Venus figurine statuette found in Dolni Vestonice in the Czech Republic (from around 29,000 to 25,000 years ago)[421]

- evidence of human cultures developing small portable stone art objects depicting recognisable images (animal and symbolic) in Europe, Africa, the Levant, and Indonesia (25,000 to 17,000 years ago)[422]

- evidence of nomadic shepherds (also referred to as pastoral nomads) found in what is now Lebanon and the Levant (believed to be from around 20,000 years ago)

- most researchers accept that North America was first settled by humans from Siberia through Asia and across the Bering Land Bridge (around 15,000 to 23,000 years ago)[423]

- pottery vessels discovered in Jiangxi, China (from around 18,000 years ago).[424]

From foragers and hunter-gatherers to farmers and pastoralists

Renowned Jewish author and journalist Arthur Koestler, in his exploration of how the human species' view of the universe has changed over time, has described the progress of science in the following way:

The progress of science is generally regarded as a kind of clean rational advance along a straight ascending line; in fact, it has followed a zigzag course, at times almost more bewildering than the evolution of political thought. … The manner in which some of the most important

---

[419] Coss (2017), pp. 27-31.

[420] Loy et al (1992).

[421] Soffer et al. (2000).

[422] SOURCE: https://www.nature.com/articles/s41562-020-0837-6.epdf?referrer_access_token=TBdrsd iZo37JcLUs1ROHUNRgN0jAjWel9jnR3ZoTv0PUtXsoSBnl3DLgWkdT-2CNbtbWQPfTHXOvh pj7b1JQPBMv6vmLspy1MsKrP1HVf_wyJLKj09MIUaKTEwGZIjKiHMjVbcQh2XqL8hKTpGK-dHlPVuS35vUHz3au8N5ZjCusftwTbMaWBvdg4ZJKSWWzMYcCV-5oYyHMLJ7m2cnCgjtxG r2j91XGFelBbfvej-YhTih6DYi6VGX6q35m6FRaPkdku0F0KJGmBK_4VbyIhEj4cjWtmYSrQH-v3kv2ZWQu7XuOeeFuYDLaozwur27Ry&tracking_referrer=www.abc.net.au.

[423] Bennett et al (2021).

[424] Except where otherwise cited, this information is compiled from a wide range of scientific sources – see Bibliography.

individual discoveries were arrived at reminds one more of a sleepwalker's performance than an electronic brain.[425]

Koestler could well have been referring to the transition from wandering foragers and hunter-gatherers to sedentary farmers and pastoralists. This transition did not occur in a logical, linear fashion and did not occur uniformly or universally over time in different geographic regions. The alignment of the tectonic plates, geomorphology, the retreating ice age, and availability of edible plants and animals in specific locations created favourable environments for different groups of the human species to develop new ways of living, surviving, cooperating, and organising.

Charles Darwin and Herbert Spencer's notion of 'survival of the fittest' did not mean that the strongest will survive, as some may think. Survival of the fittest means that the species or community that is best matched or prepared for the opportunities that emerge around them is most likely to survive.[426] This concept is best confirmed in Darwin and Spencer's parallel notion of 'natural selection'—where species with characteristics more suited to their environment have the strongest chance of survival. For specific human species families, tribes, clans, and communities in certain locations, survival and adaptation were about congruence, preparedness, and compatibility with the environmental circumstances emerging around them. Being in the right place at the right time to take advantage of a confluence of often accidental, serendipitous, or fortuitous circumstances.

There are multiple theories about how, why, and when the human species in various locations across the Middle East were the first to transition from predominantly nomadic hunter-gatherer/foraging families in primarily kin-related groups to more diverse settled/sedentary farming, pastoral and more complex communities. This happened in a piecemeal, discordant, geographically distributed, and non-linear fashion over many thousands of years.

Clarke et al. believe that significant, rapid climate change and its impact on different regions across the eastern Mediterranean contributed to the differential transition to complex social, agricultural, and sedentary urban settlements. They present evidence that the trend to urbanism was 'out of sync' across the Middle East region:

Trajectories towards social complexity were not synchronous across the region. Mesopotamia, for example, emerged at the end of the 4th millennium BC as a fully urbanised complex social

---

[425] Koestler (1959), p. 11.

[426] SOURCE: https://www.britannica.com/science/survival-of-the-fittest retrieved on 20 July 2021.

system, and so did Egypt, but urbanism in Anatolia and the southern Levant emerged at the end of the 3rd millennium BC.[427]

Maeda et al., have studied the archaeobotanical evidence from the Fertile Crescent from around 12000 BCE onwards. They have concluded that the transition to cereal domestication across the Eastern Mediterranean, including the island of Cyprus, followed diverse cultural trajectories and does not appear to be related to a specific climatic event. They claim that:

The transformations of domestication can best be appreciated as a co-evolutionary entanglement between plant adaptations, human socioeconomic systems, and technology.[428]

There are clearly many diverse theories as to why and how the transition from nomadic hunter-gatherers to settled farmers occurred. They are not mutually exclusive. The transition from foragers to farmers coalesced over time in different combinations of numerous factors in several Middle Eastern locations (the Fertile Crescent, Mesopotamia, the Levant, and the Island of Cyprus). They included:

- the Middle East and the Levant being in a geographically advantageous position historically (the prehistoric pathway out of Africa)
- the Middle East and the Levant having a distinct geomorphological advantage with the Tigris and Euphrates Rivers and their fertile plains–self-contained on all sides by the Mediterranean Sea (to the west), Zagros mountains (to the north and north-east), Black Sea, Caucasus Mountain, and the Caspian Sea (to the north), and the Arabian Desert, Persian Gulf, and Arabian Sea to the south
- climate change—a warming of the planet creating longer dry seasons favourable to annual edible crops like endemic wild cereals and an associated increase in yield from cultivated crops in some locations
- domestication (plants and animals) and agricultural practices developing in response to shortages of food and resources[429]
- availability of geographically co-located native edible crops and herdable (as opposed to huntable) animals
- the gradual development of new composite tools, technologies, and techniques

---

427 Clarke et al. (2016), p. 98.
428 Maeda et al. (2016), pp. 226-228.
429 Rindos et al. (1980), p. 752.

- human biological, cognitive, and cultural evolution that created the ability for humans to differentiate themselves from nature—no longer 'dominated by nature' but learning the 'mastery of nature'
- a related restructuring of human mentality and the emergence of symbol-making through art, communication, writing, culture, mythology, and ritual
- population increases, specialisation, demographic, and economic changes creating a need for more complex, and stable social, residential, and structural systems
- an increase in life expectancy, increasing health generally, and an increasing number of females, higher sex ratio (female to male), and associated increasing numbers of children[430]
- sustained cultural, and demographic demands on a relatively delicate landscape
- a trend away from exclusively family/kin-based households to a more widespread pooling, sharing of food, and an acceptance of responsibilities by a broader group.
- emergence of new organisational structures—from families to kinship groups to tribes to culturally aligned or ideologically similar communities
- a major change in the treatment of bodies of the dead and in attitude to nature, life, death, and ancestors—reflected in the emergence of intentional and symbolic burial practices in fixed collective locations
- a transition away from cave art towards pottery, figurines, and abstract sculptural forms
- the development of built ceremonial communal ritual structures
- a shared desire for prosperity and a new way of life.

These changes did not happen in a predictable nor in a similar fashion or pattern across all Middle East locations. They did not happen quickly. Smithsonian Institution archaeologist Melinda Zeder believes that the shaping of these disparate elements from hunter-gathering to an agricultural economy occurred over many thousands of years. She presents evidence that humans were modifying, manipulating, and exploiting plant resources and actively tilling and tending wild stands of selected endemic plants for several thousand years prior to the Neolithic Era, and the emergence of sedentary agriculture. She states:

---

[430] Eshed and Gopher (2018), pp. 103-106.

> *It is impossible to identify any threshold moments when wild became domestic or hunting and gathering became agriculture. … Drawing such distinctions actually impedes rather than improves our understanding of this process.*[431]

The piecemeal and gradual emergence of sedentary farming, crop domestication, animal husbandry, and gradual urbanisation over many thousands of years across a variety of locations in the Middle East included long periods wherein:

- some hunter-gatherers occupied fairly permanent seasonal camps—nomadic/mobile/migratory pastoralists[432]
- hunter-gatherer/foragers interacted with and exchanged food, tools, and resources with nearby emerging farming villages and pastoral camps[433]
- The Natufian 'agrotechnical revolution' (around 11000 BCE) when wild crops began to be harvested by hunter-gatherers and foragers using new tools (sickles, pestles, pounding and grinding stones)
- a 'domestication revolution' (from around 8500 BCE) involving more systematic cultivation and domestication of wild plants and animals
- the expansion into more widespread agriculture and farming communities across the Middle East (from around 7000 BCE).[434]

The emergence of farming and pastoralism occurred initially in the Middle East, but not with the birth of Cain (a farmer) and Abel (a shepherd) in 5000 BCE. It occurred circumstantially and opportunistically in a great, clumsy stumble forward across millennia (from at least 12000 BCE) and in multiple sites over thousands of years before the biblical dates of creation and the Hebrew scribes' chosen mythological date for the birth of Cain and Abel.

Beginnings of plant domestication

Our ancestors in East Africa are known to have collected and eaten wild grains for at least the last one hundred thousand years.[435] There is evidence of a Levantine sedentary hunter-gatherer camp from around 20000 BCE. It appears these inhabitants were involved in

---

[431]   Zeder (2011), pp. S222-S226.
[432]   Rollefson and Rollefson (1993), pp. 39-40.
[433]   Spielmann and Eder (1994), p. 308.
[434]   Kislev (1984), pp. 61-64.
[435]   Mercader (2009).

small-scale cultivation. The prehistoric inhabitants lived in uncovered bowl-like brush huts and harvested more than 140 plants, and there is evidence of food preparation by grinding wild wheat, barley, and oats. This is an Israeli archaeological site on the southwest shores of the Sea of Galilee referred to as Ohalo II.[436]

Archaeobotanical researchers have identified eight plant species whose wild ancestors were instrumental in the progression from forager to farmer and to crop domestication in the Levant, Anatolia, and the Fertile Crescent. These are referred to as 'founder crops' and include:

- flax (or linseed)
- emmer wheat
- einkorn wheat
- barley
- lentil
- pea
- chickpea
- bitter vetch.[437]

There are extensive archaeological excavations that highlight the emergence of early small village settlements occupied intermittently and combining nomadic pastoral and settled agricultural lifestyles throughout contemporary Israel (dated from around 10000 BCE). There is evidence of figs being the first cultivated fruit found in excavations in the Jordan River Valley from around 11,400 years ago. This was some 1,000 years before such staples as wheat, barley, and chickpeas were widely domesticated.[438] These developments were occurring five thousand years and two hundred generations or more before the HB/OT claims their God created the universe.[439]

The first archaeological evidence of widespread cultivation and domestication of animals in the Middle East has been dated to around 9500 BCE confirming this, and it is most likely that these practices began well before that date.[440]

It was a major climatic change around 10000 BCE that enabled crop domestication to spread in Anatolia, the Levant, and the Fertile Crescent. The first domesticated crops

---

[436]   Snir et al (2015).

[437]   SOURCE: https://www.worldatlas.com/articles/the-8-crops-to-be-first-domesticated-by-humans-the-neolithic-founder-crops.html retrieved on 2 March 2022.

[438]   https://www.nytimes.com/2006/06/02/science/02fig.html retrieved on 25 June 2022.

[439]   Verhoeven (2011), p. 79

[440]   https://www.britannica.com/event/Neolithic retrieved on 27 July 2021.

to emerge in these locations, at that time, included the eight 'founder crops' plus rye, figs, and olives.[441]

The Neolithic—The New Stone Age from 10000 BCE to 4000 BCE

The Neolithic Age is recognised for the emergence of the first permanent sedentary human settlements, advances in tools, and the beginnings of agriculture through the blending of domestic and wild resources into collectively managed small village-based subsistence economies. It is regarded as the time in the Middle East when hunter-gatherer communities, which were largely 'dominated by and opportunistic with nature' transitioned to agriculture and towards the 'mastery of nature'.[442] In economic terms, it is when the human species moved from gathering food (without surplus) to the organised production of food and animal husbandry (delivering a surplus for storage, and systems of production, trade, distribution, and management).[443]

The Neolithic Age was facilitated, in part, by a major climatic change. Around twelve thousand years ago, the last major ice age (which lasted from 2,580,000 to 11,700 years ago) ended.[444] The retreating ice created an advantageous climatic change in which locations across the globe experienced much longer dry seasons. What is called the Neolithic Age/Neolithic Era commenced around this time (10000 BCE) in Northern Levant (contemporary Türkiye) and lasted until around 3000 BCE.

The Neolithic Age is recognised as the last phase of the Stone Age (Greek—*neo*='new' or 'late'; *lithos*='stone'). The Neolithic cultures that have been found in the Middle East have been categorised by archaeologists into three time-based periods:

- Neolithic 1, also called Pre-Pottery Neolithic A—PPNA (beginning around 10000 BCE)
- Neolithic 2/Pre-Pottery Neolithic B—PPNB (beginning around 8800 BCE)
- Neolithic 3/Ceramic or Pottery Neolithic C—PNC (beginning around 6500 BCE).

Pre-Pottery Neolithic (PPN) represents the early Neolithic in the Levantine and upper Mesopotamian region of the Fertile Crescent, dating from around 12,000 to 8,500 years

---

[441]   Zeder (2011).
[442]   Verhoeven (2011), p. 75.
[443]   Svizzero (2014) p. 25.
[444]   SOURCE: https://www.britannica.com/science/ice-age-geology retrieved on 12 July 2021.

ago (10,000-6,500 BCE). There are multiple archaeological sites of varying sizes from this era that have been discovered in many locations in the Levant:

> *There are small (less than 0.1 hectare) temporary sites with a few huts/structures, and perma-*
> *nent, 'mega-sites' covering 10-15 hectares, usually intensively built with stone and mudbricks,*
> *creating entirely new anthropogenic landscapes.*[445]

The Neolithic Age delivered seasonal conditions to the Middle East that favoured annual plants like wild cereals.[446] In the words of Patrick McGovern et al.:

> *Following the last Ice Age, the Neolithic period in the Near East (around 10000 BCE—4500*
> *BCE) was a hotbed of experimentation, especially in the mountainous region extending west*
> *to east from the Taurus Mountains of south-eastern Anatolia through the South Caucasus and*
> *northern Mesopotamia to the Zagros Mountains of north-western Iran. … As the climate*
> *moderated and precipitation levels increased, especially between around 6200 BCE—4200*
> *BCE, humans established year-around settlements.*[447]

One of the oldest cultures to have been identified in the Levant is the Kebaran (around 15000 BCE to 12000 BCE), which was a highly mobile nomadic population in the Levant and Sinai areas composed of hunters and gatherers who used microlithic tools.[448]

The Kebaran were followed by the proto-agrarian Natufian culture, which was in the Levant from around 13000 BCE to 7500 BCE. The Natufian culture was unusual in that it supported a sedentary or semi-sedentary population even before the introduction of agriculture.

The Natufians — 10,000 years before the Israelites

The current site of Jericho in southern Palestine has provided an abundance of information about the Natufians who are regarded as one of the early hunter-gatherer cultures to establish semi-permanent settlements in the Southern Levant. The Natufians (from around 10000 BCE) had found a perennial spring in the site of Jericho and established

---

[445]   Eshed and Gopher (2018), p. 94.

[446]   SOURCE: https://www.nationalgeographic.org/article/development-agriculture/ retrieved on 12 July 2021.

[447]   McGovern et al (2017), p. E10309.

[448]   SOURCE: https://en.wikipedia.org/wiki/Kebaran.

a type of sanctuary with temporary timber shelters. The Natufians were a late Epipaleolithic archaeological culture (late Ice Age Levant culture). It is estimated that it took the Natufians at least a thousand years to shift Jericho from being a semi-permanent seasonal site to being a village of around ten acres with a surrounding wall, a tower of some thirty feet in diameter and height, and a population of around two thousand residents.[449]

The Natufians were named after a site found just north of Jerusalem. There are multiple Natufian archaeological sites throughout Israel and the Levant, several dating back to around 12000 BCE (Figure 22). The Natufians are regarded as having established themselves in the Levant as a sedentary, food-producing and crop-domesticating economy by around 7000 BCE.[450] It is possible that the Semitic language originated with the Natufians in the Levant.

The Natufians are regarded as one of, if not the originators of the transition from foraging to farming. They are regarded as the inventors of sickles, threshing floors, conical mortars, and milling utensils—all of which are essential for exploiting wild cereals.[451] The archaeobotanical evidence of their pre-agricultural plant-based subsistence lifestyles includes evidence that across a period of several hundred years, they exploited a very broad spectrum of plants to meet their required subsistence levels.[452]

Natufians harvested the wild ancestors of the eight founder crops and a wide range of 'non-founder' plants.[453] The Natufians also hunted wild gazelle. There is substantial evidence of a related bone industry involved in the making of decorative beads from gazelle bones.[454] Evidence of a Natufian burial ground has been found in the Hilazon Tachtit Cave on the northern bank of the Hilazon stream in western Galilee in Israel.[455]

Over several thousand years, the Natufian site of Jericho consolidated into a permanent settlement with well-built circular or oval mud brick houses and massive defensive walls where the Natufians largely survived on systematic gathering of wild barley and

---

[449]   Feuerstein et al (2001), p. 144.
[450]   Redford (1992), p. 6.
[451]   Eitam et al (2015).
[452]   Arranz-Otaegui et al (2018), p. 267.
[453]   Arranz-Otaegui et al (2018), pp. 279-280.
[454]   Torres et al (2020).
[455]   SOURCE: https://archaeology.huji.ac.il/hilazon-tachtit-cave retrieved on 9 March 2023.

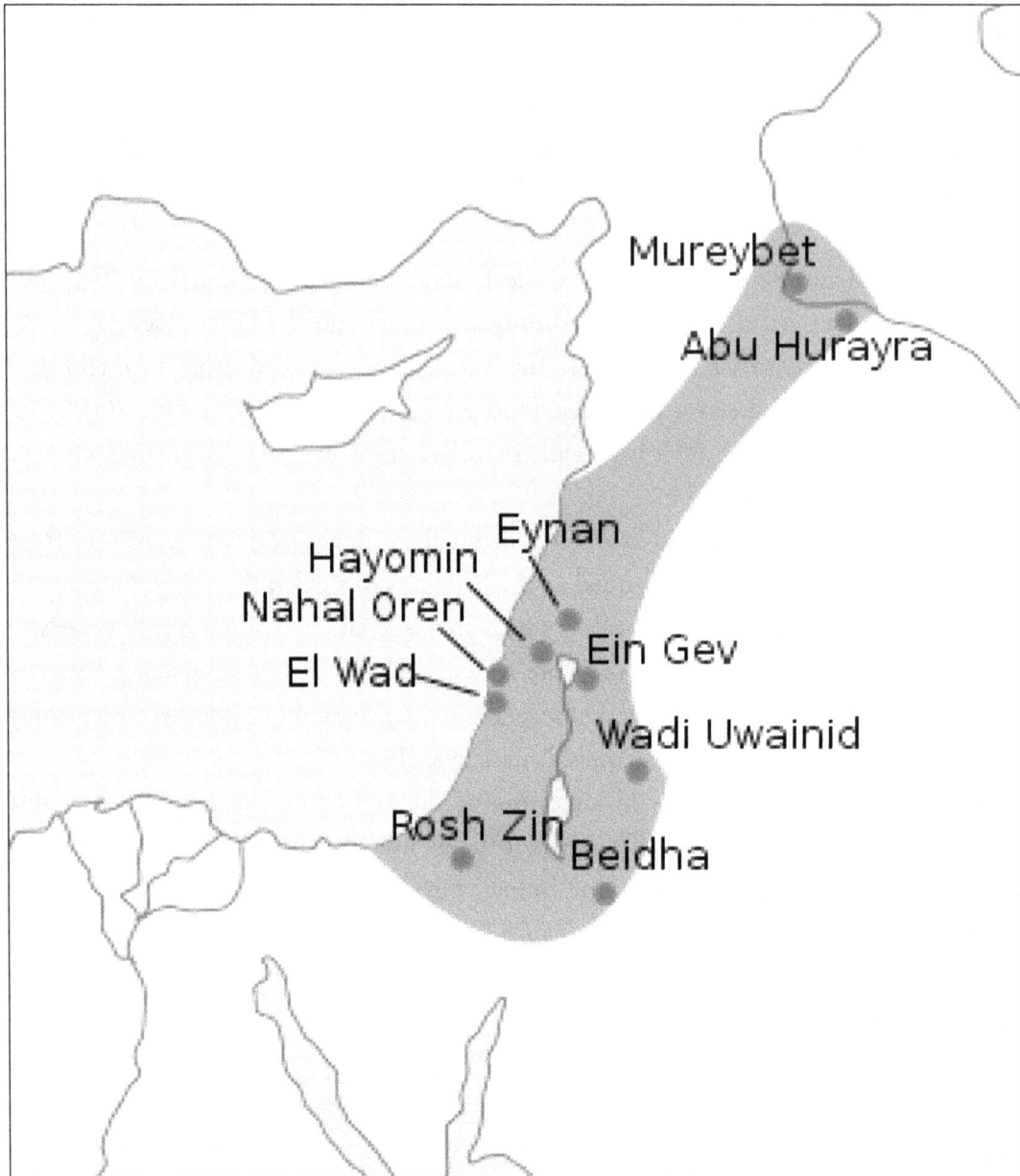

Figure 22: *Locations in Southern Levant/Israel where evidence of the Natufian culture (from 12000 BCE) has been found[a]*

---

[a]   SOURCE: By Crates—Image:NatufianSpread.png, CC BY 3.0, https://commons.wikimedia. org/w/index.php?curid=3540914 retrieved on 14 July 2021.

wild emmer wheat and hunting gazelle.[456] This site of Jericho competes with Catalhoyuk (Türkiye),[457] Uruk (Iraq),[458] and Damascus (Syria)[459] for the mantle of being the first or the longest continuously inhabited urban area/city on Earth.

Summary of key developments from 12,000 years ago to around 6,000 years ago

In the Middle East region

- The commencement of agricultural practices (systematic husbandry of plants and animals including dogs, goats, sheep, and cattle) independently emerging in several different locations where the tectonic plates had created certain geomorphological and geological advantages—including the Middle East, southeast Asia, parts of Africa, Mesoamerica, and the Andes (around 10,000 to 12,000 years ago)
- the continued consolidation of agricultural practices with the domestication of fig trees in the Middle East/Jordan Valley (around 11,000 to 13,000 years ago)
- the cultivation of cereal crops such as wheat (einkorn and emmer wheat), barley, flax, and legumes (lentils, peas, bitter vetch, and chickpeas) for the first time in southern Türkiye and Mesopotamia (around 11,000 to 13,000 years ago)
- agriculture/harvesting of crops and selective breeding of cereal grasses becomes more widespread across the Eurasian Steppe, Central Asia, and the Middle East (around 11,000 years ago)
- the discovery in the Troodos Mountains in Cyprus of a fabulously rich source of copper—the first metal smelted by humans for crafting tools and weapons and the production of the first copper ornaments (around 10,000 to 12,000 years ago)
- lapis lazuli, the deep-blue metamorphic rock ('the wisdom stone') that was highly prized across antiquity as a semi-precious stone with healing powers, is mined for the first time in the Hindu Kush mountains of Northern Afghanistan (around 9,000 years ago).
- a domesticated crop-based economy develops but then fades/is abandoned in Egypt (around 9,000 years ago)

---

[456] Tubb (1998), pp. 26-28.
[457] Shane and Kucuk (1998).
[458] Lawler (2013).
[459] https://whc.unesco.org/en/list/20/ retrieved on 8 September 2021.

- permanent farming becomes more common in Upper Egypt, including the domestication of crops and animals (around 8,500 years ago)
- the first farming sub-cultures emerge in Central Asia, west of the Indus Valley on the Kacchi Plain of Balochistan in Pakistan, where they domesticate wheat and a variety of animals, including cattle (around 8,500 years ago)
- the invention of the pottery wheel and pottery kilns in Mesopotamia (around 8,000 years ago)
- around 8,000 years ago, obsidian (volcanic glass) was being traded between Anatolia and sites in southwest Iran and the Eastern Mediterranean[460]
- wine-making and viticulture commences in the southern Caucuses where grape vines grew wildly (around 8,000 years ago)[461]
- the Copper Age begins, particularly with the widespread use of copper across the Ancient Middle East primarily with the emergence of metallurgy in the Fertile Crescent (around 7,500 years ago)[462]
- the Indus Valley becomes a thriving agricultural community, with trade networks linking this culture with related regional cultures (including trade with Sumer in Southern Mesopotamia) and distant sources of raw materials, including lapis lazuli and other materials for bead-making. Indus Valley villagers had, by this time, domesticated numerous crops, including peas, sesame seeds, dates, and cotton, as well as a wide range of domestic animals, including the water buffalo (around 7,500 to 6,000 years ago)
- around 7,000 years ago, the spectacular blue stone lapis lazuli obtained from northern Afghanistan was being traded as far west as Egypt[463]
- according to the Septuagint/Greek version of the HB/OT, the biblical God created the universe and the first humans, Adam and Eve, around 5500 BCE to 5000 BCE (approximately 7,000 years ago)
- Phoenician merchants make the first glass (around 7,000 years ago)
- the invention in several locations (from Central Europe, Southern Russia, the Eurasian Steppes to Mesopotamia) of the wheel and the wagon and the use of

---

460   Collins (2008), p. 9.
461   McGovern et al. (2017).
462   SOURCE: https://en.wikipedia.org/wiki/Chalcolithic.
463   Collins (2008), p. 9.

animals for pulling—oxen are harnessed and put to work in an almost simultaneous innovation in the Middle East and in Europe (around 6,000 years ago)

- according to the Hebrew (Masoretic) Bible, the biblical God created the Universe and the first humans in 3761 BCE (around 6,000 years ago).

Elsewhere around the globe

- Tribes in the Western and Southern Highlands of Papua New Guinea begin to cultivate taro and yam (around 13,000 years ago)[464]
- rice domestication and paddy field cultivation begin in the Yangtze River basin in China (around 8,000 and 13,000 years ago)
- pottery artefacts found from the Jomon period in Japan (from around 10,500 years ago)[465]
- Mesoamerican communities (currently central Mexico through Belize, Guatemala, El Salvador, Honduras, Nicaragua, and northern Costa Rica) begin to domesticate crops including maize (corn), beans, and squash (around 10,000 years ago)
- tribes in the Western and Southern Highlands of Papua New Guinea begin to cultivate bananas and sugarcane (around 8,000 to 9,000 years ago)
- China's Yellow River basin becomes an emerging agricultural centre with the active cultivation of foxtail millet, broomcorn millet and soybeans (around 8,000 years ago).

Ancient farming calendar in the Israeli-Levant

- One of the oldest examples of early writing from the area of Israel is the Gezer Calendar, which has been dated to the tenth century BCE. Scholars disagree on whether the language is early Hebrew or Phoenician.[466] However, it does detail the month-by-month tasks of early Levantine farmers—when to plant, when to hoe, when to harvest, and when to cultivate.[467]

---

[464] SOURCE: https://en.wikipedia.org/wiki/Agriculture_in_Papua_New_Guinea.
[465] SOURCE: https://www.ancient.eu/Jomon_Period/.
[466] SOURCE: https://www.historyofinformation.com/detail.php?id=1280 retrieved on 9 March 2023..
[467] SOURCE: https://womeninthebible.net/bible-archaeology/farming-agriculture/ retrieved on 9 March 2023.

The major achievement of the Copper/Chalcolithic Age

The discovery of copper, the locations of major sources and its flexibility in use is really the 'eureka moment' that launched major cultural, behavioural, technological, and trading innovations and political alliances in emerging cultures in and around the Levant and the Middle East. Major trade routes began to consolidate in, around, and through the Levant as pottery, copper, lapis lazuli, and cultural artefacts were traded across large distances by land and by sea.

Southern Levant in the Copper/Chalcolithic Age

There is substantial evidence that, two thousand years prior to the emergence of the Isra-elites, the Southern Levant experienced a wide range of innovations during the Copper Age (4500 BCE to 3000 BCE). This included:

> *… intensification of agricultural production, increasing social stratification, complex networks for trade in exotic items, unequal accumulation of wealth, and technological sophistication.*[468]

Larger regional centres containing coordinated social, religious, and economic activities began to emerge, as did new specialisations in the fields of ivory, pottery, and copper met-alwork. There was a mix of sedentary farming coexisting with base and seasonal campsites for nomadic shepherds.[469]

This rapid spread of innovations brought with it a range of mythological stories. Many of these stories would eventually and collectively build the foundations for the Hebrew scribes to develop their own canon and, over many hundreds of years, incorpo-rate this into the HB/OT.

The Bronze Age Ancient Middle East

The Bronze Age Middle East is probably most recognised for the pastoral, agricultural, and technological innovations that were developed originally in Anatolia and significantly enhanced by the Sumerians. These new sedentary pastoral and agricultural practices were gradually adopted across the Middle East, the Caucuses, and the Eurasian Steppe cultures.

---

[468] Clarke et al. (2016), p. 98; Rowan and Ilan (2012), p. 88.
[469] Le Dosseur (2003).

The innovations which emerged embryonically from around 13,000 years ago (approximately 11000 BCE) included the gradual transformation of wild plants and animals into domestic ones.

Depending on specific cultures and specific animals, these transformations paralleled and facilitated the Bronze Age generally to move gradually from largely nomadic hunter-gatherers to sedentary agricultural and pastoral communities and eventually to kingly theocratic states—what some researchers refer to as the transition from hunter-gatherers to foragers/food gatherers to fishers to farmers/cultivators/food producers to chiefdoms and eventually to kingdoms.[470] This transition from foraging hunter-gatherers living by hunting, collecting, scavenging, and forest gardening to pastoralism, agriculture, and a semblance of civilisation happened gradually in several locations depending in part on the endemic wild animal and plant species available in each region.

As outlined earlier, the transition to sedentarism and agriculture did not happen linearly or uniformly. For thousands of years, hunter-gatherers had developed a range of interrelated lifestyles (hunter-gathering, foraging, fishing, nomadic, sedentary, neo-domestication, pastoral, cultivating, neo-agriculture) based on climatic and subsistence pressures. Anthropologist and political scientist James C Scott sees early human species as opportunistic generalists who were agile, adaptable, and astute, depending on the immediate resource environment with multiple subsistence options available to them. The move from hunter-gatherer to sedentary agricultural and pastoral practices was non-linear, multi-dimensional, seasonally complex, and geographically dependent.[471] In Scott's own words:

> *Finally, the conventional 'subspecies' of subsistence modes—hunting, foraging, pastoralism and farming—make so little historical sense. The same people have practiced all four, sometimes in a single lifetime; the activities can and have been combined over thousands of years, and each of them bleeds imperceptibly into the next long vast continuum of human re-arrangements of the natural world.[472]*

---

[470] For example: Anthony (2007), p. 138; Bharucha and Pretty, 2010; Rowley-Conway 2014; Glassman, 2017.

[471] Scott (2017), pp. 59-63.

[472] Scott (2017), p. 71.

Growth of pastoralism and domestication of animals

The major changes that built the foundation for pastoralism and the growth and strengthening of sedentary settlements began around 10,000 to 12,000 years ago (around 10000 BCE to 9000 BCE). A key factor was the domestication of sheep in Mesopotamia (where eastern Anatolia meets western Iran)—adapted from the wild mouflon of Europe and East Asia.[473] The early domestication of sheep was most likely because of three main advantages that sheep had (apart from their availability):

- the diversity of products produced (wool, meat, and milk)
- the biological adaptability (capable of adapting to extremes of heat, and cold, and to fibrous diets and exhibiting large variation in disease resistance) to move to new environments with nomadic herders
- behavioural characteristics that facilitate ease of husbandry and management (highly selective herbivores, gregarious, follower behaviours, precocial young, promiscuous mating patterns with a dominant male, and a body size and low agility that facilitate ease of husbandry).[474]

The domestication of sheep began a cycle of growth and diversification of pastoralism in and around the Middle East typified by:

- the domestication of dogs commenced in the Fertile Crescent (from at least 13000 BCE)[475]
- the domestication of sheep in the Middle East and South West Asia from around 10000 BCE to 9000 BCE[476]
- the domestication of goats in Türkiye, the Euphrates River valley and the Zagros Mountains adapted from the wild bezoar ibex around 9000 BCE[477]
- domestication of cattle in the Eurasian Steppe, Central Asia, and the Middle East (around 8500 BCE)—this was, most likely initially as sacred or symbolically important ceremonial animal (based on the many archaeological discoveries containing cattle/bull skull bucrania, horn cores, and scapulae deliberately incorporated into platforms and walls, and decorative horns)[478]

---

[473] Anthony (2007), p. 60.
[474] SOURCE: https://www.sciencedirect.com/topics/agricultural-and-biological-sciences/mouflon.
[475] SOURCE: https://www.thoughtco.com/how-and-why-dogs-were-domesticated-170656.
[476] Chessa et al (2009).
[477] SOURCE: https://www.thoughtco.com/the-domestication-history-of-goats-170661.
[478] SOURCE: https://link.springer.com/article/10.1007/s10963-011-9045-7.

- the domestication of pigs in the Middle East (around 7000 BCE). Originally a product of the Eurasian/European wild boar, which had most likely been managed in the wild from around 9000 BCE[479]
- the domestication of oxen across the Middle East and Europe (between 7000 BCE and 4000 BCE)[480]
- the domestication of horses occurred in the Ponto-Caspian/Ukraine steppe region (today Russia, Kazakhstan, Ukraine, and Romania), which was the home of nomadic societies whose economy was based on herding, complemented by hunting and, to a much lesser degree, sporadic, itinerant agriculture sometime before 3500 BCE. Within all domestic animals, no other species has had such a significant impact on the warfare, transportation, and communication capabilities of human societies as the horse[481]
- the domestication of camels occurred in Somalia, Southern Arabia, and east of the Zagros Mountains (around 3500 BCE to 3000 BCE)
- the domesticated donkey is believed to be the descendent of the wild ass, *Equss africanus*, from the Nile regions of Somalia and Nubia. The first captivity and harnessing of the wild ass was in Egypt and western Asia dating back to around 2800 BCE to 2500 BCE.[482]

Growth of agriculture, cropping and farming

The Ancient Middle East, the Fertile Crescent, and the Sumerians, in particular, are regarded as the originators of agriculture and pastoralism. The early foundations of this emerged with hunter-gatherers in the Stone Age. Sedentary agriculture was significantly developed and enhanced during the Bronze Age, particularly in the Fertile Crescent.

The definition of the Fertile Crescent varies, but in the current analysis, it is defined as the area that spans from the Taurus Mountains (Southern Türkiye) to the Zagros Mountains (the 16,000-kilometre mountain range spanning from South-East Türkiye through Iraq and Iran) and includes the Levant. This is where agriculture and pastoralism began to emerge well before 4000 BCE. This occurred in part because of possible climatic and geomorphological reasons. At the time, the climate in these locations was more temperate than today, and the

---

[479] Giuffra et al. (2000).
[480] SOURCE: https://animals.howstuffworks.com/animal-facts/animal-domestication5.htm.
[481] SOURCE: https://www.sciencedaily.com/releases/2009/04/090423142541.htm.
[482] SOURCE: http://bioweb.uwlax.edu/bio203/s2009/wells_kels/Life%20History.htm.

Fertile Crescent had two great rivers (the Euphrates and the Tigris) higher than the surrounding fertile plains as well as hills and the mountains to the north. This fortunate geomorphological fact facilitated the construction of levees and canals between the two rivers and allowed the water to run from one river to the other by way of the many agricultural fields.[483]

The main types of grain that were used for agriculture by the Sumerians were wheat, barley, millet (most likely imported originally along the steppe corridor from China by pastoral nomads to the north of Mesopotamia), and emmer.[484] Sumerian farmers grew dates, grapes, figs, melons, and apples. Their favourite vegetables included eggplants, onions, radishes, beans, lettuce, and sesame seeds. The Mesopotamians also raised sheep, goats, and cows.[485]

Archaeological evidence about the growth of agriculture in this and associated regions includes:

- wheat first being cultivated in the regions of the Fertile Crescent around 9600 BCE. An archaeological analysis of wild emmer indicates that it was first cultivated in the Southern Levant as far back as 9600 BCE
- the earliest archaeological evidence of wild barley comes from Mesopotamia and the Levant from around 8500 BCE. Its domestication occurred in the Middle East around 10,000 years ago (circa 8000 BCE)
- the edible fig is one of the first plants that was cultivated by humans, in around 9000 BCE in the Jordan Valley
- earliest evidence of humans using wild flax as a textile comes from the present-day Republic of Georgia, where spun, dyed, and knotted wild flax fibres have been found dating back to around 30,000 years ago. However, the first domestication of flax occurred in the Fertile Crescent around 7000 BCE.
- the edible olive can be traced to the Levant, based on written tablets, olive pits, and wood fragments found in ancient tombs dating back to around 4000 BCE.
- well-known legumes include alfalfa, clover, beans, peas, chickpeas, lentils, lupins, mesquite, carob, soybeans, peanuts, and tamarind. Evidence of legume (also called pulse) cultivation has been found in Mesopotamia, the Mediterranean, and the Indus Valley dating to around 3500 BCE, with evidence of harvesting of soybeans (a legume) found in China from around 11000 BCE.[486]

---

[483] SOURCE: http://www.giftednassau.com/uploads/1/0/1/4/101418208/mesopotania_irrigation.pdf.
[484] Cunliffe (2017), p. 67.
[485] SOURCE: http://www.palmbeach.k12.fl.us/eagleslandingms/MesopotamiaAgriculture.pdf.
[486] SOURCE: Hancock (2022).

Major achievements and milestones during the Bronze Age

Whereas the Stone Age lasted a significantly long time, the Bronze Age was comparatively short—with bronze being largely and eventually replaced by iron as the primary material in metalwork by around 700 BCE.[487]

However, the Bronze Age heralded the increasing rise and spread of many diverse civilisations and the expansion of trade and exchange networks around the Levant and the Fertile Crescent. This is the age that saw the emergence and consolidation of metalworking. Bronze is around 85% copper, combined with tin and/or arsenic or other metals. Initially, the main source of copper was from Cyprus (believed to be an ancient Greek word for copper) and tin came from a variety of locations. There is archaeological evidence of small-scale mining of oxidised tin/cassiterite in Southern Türkiye, Uzbekistan, Tajikistan, Afghanistan, and Siberia, which most likely provided the metal for the Bronze being used in the Middle East.[488]

Bronze was being used in an area of what is now Serbia around 4500 BCE. However, the strongest evidence of the common usage of bronze from around 3500 BCE comes from the Sumerians in the Tigris Euphrates Valley in Western Asia.[489]

The innovation that bronze brought to prehistoric communities included the ability to cast a wide range of objects from tools, to knives to ornaments to celebratory paraphernalia (e.g., bells) to weapons. The importance of tin to Middle East Bronze Age cultures and its comparative scarcity strengthened the development of trade routes and cultural interchanges.

The emergence of Bronze Age trade routes—a network of civilisations and influence

The Bronze Age had special significance when considering the many factors that influenced the creation of the HB/OT. In the first instance, there were many massive changes and exchanges philosophically, politically, diplomatically, historically, mythologically, and culturally in and around the Levant during and prior to the Bronze Age and the emergence of Israel.

---

[487] SOURCE: http://www.makin-metals.com/about/history-of-bronze-infographic/.
[488] SOURCE: https://en.wikipedia.org/wiki/Tin_sources_and_trade_in_ancient_times#CITEREFPenhallurick1986.
[489] SOURCE: http://www.makin-metals.com/about/history-of-bronze-infographic/.

In the words of Bill Arnold:

The Levant was the crossroads of ancient Near East; a land-bridge connecting three continents. Cultural influences flowed into the southern Levant from Egypt, Mesopotamia and Syria, and numerous people groups living in this land-bridge comprised a virtual melting pot of the ancient world. We have plenty of evidence to suggest that Israel reflected that cultural diversity comfortably.[490]

From 3000 BCE onwards, the Bronze Age had witnessed a vibrant growth of influential trade routes and exchanges from the north, south, east, and west of the Levant. It was the time when the Sumerians (from around 4000 BCE) followed by the Babylonians (around 2000 BCE) built the foundations for the Fertile Crescent largely in Mesopotamia. The many innovations introduced by the Sumerians, Babylonians, Akkadians, and the Mesopotamians are what saw this region become known as the 'cradle of civilisation'.

Before the emergence of the Israelites between 1500 BCE and 1200 BCE, the Middle East had become fully integrated into an international trade system that stretched from western Iran to the Aegean Sea and from Anatolia in the north-west to the kingdoms of Nubia in the central Nile valley. Across those three hundred years, there were four major kingdoms in control—the Kassite Babylonians, the Anatolian Hittites, the Egyptians and, in northern Mesopotamia and Syria firstly, the Mittani and then the Assyrians. In addition to these, there were several smaller but powerful kingdoms—to the east were the Elamites, to the west was the state of Mycenae, and within the Middle East, the states of Syria and Palestine—all working together in a common system.[491]

The Fertile Crescent and the Levant had built dynamic and extensive exchange and trade networks in all cardinal directions throughout the Bronze Age (in line with relationships illustrated in Figure 11, page 86, and Figure 13, page 91).[492]

By 6000 BCE, obsidian (volcanic glass) was being traded between Anatolia and sites in southwest Iran and the Eastern Mediterranean. A thousand years later, the spectacular blue stone lapis lazuli was being obtained from northern Afghanistan and passed along routes until pieces had travelled as far west as Egypt.[493]

As a result, the Late Bronze Age has been described as the 'age of internationalism'. There was a wide range of economic, cultural, political, and ideological exchanges

---

[490]   Arnold (2015), p. 2.
[491]   Van der Mieroop (2007), pp. 129-130.
[492]   See for instance: Michel (2008).
[493]   Collins (2008), p. 9.

occurring between Egypt, Mesopotamia, Anatolia, the Mycenean (Greek) world, Cyprus, and the Levant.[494]

Local trading had begun in Mesopotamia in the Ubaid Period (circa 5000 BCE to 4100 BCE). This had expanded into long-distance trade by the Uruk Period (circa 4100 BCE to 2900 BCE). Trading routes across the region had flourished by the time of the Early Dynastic Period (2900 BCE to 2334 BCE).[495]

By 3000 BCE, ancient sailors were using well-established sea routes to trade with cultures all around the Mediterranean Sea. The ancient Greeks, Egyptians, Syrians, and others participated in sophisticated trading networks. Archaeologist and historian Alexander Joffe has described how the Levant, under the influence of the controlling Egyptian empire, culture and religion was embedded in, and learning from these Mediterranean trade networks:

> *Mediterranean trade was widespread, and brought the Levant into contact with 'palatial societies' of Cyprus, Crete, Western Anatolia, and the Aegean, as well as those states in Syria and Mesopotamia.*[496]

It was the emergence of metallurgy and the use of metallic bronze and the popularity of lapis lazuli that was responsible for the emergence, development, and consolidation of many of the Mediterranean trade routes. Figure 23 illustrates the primary locations of the mines for major tradeable Bronze Age metals. These locations and their adjoining towns became key points along the land-based Bronze Age trade and product exchange routes.

Bronze and lapis lazuli were not the only motivators for the expansion of the trade routes from the Phoenicians, the Levant, and the Fertile Crescent. By around 2000 BCE, Mesopotamian and Levantine traders were regularly exchanging complex administrative practices, language, writing systems, economic, political, cultural and religious systems, and mythologies with each other and with neighbouring communities such as the Caucuses, the Greeks/Mycenae, Anatolia, Syria (to the north), the Indus Valley and the Iranian Plateau to the East, Egypt, the Arabian Peninsula (Oman and Bahrain), the Dilmun culture, the Indus Valley Melukhkhans, and the Harappans.[497]

Classical scholar Richard Miles describes the eighteenth-century BCE in the Middle East, Anatolia, and the eastern Mediterranean as 'increasingly resembling a joined up cos-

---

[494] Panitz-Cohen (2013), p. 549.
[495] Mark (2022C).
[496] Joffe (2002), p. 427.
[497] Massa and Palmisano (2018), pp. 65-87.

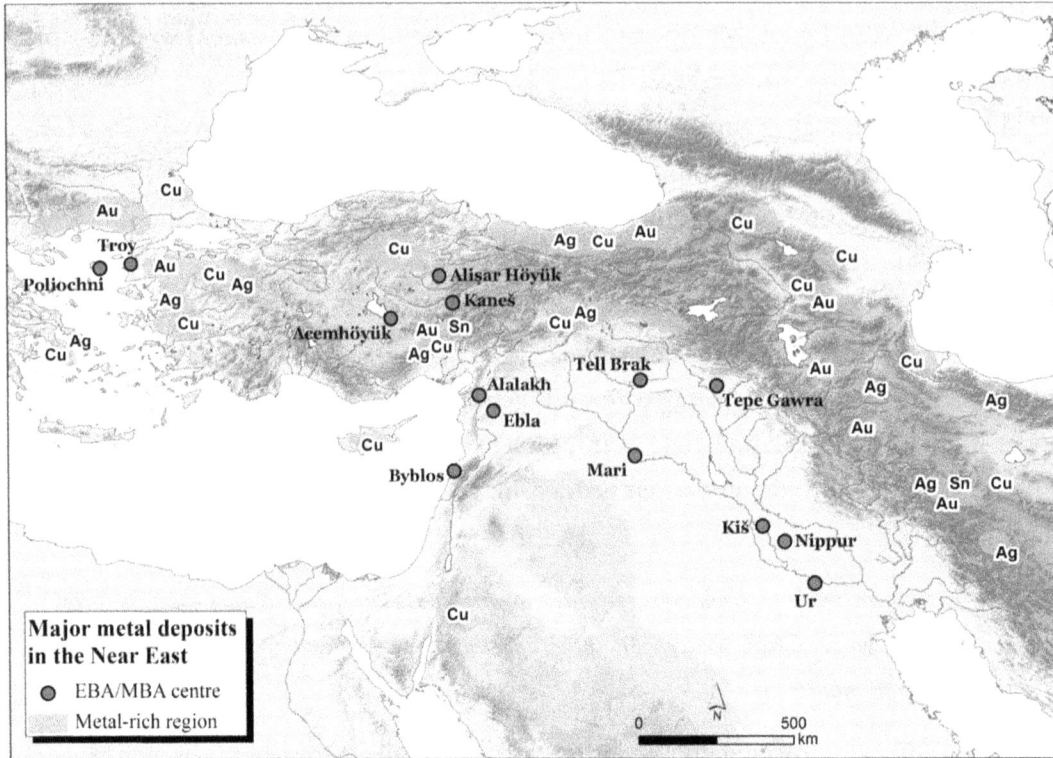

Figure 23: *Bronze Age locations of major sources of gold (Au), silver (Ag), copper (Cu) and tin (Sn)*[b]

NOTE: *EBA = early Bronze Age Centres; MBA= middle Bronze Age Centres*

---

[b] Adapted from Massa and Palmisano (2018), p. 81 and p. 83. Reprinted with permission from Dr. Michele Rüzgar Massa

mopolitan world'.[510] As an example, he cites evidence from excavations in the northern Syrian city of Mari containing:

> *… obsidian from Greece, amber from the Danube, lapis lazuli from Afghanistan, tin and silver from Cyprus, purple dye and timber from the Levant, pottery and linen from Egypt, weapons from Anatolia, onions from Palestine, honey and leather boots from Crete.*[498]

The trade route to the west was largely sea-based and stretched across the Mediterranean as far as Italy, Sicily, and Spain. The extent of these Bronze Age trade networks can be seen in the analysis of the Uluburun shipwreck, a Bronze Age vessel discovered lying off

---

[498] Miles (2011), p. 33.

the coast of Kas, Türkiye. The ship was probably originally from Phoenicia/Canaan and dates to between 1330 BCE and 1300 BCE. The Uluburun ship was carrying a full cargo of trade goods typical of the Bronze Age exchanges. It was probably from a port in the southern part of ancient Lycia (southwest Anatolia) and it was most likely on its way to the Greek mainland.[499]

The Uluburun ship's cargo included Cypriot copper ingots, tin from Afghanistan, Canaanite jars, a bronze and gold statue of a Canaanite deity, ebony logs from Nubia, glass beads, raw glass from Mesopotamia, a gold Egyptian scarab, resin, cobalt blue glass ingots, blackwood logs, ivory, hippopotamus teeth, tortoise shells, ostrich eggshells, Cypriot pottery, Cypriot oil lamps, finely glazed bronze and copper drinking cups, ivory cosmetics and ivory cosmetic boxes, a trumpet, amber beads from the Baltics, agate, carnelian, quartz, gold, a large collection of jewellery (medallions, pendants, rings), a wide range of weapons including swords and daggers from Italy and Greece (also arrowheads, spearhead, maces, axes), agricultural tools (sickles, awls, drill bits, tongs, chisels, adzes) and edible food (almond, pine nuts, figs, grapes, olives safflower, cumin, coriander, pomegranates, barley, wheat).

The sea networks to the west involved the sharing of cultural ideas and artefacts as well as trade. There is evidence of an Egyptian mummy that was wrapped in a papyrus containing the words of the Egyptian Book of the Dead. The mummy was purchased by a Croatian in Alexandria, Egypt in 1848 CE, and ended up in the Museum of Zagreb in Croatia. The mummy was wrapped in a linen funerary cloth that mystified archaeologists because it contained writing that was not Egyptian hieroglyphics. Ultimately, the words were found to be Etruscan from the third century BCE. The linen cloth wrapped around the mummy in Egypt is the longest-surviving linen Etruscan text in existence.[500]

The Etruscan culture that wrote the text emerged in what is now Central Italy, including most of Tuscany, northern Lazio, and northern and western Umbria in around 800 BCE. The Linen Book of Zagreb (also known by its Latin name, *Liber Linteus Zagrabiensis*) is further evidence of the extensive trade and cultural exchange networks across the Mediterranean at the time of the emergence of the HB/OT.

---

[499] SOURCE: https://www.ancient.eu/Uluburun_Shipwreck/.
[500] What was the mystery message written on the mummy's wrappings? (nationalgeographic.com) retrieved on 30 January 2023.

There was also a land-based trade network to the east of the Fertile Crescent involving mutual trade with the nearby Karun, Elam, and Indus Valley Harappan Civilisations. Archaeologists working in a broad arc from the Eurasian steppes through Iran and onto the Arabian Peninsula have found evidence that a complex network of cities thrived across the region at roughly the same time as the emergence of the Fertile Crescent, suggesting a dramatic new view of the emergence of dozens of civilisations and urban centres between Mesopotamia and the Indus Valley. These cities were trading commodities and, possibly, adopting each other's technologies, architecture, and ideas.[501]

Recent research has uncovered new evidence of Mesopotamians trading copper from Oman and possibly the Indus region. Omani pots have been found in Central Asia and seals from Mesopotamia and the Indus Valley region have been found in Turkmenistan. There is some evidence of carts drawn by bullocks and camels being used to facilitate trade as early as the middle of the third millennium BCE. From Mesopotamia east to the Indus Valley, archaeologists have found massive ceremonial platforms with many common characteristics.[502]

From around 2300 BCE, researchers are aware of a complementary sea-based trade route emerging up the Persian Gulf involving Mesopotamian trade with the Dilmun culture (Arabian Peninsula), the Melukhkhans, and Harappans (from the Indus Valley) (Figure 24). This sea-based trade route was apparently largely one-way, with evidence of ships from the Indus Valley docking in Mesopotamian ports but Mesopotamian ships only travelling as far as the bottom end of the Gulf.[503] Typical goods imported into Mesopotamia from the Arabian Peninsula and the Indus Valley along this trade route included a variety of objects made with shell species that are characteristic of the Indus Coast but also sesame oil, frankincense, myrrh, gold and gold dust, ebony, diorite, multicoloured birds of ivory, mes wood, aba wood, and carnelian beads.[504, 505, 506]

---

[501] Anthony (2007), p. 414.
[501] SOURCE: https://www.sciencedaily.com/releases/2007/08/070802182042.htm.
[503] SOURCE: https://www.harappa.com/answers/was-trade-relationship-between-harappans-and-mesopotamians-direct-one.
[504] SOURCE: https://en.wikipedia.org/wiki/Elam#Trade_with_the_Indus_Valley_civilization.
[505] Leemans (1960).
[506] Bottero (2001), p. 15.

In the words of David Abulafia:

The Levantine trade network (that had come into being by 1400 BCE) was buoyant enough to sustain wealthy cities in which Aegean merchant mixed with Canaanites, Cypriots, Hittites, Egyptians and other residents and visitors. The Levantine ports possessed even older links to the Nile Delta; the tomb of Kenamun (Mayor of Thebes at the time) contained a wall-painting which showed the unloading of goods at an Egyptian port, under the oversight of Canaanite merchants, and these included textiles, purple dye (a speciality of the Levantine coast, made from the murex shellfish), oil, wine, and cattle.[507]

Prior to the emergence of Israel, the Levant, the Fertile Crescent, the Middle East, Egypt, the Indus Valley, Anatolia, the Caucuses, the Eurasian Steppe, and large parts of

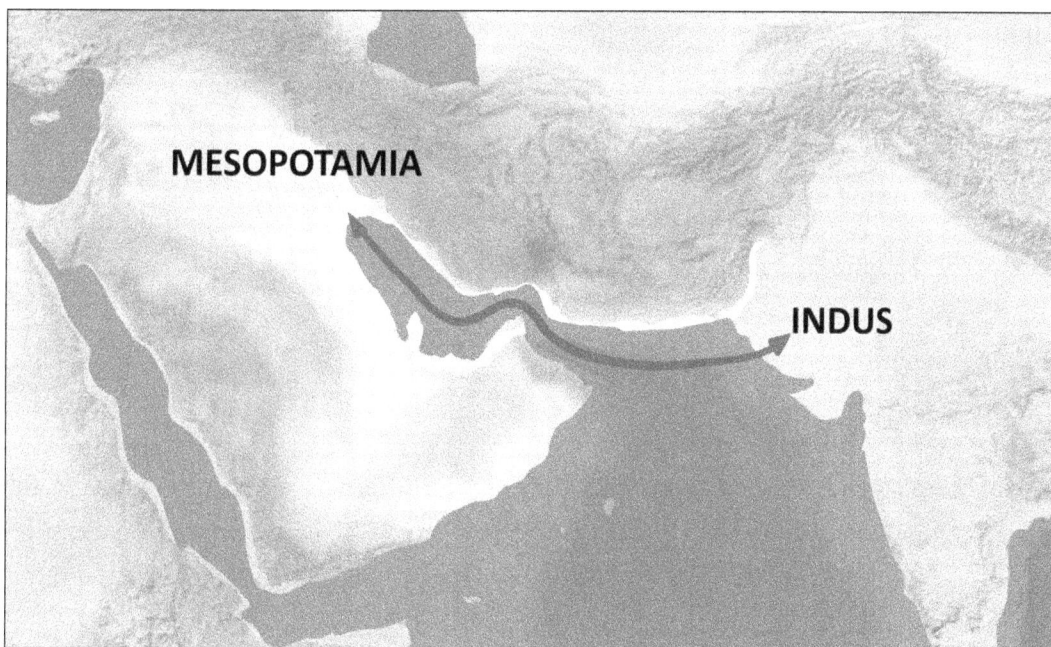

Figure 24: *The sea-based trade route to the South-East of Mesopotamia*[d]

---

[d] SOURCE: https://en.wikipedia.org/wiki/Indus%E2%80%93Mesopotamia_relations.

---

[507] Abulafia (2012), p. 35.

the Mediterranean communities had a wide range of rich cultural groups engaged in dynamic exchanges of trade, innovation, and beliefs in a single interacting system (see Figure 13, page 91).

Here was the embryonic form of today's three major industry groupings—agriculture, pastoralism, and mining—and the associated international trading systems. Linked, indeed integral to this, was the waxing and waning of political alliances, the consolidation of emerging industries, sharing of agricultural and animal husbandry practices, multiple trade networks, the growth of city-states, expansion of tool, weapon, and transport innovations, and a significant overlap in cultural mores, mythologies, and beliefs.

It was in the late Bronze Age (from around 1600 BCE) that diplomacy between a foreign power (in this case, Egypt) and lesser powers (in this case, the Ancient Middle East, Syria, Palestine, and the Levant) began to emerge.[508] By around 1400 BCE, the Amarna letters and the world's first known diplomatic system were created. The most common subjects of the Amarna letters related to negotiations of diplomatic marriage, friendship statements, and exchanged materials. In general, by around 1300 BCE diplomacy in the region had already reached a high level of geopolitical sophistication.[509]

The locations of most influence on the Hebrews and the Hebrew Bible

With the emergence of the Bronze Age, the complex intertwined trade networks in the Eastern Mediterranean and the Eurasian Steppe and the frequent territorial incursions of various empires brought with them and distributed common mythological patterns, beliefs, stories, and influences.

The group called the Israelites emerged in historical records in the Levant/Canaan around 1205 BCE. Following their emergence, and across some six hundred years, the writers of the Bible—the Hebrew scribes—developed the HB/OT, largely influenced by the beliefs and mythologies of the many previous and contemporaneous kingdoms, cultures, and mythologies around them.

---

[508]   Zangani (2018), p. 405.
[509]   SOURCE: https://www.ancient.eu/Amarna_Letters/.

Figure 25 is a schematic outline of the many kingdoms and/or cultural groups that impacted in one way or another on the emerging Israelites.

Figure 25 is schematic because it omits the time dimension (the influences on the Hebrew scribes happened at different times between around 1205 BCE and 100 BCE). It also omits the locational information about where the Hebrew scribes were mainly located when they were creating and elaborating their versions of the HB/OT (they were variously in the Levant, Mesopotamia, Egypt, Babylonia, and Persia, at different times between 900 BCE to 300 BCE).

Although the regional locations, trade routes, exiles, various empires, and associations in Figure 25 influenced the Hebrew scribes, there were four major locations that had the greatest influence. These were:

- **The Eurasian Steppe**—The Eurasian Steppe grassland cultures (Yamnaya, Adronovons, Bactria/Oxus, Scythians)—loose-knit bands of nomadic warriors and mobile herding communities whose influence, innovations and genes ultimately spread south into Mesopotamia, the Iranian Plateau, the Indus Valley, west into Europe, east into China, and ultimately into North America

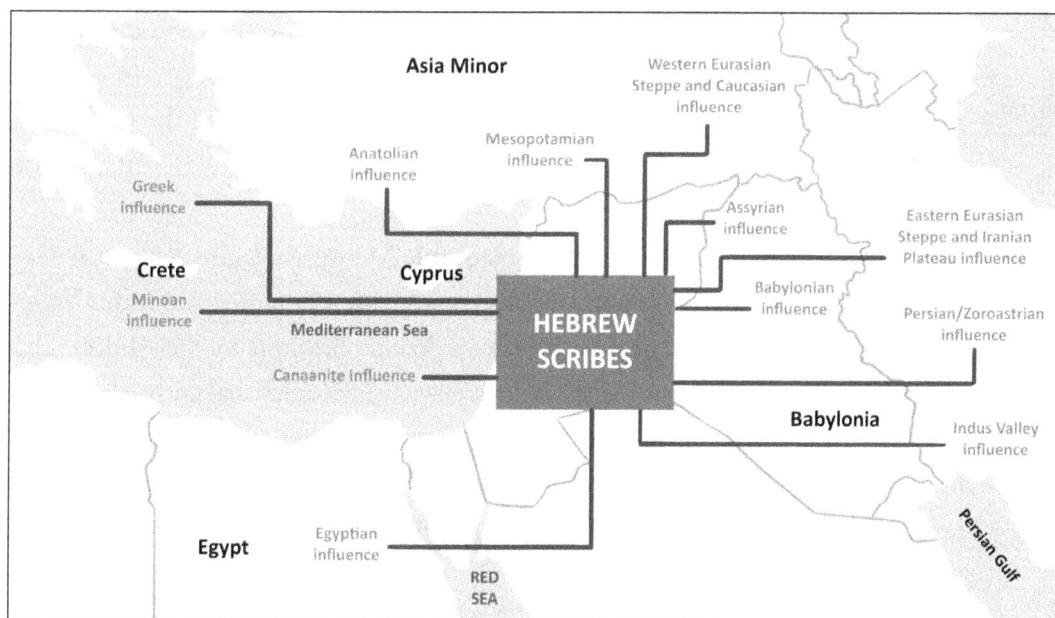

Figure 25: *Schematic outline of some of the influential sources impacting the Hebrew scribes*

- **Mesopotamia and the Fertile Crescent**—The multiple Middle Eastern cultures (Anatolia, Iran, Mesopotamia, Sumer, Akkad, Babylon, Assyria) began in and around the Tigris and Euphrates Rivers, their upper reaches, tributaries, and open plains. These locations saw the emerging sedentary farming communities and, ultimately, the first cities. It includes the Levant, where the Israelites first emerged. It includes the Iranian Plateau—the loosely defined 'plateau' extending east of Mesopotamia and encompassing most of contemporary Iran, all of Afghanistan, and parts of Pakistan west of the Indus River. The Fertile Crescent was home to many ancient cultural groups, tributary vassals and city-states, regular warfare, and conquests. Geographically, the Fertile Crescent occupied a key focal point for trade, interchange, and learnings with and from an extensive region to the north, south, east, and west. It included the Levant (Canaanites, Philistines, Phoenicians, Israelites). The Hebrews began as Canaanites, and much of Mesopotamian and Canaanite mythology and belief systems laid the foundation for the early formation of the HB/OT

- **Egypt and the Nile Valley**—The Egyptian Dynasties—commencing from around 3000 BCE. Like Mesopotamia and the Indus Valley (see below), Egypt was gifted with a river (the longest river in the world) and extensive flood plains. As a result, the ancient Egyptians were renowned as water-based traders. They traded gold, papyrus, linen, and grain for cedar wood, ebony, copper, iron, ivory, and lapis lazuli up and down the Nile River with various ports of the prehistoric and Bronze Age communities in the Mediterranean. They traded overland with the Levant and Mesopotamia

- **The Indus Valley**—The Indus Valley (Neolithic Mehrgarh, Indus Valley Civilisations, Harappan, Vedic)—along with Egypt and Mesopotamia, the Indus Valley was home to one of the three earliest recorded civilisations in the Middle East and South Asia. It was renowned for its well-planned cities, baked brick houses, elaborate drainage systems, handicrafts (carnelian products, seal carving) and metallurgy (copper, bronze, lead, and tin). It covered an area stretching from contemporary North-East Afghanistan, through much of Pakistan, and into western and north-western India

In some cases, there were only marginal differences in the shared mythologies, beliefs, and explanations of the gods and the deities in these prehistoric cultures (see later discussion).

The Hebrew scribes were essentially re-working, hybridising, and mytho-historically embedding key themes and allegories from these common mythologies into their own stories. By way of example, archaeologist and specialist in Jewish studies Carl Ehrlich described the mutual influence between the Levant and the island of Cyprus at the time in the following way:

> There is evidence of mutual cultural influence throughout the eastern Mediterranean world during the Late Bronze Age, not only with elements of Aegean or Cypriot religion found in the Levant, but also with elements of Levantine culture found on Cyprus.[510]

Indeed, these regions have played a major role in many of the concepts that are, today incorrectly, attributed to the ancient Greeks.

The true origin of Greek philosophy, poetry, mythology, and democracy

Ancient Middle East/Mesopotamian genes, philosophy, mythology, and democratic traditions dominated the Eastern Mediterranean cultures for thousands of years before the emergence of the Classical Greeks or the Israelites. The trade routes discussed above created the opportunity for emerging gene pathways, extensive cultural exchanges, and significantly more travel than might be expected considering the poor development of wheeled-vehicle transport at the time.

The Ancient Greek civilisations (also called the Aegean civilisations; Mycenaean, Minoan, Cycladic, and/or Helladic) originated from the land now known as Greece, and from the islands of the Aegean Sea, plus initially and most influentially from locations on the west coast of Asia Minor (modern Türkiye). The influence of the Greeks on the Hebrews and their Bible is usually primarily associated with the time following when the Macedonian Alexander the Great conquered and occupied large areas of land from Greece through Mesopotamia to Egypt (334 BCE to 323 BCE). However, many of the early Greek philosophers, writers and mythologists (600 BCE onwards) lived in the Ionian region on the west Coast of Anatolia (Türkiye).

The countries in this region were not isolated from each other, as sea-based travel and exchanges were quite common. There was extensive travel and exchanges of ideas and beliefs extending from Sicily, Cyprus, Crete, mainland Greece/Mycenae, the

---

[510] Ehrlich (2006-2007), pp. 47-48.

Caucuses and Egypt through Anatolia, the Levant and Mesopotamia, across the Iranian plateau to the Indus Valley and North-West Indian communities and back. Recent genomic research by the Max Planck Institute has found that the ancestors of prehistoric Myceneans (Greeks) and the Aegean Minoans (Crete) were drawn from a genetic mixture originating in ancient Western Anatolians (Türkiye), Neolithic Aegean farmers, Caucasians, and Iranians.[511]

Mesopotamian, Fertile Crescent, and Egyptian influence on the Ancient Greeks

It is a little-known fact that it was in Sumerian Mesopotamia that the Greeks first discovered the foundation for their many philosophies, mythologies, and their notion of democracy.

Along with the belief that the Greeks invented astronomy and democracy (from Greek *dēmokratia*, from *dēmos*, 'the people' + *-kratia*, 'power, rule'), the Western world tends to see the Greeks as the founding fathers of Western culture. What is seriously missing from this belief is the extent to which the Greeks borrowed and adapted many of these concepts from the Mesopotamians.[512]

Caroline Lopez-Ruiz explains the impact of the Mesopotamian region on the early Greeks in the following way:

> *The emergence of the Homeric poems in their (extremely long) written form cannot be explained without the model of the Epic of Gilgamesh; Greek cosmogony with its succession myths, its glorification of the Storm-god and his battles with monsters, even the castration of the Sky, cannot be fully understood but as a variant of the epic genre alongside the Mesopotamian, Hittite, and Canaanite variants, all of them species within a genus.*[513]

There is strong evidence that Greek philosophers prior to Socrates (470 BCE to 399 BCE) were heavily influenced by their interactions with and knowledge of the Mesopotamians. It is likely that Socrates' most famous student, Plato (428 BCE to 348 BCE),

---

[511] SOURCE: https://www.mpg.de/11419864/origins-of-minoans-and-mycenaeans retrieved on 23 March 2021.

[512] Mark (2022A).

[513] Lopez-Ruiz (2016), p. 316.

adapted his concept of the 'world soul'—the intrinsic connection between all living things on the planet—from the Mesopotamians. There is agreement amongst most classical scholars that Greek mathematics, astronomy, and the works of Pythagoras were influenced by Egypt and the Mesopotamians (Chaldeans).[514] There are Babylonian clay tablets that contain trigonometric calculations that pre-date Pythagoras by around two thousand years.[515]

Several ancient Greek philosophers who predate Socrates came from the Greek town of Miletus in the Ionian region on the western coast of Anatolia. It is widely believed that Greek philosophy began in Miletus.[516] The three founding fathers of Greek philosophy, Thales (585 BCE), Anaximander (610 BCE—546 BCE), and Anaximenes (546 BCE), were all based in Miletus.[517] From Miletus, many Greek philosophers travelled to Babylonia and Persia well before the emergence of the Greek philosophical tradition in around 500 BCE. For example, Herodotus (considered the founding father of history in Western literature), who was born on the Ionian coast in around 484 BCE, travelled extensively through Egypt, Babylonia, and Persia.[518]

Homer's *Homeric Hymns*, composed in the seventh and sixth centuries BCE, are clearly derived from the Mesopotamian Ninurta and Marduk myths.[519] The Greek poet Hesiod, whose father came from Anatolia and is recognised as 'the father of Greek didactic poetry' (active from around 700 BCE), was familiar with the traditions of the Egyptians, Babylonians, Hittites, and Hebrews. Hesoid's works, and those of Greek philosopher Thales (also from Miletus), contain close parallels with the Babylonian creation myth.

Charles Penglase has produced a thorough analysis of the influence and the embedding of Mesopotamian myths into Greek mythology. He has shown, amongst many other similarities, how the Greek legends of Aphrodite, Prometheus, and Pandora have been obviously derived from the Mesopotamian myths about the fertility goddess Inanna/Ishtar/Astarte and the god Enki respectively.[520]

---

[514] Crickmore (2009), p. 8.
[515] Mansfield and Wildberger (2017).
[516] Koestler (1959), pp. 21-25.
[517] Mark, J. J. (2020B).
[518] Clarke (1962), pp. 67-70.
[519] Schuler, (2007).
[520] Penglase (1994), p. 3; pp. 159-180; pp. 197-216.

The origins of Western astronomy can also be found in Mesopotamia via the ancient Greek mathematician and astronomer from Ionia, Aristarchus of Samos (from around 310 BCE to 230 BCE). Aristarchus is regarded in the Western world as one of the first to claim that the sun, not the Earth, was the fixed centre of the universe and that the Earth, along with the rest of the planets, revolved around the sun. Advocates of this pre-Copernican discovery, Aristarchus and his fellow ancient Greek mathematician, astronomer, and geographer Hipparchus of Nicea (190 BCE to 120 BCE), are recognised as systematically exploiting Mesopotamian (Chaldean and Babylonian) astronomical knowledge and techniques in their writings.[521]

There is a strong argument that Western medicine owes a great deal to the medical practices of the Sumerians. Hippocrates (the inspiration for the medical practitioners' 'Hippocratic Oath') has been largely regarded as the 'father of medicine'. Hippocrates was born and did most of his work on the Greek Island of Kos, which is just off the Ionian coast of Anatolia. There is substantial evidence that many of the medical practices attributed to Hippocrates were based on the medical practices of the much earlier Sumerians and Egyptians.[522]

The concept of democratic government was also appropriated by the Greeks from the wide-ranging democratic traditions in Mesopotamia. Leading Sumerian authority Samuel Kramer states that:

> *The early rulers of Sumer, no matter how great their success as conquerors, were not unbridled tyrants and absolute monarchs. On all the more important questions of state, particularly those involving war and peace, they consulted their more important fellow citizens gathered in solemn assembly.*[523]

Ronald Glassman, who has produced an extensive summary of the scope and variety of Sumerian democratic practices—from warrior assemblies and councils of elders to city-state democracies—asserts that: 'The Sumerians had tribal-democratic institutions … similar to those of Homeric Greeks, but existing millennia before the Greeks.'[524]

The success of Alexander the Great from around 340 BCE saw an increase in Greek writing and in the influence on Greek literature from exchanges with the Levant and

---

[521] Violatti (2013), p. 1.
[522] See: World History Encyclopedia, Ancient Medicine, Healing and Physicians in Antiquity—YouTube retrieved on 18 November 2021 and Mark (2023A).
[523] Kramer (1956), p. 29.
[524] Glassman (2017), p. 303.

North-western India (Figure 26). Aristotle's nephew and Greek historian, Callisthenes, was a Greek military commander in Babylonia after it was conquered by Alexander the Great.[525]

The Indus Valley influence on the Ancient Greeks

Indian scholars believe that Homer's *Iliad* and Virgil's *Aeneid* were influenced by the Mahābhārata (the ancient Sanskrit philosophical and devotional poem which is regarded as the longest poem ever written).

Peter Frankopan has explained:

> *According to Plutarch, Alexander made sure that Greek theology was taught as far away as India. … Influences and inspiration flowed in the other direction too. … [Virgil's] Aeneid was, in turn influenced by Indian texts. … Ideas, themes and stories coursed through the highways, spread by travellers, merchants and pilgrims.*[526]

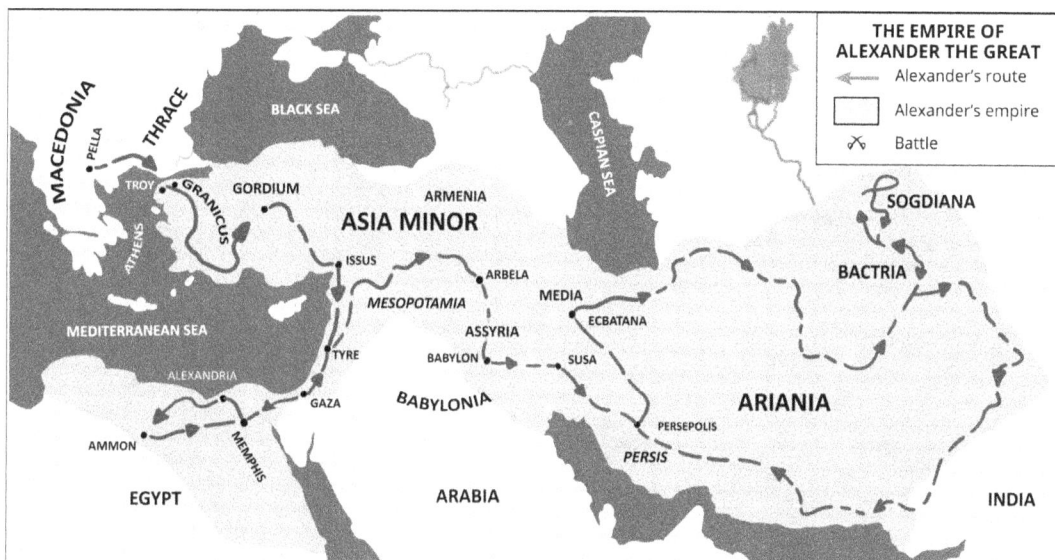

Figure 26: *The geographic coverage of the Alexander the Great Empire[e]*

---

[e] SOURCE: https://www.britannica.com/biography/Alexander-the-Great retrieved on 20 July 2021. Reprinted with permission from *Encyclopaedia Britannica*, © 2014.

---

[525] Van De Mieroop (2017), pp. 4-6.
[526] Frankopan (2016), p. 8.

Several authors have reflected on the influence of the ancient Indus Valley civilisation on Greek philosophy. Diogenes Laertius (third century CE), in writing about Greek philosophy, believed that it was necessary to determine to what extent Greek philosophy was of foreign origins. Pythagoras (sixth century BCE) increasingly acknowledged that he was transmitting knowledge and wisdom he had received from the east.[527]

It is a rarely recognised fact that the prehistoric Middle East, Egypt, and the Indus Valley prior to the emergence of the Israelites were pulsating with ideas, philosophies, innovations, and influences, many of which were unique and many of which laid the groundwork for contemporary philosophy, astronomy, democracy and religious mythologising.

---

[527] Feuerstein et al (2001), p. xvi.

Chapter 11

The Significant Historical Role of the Eurasian Steppe Grasslands

A west-to-east common latitude

In prehistory, north of the Fertile Crescent, the Eurasian Steppe is a much larger and quite different geomorphological opportunity, delivering entirely different potential for human, social, cultural, economic, mythological, and technological development.

The Eurasian Steppe stretches along roughly the same latitude some 9,000 kilometres eastwards from the Danube River through Bulgaria, Romania, Moldova, Ukraine, Western Russia, Siberia, Kazakhstan, Xinjiang, Mongolia, and Manchuria.[528] The northern boundary of the Eurasian Steppe in prehistoric times, as now, was a belt of cold boreal forests of birch, poplar, and conifers (a polar tree line) running west-to-east along the northern edge of the temperate zone in which most of the Eurasian Steppe grasslands can be found. The northern boundary of the Eurasian Steppe, the 'forest steppe', was the southern edge of the sub-polar and polar zone.

The Eurasian Steppe can be divided into two major segments—the first being the Western Steppe, a vast region that, combined with the Caucuses, had a comparatively higher genomic influence on the Middle East and Europe.[529] It stretches from the Danube River to the Altai Mountains where Kazakhstan meets Siberia and Mongolia.

The second segment is the Eastern Steppe, which arguably had a significant influence on the mythologies of Sumer and Persia and eventually the HB/OT. The Eastern Steppe extends east of the Altai Mountains to the mountains on the Pacific Coast of China.

---

[528]   Erdos et al (2018), pp. 3-7.

[529]   NOTE: Some researchers divide the Eurasian Steppe into three segments with a middle segment located roughly west-to-east across Kazakhstan.

During the Stone Age, the Altai Mountains on the Russian border with Mongolia, Siberia, China, and Kazakhstan were the home of the ancient Denisovan branch of hominids who were there with Neanderthals and early human species (modern humans). The Denisovans descended from hominids who reached Asia earlier than modern humans/human species. Archaeological evidence of Denisovans, Neanderthals, and human species has been found in the Denisova Cave in the Altai mountains making this the only place in the world where all three hominids are known to have lived and, based on genomic evidence, interbred.[530]

An innovation and genetic west-to-east pathway

There was enormous potential for unique innovations provided to the emerging prehistoric communities located in the common latitude of the Eurasian Steppe. The climate of the Steppe grasslands is semi-arid and, in prehistory, it was largely unsuitable for agriculture but good for grazing animals. The extensive grasslands are intersected here and there in a mosaic pattern by large forest patches, mountain ranges, and rivers and streams with trees along their banks. The rivers along the Steppe often tended to provide notional boundaries/obstacles that defined the different Eurasian Steppe cultural groups throughout prehistory.

In the lead-up to the Bronze Age and some two thousand years prior to the emergence of the Israelites, the Eurasian Steppe contained a complex network of loosely connected nomadic migrating cultures, influenced in their movement initially and largely by seasonal factors. These regular migratory movements, dictated by the seasons, and the needs of the nomads and their animals, shaped the economic and social networks linking the nomads to peoples on the outskirts of the steppe. These interactions facilitated the flow of goods and innovations between settled, semi-nomadic, and nomadic peoples, particularly on the southern, western, and eastern edges of the Eurasian Steppe.

Domestication and innovation along the Eurasian Steppe

By 5000 BCE, foraging groups in the Western Steppe were already herding domestic cattle, pigs, sheep, and goats, which were first domesticated in Anatolia, Mesopotamia, and northern Syria around 9000 BCE. Cereal cropping arrived in the Eurasian Steppe from the Fertile Crescent in around 4200 BCE.[531]

---

[530] Warren (2018), pp. 417-418; Callaway (2019); Krause and Trappe (2021), p. 11.
[531] Baumer (2016), p. 61.

Because of the unique geomorphology and the available native species, the prehistoric nomadic groups across the Eurasian Steppe developed a distinctly different lifestyle to that of Mesopotamia and the Fertile Crescent. The Steppe cultures tended to survive on hunting, fishing, and animal husbandry. Considering the geographic variations across the Steppe, it is not surprising that the Eurasian grassland nomads in prehistory (prior to 3500 BCE) were one of the first groups to domesticate the horse. Archaeological evidence indicates that the camel was first domesticated in Mongolia and China by the Eastern Eurasian desert nomads (in the Gobi and Taklamakan Deserts prior to 3500 BCE) and by the Copper Age, the Botai hunter-herder culture of the central steppe in Northern Kazakhstan. The earliest unambiguous evidence of horse husbandry comes from the Botai culture (around 3500 BCE to 3000 BCE), but this is likely to have been learnt from an earlier spread of Yamnaya pastoralists from the Western Steppe.[532]

The domestication of the horse in the Eurasian Steppe was a culturally transformative event. It vastly increased the possibilities and the economy of nomadic life. Subsequently, their culture emphasised horse breeding, horse riding, and nomadic pastoralism; this usually involved trading with settled peoples around the Steppe edges. The Eurasian Steppe nomads were the first to develop cavalry and horse archery. They introduced innovations such as the bridle, bit, and stirrup. The very rapid rate at which innovations crossed and spread widely along the common latitude of the Steppe lands saw their innovations being copied by settled peoples bordering the Steppes. The domestication of the horse transformed the Eurasian Steppe into an innovation, linguistic, cultural, and genetic east–west highway.

The significance and history of the domestication of the horse and the emergence of horsemanship across the Eurasian Steppe, is reflected in the widespread modern-day frequency of traditional equestrian sports across the Steppe. This includes endurance riding, *buzkashi* (in which horse-mounted players attempt to place a goat or calf carcass in a goal), *dzhigit* (a special style of trick riding) and *kyz kuu* (a horse-riding courtship race between young men and women).

Following the domestication of the horse, the three most influential inventions at this time were the wheel, the chariot, and the composite hunting bow:

- The evidence of who invented the wheel is ambiguous and contended. The Mesopotamians and the nomads of the Eurasian Steppe are most likely early

---

[532]   de Barros Damgaard et al. (2018), p. 10.

adopters and probably the actual and most likely contemporaneous inventors.[533] The wheel was in common use from around 3500 BCE.

- The Steppe nomads and the Mesopotamians are the most likely contenders for the invention of the chariot in around 1900 BCE.[534]
- Although the hunting bow made of a single piece of timber had been around for thousands of years and across many locations during the Stone Age, the Eurasian Steppe nomads were the first to invent the composite and far more effective bow in around 2500 BCE.[535, 536]

The domestication of the horse and the impact of these three inventions (the wheel, chariot, and composite bow) on the Eurasian Steppe nomads was enormous. It gave them mobility, which saw them having a major influence on culture, language, genetic pathways, innovation and the interchange of people, ideas, mythologies, and material culture across Central Asia and with the Caucuses, Anatolia, the Levant, Mesopotamia and eventually Europe. These three inventions and the domestication of the horse delivered a distinct advantage eastwards, westwards, and southwards for successful influence, warfare, and invasion of other groups within or proximate to the Central Asian region.

The regional influence of the Eurasian Steppe nomads

The Eurasian Steppe became the home of the nomadic empires, sometimes also called Steppe empires, Central or Inner Asian empires, or Steppe Warriors. They were renowned as bow-wielding, horse-riding, loose-knit nomadic cultural groups. This included the Yamnaya (3500 BE to 2500 BCE), Andronovo (2200 BCE to 1200 BCE), the Cimmerian/Kimmerian (800 BCE to 700 BCE), and the Scythian (900 BCE to 200 CE) cultural groups. Eventually, this loosely knit group of militaristic pastoral nomads occupying the Eurasian Steppe controlled large swathes of the Steppe across Eurasia from the Black Sea through Siberia to the borders of China, from 1100 BCE to around 700 BCE.

The role of the Eurasian Steppe in the emergence of innovations, technology, metallurgy, and the foundation mythologies of the region is often overlooked or misunderstood. Initially, there was a distinct west-to-east geomorphological and latitudinal advantage across the Eurasian

---

[533] Anthony (2007), pp. 65-73; Burmeister (2017), p. 69.
[534] Anthony (2007) pp. 397-405.
[535] Composite bows are usually made of a combination of at least two materials which can be laminated and include bone, horn, metal, animal skins, tree bark and sinew.
[536] Baumer (2016), pp. 35-38.

Steppe in terms of the sharing and interchange of ideas created by the common latitude, climatic change, availability of the horse, the nomadic lifestyles, and the shared and extensive expanse of grasslands. However, in the late Bronze Age (from around 1200 BCE), the Eurasian Steppe:

> … *became a bridge between the civilisations that developed on the edges of the continent of Greece, the Near East, Iran, the Indian Subcontinent, and China. Chariot technology, horses and horseback riding, bronze metallurgy, and a strategic location gave Steppe societies an importance they never before had possessed.*[537]

Inevitably, and in addition to the predominant west–east latitudinal advantage and interchange of ideas and innovations, influence from the Eurasian Steppe moved southwards rather than northwards partly for climatic reasons. The interchange of practices and innovations particularly during the Bronze Age was multi-directional.

There is substantial evidence of the prehistoric cultures of the Middle East including Mesopotamia and the Levant and the Eurasian Steppe interchanging ideas, innovations, language, and genetic inheritance. By around 5000 BCE, cultivation, domestication of animals, and the development of agriculture in settled village communities were occurring in the Fertile Crescent, the Caucuses, and intermittently in parts of the Eurasian Steppe. These practices had moved eastward into the Iranian Plateau and the Indus Valley; northwest from the Fertile Crescent into Anatolia, Mycenaean Greece (including southern Greece, Crete, and the Cyclades), parts of southwest Anatolia and ultimately as far as the Atlantic seaboard across Europe; and into the southwest to Egypt and the Nile Valley.[538]

Once cereal cropping arrived north of the Fertile Crescent, the Eurasian Steppe became the corridor for the importation of millet from China to the Fertile Crescent and, in return, wheat from the Fertile Crescent to China (in or around 3000 BCE). Here were the early beginnings of the development of the east-to-west route now called the Silk Road.

The Eurasian Steppe genomic and linguistic journey

The mobility and impact of the Eurasian Steppe nomads on modern humans have been shown in recent and diverse genomic research. As expected, and based on the findings of Jeong et al., the Western Steppe Ancient North Eurasian (ANE) ancestors' genes have been found in Caucasian hunter-gatherers, Neolithic Iranians, Native Americans, Europeans,

---

[537] Anthony (2007), p. 456.
[538] Cunliffe (2017), pp. 48-59.

Central Asians, South Asians, and some East Asians.[539] Further east, the West Siberian hunter-gatherer genetic makeup has been found to be about 30% Eastern European Hunter-Gatherer ancestry, 50% ANE ancestry, and 20% East Asian ancestry.[540]

Between 1400 BCE and 700 BCE, the genomic evidence from the central steppe region (west to east across Kazakhstan) has revealed only western lineages. After that date, around a fifty-fifty mix of eastern and western lineages has been found, highlighting the significant move of Eastern Steppe warrior nomads (largely Yamnaya and the Scythians) westwards.[541]

Genomic studies indicate that the ANE ancestral genes were introduced to Western Europe by way of the Eurasian Steppe Yamnaya pastoralists (3500 BCE to 2600 BCE) probably around 2700 BCE.[542] This westward migration introduced the Caucasus genetic component to the genetic landscape of Europe. There is significant genomic evidence of 'steppe DNA', genetic profiles of western steppe primarily male warriors largely from the Pontic-Caspian steppe arriving into Portugal and Spain from around 2200 BCE.[543] There is also strong DNA evidence that the solar-aligned neolithic stone circles at Stonehenge in England were created by a large-scale migration some four thousand years ago from Anatolia/the Western Steppe of a vanished people "who left no written language, no tales or legends, only a scatter of bones, potsherds, stone and antler tools—and an array of equally mysterious monuments".[544]

There is strong evidence that the beginnings of the universal Indo-European language, which possibly originated in Anatolia, spread with the movement towards Europe of the Eurasian Steppe Yamnaya pastoralists.[545] These events occurred approximately one thousand five hundred years or more before the earliest evidence of the existence of Israelites as an identifiably different group in the Levant (1205 BCE).

The genomic pathways from west to east and north to south along and down the Eurasian Steppe carried with it the fundamental structure and beliefs of Sumerian, Israelite, and Christian religions (adapted in part from Zoroastrianism and Hinduism in the kingdom of Bactria in the Eastern Eurasian Steppe and communities on the Iranian Plateau).[546] It is not surprising, considering the geographic location and influence of Bactria,

---

[539] Jeong et al., (2019), p. 973.
[540] Narasimhan (2019).
[541] Manco (2015), p. 140.
[542] Narasimhan (2019).
[543] Olalde et al., (2019) and Goldberg et al., (2017).
[544] SOURCE: Stonehenge was just one triumph in a surprising prehistoric building boom (nationalgeographic.com) retrieved on 21 June 2024
[545] Anthony (2007); Wade (2012); de Barros Damgaard et al., (2018).
[546] Williams Jackson (1896).

that both Zoroastrianism and Hinduism (Vedic culture), which are regarded as the oldest of contemporary religions, have similar origins, pay homage to the same spiritual seers, venerate the same gods, and even have the same verses throughout the early scriptures.[547]

The impact of the Yamnaya, Adronovons, and the Scythians

The Yamnaya

The mosaic pattern of rivers that flow across the Eurasian Steppe often tended to provide boundaries/obstacles that defined the different Eurasian Steppe social groups throughout prehistory. Prior to around 3500 BCE, there was great regional diversity and a multiplicity of cultural groups across the Eurasian Steppe.

Prehistoric populations did not set stable regional boundaries, but rather dynamic local ones in constant flow and change of interaction strategies. Semi-nomadic groups like the Yamnaya and early mobile Corded Ware communities had an even more variable control of pasture lands—at least until they settled down and became 'locals' in certain territories.[548]

Ultimately, the combination of climate change and increased mobility provided by the domestication of the horse, the need to graze larger herds of cattle, and the invention of the chariot and the oxen-drawn goods-carrying covered wagon saw a loose-knit unification of broadly similar cultures across the Eurasian Steppe.[549]

The Yamnaya culture (also referred to as the Yamnaya horizon), from around 3300 BCE to 2600 BCE, is recognised as one of the first loose-knit culturally similar groupings of tribal federations that spread east–west across the Eurasian Steppe. It was a disparate collection of Steppe communities that shared a nomadic pastoral lifestyle, similar mythological beliefs, and a related common mode of burial practices.

The complex burial practices of the Yamnaya pastoralists were a key contribution to modern religious beliefs and funerary rituals. It is most likely that the Yamnaya were the first people to ride horses. A practice which assisted them and their influence to expand both eastwards and westwards.[550] The Yamnaya are often referred to as the Pit-grave culture (Yamnaya is Russian for 'pit grave') because they are regarded as one of the originators

---

[547] SOURCE: http://www.hindupedia.com/en/Zoroastrianism_and_Hinduism retrieved on 17 November 2020.

[548] https://indo-european.eu/2020/10/east-slovakian-yamnaya-settlers-and-links-with-niche-graves/ retrieved on 3 November 2020.

[549] Cunliffe (2017), p. 95.

[550] See https://www.nationalgeographic.com/magazine/article/who-were-the-first-people-to-ride-horses-ancient-skeletons-reveal-new-clues retrieved on 19 July 2024

of the practice of burying an individual in a single grave and transporting them for burial on a wagon. And, for the first time, the wagon is buried with them to assist them in their travel to the presumed afterlife.[551]

These burial practices began a process of cultures in the Central Asian and Middle Eastern regions magnifying their conception of, and preparation for, a presumed afterlife. In Sumerian Mesopotamia (similarly in Ancient Egypt), burial practices became:

> … *intricate and beautifully fashioned subterranean palaces sunk deep into the earth and spacious enough to accommodate vast numbers of persons. Excavations of the royal graves of Ur (dating back to about 3000 BCE) revealed, in an inner chamber of one, the body of a ruler with a few intimate attendants and, in surrounding chambers, servants, ministers, dancing girls, charioteers with vehicles and animals, and other persons who had been slain to provide service in death.*[552]

Hunter-gatherer ancestor worship had transitioned into a belief that these departed ancestors could punish or reward clan members for their behaviours. With the emergence of chieftains and kingdoms, this transitioned into a far more elaborate concept of a range of deities controlling a 'conditional afterlife'. The complex prehistoric burial rituals and accompanying burial paraphernalia reflected the likelihood that the deceased person would need to be well prepared for a judgemental afterlife.[553]

Contemporary religions have elaborated this myth even further, with clearly articulated, prerequisite 'god-given' conceptual, lifestyle, moral, and ethical codes of conduct replacing the elaborate burial paraphernalia of prehistory. The Judeo-Christian belief in an afterlife, conditional on a judgmental anthropomorphic male supreme being, is the contemporary version of this ancient myth.

The cultural expansion of the Eastern Eurasian Steppe nomads

The eastern wing of the Yamnaya culture morphed into the Andronovo/Bactrian culture (1800 BCE to 1200 BCE) and then the Scythian culture (1000 BCE to around 300 BCE), although the mobility of these groups saw their boundaries being quite flexible. The Western/Pontic-Caspian Steppe morphed into the Srubnaya (Timber-grave) culture (1800 BCE to 1200 BCE).

---

[551] Cunliffe (2011), p. 170.

[552] https://www.britannica.com/topic/burial-death-rite#ref110692 retrieved on 2 November 2020.

[553] Henrich (2021), pp. 140-141.

The Scytho-Siberian world follows the Eurasian Steppe from Hungary in the west to China in the east—some 3,500 kilometres.[554] Irrespective of the long distances along the Eurasian Steppe, a broad similarity of lifestyles and mythologies had developed across these different cultural groupings.[555] The Srubnaya culture is generally considered to have been Iranian, as they shared similar mitochondrial DNA lineages with the Andronovo people and the Scythians. The Srubnaya were possibly ancestral to the Scythians. The Yamnaya, Andronovo, and Scythian cultures were convenient, loose-knit alignments of similar yet identifiably different Eurasian Steppe sub-cultures.

The Adronovo cultural groups, sometimes referred to as the Adronovo horizon, were a complex mix of similar but different communities in the Eastern Steppe (Adronovo, Sintashta, Bactria/Oxus, Bactria–Margiana Archaeological Complex). They flourished between 2000 BCE and 900 BCE in Mongolia, western Siberia, and the West Asiatic Steppe/East Eurasian Steppe. They were Indo-Iranians and were most likely the originators of the Indo-Iranian language group, which includes Iranian, Old Persian, Farsi, Kurdish, and Sanskrit—the classical language of India and the liturgical language of the Hindu, Buddhist, and Jainism religions.[556]

The Andronovo migrated southwards and south-eastwards to occupy Bactria—consolidating a geographic location south of Siberia stretching from the Caspian Sea eastwards to north-western India and straddling across modern-day Afghanistan, Tajikistan, and Uzbekistan. The scattered Andronovo communities could vary from between 50 to 250 individuals in anything from ten to forty houses in small settlements with small family kurgan cemeteries and a relatively homogenous culture across these various settlements.[557]

They were the first Eurasian Steppe nomadic warriors to establish a more settled way of life as cereal-growing, and the consumption of available edible wild plants, began to blend in with their herding economies (cattle, sheep, goats, and horses). The domesticated pig was notably absent, which is typical of a community that kept a partially mobile economy. Their settled way of life and the gradual reduction in migratory events appears

---

[554] Unterlander et al., (2017).

[555] Cunliffe (2019), p. 76.

[556] Indo-Iranian languages (also referred to as Aryan languages) are a branch of the Indo-European language family. Currently Indo-Iranian has 1.5 billion speakers, stretching from Europe, Türkiye, the Caucasus, eastward to Xinjiang and Assam and south to Sri Lanka, the Maldives and to Oceania (Fiji Hindi).

[557] Anthony (2007), pp. 448-451.

to have created the opportunity for their consolidation and the emergence of a predatory nomadic warrior elite that would eventually dominate the Eurasian Steppe.[558]

Between 1800 BCE and 1600 BCE, the Andronovo communities had already established mining of copper and tin. They were not only experienced herdsmen, but they were highly experienced miners and skilled metalworkers. They effectively had control over trade and significant economic power in minerals (copper, tin, turquoise) and pastoral products (horses, dairy, leather) across the eastern Steppe from the Caspian Sea to Siberia, Mongolia, and southwards into the Iranian plateau.[559] By around 1800 BCE, they were in regular trading relationships with communities to their south. This was partly because of their horse, chariot, and oxen-drawn goods-carrying covered wagon mobility, but also in response to the ever-increasing demand for metals, raw materials, lapis lazuli, and horses by Mesopotamia, the Iranian plateau, and the Fertile Crescent to their south.[560]

This Eastern Eurasian Steppe and, specifically, the intersection with Siberia and Mongolia, is also the most likely geographic place of origin of the Sumerians, who had moved south into Mesopotamia many years before (in around 4000 BCE)—some two thousand years before the arrival of the Andronovo horizon in the Eastern Steppe.

The emergence of the oldest continuous religions—Hinduism and Zoroastrianism

The Bactria/Oxus civilisation (also called the Greater Khorasan civilisation) (2400 BCE to 1900 BCE) was located on the southern border of the Andronovo horizon (shown notionally in Figure 27). Archaeological research indicates extensive contacts between the Bactria/Oxus civilisation and a vast region extending from the ancient Orient to the north, the Indus valley on the east, and Mesopotamia, the Persian Gulf, the Levant, and Anatolia to the west and south.[561]

Bactria and the Eastern Steppe is most likely the original location of the related mythological stories that make up Zoroastrianism, Hinduism, and Buddhism. There is some debate about when the founder of Zoroastrianism, Zarathustra (Zoroaster is the Greek form of his name) lived. Some researchers have suggested Zoroaster lived in 6000 BCE;

---

[558] Cunliffe (2019), pp. 73-76.
[559] Anthony (2007), pp. 452-454.
[560] Cunliffe (2019), p. 73.
[561] Vahdati et al (2019), p. 179.

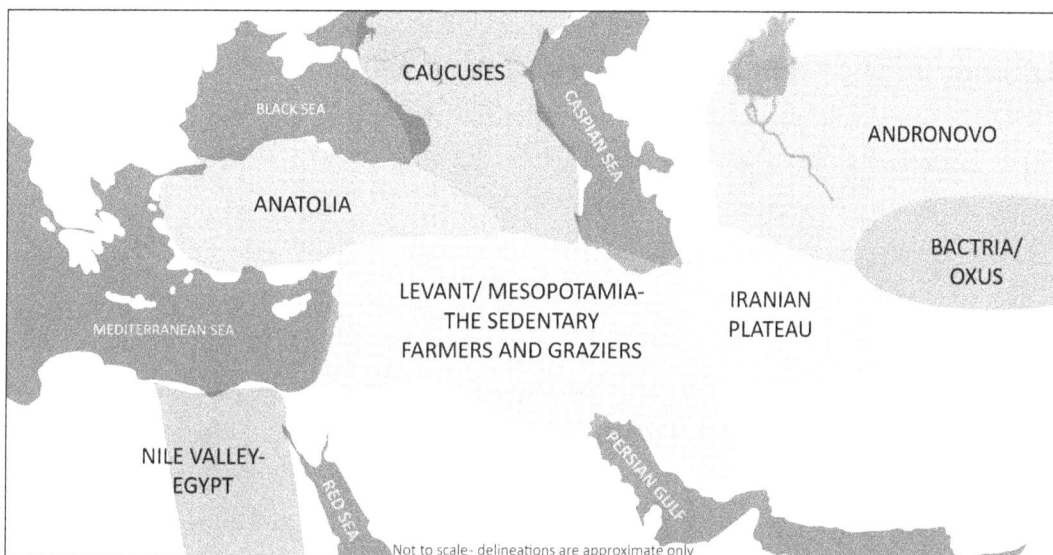

Figure 27: *Notional location of Andronovo and Bactria/Oxus civilisations[a]*

[a] SOURCE: adapted from http://wordpress-2471-39414-100555.cloudwaysapps.com/wp-content /uploads/2011/04/Hemisferio_Norte-1.jpg.

others suggest 2000 BCE; some believe that it was sometime between 1700 BCE and 1000 BCE. Others suggest he lived sometime between 1400 BCE and 1000 BCE.[562]

According to Zoroastrian doctrine, Zoroaster lived from 700 BCE to 600 BCE. Evidence of his living at least one thousand years before this time comes from the fact that parts of the Zoroastrian religious text, the Avesta, are written in a more ancient Iranian language.[563]

The close similarities between the Hindu Vedic scriptures and the Zoroastrian religious texts suggest that they were most probably developed contemporaneously or, at least, influenced by and developed from the same original source. There is circumstantial evidence that the Vedic scriptures were developed well prior to 1900 BCE and some have suggested that they were conceived prior to 3100 BCE.[564]

[562] SOURCE: http://www.avesta.org/zfaq.html retrieved on 1 March 2022.
[563] Foster and Foster (2009), p. 171.
[564] Feuerstein et al. (2001), p. xvii.

It is therefore most likely that the monotheistic Zoroastrianism religion and the Vedic scriptures can be traced back to at least the second millennium BCE. They both are regarded as having been an amalgam of the prehistoric Indo-Iranian mythological beliefs of the Andronovo and those of the Sapalli-Jarkutan Cultures (1700 BCE to 1350 BCE), which the Andronovo replaced in Bactria.[565]

The Sapalli-Jarkutan culture had access to great stores of gold, silver, tin, copper, lead, lapis lazuli, and turquoise, which created ongoing opportunities for trade and the interchange of ideas with Iran, Mesopotamia, the Fertile Crescent, and the Indus Valley.[566] The Sapalli-Jarkutans were essentially a loose affiliation of patriarchal, pastoral/agricultural clans living in communities containing housing, narrow streets, and citadels oriented to the cardinal points, with worshippers' communal religious fire temples also oriented to the cardinal points.[567] Some of these communities were protected by two-metre-thick defensive walls, designed in a form that reflected the designs that are outlined in the Zoroastrian religious text, the Avesta.[568]

Zoroaster's native country was probably Media, in North-Western Iran (possibly in modern Azerbaijan or Kurdistan), but his ministry most likely took place in eastern Iran, especially in the region of Bactria, about 1200 BC. According to Zoroastrian tradition, Zoroaster had a divine vision of a supreme being while partaking in a pagan purification rite in a river at age 30. Zoroaster began teaching followers to worship a single god called Āhurā Mazdā.

The Scythians

Unterlander et al., have described the communities scattered along the Eurasian Steppe in the following way:

> While the eastern and western populations [along the Eurasian Steppe] are separated by a distance of 2,000–3,500 km, archaeological evidence indicates that they were strikingly similar regarding their lifestyle and culture. … All of our analyses support the hypothesis that the genetic composition of the Scythians can best be described as a mixture of Yamnaya-related ancestry and East Asian/north Siberian elements.[569]

---

[565] Baumer (2012), p. 116.
[566] Baumer (2012). pp. 105-106.
[567] Askarov and Shirinov (1994), pp. 13-15.
[568] Togaev and Usarov (2017), p. 29.
[569] Unterlander et al. (2017).

Knowledge of the Scythian culture comes primarily from recent finds in burial mounds (kurgans) north of the Black Sea and in the Altai region of Mongolia. The Scythians flourished across the entire Eurasian Steppe from around 900 BCE to 200 CE. Like the Andronovo and Sumerians before them, they most likely emerged originally from the Altai Mountain region in southern Siberia (Eastern Eurasian Steppe) and have been referred to as the 'Scythian-Siberian culture'.[570] The Scythian government consisted of a confederation of tribes and chiefs, which was a common form of social organisation across the Eurasian Steppe.

The Scythians moved westward from Asia into Europe along the Eurasian Steppe corridor. Genomic researcher Mari Jarve and her colleagues have examined DNA evidence of Bronze and Iron Age Scythians and they confirm an east-to-west genetic admixture gradient, with the Scythians bringing Eastern Steppe ancestry across to the Western Eurasian Steppe. Jarve's research has confirmed that the Scythians were a genetically distinct federation of different Eurasian Steppe tribes whose genetic differences can be largely explained by geography.[571] Genomic analysis shows that Scythian genetics include a mixture of Yamnaya (Western Eurasian Steppe), north Siberian, and Han (Chinese). This research confirms ongoing and substantial gene flow across the eastern and western prehistoric Eurasian Steppe nomadic cultures facilitated by the common latitude and extensive grasslands.[572]

The Scythians were among the earliest people to master the art of riding and were feared and admired for their prowess in war and for their horsemanship. They migrated from the Eastern Steppe across to the Caucuses and the plains of the Black Sea (from around 700 BCE) forcing the resident Cimmerian (pre-Scythian) culture to vacate/escape south through the Caucuses into Anatolia and west into Europe. Eventually, the Scythians were able to largely control sections of the emerging Silk Road trading network, which is reflected in their ability to include exquisitely crafted silk and gold artefacts in their burials.[573]

The Scythian language was a branch of the Indo-Iranian language, which was a sub-branch of the widely distributed Indo-European language family that travelled along the Eurasian Steppe having originated in the Caucuses and Anatolia.

---

[570] Cunliffe (2019), p. 86.
[571] Jarve et al. (2019), pp. 2431-2434.
[572] Unterlander et al., (2017).
[573] Manco (2015), p. 140.

The impact of the Scythian religion

The Scythians were nomadic, so did not build temples or altars. They continued the development of rather elaborate burial rituals in preparation for a presumed afterlife—involving graves of dead chieftains filled with richly worked articles of gold, as well as beads of turquoise, carnelian, and amber, and many other valuable objects.[574]

The Scythians worshipped a pantheon of seven deities, as was common across Indo-Iranian mythologies of that time. Whilst the sedentary Sumerians also worshipped seven deities, theirs were based on the seven planets, and they treated the number seven as a sacred number. The Scythians had seven different gods. The Scythian gods were more related to the practicalities of their nomadic life. The supreme god/goddess (1) was Tabiti, the goddess of heat, fire, the sun, and the hearth. There were additional gods of the sky father, god of thunder, and the divine ancestor of all Scythians as told in the Scythian creation myth (2), an Earth mother goddess of fertility, water, nourishment, and healing (3), a god of war (4), a goddess of material abundance (5), a goddess of love, beauty, pleasure, passion and procreation (6), and a god of the sea, storms, earthquakes and horses (7).[575]

The Scythians sporadically invaded Mesopotamia during the collapse of the Assyrian Empire (around 650 BCE). The Hebrew scribes came to describe the Scythians in their Bible in the following way:

> Behold, a people is coming from the north country; a great nation is stirring from the farthest parts of the earth. They lay hold on bow and javelin, they are cruel and have no mercy. The sound of them is like the roaring sea; they ride on horses, set in array as a man for battle against you.[576]

Scythian shamanism sets the scene for modern-day priests and pastors

The Scythian religion was strongly influenced by the Mongolians. Many of its components have survived in modern-day religious practices and beliefs. The Scythian religion centred around a clan shaman. The clan's shaman was regarded as a bridge between the Scythian clan and the spiritual world. The Scythian shaman could communicate between

---

[574]   SOURCE: https://www.britannica.com/topic/Scythian retrieved on 17 November 2020.

[575]   This summary is adapted from several sources including Cunliffe (2019); https://en.wikipedia.org/wiki/Scythian_religion#Pantheon and https://en.wikipedia.org/wiki/Scythian_religion retrieved on 17 November 2020.

[576]   Jeremiah 6:22-23.

the upper world of the gods (modern-day 'heaven'), Earth (the middle world) and the underworld (modern-day 'hell'). Scythian shamans had such great spiritual power and access to the dead, gods, demons, and natural spirits that they had to be differentiated from society. This was done via the use of special clothing, special paraphernalia, personal adornments, and armaments. They could cure the sick, save a soul possessed by demons, have prophetic visions, control the spirits, communicate with deceased ancestors, and predict the future.[577] Here is the beginning of the formula for modern-day religious leaders.

Origin of sacred bread and wine traditions

It is not surprising, considering their origin in the Eastern Eurasian Steppe, that the Scythian mythology shared some gods and practises with Mongolians, Zoroastrians, and the Vedic religions (Hinduism and Brahmanism). Like most of the region's communities, the Scythians and the Zoroastrians used an intoxicating drink in their religious rituals.[578] The Scythians celebrated with meat and wine and the Zoroastrians with bread and wine (in the Yasna festival). The Hindu Vedic *yajña* festivals (*yajña* meaning 'divine worship') are very similar to the Zoroastrian *yasna* festival. In the Hindu festival, they drink an intoxicating plant-based drink called *soma* with small cakes called *laddo*, which are made of a mixture of sesame seeds and *jaggery* (a type of sugar). The combination of grain (bread or similar) and wine (or similar intoxicating drink) was commonly used as tributes to different deities throughout the Middle East and the Eurasian Steppe over thousands of years.

The ancient Egyptians celebrated the god Osiris by eating bread (the body of Osiris) and drinking wine (the blood of Osiris).[579] The tablets and seals found in the site of Persepolis (518 BCE to 330 BCE) the capital city of the vast Persian (Achaemenid) Empire contain references to priests giving grain (bread) and wine (the libation of the gods) as tributes to the gods.[580] This long-standing ancient tradition was a major influence on the use of bread and wine in various Jewish and Christian festal celebrations, sacrificial rituals, mythological stories, and religious ceremonies (e.g., the Jewish Passover and the Christian Eucharist).

---

[577] SOURCE: https://factsanddetails.com/asian/cat65/sub422/item2701.html retrieved on 29 March 2023.

[578] Cunliffe (2019), p. 271.

[579] SOURCE: https://mythodoxy.wordpress.com/2019/05/09/the-eucharist-of-horus retrieved on 29 March 2023.

[580] See for example, Hallock (1969), p. 639.

There is evidence of a mass migration southwards of Central Asian peoples in around 1300 BCE. Many of these headed west into Iran whilst others headed east into India.[581] Two issues eventuated—the common ancestral language came with them (Old Avestan/ early Indo-European/Sanskrit), as did the shared ideology. The influence of the Zoroastrian scriptures went west into Mesopotamia and the Levant and the related Hindu Veda scriptures went east into India.

The Eurasian Steppe origin of the Sumerians, Elamites, Persians, and the Medes

The arc of the Zagros Mountains as it folds around from the Fertile Crescent creates a row of hills intersecting with the Iranian Plateau to the east. There is evidence of organised hunter-gatherer groups (hand axes, choppers, and scrappers) along the Iranian Plateau dating back some 100,000 years.[582] There is evidence of migration of nomadic pastoralists coming down from the central and eastern Eurasian Steppe along either the Central Asian Mountain Corridor or the Khorasan/Khurasan Road or down through the Caucuses between the Black and the Caspian Seas.[583, 584, 585]

The Khorasan Road is a route that connected the Eastern Steppe region (Mongolia, Siberia and western China) across the Iranian Plateau to the Zagros Mountains and ultimately to Mesopotamia. It is conceivable that the Sumerians travelled this route or Central Asian Mountain Corridor from Siberia or from the Eastern Eurasian Steppe on their way to settling in southern Mesopotamia in around 4000 BCE.

The high country and the mountain valleys in the eastern arc of the Zagros mountains and in western Iran saw a range of nomadic warrior pastoralist communities probably related to the Scythians establish themselves here (east of Mesopotamia), in the Iranian Plateau, and in southwestern Iran near the Persian Gulf from around 3300 BCE. This included the Elamites (from around 3300 BCE), the Persians (from around 1000 BCE), and the Medes (from around 800 BCE). The Persians are believed to be ethnically related to the Bactrians, Medes, and Parthians, all of whom have links to the Scythians.[586]

---

581 Llewellyn-Jones (2022), pp. 33-37.
582 SOURCE: https://www.britannica.com/place/Afghanistan/The-arts-and-cultural-institutions#ref261364 retrieved on 14 March 2023.
583 Kurtkaya (2020); Llewellyn-Jones (2022), p. 33.
584 Van de Mieroop (2007), pp. 271-272.
585 Boyce (2001), p. 48.
586 SOURCE: https://www.livescience.com/who-were-the-persians retrieved on 14 March 2023.

The Elamites, Persians, and Medes were all renowned for their horsemanship and they also produced gold plaques decorated with recumbent stags and goats in the Scytho-Siberian style.[587] These similarities support the theory that they most probably had all travelled down originally from the Eurasian Steppe region. They were all, like the Scythians, a loose-knit collective of separate tribes or ancestral clans each with their own chieftain.

Welsh expert in Iranian ancient history Lloyd Llewellyn-Jones explained the reasons for these nomads heading south into Iran:

> *Climate change, overpopulation, and a lack of resources in ancestral homelands, combined with the military ambitions of warlords and kings, created a perfect storm for discontent and forced people to migrate.*[588]

Biblical appropriation of regional names

The name Elam came from the Mesopotamian Sumerians and Akkadians. It referred to the Zagros Mountain high country and the Iranian Plateau and not the specific nomadic tribes that inhabited those regions. Elam as an identifiable cultural group did not emerge until around 2500 BCE. As historian and Middle Eastern archaeologist Daniel Potts explains, up until then, the tribes in the Iranian highlands and plateau were a heterogeneity of native peoples. They were a:

> *… disparate collection of ethnically and linguistically diverse groups, [who] never identified themselves using the rubrics Elam or Elamites. That was a name given to the uplands east of Mesopotamia by Sumerian scribes who were simply referring to it, in a logical way, as 'highland'.*[589]

In writing the Bible, the Hebrew scribes claimed that the Elamites were descended from Elam, who they say was a son of Shem and a grandson of Noah. The Bible also claims that the Medes are descendants of Madai, who they claim was Noah's grandson. These are examples of biblical poetic licence. The Hebrew scribes often claimed that specific cultures, their people, and their geographic location were the progeny of a biblical character. This was particularly the case with biblical references to the descendants of Noah and

---

[587] Cunliffe (2017), p. 172.
[588] Llewellyn-Jones (2022), p. 35.
[589] Potts (2004), pp. 1-5.

Abraham, whose progeny were claimed to have fathered many of the cultures, towns, and communities that surrounded the emerging Israelites.

This could be done because the Hebrew scribes had used the Noah flood story to obliterate history. This created a situation for the Hebrew scribes to claim that Noah and his family were the only human survivors on Earth. The Hebrew scribes then developed a reconstruction of regional cultures and town names by claiming that these were all established, post-flood, by progeny (sons and grandsons) of Noah. Biblical advocates go to great lengths to demonstrate how most of the world's cultures and nations are descendants of Noah.[590] These claims are not supported by most scholars, or by historical or archaeological evidence. By the time of the emergence of the Israelites, the Elamites, Persians, and the Medes were known cultural groups. Whilst they were contemporaneous with the emerging Israelites, they were not related to, or the progeny of, biblical characters.

---

[590]   See, for example: https://creation.com/the-sixteen-grandsons-of-noah retrieved on 4 April 2023.

Chapter 12

The Significant Historical Role of Mesopotamia and the Fertile Crescent

The historic importance of Mesopotamia

Mesopotamia had enormous geomorphological opportunities linked to the regional mountain ranges, the rivers, and the flood plains. The word Mesopotamia comes from ancient Greek meaning 'between the rivers'. Mesopotamia is encircled by mountains on three of its sides: the Amanus and the Lebanon mountains to the north-west (running along the eastern shore of the Mediterranean), the Caucuses to the north (running between the Black Sea and the Caspian Sea), the northern Taurus/Masius mountains, from which the Tigris and Euphrates rivers originate, and the long chain of the Zagros Mountain range to the east—separating Mesopotamia from the Iranian plateau. This fertile land nestling at the base of an arc of mountain ranges, from which run two magnificent river systems, is the result of the great folded mountain belts caused by collisions over time between the African, Arabian, and Eurasian tectonic plates (Figure 5, page 50, and Figure 28, page 224).

Over thousands of years, the conquering and control of the Middle East region waxed and waned between different empires, creating significant political and cultural dependencies. Social, economic, political, linguistic, genomic, and mythological relationships were shared around the Middle Eastern region. There was a common Semitic language; the region was occupied in all or in part by several major empires and had a closely linked genetic history. Mesopotamia was part of this process, and it changed political and cultural hands many times. The empires that had the largest influence tended to be those under which the emerging Israelites were tributary vassal states. These were empires and locations under which the Hebrews were a vassal state, where they had gone voluntarily, or to which they had been exiled following their defeat in conquests between 1200 BCE and 1 CE.

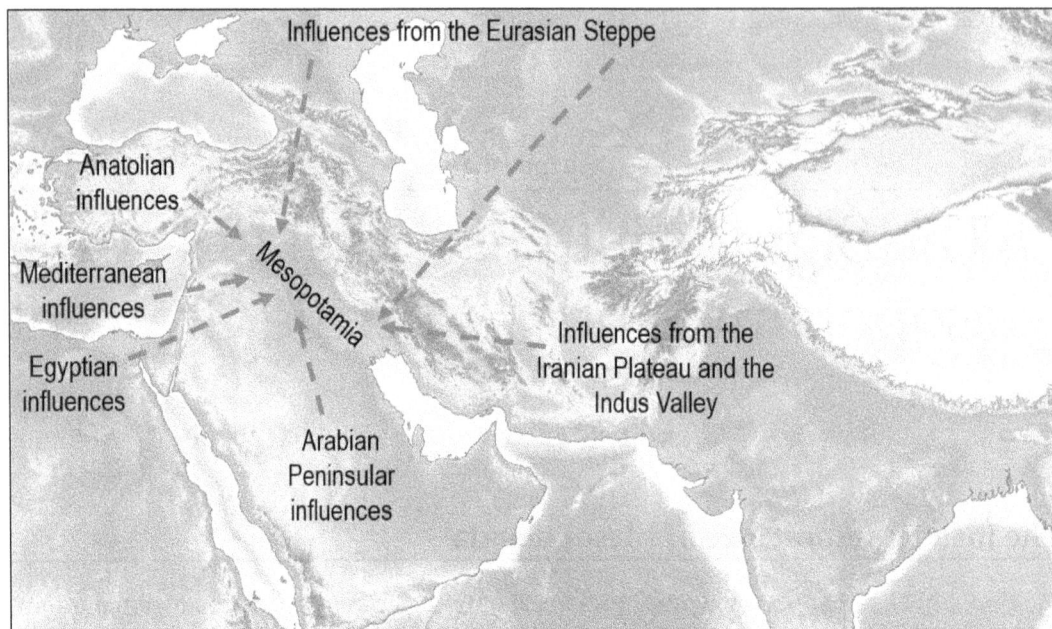

Figure 28: *Mesopotamia nestled in a tectonically created fertile and geographically central location*[a]

---

[a] SOURCE: base map by Joe Roe - Own workDataTopography/bathymetry: Amante, C.; Eakins, B. W. (2009) ETOPO1 1 Arc-Minute Global Relief Model, National Geophysical Data Center (NOAA), DOI:10.7289/V5C8276MCoastline: Natural Earth Data, CC BY-SA 4.0, https://commons.wikimedia.org/w/index.php?curid=57032013 retrieved on 9 August 2023.

Initially, the regional term Mesopotamia designated the land east of the Euphrates in north Syria. Later, the term Mesopotamia was more generally applied to all the lands between the Euphrates and the Tigris, thereby incorporating not only parts of Syria but also almost all of Iraq and south-eastern Türkiye. The neighbouring steppes to the west of the Euphrates and the western part of the Zagros Mountains are also often included under the wider term Mesopotamia. The term 'Mesopotamians' can refer to any or several civilisations that inhabited this geographic region over time. It was home to some of the most ancient states with highly developed social complexity, including six major cultural entities: the Sumerians, Akkadians, Babylonians, Assyrians, Egyptians, and Persians.

Jaan Puhvel has explained the difficulty in studying the Ancient Middle East, Mesopotamia, the Fertile Crescent, and the Levant in the following way:

The Ancient Near East at large was not one civilisation but many, more or less contiguous by geography and stretched out along a time span of several millennia. We must pick and choose among Sumerians, East Semites (Akkadians = Babylonians + Assyrians), Hurrians, and Proto-Indians in Mesopotamia, West Semites in the areas of Syria, Lebanon, and Palestine (from Ebla in the third millennium to Ugarit in the second, to Phoenicians, Canaanites, and Hebrews in the first), Indo-European speaking Hittites and Luwians in Anatolia (= Asia Minor), and likewise Indo-European Iranians in the whole vast territory between Asia Minor, Mesopotamia and India.[591]

There is some limited evidence of Stone Age humans being in Mesopotamia. By 14000 BCE, the Mesopotamian peoples were living in small settlements with circular houses. Five thousand years later, these houses formed farming communities following the domestication of animals and the development of agriculture, most notably irrigation techniques that took advantage of the proximity of the Tigris and Euphrates rivers.

Political, social, and cultural change across Mesopotamia

Mesopotamia, including the Fertile Crescent, is regarded as the 'cradle of civilisation'. So many modern-day innovations emerged initially here and, specifically, within the Sumerian culture. It is a region that has changed hands multiple times due to migration but also to warfare, invasion, and conquest. The sequence of the multiple changing of hands, different empires, and turnover of control and innovations in the region from around 5000 BCE to the time of the Hebrew scribes include:[592]

- c. 5000 BCE to 3500 BCE—the first city-states gradually develop in Southern Mesopotamia. This was entirely an achievement of the migration to the region of the Sumerian people.
- sometime between 4500 BCE and 4000 BCE, the Sumerians had settled in the region to the south on the flood plains of the two rivers.
- the Sumerians established the first known city-states, each of which was centred on a temple and each of which paid tribute to a patron god or goddess. The practice of locating the primary temple or church on a high point in the centre of each town began here with the Sumerians and is continued in religious practices today.
- c. 3500 BCE—a rudimentary form of writing is developed by the Sumerians. At first, this is based on pictograms, but over about a thousand years it evolves into a script based on wedge-shaped marks in clay (called cuneiform).

---

[591]   Puhvel (1989), p. 22.
[592]   Dates shown are approximate, some have minor disputes between archaeologists. The dates shown are presented here for the purposes of sequential chronology illustration only.

- c. 2300 BCE—the Akkadian King Sargon, moving north from the Arabian Peninsula (between Egypt and Mesopotamia), conquers and controls the region and establishes what is regarded as the first empire in history.
- the Sumerians and the Akkadians unite under one ruler and cooperate including adopting both the Sumerian and the Akkadian languages.
- c. 2100 BCE—the Sumerian city of Ur becomes the centre of Sumerian control of the Southern Mesopotamian region.
- under Akkadian and Sumerian control, the Mesopotamian region waxes and wanes between being a unified empire and a loosely connected group of city-states under different rulers with varying amounts of centralised control.
- c. 2000 BCE—with the collapse of the Sumerian rule in the city of Ur, the Assyrians take control of a large part of northern Mesopotamia.
- c. 2000 BCE—the Amorites, an indigenous people from northern and central inland Syria, conquer the Sumerians in Southern Mesopotamia and establish Babylon as their major city.
- c. 1894 BCE to 1595 BCE—Babylonia is established as an independent Amorite State.
- c. 1750 BCE—the Babylonian empire is ruled by the Amorite King Hammurabi. Hammurabi is historically renowned for developing the Hammurabi Law Code, which becomes a major influence on the Hebrew scribes' development of the Ten Commandments.
- the Anatolian Hittites (including Hatti and Hurrians) ransack Babylon in around 1595 BCE, destroying Amorite control, but the Hittites do not continue a long-term occupation of the city (Figure 29).
- c. 1530 BCE—the Kassites, a tribal group from the Zagros Mountains north-east of Babylon, take control of the region for around 400 years.
- the Babylonian scholars of the Kassite period include scribes who are writing literary texts. One of these Kassite texts, *Let me praise the Lord of Wisdom,* is a profound philosophical poem that was to influence the biblical story of Job.[593]
- c. 1500 BCE—the Mitanni, an Indo-European people from northern Syria, conquer northern Mesopotamia.

---

[593] Kuhrt (2009A), p. 347.

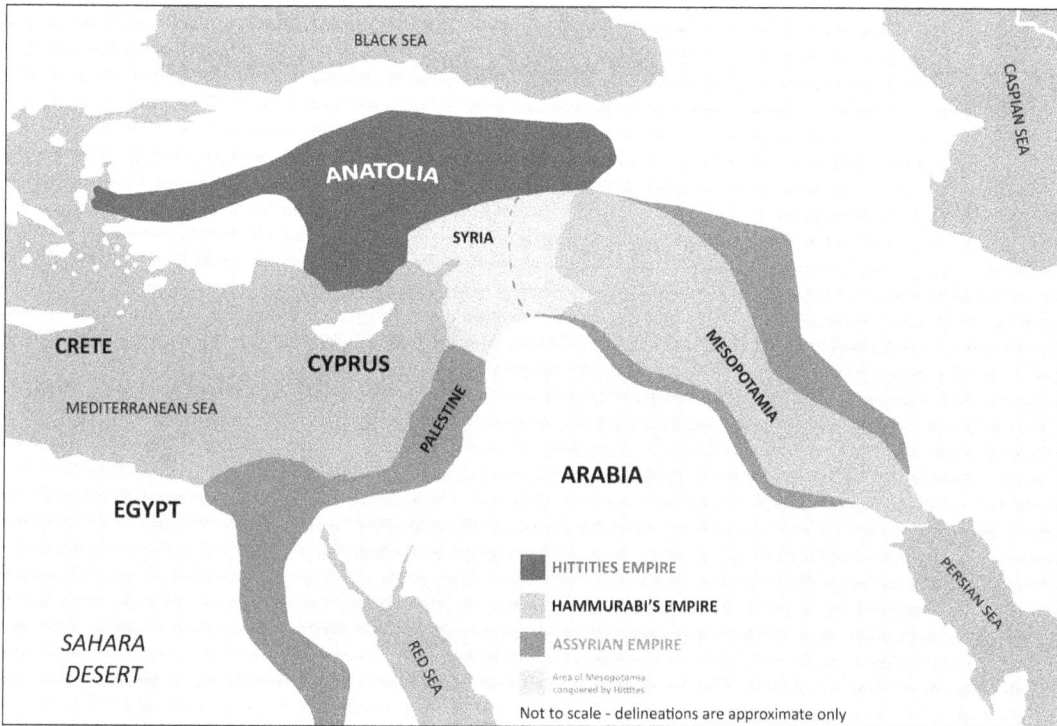

Figure 29: *Mesopotamian Empires, 1800-600 BCE* [b]

---

[b] SOURCE: https://slideplayer.com/slide/10589977/36/images/3/Mesopotamian+Empires%2C
+BCE.jpg, slide 10, retrieved on 9 August 2023.

- c. 1350 BCE—the Hittites attack the Mitanni, killing their King Tushratta. This creates an opportunity for the Assyrians who annex northern Mesopotamia from the Mitanni.

- The Kingdom of Assyria rules northern Mesopotamia from around 1350 BCE to 600 BCE.

- c. 1205 BCE—the first mention of a group referred to as Israelites is written in the Egyptian Pharaoh Merneptah Stele.

- c. 1200 BCE to 1150 BCE—the Bronze Age *'collapse'* occurs. This is when the East Mediterranean and the Aegean experience earthquakes that decimate Canaanite towns, there is famine and drought across the region, social and economic collapse and the Middle East is invaded by the Sea Peoples.

- c. 1100 BCE—nomadic peoples such as the Aramaeans and the Chaldeans overrun much of Mesopotamia.

- c. 900 BCE to 600 BCE—the Assyrian Empire controls the Fertile Crescent, Mesopotamia, and parts of Egypt. Donald Redford describes the Assyrians at this time as 'the scourge of the ancient world', controlling an empire that stretched from North-East Africa to the Caucasus and from the Mediterranean to the mountains of Iran.[594]
- c. 612 BCE—the Babylonians defeat the Assyrians and take control of parts of Egypt, the Levant, the Fertile Crescent, and Mesopotamia.
- c. 539 BCE—the Persian Achaemenid Empire defeats the Babylonians and takes control of large tracts of land from Libya through Egypt, the Levant, Anatolia, the Black Sea, parts of the east coast of Greece, all of Mesopotamia, the Iranian Plateau, north-western India and parts of northern Afghanistan.

Mesopotamian influence on the Bible

Over hundreds of years, the Hebrew scribes who wrote the HB/OT were in Canaan and were deported/exiled to or visited various other cities across the Middle East and Egypt.[595] In these activities, they were under the control of several different kingdoms and empires. Judaism got its embryonic start in the hills of Canaan from around 1200 BCE. Christianity developed from Judaism several hundred years later.

Mesopotamia is referred to in the Bible as the land of Shinar (Sumer). Mesopotamian mythology was influential across the whole of the Middle Eastern region. Much of the HB/OT was an adaptation of the mythological stories from the Mesopotamians, Canaanites, and Egyptians at the time. As Charles Penglase has pointed out, there was a great infusion of Mesopotamian mythology throughout the early archaic period, to the point that even the relatively geographically more distant culture of the Greeks derived its mythology from, or at the very least owes a great debt to, the Mesopotamians.[596]

Biblical authority Eric Cline has described Mesopotamia's influence on the Hebrew Bible in this way:

---

[594] Redford (1992), p. 338.
[595] Genomic research shows that ancient Egyptians were closest genetically related to ancient populations in the Levant. SEE: https://www.mpg.de/11317890/genome-ancient-egyptian-mummies retrieved on 25 March 2021.
[596] Penglase (1994), pp. 242-243.

Surprising as it may seem to some, it is Mesopotamia that had a tremendous impact on later biblical Israel—for this area, during the course of more than 9,000 years, from 10,000 BCE to 1500 BCE, gave rise to inventions, techniques, ideas, stories, and even laws that were still in use centuries later in Israel and Judah.[597]

Mesopotamia prior to the arrival of the Sumerians

There is sufficient archaeological evidence to establish the existence of several Neolithic cultures in Mesopotamia prior to the arrival of the Sumerians. The neolithic Hassuna culture (6000 BCE to 5300 BCE), the Samarra culture (6200 BCE to 5700 BCE), and the Halaf culture (6000 BCE to 5400 BCE) all predate the Sumerians in the Mesopotamian region. These Neolithic cultures lived in villages of mud-brick houses with provision for the penning of animals and storage bins for food. Prior to farmers settling in the alluvial plains in Southern Iraq (Mesopotamia), the flood plains of Southern Mesopotamia had been a major food source for the indigenous hunter-gatherers seeking gazelle, turtles, birds and fish.[598]

The Halaf culture (6000 BCE to 5400 BCE) is recognised as one of the first to show evidence of an increasing size and complexity of settlements and an apparent hierarchical organisational structure. It survived for one thousand years and had a wide geographic spread. In Eastern Anatolia and Northern Mesopotamia, their cultural achievements included the emergence of status objects, stamp seals, statue-like figurines, more intensive use of metals, elaborately decorated pottery vessels, and complex non-utilitarian technologies such as obsidian objects as a reflection of socio-economic status.[599]

The significant impact of the Sumerians

The Sumerians are believed to have come into the Fertile Crescent, and specifically, Southern Mesopotamia, in or around 4500 BCE to 4000 BCE.[600] They have conventionally been recognised as the foundation culture from which emerged the cradle of civilisation in Mesopotamia and the Fertile Crescent. A wide range of innovations are attributed to the Sumerians. Between 3500 BCE and 2000 BCE, they invented writing, established the first cities, and developed the first codes of law. They most likely came originally from

---

[597] Cline (2007), p. 6.
[598] Foster and Foster (2009), pp. 10-13.
[599] Ozdogan (2014), pp. 1520-1521.
[600] SOURCE: https://www.history.com/topics/ancient-middle-east/sumer.

somewhere in the eastern Eurasian Steppe. Opinions vary on their origins—although their origin from somewhere along the Eurasian Steppe does not seem to be in doubt.

Henry Rawlinson (1810-1895), who had spent many years deciphering cuneiform script and researching ancient Mesopotamia, believed that the founders of the civilisation were of Kushite (Cushite) origin (an ancient kingdom in Nubia, located in the Sudanese and Southern Egyptian Nile Valley). Rawlinson claimed that the Semitic speakers of Akkad and the non-Semitic speakers of Sumer were both black people who called themselves *sag-gig-ga*, or 'black heads.' In addition, John Baldwin wrote in his book *PreHistoric Nations* (1869), 'The early colonists of Babylonia were of the same race as the inhabitants of the Upper Nile.' This was corroborated by other scholars, including Chandra Chakaberty, who asserted in his book *A Study in Hindu Social Polity* that, based on the statuaries and steles of Babylonia, the Sumerians were:

> … *of dark complexion (chocolate colour), short stature, but of sturdy frame, oval face, stout nose, straight hair, full head; they typically resembled the Dravidians (from the Indian subcontinent), not only in cranium, but almost in all the details.*[601]

However, modern scholars now believe that it is more likely that the Sumerians either migrated south from the Eastern Eurasian Steppe—perhaps from prehistoric Siberia via the Central Asian Mountain Corridor, migrating into Mesopotamia through the Iranian Plateau east of the Caspian Sea—or from the Western Steppe (contemporary Ukraine), most likely through the Caspian littoral plain east of the Caucuses between the Black and Caspian Seas ('the Caspian corridor').[602, 603, 604]

The earliest Sumerian cities

The earliest Sumerian population was known as the Ubaid people, who are recognised as the first developers of civilisation through farming and raising cattle, social differentiation, weaving textiles, working with carpentry and pottery, and brewing beer. The dominant Ubaid culture of the time had absorbed the Halaf culture that had come before it.[605]

---

[601] Baldwin, J (1869), p. 192; Chakaberty, C. (1987), p. 33; Windsor, R.R. (1988). Cited in https://atlantablackstar.com/2014/04/16/5-ancient-black-civilizations-africa/5/.

[602] Kurtkaya (2020).

[603] Kohl (2008), p. 65.

[604] Shilov (2015).

[605] SOURCE: https://www.history.com/topics/ancient-middle-east/mesopotamia#:~:text=The%20word%20E2%80%9Cmesopotamia%E2%80%9D%20is%20formed,Map%20of%20Mesopotamia.

Sumerian villages and towns were built around Ubaid farming communities. The Sumerians were in total control of South Mesopotamia by 3000 BCE, living in city-states, which included Eridu, Nippur, Lagash, Kish, Ur, and the very first true city, Uruk. At its peak around 2800 BCE, the city of Uruk had a population between 40,000 and 80,000 people living within its six miles of defensive walls, making it a contender for the largest prehistoric city in the world. The Uruk period in Southern Mesopotamia was a period of rapid urban growth, particularly in the regions of southern and central Babylonia. The changes in the Uruk period were of such magnitude that Marc Van de Mieroop refers to this period as 'the urban revolution' on a par in importance with the nineteenth-century CE Industrial Revolution.[606] Each city-state of Sumer was surrounded by a wall, with villages settled just outside these walls and each distinguished by the worship of local deities.[607]

Sauer has described the Uruk period in Mesopotamia (3800 BCE to 3000 BCE) as being a complex network of intricate, extensive urban settlements and communications networks extending beyond Mesopotamia to include easterly-adjacent Susiana (home of the Elam and Achaemenid Empires); the Syrian Plain, south-east Anatolia, and the Iranian Plateau. The influence of these highly interactive and interconnected pathways facilitated the mediation and appropriation of innovation and knowledge involving:

> … not only the dissemination of material culture and technical and economic improvements but also the transmission of knowledge and cultural practices creating an extensively cross-linked transregional cultural landscape.[608]

Sumerian innovations

Three thousand years before the emergence of the Israelites, Mesopotamia under the Sumerians successfully consolidated many of the innovations around them into a series of vast city-states containing the first complex cities, new institutions, large fields of cereals, significant water management, and large herds of sheep. The Mesopotamian Sumerians were not necessarily the first innovators. They drew their ideas from many different places. There is an increasingly large and growing range of evidence that the Sumerians and, thereafter, the Hebrew scribes, absorbed innovations and ideas that had first emerged in

---

[606] Van de Mieroop (2007), pp. 19-20.
[607] SOURCE: https://www.history.com/topics/ancient-middle-east/sumer.
[608] Sauer (2017), p. 12.

the Eurasian Steppe, Canaan, the Middle East, Persia, and Egypt. For instance, historian and archaeologist Jean Manco has shown how:

… pottery appeared in the Far East long before it was made in the Near East. Agriculture began along the great curve of the Taurus and Zagros mountains. Metalworking too began in the hills that provided the ore. Horses were domesticated on the Steppe and donkeys in North Africa. Wheeled vehicles were probably first made in the forest-steppe zone. Wine was first produced on the southern slopes of the Caucuses, where grapes grew wild. Dairy farming first appeared around the sea of Marmara (between the Aegean and Black Seas in Türkiye). Wool sheep may have been first bred in the Caucuses, where the earliest surviving woollen textile has been discovered, dating from the 4th millennium BCE.[609]

Nevertheless, virtually every area of human knowledge was significantly advanced by the peoples of Mesopotamia and the Fertile Crescent during the Bronze Age, well prior to the emergence of the Israelites This included:

- Philosophy
- Ethics
- Democracy
- Science and technology
- Writing and literature
- Poetry
- Religion
- The first schools
- Agricultural techniques
- Horticulture
- Irrigation
- Urbanisation
- Mathematics and Astronomy
- Astrology and the development of the zodiac
- Domestication of animals
- Long-distance trade
- Social reform
- Law codes/ Justice

---

[609] Manco (2015), p. 109.

- The world's first cuisine and associated feasts
- Medical practices (including dentistry)
- Personal hygiene
- The pottery wheel
- The wheel
- The concept of time.[610, 611, 612]

The impact of Sumerian religion

Most Sumerians worked in agriculture, but a growing segment of urban society started to specialise in other activities such as pottery, weaving, metal smelting, cylinder seal production, scribal writing, sculpting, and monumental art. These specialisations required some form of centralised authority, specialised administration, and a shared ideological framework.[613]

In Uruk-period Mesopotamia, that ideology was provided by religion; goods were received by the god of the city and redistributed to the people. The temple, the house of the god, was the central institution that made the system work. Continuing a trend that had started in the early Ubaid period, temples in the Late Uruk period became the most monumental buildings in the settlements, constructed at great expense of labour as physical indicators of their prominent role within society.

Here was the emergence of the city-based cult concept united around a centralised temple. Uruk became the centre of collective cult practices, including the development of symbols and offerings to the fertility goddess Inanna. This was the beginning of the religious practice common today of locating monumental places of worship in centralised locations and ensuring they fulfil a major role in social control, religious symbolism, and religious practices.

The Sumerian religion was so influential that it survived in slightly modified forms for more than three thousand years. It was subsequently adopted with only minor modifications by the many cultures that followed the Sumerians in Mesopotamia, including the Amorites, Kassites, Assyrians, Babylonians, and Chaldeans. Indeed, key Sumerian concepts remain in the preaching of many modern-day contemporary religions. In particular,

---

610 SOURCE: https://member.ancient.eu/Fertile_Crescent/.
611 Kramer (1956).
612 Bottero (2001), pp. 43-83.
613 Van de Mieroop (2007), pp. 23-27.

the Sumerians were the first to conceive of the gods as anthropomorphic, living in a divine society but one that was largely a replica of the human society and organised in a similar manner:

> *The heavens, the earth and the netherworld were populated with gods......These gods ... had the appearances, qualities, defects and passions of human beings, but they were endowed with fabulous strength, Supernatural powers and immortality. Moreover, they manifested themselves in a halo of dazzling light, a 'splendour' which filled man with fear and respect and gave him the indescribable feeling of contact with the divine, which is the essence of all religions.[614]*

The Sumerians are renowned for being one of the first to develop the earliest forms of writing (cuneiform) along with the Egyptians (hieroglyphics). There are numerous archaeological examples of Sumerian texts. The oldest known example of literature in the world is the Sumerian Kesh Temple Hymn (from around 2600 BCE). It is a Sumerian song of praise to the goddess Ninhursag (mother goddess of the sacred mountain) and to her temple in the city of Kesh. It is accepted by most scholars that the Sumerian Kesh Temple Hymn 'influenced various passages and books of the Bible through imagery and symbolism as well as its form of praise, especially the Book of Genesis'.[615]

The emergence of a personal religion

The Sumerian city-states reflected a shift in the focus of religious belief. Centralised religion was one of the tools of management required in the transition from loosely-based tribal and kinship groups to multi-layered and more complex societies. The transition involved a growing emphasis on personal religion including concepts of sin and forgiveness, myths, magic, epic stories, hymns, laments, prayers, psalms, rituals, omen texts, and incantations.[616] Religious beliefs and practices became more structured and personal.

Danish authority on Sumerian literature Thorkild Jacobsen believes that the notion of a 'personal religion' emerged in Mesopotamia in the second millennium BCE, in Hittite communities in around 1350 BCE, and in Egypt in around 1230 BCE.

---

[614] Roux (1992), p. 87.
[615] Mark (2023B).
[616] See: https://www.britannica.com/topic/Mesopotamian-religion/Stages-of-religious-development retrieved on 15 November 2022.

Jacobsen defines the emerging personal religion that started with the city-states and centralised, structured religion in Sumer as:

> *A particular, easily recognised, religious attitude in which the religious individual sees himself as standing in close personal relationship to the divine, expecting help and guidance in his personal life and personal affairs, expecting divine anger and punishment if he sins, but also profoundly trusting to divine compassion, forgiveness, and love for him if he sincerely repents. In sum: the individual matters to God, God cares about him personally and deeply.*

Jacobsen further believes that Israel has adopted and significantly and decisively extended the Sumerian concept of a personal religion into the national realm.[617]

The relationship of Yahweh to Israel—his anger, his compassion, his forgiveness, and his renewed anger and punishment of the sinful people—is, in all essentials, the same as that of the relation between God and the individual in the attitude of personal religion. With this understanding of national life and fortunes as lived under ultimate moral responsibility, Israel created a concept of history as purposive—one that in basic essentials still governs conceptions of meaningful historical existence.

The Sumerian influence on the biblical Psalms of praise and lament

The oldest available Sumerian religious literature, of which the Kesh Temple Hymn is an example (see middle paragraph 234), relates to songs of praise and lament. In the words of Jacobsen:

> *The literature of praise includes hymns to gods, temples, or deified human rulers, as well as myths, epics, and disputations. … The literature of lament, on the other hand, was directed to powers lost, difficult or impossible to regain.*[618]

Two thousand years later, the Hebrew scribes continued this tradition in their compilation of many of the biblical Psalms. Whilst the content varies because the Hebrew scribes were essentially dealing with one god and the Sumerians were dealing with several deities, the underlying principles remain. The HB/OT contains eleven Psalms of praise—namely Psalms 18, 21, 30, 32, 34, 40, 41, 66, 106, 116, and 138. The HB/OT contains eight Psalms of communal lament—namely Psalms 44, 60, 74, 79, 80, 85, 86, and 90.

---

[617]   Jacobsen (1976), pp. 147-164.
[618]   Jacobsen (1976), p. 15.

The overall impact of Sumerian religion on the Hebrew Bible

The Sumerians were so influential across the Middle East that Samuel Kramer believes that the impact of Sumerian cultural and spiritual beliefs on the Akkadian, Assyrians, Babylonians, Hittites, Hurrians, Canaanites, Hebrews, and Greeks cannot be overestimated.[619] Kramer has itemised fifteen examples where the Hebrew scribes were obviously influenced by Sumerian mythology. These are the biblical stories about:

1. The creation of the universe
2. The creation of man
3. The creation techniques used
4. The concept of paradise
5. The flood
6. The Cain and Abel story
7. The Tower of Babel and the Dispersion of Mankind
8. The Earth and its Organisation
9. The personal God
10. Law
11. Ethics and Morals
12. Divine Retribution and National Catastrophes
13. The notion of plagues from God
14. Human Suffering and Submission
15. Death and the Nether World.[620]

The role of the Akkadians

The Akkadians were a Semitic people from the Arabian Peninsula who, under population pressure, moved north to conquer the Sumerians (2350 BCE to 2150 BCE). The Akkadian Empire is regarded as the first empire. The Akkadians were the first to claim to be ruled by a god-king and the first to establish a professional military force.[621] The Akkadian Empire united Assyria, Babylonia, and the Sumerians under one ruler. It was able to maintain influence over trade routes and communities in Anatolia and the Levant in the

---

[619] Kramer (1963), p. 166.
[620] Kramer (1971), pp. 292-296.
[621] Matyszak (2020), p. 19.

west, the Arabian Peninsula and the Persian Gulf to the south, and east to Mesopotamia by sending out military expeditions.[622]

The Akkadian leader was Sargon the Great, who established his base in the city of Akkad (also known as Agade) on the western shores of the Euphrates River. Sargon united the various Mesopotamian city-states under his rule as a large territorial kingdom with a massive shift from agricultural villages to urban centres. He abandoned the ancient regime of city-states, destroyed the walls around each of the cities, built a standing army, and conquered and commanded loyalty from the local kings or replaced them with a governor who supported Sargon.[623] For around two hundred years, the empire continued to expand.

Although they generally worked well together, Assyriologist Gwendolyn Leick described the differences between the Sumerians and the Akkadians in the following way:

Much has been made in the past of the alleged differences between Sumerians and Semitic Akkadians, contrasting the free-spirited if cruel Semites with the bureaucratic and parochial Sumerians, the former producing leaders that were typical empire builders like Sargon while the stereotypical Sumerian ruler was a bald and 'spiritual' priest-king.[624]

The Akkadian Empire, under the control of Sargon's grandson, Naram-Sin ('beloved of the moon god'), eventually fell to a combination of an invasion by outsiders (primarily the Gutian vassal state from the Zagros Mountains to the north-east), the windy, winter dust storms (*shamals*), lack of rainfall, and prolonged cold winter seasons, which impacted on agriculture and lifestyle. By 2300 BCE, the climatic conditions, and residual mineral salts in the soil from the evaporated irrigation and related agricultural practices had left the soil in Mesopotamia no longer able to produce crops.[625] Agricultural production significantly decreased and, together, these conditions led to famine. These were the combined causes of the collapse of the Akkadian Empire in 2154 BCE.[626]

After the Akkadian Empire fell, there was a brief period of control (around two hundred years) by the Gutian Dynasty of Sumer, about whom there is very little surviving information.[627] Eventually, two kingdoms were formed: Assyria, which was in the north,

---

[622] Mark (2011A).
[623] Holland (2010), pp. 100-101.
[624] Leick (2002), p. 98.
[625] SOURCE: http://www.palmbeach.k12.fl.us/eagleslandingms/MesopotamiaAgriculture.pdf
[626] SOURCE: https://www.sciencedaily.com/releases/2019/10/191024093606.htm.
[627] Captivating History (2022), pp. 101-102.

and Babylonia, which was in the south.[628] The tribal areas that formed the Assyrian home-land are parts of present-day northern Iraq (Nineveh Plains and Dohuk Governorate), South-Eastern Türkiye (Hakkari and Tur Abdin), north-western Iran (Urmia) and, more recently, north-eastern Syria (Al-Hasakah Governorate).[629]

Impact of the Akkadians on contemporary religion

The Akkadians largely continued the Sumerian religious beliefs. However, Sargon did not continue the Sumerian association of a specific god with each city. He elected to establish a new capital city, Akkad (Agade), which was not created by a god but by the emperor himself. Sargon was religious in the sense that he saw himself as divinely inspired. He strengthened the widely held Sumerian belief in priest- or god-kings. He believed, along with most Sumerians and Akkadians, that the success of major empires and the defeat of smaller vassal states was linked to the leader's special relationship with an appropriate god or goddess.[630]

Philip Matyszak explains the underlying foundation of Akkadian religion in this way:

The Akkadians had an interest in omens and a fear of witchcraft and demons. Akkadian sculpture was used for propaganda purposes, showing the Akkadian king conquering his enemies or consorting with the gods.[631]

The belief in demons, witchcraft, and omens and the power of sculptured figurines was a powerful and influential idea across Mesopotamia at the time. It resulted in a belief in incantations to repel evil and a belief that statues were a true presence of a person or a god.[632] Both concepts continue in contemporary religions—modern-day prayers are often incantations to remove a perceived evil, and religious statues, medals, or pictures are often regarded as being the actual presence of a god or a saint rather than just a symbol or representation of them.

Sargon's goddess protector was Ishtar, the goddess of war, love, procreation, lust, and fertility. During his lifetime, and for centuries later, Sargon was regarded as a semi-sacred legendary figure. Multiple epic mytho-historical stories were written about his victories

---

[628] SOURCE: http://www.differencebetween.net/miscellaneous/politics/difference-between-syria-and-assyria/.

[629] Skutsch (2013), p. 149, cited in https://en.wikipedia.org/wiki/Assyrian_people#cite_note-Skutsch 2013-45.

[630] Matyszak (2020), p. 20.

[631] Matyszak (2020), p. 22.

[632] Bottero (2004), p. 116 and pp. 192-194.

over enemies with divine assistance.[633] This special link between a leader and their god is the foundation for the belief in the Catholic Church of the divine power and relationship with their God of their elected popes. It is also a fundamental idea in the famous Bob Dylan song, *With God on Our Side*.

However, the most frequently cited link of Sargon to Judaism relates to Sargon's birth myth. Written hundreds of years before the emergence of the Israelites, Sargon's birth myth was a major inspiration and source for Moses' birth story in the Hebrew Bible.

The Rise and Fall of Mesopotamian Empires

George Roux has explained how the rise and fall of the Akkadian Empire set the scene for a pattern that occurred across Mesopotamia for thousands of years:

> *Rapid expansion followed by ceaseless rebellions, palace revolutions, constant wars on the frontiers, and in the end, the 'coup de grâce' by the highlanders: Gutians now, Elamites, Kassites, Medes or Persians tomorrow. A civilisation based on agriculture and metal work in a country like Iraq required, to be viable, two conditions: perfect cooperation between the various ethnic and socio-political units within the country itself, and a friendly or at least neutral attitude from its neighbours. Unfortunately, neither one nor the other lasted for any length of time.[634]*

The Assyrians, the Amorites, and the Babylonians

The Assyrians were Semitic people who lived in what is now modern Syria and present-day Iraq before the Arabs came to live in Assyria. The ancient Assyrian civilisation existed between 2300 BCE and 608 BCE; it was in Northern Mesopotamia (now modern Iraq) on the Tigris River and came into existence after the fall of the Akkadian kingdom. From around 2000 BCE, with the collapse of the Sumerian rule from the city of Ur, the Assyrians took control of a large part of northern Mesopotamia.

British archaeologist Barry Cunliffe described the Assyrians in the following way:

> *The Assyrian Empire was quite different from anything that had gone before. It was a single militaristic state that maintained itself by feeding off the energy and the spoils of constant expansionist warfare. After the mid-eight century conquered states were incorporated as*

---

[633] Pryke (2017), pp. 134-135.
[634] Roux (1992), p. 159.

provinces ruled through a centralised bureaucracy. What drove the relentless expansion is dif-
ficult to say, but the social structure, which expected the king to be a successful military leader,
had a significant part to play. So, too, did religious ideology. The kings believed they were
required by the god Ashur to expand the domain, though this may have been justification
rather than a driving force.[635]

Specialist in ancient Middle Eastern history, Amelie Kuhrt, asserts that any attempt to reconstruct events in the ancient Middle East during the period from around 900 BCE to 610 BCE (a period when the Hebrew scribes were most active) must take account of Assyrian political dominance and must also rely 'to a significant extent' on Assyrian evidence.[636]

The Assyrian dynasty originated around 1900 BCE in the city of Ashur, which was located on a plateau above the Tigris River in northern Mesopotamia. The city lay on a trade route connecting Mesopotamia with the Levant and Anatolia. The city's name reflects the Sumerian practice of each city having a specific god to worship. In this case, the god Ashur was represented as a winged sun disc and was worshipped as a national and supreme god by Sumerians, Akkadians, and Assyrians. The principal shrine/temple to the god Ashur was called Esarra (Temple of the Universe) and was placed on the highest northernmost point of the city's escarpment overlooking the Tigris River.[637]

From around 2000 BCE, the Assyrians frequently battled with the Amorites in northern Syria. The Amorites were a group of fierce nomadic Bedouin pastoralists who roamed the Syrian desert and parts of Syria and Canaan. They frequently grazed their flocks in the steppes of Mesopotamia.[638] Eventually, under pressure from the Assyrians, the Amorites settled permanently in many of the smaller kingdoms within Mesopotamia. The Amorites claimed the Mesopotamian city of Mari on the Euphrates as their capital.[639]

Babylon was a key Sumerian, Akkadian, and Assyrian city. The name originates from *bav-il* or *bav-ilim*, which in Akkadian meant 'gate of god' (or 'gate of the gods'). It was founded during the reign of Sargon of Akkad (2334-2279 BCE).[640]

The Amorites eventually conquered Sumer and parts of Assyria. The Mesopotamian era under the control of the Amorites from around 2000 BCE to 1600 BCE saw many

---

[635] Cunliffe (2017), pp. 161-162.
[636] Kuhrt (2009B), p. 473.
[637] SOURCE: Based on materials prepared by Eleanor Robson for the UK Arts and Humanities Research Council (AHRC)-funded Nimrud project.
[638] Roux (1992), pp. 175-176.
[639] Matyszak (2020), pp. 25-26.
[640] Mark (2022E).

significant changes. The sixth Amorite King was Hammurabi. Hammurabi reigned for forty-three years from 1792 BCE to 1750 BCE. He unified Mesopotamia and made the Assyrians a vassal state. Hammurabi introduced significant cultural change. He made Babylon a major city and introduced a code of law that influenced the Hebrew scribes' writing of the Ten Commandments. Hammurabi made major changes to art, language, literature, justice, and philosophy. Under Hammurabi's control, there were significant developments in astronomical measurements, technological developments, and mathematics.[641]

The religious influence of Hammurabi

It was during Hammurabi's reign that Sumerian scribes completed the stories of the Atrahasis (creation and flood myth), the Gilgamesh epic, and the Babylonian creation myth Enuma Elish (also known as the Seven Tablets of Creation). These three Babylonian documents were to have a significant influence on the Hebrew scribes developing the HB/OT.

During Hammurabi's time, the Sumerian system of temples, city-states, land, and kings, once the focus of various gods and kings, was replaced by a new societal structure featuring large farms, free citizens, and enterprising merchants.[642]

The people of the area continued to worship the Sumerian gods, and the older Sumerian myths and epic tales were piously copied, translated, or adapted. Mesopotamian religion continued its evolution from one characterised by many local deities to a regional pantheon of major and minor gods. By the time of Hammurabi, a major religious change was occurring. The storm-god Marduk came to assume the role of chief deity, and the story of his rise to supremacy was dramatically told in the epic myth known as the Enuma Elish.

The origin of penitential psalms

Hammurabi's reign was the time when there was a shift in emphasis from centralised city-based gods, temples, and cults to personal relationships with a god and the growth of wisdom literature:

> *As witnessed by innumerable clay figurines or votive plaques representing gods and demons and by moving prayers, 'letters to the gods' and street corner chapels. ... The Mesopotamians*

---

[641]   SOURCE: https://member.ancient.eu/Fertile_Crescent/ retrieved on 15 March 2023.

[642]   SOURCE: https://www.newworldencyclopedia.org/entry/Amorites retrieved on 15 March 2023.

began to wonder, to doubt and to ponder the great mysteries of Life and Death or Good versus Evil.[643]

Personal prayer and an expression of the relationship with the gods had been emerging in Mesopotamia, Assyria, and Babylonia for some time. Under Hammurabi, the individual's relationship with a god was expressed in what are now referred to as penitential psalms. The Bible is full of them, but this is where they began. Penitential psalms are expressions of regret or sorrow for sins. Edwin Oliver James, a specialist in the history and philosophy of religion, describes them as expressing sorrow for sins through an intermingling of ethical concepts with ritual holiness. James cites an example of a prayer to the goddess Ishtar—'forgive my sins, my iniquity, my shameful deeds, and my offence: overlook my transgressions, accept my prayer'.[644] A typical example of a penitential psalm from the Bible is Psalm 142:1: 'Lord, hear my prayer, listen to my cry for mercy; in your faithfulness and righteousness come to my relief.'

The Elamites, Hittites and Kassites

The Elamite city-state was in southwestern Iran close to Southern Mesopotamia. Like the Sumerians, the Elamites spoke a unique language unrelated to any other known language. The Elamites most probably came into southwestern Iran from the Eastern Eurasian Steppe in around 3300 BCE.

There is limited archaeological information available about the Elamites. From around 2700 BCE, they came into violent conflict with the Sumerians and were initially a vassal state under Sumerian control.[645] Like most of the Middle East at the time, fortunes waxed and waned between the different city-states and different cultural groups. They would trade and cooperate but also regularly conquer each other.

There was a great deal of trade and influence between Mesopotamia and Iran at this time. George Roux saw this region as being under a current of three major trade influencers—Akkadians, Sumerians, and Elamites.[646] The common trade was evidenced by the widespread popularity and trading of lapis lazuli, which came from the Hindu Kush mountains of Northern Afghanistan.[647]

---

[643] Roux (1992), p. 196.
[644] James (1999), pp. 267-268.
[645] Matyszak (2020), p. 37.
[646] Roux (1992), p. 185.
[647] Cunliffe (2017), p. 119.

The regional cross-cultural influence was also reflected in the widespread use of kaunakes/gaunaka as a popular piece of nomadic clothing. The kaunakes was a unisex wraparound cloak made of either sheep skin, sheep's wool, or goat's skin woven into a feather or leaf-like pattern. During the Uruk period in Sumer (4100-2900 BCE), men and women wore ornamented kaunakes as knee-length or ankle-length skirts accessorised with hats, headbands, and jewellery.[648] The kaunakes became popular regionally from around 2800 BCE and were commonly worn in Sumer, Mesopotamia, Elam, and Persia. It was commonly shown as the garb on female goddess statuettes.[649]

Despite these cultural similarities and the close trade links, there were regular military conflicts between the Elamites and the Southern Mesopotamian cities. Elam lay on the south-eastern boundary of Sumer, close to the Sumerian city-state of Lagash. Power and control of the Elamite and Southern Mesopotamian territories shifted backwards and forwards between 2600 BCE and 1308 BCE.[650]

The Elamites controlled resources arriving through the Persian Gulf and the trade in Iranian tin, which was in high demand as a major ingredient in the production of bronze.[651] From around 2270 BCE, this southern Iranian region is referred to as *Elamite Anshan* by the Akkadian King Manishtushu, who tells of re-subjugating Anshan after a local ruler there revolted from the empire created by Sargon.[652] Like many locations in the Levant, Mesopotamia, and Iran, Anshan had been conquered and become a vassal state to several empires over time. In 2700 BCE, the Elamites were defeated by the Sumerians and they became a vassal state under Sumerian control.

This set the stage for a period of back-and-forth warfare, diplomacy, and trade during which the Elamite Awan dynasty of kings conquered Sumer, was then crushed by Sargon of Akkad, regained control of Southern Mesopotamia, and was finally defeated by the kings of the resurgent city of Ur.[653]

Throughout the period during which the Akkadians controlled Mesopotamia (2350 BCE to 2150 BCE), the Elamites were on friendly terms with the Akkadians. With the collapse of Akkadian control of Mesopotamia, the Elamite governor Puzur-Inshushinak

---

[648]   Mark (2023C).
[649]   Baumer (2016), pp. 109-112.
[650]   See for example, Potts (2004), pp. 89-90.
[651]   Van de Mieroop (2007), pp. 101-103.
[652]   SOURCE: https://www.iranicaonline.org/articles/anshan-elamite-region retrieved on 22 March 2023.
[653]   Matyszak (2020), p. 37.

declared Elam as independent, replaced the Akkadian language with Elamite, and declared himself the 'king of the universe' (around 2100 BCE).[654]

In 1595 BCE, Babylon fell to the Anatolian Hittites, who came in from the west. The Hittites then retreated north and left Babylonia in a state of political chaos. The Kassites were a nomadic tribal group based in the green river valleys of the Zagros Mountains in Northern Babylonia. They had occasionally fought alongside the Amorites in defence of Babylonia but, on this occasion, they took control of Babylonia. They renamed Babylon, Karanduniash, and they became a major force in the region for some four hundred years.

From around 1300 BCE onwards, the Elamites consolidated in southern Iran as a relatively sophisticated political power. Towns grew, ziggurats were built, trade increased, and the territory under Elamite control expanded.[655]

Power and control over this region waxed and waned. Ultimately, in around 1185 BCE, the Elamites conquered the Kassites in Babylon. In the process, they stole both the famous stele inscribed with the Laws of Hammurabi and the sacred statue of the Sumerian god-protector of Babylon, Marduk. These were rededicated to Elamite gods with supporting inscriptions. Across the Middle East, the removal and reappropriation of religious icons was a common practice. This was a device to show that a city, a community, and its religion had been conquered because the conqueror's god was more powerful than the god of the defeated.

The Elamite Kingdom of Susa and Anshan was defeated by the Southern Mesopotamian King Nebuchadnezzar I. Nebuchadnezzar I was the fourth king of the Second Dynasty of Isin and Fourth Dynasty of Babylon (1121 BCE to 1100 BCE).[656]

The Return of the Assyrians

The Assyrians retook control of Babylonia from 911 BCE to 608 BCE. By around 850 BCE, the Assyrian King Shalmaneser III had made many of the existing Mesopotamian city-states, including Israel, as vassal states under Assyrian control. The Assyrians had also conquered parts of Iran (around 843 BCE) where they first came across the Medes and the Persians, who they subjugated.[657]

---

[654] Roux (1992), pp. 157-158.
[655] Kuhrt (2009A), pp. 368-370.
[656] Potts (2004), p. 188.
[657] Manco (2015), pp. 137-138.

The Assyrian kings that followed Shalmaneser III during the time of the known existence of ancient Israel included Tiglath Pileser III (745 BCE-727 BCE), Sargon II (722 BCE-705 BCE), Sennacherib (705 BCE-681 BCE), Esarhaddon (681 BCE-669 BCE) and Ashurbanipal (668 BCE-627 BCE).

The widespread use of deportation and exile

The Assyrians were intolerant of other cultures and sought regional power and the assimilation of their foes. Vassal states were no longer controlled by their kings. The upper echelons of their societies were deported to other locations within the Assyrian empire. From 745 BCE, under the control of military general Tiglath-Pileser III, who usurped the kingship, the Assyrians had begun indiscriminate use of mass deportations of the ruling class from the cultures they had conquered.[658] Tiglath-Pileser III sent the Israelite upper classes into exile in northern Mesopotamia between 734 BCE and 732 BCE.[659] The vassal states were placed under the control of the Assyrian overseers but could retain their existing administration. The Assyrian deportation strategies appear to have had several main objectives:

- to weaken the authorities by removing and relocating the ruling class and the potential source of leaders thereby reducing the likelihood of an organised revolt in the defeated cities
- to dismantle the conquered community's political and cultural unity
- to relocate the leaders/king/emperor of the conquered so they could learn the significance of the culture and religion of the conquerors and thus become more loyal [660]
- to diminish the local religion in the conquered locations by removing and reappropriating their religious icons into the conqueror's religion
- to populate the conqueror's own cities
- to build a slave workforce within the empire
- to place an Assyrian governor to rule and control the vanquished.[661]

The deportations included female captives, many of whom became concubines for the Assyrian kings or were deported for their reproductive potential. According to

---

[658]   Redford (1992), p. 341.
[659]   SOURCE: https://www.baslibrary.org/biblical-archaeology-review/29/6/6 retrieved on 31 March 2023.
[660]   See for example, Llewellyn-Jones (2022), p. 44.
[661]   Holland (2010), p. 106.

Llewellyn-Jones, Assyrian King Esarhaddon (681-669 BCE) brought the following female captives to his harem in the Assyrian capital city of Nineveh:

36 Aramean women; 15 Kushite women; 7 Assyrian women; 3 Tyrian women; Kassite women, female Corybantes; 3 Arpadite women; 1 replacement; 1 Ashdodite woman; 2 Hittite women; in all, 94 women and 36 maids of theirs. ... In all 140 women and an additional 61 female musicians.[662]

In addition to massive deportations, the Assyrians were regarded as particularly cruel. They had a reputation for terror and torture. This was possibly because of their geographical position—being surrounded on all sides and from within by enemies who were continually threatening them—although Samuel Kramer has suggested that:

... a good deal of Assyria's dependence on sheer physical power and brutality also stemmed no doubt from a feeling of cultural inferiority to neighbouring Babylonia, from which it had borrowed writing, literature and many religious, economic, and legal ideas and practices.[663]

In 721 BCE, Sargon II was the Assyrian king and he deported around 27,900 from the top layers of Israelite society to northern Mesopotamia and replaced them with Assyrian nobility.[664] This occurred on two occasions, between 729 BCE and 724 BCE and between 716 BCE and 715 BCE. Across these several hundred years, the Assyrians were responsible for multiple deportations of the top layers of Israelite society, including the Hebrew scribes. The positive outcome of these deportations was the exposure that the Hebrew scribes had to the many different mythologies across the ancient Middle East region. This created the perfect writer's palette for the Hebrew scribes as they began their role in the ethnic differentiation of the Israelites from their Canaanite and regional brothers and sisters.

The important contribution of the Assyrian King Ashurbanipal

By around 670 BCE, the Assyrian empire was at its most powerful (Figure 30). The Assyrians controlled from Elam in the east to Anatolia in the north-west down to Egypt in the south.[665]

The Elamites had been conquered by the Assyrian King Ashurbanipal (668-627 BCE). Those Elamites who were not massacred were forcibly distributed as exiles around the Mesopotamian region.[666]

---

[662] Llewellyn-Jones (2022), p. 178.
[663] Kramer (1968), p. 57.
[664] Holland (2010), p. 197.
[665] Cunliffe (2017), p. 160.
[666] Matyszak (2020), p. 41.

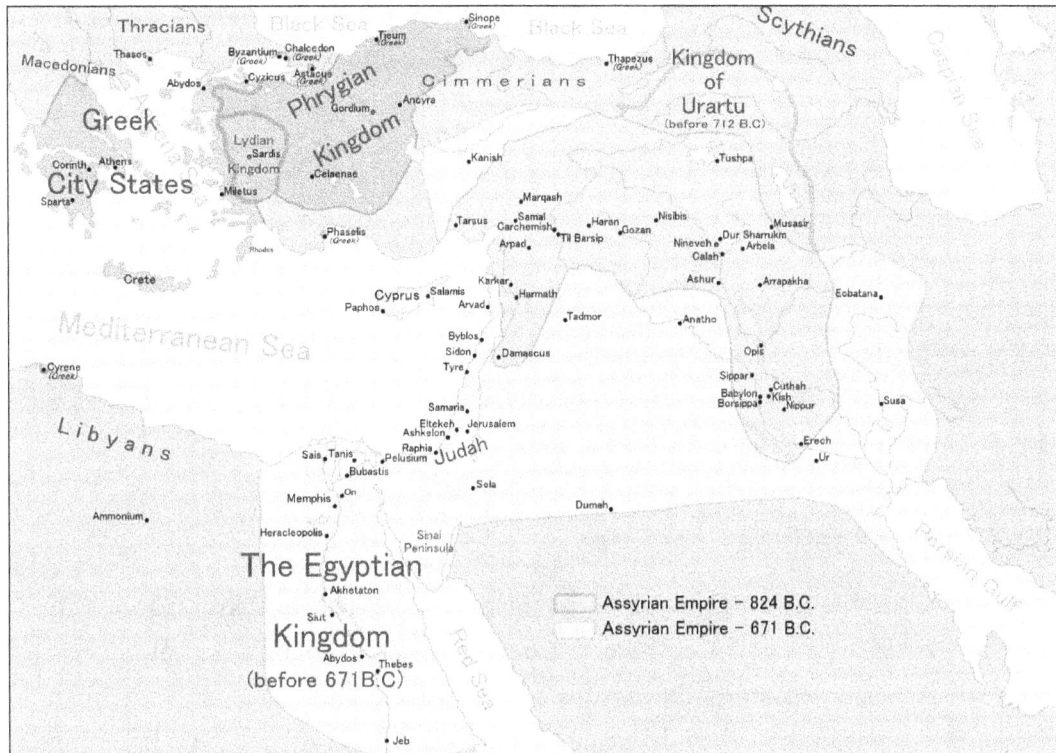

Figure 30: *The Assyrian Empire from 824 to 671 BCE*[c]

[c] SOURCE: https://member.worldhistory.org/uploads/images/117.png?v=1678299903 retrieved on 9 August 2023. Reprinted with permission from World History Encyclopedia

Ashurbanipal valued knowledge so highly that he established The Royal Library of Ashurbanipal, which stored many literary works from across the region. This included Sumerian texts such as the Epic of Gilgamesh (written around 1800 BCE), which was very well-known in Mesopotamia, Egypt, Hatti, and Canaan.[667] The Epic of Gilgamesh would become a major influence on the Hebrew scribes and, in particular, a major source for their Noah flood story.

Ashurbanipal was particularly ruthless towards the Elamites, diminishing them to such an extent that they never regained their position as a powerful empire:

Ashurbanipal attacked Susa, the Elamite capital and decided to make of it an object lesson: he stripped the palaces of everything of value, demolished the temples, destroyed the ziggurat, smashed the statues of previous Elamite kings and desecrated their tombs. Then he turned his

---

[667] Collins (2008), p. 56.

attention to the Elamite hinterland. 'In a month of days, I levelled the whole of Elam. I deprived its fields of the sound of human voices, the tread of cattle, and sheep, the refrain of joyous harvest songs. I turned it into a pasture for wild asses, gazelles, and all manner of wild animals'.[668]

This action by the Assyrian King Ashurbanipal effectively destroyed the Elamites, but it created a power vacuum on the eastern flank of Mesopotamia; a power vacuum that was quickly filled by the Medes and the Persians. Ashurbanipal's destruction of the Elamites was largely responsible for the eventual fall of the Assyrian empire by the Chaldeans in a coalition with the remaining Elamites, the Medes, the Parthians, the Persians, the Scythians, and the Cimmerians. This coalition of forces had eliminated the Assyrians from Mesopotamia by 605 BCE.[669]

The Arameans and the Chaldeans

Much of the Middle East region was under the control of the Assyrians on and off from around 2300 BCE to 608 BCE. Several different cultural groups were able to survive under the Assyrian hegemony during this period. This included two nomadic pastoral groups: the Arameans and the Chaldeans. Prior to the Assyrians retaking Babylonia in 911 BCE, in the eleventh century BCE, in the aftermath of the Bronze Age collapse, the communities of Greece, Anatolia, Syria and Canaan were in disarray. A group of unstable principalities and tribal groupings, including the Canaanites, Phoenicians, Philistines, and the emerging Israelites, were competing for territory and resources. In amongst this,

as central and southern Syria fragmented into small, widely spaced, urban enclaves much of the plains were claimed by local tribal groups who spoke the Aramaic language. Although Arameans populated the cities and farming villages, a large number were pastoral nomads, moving their animals across grazing lands. … Despite his triumphal march across Syria to the Mediterranean, Tiglath-pileser of Assyria was faced by the continued menace of Aramean groups.[670]

The Arameans

The Assyrian policy of displacement and relocation of the upper echelons of society impacted the Arameans. Under Tiglath-Pileser, the Arameans were conquered and widely

---

[668] Kriwaczek (2010), pp. 257-258.
[669] Matyszak (2020), pp. 121-122.
[670] Collins (2008), pp. 107-108.

resettled across the ancient Middle East. An unexpected consequence of this was the wide distribution of the Aramaic language. As Foster and Foster have observed about the Assyrian deportation strategy:

> The result was the creation of a polyglot population of Mesopotamia comprising peoples of many lands, among whom Aramaic was the most widely spoken and understood idiom. This gave rise to its role as the great world language of the Persian Empire and as the primary language of Judaism and Christianity.[671]

The Aramaic language had gradually become the common language of public life and administration across the Middle East, replacing Sumerian and Akkadian. Most biblical scholars believe that Aramaic was the language of Jesus some six hundred years later because, by then, Aramaic had become the common language of Judea.

The Chaldeans

The Chaldeans were a Semitic-speaking semi-nomadic tribal group from the Levant who migrated into Mesopotamia in around 900 BCE following the chaotic Bronze Age collapse and subsequent territorial and resource conflicts in the Southern Levant. The Chaldeans settled in the southernmost part of Mesopotamia referred to as Sealand. Sealand is a term that refers to the swampy area in the southeastern corner of Sumer around the mouths of the Tigris and Euphrates Rivers—a relatively poor area where the river mouths occasionally silted up. It was a location that controlled large plantations of date palms and the trade links coming through the Persian Gulf.[672]

In 626 BCE, massive, brutal internal civil wars broke out in Assyria. This could well have been because of the brutality of the regime but the net effect was the collapse of their control over Babylonia. After the collapse of the Assyrian regime, in 622 BCE, the Chaldean King Sheikh Nabopolassar took control of Babylon. Nabopolassar's son, Chaldean King Nebuchadnezzar ll (604 BCE to 562 BCE), also known as Nebuchadnezzar the Great, succeeded his father and continued military campaigns to strengthen the Chaldean empire and gain control across the Middle East and Egypt. Nebuchadnezzar ll secured major victories to the west over Egypt, which was now a primary territory for conquest and to the east over the Medes.[673]

---

[671] Foster and Foster (2009), p. 115.
[672] Collins (2008), p. 117.
[673] Holland (2010), pp. 108-109.

The Chaldean aggression included once again defeating the Elamites, retrieving the sacred statue of Marduk that the Elamites had carried off from Babylon, and laying siege to and capturing Jerusalem (597 BCE and 586 BCE). Nebuchadnezzar ll dealt harshly with those states who fought against him. He carried on the Assyrian policy of deportation of the upper echelon of the states he had conquered. As a result, during his reign he exiled some three thousand leading citizens of Israel (professionals, priests, scribes, craftsmen, and the wealthy) to 'the rivers of Babylon' on two occasions (598 BCE and 582 BCE—although biblical accounts vary on the dates and numbers).[674]

Under the control of the Chaldeans, Babylonia underwent a significant religious revival:

To the rebuilding of sanctuaries, the restoration of age-old rites, the celebration of religious festivals with increased ceremonial display, the Chaldean kings devoted much time, energy, and money.[675]

The origin of the Tower of Babel story

One of Chaldean King Nebuchadnezzar ll's original reasons for deporting the conquered Judaeans and others to Babylon was to assist him in repairing the damage that had been done to the ziggurats in Babylon by the Assyrians. The Assyrian King Sennacherib had plundered and burned the Babylonian ziggurats in 689 BCE. To the Sumerians, the ziggurats were a tribute to the city's patron deity, Marduk. They represented the mountain of creation, linking man with god and symbolising the bond between heaven and Earth. The Sumerian names for the two main ziggurats dedicated to the god Marduk were Etemenanki, which meant 'temple of the foundation of heaven and Earth', and Esangil, which meant 'temple whose top is lofty'.

The mythological biblical story of the Tower of Babel (Genesis 11:1–9) was inspired by the Babylonian attempted rebuilding of the ziggurats Etemenanki and Esangil. Babylonia was called Bab-ilu ('Gate of God'), Hebrew form Babel, or Bavel. The similarity in pronunciation of Babel and *balal* ('to confuse') led the Hebrew scribes to create a story with two main objectives—to demonstrate the weakness of the Babylonians and to explain that the Babylonians wanted to make a name for themselves by building a mighty

---

674 Holland (2010), p. 108.
675 Roux (1992), p. 389.

city 'with its top in the heavens'. According to the biblical account, God disrupted the work by confusing the language of the workers so they could no longer understand one another.[676]

Graves and Patai believe that the transported Judaeans would have been astonished by the number of different dialects among their fellow deportees in Babylon. The deportees had been deported from all over the Middle East. Evidence from the Assyrian city of Nippur south of Babylon, for instance, indicates that the deportees to that city included:

> *Lydians and Phrygians from western Anatolia … Urartians and Melidans from central and eastern Anatolia … Greeks, Tyrians and Philistines from Gaza; as well as possibly Judaeans.*[677]

The deportees from across the empire were enslaved to rebuild the Babylonian ziggurats under Nebuchadnezzar ll's cruelly enforced rebuilding regime.[678] These three facts—the ziggurats, their demise, and the many languages of the enslaved workers—were most likely the material woven into the biblical story of the Tower of Babel.[679]

The Tower of Babel myth claims that God destroyed a mighty tower being built by the Babylonians 'with its top in the heavens'. The angry deity then replaced the one common language with seventy different languages. Sumerian authority Samuel Noah Kramer believes that there were two additional inspirations for the Hebrew scribes' Babel story.

The Hebrew scribes, in common with an oft-repeated theme in the Hebrew Bible, saw the devastation of the Mesopotamian ziggurats caused by the Assyrian King Sennacherib as 'symbols of man's feeling of insecurity and the not unrelated lust for power that brings upon him humiliation and suffering' (a typical biblical theme). Secondly, Kramer believed that the biblical story of an angry deity ending the use of one common language is an adaptation of the Sumerian golden age myth 'Enmerkar and the Lord of Aratta', which mentions a godly intervention to disrupt the unity of the languages of mankind.[680]

---

[676] https://www.britannica.com/topic/Tower-of-Babel retrieved on 2 December 2021.
[677] Leick (2002), p. 145.
[678] The Bible claims that the king at the time was Nimrod who was Noah's grandson. Most scholars accept that there is no evidence of a king of this name at that time in Mesopotamia.
[679] Graves and Patai (1964), p. 128-129.
[680] Kramer (1971), pp. 293-294; and Shilov (2015), p. 427.

The Hebrew scribes seek favour with their Chaldean captors

The Bible states that the Israeli's founding patriarch, Abraham, was born in Ur of the Chaldeans in 1996 BCE as the son of Terah.[681] In 1996 BCE, Ur was not under the control of the Chaldeans. It was a major Sumero-Akkadian urban centre located in the marshy land in the far southeastern corner of Mesopotamia. At that time (1996 BCE), Ur was controlled by the Sumerians and had been under Sumerian control on and off for about two thousand years since around 3800 BCE.

The Chaldeans did not move to Southern Mesopotamia until around 940 BCE and did not control Southern Mesopotamia and the city of Ur until around 622 BCE. Any mention of the Chaldeans being in control of Ur suggests that this biblical text describing the birth of Abraham could not have been written before 940 BCE. It was most probably written when the Hebrew scribes were exiled to Babylon under Chaldean control from around 598 BCE. Gary Greenberg, amongst many other biblical authorities, suggests that the text attributing Abraham's birth to the Ur of the Chaldeans is an anachronism inserted at these much later dates by biblical scribes. Greenberg suggests that this part of the biblical text was most likely written by the Hebrew scribes during the Babylonian Captivity (after 587 BCE) to find favour with their then-Chaldean conquerors.[682]

The Persians, Elamites, and Medes

The Persians, Elamites, and Medes had all migrated at different times into Iran from the Scytho-Siberian horizon/Eurasian Steppe. They were nomadic, had a common history, mutually intelligible Iranian-related languages, common horse and pastoral skills (cattle, sheep, and goats), similar burial practices, and generally similar customs.[683] However, like the Scythians, each group was still not a united people but largely a federation of separate tribes.

The Persians were initially referred to as the Parsua by the Assyrians (843 BCE). Along with the Elamites, the Parsua occupied the kingdom of Anshan in southern Iran (modern-day Fars Province) along the eastern edge of the Persian Gulf.[684] The Elamites and the Persians formed a strong cultural bond in Anshan, although the Elamites were

[681] SOURCE: https://biography.yourdictionary.com/abraham.
[682] Greenberg (2008), pp. 135-136.
[683] Golden (2011), p. 24.
[684] Manco (2015), p. 138.

the more sophisticated and culturally dominant. Lloyd Llewellyn-Jones has described it in this way:

> *There can be little doubt that the Elamites form the 'missing link' in the chain of Persian ideological development; that is to say, the way in which the Persians developed a distinct culture. The Persians were the true heirs of the Elamites.*[685]

The Elamites had suffered a devastating defeat at the hand of the Assyrian King Ashurbanipal and were comprehensively defeated by the Chaldeans. In southwestern Iran and, specifically, in Susa and Anshan, Persia became a small vassal state of the Medes, to whom they paid tributes for protection and to maintain some independence.[686]

In assisting the Chaldeans in destroying the Assyrians, the Medes had been particularly destructive in their demolishing of the Assyrian capital city, Nineveh (612 BCE).

The Medes carried out such thorough slaughter, destruction, and plundering that nothing of Assyrian might and culture remained visible, including the library of Ashurbanipal, which was smashed into thousands of fragments. It is likely the Medes even mutilated a life-size, cast copper head of an Akkadian ruler, for archaeologists found the heirloom sculpture in the ruins, deliberately disfigured in just the way the Medes treated enemy notables.[687]

The Chaldean King Nabopolassar rewarded the Medes by giving them control of Anatolia and the northern parts of Mesopotamia. Here, the Medes battled unsuccessfully against the Anatolian Lydians, who had taken over parts of Anatolia after the collapse of the Hittite Empire.[688] The unsuccessful war led to a truce with the Lydians in 585 BCE. The various battles had taken a great toll on the Medes, who retreated into Anshan.

The emergence of the Persian Empire

The ruling family of the comparatively small Persian tribe that was in southwestern Iran at the time was the Achaemenids, named after their founder Achaemenes (705 BCE to 650 BCE).[689] The Persians were in southwest Iran, south of where the Elamites and the

---

[685] Llewellyn-Jones (2022), p. 43.
[686] SOURCE: https://www.khanacademy.org/humanities/world-history/ancient-medieval/ancient-persia/a/the-rise-of-persia retrieved on 30 March 2023.
[687] Foster and Foster (2009), p. 126.
[688] Kriwaczek (2010), p. 258.
[689] Llewellyn-Jones (2022), p. 7.

Medians had located.[690] The Persian tribes were vassals of the Medes.[691] Achaemenes' great-great-grandson Cyrus ll (Cyrus the Great) was born sometime between 600 BCE and 590 BCE.[692] Cyrus became the heir to the throne of Anshan when his father Cambyses, who was King of Persia, died in 559 BCE.[693]

Not long after Cyrus was appointed leader of the Persians, there was a rebellion of the Median army against the Medes King Astyages. Cyrus rallied the Persian tribes around him, gaining the support of the Babylonian King Nabonidus and many disgruntled Median nobles.[694] Taking advantage of the rebelling Median army and the support of the Persian tribal leaders and Median nobles, Cyrus took control of the Persian and Median Empires, including the Median territory, in Anatolia in 550 BCE.[695]

Cyrus then began several campaigns moving both eastward and westward. He conquered the Lydians in eastern Anatolia, ancient Armenia in the Caucuses, the Bactrians, the Scythians, and the Babylonians, and took control of most of Mesopotamia, Anatolia, the Levant, and parts of Egypt. By the time of his death in 530 BCE, Cyrus had created an empire that controlled the entire Middle East from Egypt to Iran.[696]

A significant change in relationships within the Middle East

There was a major difference between the control of the Middle East under Cyrus compared to the practices of the Assyrians or Chaldeans. Cyrus understood the importance of cultivating a good public image.[697] He was a humane and enlightened leader.[698] All provinces were still required to pay tributes (gold, silver, lapis lazuli, ebony, ivory, horses, cattle, grain, building materials), taxes, and military levies to the king for royal projects and royal treasuries. However, under Cyrus and subsequent Persian kings, the cultural, political, and religious traditions of the people they had conquered were respected. These practices were adopted to bring unity to the emerging empire and for

---

[690] Van de Mieroop (2007), p. 287.
[691] Roux (1992), p. 383.
[692] The Cyrus birth story and his relationship to Achaemenes is disputed by some academics – see Nijssen (2018).
[693] Bauer (2007), p. 459.
[694] Llewellyn-Jones (2022), p. 55.
[695] Van de Mieroop (2007) p. 273; Cunliffe (2017), p. 204.
[696] Nijssen (2018).
[697] Llewellyn-Jones (2022), p. 67.
[698] Foster and Foster (2009), p. 142.

the kings to be seen and respected as tolerant leaders and unifiers of diverse peoples. In Susan Bauer's words:

> *The newness of Cyrus's empire lay in his ability to think of it, not as a Persian nation in which the peoples must be made more Persian, but rather as a patchwork of nations under Persian rule.*[699]

Cyrus discontinued the Assyrian and Chaldean practice of deportation. He, and subsequent Persian kings, did not attempt to impose Persian traditions on their provincial subjects.[700] Cyrus respected local cults, allowing exiled members of vassal states to continue worshipping their own gods in their homelands and allowing the rebuilding or restoration of their temples. He guaranteed and took part in their religious rituals. He respected and supported their worship of their gods. In Babylonia, he restored the temples and public buildings and reinstated the displaced cult statues to their original temples.[701] Despite being a devout Zoroastrian, Cyrus claimed that his success in capturing Babylon was attributable to the support he had from the Babylonian's patron god Marduk.[702] This was partly true, as his success in conquering Babylon was supported by an internal revolt within Babylon by the priests of Marduk.[703]

The Greek father of history, Herodotus of Halicarnassus, wrote of the empire under the control of Cyrus the Great:

> *And although it was of such magnitude, it was governed by the single will of Cyrus; and he honoured his subjects and cared for them as if they were his own children; and they, on their part, revered Cyrus as a father.*[704]

Cyrus's successors continued to build the Persian Empire—his son, Cambyses (king from 525 BCE) conquered Egypt and Darius (king from 521 BCE) conquered parts of Greece (in battles extending from 499 BCE to 449 BCE). This included claiming Macedon as a vassal state (492 BCE) and burning down the Acropolis in Athens in 480 BCE. As a result, Greek city-states united and Greece became the major rival of the Persians for control of the Middle East. Greece was united under the military monarch Philip of Macedon in

---

[699] Bauer (2007), p. 468.
[700] Kriwaczek (2010), p. 277.
[701] Leick (2002), pp. 271-272.
[702] Van de Mieroop (2007) pp. 295-296.
[703] Holland (2010), p. 109.
[704] Cited in Miles (2011), p. 132.

359 BCE. Philip's son, Alexander the Great (336 BCE to 323 BCE), eventually defeated the Persians and within a short period of some thirteen years established 'a vast empire extending from Macedonia in the west to the Indus Valley in the east, from Armenia and Bactria in the north to Egypt and Arabia in the south'.[705]

A key influence on the role of contemporary religious leaders

The ancient Persians, Medes, Parthians, and Bactrians believed in the cult of Mithra—a religion related to the Zoroastrian Avesta scriptures and the Hindu Veda scriptures. The holy men were known as Magi (also Magoi, Zaotar). The Magi were one of the six tribes within the Medes. They were a close-knit fraternity of missionary priests who were influential with Persians, Medes, and Parthians. They were probably partly responsible for the spread of Zoroastrianism within Iran.[706] The Magi were hereditary priests who chanted divine hymns of praise.[707] They interpreted and administered the law, and were relied on to perform at initiations, deaths, marriages, special family, community, and religious events.[708]

The Magi were the source of the New Testament story of the three wise men visiting Jesus. The Magi set the scene for many priest figures to follow, even up until modern times. They were regarded as intermediaries who could commune with the gods. They were an elite class of religious observers and performers of important rituals at royal funerals and investitures, undertaking animal sacrifices, preparing sacred drinks, performing ritual offerings of food (grain and wine) as tributes to deities, and acting as dream interpreters and soothsayers.[709] Here was the model for strengthening and giving greater definition to the roles of the contemporary 'holy men' who followed—sages, priests, bishops, popes, and pastors.

The Hebrew scribes seek favour with Cyrus the Great

In 538 BCE, Cyrus issued an edict for the Jews to be released to return to their homeland and rebuild their temple. However, most of the Jews decided to stay.[710] Many Jews had

---

[705] Holland (2010), p. 198.
[706] Boyce (2001) pp. 48-49.
[707] Llewellyn-Jones (2022), p. 214.
[708] Boyce (2001), p. 46 and p. 140.
[709] Llewellyn-Jones (2022), pp. 214-215; Potts (2004), p. 346.
[710] Armstrong (1993), p. 62.

been integrated into Persian society. For example, Jewish soldiers and their families were serving in the Persian army as far away from Mesopotamia as on Elephantine Island on the Nile River in Upper Egypt.[711]

When Cyrus encouraged the Jews to return to their homeland, he encouraged those who chose to return to rebuild their temple in Jerusalem.[712] The Hebrew scribes were apparently happy with Cyrus the Great and, as they did with the Chaldeans, they wrote positively about him. The Hebrews referred to Cyrus as the Messiah, Anointed One, or Anointed of the Lord—a nomenclature that exiled Jews would only use if they were speaking of a God-sent saviour or a redeemer.[713] The Hebrew Bible claimed (Isaiah 44:28-45:4) that their god Yahweh chose Cyrus to rebuild their temple in Jerusalem. They wrote in Isaiah 45: 1-3:

> This is what the Lord says to his anointed, to Cyrus, whose right hand I take hold of to subdue nations before him and to strip kings of their armor, to open doors before him so that gates will not be shut: I will go before you and will level the mountains; I will break down gates of bronze and cut through bars of iron. I will give you hidden treasures, riches stored in secret places, so that you may know that I am the Lord, the God of Israel, who summons you by name.

The origin of the myth of a child miraculously saved

Persian King Cyrus the Great's birth story tells of his grandfather, the Median King Astyages, being concerned that he did not have a son and heir. His Lydian wife, Aryenis, had a daughter, Mandane. Astyages accepted that his heir would have to be his grandson and that his daughter needed a compliant husband who would not be concerned if his son, and not he, became the king. Astyages convinced Mandane to marry a loyal Persian vassal, Cambyses, who successfully fathered a son, Cyrus.

After a prophetic dream, Astyages decided that Cyrus would have to be killed, as the dream foretold that the child would take control of the Median kingdom. Astyages arranged for Cyrus to be killed. However, a stillborn child was put in his place and Cyrus survived to become the King of Persia.[714]

---

[711] Kuhrt (2009B), p. 651.
[712] Cunliffe (2017), p. 209.
[713] Llewellyn-Jones (2022), pp. 71-72; Bauer (2007), p. 467.
[714] Bauer (2007), pp. 455-457.

A god-child being surreptitiously born and hidden or saved was a common mythological theme across India, the Middle East, and Egypt. The Hindu god Krishna (3200 BCE) was carried in a basket across a river to hide him from potential danger.[715] The Ancient Egyptian myth on the birth of Horus (the god of kingship and the sky) has his mother Isis (goddess of kingship and protection of the kingdom) giving birth to Horus in the Nile Delta marshes.[716] This mythological storyline involving a miraculous escape of a young soon-to-be leader includes the birth stories of Sargon the Great and Moses (each was afloat in a basket on a river) and Jesus (fleeing into Egypt with Mary and Joseph because King Herod wanted to kill him).

Susan Bauer states about the Cyrus birth story:

> *It is clearly a reprise of the standard peril that also shows a king's divine appointment: a baby, miraculously preserved, grows to be a great leader, thanks to the supernatural providence that so clearly lay upon his early life.[717]*

Canaan and the Levant

The term 'Canaan' refers primarily to a geographical location and not to a specific ethnic or cultural group. It is a loose term for the geographic location on the eastern coastline of the Mediterranean that is the ancient equivalent of the Levant. In modern-day terms, it includes Syria, Lebanon, Israel, parts of Jordan, and Palestine. The Levant is the narrow land bridge (the 'Levantine corridor') linking Africa and Eurasia. It was the main pathway for modern humans to leave Africa around 100,000 years ago. It has along its coastline 'the oldest road in the world'. This is the ancient military road along which ancient Canaanites travelled down into Egypt. It is the northbound land-based route along which the Egyptians traded northwards with the Levant and Mesopotamia. It was the land route for the punitive Pharaonic attacks and conquests of the Levant and other kingdoms/invaders (Shasu, Apiru, Hyksos/Canaanites, Hittites, Mitanni, Persians, Scythians, Greeks). The Egyptians travelled along it in parallel with their sea fleets.[718]

The names Canaan and Canaanite occur in cuneiform, Egyptian, and Phoenician writings from the Late Bronze Age (1600 BCE to 1200 BCE). From around 1200 BCE

---

[715] https://www.britannica.com/topic/Krishna-Hindu-deity retrieved on 3 September 2022.
[716] Shaw (2014), pp. 84-85.
[717] Bauer (2007), p. 456.
[718] Gardiner (1920); Grabbe (2018C), p. 9.

onwards, the Canaanites were referred to as Phoenicians.[719] There is a growing consensus among Egyptologists, biblical scholars, and archaeologists that most of the early Israelites were Canaanites.[720] Canaan is mentioned in the HB/OT, although most researchers regard many of these biblical references to be mytho-historical.[721]

There is no academic or archaeological consensus on the origin or meaning of the word Canaan.

- Susan Bauer claims that Canaan is 'an anachronistic name … that appears to be an uncomplimentary reference to roving bandits from somewhere around the Jordan river'.[722] This is supported by Thomas Beyl, who claims that the earliest attestation to a region called Canaan occurs in the eighteenth-century BCE where the term is used to describe a group of brigands[723]

- the name 'Canaan' appears in various ancient texts from Egypt to Mesopotamia and appears to have been used as a designation for what was then Egypt's Levantine Asiatic province.[724] The Semitic word means 'to be low, humble, subjugated', which could be metaphorically referring to the lowlands of the Levant, in contrast to the highlands, or it could also be a metaphor for 'the subjugated' reflecting its role as Egypt's province in the Levant

- the name could also come from an old Semitic/Hurrian word *kinaḫḫu*, denoting 'reddish-purple,' referring to the rich purple or crimson dye produced from various types of snails found off the coasts of the Levant. The Canaanites produced and traded highly valued wool fabrics coloured with this dye. The name Phoenicia also means 'purple land' in Greek

- the Bible claims that Canaan was named after a grandson of Noah (Genesis 10:6). All Canaanites would, according to the HB/OT be descendants of Noah's grandson, Canaan. Canaan was regarded as the 'promised land'—God's gift to Abraham (Genesis 12:1-6).

The Canaan region is an interesting geographic location. In many ways, it was a meeting or transit place for the ideas, discoveries, cultures, and communities from Europe, western

---

[719] Source: https://jewishweek.timesofisrael.com/blue-heaven-2/ retrieved on 11 May 2021.
[720] SOURCE: https://www.nytimes.com/1990/09/04/science/battle-scene-on-egyptian-temple-may-be-earliest-view-of-israelites.html retrieved on 5 March 2021.
[721] Grabbe (2018A), pp. 11-16.
[722] Bauer (2007), pp. 129-130.
[723] Beyl (2013), p. 16.
[724] Mark (2018B).

Asia, the Eastern Mediterranean, the Middle East, and North and North-East Africa. The Caucuses formed a bridge between Mesopotamia in the south and the Eurasian Steppe in the north. The Levant was linked to the historical path of the Silk Road (the trans-Asian east–west trade route) and to the Eurasian Steppe (connecting Eastern Europe, Central Asia, Eastern Asia, Southern Asia, and the Middle East economically, politically, and culturally).

Archaeological and genetic evidence explains that, because of this geographic location, people came to and through Canaan/the Levant from the north, north-east, south, and north-west across tens of thousands of years—well before the biblical appearance of Noah and Abraham. The region was among the earliest in the world to see human habitation, agricultural communities, and civilisation. The earliest humans in the Levant made some of the earliest stone tools made by *Homo erectus* after they left Africa. These have been found at a handful of known sites in Israel, Syria, and Jordan from some 1.7 million years ago. Stone tools were used to process plants and butcher animals for food.

Encyclopedia Britannica explains that:

> *… the human habitation of coastal Canaan can be traced back to Paleolithic and Mesolithic times, and excavations have revealed that a settled community and an agricultural way of life existed at the site of Jericho by 8000 BCE. More widespread settlement in fixed towns and villages appears not to have occurred until the Neolithic Period (c. 7000 BCE to c. 4000 BCE). The following period, called the Chalcolithic Age (c. 4000 BCE to c. 3000 BCE), was characterised by the use of pottery and copper and by houses of uncut stones, with walls of mud brick.*[725]

Canaan and archaeological evidence from Southern Levant

Northern and Southern Levant are traditionally differentiated by a line drawn from Damascus to Beirut. The Canaanites were the indigenous peoples of the ancient Levant, living primarily along the Mediterranean coast and in the fertile valleys of the Southern Levant. Modern Israel is located entirely in the Southern Levant (Figure 31).

There is a substantial body of archaeological evidence of ancient hominin and human species habitation in the Southern Levant hundreds of thousands of years before the emergence of the Israelites and the biblical date of creation. Stone Age human hunter-gatherer

---

[725] See: https://www.britannica.com/place/Canaan-historical-region-Middle-East retrieved on 11 May 2021.

Figure 31: Modern Israel located on a map of the Ancient Middle East Southern Levant [d]

---

[d] Base map source: https://www.pinterest.com.au/pin/561331541032592914/ retrieved on 9 August 2023.

cultures were in the Fertile Crescent, the Levant, and Israel (Southern Levant) dating back tens of thousands of years (Figure 32).

Some two to three hundred thousand years ago, there were human-like ancestors in Mugharet el-Zuttiyeh ('the Cave of the Robbers') in Upper Galilee, Israel. Phylogenetic analysis of remains from the Cave of Robbers demonstrates that, even hundreds of thousands of years ago in the Levant, groups of early hominins were interacting. Specifically, Levantine and East Asian hominins from two hundred to three hundred thousand years ago share similar morphological features.[726]

Mousterian/Mode III (top row, Figure 32) is a term used by archaeologists to group together Stone Age Neanderthal and human species hunter-gatherers. This terminology is

---

[726] Sohn and Wolpoff (1993) pp. 344-345.

261

Approximate date in the Near East	Location of evidence from archaeological site/s	Levantine culture	Characteristics of this period
50000 BCE to **40000** BCE	throughout Israel	Mousterian/ Mode III	Stone Age hunter gatherers. Using stone tools, hand axes and grinders.
40000 BCE to **30000** BCE	throughout Israel	Emiran Culture	Stone Age hunter gatherers indigenous to the Levant. Using numerous stone blade tools, including curved knives.
30000 BCE to **18000** BCE	Judean Desert, Israel	Masraqan/ Ahmarian	Stone Age hunter gatherers. Likely originators of complex stone chipping techniques producing implements made of shaped stone blades with handles, creating the first composite tools and high velocity weapons.
18000 BCE to **12000** BCE	Israel and the Levant	Kebaran Culture	Highly mobile nomadic Stone Age hunter gatherers using microlithic/ small stone tools.
12000 BCE to **10000** BCE	Israel, Jericho and the Levant	Natufian Culture	semi-sedentary hunter gatherers and foragers with some cereal (rye) cultivation/harvesting; the beginnings of small permanent settlements/ villages and possibly the first known makers of bread and beer.
10000 BCE	The last major ice age ends. The retreating ice creates a major advantageous climate change where locations across the globe experience much longer dry seasons. In the Near East this climate change favours annual plants like wild cereals.		
10000 BCE to **8600** BCE **(Neolithic Age)**	Israel, Jericho, the Levant and Northern Mesopotamia	Khiamian Culture	Hunter gatherers transitioning to semi-permanent and permanent villages; experimenting with early agriculture and above ground housing, religious iconography (female figurines) and centralised places of worship.
10000 BCE to **8800** BCE	extensive archaeological finds throughout Israel, Jericho, Lebanon, Jordan, Syria, Turkey, the Levant and Mesopotamia	Pre-Pottery Neolithic (PPNA)	the world's first town Jericho appears in the Levant
8800 BCE to **6500** BCE		Pre-Pottery Neolithic (PPNB)	small settlements emerge including greater use of domesticated animals, new technologies and tools, and new architectural styles.
6500 BCE to **5000** BCE		Ceramic or Pottery Neolithic - Yarmukianculture	distinctive cultures emerge with distinctive ceramic pottery decorated with abstract geometric patterns and ornaments, female fertility figurines and stylistic stamp seals

Approximate date in the Near East	Location of evidence from archaeological site/s	Levantine culture	Characteristics of this period
6200 BCE	Cyprus, Anatolia, the Southern Levant (modern-day Israel, Jordan, Lebanon, the Palestinian Territories and Syria), Mesopotamia and parts of North Africa.		sudden, rapid decrease in global temperatures and increased regional aridity persisting for two to four hundred years leading to changes in modes of subsistence, social organisation and settlement patterns
5000 BCE	Hebrew Bible/Christian Old Testament claims that their god created the Universe around this time		
5000 BCE to **3300** BCE	Fertile Crescent, Sumer, Egypt, Crete, Indus Valley	Copper/ Chalcolithic Age	transitional period between the Neolithic and the Bronze Age. The first state societies emerge - large-scale, populous, politically centralized, and socially stratified polities/societies governed by powerful rulers
4000 BCE to **3000** BCE	periods of intermittent, often rapid climatic, environmental change resulting in cultural disruption, social and economic change across many Near Eastern cultures		
3300 BCE to **1200** BCE	multiple, multi-faceted evidence available from sites across Turkey, Syria, Jordan, Israel, Iraq, Iran, Afghanistan, Egypt	Bronze Age	extensive and diverse archaeological, linguistic, written and genomic evidence available across the Near East from these periods onwards
1200 BCE to **550** BCE		Iron Age	

Figure 32: *Archaeological evidence of habitation in the Middle East before and after the biblical creation date* [a]

[a] Adapted, in part from Goring-Morris and Belfer-Cohen (2011), p. S196; Cauvin (2003); Clarke J. et al. (2016); Tejero et al. (2021).

based on the similarity of stone tools found in specific sites. The term originates from the Le Moustier archaeological site in the Dordogne in France where stone tools were found that have also been found in other parts of Europe (used by Neanderthals) and the Middle East, the Levant, and North Africa (used by archaic human species). The Levantine Mousterian have left archaeological evidence of their presence in the Levant in locations in Lebanon, Syria, Israel, and Jordan dating back to around 50,000 BCE.[727] Skull fragments

---

[727] Shea (1998), p. S46.

from an early hominin have also been found in a quarry in central Israel dating back some 120,000 to 140,000 years.[728]

There is substantial archaeological evidence of the earliest Canaanites/Natufians establishing themselves in and around Jericho in the Southern Levant from around 10000 BCE. Initially, the Natufians were nomadic hunter-gatherers and fishers using seasonal sites like Jericho, where they had access to a perennial spring. By around 2000 BCE, Jericho had become a medium-ranked but prosperous Canaanite city.[729] Jericho's name in Hebrew, *Yerih̲o*, is generally thought to derive from the Canaanite word *reah* ('fragrant'). The Arabic name, *Arīḥā*, means 'fragrant'. However, other theories hold that the name originates in the Canaanite word for 'moon' (*yareah*) or the name of the lunar deity Yarikh, for whom the city was an early centre of Canaanite moon god worship.[730]

Archaeologist Jonathon Tubb believes that the many communities identified as 'Canaanite' had moved to the region and settled in farming villages around the eighth millennium BCE and that their identities had been subsumed under other names such as Ammonites, Moabites, Phoenicians, and Israelites.[731]

They emerged initially as a loose-knit collection of decentralised Levantine nomadic pastoral communities, extended chiefdoms, and city-states sharing genetic similarities, many similar cultural practices, material culture and patterns of daily behaviour, including religious beliefs and behaviours.[732] They spoke variations of the same Semitic language that most likely originated with the Natufians in the Levant or in Northern Mesopotamia. The regional variations of this Afro-Asiatic language family included Akkadian, Eblaite, Amorite, Ugaritic, Canaanite, Aramaic, Hebrew, North Arabian, Arabic, South Arabian, and Ethiopian.[733]

It is near impossible to isolate the numerous ancient Canaanite communities from each other because of the small number of identifiably different material remains uncovered by archaeologists.[734] Most were nomadic pastoralists and their archaeological footprints are, by nature, almost impossible to find.[735]

---

[728] SOURCE: https://www.nationalgeographic.com/science/article/puzzling-skull-discovery-may-point-previously-unknown-human-ancestor? retrieved on 1 July 2021.
[729] Matyszak (2020), p. 31.
[730] SOURCE: https://en.wikipedia.org/wiki/Jericho retrieved on 5 August 2021.
[731] Tubb (1998), pp. 13-14.
[732] Gzella (2014), p. 29.
[733] Rendsburg (2003), p. 71.
[734] Tubb (1998), p. 13.
[735] Levy et al (2004), pp. 68-71.

Across millennia, because of their focal geographical location, the Canaanite communities witnessed and learnt from agricultural, technological, cultural, historical, and mythological customs and beliefs that converged from all cardinal directions throughout history and prehistory.

The Canaanites, as tributary vassals of much larger Middle Eastern Kingdoms, were heavily influenced by the various Mesopotamian kingdoms.

The Canaanites had a cuneiform script, their schools followed the Mesopotamian curriculum, and their culture was deeply imbued with Mesopotamian thought and belief.[736]

The Canaanite communities remained as independent states that were never united into a Levantine regional empire (Figure 33). Archaeologist and historian Alexander Joffe has described the Canaanite city-states as being numerous in number, flimsy, under palatial control, and often barely capable of projecting their authority beyond the confines of their specific city. Whilst some on the Mediterranean coast and in the largest inland site were wealthy, the majority were poor and living in unfortified cities.[737]

For centuries, Canaan remained this group of separate ununified vassal states under the control of a range of major empires including the Assyrians (c. 2300 BCE and 1700 BCE), Hyksos (c. 1720 BCE to 1570 BCE), Mitanni (c. 1600 BCE to 1260 BCE), Egyptians (c. 1550 BCE to 1000 BCE), Bronze Age collapse (c. 1200 BCE to 900 BCE), Assyrians (c. 911 BCE to 608 BCE), Babylonians (c. 605 BCE to 550 BCE), Persians (c. 550 BCE to 330 BCE), and Greeks (c. 340 BCE to 116 CE).

The urban development of Canaan lagged considerably behind that of Egypt and Mesopotamia. During the Early and Middle Bronze Ages, independent Canaanite city-states were beginning to form. They were influenced by the surrounding civilisations of Mesopotamia, Phoenicia, Minoan Crete, Syria, and ancient Egypt, which ruled the area in the Late Bronze Age (1550 BCE to 1000 BCE).

---

[736] Kramer (1968), p. 158.
[737] Joffe (2022), p. 428.

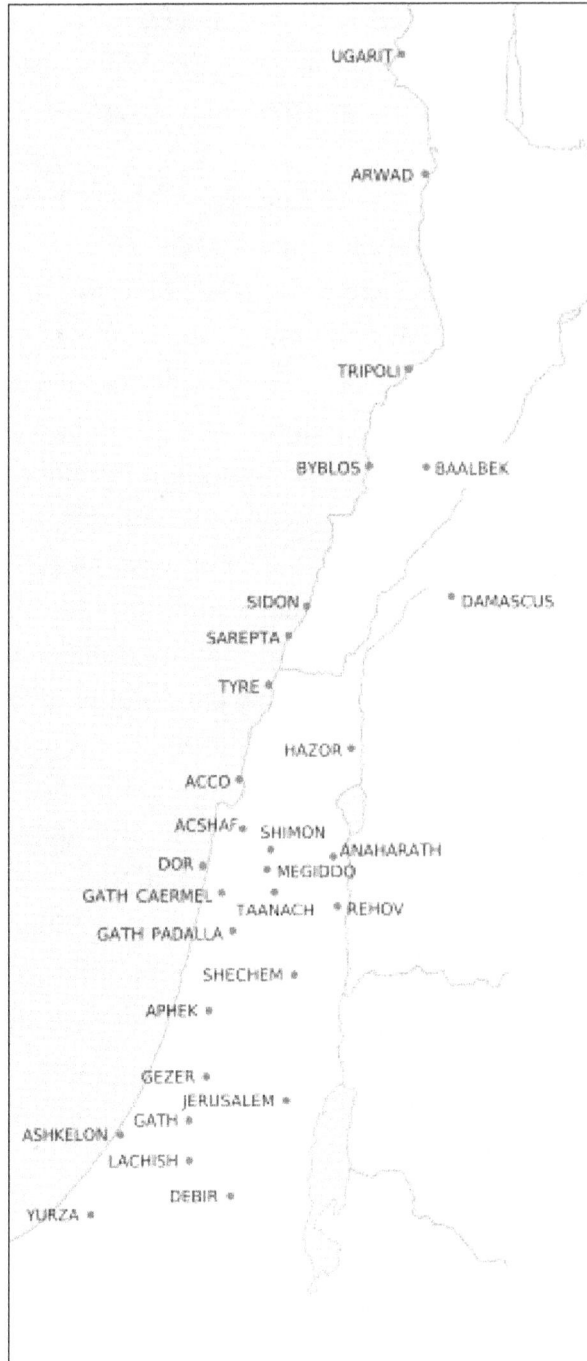

Figure 33: *The Bronze Age Canaanite city-state* [b]

[b] SOURCE: https://commons.wikimedia.org/wiki/File:Canaanite_City_States_In_The_Bronze_Age.svg

Chapter 13

The Significant Historical Role of the Ancient Egyptians

The importance of the Nile Valley

The Nile Valley is one of the five locations where the movement of the tectonic plates created the geomorphological conditions for the emergence of one of the world's 'cradles of civilisation'. The region is an oasis in the desert located along the longest river in the world. It commenced as a series of fishing, hunting, and agricultural communities stretched out along the Nile River. Richard Miles defines the unique characteristics of this location in the following way:

> Though land locked on three sides, ancient Egypt was essentially a ribbon-shaped island, protected from its neighbours by mountains to the south and deserts to the east and west. Its frontier to the north was defined by the marshy delta of the Nile, the river which shaped the civilisation which developed there.[738]

Egypt is regarded as:

> The largest and naturally most fertile oasis in north Africa, because the Nile has cut here a relatively broad flood-plain through the lime and sandstone. … The Nile Valley marks Egypt off from the deserts to east and west. … Given the severely limited area available for agriculture, it was generally (although not always) the case that settlements and fields were located in this irrigable land, while burials were cited in the desert.[739]

Ancient Egypt was divided into Upper and Lower Egypt, and each of these locations developed differently during prehistoric times (Figure 34). They were eventually unified

---

[738]   Miles (2011), p. 21.
[739]   Kuhrt (2009A), p. 118.

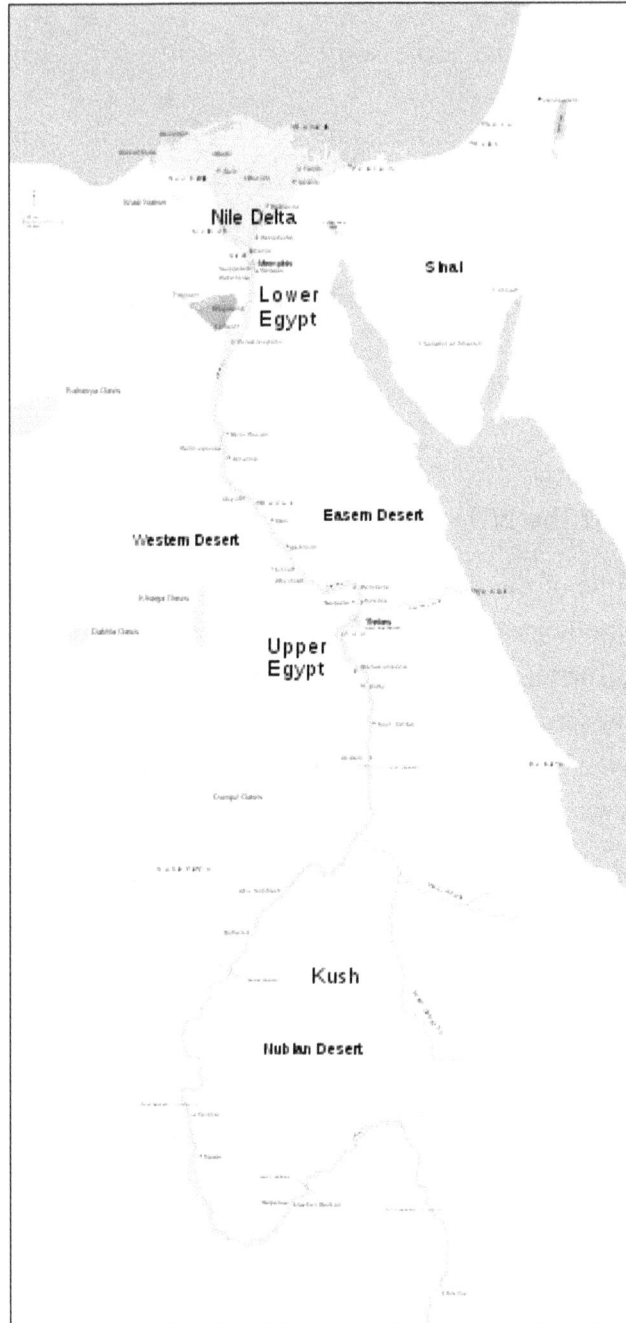

Figure 34: *Upper and Lower Egypt* [a]

[a] SOURCE: By H.Seldon—The map was made from file Ancient_Egypt_map.svg. This file was made by Jeff Dahl. For Faiyum_oasis.svg was used information from book: Ian Shaw: Dějiny starověkého Egypta, ISBN 80-7257-975-4., CC BY-SA 3.0, https://commons.wikime-dia.org/w/index.php?curid=3948636 retrieved on 24 April 2023.

into one kingdom during the Early Bronze Age by the First Dynasty King Menes (around 3100 BCE).

The Nile River Valley played two important roles in the emergence of the human species—it was the main dispersal corridor, 'the natural route', for ancient hominins in their journey out of Africa and its north-eastern end (the Levant, Fertile Crescent, and Mesopotamia) became a major source for the dispersal of ancient hominins and human species and agricultural and pastoral practices back into Africa.[740]

Archaeological evidence shows that human ancestors' habitation in the Nile River Valley began some three hundred thousand years ago.[741] There is evidence of Old Stone Age (Upper Palaeolithic) hunter-gatherers (e.g., Sebilians) in the Nile River Valley from 30000 BCE to 10000 BCE. The Sebilians were hunters and fishermen who survived on freshwater molluscs, fish, river animals, plains animals, and wild-growing cereals.[742] Neolithic (New Stone Age) hominins inhabited the Valley from around 7000 BCE to 4500 BCE. Most of the initial inhabitants came from the south (Nubia—now southern Egypt and northern Sudan), the west (now Libya), and the north-east (now the Middle East).

Impact of Mesopotamia on the Nile Valley

Even though the Nile River valley was rich in native wild animals (gazelle, antelope, ox, fish, hippopotamus, waterfowl) and plants, the ancient Egyptians were already in the process of domesticating selected plants and animals. Around 6000 BCE, this indigenous process was interrupted by the arrival of domesticated strains of wheat and barley and domesticated sheep and goats from Mesopotamia.[743]

Once sedentarism and domestication of animals and plants had arrived, farming communities rapidly spread across the Nile Delta and the Nile River Valley, displacing the hunter-gatherers.[744] By around 5000 BCE, communities involved in domesticating wheat, barley, sheep, goats, pigs, and cattle were well established in Egypt. As occurred in Mesopotamia, the ancient Egyptians were now collectively harnessing and exploiting

---

[740]   SOURCE: https://www.frontiersin.org/articles/10.3389/feart.2020.607183/full retrieved on 23 April 2023.

[741]   Redford (1992), p. 3.

[742]   Hayes (1965), pp. 59-60.

[743]   Redford (1992), pp. 5-7; and https://what-when-how.com/archaeology-of-ancient-egypt/neolithic-cultures-overview-archaeology-of-ancient-egypt/ retrieved on 23 April 2023.

[733]   SOURCE: https://what-when-how.com/archaeology-of-ancient-egypt/neolithic-cultures-overview-archaeology-of-ancient-egypt/ retrieved on 23 April 2023.

the floodplain soils, which were enriched by the annual flooding of the Nile. Centralised power structures and social differentiation began to emerge.[745]

Geographical circumstances allowed dominating elites to harness the power of collective activity, propelling the growth of the first cities, states, and empires.

The Metropolitan Museum of Art in New York describes developments in the Nile Valley after 4500 BCE in the following way:

> *In the ensuing millennia many forms of art flourish, including jewellery (faience beads), ceramic vessels, geometric figures, and pottery, much of which is found in tombs. Hierakonpolis in the south, the largest Predynastic settlement known, is the center of political control. The pyramids of Giza and Saqqara arise in the Old Kingdom (ca. 2649–2150 BC), one of the most dynamic and innovative periods in Egyptian culture. Power decentralizes during the First Intermediate Period (ca. 2150–2030 BC), only to be unified again by the Theban king Mentuhotep II in the Middle Kingdom (ca. 2030–1640 BC).*[746]

Prehistoric development in Egypt was influenced by the dispersal of people and ideas back from the Levant and Mesopotamia into north-eastern Africa, specifically, into the Nile Delta. Sedentarism and the domestication of plants in Egypt were heavily influenced by Mesopotamia, and exotically decorated items emerging in fourth-millennium-BCE Egypt contain largely Mesopotamian and Elamite motifs.[747]

The unification of the Upper Egyptian communities began gradually under the Gerzean (Naqada II–III) culture from 3500 BCE to around 3100 BCE. Here the various chief or ruling family-based communities began to unify but were not yet a state-based collective. There was a gradual uptake of uniformity and homogeneity in farming, pastoralism, the use of the plough and draft animals, symbolism, decorative arts, leadership, trading, social stratification, alliances, weapons, military capabilities, mythological beliefs, cult, and burial practices.[748]

Not long after, Ancient Egypt was unified 'dynastically' under pharaonic monarchies (from around 3100 BCE). From here onwards, the pattern of influence from the northeast was reversed somewhat. The Egyptian dynastic empires became some of the most important empires, major invaders, controllers, and influencers on the Levant, and ultimately, on the content of the Hebrew Bible. The land route through the Levant and the

---

[745] Matyszak (2020), p. 15.

[746] The Metropolitan Museum of Art (2000).

[747] Kuhrt (2009A), p. 133.

[748] Kuhrt (2009A), pp. 130-134.

sea route to Byblos were the most likely major routes for the invasions and cultural, intellectual, and mythological exchanges between Egypt and the Levant.[749]

The Dynasties of Egypt

Encyclopedia Britannica defines the word *dynasty* as: 'a family or line of rulers, a succession of sovereigns of a country belonging to a single family or tracing their descent to a common ancestor'.[750] The term is largely used when referring to the history of Egypt. The ancient Egyptians did not have a commonly agreed calendar or lunisolar dating system. They recorded history based on a list of the continuous reign of their kings beginning with the reign on Earth of their sun god, Ra.[751]

Modern scholars have divided some thirty Egyptian dynasties occurring between the first dynasty and the biblically determined time of Jesus into the following kingdoms and approximate dates:

- **The Archaic Period** (414 years)—Dynasty I and Dynasty II—3100 BCE to 2686 BCE

- **The Old Kingdom** (505 years)—Dynasty III to Dynasty VI—2687 BCE to 2181 BCE

- **The First Intermediate Period** (126 years)—Dynasty VII to Dynasty X—2181 BCE to 2040 BCE,

- **The Middle Kingdom** (405 years)—Dynasty XI to Dynasty XIII—2130 BCE to 1649 BCE

- **The Second Intermediate Period** (100 years)—Dynasty XIV to Dynasty XVII—1725 BCE to 1550 BCE,

- **The New Kingdom** (481 years)—Dynasty XVIII to Dynasty XX—1550 BCE to 1077 BCE

- **The Third Intermediate Period** (322 years)—Dynasty XXI to Dynasty XXV—1069 BCE to 656 BCE

---

[749] Redford (1992), pp. 21-23.
[750] SOURCE: https://www.britannica.com/topic/dynasty retrieved on 25 April 2023.
[751] NOTE: the absence of a calendar and the reliance on king lists makes the exact determination of historical dates difficult. There is some dispute amongst scholars over the exact dates of each Egyptian Dynasty and the reign of specific kings.

- **The Late Period** (415 years)—Dynasty XXVI to Dynasty XXXI—664 BCE to 332 BCE—Persians ruled Egypt from 525 BCE to 404 BCE and again between 343 BCE and 332 BCE

- **The Greco-Roman Period**—from the Greek Argead Dynasty to the Greek Ptolemaic Dynasty—332 BCE to 30 BCE—the Persian control was lost to the Greeks under Alexander the Great from 332 BCE

- **In around 63 BCE**, Canaan/Israel was incorporated into the Roman Empire. In 30 BCE, Egypt was incorporated into the Roman Empire.[752]

The Egyptians believe that the first mortal king and first Pharaoh after Ra was called Menes. However, there is significant confusion over whether the first king was named Menes or possibly Scorpion, Narmer, or Hor-Aha.[753] It is accepted that the first king was responsible for unifying Upper and Lower Egypt into one kingdom.

Pharaoh means 'great house', which is a reference to the palace where the Pharaoh/king lived.[754] The Egyptians believed in a divine monarchy, where the Pharaoh king was the earthly embodiment of Horus, the falcon-headed god of war and the sky. The Pharaoh king was believed to be able to guarantee the fertility of the Nile River and the surrounding soils.[755] The king was regarded as omnipotent. He guaranteed and safeguarded the cosmic and earthly order known as Ma'at—the correct balance/truth.[756]

First-Dynasty unified Egypt was an homogenous cultural identity differentiating itself from its neighbours. Hieroglyphic writing expanded enormously to celebrate royal exploits as trade with the Levant/Southern Palestine and Mesopotamia intensified.[757]

It was in the Old Kingdom period (Dynasty III to Dynasty VI), that the art and architectural symbols of Egypt took a leap forward. Stone began to be used in the production of life-sized statues and monumental buildings. The very first Egyptian pyramid, the Pyramid of Djoser (2670 BCE–2650 BCE) was a step pyramid shape and was most likely influenced by the stepped ziggurats in Iran and Mesopotamia.

It was during this period of rapid growth that Egypt lacked an essential building material—timber. It built a strong link by sea to the Canaanite port town of Byblos,

---

[752] SOURCE: https://discoveringegypt.com/ancient-egyptian-kings-queens/egyptian-old-kingdom-dynasties / and https://en.wikipedia.org/wiki/Dynasties_of_ancient_Egypt both retrieved on 25 April 2023.

[753] Greenberg (2019), p. 34.

[754] SOURCE: https://education.nationalgeographic.org/resource/pharaohs/ retrieved on 25 April 2023.

[755] Redford (1992), p. 24.

[756] Miles (2011), p. 23.

[757] Kuhrt (2009A), pp. 134-135; Mumford (2014), pp. 71-72.

from which it imported pine, cypress, and cedar from the forests of what is now Lebanon. Egyptian diplomacy and cultural influences spread along the Canaan coast from there.[758]

Ancient Egypt's shortage of other key resources was largely responsible for their peaceful and diplomatic relationships with these more distant foreign lands. Ancient Egypt had a demand for other commodities, including pitch, bitumen, oils, metals, wine, trade skills, seafaring skills, military service, and craftmanship such as viticulture and wood- and metalworking. Peaceful trade was established with the Levantine port cities of Tyre, Arwad, Byblos, and Sidon, and with the Libyans to the west and the Nubians to the south.[759]

The long-term relationship between Egypt and the Levant

The relationship between ancient Egypt and the Southern Levant had already existed for thousands of years. Trade between Egypt and the Southern Levant began in around 6000 BCE and intensified from 3100 BCE onwards. Egyptologist and specialist in Middle Eastern archaeology, Gregory Mumford, has outlined evidence of Egyptian influence, and imports from and exports to the Levant, in almost a continuous pattern from 4500 BCE to 332 BCE.[760] There were political, trade, economic, and mythological exchanges between the two locations for more than four thousand years before the HB/OT was canonised. In the second millennium BCE, there were major exchanges of people, objects, ideas and:

> … increased interactions and interconnections between Egypt and the regions of the southern Levant. Mobility and movement between and among these regions were key factors in the exchange of ideas, technologies, and values and, therefore, were essential components of the evolution of both societies.[761]

The archaeological and textual evidence indicates at least four main ways in which Egyptian influence penetrated the Levant and the Israelites—through trade, political dictate, cultural appropriation of Egyptian ideas by Levantine communities, and objects and practices imported, utilised, and/or undertaken by the Egyptian military

---

[758] Roux (1992), pp. 237-238.

[759] Bietak (2018), pp. 68-72.

[760] Mumford (2014), pp. 69-71.

[761] Cohen and Adams (2019), p. 1.

and administrators whilst in control of the Levant.[762] Regardless, there is ample evidence of the intermingling of material and intellectual aspects of both cultures prior to the emergence of the Hebrew Bible.

The most influential Pharaonic periods for the impact of Egypt on the Southern Levant and subsequently on the HB/OT covered the second millennium BCE, including the Egyptian Second Intermediate Period, New Kingdom, Third Intermediate Period and Late Period, extending from around 1725 BCE through to 332 BCE:

- The Canaanite Hyksos invaded and successfully dominated the Nile Delta from 1720 BCE to 1595 BCE. During this time, there was intensive trade between Egypt, the Levant and Mesopotamia,[763] including goods from the Levant into Egypt (jewellery, pottery, olive oil, wine, wheat, perfume, lazuli, turquoise, silver, battle axes, oils, fats, honey, cedar, and precious woods). Once the Hyksos were defeated, they returned to Canaan and adopted 'aspects of Egyptian culture and relay Egyptian and Egyptian-style materials, products, and motifs abroad (e.g., "Hyksos" scarabs)'[764]

- Egypt controlled the Levant between 1500 BCE and 1000 BCE. During this time, the Southern Levant was under the control of the Egyptian military and Egyptian administration, with the Levant, including Israel, being vassal states of the Egyptian Empire

- Between 1353 BCE and 1334 BCE, the Egyptian Pharaoh Akhenaten introduced the concept of monotheism to the Egyptian religion. This was some one thousand years before the HB/OT was finalised, including the Jewish concept of monotheism

- In 1205 BCE Egyptian Pharaoh Merneptah claims he has conquered the Israelites—'Israel is laid waste; his seed is not.'

- During the Persian occupation of Egypt, there are many Hebrews living in Egypt. In 538 BCE, when Cyrus issued an edict for the Jews to be released to return to their homeland and rebuild their temple, many Jewish soldiers and their families remained on Elephantine Island on the Nile River in Upper Egypt.

---

[762] Jeske (2019), pp. 31-32.
[763] Bietak (2018), p. 79.
[764] Mumford (2014), p. 69.

The Ancient Egyptian religion

The ancient Egyptians saw the divine world as being inhabited by a vast array of gods. The Egyptian pantheon included nine gods, who were the first products of creation; there were multiple sun gods, gods involved in elements of creation or natural phenomenon; gods who represented different cosmic elements; goddesses associated with joy, erotic love, and pleasure; goddesses associated with fertility and agriculture; national, regional, and local gods; gods associated with different occupations; funerary deities; and gods of the underworld.[765]

Ancient Egyptian influence on biblical Proverbs

It is near the Pyramid of Djoser in Sakkara that an important tomb has been found. It was the tomb of the author who some believe wrote the oldest book in the world, the Prisse Papyrus. The tomb belonged to an Egyptian scribe called Ptahhotep, who is believed to have lived sometime between 2396 BCE and 2356 BCE.[766]

The book was written for another Egyptian scribe and contains thirty-seven teachings or instructions. Written two thousand years before the finalisation of the Hebrew Bible, the Book of Ptahhotep has an uncanny similarity to many concepts in biblical Proverbs. For example:

- the Book of Ptahhotep—*Follow your heart as long as you live. Do no more than is required. Do not shorten the time of 'follow the heart'.* Proverbs 4:23—*Guard your heart above all else, for it determines the course of your life.*
- the Book of Ptahhotep—D*o not be proud and arrogant with your knowledge.* Proverbs 11:2—*When pride comes, then comes disgrace, but with humility comes wisdom.*
- the Book of Ptahhotep—*If you plow and if there is growth in your field and God lets it prosper in your hand, don't boast to your neighbour.* Proverbs 27:1-2—*Never boast about tomorrow. You don't know what will happen between now and then. Let other people praise you—even strangers; never do it yourself.*

---

[765]   Holland (2010), pp. 19-25.
[766]   Hilliard et al (1987), pp. 6-7 and 17-22.

Prehistoric Precedence

The Ancient Egyptian concept of paradise and life after death

Ancient Egyptian mythology had a concept of life after death that has some similarities with the concepts found in both Judaism and Christianity. Even in prehistoric times, there is evidence of an ancient Egyptian belief in an afterlife. A key ancient Egyptian concept of the afterlife, adopted by Judaism and Christianity, was that it was essentially, a continuation of a person's earthly life, but would be much better, without sickness or death.[767]

Murry Hope has shown how burials in prehistoric Egypt had bodies placed crouched on their side as if waiting to give birth and being surrounded by material possessions and artefacts to see them into an afterlife.[768] For Dynastic Egyptians:

> *Life on earth was only one aspect of an eternal journey. The soul was immortal and was only inhabiting a body on this physical plane for a short time. At death, one would meet with judgment in the Hall of Truth and, if justified, would move on to an eternal paradise known as The Field of Reeds which was a mirror image of one's life on earth. Once one had reached paradise one could live peacefully in the company of those one had loved while on earth, including one's pets, in the same neighbourhood by the same stream, beneath the very same trees one thought had been lost at death. This eternal life, however, was only available to those who had lived well and in accordance with the will of the gods in the most perfect place conducive to such a goal: the land of Egypt.[769]*

The Egyptian version of monotheism

The ancient Egyptians had worshipped a sun god using a variety of names since the third millennium BCE (Amun, Atum, Bast, Hathor, Horus, Khepri, Ptah, Ra, Sopdu, Aten). There is archaeological evidence of solar cults, solar temples, and solar obelisks being built for hundreds of years before the emergence of monotheism in Egyptian mythology.[770]

The Egyptian Pharaoh Akhenaten (1353 BCE to 1336 BCE) introduced monotheism to Egyptian mythology. He is accredited, along with the Zoroastrians, as being one of the influences on the Hebrew scribes' version of monotheism. Akhenaten developed his version of monotheism by reducing all the Egyptian deities into a cult of the one sole heavenly sun god, Aten.

---

[767]   Mark (2023E), p. 20.
[768]   Hope (1996), p. 24.
[769]   Mark (2009A).
[770]   See: Nuzzolo and Krejei (2017).

Ancient history authority Amelie Kuhrt believes that this move to monotheism did not come out of the blue. It was the culmination of a trend that was already occurring in the Egyptian religion. During the eighteenth dynasty (1550 BCE to 1292 BCE), the Egyptian sun god Re had begun to absorb many of the features of the other Egyptian deities creating 'a kind of syncretistic monotheism' with other gods being regarded as various manifestations of Re. It was not that difficult for Akhenaten to then abandon traditional Egyptian polytheism and introduce worship centred on Aten as the sole heavenly king.[771]

In many ways, Akhenaten continued the pursuit of one supreme monotheistic god at the expense of all or any other religions, religious symbols, or any other gods. Akhenaten embarked on a series of strategies to exterminate memories of or devotion to any other gods than his supreme deity, Aten. This involved him in ideologically-driven editing of numerous inscriptions, demolishing temples and destroying or defacing images of other Egyptian gods such as Amun, Horus, Osiris across the empire.[772]

This practice of suppressing other gods and other religions was not unique to Akhenaten. It was also a common strategy of the Assyrians (from around 2300 BCE) and the Akkadians in Mesopotamia (from around 1180 BCE). Suppression of other religions or beliefs eventually became an ongoing practice for several of the religions that emerged from these Egyptian and Mesopotamian practices – particularly the three Abrahamic religions.

In contradistinction to Judaism and Christianity, Aten was not represented in anthropomorphic form but as a sun disk.[773] Aten was associated with previous sun gods Amun and Ra. The sun god cult had multiple hymns praising the sun disc, which came to represent Aten. Hymns and poetry about and to the sun disc abound. They focus on the dependence of life on the god and the sun; its transcendence, creativity, and absolute power. There are various inscriptions that refer to the 'eternal lord' and 'image of the Lord', phrases and concepts that were to become common in both Judaism and Christianity. While King Akhenaten was the chief worshipper of the disc, it was served by a 'first prophet' and 'chief seer'.[774] This is an ancient tradition that has continued in modern times with the Chief Rabbi of Judaism, Christian Pope, and the Church of England's Archbishop of Canterbury.

---

[771] Kuhrt (2009A), pp. 200-201.
[772] See: Jack (2016).
[773] Holland (2010), p. 29.
[774] Redford (1980), p. 22-28.

Chapter 14

The Role of the Ancient Indus Valley Civilisation

The ancient Indus Valley is a location where the movement of the tectonic plates and the resultant geomorphology created opportunities for complex human habitation dating back several thousand years. The Indus Valley is regarded as one of six possible 'cradles of civilisation'. Like the Tigris, Euphrates, and Nile, the Indus River had a fertile alluvial flood plain partly surrounded by mountains. It had five tributaries feeding down from the Himalayas and the Hindu Kush mountains in the north, the Kirthar and Sulaiman Ranges to the west, and the Thar or Indian Desert to its east.

Archaeological evidence indicates that there was a flourishing Indus Valley civilisation from around 7000 BCE until 600 BCE.[775] It is highly likely that the Indus Valley civilisation predated the Sumerian and Egyptian civilisations by at least one thousand years.[776] In fact, the earliest terminology used by archaeologists to describe this civilisation was Indo-Sumerian, owing to the obvious affinities with the Sumerian civilisation of the third millennium BCE. It is now largely accepted that the Indus Valley civilisation, usually referred to as the Harappan Civilisation is one of the world's three most ancient civilisations, along with Mesopotamians and Ancient Egyptians. The Bharatiya Vidya Bhavan Institute describes it in this way:

> *India now takes her place, side by side with Egypt and Mesopotamia, as a country where we can-trace the dawn of human civilization and the beginnings of those thoughts, ideas, activities and movements which have shaped the destinies of mankind all over the civilized world.*[777]

---

[775] Mark (2020C).
[776] SEE: https://www.youtube.com/watch?v=jn-mnkLkVFQ&ab_channel=UniverseInsideYou retrieved on 1 May 2023.
[777] Bharatiya Vidya Bhavan (2018), Section 01, p. 37 and p. 70.

The Harappan Civilisation

The Harappan Civilisation was the first urban civilisation on the Indian sub-continent. It covered a larger geographic area than either ancient Egypt or Mesopotamia. It covered what is now most of Pakistan, North-East Afghanistan, and North-West India. Its two most famous ancient cities were Mohenjo-daro and Harappa.[778] In many ways, the historical fascination with ancient Egypt, Mesopotamia, and Greece has meant that the many prehistoric achievements of the civilisations of the Indus Valley have been overlooked. Yet for their time, these were very advanced civilisations.

Farmers raised crops and livestock in the fertile plains of the Indus River and other waterways. Artisans created beautiful pottery, jewellery, and stone and metal sculptures. Merchants traded with faraway lands. They marked their goods with square stone seals carved with images and a type of writing that has yet to be deciphered. The Indus Valley people also built large, walled cities, including Mohenjo-daro and Harappa. These cities had straight paved streets, well-built brick houses, and a sophisticated system of private baths and sewers.[779] There is extensive archaeological evidence of Indus Valley trade with Mesopotamia, Anatolia and Egypt dating back to at least the seventh millennium BCE. This includes evidence of Indus Valley traders and families living and worshiping in ancient Mesopotamia and Babylonia. Trade between the advanced prehistoric communities of the ancient Indus Valley and Mesopotamia and Egypt occurred both overland and via the Indian Ocean through the Persian Gulf and the Red Sea. Traded goods from India included carnelian, teak, marble, ivory, distinctive Indus Valley cooking utensils, shell jewellery, toys, silk, spices, and Indian pepper.[780]

Religion of the Indus Valley

Excavations across the Indus Valley determined that the religious practices in the ancient Indus Valley did not include temples or other centralised religious structures. However, there is archaeological evidence of terracotta figurines, seals containing images of animals and trees, and geometric and decorative motifs that some have linked to cultic beliefs.[781] The Harappans celebrated the Northern Hemisphere vernal equinox as the time of the birth of their god of war and leader of their god's army, Skanda-Kartikeya.

For centuries, this region had been a focus for a range of different cults, beliefs, and mythologies.[782] Bactria, eastern Iran, the Indus Valley, and Nepal, were where Zoroastrianism,

778 SOURCE: https://member.ancient.eu/hinduism/ retrieved on 9 May 2023.
779 Schomp (2005), pp. 5-6.
780 Dalrymple (2024), pp.58-61
781 SOURCE: https://encyclopedia.pub/entry/32926 retrieved on 1 May 2023.
782 Harmatta et al., (1996).

Hinduism, and Buddhism first emerged. It is generally accepted that Hinduism began in the Indus Valley and was well established by around 1500 BCE:

> *What has come to be called the Hindu faith, tradition, or religion is the result of a rich blend of human civilization, including many different practices and expressions of religious life. Many religious cultures, who spoke many languages and held many different concepts about the nature of the Divine, have contributed to its development and evolution.*[783]

The Hindu religious narratives

Hinduism is currently the world's third-largest religion. Prior to the emergence of the narrative texts that eventually became the HB/OT, east of the Levant, in north-western India, there was a wide range of different tribal groups whose scribes were articulating the foundational texts of the Vedic culture (around 1600 BCE to 700 BCE).[784] The Vedic culture produced the oldest Hindu writing, which was finalised at around the same time as the early work of the Hebrew scribes—from around 800 BCE to 500 BCE.

Hindu scribes wrote the Vedas (the Sanskrit word *véda* means 'knowledge, wisdom, insight, sacred writings'), which predate the HB/OT and are considered among the oldest, if not the oldest, religious texts in the world. They are Hinduism's scriptures dealing with meditation, knowledge, philosophy, existence, reality, and the nature of being.

The Vedas had been orally transmitted since the second millennium BCE. However, followers believe that the Vedas have existed forever and have been passed down through the ages. Hindus consider the Vedas to be *apauruṣeya*, which means 'not of a man, superhuman'. The Hindu Vedas are considered revelations seen by ancient sages after intense meditation.[785] Their followers believe them to be the actual words of God. (see *The origin of the biblical "Word of God"*, page 379).

The Indus Valley's link to biblical hymns and scripture

Rig Veda, one of the four sacred Hindu canonical texts, has a pattern of deification that was common across the Middle East, at the time. It contains various hymns for praying

---

to Vedic Gods such as Agni (the fire god), Indra (the lord of heavens), Mitra, Varuna (the water god), and Surya (the sun god). As also occurred with the HB/OT stories, there are deep secrets and allegories about gods, the universe, spiritual knowledge, and rituals woven into the Vedas.

The ancient Mahābhārata, one of the two major Sanskrit epics of ancient India, was most likely written around 400 BCE. The Mahābhārata is the longest poem ever written. It contains eighteen books and twenty-four thousand verses recounting the struggle between two groups of cousins and contains Hindu philosophical and devotional texts and a list of the four goals of life.[786]

- Dharma: righteousness, moral values
- Artha: prosperity, economic values
- Kama: pleasure, love, psychological values
- Moksha: liberation, spiritual values.

The Indus Valley link to the Jesus story

The virgin birth attributed to being impregnated by a god has parallels in the ancient Indus Valley. The ancient Vedic (Zoroastrian, Hindu, and Buddhist) action and storm god Indra (around 1500 BCE) was conceived by a virgin who was impregnated by Spenta Mainyu (the Zoroastrian Holy Ghost).[787]

The Indus Valley link to the Noah flood story

Prior to the biblical Noah story, flood stories involving the wiping out of civilisation pervaded the prehistoric Middle Eastern, Egyptian, Anatolian, and Indus Valley cultures.[788] Hindu mythology relates the story of the first king of India, Manu Vaivaswata (3102 BCE), who is warned by a fish of an impending flood in the Indus Valley—the location of the merging of five Indus River tributaries (Punjab, from *panj-ab*, 'five rivers'). Manu is warned that the flood would sweep away the heavens and the Earth. He builds a wooden ark and invites seven wise sages to join him. They survive the flood and Manu becomes the first king of India.[789]

---

[786] SOURCE: https://worldhistory.org/Mahābhārata/ retrieved on 6 October 2021.
[787] Boyce (2001), p. 21.
[788] Bierlein (1994), pp. 121-135.
[789] Leeming (1990), p. 55.

Chapter 15

The Impact of the Bronze Age Collapse

During the second millennium BCE, under Egyptian New Kingdom control, Canaan contained competing city-states controlled by headmen or mayors and councils of elders. The Bronze Age collapse in around 1200 BCE provided an opportunity for the failure of imperial domination and the strengthening of these Canaanite city-states. This included Ugarit, Phoenicia, Israel, Judah, Ammon, Moab, and Edom. It was around this time that Egypt, which had been controlling the Levant since around 1500 BCE, withdrew from the Levant, and these groups and the invading sea peoples seized the opportunity to claim territory.

Two of the groups that emerged in the Levant, at this opportunistic time, were the Israelites and the Philistines.[790] Both newly emerging ethnic entities were taking advantage of the conjunction of circumstances facilitating their expansion territorially and culturally. This included the collapse of the dominant kingdoms, the parallel collapse of the major trading networks, the resultant regional disorganisation, major people movements/demographic changes, the withdrawal of the Egyptians, the emergence of the Iron Age, and the availability of written communication.

The once-dominant kingdoms broke into smaller territorial and ethnocultural claimants, a mixture of locals (Assyrians, Canaanites, Phoenicians, Egyptians) and newcomers (Cypriots, Minoans, Anatolians, Asia Minor, Aegeans), regional reuse and resettlement, new villages and hamlets, and a revival of small Canaanite cultic buildings and unfortified village layouts with very little evidence of integrated settlement hierarchies.[791]

---

[790] Horwitz et al., (2017), p. 97
[791] Gilboa (2014), pp. 635-640.

283

The Levant saw the emergence of new forms of local identity, administration, and organisation focused on certain behaviours, symbols, and historical and ethnic mythologies.[792]

In around 800 BCE, when the Hebrew scribes were beginning to develop the main themes in the HB/OT, the Levant saw the emergence, post-collapse, of a range of small kingdoms. In the northern Levant, this included the Phoenicians, the Kadmonites/Nabateans, and remnants of the once-dominant Hittites. In the Southern Levant, the newly formed kingdoms included the Edomites, Kenites, Moabites, Medians, Philistines, Northern Israel, and Southern Judah. This rich tapestry of different kingdoms that evolved following the Bronze Age collapse gave the Hebrew scribes material (historical, geographic, and mythological) that they wove into their biblical stories. This included linking the origin of many of these kingdoms to the sons or grandsons of Noah.

Jonathan Tubb describes the creative storytelling by the Hebrew scribes as they constructed a mytho-history of the Israeli kingdom (written largely whilst in Babylonian exile around 580 BCE). They dated their kingdom back to a presumed united monarchy in 1050 BCE:

> It is important to look at the biblical texts, and to appreciate that they were not written, or at least edited until at least four hundred years after the events they refer to. At this time, perhaps during the exile, the motivation for their composition was surely to create an historical 'golden age', a past glory which would give hope and inspiration to the exiles.

A key device in the appropriation of the names of the Canaanite kingdoms as progeny of Noah was to strengthen the myth that the great flood destroyed all humans except Noah's family, from which all of humanity then evolved. It provided an opportunity to give meaning to the developing mythology by referring to locations with which their emerging followers were familiar but rebranding them as the progeny of Noah.[793]

The Phoenicians

Three different sea peoples settled on the southern Canaanite coast—the Philistines, the Sikila/Tjekker, and the Shardana. The sea peoples' occupation of the Southern Levant saw the southern coastal plain of Canaan divided into two discrete entities and territories: the

---

[792] Joffe (2002), p. 426.
[793] Tubb (1998), p. 114.

sea peoples' territories on the southern Canaan coastline and the indigenous Canaanite Phoenicians along the northern coastline.[794]

The Phoenicians called themselves Canaanites.[795] By all available evidence, the Phoenicians were a creative, inventive, maritime, and economically active culture. It is likely that they were participants, with other Canaanites, in the Hyksos invasion and successful migration into and control of the Nile Delta from 1720 BCE to 1595 BCE.[796] Their maritime skills were recognised across the region. Following the Bronze Age collapse, and free from Egyptian control, Phoenicia began a major renaissance and emerged as a distinct culture. The Assyrian kings Tiglath-Pileser I (1114 BCE to 1076 BCE) and Ashurbanipal (668 BCE-627 BCE) both record that they were paid tributes from established, major Phoenician harbour towns and city-states at Arwad, Byblos, and Sidon to avoid being attacked by the invading Assyrian armies.[797]

No peoples dominated the Mediterranean Sea trade networks more than the Levantine Phoenicians. The Phoenicians became a trading-based culture and were such prolific traders and influencers that their alphabet eventually became the de facto language of international trade at the time. It subsequently became the basis for the alphabet in use to this day.[798]

The Phoenician religion was largely inherited from the Mesopotamians. Like the early Israelites, they believed in a supreme god (Ba'al) and a group of lesser gods to whom they performed religious rites and rituals to ensure productive agriculture, prosperity, and health. They shared a priesthood and mythology with their Canaanite neighbours.[799]

The Philistines

There is some debate about the origin of the Philistines, but it is generally accepted that they were not native Canaanites. Some believe that they were most probably part of the invading 'sea peoples' and possibly from somewhere in the Aegean[800] or perhaps from ancient Crete, Cyprus, and/or southern Italy.[801] They came via land and sea and settled

---

[794] Gilboa (2005), pp. 47-52.

[795] Kuhrt (2009B), p. 403.

[796] Redford (1992), p. 100.

[797] Stieglitz (1990), p. 279; Bauer (2007), pp. 337-338.

[798] SOURCE: https://study.com/academy/lesson/mediterranean-sea-trade-origins-routes.html

[799] Captivating History (2019B), p. 8.

[800] Birney (2007), pp. 433-440.

[801] Horwitz et al (2017), p. 97.

in and around the ancient Southern Levant city of Ashkelon, which is now a major Israeli city.[802]

DNA analysis of skeletons from ancient Ashkelon excavations gives some weight to the Philistines' migration from southern Europe. However, linguistic analysis suggests the 'invaders' may have included some Hittites from the northern Levant and/or Anatolia (the sea people's land route). Their pork-eating practices may also link some of them to mainland Greece (the sea people's sea route).[803]

Notwithstanding their place of origin, it is most likely that the group referred to as the 'Philistines' were, as were the Israelites, an emerging opportunistic confederation of peoples from a variety of locations who had migrated to or were already in the Levant during and after the Bronze Age collapse.

The Levant has predetermined geomorphological conditions that limit the likelihood of the region being under the control of one locally-based empire. Donald Redford describes it thusly:

> *In Palestine the genesis and growth of communities with a manifest destiny to control vast tracts of land were impossible. The mountains divide the land into circumscribed regions—valley, upland, steppe, coast—and prevent the development of anything beyond a canton.*[804]

Today, the land between the west of the River Jordan and the Mediterranean Sea in the Southern Levant is referred to as Cisjordan, based on the neo-Latin language for 'on this side of the river Jordan'. The land to the east of the Jordan River is referred to as Transjordan based on the Latin word 'trans', which can mean either across or beyond (Figure 35).

From around 1300 BCE to 1100 BCE, the Philistines settled down in the southern coastal plains of the Levant and immediately wanted to expand further eastwards. They were but one of the new ethnic entities in the region that were battling each other for identity formation, recognition, and territory along with the remaining Canaanite indigenous groups who occupied a narrow zone just below the highlands (in or near the trough valley/s). and the emerging Israelites (occupying the hill country but wanting to expand westwards).[805, 806] (Figure 35).

---

[802] Matyszak (2020), pp. 78-83.
[803] Horwitz et al (2017), pp. 99-102.
[804] Redford (1992), p. 15.
[805] Bryce and Birkett-Rees (2016), p. 181.
[806] Faust (2018), p. 280.

Figure 35: *Schematic map showing: Early Iron Age locations of the Philistines, Canaanites, and Israelites in southern Canaan (on the background of the main geographical regions)* [a]

---

[a]   SOURCE: modified from Faust and Katz, 2011, p. 232; the use of the base-map, courtesy of Avraham Faust

Palestine

The name Palestine has been used historically as an alternative name for the region of Canaan and the land of Israel. There is ambiguity around the origin of the name. The ancient Egyptians referred to one of the invading sea peoples as 'Prst' or 'Plst', which has been translated from hieroglyphics as 'Peleset'. Most scholars believe that this term was referring specifically to the Philistines.[807]

The Assyrians called the same region 'Palashtu/Palastu' or 'Pilistu' and the fifth- century Greek historian Herodotus wrote about the region between Phoenicia and Egypt as Palestine.[808]

---

[807]   Matyszak (2020), p. 57 and p. 79.
[808]   https://en.wikipedia.org/wiki/Timeline_of_the_name_Palestine retrieved on 12 April 2023.

Since the time of Herodotus, the term Palestine has been applied to the whole of the Southern Levant from the Dead Sea to the Mediterranean coast. From the fifth century BCE onwards, Palestine was regarded as all the land of Israel, including the occupied territories and not only the parts controlled by the Philistines or the coastal parts of Israel's 'holy land'.[809]

Palestinian academic, Nur Masalha has completed a lengthy documentation of the history of Palestine. He claims that Palestine has existed as an identifiable region, named country and a geo-political unit for at least three thousand years (from around 1300 BCE onwards). He further asserts that the term Palestine was more commonly used in ancient times to describe the region than the word Canaan.[810]

Modern-day researchers, historians, and authors also generally use the term Palestine to refer to Canaan or the whole of the Southern Levant. Broshi and Gophna and Broshi and Finkelstein, for instance, explore the archaeological evidence of settlements in 'Palestine'. They define Palestine as covering from the River Jordan west to the Mediterranean Sea and from the Plains of Arad and Beersheba in the south to Upper Galilee and the Huleh Valley in the north.[811]

---

[809] Jacobson (1999), p. 69.
[810] Masalha, (2018), p. 2, p.16 and p. 18.
[811] Broshi and Gophna (1986), p. 74; Broshi and Finkelstein (1992), p. 49.

Chapter 16

The Origin of the Israelites

Origin and use of the word—Israel

The word *Israel* has a long history. By 3000 BCE, the personal name Israel was already a popular personal name in the Middle East. This was well before the initial writing of the HB/OT (from around 900 BCE). Israel is an early Semitic language word in Eblaite that, along with Akkadian, is the oldest known Semitic language. The Eblaite language was discovered from archaeological excavations in and around the town of Ebla, which was part of Mesopotamia in the third millennium BCE (Figure 36). Other Semitic and Mesopotamian language documents—Sumerian, Ugaritic, and Akkadian—were found in archaeological excavations, as well as the Eblaite language documents. Because of its use in the Levant, Eblaite was initially described by scholars as a Paleo-Canaanite language.

Israel was also a personal name used in the extinct Semitic Amorite dialect of Ugaritic. Ugarit was a major fortified port, trading, and diplomatic relations town in Northern Syria that had been established around 6000 BCE (Figure 36).

Researchers differ on the literal meaning of the word 'Israel'. *El* or *il* is a North-West Semitic (Ugaritic, Ebla, Phoenician, Old Akkadian, and Amorite) word meaning 'god' or 'deity'. The Semitic word *el* or *il* could be used to describe any god, but for the Canaanites and the ancient Levantine region, El was the supreme god, the father of mankind and of all creatures. Across ancient Semitic religions at the time and prior to the emergence of Israel, El was regarded as the husband of the consort/mother goddess Asherah.

There is archaeological evidence of Israelite families in the eighth century BCE keeping naked figurines of Yahweh's consort, the goddess Asherah, in their homes as part of complex cultic rituals to appeal to the heavenly goddess for fertility and wellbeing.[812]

---

[812]   Finkelstein and Silberman (2002) pp. 240-242.

Figure 36: *Location of the Northern Syria extinct Eblaite and Ugaritic Semitic languages* [a]

---

[a] SOURCE: By Sémhur—File:Near_East_topographic_map-blank.svg, CC BY-SA 4.0, https://commons.wikimedia.org/w/index.php?curid=37448043 retrieved on 18 February 2021.

The Sumerians adapted the Semitic word for god, *il*, in naming their supreme god Enlil. The Sumerians, who spoke their own unique language, developed their word for god by combining two Semitic words—the title *en* combined with the word *lil* meaning 'wind' or 'ghost'. The Sumerians' supreme god Enlil was 'Lord Air'.[813]

A *theophorous name* is a name that has the name of a god embedded somewhere within it. The use of theophorous names was popular across Semitic-speaking cultures in prehistory and remains a common practice within Jewish communities today. The aim is to invoke and display the protection of that deity. Porten et al. have explored the use of theophorous personal names in Egypt (around 300 BCE) within a broad sample of Semitic languages, including Ancient Hebrew. They specifically examined archaeological

---

[813] Leick (2002), pp. 151-152.

documents found on Elephantine Island in the Nile River, where a large early Hebrew community was located.[814]

The name Israel, in the Semitic languages, means 'to contend, fight or wrestle (*isra* from *sarâ*) with god (El)'. The Hebrew scribes, when they wrote the Bible, described how their patriarch Jacob, regarded as the father of the twelve founders of the tribes of Israel, was renamed Israel after he had wrestled with an angel of God. The name Israel was adopted by the Hebrew scribes to define the father of their founders and, thereafter, their collective name, because it is a metaphor for much of the messages and allegories in the HB/OT.

Biblical stories tend not to be about a passive relationship of blind obedience to a god but what Jonathan Lipnick of the Israel Institute of Biblical Studies has defined as an 'active relationship of struggle, confrontation and dialogue'.[815] The word Israel is a metaphor for the essence and nature of the relationship with God being conveyed by the Hebrew scribes throughout the HB/OT.

First historical mention of the Israelites

A key issue for almost all biblical researchers has been to answer the question, 'Where did the Israelites originally come from?'

The Egyptians occupied the Levant from 1500 BCE to 1000 BCE. During that time, they referred to the scattered tribal groups in the mountains of Canaan with the generic term *shasu*, meaning 'tent dwellers'. In some of these tribal settlements, the Egyptians referred to these tent dwellers as *apiru* (also referred to as *habiru*), a term that meant 'outlaws' or 'economic refugees'. This seems to align with the most likely meaning of the word *canaan* as a 'roving bandit' or 'brigand'.

It was in the late Bronze Age that the first evidence appeared of the emergence of the tribal name 'Israelites'. The earliest record to mention Israel is in the Merneptah Stele (dated around 1205 BCE). The Merneptah Stele has also come to be referred to as the 'Israel Stele' because it contains the earliest textual reference to Israel and the only reference from Ancient Egypt. Unlike most of the other cultures that existed in the Middle East region, at and before this time, there is almost no archaeological evidence of Israel prior to

---

[814] Porten et al (2016), pp. 2-3.
[815] SOURCE: https://www.youtube.com/watch?v=VxxhgzDOd58 retrieved on 18 February 2021.

their first and almost insignificant mention in a relatively obscure Egyptian archaeological record in 1205 BCE.

The phrase found on the ancient Egyptian Merneptah stele was written in Egyptian hieroglyphics and was part of a victory hymn celebrating an Egyptian pharaoh's military conquests. The phrase that archaeologists have interpreted as mentioning Israel for the first time relates to Pharaoh Merneptah's victories in locations extending from Libya to Canaan. The hieroglyphic phrase has been translated as 'Israel is laid waste (and) his seed is not'.[816] The phrase 'their seed is not' was apparently a common phrase used by Egyptian pharaohs to claim that an enemy has been vanquished. For instance, Pharaoh Ramesses III (1187 BCE to 1156 BCE) used this phrase to describe his vanquishing of the sea peoples.[817]

The mention in the Merneptah Stele is brief and is part of the Egyptian Pharaoh Merneptah's listing of his military conquests of the time. The term Israel is written with a special pharaonic sign indicating it was referring to a people rather than a place.[818] It is accepted by most researchers that Israel as mentioned in the stele was not a nation but, most likely, a nomadic pastoral and agriculturally-based semi-sedentary socio-ethnic entity, a people, or political entity significant enough to be mentioned but distinguishable from the regional urban city-states and probably located in small settlements somewhere in the hills of Canaan.[819]

That Israel is recognised as distinct from Canaanites is reflected in the wording of the Merneptah Stele. Both Canaan and Israel are separately identified in the Stele, along with several other groups:

> *Desolation is for Tehenu; Hatti is pacified*
> *Plundered is the Canaan with every evil*
> *Yanoam is made as that which does not exist*
> *Israel is laid waste; his seed is not*
> *Hurru is become a widow for Egypt*
> *All lands together, they are pacified*
> *Everyone who is restless, he has been bound.*[820]

---

[816] Hoffmeier (1999), pp. 25-33.
[817] Finkelstein and Silberman (2002), p. 88.
[818] Cline (2014), p. 6.
[819] Halpern (2006-2007), p. 20; Hasel (1994), p. 54.
[820] Smith, R. (2002), pp. 25-26.

The Tehenu was a Berber tribe in Libya, the Hurru (Hurrians) were in Anatolia and northern Mesopotamia, and Yanoam, Canaan, and Israel are regarded as separate entities located in Canaan at the time.

There has been an interesting alternative proposition put forward about the word Israel in the Merneptah Stele by biblical scholar Othniel Margalith. Margalith suggests that the reference to the name Israel is an error by Egyptian scribes who were referring to the fertile Yezreal Valley in the northern Levant. The word Jezreel/Yezreal comes from Hebrew and means 'God sows' or 'El sows', which explains the comment in the Merneptah stele that 'the seed is not laid waste'.

If Margalith is correct—and many dispute his proposition—then the first historical mention of Israel as a people did not happen until around 840 BCE on the Mesha/Moabite Stele. This stele records the victory of the Moabite King Mesha over the Israelites.[821] It contains a reference to 'Omri, the king of Israel'. The Bible describes Omri as the ruler of the Northern Kingdom of Israel during the ninth century BCE.[822] Finkelstein and Silberman believe that, apart from the mention of the word Israel in the Merneptah Stele, the next extra-biblical mention of Israel is in an account of the Northern Kingdom of Israel and the Omride Dynasty in the Mesha Stele.[823]

The victorious listing of military conquests on the Merneptah Stele raises a major credibility issue. Cline and O'Connor, in discussing the various attempts at reconstructing events that happened in Late Bronze Age, make it clear that textual evidence is likely to be the least reliable. The victories of Pharaoh Merneptah outlined in the stele could very well have been propaganda—fabrications of imagined or quite different victories in time and place. Cline and O'Connor recommend that it is more important to isolate relevant material culture (e.g., pottery and other dateable artefacts), for these are the primary source material for an understanding of cultural and population change and movements at the end of the Late Bronze Age.[824] And yet there is none of this evidence of the Israelites in pottery or dateable artefacts prior to 1205 BCE.

Accepting both the Merneptah Stele (late thirteenth century BCE) and the Mesha Stele (late ninth century BCE), there are still just half-a-dozen references to Israel mentioned in the four hundred years between these two finds (excluding the biblical stories).[825]

---

[821] Cited in Hasel (1994), p. 296.
[822] Cline (2009), pp. 16-17.
[823] Finkelstein and Silberman (2002), pp. 170-172.
[824] Cline and O'Connor (2007), p. 134.
[825] Redford (1992), p. 257.

Some biblical scholars claim to have discovered an earlier reference to Israel on a broken statue pedestal containing hieroglyphic name-rings in the Egyptian Museum of Berlin that is dated at 1400 BCE, but this has yet to receive widespread support from archaeologists.[826]

The absence of any archaeological evidence of the Israelites prior to around 1200 BCE has led to much speculation on how their presence might be confirmed prior to this date. Several researchers have focused on possible differences found in prehistoric Canaanite groups' artefacts (e.g., pottery design, burial practices, house designs, settlement patterns), dietary evidence, ethnic markers, or mythological practices (e.g., men being bearded or not, types of beards, eating or not eating pork, circumcision), and technical skills (military, weaponry, metallurgy). Elizabeth Bloch-Smith has examined this research and has not been able to unambiguously nor convincingly demonstrate the emergence of a group that can easily differentiate the prehistoric Israelites on these criteria from the Philistines or the Canaanites at that time.[827]

Most scholars now believe that the Israel mentioned in the Merneptah Stele is probably, in some way, related to the Israel in the HB/OT but the extent of this and exactly who they were is not clear.[828]

Whichever date for the emergence of Israel is chosen, reliable records of their existence did not emerge until the Late Bronze Age. This is a time when, despite there being a wide range of archaeological and artefactual evidence from the various other communities, tribes, nations, cultures, leaders, and religions present, there appears to be no archaeological or reliable artefactual evidence of the Israelites prior to that date. This is strange considering that archaeologists have amassed around half a million cuneiform tablets documenting the life of the Mesopotamians during and well before this same time in prehistory.[829] There is a wealth of archaeological evidence from prehistoric Egypt since the discovery of the Rosetta Stone (1799 CE), Tutankhamen's tomb, the Valley of the Kings (1922 CE), and excavations in and around the Pyramids at Giza.[830]

So, it is not clear from the text in the Merneptah Stele, and the absence of any supporting archaeological evidence, just who the prehistoric Israelites were or exactly from

---

[826] SOURCE: https://www.biblicalarchaeology.org/daily/ancient-cultures/ancient-israel/does-the-merneptah-stele-contain-the-first-mention-of-israel/.

[827] Bloch-Smith (2003).

[828] Hasel (1994), p. 47; Grabbe, 2018.

[829] Bottero (2001), p. 65.

[830] SOURCE: https://www.history.com/news/ancient-egypt-10-best-discoveries-king-tut-pyramids.

whence they came. Multiple sources indicate that it is most likely that the Israelite people emerged as a loose-knit collection of tribal groups somewhere in the Eastern Mediterranean, and probably from the hills and opportunistically after a major, chaotic, and catastrophic decline of kingdoms, principalities, communities, and tribal groups in that region during the Bronze Age.

Hebrew/Israelites — genomic evidence

The preceding combination of archaeological evidence highlights the mobility of the peoples, cultures, and gene pool during the early Bronze Age prior to the emergence of the Israelites. Another major source of evidence relates to the genetics of persons found in ancient burials. It is difficult to accurately identify which of the post-1205 BCE burial offerings found in what is now Israel can be confidently or accurately linked genetically to the Bronze Age Israelites who were first identified in the Merneptah Stele (1205 BCE).

Currently available genomic evidence from Southern Levant/Northern Israel excavations confirms that the prehistoric Levant Copper Age/Chalcolithic peoples' and Bronze Age Canaanite people's genes show substantial ancestry from northerners. There are genetic links to the Caucuses, Zagros Mountains, Türkiye (ancient Anatolia) and the Iranian plateau dating back to at least six or seven thousand years ago.[831, 832]

In the words of Liran Carmel of the Hebrew University of Jerusalem, following her team's genome-wide analysis of ancient DNA collected from 73 Middle-to-Late Bronze Age individuals from five archaeological sites across the Southern Levant:

> *Populations in the Southern Levant during the Bronze Age were not static. Rather, we observe evidence for the movement of people over long periods of time from the north-east of Ancient Middle East, including modern Georgia, Armenia, and Azerbaijan, into the Southern Levant region.*[833]

Genomic research by Tel Aviv University, the Israelite Antiquities Authority, and Harvard University has found that the Chalcolithic (Copper Age) culture in the Upper Galilee

---

[831] SOURCE: https://www.eurekalert.org/pub_releases/2018-08/afot-dao082018.php retrieved on 8 February 2021.

[832] Agranat-Tamir et al. (2020) pp. 1153-1155.

[833] SOURCE cited in https://www.sciencedaily.com/releases/2020/05/200528115829.htm retrieved on 8 February 2021.

region of the Levant some six to seven thousand years ago was populated by waves of migrations from the north—from Anatolia and the Zagros Mountains.[834]

Liran Carmel's research has found that there is a broader Middle Eastern component, including genetic links with populations from the Caucuses and the Zagros Mountains that account for around 50% of the ancestry of many Arabic-speaking and Jewish groups living in the region today. This research confirms the uniformly held view amongst genomics researchers that there is a remarkable genetic uniformity amongst modern Jews—a uniformity that has:

- strong genetic links to and common paternal lineages with other Middle Eastern groups including Palestinians, Syrians, and Lebanese[835]
- local genetic founder links/shared genetic history with Bedouins and Druze.[836]

Lily Agranat-Tamir and her team at the Hebrew University of Jerusalem, after analysing the genetic evidence from 71 Bronze Age and 2 Iron Age individuals spanning some 1,500 years, supplemented by datasets from 93 individuals and nine sites across present-day Israel, Jordan, and Lebanon, conclude that:

> *The genomes of present-day groups geographically and historically linked to the Bronze Age Levant, including the great majority of present-day Jewish groups and Levantine Arabic-speaking groups are consistent with having 50% or more of their ancestry from people related to groups who lived in the Bronze Age Levant and the Chalcolithic (Copper Age) Zagros.*[837]

The possible loose-knit Middle Eastern tribal groups that formed the Israelites

Various academics claim the emergence of the Israelites as a unified group in the Canaanite hill country was a loose-knit collection of tribal groups based on the following:

---

[834] SOURCE: https://www.sciencedaily.com/releases/2018/08/180820104204.htm retrieved on 15 February 2021.

[835] SOURCES: https://en.wikipedia.org/wiki/Genetic_history_of_the_Middle_East retrieved on 9 February 2021; https://wiki2.org/en/Archaeogenetics_of_the_Near_East retrieved on 15 February 2021; https://en.wikipedia.org/wiki/Genetic_studies_on_Jews retrieved on 15 February 2021.and, https://www.sciencedaily.com/releases/2000/05/000509003653.htm retrieved on 17 February 2021.

[836] Atzmon et al. (2010), p. 858.

[837] Agranat-Tamir et al. (2020) p. 1147.

- there is evidence that thousands of years ago, many Levantine Canaanite Semitic-speaking peoples were living in Egypt because of the rich harvests and the role of the Nile valley as a major source of food.[838]

- Levantine West Semites have lived in the Eastern Delta of Egypt since the second millennium BCE.[839]

- the Canaanite Semitic tribal group referred to as the 'Shepherd Kings' or the Hyksos were a mix of members of the vassal dynasties under Egyptian control. They successfully migrated into the Nile Delta in 1720 BCE. The Egyptians named them the Hyksos (Heka Khasut), which translates as 'rulers of foreign lands/hill countries'. The Hyksos introduced the composite bow and the chariot to Egypt. Based on this and other evidence, they were most probably a mixed group of Canaanites, Phoenicians, Hurrians, and Anatolians. The Egyptians successfully overthrew the Hyksos in around 1595 BCE. This was around the same time that the Kassites successfully took control of Mesopotamia. The Canaanite Hyksos group that was expelled from Egypt when they returned to the Canaanite hill country could have been one source for the Hebrew scribes' Exodus story.

- the HB/OT claims that the Jews have descended from Abraham who, according to the Bible, was not an Israelite but an Aramaean. Like the Israelites, there is no historical, archaeological, or linguistic evidence of the existence of the Aramaeans prior to the Bronze Age collapse (1200 BCE to 900 BCE). What evidence does exist outside of the Bible suggests that the Aramaeans were a north-western Mesopotamian Semitic-speaking (Aramaic) group of nomadic pastoralists who belonged to the Ahlamu.

- the Ahlamu was a loose confederation of wandering tribes of various origins that most likely included the Aramaeans, the Amorites, the Habiru, the Shasu and the Suteans. They were renowned for their plundering and fighting ability. They became participants in the upheavals and the mass movement of people that followed the Bronze Age collapse. From there, they managed to spread throughout and settle in locations largely in Assyria but also in Anatolia, Mesopotamia, Babylonia, and the Levant.

---

[838] Bohstrom (2021).
[839] Mazar (2007), p. 59.

- the Amorites (biblical Aramaeans), Habiru (Apiru), and the Shasu were living outside the mainstream Canaanite society. They have been linked to the emerging Israelites who have also been regarded as Canaanite outsiders.[840]

From the eleventh century BCE onwards, a series of separately governed but united Aramaean city-states had been established in a region that became identified as Aram or Aramea. Aram extended across parts of Anatolia, Assyria, the Levant, and Mesopotamia. The Aramaeans eventually spread throughout the Levant. The Christian Bible claims that Jesus spoke Aramaic, which was the most common language spoken across the Middle East around that time.

It is unlikely that the Israelites have descended uniquely from the Aramaeans. As discussed above, genomic research demonstrates that the Israelites and the Arabs have the same or very similar genetic identities, including ancient Levantine, Persian, and Zagros origins. The modern-day Arabs and the Israelites are genetically and essentially closely related to the historical Canaanites.[841]

Donald Redford has referred to the culture of the ancient Hebrews as having their roots:

… in their nomadic, Shasu past, borrowed heavily from Canaan and their congeners who lived in Syria and on the (Mediterranean) coast. Israel was a community of speakers of the Canaanite language of the West Semitic subfamily, and their way of life and material culture were endemic to the Levant.[842]

Levy et al., claim that the word 'Shasu' does not refer to a specific ethnic group but that the word refers to an ancient social class, a generic socioeconomic subsistence level class of pastoral nomads, equivalent to the term Bedouin.[843]

The only other alternative story of the emergence of Israel as a dominant and influential religious entity comes from the Bible which, by all accounts, was written sometime after the development of systems of writing and the emergence of Hebrew scribes—most probably finalised around 300 BCE. Some scholars claim that the main structure, content, and finalisation of the HB/OT as it is now known was more likely to have been

---

[840] Roux (1992), pp. 239-240; Matyszak (2020) pp. 48-53; Hoffmeier (1996), p. 124; Zevit (2001), pp. 113-115; Finkelstein and Silberman (2002), pp. 102-103.
[841] Agranat-Tamir et al. (2020), p. 1154.
[842] Redford (1992), p. 365.
[843] Levy et al., (2004), p. 66.

developed, written, and finessed by around 550 BCE or much more recently than that.[844] This is significantly later than the extensive archaeological evidence showing the human species being in the Levant hundreds of thousands of years before the dates identified as significant in the Hebrew Bible.

There is thus a growing consensus among Egyptologists, biblical scholars, geneticists, historians, and archaeologists that most of the Israelites and their Arab counterparts were originally Canaanites.[845] The Israelites mentioned in the Mernepath stele were most likely a semi-nomadic Canaanite group in the Canaanite hill country, Galilee, and north and east Syria. The scientific consensus and the linguistic and genomic evidence give credence to the archaeological and historical speculation that the Israelites first ever mentioned in the Merneptah Stele were most likely:

- emerging mobile tent-dwelling shepherds, part agriculturally-based semi-sedentary socio-ethnic Canaanite cult (with no prior unique or yet-to-be-found archaeological evidence of their existence or differentiation from other Canaanites)
- ethnically, culturally, and spatially of the same stock as the Canaanites evolving out of prehistoric Canaanite and Middle Eastern cultural and mythological practices, with shared genetic and interconnected links to other middle eastern cultures (Palestinians, Syrians, Lebanese, Bedouins, and Druze)
- speakers of a language that was derived from the ancient Canaanite group of Semitic languages and is shared with their contemporary Middle Eastern Arabic counterparts
- having the same Middle Eastern genetic pathway and ancestry as most of today's Middle Easterners (including some genetic components from the Caucuses, Zagros Mountains, Prehistoric Levantine, ancient Anatolia, and the Iranian plateau)
- possibly a loose-knit mix of Canaanites, Hyksos, Habiru, Shasu Bedouins, Amorites and early Palestine hill country nomadic pastoralists[846, 847]

844 Gnuse (2014), p. xv.
845 SOURCE: https://www.nytimes.com/1990/09/04/science/battle-scene-on-egyptian-temple-may-be-earliest-view-of-Israelites.html.
846 Redford (1992), p. 412.
847 Kuhrt (2009B), p. 426; Gilboa (2014), p. 644; Cline (2007), pp. 114-119.

- to have most probably started to differentiate themselves from their Canaanite origins and neighbouring regions through emerging ideological, mythological, food and religious taboos, cultural beliefs, and tribal affiliations (see chapter 17)
- significant enough at the time (around 1205 BCE) to be mentioned in an Egyptian Pharaoh's military conquests as a political entity, but not yet a nation nor as an existing regional urban city-state
- to have begun as an emerging loose-knit socio-cultural grouping (from possibly around 1500 BCE) that, over time, differentiated itself as a separate ethnic entity (first recognised in 1205 BCE), transitioning into two political kingdoms in the 'united monarchy' of Judah and Israel (around 900 BCE).[848] It was around this time (900 BCE) that the Hebrew scribes commenced writing the Hebrew Bible.

---

[848] Smith, M.S. (2011), p. 245; Finkelstein (2010), pp. 19-23.

Chapter 17

The Hebrew Scribes' Use of Ethnic Markers and Ethnic Differentiation

Most emerging ethnic entities create a variety of ways to discriminate themselves from other contending cultures. This occurs even in contemporary times. Brad Gregory has outlined how even within the same religion, in this case, Christianity, factional ethnic marking through contrasting rituals evolved from doctrinal disagreements on what is and what is not God's word. Commencing with the Reformation in early 1500 CE, religious differentiation led to several identifiably different Christian denominations (Lutherans, Catholics, Anglicans, Methodists, Protestants, Baptists, Pentecostalists). This was based on what they each regarded as meaningful differentiating factors in defining and adhering to their religious beliefs. Gregory states:

> *Doctrinally, socially, and politically divisive disagreements about what is true, how one ought to live, what matters in life and so forth emerged within a Christian context and character-ised the Reformation era from its outset in the early 1520s.*[849]

In establishing their individual ethnic markers, religious groups intend these markers to fulfil two main functions:

- an internal function that specifies and unifies believers around an agreed and specified canon
- an external function that contrasts their beliefs against other mythologies, denominations, religions, and cultures.

---

[849] Gregory (2017), p. 28.

This is a codification of cultural beliefs and differences. Quoting William Temple, Gregory sees the use of these differentiating factors as subjectivising, interiorising, and compartmentalising each religion.[850]

Norwegian social anthropologist Frederik Barth has hypothesised that the incremental change that gradually differentiates two cultures from what was originally a common culture involves three aspects of cultural creativity:

- conceptual clarifications
- enrichment of idioms
- harmonisation between the connotations of key symbols.[851]

From around 1200 BCE onwards, the Hebrew scribes went to great lengths to differentiate their emerging community and culture from their fellow Canaanites and territorial enemies to their west, the Philistines. Genomic research confirms that the Philistines most probably originally came from Southern Europe. Yet, the genetic distinction they brought with them had largely dissipated within two centuries. This provides evidence of two main factors—the strength of the local Levantine gene pool and the inter-marrying of the Philistines into the Levantine cultures.[852]

As the Israelites emerged post-1205 BCE, the Hebrew scribes used a variety of techniques to differentiate themselves from the other cultures in the Levant. Over some six hundred years of writing, rewriting, and reshaping, the HB/OT evolved into the 'road map', the specification for their uniqueness through a wide range of ethnic markers. The two markers that tend to differentiate the Hebrews from regional neighbours, in popular conversations, are their taboo on pork and the biblical God's command for the ritual circumcision of all male Jews.

The mythological use of food taboos

Globally and historically, food is regarded as more than sustenance. For many religions, including Judaism, the communication of their ideology and mythology includes cultural differentiation and prohibitions involving food.

Unique beliefs about food assist religions in differentiating themselves. Foods are frequently embedded in rituals that reflect and reinforce a shared ideology, belief system,

---

[850]   Gregory (2017), p. 46.

[851]   Barth (2007).

[852]   Feldman et al., (2019), p. 6.

and religiously sanctioned lifestyle. Dietary laws covering the preference or prohibitions around food assist a religious community or a culture to communicate their separate identity. Beliefs about what should and should not be eaten, how and when contribute to, are symbolic of, and are usually integrated with, cultural and religious differentiation.

Dietary prohibitions were common across the ancient Middle East prior to the emergence of the Israelites and the Hebrew scribes. Zoroastrians followed spiritual guidelines involving the protection of animals, which included a prohibition on eating the flesh of the cow, ox, bull, steer, cattle, deer, caribou/reindeer, moose, and elk.[853] Ancient Mesopotamians had a prohibition on the eating of various foods (mainly pork and beef) during specific months of the year to avoid negative spiritual consequences.[854]

In modern times, devout Catholics do not eat meat on Fridays during Lent, in memory of Good Friday, the day their New Testament Bible says Jesus died on the cross. The Christian religions generally associate bread and wine with the body and blood of Jesus.[855] Muslims fast during Ramadan, which to them is the month during which the Quran, the Islamic holy book, was given from God to the prophet Muhammad. The Muslim food-based ritual involves fasting during daylight hours—eating and drinking before dawn and after sunset. For Muslims, eating pork is strictly forbidden in the Quran. Followers of Buddhism, Hinduism, and Jainism, religions that derive in part from Zoroastrianism, are vegetarian because of a doctrinal belief in non-injury or nonviolence. Practising Jews tend to follow biblical dietary laws, commonly referred to as the 'kosher diet'.

Hebrew pastoralists, pigs, the kosher diet, and the pork taboo

The Pastoralists

The HB/OT contains many references to the Jewish patriarchs as being primarily tribal pastoralists.[856] It is generally accepted that the emerging Israelites were largely pastoral Canaanite nomads moving cyclically or periodically around a relatively defined territory in the Levantine hill country that was not conducive to agriculture. They were most likely

---

853 https://authenticgathazoroastrianism.org/2012/03/05/zoroastrian-dietary-laws-animal-friendship -and-stewardship/ retrieved on 14 June 2021.
854 Guillaume (2018), p. 155.
855 This is an adaptation of a Jewish Passover practice of eating of unleavened bread. The Passover and the Christian celebration of the death and resurrection of Christ both occur at the same month as the lunar-solar March/April equinox.
856 Mathews (1981).

a tribal confederacy of locationally scattered sheep and goat-herding pastoralists moving their livestock seasonally in search of fresh pastures on the desert steppes to the south and east of Canaan.[857] They were likely moving from one interim tent encampment to another, depending on the pastoral and seasonal opportunities—moving livestock from one grazing ground to another in a seasonal cycle, typically moving herds to lowlands in winter and highlands in spring or summer.[858]

The origin and domestication of pigs

There are currently two main morphologically different pig breeds—Asian and European. Genomic analysis shows that they diverged from the same Eurasian wild boar species some 500,000 years ago and that domestication of pigs occurred independently in several locations—a major one of which was in the Middle East (around 7000 BCE).[859] This timing corresponds with the earliest evidence of the transition of the human species from groups of hunter-gatherers and forest foragers through nomadic pastoralists to sedentary agricultural farming settlements in Anatolia, the Fertile Crescent, and the Levant (commencing from around 9000 BCE onwards).[860]

Unlike cattle, sheep, and goats, which were common to the nomadic pastoralists, pigs are not usually herding animals. A pig's instinct is to act individually when under pressure, whereas herding animals tend to work as a group to challenge a perceived threat. However, pigs do not like to be left alone for long. They will usually group together but do not like being moved. In many ways, pigs are symptomatic and reflective of the prehistoric emergence and consolidation of sedentary farming.

According to the United Nations Food and Agriculture Organisation, pork is currently the most widely eaten meat in the world, accounting for over 36% of the world's meat intake (poultry is 35% and beef 22%).[861] However, pork appears to be the meat that attracts the most attention for its prohibition by different religious groups. Whilst the reasons for not eating pork vary, several contemporary religions specifically prohibit the eating of pork—namely Judaism, Islam, Buddhism, Hinduism, Jainism, and some Christian religions (e.g., Seventh Day Adventists).

---

[857] Silberman (1992), pp. 27-30.
[858] Finkelstein (1990), pp. 42-43.
[859] Giuffra et al., (2000).
[860] Van Der Crabben (2021).
[861] http://www.fao.org/ag/againfo/themes/en/meat/backgr_sources.html retrieved on 14 June 2021.

The HB/OT (in the books of Leviticus and Deuteronomy) contains a wide range of laws relating to which foods, which animals, which parts of animals, and which food preparation methods are either supported or prohibited. This has laid the foundation for what is referred to as the Jewish kosher diet. The prohibition on eating of pork is just one part of the kosher diet. The belief comes mainly from Leviticus (11:1–8), which articulates the Hebrew scribes' notion of 'clean and unclean food':

> *You may eat any animal that has a divided hoof and that chews the cud. … There are some that only chew the cud or only have a divided hoof, but you must not eat them. … The pig, though it has a divided hoof, does not chew the cud; it is unclean for you. You must not eat their meat or touch their carcasses; they are unclean for you.*

Prehistoric pork consumption

There is zooarchaeological evidence of a high abundance of pig domestication in the Jordanian highlands and in the Northern Jordan Valley in the Southern Levant from around 8000 BCE. This is some seven thousand years before the emergence of the Israelites. These locations correspond to habitats where wild boars thrived. A zooarchaeological analysis of bone specimens from these locations determined that, at that time, pigs/boars at 18% were the second most exploited domesticated animal after goats (around 53%) with sheep bones being a relatively low percentage (8%) of the specimens. The remaining specimens were from cattle (7%), gazelles (7%), and other less common animals (fox, ass).[862]

By around 4000 BCE, there is extensive zooarchaeological evidence of a change in the significance of pig husbandry across the Middle East, where pig bone specimen numbers were below the levels of horses, camels, cattle, sheep, and goats. By this time, in the Bronze and Iron Age Middle East (across Anatolia, the Fertile Crescent, and the Levant), as a percentage of livestock, pigs rarely exceeded 10% to 15% and, on average, were around 7% or below in estimated domesticated stock numbers.[863]

During the Bronze Age and early Iron Age, there is evidence of comparatively large amounts of pig consumption on the Mycenae/Greek mainland, with many sites having faunal remains indicating ten percent or more and up to in excess of fifty percent presence of pigs. Several researchers believe that this fact, along with a similarly high incidence of pigs in early Iron Age Philistine sites in the Levant, confirms the most likely importation

---

[862] Makarewicz (2016), p. 152.
[863] Sapir-Hen et al (2003), pp. 4-7.

of pigs from the Greek mainland by the Philistines. Recent genomic analysis demonstrates that the importation and breeding of the European pigs in the Levant during the Bronze and Iron Ages has led to the situation where modern-day pigs in the Levant no longer show a link to the originally endemic Asian pig. Contemporary Levantine pigs and their wild boar cousins are genomically linked to the European pig.[864]

There is evidence that in around 800 BCE, prior to the unification of the northern Kingdom of Israel and the southern Kingdom of Judah, pig consumption was common in the northern Kingdom (up to 7.8%) whilst pig remains are entirely absent from sites of the ancient Kingdom of Judah. This has led to some proposing that the biblical taboo on pork was important in the merging of the accepted practices of the two kingdoms.[865] It is possible that the frequency of pig specimens relates to differentiation in cultic animal sacrificial practices and feasting across the Levant.[866] This would add another layer to the Hebrew scribes' desire to discriminate themselves from the cultic practices of both the Philistines and the Northern Israelite Kingdom, where different cults were common prior to unification.

During the 1980s, when zooarchaeological studies of faunal remains in the Levant became a key area of research, researchers noticed that pigs were completely absent from early Israelite archaeological sites but quite numerous in sites that were then under the control of the Philistines.[867]

Israeli archaeologist Avraham Faust has undertaken a comprehensive analysis of the trends in pork consumption over time in the Levant during the late Bronze Age and the Iron Age. He has found that pork consumption in the early Philistine period in the Levant was comparatively high and, for the first 150 years, was increasing when compared to the emerging Israelites or the indigenous Canaanite communities. Faust found that as the Philistines 'acculturated' to the Levant, their pork consumption declined.[868]

The origin of the biblical taboo

The biblical prohibition on the consumption of pork was most probably written by the Hebrew scribes during the Babylonian exile/Persian era (around 590 BCE to 530 BCE).[869]

---

[864]   Horwitz et al (2017), p. 103.
[865]   Sapir-Hen et al (2003), p. 95.
[866]   Niesiolowski-Spano (2015), pp. 113-114.
[867]   Faust (2018), p. 276.
[868]   Faust (2018), p. 293.
[869]   Guillaume (2018), p. 160.

Apart from religious dictates, the main reasons that have been postulated for any prohibition on eating pork include the animal's nature and behaviour, ecological requirements, political-economic decisions, and the pastoral-nomadic background of the societies in question.[870]

Mary Douglas was the first to offer the most cogent interpretation of the Bible's food prohibition laws in her book, *Purity and Danger*.[871] She suggested that the notions of defilement are rules of separation that symbolise and help maintain the biblical notion of the distinctness of the Hebrews from the other societies.[872]

The Hebrew scribes used a variety of mechanisms such as this to specifically distinguish themselves ethnically from the Philistines. The biblical prohibitions include circumcision, pork consumption, and excessive wine drinking. The Philistines had a unique style of decorated pottery for wine drinking and a large industry in fermented drink including breweries, wineries, and retail shops marketing beer and wine.[873]

There has been an ongoing debate on the issue of whether pork consumption was used by the Hebrew scribes as a defining factor in establishing ethnic and territorial boundaries. Supporters see the prohibition as part of a package involved in the crystallisation of Israelite ethnic identity and the demarcation of geographic and cultural boundaries through clearly differentiated beliefs, lifestyles, and practices (the HB/OT overall). The biblical book of Proverbs states, in what is no doubt a reference to the Philistines:

> *Do not join those who drink too much wine or gorge themselves on meat, for drunkards and gluttons become poor, and drowsiness clothes them in rags. (Proverbs 23:20)*

HB/OT scholar Phillipe Guillame claims that the archaeological evidence from the late Bronze and Iron Ages does not support the notion that the biblical taboo on pork was developed as part of ethnic differentiation. He claims that the archaeological evidence is more likely to be associated with economic (high versus low socio-economic eating habits) and locational factors (rural versus urban locations pork availability) rather than any obvious or defensible association with the Israelites of the time.[874]

---

[870] Sapir-Hen et al (2013), p. 13.
[871] Douglas (1966).
[872] SOURCE: https://www.britannica.com/topic/dietary-law/Rules-and-customs-in-world-religions retrieved on 9 June 2021.
[873] Niesiolowski-Spano (2015), p. 110.
[874] Guillaume (2018).

Most researchers disagree with Guillame. They suggest that it is most likely that the prohibition on pork consumption in the HB/OT was influenced by three factors:

- the pastoral background of the prehistoric Hebrews (pigs are not herding animals)
- the desire for ethnic unification into one kingdom of Judah (which had a prohibition on pig consumption) with the Northern Kingdom of Israel (where there is evidence of routine pig consumption), and
- the desire to ethnically differentiate the new Hebrew Kingdom from their Philistine neighbours and antagonists (who, at the time, were regularly consuming pork).[875]

Faust has completed the most recent and most comprehensive analysis of the literature and the available data on this topic to date. He has concluded that both the Philistines (increasing their consumption) and the Israelites (prohibiting pork consumption) were clearly using pig consumption as an ethnic marker and a critical component of ethnic negotiation and cultural differentiation.[876] The Hebrew scribes during the Babylonian exile/Persian era were merely embedding this ethnic differentiation device into a biblical taboo. It is but one of a wide range of devices used by the Hebrew scribes in attempting to unify their community and their mythology around a range of strictures that included tactical food taboos.

Circumcision as a biblical ethnic marker

The origin of the mythological use of circumcision

Circumcision as a cultural and/or religious dictate was widespread across the Middle East and Africa many centuries before the emergence of the Israelites. As a practice globally, it predated the Bible by hundreds of thousands of years. Cox and Morris estimate that the practice probably began in the Stone Age, that it was ubiquitous across many prehistoric cultures, and that it was in Egypt (well before 4000 BCE) that it most likely first became a religious requirement. They cite the example of the Egyptian sun god Ra, circumcising himself and, from the spilt blood, two other gods come into being. Thereafter, male circumcision became close to the norm for young males in Egyptian society.[877] Other researchers have found evidence of young boys in an Egyptian circumcision scene, dating

---

[875] Sapir-Hen et al. (2031), pp. 12-13.
[876] Faust (2018), p. 294.
[877] Cox and Morris (2012), p. 249.

back to around 2500 BCE—some 1300 years before the emergence of the Israelites and some two thousand years prior to the finalisation of the HB/OT.[878]

In prehistoric times, Egypt was very influential across the Levant and, specifically, with the Canaanites. This varied from trading and commerce as a regional neighbour to being a conquering foreign power occupying and influencing the region (from around 1550 BCE to 1000 BCE).[879] The regional frequency of circumcision in the Middle East may have been, in part, the influence of the Egyptians. However, there is evidence of the practice being common in the region much earlier than during the Egyptian control of the Levant. For example, inhabitants of northern Syria practised circumcision from around 3200 BCE.[880] By the time the Hebrews were exiled to Babylonia, circumcision was widespread across Egypt and parts of Mesopotamia and was equally the subject of harsh condemnation from the emerging Greco-Roman societies.[881] Whatever the origin, circumcision remained a common practice across the Levant prior to the emergence of the Israelites, except amongst the recently arrived Philistines!

The Philistines were an emerging opportunistic confederation of peoples from a variety of locations, including some representation from mainland Greece. This is an interesting place of origin, as the Greeks of the time were strongly opposed to circumcision, as were the Philistines when they arrived in the Southern Levant. Frederick Hodges has shown how the ancient Greeks idealised the penis and the foreskin and regarded circumcision as genital mutilation.[882]

Biblical mandating of circumcision

The Egyptian myth of their sun god Ra circumcising himself was the instigation of the Egyptian practice of circumcision. The Hebrew scribes probably borrowed from this myth. They wrote of how the founder of their religion Abraham came to be circumcised through a covenant of circumcision with their God. According to the HB/OT, Abraham was able to father a son, Ishmael, with his Egyptian maid, Hagar, but he was unable to do so with his wife, Sarah. The biblical text states that God spoke to him (Genesis 17:1–14):

---

[878] Megahed and Vymazalova (2011), pp. 155-156.
[879] Morris (2005), pp. 144-145.
[880] Sasson (1966), p. 476.
[881] Jacobs (2011), p. 563.
[882] Hodges (2001).

This is my covenant with you and your descendants after you, the covenant you are to keep: Every male among you shall be circumcised. You are to undergo circumcision, and it will be the sign of the covenant between me and you. For the generations to come every male among you who is eight days old must be circumcised, including those born in your household or bought with money from a foreigner—those who are not your offspring. Whether born in your household or bought with your money, they must be circumcised. My covenant in your flesh is to be an everlasting covenant. Any uncircumcised male, who has not been circumcised in the flesh, will be cut off from his people; he has broken my covenant.

According to the Hebrew scribes, Abraham, aged in his nineties, gets circumcised and Sarah bears him a son, Isaac. The Bible then proceeds to contain many references to circumcision, and often contrasts this with the Philistines, who are not circumcised. Probably the most applicable example of such biblical references reflecting the antipathy between the early Israelites and the Philistines is in 1 Samuel 18:25–27:

Say to David, 'The king wants no other price for the bride than a hundred Philistine foreskins, to take revenge on his enemies.' Saul's plan was to have David fall by the hands of the Philistines. When the attendants told David these things, he was pleased to become the king's son-in-law. So, before the allotted time elapsed, David took his men with him and went out and killed two hundred Philistines and brought back their foreskins. They counted out the full number to the king so that David might become the king's son-in-law. Then Saul gave him his daughter Michal in marriage.

Biblical reason for the ritual of male circumcision

Across the Middle East, prior to the Hebrew scribes, circumcision was a generally held fertility rite associated with puberty and marriage.[883] The Hebrew scribes shaped this practice into an internal indicator of cult membership and an external ethnic differentiator. The Dead Sea Scrolls, which are the oldest existing examples of the HB/OT (dating from around 300 BCE) and most of which represent widely accepted Jewish beliefs and practices, contain no reference to male circumcision.[884] Where the word circumcision occurs in the Dead Sea Scrolls, it is used exclusively as a metaphor. For example:

---

[883] Fox (1974), p. 590.
[884] Vermes (1965), p. 44.

No one should walk in the stubbornness of his heart in order to go astray following his heart and his eyes and the musing of his inclination instead he should circumcise in the Community the foreskin of his tendency.[885]

The biblical pork taboo and circumcision have been used throughout the HB/OT as ethnic markers differentiating the emerging Israelites from their Philistine opponents. With circumcision being common across many cultures in the Middle East, the biblical use of it as a cultural differentiating factor can only have been to differentiate themselves from the Philistines. Biblical researcher Ziony Zevit has described it in the following way: 'Circumcision seems to have been a rather straightforward matter, more technical than cultic and more an indication of ethnic affiliation than not.'[886]

Avraham Faust described it thusly: 'It is clear that circumcision was viewed as a marker when Israelites and Philistines interacted.'[887]

---

[885] From Dead Sea Scroll 1QS V:4-6, quoted by Jacobs (2011) p. 571.
[886] Zevit (2001), p. 665.
[887] Faust (2015), p. 276.

Chapter 18

The Emergence and Impact of Written Communication

The human species was communicating visually over thousands of years prior to the emergence of written communication. Some 30,000 to 40,000 years ago, some early prehistoric communities made carved-engraved bone plates of mobiliary art.[888] They have markings that represent hunting tallies (a mathematical counting system) or lunar notations that correspond to the monthly cycle of the moon or sun and/or the yearly solar path.[889] These artefacts are some of the first evidence of symbolic, abstract expression by ancient human ancestors.

There is evidence of Stone Age hunters producing an early map engraved on a mammoth tusk some 17,000 years ago that included seven rows of images illustrating the territory on which the original hunters resided (Figure 37).

From these very early beginnings of visual communication, the earliest forms of written communication appeared around 6,000 years ago. However, it took an additional two to three thousand years to elapse before a generally accepted alphabet and widely adopted written communication would emerge in the Middle East.

---

[888] George (2021).

[889] SOURCE: https://www.researchgate.net/publication/233529929_Prehistoric_astronomers_Ancient_knowledge_created_by_modern_myth retrieved on 10 May 2021.

Figure 37: *17,000-year-old hunter-gatherer map of their territory in prehistoric Ukraine* [a]

---

[a] **SOURCE** Cartwright (2021): https://www.worldhistory.org/collection/122/a-gallery-of-historical-maps/

Notation on clay was occurring across the Middle East during the fourth millennium BCE.[890] Writing as a recording system, the visual representation of language, was initially developed by the Sumerians and Egyptians in rudimentary forms. The Sumerian cuneiform writing system was logo-syllabic, where symbols could represent sounds, syllables, a word or word part, or a word clue (morpheme).

The Egyptian system consisted of logo-consonantal hieroglyphics, where symbols could represent alphabetic elements, consonants, syllables, a word or word part, or a word clue (morpheme).[891] It was most probably around 3500 BCE that Sumerians first invented writing. Cuneiform comes from the Latin for 'wedge-shaped' because the images

---

[890] Kuhrt (2009A), p. 10.
[891] Weninger (2011), p. 761.

were made from wedge-shaped marks in clay. Sumerian cuneiform was used initially for economic and administrative records and was written on clay.[892]

Joshua Mark believes that:

The development of long-distance trade during the Ubaid and Uruk periods led to the invention of writing in the form of cuneiform script by c. 3500 BCE so that merchants could communicate with clients in foreign regions or distant Mesopotamian cities.[893]

The Sumerian cuneiform script took many hundreds of years to develop. It began in around 3500 BCE primarily as an accounting system with clay tablets containing just two signs—one for products (e.g., an image of a sheep's or goat's head) and one numeric symbol signifying details of the specific transaction.

As trade and internal resource sharing became more complex in Mesopotamian city-states, tablets began to contain multiple symbols of products or resources with multiple numeric symbols including additional symbols referring to the institution or the individuals involved in a transaction. As the number of interactions and complexity of symbols increased, a need emerged for a skilled 'decoder' who was assisted by a new arrangement where the symbols were now structured into rows and columns to assist interpretation. This was the beginning of the profession of 'scribe', a spatial syntax, and a more detailed set of symbols so the production and distribution of goods could be more easily tracked and accounted for.[894]

The first scribes or 'decoders' were documented professional writers using glyphs (pictograms, ideographic, and syllabic cuneiform images) but not alphabet script (which emerged much later). Cuneiform writing was complicated, involving hundreds of signs, each of which could have several possible values (Figure 38). As explained by Assyriologist Jean Bottero:

Depending on choice and context, the outline of a human foot could designate any behaviour, movement, or attitude in which this extremity was involved (standing, local movement, walking, progress, carrying or transporting); and the outline of a star could represent everything to be found in the heavens: superior, sublime, dominant, divine.[895]

---

[892] Kramer (1956), p. xxi.
[893] Mark (2022C).
[894] Maiocchi (2019), pp. 399-406.
[895] Bottero (2001), p. 188.

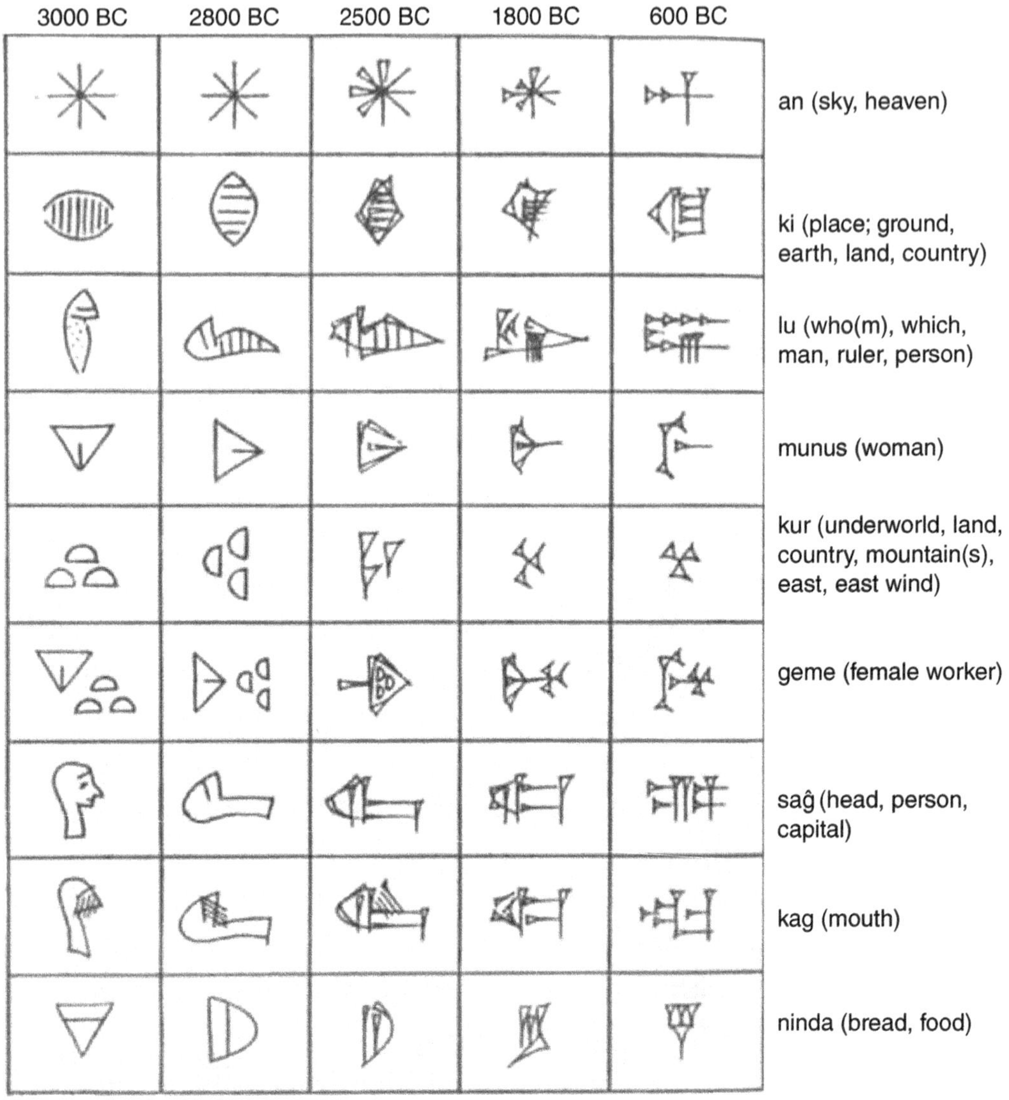

3000 BC	2800 BC	2500 BC	1800 BC	600 BC	
					an (sky, heaven)
					ki (place; ground, earth, land, country)
					lu (who(m), which, man, ruler, person)
					munus (woman)
					kur (underworld, land, country, mountain(s), east, east wind)
					geme (female worker)
					saĝ (head, person, capital)
					kag (mouth)
					ninda (bread, food)

Figure 38: Sumerian cuneiform script over time [b]

---

[b] SOURCE: Ager, Simon. "Omniglot - writing systems and languages of the world": https://omniglot.com/writing/sumerian.htm retrieved on 9 August 2023.

Emerging sometime later, and possibly influenced by the Sumerian cuneiform symbols, Egyptian hieroglyphics began as pictograms. Egyptian hieroglyphics evolved over time from hieroglyphics through a cursive writing phase (hieratic) that was largely used by the elite and priests as a symbol system that related to common day language (demotic) (Figure 39).

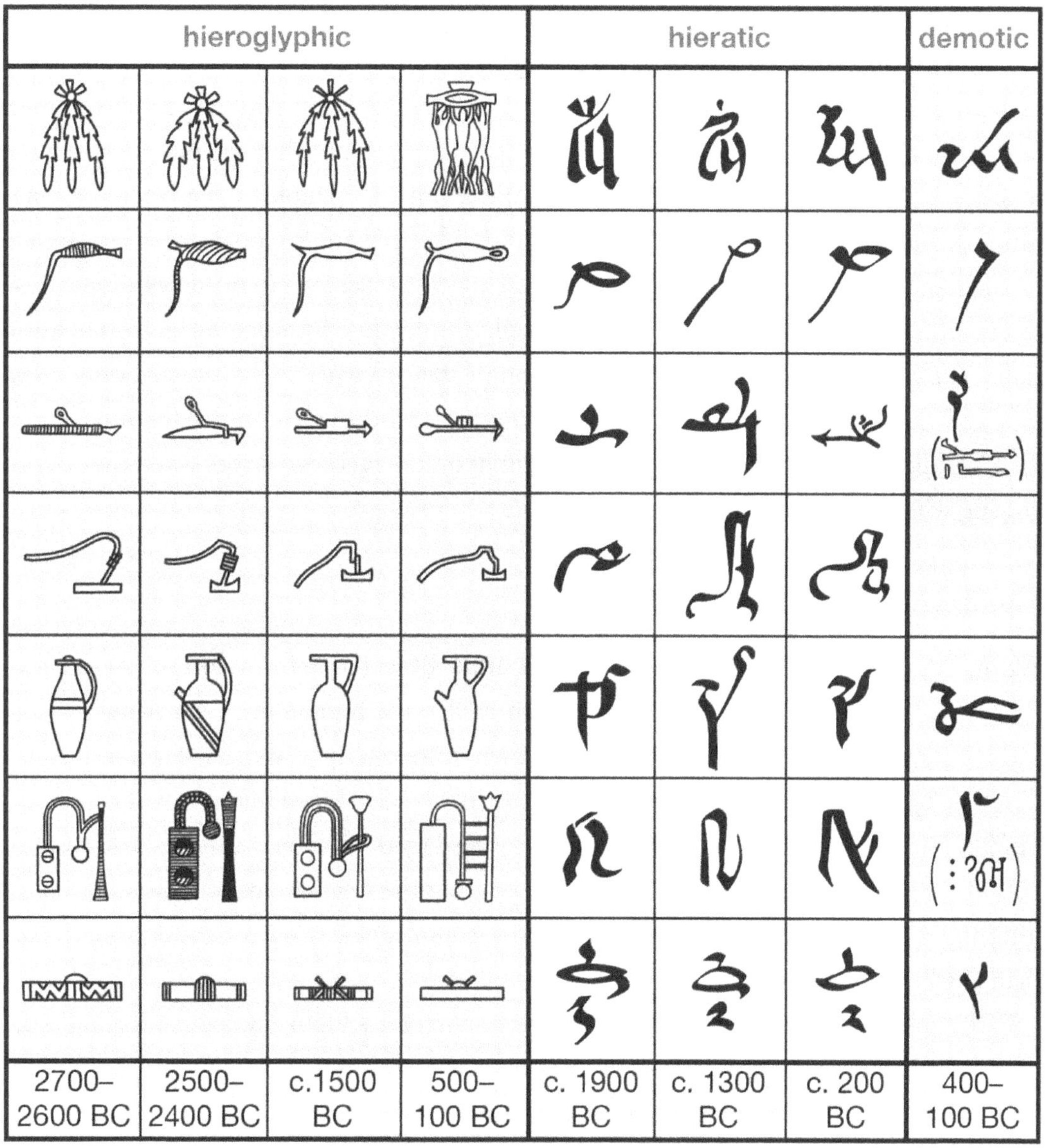

hieroglyphic				hieratic			demotic
2700– 2600 BC	2500– 2400 BC	c.1500 BC	500– 100 BC	c. 1900 BC	c. 1300 BC	c. 200 BC	400– 100 BC

Figure 39: Egyptian written communication evolving over time

Sumerian cuneiform and Egyptian hieroglyphics began as pictorial representations and transitioned to representing phonetic signs that stood for specific sounds and related words. For example, if adopted in contemporary English, a picture or symbol of a bee could be used to refer to the verb 'to be' or to the insect. Both cuneiform and hieroglyphics were clumsy systems. One improvement in Sumer and Egypt was to use a symbol (a determinant/determinative) ahead of each hieroglyphic image to clarify the meaning of an ambiguous hieroglyphic symbol.[896, 897] It was the use of a determinant in the hieroglyphics in the Merneptah Stele that allowed researchers to understand that the first hieroglyphic mention of Israelites was not referring to a nation but to a people or political entity significant enough to be mentioned but distinguishable from the regional urban city-states.

James Scott, citing the work of Hans Nissen (1985), believes that the widespread use of cuneiform in Sumerian administration took around five hundred years to transition into a common mechanism for self-promotion of state-centric, civilisational glories, king lists and genealogies, chronicles, founding myths, praise hymns, and religious texts.[898] This Middle Eastern tradition was very influential on the Hebrew scribes when they began writing what was to become the Hebrew Bible.

The development of an alphabet

Written documentation commenced around 4000 BCE (cuneiform and hieroglyphics). By the early Bronze Age (3000 BCE to 2100 BCE), the Sumerians, Egyptians, and the Indus Valley civilisation had developed their own unique scripts. Written communication developed gradually into a more widely used alphabet—developed initially by the Canaanites (around 1900 BCE to 1600 BCE) and improved by the Phoenicians (by 1100 BCE to 1000 BCE). The significance of an alphabet was that the new system of representation of information was now based on words to describe sounds, places, objects, and things rather than abstract pictures or symbols.

The transition from either the cuneiform or the hieroglyphic system to the alphabet of today is the subject of much debate amongst leading scholars. Evidence suggests that the evolution of the alphabet involved a merging of the early Egyptian and Sumerian concepts in various groups within Canaan. The Egyptian logo-consonantal hieroglyphics included twenty-four signs for consonants. But the Ancient Egyptians never progressed to a purely consonantal alphabet—preferring to maintain their link to pictorial images or their combination in pairs or trios to form signs or symbols.[899]

---

[896] Diamond (2005), p. 220; also called the rebus principle.
[897] Bauer (2007), pp. 46-47.
[898] Scott (2017) p. 13 and p. 141.
[899] Diamond (2005), p. 226.

The Sumerian cuneiform scribal culture spread rapidly across the Middle East Semitic communities. This led to many variations of cuneiform influenced by the Egyptian approach. This included Sumerian, North Semitic, Ugaritic, Phoenician, and Akkadian cuneiform, each differing subtly from the others.[900]

Canaanites were renowned for their artistic and sophisticated composition of different motifs and symbols on bowls, utensils, jewellery, and ivory carving.[901] They were influenced by Egyptian, Mesopotamian, Syrian, and Aegean motifs. Tubb believes that this sophisticated artistic background was influential in the Canaanites (North Semites, Ugaritic, Phoenician) attempting to develop the first workable alphabet to replace the cumbersome cuneiform system as they inscribed on various bowls, inscriptions, and artefacts.[902]

The breakthrough in the development of the modern-day alphabet most likely came from the Phoenicians.[903] Like the emergence of the Sumerian cuneiform, the Phoenician consonantal alphabet was necessitated by the need to communicate and document administrative and economic information. The need for a better system of writing was motivated by the Phoenicians' extensive levels of trade in the Middle East, Egypt, the Mediterranean, North Africa, and Mycenean/Greek communities (Figure 40).

From around 1400 BCE, the native alphabets that emerged from the Canaanites, Ugarit, and Phoenicians were consonantal systems (containing no vowels).[904] Multiple consonant-based alphabets emerged in Ugarit, Canaan (Beth Shemesh), Egypt, and South Arabia. Each of these contained somewhere between twenty-five and thirty consonants.[905] All appear to have been influenced by the Canaanite/Phoenician/Semitic emerging consonantal alphabet.[906] From around 1700 BCE, the native alphabets that emerged from the Canaanites, Ugarit, and the Phoenicians were consonantal systems.[907] The consonantal alphabets of the time contained cuneiform signs, but they were now alphabetic rather than syllabic values.[908]

---

[900] Hoffman (2004), p. 28.
[901] SOURCE: https://www.britannica.com/topic/Canaanite-inscriptions retrieved on 18 April 2023.
[902] Tubb (1998), pp. 66-67.
[903] SOURCE: https://www.britannica.com/topic/alphabet-writing retrieved on 18 April 2023.
[904] Weninger et al (2011), pp. 97-98.
[905] Haring (2015), p. 195.
[906] See: Schneider (2018).
[907] Weninger et al (2011), pp. 97-98; Diamond (2005), p. 227.
[908] Tubb (1998), p. 73.

Figure 40: *The extensive Phoenician trade network* [d]

---

[b] SOURCE: http://www.civilization.org.uk/intermezzo/phoenicians/ retrieved on 18 May 2021.

Jared Diamond has proposed that the evolution of the alphabet from the more pictorial or symbolic representations (cuneiform and hieroglyphics) involved three major steps:

- the abandonment of abstract pictorial representations as a means of communication
- placing the consonant representations in a fixed sequence for ease of memorisation and giving them easy-to-remember names
- providing vowels.[909]

---

[909] Diamond (2005), p. 227.

While it is largely accepted that the modern-day alphabet has Semitic origins, there is some disputation on the origin of vowels. Most accept that vowels were first developed by the Greeks. From around 1400 BCE, the Mycenean Greek (Cypriot and Ionian) syllabic script was influential in the use of vowels and in the overall development of the contemporary alphabet.[910]

The Origin of the Hebrew word 'Yahweh'

Contrary to most scholars who see the Greeks as inventors of vowels, Ancient Hebrew authority Joel Hoffman believes that there is ample evidence that the Hebrew scribes, and possibly the neighbouring Moabites, were the first to introduce the use of vowels into alphabets. He believes that the introduction of the vowels played an important role in the naming of the Hebrew God.

Before the emergence of the Israelites, the Sumerians and the Egyptians believed that the gods invented writing. For the Sumerians, writing contained a divine essence and was devised to assist the transmission of gods messages to the believers. It was the Sumerian god of wisdom, fresh water, intelligence, mischief, healing, creation, fertility, and art—Enki—who invented writing. For the Egyptians, it was Thoth, the god of the moon, sacred texts, messenger and recorder of the deities, master of knowledge, and patron of scribes, who invented writing.[911]

The Hebrew scribes continued the Middle Eastern and Egyptian linking of writing to a god or gods. Hoffman explains how the Hebrew scribes regarded vowels as divine. They used vowels as a name for their god and a mechanism for ethnic differentiation. He claims that:

- the Hebrews invented vowels
- the vowels were a gift from God
- vowels were inserted into the otherwise consonant-only names of the biblical characters. Thus, *brm* becomes *Abraham* and his wife *sry* becomes *Sarah*
- the ancient Sumerian and Egyptian belief in writing as a gift from god was continued by the Hebrew scribes.

Hoffman has hypothesised that the Hebrew scribes, in recognition of the importance of the invention of vowels and their association with the divine, created a word for their god.

---

[910]   Theodorides (2022); Diamond (2005), p. 227.
[911]   Gong et al. (2009), pp. 139-140.

This word was composed entirely of the newly invented 'magic' and divine vowels. This invention is the word for god consisting entirely of the Hebrew vowels—*yhwh*—*Yahweh*. Hoffman explains:

> *The letters yhwh were chosen not because of the sounds they represent, but because of their symbolic power in that they were the Hebrews' magic vowel letters that no other culture had. … The letters … were chosen for their symbolic value rather than for their pronunciation.*[912]

The origin of not mentioning God's name

Subsequently, many Jews will not say the name, Yahweh, aloud. This is because it is believed to be too holy to be spoken. Hoffman suggests that this has occurred because, when the vowels were invented, they came from the Hebrew God and they did not come with a pronunciation.[913]

However, the idea of not speaking the actual word for god originated thousands of years before the emergence of the Hebrew scribes. In prehistoric Siberian and Mongolian shamanism, mountain-based deities were regarded as being so numinous (having a strong religious or spiritual quality) that their names were never mentioned. Siberian and Mongolian gods' names were replaced by phrases such as 'the high', 'the holy' and 'the beautiful'.[914] In the Indus Valley, the Hindus also had a notion of the 'ultimate reality'— the nameless one, which is a sense of a genderless, infinite-eternal truth, and cause of all things.[915]

The Hebrew scribes adopted this prehistoric shamanic and Vedic practice from the Altaic/Turkic (Siberia and Mongolia) and Vedic/Sanskrit (north-western India) mythologies, which they experienced when they were in exile in Babylonia.

The impact of the written word

It is not possible to overestimate the impact of an alphabet and the introduction of the first widely used methods of written record keeping and communication. It has delivered to academics and researchers direct and more reliable written records as the major source of historical investigations. Prehistory's reliance on scientific interpretation, guesswork

---

[912] Hoffman (2004), pp. 39-45.
[913] Hoffman (2004), p. 45.
[914] Ashe (2018), p. 48.
[915] Feuerstein et al (2001), p. 198.

and imagining from carbon dating, ancient built structures, excavations, stone tools, art, artefacts, ruins, and funerary and burial practices faded into the background as written evidence laid the foundation for significantly improved historical research.

Middle East historian Massimo Maiocchi has described the impact of writing in the following way:

> *Writing effectively extends cognitive facilities by allowing the externalization of previously embodied meaningful information clusters in the form of linguistic symbols, which in turn can then be easily compared at a glance. … Writing assists in identifying associations, shaping thought, and intensifying the cognitive apparatus in a reciprocal feedback process, which can produce cascade effects on other techniques and fields of knowledge.*[916]

The invention of written communication was as profound as the impact of the invention of the first printing press by German goldsmith Johannes Gutenberg in 1440 CE. Gutenberg's invention had a profound impact on the global distribution of information and knowledge. This was recognised in 1962, by Canadian professor of English literature Marshall McLuhan, in his classic book, *The Gutenberg Galaxy: The Making of Typographic Man*. McLuhan claimed that there have been four epochs of history transitioning from pre-alphabetic tribal times to the electronic age. The four epochs involved the 'externalisation of our senses'.[917] This became the platform from which McLuhan explored the historical impact of different communication technologies on communities and cultures:

1. **The Oral Tribal Age/Oral Tribe Culture**—Stone Age
   - McLuhan describes this as primarily 'an acoustic community', where the senses of hearing, touch, taste, and smell were more advanced than visualisation.
2. **The Manuscript Culture/The Age of Literacy**—Bronze Age
   - Literacy, the invention of the alphabet and widespread handwriting capabilities moved people from collective tribal involvement to private detachment. It encouraged logical, linear thinking, and fostered mathematics, science, and philosophy.

---

[916] Maiocchi (2019), p. 395.
[917] McLuhan (2010), pp. 49-51.

3. **The Print Age/Gutenberg Galaxy**—Middle Ages
   - The printing press made visual dependence widespread. The development of fixed national languages produced nationalism. McLuhan regarded the fragmentation of society as the most significant outcome of print.
4. **The Electronic Age/Era of Technology**—Modern times
   - McLuhan (somewhat prophetically and well before the internet!) believed that the electronic media would re-tribalise humanity—that, in an electronic age, privacy would be a luxury or a curse of the past and that linear logic would be useless in the electronic society as the focus moves to feelings.[918]

McLuhan proposed in 1962 that new technologies (like the invention of the alphabet, printing presses, and even speech itself) exert a gravitational effect on cognition, which in turn affects social organisation and culture.[919]

The emergence of a scribal culture

The invention of the alphabet in the Levant around 1400 BCE led to the consolidation of an emerging scribal culture across the Middle East. The scribal culture had begun in Mesopotamia under the Sumerians from around 3500 BCE. It was initially based on the earliest forms of writing (cuneiform) and tended to focus on proverbs, riddles, aphorisms, incantations, and magical spells.[920] With the invention of a communicable alphabet, there was an unprecedented spread of writing and written culture. Initially, the Sumerians recorded lists of things—grain, barley, manpower, labour standards, taxes, captives, slaves, their population—in terms of location, age, and gender—and lists of books.[921, 922] Scribal schools to train scribes were invented by the Sumerians, but they became common across most of the Middle East, Egypt, and Indus Valley cultures.

Sumerian scribes

The first Sumerian scribes were a small number of elite masters and 'decoders' of the cuneiform symbols. Civilisations of the Ancient Middle East were primarily oral cultures

---

[918] SOURCE: https://www.coursehero.com/file/p5qvrhr/McLuhan-divided-human-history-into-4-periods-or-epochs-1-The-Tribal-Age-An/.

[919] SOURCE: http://www.historyofinformation.com/detail.php?id=792.

[920] Leick (2002), p. 69.

[921] Scott (2017), pp. 142-143.

[922] Kramer (1981), pp. 250-254.

because levels of literacy were somewhere around 5% to 10% of the population. This ensured that the scribe's task was documenting and recording information, court depositions, legal texts, loans, commercial notes, rules, literary texts, magical incantations, and mythological stories for trade, administration, government, kings, and priests.[923]

Bottero described the task of the Sumerian scribes thus:

In ancient Mesopotamia, the system of writing—not all alphabetic but simultaneously ideographic and syllabic, with several hundred signs each having possible values—was terribly complicated and, if it was to be mastered, called for many years of exercises and studies which could be tackled only by an elite or members of a professional body as restricted as those of lawyers or doctors nowadays.[924]

Sumerian scribal schools

The invention of the cuneiform system of writing was the main reason for the emergence of Sumerian schools as early as 3000 BCE. Writing and learning evolved together in these schools. Sumerian authority Samuel Kramer explains that it was in the last half of the third millennium (BCE) that the Sumerian school system, with the specific and primary task of teaching the writing of the Sumerian language, matured and flourished.

There were junior and 'high' scribes, royal and temple scribes, scribes who were highly specialised for particular categories of administrative activities, and scribes who became leading officials in government.[925]

The social structure across the Middle East was very similar, from Bactria in the north-east (2400 BCE to 1900 BCE) through Mesopotamia to the Levant. The Bactrians had a social hierarchy consisting of:

1. Male city rulers/leaders (palace people, priest-kings, god-kings)
2. Religious ideology servants (temple people)
3. Military people (the original Steppe warrior culture)
4. Handicraftsmen (potters, blacksmiths, weavers, jewellers)
5. The general population (peasants, stock-breeders, farmers, merchants)
6. Poor people with no rights (labourers, slaves)

---

[923] Highcock (2017).
[924] Bottero (2001), p. 61.
[925] Kramer (1956), pp. 3-4.

The Sumerians' social structure was very similar. The Sumerian scribes, like the priests and other temple people, held a comparatively high position in Sumerian society:

1. The god-king
2. High priests and nobles
3. Officials, scribes, and minor priests
4. Craftsmen
5. Labourers and peasants
6. Servants and slaves.

From 3000 BCE onwards, the Sumerian school system for training the scribes matured and developed. The schools were called *edubba*, 'tablet house'. Their main purpose was for the scribes to develop the writing skills and background knowledge to satisfy the economic, administrative, and religious needs of the temple and the palace.

The schools were not simply places of learning and the development of administrative, judicial, and trade-based records. They became centres of creative and religious writing. Literature of the past was studied, copied multiple times, modified, and new versions composed. The curriculum had two main streams—the semi-scientific and scholarly stream that focused on textbooks linked to learning, copying, and memorising the cuneiform alphabet, the grammar, words, phrases, and lists (historical, botanical, zoological, geographical, mineralogical) in the Sumerian language; and the literary and creative stream that focused on myths, epic tales, poems, wisdom compositions, proverbs, fables, and essays.[926]

Kramer cites German cuneiformist Nikolaus Schneider as discovering that, in around 2000 BCE, more than one thousand years before the emergence of Hebrew scribes:

Fathers of the (Sumerian) scribes—that is, of the school graduates—were governors, 'city fathers', ambassadors, temple administrators, military officers, sea captains, high tax officials, priests of various sorts, managers, supervisors, foremen, scribes, archivists, and accountants.[927]

The role of a Sumerian scribe could start at a very young age:

At the Sumerian scribal school, students as young as 8 years old would begin their education in mastering cuneiform script as well as the various fields of knowledge they would be expected to write about, ranging from mathematics and accounting to botany, agricultural and tax records, literature, religion, and other subjects. The students were almost uniformly male,

---

[926] Kramer (1971), pp. 230-231.
[927] Kramer (1956), p. 5.

although girls from prestigious families were allowed to attend if their parents wanted them to
become doctors, priestesses, or participate in the family business at the highest levels.[928]

There are literally thousands of documents now available to scholars from the work of Mesopotamian scribes (Sumerian, Akkadian, Assyrian, Babylonian, Elamite, Hittite). Glassner has described this wealth of ancient material in the following way:

The diversity of these works and the richness and variety of the information they contain make
them works of reference, and the sheer bulk of their achievements inspires admiration.[929]

The Hebrew scribes

Like their Sumerian, Egyptian, and Indus Valley counterparts, the Hebrew scribes were storytellers, story adapters, story keepers, and story promoters. They were not unique in their time. Prehistoric cultures in and around the Levant had much in common in their religious practices and beliefs. Most of the priests, priestesses, kings, pharaohs, and shamans in the surrounding cultures at the time, were influenced by several similar, common, widely distributed, and collectively believed mythologies. Once a writing system was invented and widely distributed, most cultures adopted the Sumerian practice of training and establishing a team of official scribes whose task was to develop and communicate official and religious information.

The role of the Hebrew scribes, adopted from the Sumerians, was to write, rewrite, and adapt stories to convey and elaborate on administrative practices and their interpretation of what imagined gods, goddesses, and ancient prophets may or may not have said and what, why, and how the world existed. The analysis of the script, writing style, and different languages (Hebrew, Aramaic, Greek, or Nabatean) in the oldest versions of the Hebrew Bible—the Dead Sea Scrolls—clearly demonstrate that there were many different authors.[930]

The Hebrew scribes were simply harvesting, adapting, modifying, retelling, and reshaping stories from the mythologies they had personally experienced in the Levant, Babylonia, their times in Egypt, and during the Egyptian occupation of the Levant. These mythologies themselves had been influenced by and adapted from mythologies and common beliefs across a much wider range of interacting cultures—Anatolia, the Caucuses,

---

[928] Mark (2023D).
[929] Glassner (2004), p. xix.
[930] See: Who wrote the Dead Sea scrolls? Science may have the answer. (nationalgeographic.com) retrieved on 3 August 2022.

the Eurasian Steppe, Central Asia, the Iranian Plateau, Siberia/Mongolia, the Indus Valley, Northern India, Greece, and the Mediterranean islands.

The major influences on the writing of the Hebrew scribes

The content, structure and style of the Sumerian literary works were a significant influence on the literature of the entire ancient Middle East, including the Akkadians, the Assyrians, the Babylonians, the Hittites, the Hurrians, the Canaanites, the Israelites, and the Greeks.[931]

As was the practice across most of the Middle East, the initial writings by the Hebrew scribes were largely to communicate with other scribes. Dutch authority on ancient religions, Karel van der Toorn explains:

> *The text of the Hebrew Bible was not part of the popular culture. The Bible was born and studied in the scribal workshop of the temple. In its fundamental essence, it was a book of the clergy. … The story of the making of the Bible is the story of the scribes behind the Bible.*[932]

The Hebrew scribes were educated members of the Jewish elite, often working in temples and palaces where they would be involved in writing letters and contractual documents. However, like the Sumerian scribes, they were often involved in issues such as cosmology, rituals, prayers, laws, and revelations. Their writing style varied accordingly. The Hebrew scribes would also often attribute their work to ancient luminaries.[933]

They drew on four main sources for the content of their mythological writing. They relied on:

1. **The surrounding pre-existing and widely held regional mythological beliefs and practices**:
   a) **Regional mythological influences.** The long-term beliefs passed down from the regional mythologies around them. Absorbing the cultural and mythological beliefs and practices of the ancient Middle Eastern and associated regions (Zoroastrians, Sumerian, Mesopotamian, Assyrians, Anatolians, Babylonians, Hittites, Mitanni, Iranian, Persians, Eurasian Steppe, India Harrapan), which had been developing and shared from around 4000 BCE onwards.

---

[931] Kramer (1971), p. 166.

[932] Van Der Toorn (2007), p. 2.

[933] SOURCE: https://www.bibleodyssey.org/en/tools/bible-basics/how-does-the-hebrew-bible-relate-to-the-ancient-near-eastern-world.

b) **Local regional influences.** Beliefs adapted from their own Canaanite region. Inter-mixing with their Canaanite cultures including Canaanites, Phoenicians, and Philistines (from around 1205 BCE to 340 BCE).

c) **Beliefs learnt and adapted when in exile.** The scribes were exiled with the skilled and upper-class Israelites from Samaria into upper Mesopotamia (modern-day Syria and Iraq) by the Assyrians. Initially in around 734 BCE, and secondarily in around 722 BCE, they were exiled with the ruling classes of Judah into Babylon by the Babylonians on two occasions between 590 BCE and 538 BCE.[934]

d) **Beliefs developed when under conquest/vassal state arrangements.** They were under the control of the Egyptian Empire (from around 1500 BCE to 1000 BCE), were a vassal state under the control of the Assyrian Empire (from around 900 BCE to 600 BCE), a vassal state under the control of the Babylonian Empire (from around 600 BCE to 500 BCE), a vassal state under the control of the Persian Empire (from around 900 BCE to 300 BCE), a vassal state under the control of the Greek Empire (Alexander the Great, Ptolemaic and Seleucids) from around 332 BCE to 100 BCE, and a vassal state under the control of the Roman Empire (from around 305 BCE to 1 CE)

2. **Lunisolar and planetary annual patterns**. Many of the Hebrew and Christian holy days and celebrations are a repackaging of celebrations of the four significant ancient Northern Hemisphere annual lunisolar events—spring/March equinox; summer/June solstice; autumn/September equinox; winter/December solstice. These are adjusted to take account of the waxing and waning of the moon and have close links to the barley/wheat cropping and lamb breeding cycles.

3. **The barley cropping and lamb breeding cycle**. The two main crops were barley and wheat, and the primary domesticated and food animals were sheep. Many of the Hebrew and Christian holy days and celebrations are a repackaging of celebrations relating to lamb breeding, crop planting and crop harvesting. For example:

---

[934] SOURCE: https://www.thetorah.com/article/assyrian-deportation-and-resettlement-the-story-of-samaria retrieved on 13 March 2023.

a) The Feasts of Passover and Unleavened Bread were celebrated at the beginning of the barley harvest.

b) Fifty days later came the Feast of Weeks, or Pentecost, when the wheat harvest began.

c) The Feast of Tabernacles, or Ingathering, took place when the harvest was complete.[935]

4. **Their own imagination/mythological beliefs.** They had a desire to differentiate themselves ethnically and culturally and to position themselves as the one true religion.

These experiences contributed significantly to the stories that make up the HB/OT. The Bible does not only contain appropriations from many of these previous cultural and mythological experiences. Throughout the Bible, the Hebrew scribes have a recurring theme. A predominant biblical theme is that the various exiles and diasporas were essentially God's punishments imposed on Israel for idolatry and unbelief. This theme is one of an ethnic struggle against God and circumstance. It is a metaphor for the whole of the Jewish religion—reflected in the word Israel itself, which is a metaphor for the essence and nature of this relationship with God. The exodus and exilic stories continue this metaphor of struggle with and response to their god.

The writing styles and traditions that influenced the Hebrew scribes

The Bronze Age and the invention of the alphabet and writing were typified by the emergence of what McLuhan calls Manuscript Culture and the Age of Literacy. The widespread use of the alphabet exerted a gravitational effect on cognition, which in turn affected social organisation, culture, and mythological writing. The written expression of historical and mythological beliefs began to emerge, be elaborated/consolidated, shared, and was spread across South-eastern Europe, the Eurasian Steppes, the Caucuses, Egypt, the Middle East, and Northern India.

It was during the Bronze Age that this regular contact and regular sharing of ideas operated in a dynamic intellectual, intercultural, and influential network that transcended political and cultural boundaries. Ancient Middle Eastern Studies scholar Beate Pongratz-Leisten has described it in this way:

---

[935] SOURCE: https://womeninthebible.net/bible-archaeology/farming-agriculture/ retrieved on 9 March 2023.

The ancient Near East (was) an intellectual community that, despite linguistic, regional, and local distinctions, displays features of cultural cohesion, drawing upon a common reservoir of religious practices, tropes, ideas and cultural strategies and institutions generated by intense and repeated demographic shifts throughout history. The political geography of the region, empire-building, commerce, and diplomacy all encouraged interconnectivity between the great powers, contributing to the creation of an osmotic cultural space in which the multilingual education of the scholarly elites nurtured intense communication and allowed for the diffusion as well as the conscious reception of ideas.

Pongratz-Leisten goes on to confirm that this dynamically networked environment promoted a relatively wide circulation of religious tenets, texts, and religious experts and the dissemination of shared writing systems, ideas, and ideological frameworks.[936]

The Bible reflects and is typical of these times. The Hebrew scribes were writing in, and influenced by, many different locations, mythologies, languages, and cultures across their region. The resulting document contains prose, poetry, metaphors, laws, narratives, fables, autobiographical stories, third-person accounts, wisdom, myth, mysteries, facts, fiction, and fantasy. It contains the same variety of literary styles that pervaded the Middle East and surrounding regions during the hundreds of years when the Hebrew scribes were writing.

Hebrew Bible as a typical example of Middle Eastern Bronze Age literature

There were literally hundreds of scribes, hundreds of years, and many influences involved in the writing of the HB/OT. It is not surprising, therefore, that the result contains a range of Middle Eastern literary styles or genres. Biblical advocates and scholars have identified the following literary genres within the Hebrew Bible:

- Historical narrative
- Wisdom and poetry
- Law
- Prophecy.[937]

---

[936] Pongratz-Leisten (2011), pp. 3-4.
[937] See: https://www.biblestudywithrandy.com/2015/10/why-genre-is-important-in-bible-study/ ; https://myprintablefaith.com/genres-in-the-bible/ and https://static1.squarespace.com/static/570bc781b6 aa60017e66cca4/t/5c6c4f40eb393136fc7d0e70/1550602049454/Quick+Guide+to+Biblical+-Genres.pdf retrieved on 10 November 2022.

These literary styles owe a great deal to the historical, religious, and philosophical writing traditions that were common across Egypt, the Middle East, and the Indus Valley during the hundreds of years during which the Hebrew scribes were writing their texts. The eight literature traditions that influenced the style of the HB/OT were:

1. The Middle Eastern, Indus Valley, and Egyptian writing styles
2. The practice of writing self-promotional stele and inscriptions
3. The Ugaritic/Canaanite narrative poetry tradition
4. The Mesopotamian Naru literature tradition
5. The Middle East's divination texts and omen literature tradition
6. The use of ancient eponym chronicles
7. The Middle Eastern tradition of 'wisdom literature'
8. The law codes of the Ancient Middle East.

The Middle Eastern, Indus Valley and Egyptian writing styles

The oral style of writing

The low levels of literacy across the Middle East had a major influence on the writing style of all Middle Eastern scribes. Most of the communities were illiterate and were accustomed to the oral communication of religious myths, epics, maximums, truisms, adages, paradoxes, legends, hymns, prayers, prophecies, and poems. Outside of the documentation and messages for the elites, the scribes were writing primarily for an oral society. The scribes were not simply slavishly creating and writing abstract texts. The Sumerian scribes, specifically within the literary and creative stream, were writing in a range of styles that respected the aesthetics of oral communication. The low levels of literacy caused scribes to change the transmission process to a more creative, oral style of storytelling, which was one of the major techniques adopted by the Hebrew scribes.[938]

The ancient writing styles generally

The emergence of written recording, firstly in cuneiform, hieroglyphics and eventually through the alphabet saw the emergence of various writing styles, storytelling, and literary traditions. McLuhan described this era as the Manuscript Culture/Age of Literacy and from it emerged a plurality of literary styles. As a result, the Middle East at the time

---

[938] Person Jr (1998), p. 602.

of the emergence of Israel had already adopted a wide-ranging manuscript culture and writing styles. This was facilitated by the availability of an alphabet, a scribal culture, and the growing popularity of training centres and scribal schools (*edubba*) for students, apprentices, and influential master scribes.

There are tens of thousands of cuneiform Sumerian clay tablets containing documentary evidence of the Sumerian culture, economy, trade, mythology, spiritual and intellectual life, administrative systems, social organisation, and day-to-day life. The archaeological evidence of the Sumerian literature tradition reflected in these thousands of clay tablets is the oldest significant amount of ancient written literature yet to be found.

Samuel Kramer has identified the Sumerians as the first to establish and expand literary imagery. He has described the Sumerian literary legacy as:

- 20 myths varying in length from just over 100 to close to 1,000 lines
- 9 epic tales varying in length from just over 100 lines to 500 lines
- over one hundred hymns royal and divine varying in length from under 100 lines to close to 500 lines
- a score or so of lamentations and lamentation-like texts with about 3,000 lines
- 12 disputations and school essays with about 4,000 lines
- a dozen or so collections of proverbs and precepts of some 3,000 lines
- overall, a total of some 28,000 lines of Sumerian literary imagery.[939]

Over time, the Sumerian, Mesopotamian, and Middle Eastern manuscript cultures delivered a range of writing and storytelling styles that had a significant influence on biblical writing. The Hebrew scribes were typical of their time. As mentioned earlier, the other seven ancient writing styles/literature traditions directly influencing the tone, the stories, the narrative, structure, and style of the HB/OT were:

- self-promotional stories of Egyptian and Middle Eastern conquests written on cylinder seals, stelae, and inscriptions linked to specific empires, gods, kings, and leaders
- the Ugaritic/Canaanite narrative poetry tradition
- the Mesopotamian Naru literature tradition
- the divination texts and omens of the Sumerians, Mesopotamians, and Assyro-Babylonians
- ancient eponym chronicles

---

[939]   Kramer (1956), p. 289.

- the Middle East tradition of wisdom literature
- the legal traditions of the Ancient Middle East.

The self-promotional stele and inscriptions

Kings, pharaohs, and scribes regularly embellished their stories. The Egyptian Pharaoh Merenptah, whose stele first mentions Israel, is suspected of creating imaginary lands (pseudo-geographic entities with distinctive inhabitants and cultures) in order to meet religious, intellectual, and emotional needs. The mixing of some historical information into fictional stories with imagined conquests, exaggerated enemies, legendary heroes, and mythological locations was commonly used as self-promotional propaganda. The creation of mysterious locations and legendary stories to convey symbolic and mythological messages occurred in Egypt and across the Middle East in the Late Bronze Age. It is not surprising, then, that scholars disagree, sometimes vehemently, about the locations and cultures of some important but geographically disputed conquests and lands covered in any of these Late Bronze Age texts.[940]

The biblical claims of the Israelites conquering the Canaanites following their claimed exodus from Egypt and the claim that Joshua attacked and destroyed Jericho are examples of this tradition (Joshua 6:1–27). The archaeological evidence confirms that neither of these events occurred as described in the Bible. Both stories are now largely confirmed as nationalist propaganda in keeping with this ancient self-promotional tradition.

The Ugaritic/Canaanite narrative poetry tradition

Ugarit is an ancient Canaanite coastal port that is known to have existed since at least 6000 BCE. It was a key link to the inland trade networks from the Mediterranean to the Fertile Crescent. Ancient Ugaritic texts predate the Hebrew Bible by more than one thousand years, but they contain many parallels with the Hebrew Bible. Large numbers of Ugaritic clay tablets have provided archaeologists with some of the only examples of indigenous texts relating to the ancient Canaanites.[941] Ugaritic texts contain poems, narratives, myths, and legends relating to the epic adventures of kings, gods, and goddesses.

---

[940] Cline and O'Connor (2007), pp. 133-134.
[941] Tubb (1998), p. 73.

The biblical writers were influenced by the poetic style of these early Canaanites. Simon Parker explains how the biblical poetry of the latter prophets (Isaiah to Malachi), the Psalms, and the Books of Job and Proverbs reflect this Canaanite literature tradition:

> *The major difference between the two literatures is that virtually all poetry in Ugaritic is narrative, while there are only occasional short passages of narrative in biblical poetry. However, the Ugaritic narrative poems illustrate the antecedents of biological literature with narrative episodes, scenes, and motifs; mythological motifs and schemes; and imagery, formulae and other poetic devices. To recognise these connections is also to sharpen our perception of how biblical writers adapted the tradition to their own purposes.*[942]

Mesopotamian Naru literature

Another influential writing tradition adopted by the Hebrew scribes was the Mesopotamian Naru style. The word *naru* originally referred to a boundary stone, monument, or engraved stele. In his 1933 dissertation, German-American Hittitologist Hans Gustav Güterbock introduced the term 'naru-literature'.[943] Naru literature is regarded as the world's first historical fiction. The story is most often an heroic first-person narrative based on well-known popular historical or semi-mythic kings or famous persons. The historic, partly autobiographical facts are embellished by anonymous authors with fictional and symbolic additions. The fictional and symbolic additions are used as vehicles to emphasise messages usually about religious, moral, life lessons, ethical or cultural values.

Naru literature was an adaptation of the typical self-promotional stele inscriptions on which kings boasted about their various conquests and victories (above) but written by anonymous authors expanding the narrative into a purposeful blend of historical fact and carefully constructed fiction. A major difference between the self-promotional stele (above) and Naru literature is that Naru literature deviates significantly from the stele inscriptions to include the struggles and failures being confronted by the king/person who is the subject of the story. Naru literature almost always includes a focus on interactions with and the will of the gods.[944]

---

[942] Parker (2000), p. 229.

[943] See: https://oi.uchicago.edu/research/projects/chicago-hittite-dictionary-project/people/founders-and -former-editors/hans-gustav-gueterbock retrieved on 1 November 2022.

[944] The History of the Mesopotamian Naru Literature—World History Encyclopedia retrieved on 1 November 2022.

Naru literature tells of symbolic as opposed to factual memories. The genre has been referred to as poetic narratives, pseudo-autobiographies, or fictitious autobiographies.[945] Joshua Mark described Naru literature in this way:

Mesopotamian Naru Literature was a literary genre, first appearing around the 2nd millennium BCE, which featured a famous person (usually a king) from history as the main character in a story that most often concerned humanity's relationship with the gods. These stories became very popular and, in time, seem to have replaced the actual historical events in the minds of the people.[946]

Three epic Mesopotamian Naru literature stories were the sources of the biblical story of Noah and the flood. The sources for the biblical flood story were the Sumerian *Epic of Ziusudra* (2900 BCE), the Sumerian/Babylonian *Epic of Gilgamesh* (2150—1400 BCE) and the Akkadian *Atra-Hasis* (1800 BCE).

The biblical flood story is not the only Naru literature source or influence in the Hebrew Bible. There are several books of the Bible where the influence of Naru literature, the use of the first-person narrative, and the Naru autobiographical style appear. These include:

- The Book of Nehemiah
- The Book of Ecclesiastes
- The Book of Ezekiel
- The Book of Habakkuk
- The Book of Second Chronicles
- The Book of Zechariah from 1:8 through to the end of the book
- The Book of Revelation 1:9—22:18
- Chapter 6 of the Book of Isaiah
- The Book of Jeremiah 1:4—7:30; 11:5b—19:13; 24: 1—10; 25: 15—38 & 31:26—32:15
- The Book of Ezra chapters 7:27—9:15.[947]

The Middle East's divination texts and omen literature

There is written (cuneiform) evidence dating back to Mesopotamia in the third millennium BCE of a belief in signs or portents observed in the physical and social world

---

[945]   Westenholz (1983), p. 327.

[946]   Mark (2014).

[947]   SOURCE: https://www.academia.edu/7110697/POV_in_the_Bible retrieved on 1 November 2022.

indicating the will of supernatural agents and providing humans with divine predictions of future events or divine intent.[948]

Mesopotamian/Assyro-Babylonian omen literature and divination texts exist in some tens of thousands of tablets, seals, or incantation bowls discovered by archaeologists. They show that the ancient Mesopotamians believed that signs from the gods could be found everywhere. Divination texts represent one of the more difficult and intriguing literary genres from Mesopotamia.

The Mesopotamians and, in particular, the Babylonians and Assyrians were highly organised in their management of divination. The forerunners to the Hebrew scribes were specially trained Mesopotamian divination/omen priests attached to the staff of many temples. These were the individual scholars/scribes responsible for the vast collection of Mesopotamian omen texts that have been found.[949] The Mesopotamians had scholarly centres where individual scholars had the freedom to choose which omen to write about from a given list of possible topics including celestial, meteorological, terrestrial, life and living, gods, ghosts, supernatural entities, and human and animal bodily and intestinal characteristics.[950]

Because of the plurality of modes/genres of Mesopotamian literature, Assyriologist Jacob Finkelstein has suggested that modern understandings of history are inadequate in explaining the Mesopotamian approach to writing history. History is an intellectual form in which civilisations render accounts to themselves of their past (after Dutch historian Johan Huizinga).[951] Jacob Finkelstein sees Mesopotamian omen texts as being the closest to this definition. Despite abounding in allusions, the omens have a ring of authenticity about past historical events and observable daily occurrences.[952]

The Mesopotamians developed lengthy catalogues containing lists of omens and their meanings.[953] Some omens were based on the gods' responses to specific questions and others that the gods had sent as portends without a prior human request.

The Mesopotamian omens usually were conditional statements of the form 'if this … then this'. Examples from the Mesopotamian celestial omens (from *enuma anu enlil*) include:

---

[948] Annus, A. (2010), p. 1.
[949] Hooke (1955), pp. 330-331.
[950] Fincke (2013), pp. 583-585; Rochberg (1999).
[951] Huizinga (1936).
[952] Finkelstein J.J. (1963), p. 462.
[953] Geers (1926); Jacobsen (1946B), p. 189.

- 'If the sun is eclipsed in the month of Nissan on the first day, the King of Akkad will die.'
- 'If the sun rises early and the west wind blows all day there will be an eclipse.'
- 'If it is eclipsed on the sixteenth day, a pregnant woman will miscarry.'[954]

This conditional 'if … then' style was one of the styles adopted by the Hebrew scribes. The only difference was that the focus of the Mesopotamians on multiple deities in the heavens (sun god, moon god), transitioned over the centuries of Hebrew scribes' versions into the concept of 'if … then' being linked to a belief in a singular anthropomorphic god in the heavens. Biblical examples of the Middle East's omen tradition include:

- 'Now therefore, if ye will obey my voice indeed, and keep my covenant, then ye shall be a peculiar treasure unto me above all people: for all the earth is mine.' (Exodus 19:5)
- 'My son, if you accept my words and store up my commands within you, turning your ear to wisdom and applying your heart to understanding—indeed, if you call out for insight and cry aloud for understanding, and if you look for it as for silver and search for it as for hidden treasure, then you will understand the fear of the Lord and find the knowledge of God.' (Proverbs 2:1-5)
- 'If my people who are called by my name humble themselves, and pray and seek my face and turn from their wicked ways, then I will hear from heaven and will forgive their sin and heal their land.' (2 Chronicles 7:14).

Ancient Eponym Chronicles

Eponym chronicles are historically sequential stories where each notable annual event refers to a specific leader or official. An eponym (ancient Assyrian word *limu*) describes a word that has been adapted from the name of an official person. A simple example is the word for the Australian city of Gladstone, which was named after the British Chancellor of the Exchequer, William Ewart Gladstone. Chronicles are, by definition, written records of historical events arranged in order of time usually without analysis or interpretation.[955] With the advent of writing and the development of families of scribes and scribal schools in Mesopotamia, eponym chronicles proliferated. The eponyms were a technique used to

---

954   Rutz (2006), pp. 80-82.

955   SOURCE: https://www.merriam-webster.com/dictionary/chronicle#:~:text=chron%C2%B7%E2%80%8Bi%C2%B7%E2%80%8Bcle,chronicle%20of%20the%20Civil%20War retrieved on 21 November 2022.

assist in distinguishing one year from the next. In the development of the Ancient Middle East chronological records, three methods for distinguishing the years evolved over time:

- from around 3000 BCE in Egypt and until 2400 BCE in Babylonia, each year was named after an important event
- from around 2150 BCE in Egypt and 1595 BCE in Babylonia, the chronology was recorded by stating the number of years of each king's reign
- finally, at a date still not determined (possibly earlier by the Sumerians than elsewhere), each year was named after a holder of a high office.[956]

Jean-Jacques Glassner has compiled translated versions of Mesopotamian, Sumerian, Akkadian, Assyrian, Babylonian, Persian and Hellenistic eponym chronicles commencing from around 2200 BCE until around 140 BCE. The Preface of Glassner's book describes the Assyrian eponym chronicles in the following way:

[They] list year after year, from the beginning of the second millennium to the middle of the first BCE, the accessions and deaths of kings, the names of high officials of state as well as their subordinates, and the annual objectives of military campaigns.[957]

Initially, the desire to be able to refer to and distinguish specific years was required by administrative, legal, and business documents. This required the making of correct sequential lists of the order of each eponym so that documents could be correctly date-ordered.[958] Archaeological records now include eponym chronicles that tell of the event and the leader and eponym lists that place all Middle Eastern eponyms in a chronological sequence. The Middle Eastern eponyms usually followed the same order, with the name of the king first and then next the military commander-in-chief, followed by the chief of the palace, the head priest, and then the names of military attendees of the king, followed by the governors of various towns.[959]

The biblical Book of First Chronicles is largely an eponym list in the Middle Eastern tradition. Second Chronicles is closer to the Middle Eastern eponym chronicles in style and content.

The existence and discovery of correctly date-ordered events in the Assyrian eponym lists (first published in 1862),[960] particularly highlighting events and dates between 900 BCE and 300 BCE, led almost immediately to commentary and research on whether the

---

[956] Millard (1994), p. 1.
[957] Glassner (2004), p. xix.
[958] Millard (1994), p. 1.
[959] Smith, G. (1875); p. 24.
[960] Rawlinson (1862).

date order in the Assyrian eponym lists confirmed the biblical chronologies available by analysing First and Second Chronicles and the Second Book of Kings.[961]

However, the ancient eponym chronicles and, indeed, the biblical stories were not necessarily entirely factual. The writers of eponym chronicles were not simply creating an historical record—they were also selectively elaborating, fictionalising, and editorialising. They were ideological and religious. They were either subliminally or consciously promoting and sustaining the status quo and a particular version of history. There are many similarities between the Mesopotamian eponym chronicles and the Mesopotamian Naru literature. The differences between the two literary styles are threefold:

- The chronicles, like annals, cover many year-by-year events and many different leaders. Naru literature had a narrower focus.
- The chronicles serve an important purpose in the ability to distinguish/confirm events chronologically. Naru literature did not serve as a chronological datum.
- The chronicles, whilst containing embellishments, tend to be slightly more objective and factual than Naru literature, although there is some evidence that the chronicles (specifically the Assyrian eponym lists) were less factual than the Assyrian omen texts.[962]

Glassner refers to the writers of the Mesopotamian eponym chronicles as 'chroniclers'. He documents the evolution of their writing styles over time. He observes that the Neo-Babylonian chroniclers had developed:

> … an archetypal view of history and a way of thinking that saw in events the 'repetition' of exemplary types … the same ponderous style, the same tedious repetitions, the deliberate strategy of saying the same things in exactly the same words and a desire to note the same developments by means of the same expressions … and the same word order, such as concerning the extent or significance of pillage … or scope of defeats. Such cliches greatly ease the reading of the texts and assist the reader in understanding them.[963]

The ancient Middle Eastern tradition of using eponym chronicles as a means of identifying and embellishing sequential years was adopted by the Hebrew scribes in their writing of the Bible. The ponderous style and mix of specific word repetition can be most clearly seen in First Chronicles and Second Chronicles. An example of the application of this technique from First Chronicles (11:22–24) is where the Hebrew scribes are describing one of King David's commanders, Benaiah:

---

[961] See for example: Smith, G. (1875); Badger (1886).
[962] Millard (1994), p. 6.
[963] Glassner (2004), p. 83.

... and Benaiah, the son of Jehoiada was a valiant man of Kanzeel, a doer of great deeds. He struck down two heroes of Moab. He also went down and struck down a lion in a pit on a day when snow had fallen. And he struck down an Egyptian, a man of great stature, five cubits tall. The Egyptian had in his hand a spear like a weaver's beam, but Benaiah went down to him with a staff and snatched the spear out of the Egyptian's hand and killed him with his own spear.

This example, like many in First Chronicles, Second Chronicles, and the Second Book of Kings is the chroniclers' creative elaboration on events and people—in this case, around the unfolding stories about the reigns and battles of the biblical King David and his son, King Solomon.

The Middle Eastern tradition of 'wisdom literature'

Across Central Asia, the Middle East, Egypt, and the Indus Valley, most prehistoric mythologies had gods or symbols of wisdom. The Zoroastrians had Āhurā Mazdā ('Lord Wisdom') and the Faravahar icon (age and wisdom), the Mesopotamians had Nabu, the Akkadians had Ea, the Sumerians had Enki, the Egyptians had Thoth (and his associate goddess Maat) and his consort Seshat, the Greeks had Athena, and the Hindus had Saraswati and Ganesha.

In some cases, these gods of wisdom were also gods of justice, truth, literature, language, knowledge, learning and/or writing. The much sought-after spiritual stone lapis lazuli (7000 BCE onwards) was regarded by these prehistoric cultures as a highly valued stone of wisdom, good judgement, and healing.

Paul Kriwaczek has explained the significance to the Sumerians of their god of wisdom, Enki in the following way:

Mesopotamians recognized Enki as the god who brings civilization to humankind. It is he who gives rulers their intelligence and knowledge; he 'opens the doors of understanding'. ...
Enki, the Lord of abundance, of trustworthy commands,
The Lord of wisdom who understands the land. [964]

The ancient search for wisdom, and the presence of mediators such as shamans, sages, scribes, astrologers, diviners, prophets, seers, exorcists, and priests, reflected the human desire to respect their god/s, to behave correctly, to live virtuously, and to better explain the mysteries of life. The work of this variety of prehistoric mediators can be found in omen texts, divinations, inspirations, instructional texts, dreams, hymns, epic stories, legal documents, cult lore, magic, proverbs, and fables. Their key role was to provide guidance and instructions on

---

[964] Kriwaczek (2010), p. 30.

how to behave ethically, live in society, understand the cosmos, and respect the god/s. These literary devices were tools applied by the Hebrew scribes in creating their biblical stories.

Sara Denning-Bolle has suggested that ancient wisdom can be categorised into two types:

- practical, down-to-earth wisdom, where advice is offered on how to conduct one's life, and

- a more abstract type of wisdom, where one finds an enquiring into the enigmas of life and an attempt to answer some of these mysteries.[965]

In recent times, the term 'wisdom literature' has almost uniformly been applied and almost exclusively to the HB/OT. This is even though:

… the biblical wisdom writers drew upon a long-established generic tradition in the region, a type of didactic or advice literature that had existed in the ANE (Ancient Near East) for over thousands of years.[966]

Encyclopedia Britannica confirms the ancient origin of wisdom literature:

Wisdom literature flourished throughout the ancient Near East, with Egyptian examples dating back to before the middle of the 3rd millennium BCE. It revolved around the professional sages, or wise men, and scribes in the service of the court, and consisted primarily in maxims about the practical, intelligent way to conduct one's life and in speculations about the very worth and meaning of human life.[967]

The Sumerians were the first to develop an extensive wisdom literature. It included legendary tales, long and short essays, disputations, debates, battles of words, collections of precepts and proverbs. They established scribal schools where literature was studied, copied, duplicated, and varied by thousands of students and specialist scribes.[968] The format and intent of the Sumerian wisdom literature have been described by Samuel Kramer in a way that could well be applied to the Hebrew Bible:

As for the poetic compositions, and especially the epic tales, these contain at best a kernel of historical truth, and the modern scholar usually finds himself hopelessly frustrated in his efforts to separate the wheat from the chaff, the real from the imagined, and thus isolate the historically significant residue.[969]

---

965 Denning-Bolle (1987), p. 217.
966 Dell et al (2022), p. 206.
967 See: https://www.britannica.com/topic/biblical-literature/Proverbs#ref597827 retrieved on 25 October 2022.
968 Kramer (1981), p. 3.
969 Kramer (1971), p. 38.

The Sumerian wisdom literature was a stylistic device to instil piety, virtue, and moral and ethical standards, and to promote wise, effective, and community-standard behaviour. One of the oldest examples of the Sumerian wisdom literature is *The Instructions of Shuruppak to His Son Ziusudra* (from around 2000 BCE). Kramer quotes from this Sumerian document to highlight the much later 'biblical flavour' of this style of writing as it was continued centuries later by the Hebrew scribes:

> *My son, I would instruct you, to take instructions,*
> *Ziusudra, I would utter a word to you, give heed to it*
> *Do not neglect my instruction,*
> *Do not transgress the word I uttered,*
> *The father's instruction, the precious, carry out diligently.*[970]

Centuries before the emergence of the Israelites, Ancient Egyptian wisdom literature, namely *Maxims of Ptahhotep* (circa 2300 BCE) and the *Instruction of Amenemope* (circa 1200 BCE), contained teachings and instructions on successful living, ethics, divinity, and virtue. The Akkadians (2350 BCE to 2150 BCE) are also recognised as promoters of what is now referred to as 'wisdom literature'. The Babylonian/Akkadian *Counsels of Wisdom* (around 1500 BCE) is a list of moral exhortations to a 'son' that has striking similarities to the biblical Book of Proverbs.[971] The Akkadian poem, *Ludlul bel nemeqi* ('Let me praise the Lord of Wisdom') is regarded as a major influence on the Hebrew scribes when they wrote the Book of Job.[972]

These various ancient wisdom texts are regarded as the most likely source of the inspiration for the seven biblical books that are commonly called wisdom books. The biblical 'wisdom books' are the Books of Proverbs, Job, Psalms, Ecclesiastes (Qoholeth), Song of Songs, Wisdom, and Sirach (Ecclesiasticus).

The influence of these ancient wisdom texts and the ancient legal traditions (see below) written centuries before the Hebrew Bible can be seen in the wording of the biblical Ten Commandments. The Hebrew scribes have Moses advising his people about the ten commandments in the following way:

> *Observe them carefully, for this will show your wisdom and understanding to the nations, who will hear about all these decrees and say, 'Surely this great nation is a wise and understanding people.' (Deuteronomy 4:6).*

---

970   Kramer (1963), p. 224.
971   See: https://mostlydeadlanguages.tumblr.com/post/132233974443/counsels-of-wisdom-bwl-96ff-21-80 retrieved on 19 October 2022; and, https://www.ewtn.com/catholicism/library/wisdom-literature-12473 retrieved on 8 November 2022.
972   See: https://www.britannica.com/topic/Ludlul-bel-nemeqi retrieved on 2 November 2022.

Modern examples of the biblical writing style

There have been much more recent examples of this style of writing that exemplify what may have been the intention of the Hebrew scribes.

A contemporary example of this type of creative writing is a book by Italian writer Italo Calvino.[973] In 1972, Calvino produced a wonderful book wherein he imagines that Marco Polo is describing the many cities he has visited to the all-powerful emperor of the Tartars, Kublai Khan. The cities and the stories are illusional and breathtaking—cities hung between hills in hammocks; subterranean cities like sewer systems; spiderweb cities; cities with earth in place of air; cities within cities within cities. The descriptions encourage Kublai Khan's imagination because he is, himself a conqueror. However, Marco Polo (via the hand and the imagination of Calvino) is really creating the myriad possible forms a city might take as exemplars for one city—Venice, which, at the time, was in total disarray.

The use of these literary mechanisms, metaphors, and poetic and allegorical stories are the same mechanisms that were used by the Hebrew scribes as they constructed the mythological story of the exodus of the Israelites from Egypt. Most of the names (and the sequence) of the exodus stations are probably illusional. But they convey a message about the values, beliefs, and behaviours that combine to reinforce the overall cultural objective of the scribes when writing the HB/OT.

The ten commandments and the law codes of the Ancient Middle East

With the emergence of large sedentary and largely agricultural communities across the Middle East in around 3000 BCE, systems needed to be put in place to manage and control the new and emerging city-states. The transition to city-states was most often led by a king who claimed a direct link to one of the gods. This god became the identified protector of each city.

To strengthen the control needed in each city, law codes were introduced from around 2300 BCE. The law codes fulfilled two main functions: they reflected the transition of religious beliefs from an individual being embedded in a complex spiritual universe to one where the individual was in a personal relationship with a specific deity.[974] They also itemised the rules to be followed in the personal relationship with the city god, doubling as a means of maintaining social order. In many ways, the emergence of law codes in ancient Sumer is the hallmark of the commencement of 'civilisation'.

The Mesopotamian law codes' influence on Mosaic law

The Urukagina Code (2350 BCE) is the first known example of a legal code in recorded history. Urukagina was a god-king ruler and social reformer of the city-state of Lagash in Meso-

---

[973] Calvino (1979).
[974] Jacobsen (1976), pp. 147-164.

potamia. Unfortunately, the actual text of the Urukagina Code has never been discovered, and much of the Code's content is assumed from references to it in other archaeological discoveries. From the fragmentary evidence available, the Urukagina Code focused on government reform, limiting the power of priests, the elite, and large-scale property owners, introducing legal rights of citizens and measures to limit corruption, hunger, theft, and murder.[975]

The oldest surviving law code was made by Ur-Nammu (Ur-Namma), the founding king of the last Sumerian dynasty (2100 BCE to 2094 BCE and 2047 BCE to 2030 BCE).[976] The archaeological evidence of the Ur-Nammu Code is incomplete, but the Code articulates the rules that would free the land of thieves, robbers, and rebels. It achieved this by specifying how a crime would be dealt with—by death, mutilation, or payment of shekels of silver (the weight of which was determined by the gravity of the crime).[977]

The Laws of Eshnunna (around 1930 BCE), were developed for the Mesopotamian city of Eshnunna—a city located on the banks of the Diyala River, an eastern tributary of the Tigris River. The Laws of Eshnunna are believed to have been the origin of the conditional phraseology of subsequent Laws—'If A, then B' or 'If a man does something … then this will happen'. It covered five main offences:

1. Theft and related offences
2. False distraint
3. Sexual offences
4. Bodily injuries
5. Damages caused by a goring ox and comparable cases.[978]

These offences were dealt with in a similar way to the Ur-Nammu codes—pecuniary fine or death.

The Code of Sumero-Akkadian-Amorite god-king Lipit–Ishtar (1868 BCE to 1857 BCE) exists only in archaeological fragments. It is written in Sumerian and is regarded as originally being the full Sumerian Law Code, including a prologue and epilogue. Topics covered included the emancipation of slaves, equitable family relations, rules on the use of boats, and legislation dealing with real estate, orchards, inheritance, and marriage. This is the code that contains the oldest historical example of the principle of 'an eye for an eye'—wherein punishment for an injury or for damages is equivalent to what has been inflicted by the perpetrator (later adopted in biblical and Roman Law).[979]

---

[975] See:https://en-academic.com/dic.nsf/enwiki/175293andhttp://sumerianshakespeare.com/70701/77001.html retrieved on 8 June 2022.

[976] Kramer (1971), p. 68 and 83-84.

[977] Roux (1992), p. 162.

[978] Adapted from https://dbpedia.org/page/Laws_of_Eshnunna retrieved on 7 June 2022.

[979] Steele (1948), pp. 427-430.

The Babylonian Code of Hammurabi (1755 BCE to 1750 BCE) is currently regarded as the longest, best-organised, best-preserved prehistoric legal text and the one that was most influential on the Hebrew scribe's writing of Mosaic Law. Well before the Moses story, legend has it that Hammurabi received his code of laws directly from Shamash, the Mesopotamian god of the sun, justice, light, life, and the universe. As well as the Hammurabi code influencing the Mosaic Law, the name Shamash has been adopted into Judaism to signify the person who is the custodian of a synagogue. Shamash has also been adopted as the Hebrew term used to describe the ninth light of the multi-branched candelabra (the menorah) that is used in the religious rituals of Judaism including during the eight-day December (winter solstice) festival of Hanukkah.

The Hittite Code of the Nesilim was used in Anatolia during the reign of the Hittite kingdom (1650 BCE to 1180 BCE). The Hittite laws reflected the kingdom's social structure (a rural economy and a feudal aristocracy), sense of justice, and morality, addressing common outlawed actions such as homicide, injuries, kidnapping, runaway slaves, marriage, land administration, animals' injuries, theft, fire, prices and wages, and inappropriate sexual behaviour. The Hittite Code was another major influence on the Hebrew scribes writing the Mosaic Law.[980]

The Hindu law codes' influence on Mosaic law

The Hindu law code Manusmṛiti, which is also known as the Laws of Manu, has been dated to around 1200 BCE. These are the Hindu sacred texts that are believed to have been handed down by the Hindu god Brahma to Bhrigu, one of Hindu's seven great sages.[981]

Egyptian influence on the Mosaic laws

The Mosaic Law was also influenced by the Egyptian Book of the Dead (ca 1700 BCE).[982] The ancient Egyptians believed that the Book of the Dead, which was also referred to as the 'Book of Emerging Forth into the Light', was written by Thoth, the Egyptian god of the moon, wisdom, writing, hieroglyphs, science, magic, art, and judgment.[983] The Ancient Egyptians believed that life and death were just the first steps in the journey to immortality and the afterlife. The Book of the Dead contained instructions for the person's soul, the spiritual element of themselves, to navigate this journey. Over time, the Book of the Dead existed in various forms,

---

[980] See: Hoffner Jr. (1969).
[981] Schomp (2005); Shah (undated) https://www.academia.edu/8301757/Ancient_Law_Givers retrieved on 2 September 2022.
[982] Castellano (2019) and Wallis Budge (1967), p. xiii.
[983] Wallis Budge (2010), pp. 9-10.

but it essentially documented the various priestly spells, incantations, spiritual powers, magical texts, and funerary rituals to assist the deceased in their passage to judgement in the afterlife.

The link of the Ten Commandments to Mesopotamian Ritual and Liturgical Incantations

From around 1350 BCE to 1050 BCE onwards, the Mesopotamian incantations surrounding the death of a person tended to include a soothing of the gods by summarising a long list of the wrongdoings of the person who had died. The following extract is taken from the Mesopotamian Shurpu (also Shuru) ceremony's incantation of a list of a deceased person's wrongdoings. It has an uncanny similarity to the HB/OT version of the Ten Commandments written at least one thousand years later:[984]

> *He scorned the god, despised the goddess,*
> *his sins are against his god, his crimes are against his goddess.*
> *He is full of contempt [against] his father, full of hatred against his elder brother.*
> *He despised his parents, offended the elder sister,*
> *gave with small (measure) and received with big (measure),*
> *her said "there is", when there was not,*
> *he said "there is not" when there was,*
> *s[poke] unseemly things, spoke [i]mprope[r] things,*
> *he spoke insolent things, [he spo]ke [. . .]*
> *he us[ed] an untrue balance, (but) [did not us]e the [true balance],*
> *he took money that was not due to him, (but) [did not ta]ke mo[ney due to him],*
> *he disinherited the legitimated son (and) [did not est]ablish (in his rights) the le[gitimated] son,*
> *he set up an untrue boundary, (but) did not set up the [tr]ue bound[ary],*
> *he removed mark, frontier and boundary.*
> *He entered his neighbor's house,*
> *had intercourse with his neighbor's wife,*
> *shed his neighbor's blood,*
> *put on (var. took away) his neighbor's clothes,*
> *(and) did not clothe a young man when he was naked.*
> *He ousted a well-to-do young man from his family,*
> *scattered a gathered clan,......*

In content and in the sequence of the issues being presented to the gods, the ancient Mesopotamian funeral incantation mirrors almost exactly the Ten Commandments.

---

[984]   SOURCE: Pongratz-Leisten (2023), pp. 427-428 adapted from Shurpu Tablet II 33–53; Reiner 1958, 14.

The integration of previous law codes into Mosaic law

These precedents highlight the fact that, thousands of years before the emergence of the Israelites, the region had established a common, top-down process of documenting various god-given legal, moral, and social codes as a means of managing, controlling, and unifying a cultural group. The Mosaic Law followed suit. It covered the Ten Commandments (significantly influenced by these earlier Ancient Middle East codes and the Egyptian Book of the Dead), but it also includes instructions relating to morality, social issues, food, feasts, purity, sacrifices, tithing, and the future of Israel.

The Mosaic Law (900 BCE to 300 BCE) is regarded as the law that God gave to the Israelites through Moses. Mosaic Law covers the Ten Commandments and the rules and religious observances in the first five books of the HB/OT (the Torah). Mosaic Law is significantly influenced by the general trend and the contents from previous laws and codes made across the Middle East (Urukagina Ur-Nammu, Eshnunna, Lipit–Ishtar, Hammurabi, Hindu, and Hittite). These previous codes had been in existence for thousands of years before the drafting of the Ten Commandments. They highlight the regional commonality of these beliefs and these practices.

There is one distinct difference between the earlier precedents and the Mosaic Law.[985] The earlier Ancient Middle East codes focused on establishing and managing social order and fairness—largely around how people should relate to each other. The Egyptian Book of the Dead focused on preparing the deceased for their passage to judgement. The Mosaic Law appears to blend influences from the Middle East, Hindu, and Egyptian precedents. Mosaic Law is more focused on morality, religious purity, and the individual's ongoing relationship with the Jewish god.

In summary, the archaeological evidence confirms that the notion of a set of guiding principles linked to a deity began with the Sumerians and Mesopotamians, was adopted and then adapted by the Akkadians, Babylonians, Hindus, and Hittites, became a regionally common practice, and was further enhanced by the Hebrew scribes. Each cultural variation involved customisation to reflect the social, moral, and religious intention of the various leaders/priests/ scribes/god-kings. The Mosaic Law and the prehistoric Middle Eastern legal codes from which it was largely derived have been analysed by Rebecca Denova into their common component parts:

- A story that outlines the historical context that led to a treaty with the deity/ies
- Specific details of the ordinances and required rituals
- Reading the text or publicly announcing its details to the group
- A list of blessings for obedience followed by curses or violence when the treaty is broken. In this sense, a 'sin' was defined as a violation of a god's commandments.[986]

---

[985]   SOURCE: https://www.britannica.com/topic/Ten-Commandments retrieved on 14 December 2020.
[986]   See: Denova (2021D).

Chapter 19

Biblical Authorship

The HB/OT was not written in isolation and was not written linearly from the first to the last page. It was an orchestrated, frequently restructured, edited, and rewritten document—a product of its times. There were three main influences on the Hebrew scribes:

- The collectively held (and believed) mythological storyline that was common across many prehistoric and Bronze Age cultures, at that time. Divine intervention to create heaven and Earth from chaos and humans from clay.
- There were various mythologies and literary traditions with which the Hebrew scribes were familiar—Sumerian, Mesopotamian, Babylonian, Indus Valley, Egyptian, Persian, and Greek. The Hebrew scribes cherry-picked bits and pieces of these and customised them into their own emerging mythological stories.
- A conscious effort to include cultural narratives that could easily identify them as having primacy and differentiation from their neighbours. They were constructing the codification of a culture that would discriminate and differentiate themselves as a separate ideological and territorial entity.

The Hebrew scribes were surrounded historically and contemporaneously by similar, overlapping cultures, mythologies, gods, myths, rituals, and beliefs. Like most scribes in the region at the time, they were involved in mythological assimilation—adapting their writings to incorporate the indigenous cultures, the mythologies, the towns, and the landscapes around them. They were embedded in a diffusion of cultures, reflected in their harvesting, re-writing, and interpreting of the shared mythological stories across hundreds of years of creating the HB/OT.[987]

---

[987] Raglan (1956), p. 149.

The Hebrew scribes were not plagiarists or fraudsters. Like most of the scribes across the Middle East, they were myth-makers and myth-appropriators who wove significantly exaggerated claims into an ethnic group's emerging narrative. The resulting Hebrew Bible and the Christian Old Testament are largely a reworking, coalescence, pastiche, and hybridisation of the cultural, spiritual, and mythological beliefs common to the region and the communities around them as they wrote.

The Hebrew scribes, like all scribes across the Middle East, Greece, the Mediterranean, and the Indus Valley in the late Bronze Age, were versed in the routine use of symbolism, iconography, storytelling, and allegory as devices for communicating legends, values, and beliefs to justify and indeed mystify the world around them. In the words of Jaan Puhvel:

> *Diffusion is the key word in ancient Near East mythology in general and in the creation myth in particular. Even the best-known specimen of the latter, the Hebrew Genesis, reeks of diffusionary regional motifs ultimately traceable to the Sumerians, who have left us their paradise myth of the pure and bright land of Dilmum, the tale of Dumuzi the petulant shepherd's antagonism toward Enkimdu the peaceful farmer, which is inversely reminiscent of the Cain-Abel conflict but does not culminate in murder, and the story of the flood hero Ziusudra, which has replicated itself in Utnapishtim of the Gilgamesh epic and Noah of Genesis.*[988]

They were theological rather than calendrical, which was the modus operandi for all scribes across the region at the time. The accuracy of past dates, years, and names and ages of key kings and prophets was secondary to the application of creative devices that would reinforce the mythological messages.

High on this list of devices was the creation of the myth of being the only group that can demonstrably trace their origins to the date of the creation of the world (referred to as 'primacy' or 'religious exclusivism'). This includes claims of having shared descent and kinship with imagined patriarchs through a common and largely fabricated ancestry. The patriarchs' names were appropriated from cultures, towns, or communities that predated the emergence of the Israelites. These devices were essential to the gradual and very successful process of crafting a history in the cause of constructing a sustainable and believable ethnic and spiritual identity.

---

[988] Puhvel (1989), p. 23.

Hybridisation by Jewish scribes around 500 BCE

The Hebrew scribes were presented with the perfect palette of experience, ideas, mythologies, and opportunities to create their Bible. James Carroll has described the role of the Jewish scribes in adapting the mythologies of their time in the following manner:

> *The composers of the scripture were a community of people. … Someone told a story, and someone else repeated it, and someone else elaborated it. An early interpreter read the story as a one-note signal about the Lord, then a later interpreter found in it second and third notes. Harmonies, melodies—a symphony. Thus myths, laws, songs, proverbs, dirges, oral traditions, stories told around fires, rhyming and rhythmic verses, heroic legends, into which youngsters were initiated in generation after generation—all of it became scripture.*[989]

The scribes were able to:

- reflect the generally held regional view about creation and the universe
- repackage the astronomical origin of prehistoric mythological beliefs
- embed seasonal agricultural celebrations into their mythological narrative
- creatively appropriate mythologies and/or cultural practices from surrounding city-states and empires
- reimagine events from their own history and embellish these events into mythological storytelling
- differentiate themselves from historical and emerging competitive cultures and mythologies
- conceptualise and codify a new set of values and beliefs in language, rites, rituals, and social and cultural organisation to demark their own ethno-religious identity.

The Hebrew scribes spent many years in Babylonia, where they had access to an extremely large range of documents from Mesopotamia, Sumer, Akkad, Assyria, Anatolia, and the Levant. Libraries had existed in Mesopotamia for some two thousand years before the arrival of the Hebrew scribes. They had existed as early as the mid-third millennium BCE. Temples, palaces, and scribal schools kept collections of literary works, practical handbooks—such as lists of dates and manuals for drawing up contracts—and scholarly works, such as magical procedures.

Jean Bottero believes that the many stories in the Bible relating to the creator's control of the sea (Exodus 14:21; Job 26:12; Psalms 72:8; Psalms 74:13–17) were influenced by

---

[989]   Carroll (2011), p. 55.

their experiences in Mesopotamia. They were developed by the Hebrew scribes based on the Mesopotamian epic of creation, in which the Mesopotamian chief god Marduk has victory over the terrifying seas. He states:

> *All these passages were composed after a certain class of Israelites had been in Mesopotamia for a long time during the great exile (sixth century). We are thus quite reasonably to believe that those Israelites who would have encountered, appreciated, and adopted, in their own way, the mythological representations of the creation of the world that they found there.*[990]

The renaming of places to strengthen the mythology

The Hebrew scribes were at pains to explain not only how creation happened, but how their god had created all known peoples and places. Prior to the emergence of the Israelites, it was common for hunter-gatherers to assign meaning, spirituality, and legendary stories to nature and the planets. The Hebrew scribes extended this practice further by creating their own legends and myths and assigning them to the names of the cultures that were around them, even though some of these cultures predated the Israelites by thousands of years. They used a variety of allegorical techniques.

Linking Noah's sons to existing people and places

For instance, in referring to the then-known three large-scale racial groupings within and surrounding the Levant, they named Noah's three sons Shem (meaning 'dusky' in Hebrew), Ham ('black'), and Japeth ('fair'). Shem refers to the Semitic-speaking peoples (largely the 'dusky' peoples of the Levant and Arabia), the Land of Ham was the Israelites' term for Egypt (the 'black' people), and Japeth refers to the white people (largely from the north—the Caucuses).

Linking Noah's grandsons to existing people and places

The Hebrew scribes claimed that Noah's grandsons and great-grandsons were founders of the surrounding and most influential cultures known to them at the time—Noah's grandsons were ascribed the names of Elam (the Elamites), Ashur (the Assyrians), Aram (the Aramaeans), Cush (the Cushites), and Canaan (the Canaanites). Noah's great-grandsons

---

[990]   Bottero (2004), pp. 206-207.

(sons of Canaan) were given the names of Heth (the Hittites), Jebus (the Jebusites), and Amorus (the Amorites).

Linking Lot's sons to existing people and places

The Hebrew scribes wrote that the regionally adjoining cultures of the Moabites (who were located on the rich highlands to the east of the Dead Sea) and Ammonites (living to the west in what is now Palestine) were descendants of Lot's sons (Moab and Ammon), born of a drunken Lot's incest with his daughters. (Genesis 19:37–38). The Hebrew scribes were transforming the landscape and the cultures around them into a cultural landscape that reinforced their emerging religious ideology and ethnic differentiation.

The use of artificial lineages

The practice of creating artificial lineages was a device used extensively by the Babylonian scribes prior to the emergence of the Hebrew scribes. It was a common practice in prehistoric mythologies to rationalise myths into artificial lineages, historical stories, and/or by geographic appropriation.[991]

Even today, most occupying forces will rename locations in their own language, reflecting their own view of history and often reinforcing their values, beliefs, and their mythology. Colonial appropriators, such as the British Empire, had a significant track record in this field of political geography—most notably in places like Australia, where the community still struggles to have some acceptance and recognition of the previous Indigenous names for places.

The Hebrew scribes used this largely subliminal process of reinforcing power and control by distributing explicit indicators of the link between political control and the spatial distribution of culturally-endorsed names across the landscape. It is a method that symbolises a collective rejection or negation of the previous cultures and any historical legacy that is not related to the ideological and political legends that are being created.

Cohen and Kliot have shown how modern Israel has used a similar process of renaming places with Hebrew names as a mechanism that is inextricably linked with their nation-building and state formation. The new names are 'symbolic expressions of Israelite nationalism'.[992]

---

[991] See: Puhvel (1989); Blenkinsopp (2011).
[992] Cohen and Kliot (1992), pp. 653-654.

Appropriating surrounding cultures

To the minds of the Jewish scribes writing in around 500 BCE, their immediate attention was drawn to explaining just how a few of the many and varied cultures that existed at the time were generational offspring of their nominated spiritual leaders. The Hebrew scribes explained that their god created these geographic locations and these peoples. This was a somewhat myopic view, as it only refers to the then-known world of the Hebrews. It covers a very small number of the many locations and cultures that, at the time, existed globally or were in geographic proximity, influential, in cultural exchange and/or sometimes even in conflict with the Hebrews.[993]

Geographic locations/cultural groups used in the invention of Noah's family names:

- The Caucuses to the north
- The Semites—in and around the Levant, the Fertile Crescent and parts of Arabia
- The Egyptians to the south and south-west.

Potential Cultural protagonists used in the invention of Noah's family names:

- The Canaanites in the Levant
- The Hittites in the Levant
- The Jebusites (who were a Canaanite tribal group) in the Levant
- The Amorites, who were in Syria, Mesopotamia, and the Levant
- The Assyrians to the north in Syria, and in the Levant
- The Aramaeans to the north in Syria
- The Elamites to the East on the Iranian Plateau.

The use of location names as a literary device

The literary device of appropriating or creating place names to strengthen the biblical narrative occurs throughout the HB/OT. This allowed the Hebrew scribes to claim that those towns or communities were created by or descended from their biblical heroes. This device of building believability into tribal records by assigning the names of legendary enemies or heroes to the names of towns was a device commonly used in the region at the time of the Hebrew scribes. For instance, as early as 1956, Lord Raglan had shown how in Homer's *Iliad* (around 630 BCE), the names of men allegedly slain by heroes of the

---

[993]   See Figure 13.

Iliad are town names from the island of Crete from which the Greek fighters had allegedly come.[994]

The symbolism involved in appropriating geographic locations and names in constructing an ethnic identity and territorial ownership was a key underlying factor in the Abraham story. The Abraham story is largely a reflection of the past Northern Israel and Canaanite moon-worshipping cult. Abraham's journey and his family names reflect and respect this cult something that would have been clear to all at the time of it being written.

Whilst several of Abraham's and his father Terah's family names were linked to the Mesopotamian moon god, others were given names by the Hebrew scribes based on towns that were already flourishing in that region. Paul Kriwaczek explains:

> *Serug, Terah's grandfather, corresponds with Sarugi—Seruj today; Nahor, Terah's father and also the name of his second son, with Nahur on the Habur River; Terah himself has been identified with Til Turahi on the Balikh River; his third son, Haran, matches the name of the city itself, … Believers propose that the names of these towns record settlements founded by the figures mentioned in the Bible.*[995]

Finkelstein and Silberman, elaborating on the work of German biblical Scholar Martin Noth, claim that the Abraham story is an example of the use of geographical references to reinforce political unification. They believe that the linking of Abraham to Hebron and Jerusalem was a literary device to emphasise the importance of the southern kingdom of Judah over the northern kingdom of Israel. Abraham's journey to the southern kingdom via the Northern Kingdom moon god cities is used as a metaphor for the transition away from the Northern Kingdom moon god cult towards the beliefs of the southern, kingdom of Judah. Finkelstein and Silberman believe that this aspect of the Hebrew Bible was most likely written around 500 BCE, after the Northern Kingdom had been vanquished by the Assyrians (720 BCE) and Judah was consolidating as God's intended divine centre for the Israelites.[996]

The origin of the Torah/Pentateuch

The first five books of the Bible are Genesis, Exodus, Leviticus, Numbers, and Deuteronomy. In the Jewish religion, they are called the Torah, or the written Torah; in Christian religions, they are called the Pentateuch, which means 'five books'.

---

[994] Raglan (1956), p. 119.
[995] Kriwaczek (2010), p. 163.
[996] Finkelstein and Silberman (2002), pp. 43-44.

Modern scholars generally see the completed Torah as a product of the time of the Persian Achaemenid Empire (probably 450 BCE to 350 BCE), although some would place its production in the Hellenistic period (333 BCE to 164 BCE), after the conquest of the Levant and the Fertile Crescent by Alexander the Great.

The Bible claims that the first five books were written by the prophet Moses. However, there are several alternative scientific theories about the authorship of the Torah/ Pentateuch:

- some scholars believe in a *fragmentary hypothesis*, in which the Pentateuch is seen as a compilation of short, independent narratives, which were gradually brought together into larger units in two editorial phases by many different authors: the Deuteronomic and the Priestly phases
- other scholars believe in a *supplementary hypothesis*, which proposes that the Torah is the result of two major additions—Yahwist and Priestly—to an existing corpus of work
- other scientific researchers have developed what is referred to as 'the *documentary hypothesis*'. They claim that the Torah/ Pentateuch was written over hundreds of years, in several different versions, based on several pre-existing texts and written by multiple authors and not by Moses.

The Documentary Hypothesis

The Documentary Hypothesis emerged from a systematic literary analysis of the Torah/ Pentateuch.[997] This literary analysis explores continuity, style, linguistics, dialect, terminology, plot, contradictions, and repetition across the narrative across all five books to gauge the likelihood of either a single or multiple authors.

The literary analysis found that there is little doubt that there have been several different authors and several different sources and that the first five books of the Bible were created at different times.[998] The Documentary Hypothesis claims that the Pentateuch is a composite of four separate documents ('J', 'E', 'P', and 'D') and that a final group of redactors R (Ezra) compiled these into the final product (Figure 41):

---

[997] SOURCE: https://kevinbinz.com/2018/06/19/documentary-hypothesis/.
[998] See: Friedman, 1997 for a comprehensive explanation of the Torah/ Pentateuch authorship. see in particular pp. 158-159.

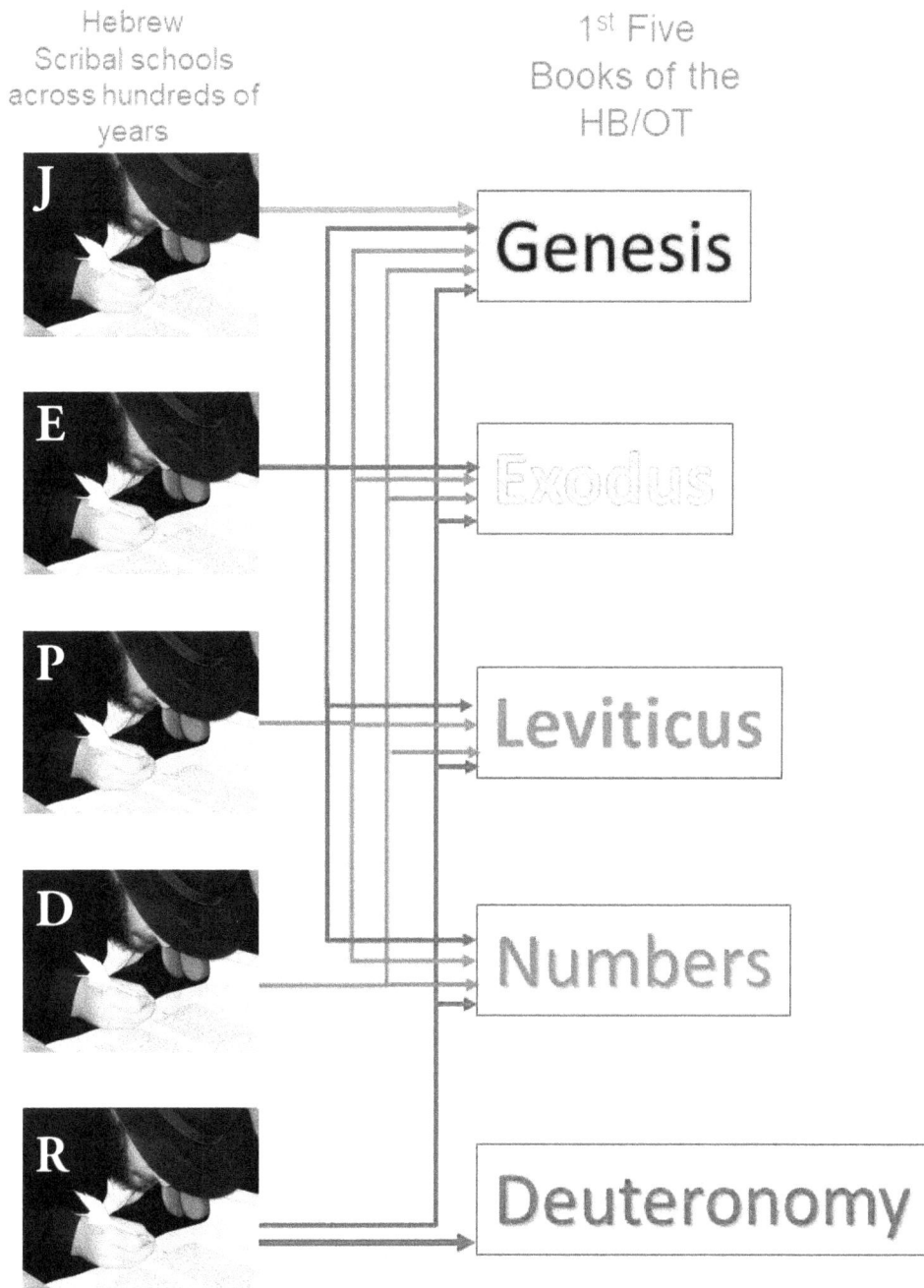

Figure 41: *The hypothesised sources of the first five books of the Bible* [a]

---

[a] SOURCE: based on https://kevinbinz.com/2018/06/19/documentary-hypothesis/.

- J — the Yahwist. J gets its name because it uses and allows humans to use the name (Jahwe in German) before Israel existed (see Genesis 4:26; cf. E and P, below). J appears to have been composed in Judah, perhaps during Solomon's day, around 950 BCE.
- E — the Elohist. The name is derived from E's use of Elohim (Hebrew for 'God') rather than YHWH in the early period. E reserves the name Yahweh for the time from Moses on (see Exodus 3:13-15). E appears to have been written in the north, around 850 BCE.
- P — the Priestly source. P is especially concerned with stories and laws relevant to priests. Like E, it reserves the name YHWH for the period from Moses on (see Exodus 6:3). Many scholars date P either during the exile (sixth century BCE) or shortly after (Fifth century BCE). Others date it as early as the beginning of the seventh century BCE.
- D is essentially the book of Deuteronomy. It is not mingled with J, E and P.

The Documentary Hypothesis has been challenged by several key biblical scholars. These challenges have largely been about the relative importance or role of a specific source (J, E, P or D) and the likely dates of the writing of each of the sources. However, apart from the biblical account, most biblical scholars accept that the first five books of the Bible are not a unified work by one author. These five books have come from several earlier sources repackaged and revised over several centuries and by many hands. The consensus remains that the Torah/ Pentateuch was most probably woven together as a literary and ideological unity from earlier sources by a range of Hebrew scribes over several hundred years and brought together in its next-to-current form as a composite work probably no earlier than 300 BCE.

Written over hundreds of years by hundreds of scribes, it is most likely that the final canonically endorsed Hebrew Bible was a mixture of all three of the fragmentary hypothesis, supplementary hypothesis, and the Documentary Hypothesis.

The influence of previous Hebrew texts

There is strong archaeological and biblical evidence of the existence of pre-biblical Hebrew texts, all of which have disappeared or have been lost or suppressed. Were they available, and if they did exist prior to the HB/OT being written, these lost documents would provide a clearer understanding of the Hebrew mythology prior to the compilation of the Bible in its current form. These missing pre-biblical texts could probably give greater insights into the extent of borrowing from the surrounding mythologies as they appear to have been the sources from which parts of the biblical account were drawn and are referenced in the Bible. The lost pre-biblical documents mentioned in the Bible include:

- The Book of the Story of Adam (Genesis 5, 1)
- The Chronicles of the Kings of Levi (Exodus 6, 16-25).
- The Book of the Wars of Yahweh (Numbers 21, 14)
- Book of Yashar/Jashar (Joshua 10, 14)
- A book describing the cities of Canaan (Joshua 18, 9)
- The Acts of Solomon (1 Kings 11, 41)
- The Chronicles of the Kings of Judah (1 Kings 14, 29)
- The Book of Genealogy (1 Chronicles, 1)
- The Book of Yahweh (Isaiah 14, 16)
- The Chronicles of the Kings of Israel (referred to several times in the HB/OT).[999]

The Hebrew Scriptures are traditionally divided into three sections: Torah (the first five books, assigned to Moses), the Prophets (Nevi'im—including Joshua, Judges, Samuel, Kings, Isaiah, Jeremiah, Ezekiel, and the Twelve Minor Prophets), and Writings (Ketuvim—including Ruth, Psalms, Job, Proverbs, Ecclesiastes, Song of Solomon, Lamentations, Daniel, Esther, Ezra (which included Nehemiah), and First and Second Chronicles).

The HB/OT was not written overnight in one sitting or by one author—but the stories told therein have been retold, embellished, and hybridised over literally hundreds, perhaps thousands, of years. In the words of Middle Eastern archaeologist Kathleen Kenyon:

> *All reputable modern scholars accept as certain that the Pentateuch, as well as the Books of Joshua, Judges and others early in the sequence, only acquired the form in which they have reached us by a very long process of the combination of oral and tribal records, of editing and redactions. … The complete canon of the Old Testament is probably not earlier than 300 BC.*[1000]

Prior to the discovery of the Dead Sea Scrolls, early evidence of the text of the HB/OT is scant. There is some fragmentary evidence of Hebrew writing in the form of pottery inscriptions dating back to around 1000 BCE but, there are just two tiny silver scrolls dating to around 600 BCE containing parts of the text from the Book of Numbers

---

[999]   Graves and Patai (1964), p. 11.
[1000]   Kenyon (1978), p. 7.

and a range of fragments containing biblical text written in Greek, dating from around 150 BCE. The Dead Sea Scrolls only contain fragments of the HB/OT and are dated from around 150 BCE. The Dead Sea Scrolls contain texts, psalms, and prophecies that are not part of current versions of the Hebrew Bible nor part of the Christian Old Testament.

The Aleppo Codex, the oldest HB/OT in existence today, also known as the Crown of Aleppo, was written by scribes called Masoretes in Tiberias, Israel, around 930 CE.[1001] Thus, the oldest HB/OT in existence today was written some 1,200 years after the biblical canon is claimed to have been originally formulated.

[1001] SOURCE : https://www.biblicalarchaeology.org/daily/biblical-topics/hebrew-bible/the-aleppo-codex/ retrieved on 5 August 2020.

Chapter 20

The Influence of Selected Prehistoric Mythologies

Samuel Noah Kramer, one of the world's leading Assyriologists and world-renowned expert in Sumerian history, literature, and language, has shown the extent to which the biblical texts have drawn heavily from the earlier mythologies of the Middle East, specifically, from Sumerian mythologies.[1002] Since Kramer's passing (1990 CE), the evidence of the multiple sources influencing the Hebrew scribes has expanded.

Commonly shared mythological storylines

The ubiquity of religion supports Yuval Noah Harari's theory that there is a human characteristic to imagine or continuously invent the unknown. Mythologist JF Bierlein has undertaken a comprehensive analysis of the various mythologies from across the world and has determined that myth is constant amongst all human beings at all times. There are significant commonalities and fascinating parallels among the myths of widely different and separated cultures. Bierlein believes that myth is like a language involving the telling of stories—a thread that holds the past, present, and future together. It may well reflect a structure of the unconscious mind that is encoded in an individual's genes.[1003]

[1002]   Kramer (1956), pp. 141-167.
[1003]   Bierlein (1994) pp. 5-6.

Bierlein identifies the recurrence across many cultures historically and globally of a creation myth, the recurrence of the snake, a flood myth, myths about a fall from grace, love myths, myths about historical heroes, myths about brothers or twins, myths about the existence of and journeys to the underworld, and apocalyptic myths.

The practice of sculpting females was a commonly shared practice across prehistoric hunter-gatherer societies. There are multiple sites across many prehistoric European cultures where similar mythological female figurines have been found dating back some 30,000 years[1004]. Shamanism (spiritual mediators) was commonly practised by European, Eurasian, Middle Eastern, and Central Asian prehistoric hunter-gatherers thousands of years before the emergence of modern religions.

Comparative linguist E.J. Michael Witzel has used the combined sciences of archaeology, linguistics, and genetics to propose the existence of parallels in prehistoric mythological storytelling.[1005] Like Bierlein, Witzel undertook a comprehensive, comparative analysis of prehistoric mythologies and concluded that, across the Northern Hemisphere, the various prehistoric mythologies had the same or a very similar underlying pattern of stories.

The ancient storylines emerged across the Northern Hemisphere from possibly as far back as 40,000 years ago. Well before the emergence of the Israelites, the storylines had travelled west and east along the Eurasian Steppe and southwards into Mesopotamia and the Levant. They may have originated in embryonic forms, most likely in Western Asia or Siberia, from where shamanism is thought to have originated.

Most Northern Hemisphere prehistoric mythologies included these storylines as a metaphor for the human condition—how life began mysteriously from chaos, how humans emerged, how divine intervention would occur (from a god or a group of gods), and that there would be an ominous ending. The storylines metaphorically encoded and enshrouded an answer to the eternal question of 'Why we are here?'[1006]

Witzel's work has its supporters and detractors—in the latter case, there has been strong and reasonable criticism of many of his assumptions and specifically the fact that he uses his otherwise defensible evidence on comparative mythologies to make judge-

---

[1004] SOURCE: https://www.nationalgeographic.com/history/history-magazine/article/who-were-these-queens-of-the-stone-age? retrieved on 28 January 2022.

[1005] See also: Bierlein, J.F. (1994).

[1006] Witzel (2012), p. 422.

ments about the worthiness or otherwise of different mythological traditions.[1007] There are those who see some weaknesses in his methods and his conclusions, but they are equally adamant that his research, his methods, and his concept of unifying prehistoric mythological storylines have a great deal of merit.[1008]

According to Witzel, no single prehistoric Northern Hemisphere mythology contains all myths in the underlying prehistoric storylines and not always in the same sequence. The component stories are hybridised, scattered, and customised by location, circumstance, and cultural intent. Witzel does not stand alone. The portfolio of component myths in the common Northern Hemisphere underlying mythological storylines are (combining evidence from the works of Puhvel, Leeming, Campbell, Bierlein, Wilkinson, and Witzel):

- there is a 'genesis'—wherein the origin of the universe and the Earth are explained

- depending on the specific prehistoric culture, the world was created from nothing, from darkness, from primordial waters or out of chaos

- the floating Earth emerged from primordial waters

- heaven and Earth were separated by a large mountain, a giant, a large pole/pillar, or a large tree

- there was a primordial mountain, mound of earth, hill, or island

- there was a father deity (the sky/heaven/the sun/supreme being) and a great mother (the Earth Mother)

- there were high god/s and lower gods up above in 'heaven' (sky gods) who are related to or embody the sun the moon, the planets, and the stars

- there was a bull, a serpent, a large cosmic egg, or giants who predate humans. In the HB/OT the giants are referred to as Nephilim (Genesis 6:1–4)

- current god/s have defeated or killed previous god/s in a sacred combat

- humans were created from trees and clay or rock and, occasionally, are descended from or created by the sun god/the supreme god/'god the father'

- there are trickster deities

- rituals and early forms of worship are linked to two annual solstices and the full moon cycles. The winter solstice (emergence of the sun or of light) and the summer solstice (with the killing of the dragon)[1009]

[1007] See for example, Thompson (2013); Lincoln (2015).
[1008] Smith, F.M. (2013); Kaufman (2013); Finnchuill's Mast (2018).
[1009] Witzel (2012), pp. 153-157.

- there is often a mythological hero who can have one mortal and one divine parent (cf. the Christian Jesus). The hero will journey on a series of adventures, perhaps into the supernatural, to recover what has been lost and overcome those who would destroy him, and returns with new knowledge and power[1010]
- there is a heavenly/sacred drink—wine in the Middle East and Indo-European religions; the Sumerians had fermented cereals (an early form of beer); fermented rice in north-western India; the Hindus have a plant-based drink called soma; fermented honey is the sacred drink in Greece; the Zoroastrians had a sacred drink from the *haoma* tree; rice beer and barley beer were sacred in Tibet and Nepal
- humans are good but are punished by God/the gods for misdemeanours
- there is a final destruction of the world and a new heaven and Earth emerge.[1011]

The blueprint for the three Abrahamic religions

The ancient mythological storyline identified by Witzel in its various manifestations was most likely taken for granted by the Hebrew scribes when they began writing the HB/OT. It pre-existed them in a variety of forms for millennia across and around their region. Different cultures had embellished and adapted it over hundreds of years and in different ways.

The Babylonian creation myth, called Enuma Elish, was named after the opening words of the myth—translated as 'when on high'. The Enuma Elish myth had a major influence on the HB/OT.[1012] However, Enuma Elish and the Hebrew Genesis story both follow the same mythological storyline found in the ancient Sumerians, Assyrian, and Babylonian creation myths[1013]—a common storyline across the Middle East, at that time, which has been articulated by E.J. Michael Witzel (above).

The fundamentals of the mythological 'plot' or underlying storyline in the HB/OT are simply customisation of this shared storyline as best it suited their ideological and cultural differentiation agenda. From then on, the prehistoric storyline has continued as the mythological blueprint and the underlying structure/plot for the three major contemporary Abrahamic religions.

[1010]   Campbell with Bill Moyers (1991), p. 152; Leeming (1990), p. 217.
[1011]   See: Puhvel (1989), Leeming (1990), Bierlein (1994), Wilkinson (2009) and Witzel (2012).
[1012]   See: Mark (2018C).
[1013]   Leick (2002), p. 20, pp. 214-215, and pp. 252-253.

The metaphor for an historical religious journey

In the biblical narrative, there was a need to create a story around the motif of migration as preparation for a religious destiny—a journey that would lead to the 'promised land'. The notion of around two million people (men, women, and children), wandering lost in a desert between Egypt and Canaan for forty years to be eventually guided by God to their destination, is a fascinating rendition of this objective!

The biblical exodus story is not the only overland journey presented in the HB/OT. The Bible contains many examples of religious leaders having to travel distances under the direction of their god. For example, after the flood, Noah's descendants are told to migrate from Mount Ararat to Babel, Abraham is told to travel from Ur of the Chaldees to the land of Canaan, Abraham then must leave Canaan and go to Egypt, and Joseph and his family flee the drought in Canaan to live in Egypt. These journeys are metaphors for the divine journey of acquisition of the faith and gradual discovery of Yahweh.

According to the HB/OT, Yahweh said to Abraham, '*Lekh Lekha* (go forth, but literally 'go to yourself') from your land and from your birthplace and from your father's house, to the land that I will show you.' (Genesis 12:1) This idea has been extended into the modern-day commonly held religious belief in 'life ever after' for those who walk with the Lord (Book 1 Psalm 1-6).

The metaphor of a god-directed spiritual journey originated with the Siberian shamans, who claimed to have spirit guides guiding them through the spirit world. In the words of Angela Roothaan, 'The human being who communicates with a spiritual or divine being is often said to have made some kind of ascent or journey to the "higher" level of the spiritual.'[1014]

Mesopotamian mythology contained many examples of similar necessary spiritual journeys. Probably the most important one related to the journeys of Mesopotamia's most important goddess, Inanna/Ishtar, who was associated with the moon, love, beauty, sex, fertility, war, justice, and political power. Inanna's spiritual journey took her down and back to the underworld to gain power—this journey took her along the course of the Euphrates through the Mesopotamian cities of Uruk, Badtibira, Zabalam, Adab, Nippur,

---

[1014] Roothaan (2015), p. 143.

Kish, and Akkad to the Zagros mountains—described by Charles Penglase as a 'cultic traditional divine journey'.[1015]

The exodus story and the many other god-directed journeys in the HB/OT are metaphors for this journey of religious discovery. The Buddhists call this journey the path to 'enlightenment' (*bodhi*). Hindus call it the three paths to 'liberation' (*moksha*). The Zoroastrians call it the 'awakening' (*ushta*). Christians call it 'revelation'.

These journeys are literary artefacts, or metaphors, and are not historical facts. The many god-directed journeys in the HB/OT are spiritual journeys written using repetitive metaphors of real-world journeys to convey the nature of religion and the effort required to attain godliness and communion with the divine.

Roothaan points out that the Christian story of Jesus ascending into heaven as told in the Christian New Testament and the stories of Muhammad's celestial journeys as told in the Koran are most likely the continuation of the divine journey metaphor that began originally with the Siberian shamanic spiritual journey.[1016]

Shamanism's separation of myth and religion from facts

Shamanism is the origin of many modern-day religious practices. Shamanism is the first documented example of differentiating between empirical and spiritual systems of belief. The shaman's methodology consisted of examining evidence from the past or the present and using this to predict the future. This is possibly the first time that empirical evidence or observations (a sheep's liver, celestial events, illnesses, social facts, natural occurrences) become a stimulus for divination and prophecy.

These factual observations become a lever for the creation of omens, rituals, and predictions of the future. The empirical culture of evidence is separated from the separate system of the shaman/diviner's thoughts and spiritual interpretations. In the words of Mesopotamian scholar Jean-Jacques Glassner, 'The diviner's thought was disconnected from empirical knowledge and was established as a separate system.'[1017] This is the foundational principle for the separation of myth and religion from science and facts. It continues as a fundamental principle in all religions today.

[1015]   Penglase (1994), pp. 24-25.
[1016]   Roothaan (2015), pp. 143-147.
[1017]   Adapted from Glassner (2004), pp. 9-10.

The origin of religious medals, medallions, holy days, and ornaments

Shamanism was the first to introduce the concept of packaged reminders of their follower's relationship with and acquiescence to the spiritual world. This is what contemporary psychologists call 'primes'. A prime is a symbol that is associated with something else and stimulates a memory and a reaction to the thing that it represents.

The shamans introduced the concept of symbolic reminders or primes that carried meaning about the spiritual world. The shamanic practice of identifying specific objects with spiritual meaning (antler horns, specific hats, special staffs, adornments) set the scene for many modern religious practices.

The wearing of medallions or amulets and other objects depicting protective deities was common across prehistoric Egypt and Mesopotamia. As in the modern-day continuation of these practices (the wearing of medals depicting Christian saints, for example), the wearers believed that these objects, which most often contained an image of a specific deity, would protect them from various harms.[1018]

Evolutionary biologist Joseph Henrich has outlined the extensive use of 'primes' that are common in contemporary religions. They are unconscious or subliminal reminders of a person's god, their religious obligations, and their faith.

Modern-day religious 'primes' include religious dress (liturgical attire, 'dog collars'); adornments (crosses, bells, specific hats, incense, rings); personal artefacts (rosary beads, cross necklaces, and brooches); holy days (Friday, Sunday, sabbath); saints'/other holy days, annual celebrations (Christmas, Easter, Ramadan); religious phraseology in common language ('thank god', 'god only knows', 'god willing'); daily devotions (prayers before meals and before bed); daily behaviours (signs of the cross, facing Mecca); temples, churches, mosques, or synagogues in strategic locations; and sounds, music, and chants (cathedral bells, calls to prayer).

Each of these is a symbol, some assumed to have supernatural powers (e.g., rosary beads, crucifixes, signs of the cross) which, when packaged together, deliver continuous, subliminal, subtle (and sometimes less-than-subtle) reminders of a person's faith, reinforcing their belief in the supernatural and the need to continuously defer to their god.[1019]

The use of a variety of symbols/primes that reflect a belief in being able to communicate with the divine dates back to shamanism.

[1018] See: https://worldhistory.org/article/2054/family-planning-in-the-ancient-near-east/ retrieved on 3 August 2022.

[1019] Adapted from Henrich (2021), pp. 124-127.

Influential Zoroastrian and Hindu beliefs

The Eastern Steppe's geographic location, frequent trade, and Bactrian mythological beliefs influenced the Mesopotamians and the Indus Valley (Hinduism/Vedic Culture) communities (from around 1800 BCE). It led to the Persian Empire's adoption of Zoroastrian mythology (from around 550 BCE onwards) and the hybridisation of many Zoroastrian ideas by the Hebrew scribes into beliefs in the HB/OT.

Zoroastrianism and Judaism are monotheistic, whilst Hinduism is henotheistic—worshipping one god who can appear in many forms. There is some debate about which of the Zoroastrian and Hindu mythologies was first developed and communicated. Most historians believe that both Zoroastrianism and Hinduism were developed in roughly the same geographic area and within one hundred or so years of each other in the second millennium BCE. Both religions developed at least one thousand years before the emergence of Israel.

A key Zoroastrian belief that translated into contemporary religions included monotheism/a belief in a singular divine being and notions of good and evil deities. The Zoroastrians were responsible for several of the Sumerian mythological stories that moved south with the Sumerians when they migrated into Mesopotamia around 4000 BCE, probably from the Eastern Steppe/Siberia. Thereafter, the Sumerian and the Zoroastrian mythological beliefs influenced and were hybridised into many of the HB/OT stories.

For example, the early creation stories from the Eastern Steppe (Mongolia/Siberia) and Bactria, and of Buddhism, involved the creator sitting on top of a golden mountain in the middle of the sky prior to creating the cosmos. In Hinduism and Buddhism, this mountain, central to their beliefs of creation, is called Sumeru; in Mongolian, it is referred to as either Sumer or Sumeru.[1020]

The mythological link between a mountain and a god was a generally held and influential belief regionally. The primeval hill was seen by the Egyptians as the location from which the creator-god made his appearance and from which he created the world order. It is most likely that this widely held belief is why the Hebrew scribes had God meeting Moses on a mountaintop to deliver his commandments to the Israeli people during the biblical story of the Exodus from Egypt.

[1020] Ashe (2018), p. 48.

Biblical scholar James Barr has accepted that Zoroastrian/ancient Iranian beliefs, although not directly copied, were influential on the Hebrew scribes. This was particularly evident when the Hebrew scribes were exiled to Babylon and the Babylonians and then the Persians were controlling Babylon and the Levant (from around 550 BCE to around 330 BCE).

Barr and many other scholars agree that the prehistoric Zoroastrian mythological beliefs, such as a creation myth, adoration of a single supreme being ('the one true god'), opposing forces of good and evil deities (duality), angels and demons, messianism, belief in a soul, free will, judgment after death, heaven and hell, and the final revelation of the world were influential on the Hebrew scribes.[1021] Many of these originally Zoroastrian/ancient Iranian beliefs had a major influence on other belief systems, including Judaism, Gnosticism, Greek philosophy, Christianity, Islam, the Baha'i Faith, and Buddhism.

Barr concludes:

It is intelligible that Jews might find stimulus in an element or pattern of Iranian religion, such as its dualism, its idea of resurrection, or its picture of the dethroned powers penetrating back into the cosmos, even if they did not take over or even understand the inner bonds of cause and meaning that held these same things together within Iranian religion.[1022]

A virgin birth, Satan, and a book of judgement

Three other myths of Zoroastrianism were adapted into Judaism and Christianity. These were that:

- there was an evil god who battled with the good god
- a virgin would bear a child who would save the world
- there is a book of judgment that records the acts of people on Earth, who would face a judgment day and be resurrected to an earthly paradise.

The origin of the devil/evil god concept

The belief that there are two main religious protagonists—god and the devil—goes back to the Zoroastrians. Zoroastrianism was the religion of the Persians in Babylon when the

---

[1021]   SOURCE: https://member.ancient.eu/Ahriman/ retrieved on 17 November 2020.
[1022]   Barr (1985), pp. 219-230.

Hebrews were exiled there and were writing and rewriting much of the biblical stories. The entire faith of Zoroastrianism is predicated on the struggle between God and the forces of goodness and light. This is represented by the Zoroastrian Holy Spirit, Spenta Manyu—who protects the sky, water, earth, plants, and children yet to be born—and Ahriman—the lord of darkness and chaos and the source of human confusion, disappointment, and strife—who presides over the forces of darkness and evil.[1023]

The largely accepted origin of the biblical concept of a devil/satan comes from the Hebrew scribes' adaptation of this Zoroastrian myth. The Hebrew scribes were in Babylon under the control of Persia and Zoroastrianism from around 550 BCE to 539 BCE. It is accepted that the biblical book of the Chronicles, which is often cited as identifying Satan as an evil god, was written after they returned to Jerusalem in around 515 BCE.[1024]

Biblical scholar Marvin E Tate provides an extensive analysis of the use of the term *satan* throughout the Hebrew Bible/Old Testament. He concludes that the word *satan* is never used to refer to an evil divine being in the Old Testament. Where the word *satan* does occur, it is essentially used to designate a function (adversary/accuser/ opponent) but never as a personal name.

Joseph Campbell describes the Zoroastrian influence on contemporary beliefs about the existence of an evil god thusly:

> *The only mythologies in which you have an absolute duality are those that stem from the Near East after the time of Zoroaster. With Zoroastrianism, you have the idea of a god of light and a god of darkness who are in competition and their competition has created the world that we have now.*[1025]

An erroneous use of experience in the Persian exile

The Hebrew scribes used their experience and observations of Persian culture to create elaborate fictional stories. A typical example relates to the biblical Book of Esther. This biblical Book tells the story of an orphaned Hebrew woman (Hadassah but known as Esther) living in Persia who becomes the queen of Persia. Llewellyn-Jones describes this biblical story as 'closer to a fairy tale than to history' because Persian monarchs never took

---

[1023] SOURCE:https://www.bbc.com/culture/article/20170406-this-obscure-religion-shaped-the-west retrieved on 17 November 2020.
[1024] Denova, R. (2021A).
[1025] Campbell (2004), p. 234.

foreign consorts and 'the prospect of a Jewish girl, no matter how beautiful, reaching the rank of a royal wife was negligible'.[1026]

The origin of the Star of David and the Jewish flag

The Jewish word for the blue/blue-violet dye derived from a Canaanite snail is *tekhelet*. This dye is originally a rich purple or crimson colour. Over time, it fades to a blue-violet. *Tekhelet* is highly prized in the Jewish religion. It is mentioned 49 times in the HB/OT and is recommended for use in the clothing of the Jewish high priest, the tapestries in the Tabernacle, and the tassels on the four-cornered garment usually worn during Jewish prayer. It is highly likely that the blueish colour on the modern Israeli flag was an historical reference to this original Canaanite blue/violet.

The Star of David in the centre of the Israeli flag has been borrowed from the identical symbol in the Hindu heart chakra (Anahata). Anahata represents the centre of love for oneself and others, compassion, empathy, and forgiveness. This hexagram symbol emerged throughout the Early Vedic Period around the Indus Valley (1500 BCE—1000 BCE). To the Hindus, it has multiple religious meanings around balancing two opposite forces. It is based on two equilateral triangles with the same centre—one triangle pointing to the heavens and the other to the Earth to symbolise matter and the spirit—with humanity's role in the centre.

The Hindu chakra shape refers to the meeting point of male (upwards-pointing triangle) and female (downwards-pointing triangle). The Hindus most likely borrowed the notion of chakras from the Zoroastrians whose 'Fourth (Heart) Chakra' is also regarded as the energy centre for love, both human and divine. Hinduism and Zoroastrianism were two religions that developed contemporaneously and well before the emergence of Judaism.

[1026]   Llewellyn- Jones (2022), pp. 187-188.

Chapter 21

The Origin of Specific Biblical Stories

The origin of the Hebrew anthropomorphic god

There is strong archaeological and biblical evidence that the Hebrews, in line with most other cultures in and around their region, initially believed in the existence of many anthropomorphic gods, but consistently worshipped just the one primary deity, Yahweh.[1027]

Many independent scholars of prehistory are of the opinion that Yahweh was originally a god of the Midianites, a nomadic tribe that inhabited the Sinai Peninsula in the north-west of the Arabian Peninsula, on the east shore of the Gulf of Aqaba and the northern tip of the Red Sea.[1028] Yahweh was worshipped by other Canaanites, including the Edomites, Kenites, and Moabites. The scientific consensus is that Judaism evolved specifically out of Midianite, Mesopotamian, and Ancient Canaanite polytheism.

Ancient Hebrew authority Joel Hoffman believes that there is evidence that the Hebrew scribes, and possibly the neighbouring Moabites, were the first to introduce the use of vowels into alphabets. He believes that the introduction of the vowels played an important role in the naming of the Hebrew god (see *The Origin of the Hebrew word Yahweh*, page 321).

Joshua Mark has shown that:

Initially, the people of Canaan, including the Israelis, practised a form of ancestor worship … [and] … in time this practice evolved into worship of deities such as El, Asherah, Baal, Utu-Shamash and Yahweh among others.[1029]

[1027] a belief system defined as Monolatrism.
[1028] Luckenbill, 1918, p. 27.
[1029] Mark (2018A), p. 5.

Mark has explained that:

The biblical narrative … is not as straightforward as it may seem as it also includes reference to the Canaanite god El … the chief deity of the Canaanite pantheon and the god, who according to the Bible, gave Yahweh authority over the Israelis [1030]

There are many references in the HB/OT to the existence of other gods:

- references to other gods, such as the 'gods of the Egyptians' in the Book of Exodus
- the first of the Ten Commandments—'Thou shalt have no other gods before me.'
- Psalms 86:8 reads, 'There is none like you among the gods, O Lord, nor are there any works like yours.'
- Psalm 82 reads, 'God has taken his place in the divine council; in the midst of the gods he holds judgement.'[1031, 1032]

The Hebrew scribes borrowed the notion of a human-like monarchical deity governing the universe directly from the mythologies in the regions and cultures around them. Although the Hebrew god, Yahweh, had no visible shape or form and was clearly known to be all-holy, transcendent, self-sufficient, and spiritual, throughout the HB/OT, Yahweh is described as:

… having eyes, ears, hands, and feet. He moulds man out of the dust, plants a garden, takes His rest. He speaks, listens, and closes the door of Noah's ark; He even whistles. Other expressions credit God with human emotions: He laughs, rejoices, becomes, disgusted, regretful, and revengeful. Very frequently He is declared to be a jealous God.[1033]

Belief in one single supreme god

The notion of a supreme god in heaven is a legacy of the prehistoric belief that the sun was a god. Over centuries, this concept gradually metamorphosised into an anthropomorphic god, but one that was (and is) still located, like the sun, up in heaven.

For example, Hindus worship Brahman, who is regarded as the single supreme entity that created existence. Brahman is regarded as being so great and difficult to comprehend by humans that he is existence itself. The ancient mythological concepts of a single Zoroastrian

---

[1030]   Mark (2018A), p. 4.
[1031]   See also https://www.firstthings.com/web-exclusives/2014/01/the-bibles-many-gods.
[1032]   SOURCE: https://www.newworldencyclopedia.org/entry/Monolatrism#Examples_of_Monolatrism.
[1033]   SOURCE: https://www.encyclopedia.com/religion/encyclopedias-almanacs-transcripts-and-maps/anthropomorphism-bible.

monotheistic god, called Āhurā Mazdā ('Wise Lord'), who is compassionate, just, and is the creator of the universe; and of a Hindu god (Brahman) who is the single supreme entity, both influenced Judaism and Christianity. Judaism and Christianity emerged much later but derived a concept of a similar single supreme being who was the creator, omnipotent (all-powerful), omniscient (all-knowing), and omnipresent (everywhere at all times)—what Christian polemicist Bishop Eusebius in 325 CE called 'the oneness of God'.[1034]

Leeming believes that the transition from the sun god into a sky god and into the all-pervasive 'supreme being' in heaven reflected the transition towards the male-dominated patriarchy:

> *In literature as well as in the other arts, including architecture, the Supreme Being archetype would seem to inform and provide metaphorical support for the tendency toward the patriarchal, the authoritarian, or the monumental. The myth of the Supreme Being is the most universal of archetypes; it is as common as fatherhood and the idea of God. It is realized literally everywhere.*[1035]

The origin of the biblical creation story

Creation stories abound across the mythologies of prehistoric and more contemporary cultures. Mythologist JF Bierlein has identified different, sometimes conceptually related, creation myths in more than a dozen cultures across history and globally. These vary from Babylonia to Iran, Greece, India, Africa, Nordic countries, Japan, Egypt, Judaism and Christianity, Polynesia, and North American Indians.[1036] Religious studies Professor Glenn Holland has identified four underlying themes in creation stories:

1. Creation by making—where a god brings order to primordial matter by his actions (e.g., Sumerian Enki, Hebrew Bible's god of creation)
2. Creation through conflict—where a god battles some personified being whose defeated body becomes the primal matter to create a divinely ordered cosmos (e.g., Babylonian god Marduk and Tiamat; Zoroastrians' Ormazd and Ahriman)
3. Creation through sexual generation—where a god and goddess engage in sexual intercourse and the goddess gives birth to elemental gods (e.g., Greek goddess Chaos giving birth to Gaea, the Earth, and Tartarus, the underworld)

[1034] SOURCE: Eusebius on Christianity—World History Encyclopedia retrieved on 23 October 2021.
[1035] Leeming (1990), p. 124.
[1036] Bierlein (1994), pp. 37-80.

4. Creation by word—where god's spoken word creates divine spirit, which once spoken becomes a substantial reality (e.g., Egyptian god Ptah).[1037]

The Hebrew scribes commenced the HB/OT with the book of Genesis, which outlined their belief in the process of God's creation of the world and the universe. This was 'creation by making' and how the foundation of their religion began.

The biblical claim for primacy and prophetic visions

Being able to claim a heritage as far back as the time of creation is a key tool for all religions, illustrating that they have 'primacy'—they were the first—and that they alone can trace their beginnings all the way back to the imagined beginning of the world. The Greeks used this technique when they recounted the mythologies of the Scythians. Herodotus (484 BCE to 425 BCE), in writing about Scythian mythology, ensured that the Greek gods Zeus or Hercules were inserted as the lovers of the Scythian goddesses to reflect the fact that the Greek nation and the Greek gods pre-existed and were older than the Scythians.[1038]

Placing events in the past was a technique frequently used throughout the Ancient Middle East in order to allow for a 'prophetic vision' to attribute to transcendental, mythical characters who emerge later—such as the patriarchs of the Israelites who emerge later in the biblical text. This form of narrative was commonplace in the genre now known as Mesopotamian Naru literature—first appearing around the second millennium BCE, when historical events or individuals were treated with poetic license in order to make a point.[1039]

The origin of the biblical days of creation

Biblical scholar Rabbi Yossi ben Halafta, in the second century CE, declared that God created the world on 6 October 3761 BCE and humanity commenced with God's creation of Adam and Eve, at that time (around 6,000 years ago). Twelfth Century Jewish philosopher and scientist Maimonides re-calculated the year of God's creation of Adam and Eve based on biblical evidence and confirmed that according to the Hebrew Bible

---

[1037] Holland (2010), pp. 31-32.
[1038] Cunliffe (2019), p. 267.
[1039] Mark (2016), p. 1.

(Old Testament), the first humans were created by God in 3761 BCE (confirming a date around 6,000 years ago).

Followers of the Septuagint version of the Jewish Bible tend to locate the date of the biblical God's creation of the universe and of Adam and Eve as sometime in early to mid-5000 BCE.

What has fascinated many biblical researchers is the illogical sequence of creation as outlined in the Book of Genesis. According to Genesis, God created vegetation (third day) before he created the sun and the moon (fourth day). There is an historical reason for this strange sequence—it occurred because the book of Genesis is, in part, an adaptation of the dominant Sumerian/Babylonian/Akkadian creation myths.

The naming of the seven-day week originated from the Sumerians' mythological link of the planets to the ancient Babylonian gods. The Sumerians created the 'week' by dividing the lunar month (its 29-day monthly orbit of the Earth) into four lots of roughly seven days each.[1040] The seven days were then linked to seven of the Sumerian gods. The days of the week were then named after the seven planets (the sun, moon, and the five sacred planets) and the associated gods.

The biblical creation story, and thus the order of creation, was based on the order of the seven planetary gods and the order of the seven days in the Sumerian/Babylonian week (Figure 42).

In the late Babylonian period, the third day of the week (the planet Mars) was Nergal, the pastoral god, god of the desert, and god of the underworld, and the fourth day was Nabu (the planet Mercury), the god of astronomy, wisdom, and writing. When the Jewish scribes were compiling their version of the seven days of creation, they translated across the sequence of Babylonian weekdays and the associated concepts—vegetation created on the third day (Nergal) and sun and moon created on the fourth day (Nabu).

It was this Sumerian and Babylonian pre-existing link between the sacred planets and the weekdays that influenced the biblical scribes to write the strange sequence (vegetation existing before the sun) in their story of how their god created the world (Figure 42).

[1040]   SOURCE: https://www.friesian.com/week.htm.

Week day	Planet associated with the gods	Sumerian god	Babylonian god	Babylonian god's realm	link to Biblical Genesis	Underlying concept	Biblical day of creation
Sunday	Sun	Utu	Shamash	Son of Sin, god of the sun who protects the poor and travellers	let there be light: creating day and night	creating day and night	day 1
Monday	Moon	Nanna	Sin	Moon god	creating heaven/ evening and morning	creating heaven and earth	day 2
Tuesday	Mars	Gugalanna	Nergal	vegetation; pastoral god; god of the underworld of war and pestilence	earth, the seas and vegetation	letting the earth sprout vegetation, plants yielding seed, and fruit trees bearing fruit	day 3
Wednesday	Mercury	Enki	Nabu (Nebo)	god of astronomy; god of writing and wisdom	sun, moon, stars and the seasons	and god made the two great lights – the greater light to rule the day (sun) and the lesser light to rule the night (moon) – and the stars	day 4
Thursday	Jupiter	Enlil	Marduk	water, fertility and vegetation, judgment, and magic	sea-beasts, fish & birds	letting the waters swarm with ..living creatures and letting the birds fly	day 5
Friday	Venus	Inanna	Ishtar	goddess of passion, war, prostitution	land beasts, creeping things & mankind	letting the earth bring forward living creatures including cattle....and making man in god's image and likeness with dominion over all creatures	day 6
Saturday	Saturn	Ninurta	Ninurta (Ninib)	farmer and a healing god	day of rest	job is done/creation complete - rest	day 7

Figure 42: The biblical Genesis story linked to the Sumerian/Babylonian gods and weekday sequence [a]

[a] Adapted from https://www.friesian.com/week.htm.

The origin of the Sabbath

The Babylonians held the number seven as sacred, which was most likely influenced by their reference to the seven visible planets. They believed that the seventh, fourteenth, twenty-first, and twenty-eighth days were holy days, which were sometimes called 'evil days', on which certain activities were prohibited. The Babylonian Akkadian word *sapattum* or *sabattum* means 'full moon' and the Sumerian word *sa-bat* means 'mid-rest'.

Professor of Divinity and Biblical Criticism Thomas Nicol found as early as 1899 that 'in a lexicographical tablet in the British Museum the word Sabattu, the Sabbath, is found and is explained by words that mean "a day of rest for the heart"', and further that 'In these old Babylonian calendars we have the Sabbath rest and abstinence from work expressly prescribed: 'The seventh day is a resting day … a holy day, a Sabbath'.[1041]

The Hebrew scribes did not only use the Sumerian/Babylonian weekdays to build their conception of the creation of the universe (see above), but they also adopted the Babylonian concept of the day of rest on the seventh day. The time the Hebrew scribes spent in exile in Babylon had a significant influence on their writing. Isaac Asimov, in his step-by-step analysis of the Bible, highlights the impact of the time spent in exile in Babylon on the Israelite's changing attitude to the sabbath:

> *In pre-Exilic times the Sabbath is barely mentioned and seems to have been of little consequence among the Israelis. In post-Exilic times, its observance was of the greatest importance and Jews died rather than violate that observance.*[1042]

The origin of the biblical 'Word of God'

A popular ancient creation story is based on a belief that a supreme being had the power to create the universe and everything that existed by the power of words, where god's spoken word creates divine spirit—once spoken, the word becomes a substantial reality.

It was an ancient Egyptian belief that the god Ptah, who created the world, brought it into being by the creative power of the spoken word.[1043] The Hindus believe that the entirety of their religious texts, the Vedas, are the word of god. This is reflected in their alternative word for the Vedas, *shruti*, which means 'to hear'.[1044]

The notion that god worked not by aggression but by the power of words comes from Mesopotamian mythology. The Mesopotamians believed that their god's words had power; their authority was inherent in their commands and must be obeyed.[1045]

[1041] Nicol (1899), p. 60.

[1042] Asimov (1981), p. 19.

[1043] Shaw (2014), p. 25.

[1044] SOURCE: https://www.bbc.co.uk/religion/religions/hinduism/texts/texts.shtml retrieved on 13 April 2023.

[1045] Jacobsen (1946A), p. 174.

The HB/OT contains multiple occasions in which the authors promote the infallibility of the 'word of god' as expressed in the biblical text. This includes:

- For the word of God is alive and active. Sharper than any double-edged sword, it penetrates even to dividing soul and spirit, joints and marrow; it judges the thoughts and attitudes of the heart. (Hebrews 4:12)
- As for God, his way is perfect: The Lord's word is flawless; he shields all who take refuge in him. (Psalm 18:30)
- For the word of the Lord is right and true; he is faithful in all he does. (Psalm 33:4)
- Your word is a lamp for my feet, a light on my path. (Psalm 119:10)
- How can a young person stay on the path of purity? By living according to your word. (Psalm 119:95)
- The grass withers and the flowers fall, but the word of our God endures forever. (Isaiah 40:8).

This concept is strengthened even further in the Christian New Testament, where the author of John's gospel states:

- In the beginning was the Word, and the Word was with God, and the Word was God. (John 1:1).

Barbara Walker has explained how the Christian adoption of the notion that Jesus was 'God's word made flesh' was itself an adaptation of the ancient practice of associating sacred kings and saviour gods with holy words.[1046] The creative power of the divine word in Sumerian mythology influenced the Hebrew scribes. Samuel Kramer, the world's leading expert on the Sumerians, described it thus:

> *As for the technique of creation attributed to (the) deities, our Sumerian philosophers developed a doctrine which became dogma throughout the Near East, the creative power of the divine word. All that the creating deity had to do, according to this doctrine, was to lay his plans, utter the word, and pronounce the name.*[1047]

These examples, the biblical creation story, the adoption of the sabbath (above), and the sanctity of the word of God, exemplify a commonly held view amongst most

---

[1046] Walker (2010), p. 47.
[1047] Kramer (1971), p. 115.

modern scholars. This collectively held view is typified by the words of Kenton Sparks, who is a highly regarded American scholar of the early books of the HB/OT:

> *The earliest part of Israel's history in Genesis is now regarded as something other than a work of modern history. Its primary author was at best an ancient historian (if a historian at all), who lived long after the event he narrated, and who drew freely from sources that were not historical (legends and theological stories); he was more concerned with theology than with the modern quest to learn 'what actually happened'.*[1048]

The origin of the myth of heaven

Buddhism and Confucianism have a concept of heaven, even though neither religion believes in a supreme deity. In Buddhism, there are several heavens. If a person has good karma, they may go to one of the heavens temporarily on their way to being reborn. Confucianism has an abstract idea of heaven as the supreme source of wisdom and goodness without the existence of any gods or deities.

This belief in a parallel invisible 'other world' originated with Shamanism in prehistoric Siberia. It became a widely held belief across the prehistoric world well before the emergence of the Israelites. Polish Archaeologist Andrzej Rozwadowski has described the shamanic worldview in this way:

> *Apart from the visible world, there is another reality, for shamanic cultures truly real (not an illusionary or imaginary). Access to this other world is not easy, however, it requires special knowledge and skills that are the domain of shamans. The social need to have a shaman in society stemmed from the belief that everything that is happening here and now is closely linked with and depend on the spirits who populate the invisible world. The shaman played thus the role of an intermediary between the human world and the spirits.*[1049]

The HB/OT was written well before the emergence of science, chemistry, physics, medicine, astronomy, and global communication and was heavily influenced by Shamanism and the Sumerian, Babylonian, and Egyptian conceptions of creation, death, heaven, and hell.

In 1902, Lutheran pastor Dr Alfred Jeremias explained that there was:

> *A surprising correspondence between the Babylonian ideas concerning death and Hades and the Jewish notions of the same. … The connection of Israel with Babylonia was indeed of the*

[1048]   Sparks (2007), p. 587.
[1049]   Rozwadowski (2019), p. 177.

closest …[and] that Babylonian thought had spread over the land of Canaan before it was conquered by the Hebrews. At the time … there stood in Jerusalem a temple of the Babylonian Storm-god Ninib.[1050]

The Sumerians believed that heaven and Earth were originally united in an eternal primal sea. The Sumerian creation story involved a metaphor of a cosmic mountain emerging from the eternal primal sea—a mountain whose 'base was the bottom of the Earth and whose peak was the top of the heaven', and:

The lord whose decisions are unalterable,
Enlil, who brings up the seed of the land from the earth
Took care to move away heaven from earth,
Took care to move away earth from heaven.[1051]

Enlil was the chief deity of the Sumerian pantheon and was associated with wind, air, earth, and storms and watched over humanity and cared for their wellbeing. The Sumerian's supreme god was An/Anu, the divine personification of the sky, the supreme god, the utmost power, source of all authority, and ancestor of all the deities with authority over and legitimisation for all mortal rulers across Mesopotamia. Enlil was the child of An (heaven) and the goddess Ki (Earth)—and the Sumerian name for the universe was Anki.

In the HB/OT, the universe is commonly divided into the same two realms: heaven (*šāmayim*) and Earth (*'ereṣ*), with a third realm often added: either 'sea' (like the Sumerian concept of the primal sea) (Exodus 20:11, Genesis 1:10) or 'water under the earth'. (Exodus 20:4, Deuteronomy 5:8).[1052]

The collective belief in Mesopotamia, in ancient Israel, and across the Middle East and the Mediterranean was that the Earth was a flat disk floating in the ocean with a hemispherical sky-dome or domes above it, that the planets were gods, and multiple gods were controlling resources and life (Figure 43). The Mesopotamians believed that the sky was a series of domes (usually three, but sometimes seven) each made of a different precious stone. The highest, outermost dome was the home of the supreme god, An.

Arthur Koestler explains this collectively held concept of the universe in the following way:

[1050] Jeremias (1902), p. 3.
[1051] Kramer (2007), p. 58.
[1052] https://en.wikipedia.org/wiki/Heaven accessed on 28 July 2020.

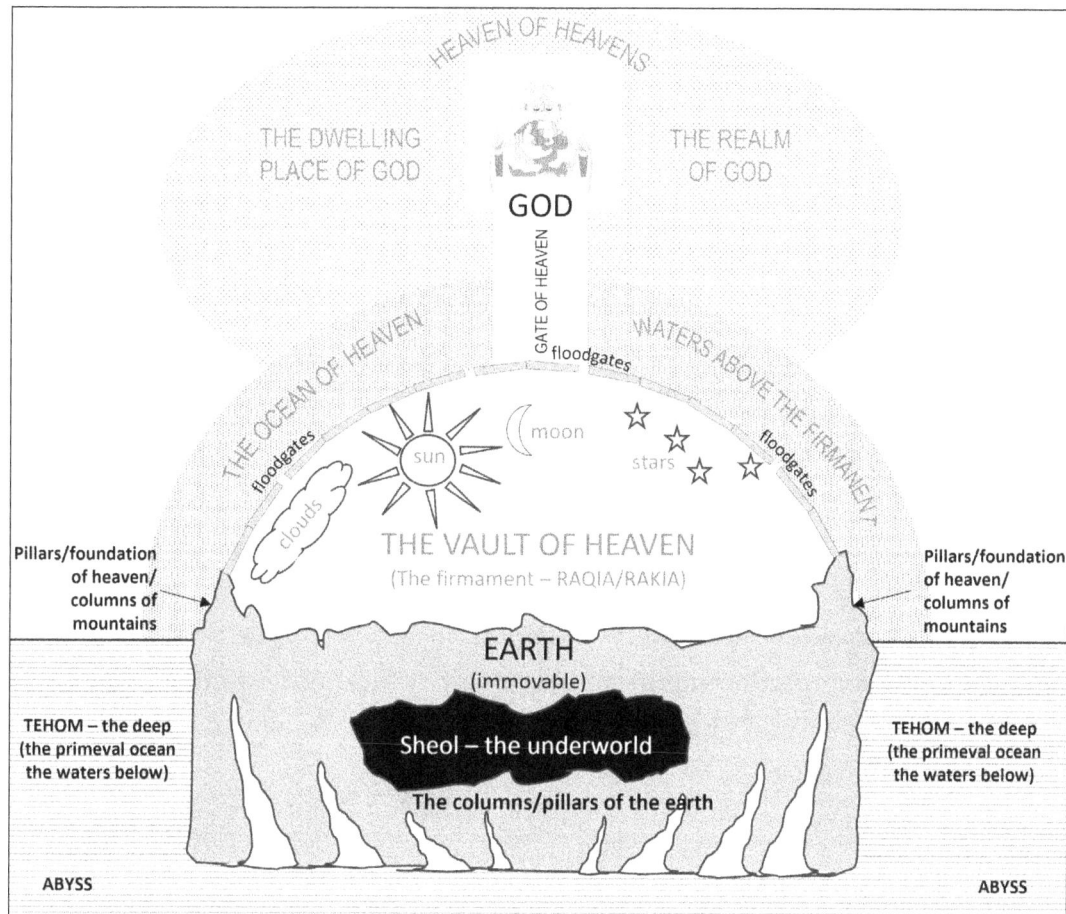

HEAVEN OF HEAVENS

THE DWELLING
PLACE OF GOD

GOD

THE REALM
OF GOD

GATE OF HEAVEN

floodgates

THE OCEAN OF HEAVEN

WATERS ABOVE THE FIRMAMENT

floodgates

floodgates

sun

moon

stars

clouds

THE VAULT OF HEAVEN
(The firmament – RAQIA/RAKIA)

Pillars/foundation
of heaven/
columns of
mountains

Pillars/foundation
of heaven/
columns of
mountains

EARTH
(immovable)

Sheol – the underworld

TEHOM – the deep
(the primeval ocean
the waters below)

TEHOM – the deep
(the primeval ocean
the waters below)

The columns/pillars of the earth

ABYSS

ABYSS

Figure 43: The ancient Middle East conception of heaven and earth [b]

---

[b]   Adapted from: Esparza (2016) : https://aleteia.org/2016/07/07/when-the-earth-was-
       flat-a-map-of-the-universe-according-to-the-old-testament/ accessed on 28 July 2020.

*The world of the Babylonians, Egyptians and the Hebrews was an oyster, with water under-
neath, and more water overhead, supported by the solid firmament. It was of moderate dimensions, and as safely closed in on all sides as a cot in the nursery or a babe in the womb.* [1053]

This simple, safe, dependable, predictable, and entirely mythological conception of the
universe remains the basis for most of the religious beliefs in the modern world.

The Sumerian supreme deity An's Semitic and Hebrew equivalent was El—the
supreme god who, according to the Bible, appointed Yahweh as the chief god of the

---

[1053]   Koestler (1959), p. 19.

Israelites. It was a commonly held belief across the Ancient Middle East that the supreme god (Sumerian An, Babylonian Marduk, Akkadian Anshar, Assyrian Ashur, Egyptian Horus, and Hebrew El) lived above the dome and watched down on humanity from this vantage point (Figure 43).

This is the mythical foundation for religious followers throughout the ages pointing up to the sky when referring to 'heaven'. It comes from a mythological belief that a prehistoric supreme god is sitting on the highest dome of the sky watching down on humanity.

The universality of the tripartite universe

Biblical scholar John R Roberts has shown how most of these prehistoric cultures and subsequently the Hebrew scribes 'conceived of the world in terms of a three-tiered cosmos consisting of the Earth as a flat disk in the middle … floating on water, with heaven above and the underworld beneath'.[1054]

Polish Archaeologist Andrzej Rozwadowski has identified the Siberian shamans as the origin of the notion of a three-tiered world heaven-Earth-the underworld.[1055] Kit Wesler claims that the three-tiered belief of Earth, heaven, and hell can be traced back to Stone Age shamanism. She states:

Shamanism seems to be a basic substratum of human perception, linked in part to biological processes that cause our brains to misperceive reality under certain stimuli—or that allow our brains to perceive the supernatural in certain conditions. Shamanism in a broad sense appears to be nearly universal among non-agricultural peoples, and elements of the belief system, such as the three-tiered world view persist into the heavens and hells of modern religions.[1056]

The Sumerians took these concepts much further. Some two thousand years before the emergence of the Israelites, and some two thousand five hundred years before the Hebrew scribes started to write the HB/OT, the Sumerians had laid a mythological template for explaining the universe. This became the accepted creed and dogma for most of the ancient Middle East from around 3000 BCE onwards. The Sumerian word for the universe was *an-ki*, which is a composite word meaning *heaven-earth*. They imagined a pantheon of deities who were manlike but superhuman, immortal, and invisible to the eye. These anthropomorphic superhuman gods governed different parts of the universe according to

---

[1054]   Roberts (2020), p. 1.
[1055]   Rozwadowski (2019), p. 177.
[1056]   Wesler (2012) p. 272.

well-laid plans and duly prescribed laws. The Sumerians believed that the primeval sea was the first cause/prime mover and that the universe emerged from this. They believed that:

> *… heaven-earth consisted of a vaulted heaven superimposed over a flat earth and united with it. In between, and separating heaven from earth was the moving and expanding 'atmosphere'. Out of this atmosphere were fashioned the luminous bodied—the moon, sun, planets and stars. Following the separation of heaven and earth—and the creation of the light-giving astral bodies—plant, animal and human life came into existence.[1057]*

This dominant archaic mythology about the nature of the world as a tripartite, three-tiered cosmos (heaven, Earth, and under the earth) significantly influenced the Hebrew scribes as they hybridised and scattered it into multiple sections of the HB/OT (Figure 43). Roberts cites several examples where this conception has been woven into the HB/OT, for example in Exodus (20:4), Deuteronomy (4:18) and Revelation (5:3). Roberts claims that there are multiple examples in the Hebrew scriptures that make no sense without the assumed and mythological tripartite explanation of the world, for example, Genesis 1:1 to 2:3.[1058]

Roberts adds further that:

> *While many scriptures confirm the biblical cosmos is conceptualized as being three-tiered there is no scripture that indicates the biblical earth is conceptualized as a globe suspended in space. If there were then it would contradict the rest of the Bible. This concept would have been unknown to the original author and audience.[1059]*

This prehistoric belief in a tripartite cosmos that originated with the Sumerians some five thousand years ago is the origin of the contemporary mythological belief, common across the three Abrahamic religions, that heaven (God's paradise) is up there (pointing to the sky) and hell (the underworld) is down there (pointing to the notional underground).

The model is reinforced in biblical passages such as this from Isaiah 40:22:

> *He sits enthroned above the circle of the earth, and its people are like grasshoppers. He stretches out the heavens like a canopy, and spreads them out like a tent to live in.*

The notion of the underworld as being a place of punishment for misdeeds did not enter the writings of the Jewish scribes until after the arrival of Alexander the Great. From

---

[1057]   Kramer (1956), pp. 76-77.
[1058]   Roberts, John R. (2020), pp. 1-3.
[1059]   Roberts, John R. (2020), p. 4.

around 330 BCE, the Jewish scribes adopted the Hellenistic notion that only the righteous would inherit and enjoy the afterlife in heaven while those who deserved punishment would suffer in hell.

The origin of baptism and the thirty-year-old messiah

At the age of thirty, Zoroaster entered a river and received a spiritual revelation that formed the major foundations for his preaching. This is the beginning of the Jewish and Christian notion of baptism by water as a spiritual event in which a child/person is bathed in sacred water to represent cleansing and purification.

The Zoroastrian tradition of a messiah commencing ministry at the age thirty influenced Buddhism and the Old and New Testament stories hundreds of years later.

According to the legend, Siddhartha Gautama (Buddha) was born to a Hindu king who, in response to a prophecy that claimed the child would become a great king or spiritual leader, protected his son from any form of suffering for the first 29 years of his life.[1060]

The Hebrew Bible/Old Testament states that a priest had to be 30 years old before he took up the mature, senior office of priest:

The lord said to Moses and Aaron, 'Take a census of the Kohathites among the Levites by their clans and families, men from thirty to fifty years old—everyone who is qualified to serve in the work at the Tent of Meeting'. (Numbers 4:2-3).

The Christian Bible/New Testament states that after Jesus was baptised by John the Baptist (purified like Zoroaster), 'Now Jesus himself was about thirty years old when he began his ministry'. (Luke 3:21).

The origin of the trinity

The trinity concept is a very ancient mythological belief. It was originally based on the sky (the heavens), the Earth (fertility goddesses), and the sun (the supreme deity). Prehistoric Zoroastrians, Hindus, and Egyptians were 'trinitarian' worshippers.

The Zoroastrians had a trinity consisting of Āhurā Mazdā (the supreme being in heaven), Apam Napat (a water deity and goddess of fertility, health, healing, and wisdom), Mithra (god of the rising sun, contracts, covenants, and friendship). The Zoroastrians

---

[1060]   Mark (2020B).

believed that these three divinities acted together to represent and protect divine truth and righteousness.

The link between the Zoroastrian and Christianity trinities sees God the Father as an adaptation of Āhurā Mazdā, Christ as a variation on Mithra, and the Holy Spirit as an adaptation of Apam Napat.

Hinduism had a belief in a triple deity of supreme divinity consisting of three gods who were responsible for the creation, upkeep, and recreation of the world (the Trimūrti). These were avatars—incarnations of the Hindu single supreme deity Brahman. The first avatar was Bramha, the creator of the universe, who developed the four Vedas and is the god of creation and knowledge; the second was Vishnu, associated with light and the sun, and who was regarded as the preserver and protector of the universe; and the third was Shiva, a god of wisdom and insight, whose role was to destroy the illusions and imperfections of this world, paving the way for beneficial change.[1061]

Hinduism also has a trinity of three female goddesses (the Tridevi)—Saraswati (wife of Bramha), the goddess of knowledge, music, art, speech, wisdom, and learning; Lakshmi (wife of Vishnu), the goddess of wealth, fortune, power, beauty and prosperity; Parvati (wife of Shiva), the goddess of fertility, love, beauty, bravery, harmony, marriage, children, and devotion.

The Mesopotamians believed in a three-god trinity that ruled the heavens, the earth, and the seas. The highest god was Anu, the god of the heavens. Enlil was the god of wind and agriculture, and Enki (or Ea) was the god of water and knowledge.

The Egyptian (3000 BCE) trinity included Asar (Osiris), the god of life, death, fertility, and the underworld; Aset (Isis), the goddess of salvation, protector of rituals, healer, wise person, mother, and nurturer; and Heru (Horus), god of the sun, moon, the sky, the heavens, and power. Heru was regarded as the son of Asar and Aset. Jennifer Williams claims that the Egyptian trinity is the source from which the Christians developed their concept of the trinity: Asar was the source of God the Father, Heru was the source of God the Son/Jesus, and Aset was the source of the Holy Spirit and of the Virgin Mary.[1062]

The Pharoah Akhenaten (1353 BCE to 1363 BCE) who introduced monotheism into Egyptian religion also had a concept of a holy trinity. It was made up of Aten (the sun god), Akhenaten (the Pharoah portraying himself as the Egyptian god of air and wind,

---

[1061] SOURCE: adapted from World History Encyclopedia, Introduction to the Vedas: the Religious Texts from Ancient India—YouTube retrieved on 21 October 2021.

[1062] Williams (2014), p. 107 and pp. 118-119.

Shu) and Nefertiti (his wife being linked to the Egyptian goddess Tefnut – the goddess of moisture, dew and rainfall, the twin sister and consort of Shu,). A trinity of gods was not unique in ancient Egypt. As philosophy student James Jack has observed:[1063]

> *the grouping of gods into triads was reasonably common, with one new kingdom text even declaring 'all the gods are three'.*

The HB/OT does not specifically contain a reference to, or a word for, 'the trinity'. Although there is substantial dispute and disagreement amongst Jewish authorities, there are some leading authorities who claim that trinitarianism is a Jewish concept.[1064] In Kabbalah (traditional Jewish mysticism), the triangle of divinity is the three *sephirot* (emanations) at the top of the Kabbalistic tree of life. The three represent the crown, wisdom, and understanding/intelligence.

The Gnostics, a Jewish sect, maintained a belief in a trinity that involved the Father, Son, and Holy (Mother) Spirit. The Christian (father, son, and holy spirit) and Jewish concepts of a trinitarian god who exists as three persons but is one being who has a single divine nature was a continuation of the ancient trinitarian beliefs adapted from prehistoric Zoroastrian, Hindu, and Egyptian mythologies.

The origin of the concept of a soul

Austrian priest, linguist, anthropologist, and ethnologist Wilhelm Schmidt postulated as early as 1931 that prehistoric matrilinear agricultural societies, the affinity of women with fertility, nature, and planting cycles, and the close link to lunisolar and planetary annual patterns influenced and strengthened the belief in the existence of a 'soul' in all things—humans, inanimate and animate—a belief system that scientists refer to as 'animism'.[1065]

In the Cis-Baikal regions of Siberia, in around 6000 BCE, there is evidence of animal burial practices (dogs, wolves, reindeer, elks) that suggest that the animistic culture there regarded these animals as having unique souls that would cycle back to their species.[1066]

Wilhelm Schmidt observed that the Babylonians, Assyrians, and Egyptians in or around 1900 BCE collectively transitioned from animism to mythology based on nature

---

[1063] Jack, (2016), p. 14 citing Papyrus Leiden I 350, 4.21-26 (trans. Allen); Sigfried Morenz (trans. Ann E Keep), Egyptian Religion (London: Methuen, 1973), pp. 142-144.

[1064] See: https://www.hebrew4christians.com/Names_of_G-d/Trinity/trinity.html retrieved on 21 October 2021.

[1065] Schmidt (2014), pp. 85-86.

[1066] Losey et al., (2011), p. 175.

myths and star/planetary myths, a transition that included the carrying over of a belief in the notion of multiple external souls.[1067, 1068]

The ancient Egyptians believed the soul (the *ka*) was a detached part of a person's personality that could protect, intermediate, and sustain him/her. The Egyptians believed that an individual could talk to and seek advice from their soul. Egyptologist John A Wilson relates the story of an Egyptian man who was considering suicide having a lengthy discussion and debate with his soul about the relative merits of life and death.[1069]

Irving Finkel suggests that the Mesopotamian mythological notion of human beings having a 'spirit' can be traced back to the Mesopotamian creation story. The Mesopotamians believed that the first humans were created from clay but that the clay was mixed with the blood of the intelligent god We-ilu (also known as Ilawela or Geshtu/Geshtu-e). We-ilu's divine blood and divine intelligence blended god and man into the clay to produce the human heartbeat and the human spirit.[1070]

Finkel's extensive exploration of the ancient Mesopotamian concept of ghosts has outlined what is essentially the groundwork for much of the contemporary religious mythologies around an individual's soul. The Mesopotamians believed that a part of an individual survived beyond their death and that these ghosts/spirits were ever-present. Depending on their origin, they could be expressed in different words to describe a simple ancestor spirit, an evil demon, a ghost, a phantom, a breeze or wind, nothingness, or foolishness.[1071]

Mesopotamian authority Jean Bottero explained the Mesopotamian concept of the soul at length in the following way:

> *The human was not, as had been thought, simply a body, a carnal mass: to animate and enhance him he above all had a 'spirit', in itself independent from the body, a 'soul' existing by itself, created foremost by the divine stars in their celestial dwellings, one of those layers in the sky that were assigned to each of them. At birth the soul descended to join the material body, itself formed by earth. As it descended toward its earthly goal, the soul crossed through successive circles belonging to the various stars, thereby acquiring at the whim of those stars, the qualities, the peculiarities, and the talents unique to them which they thus bestowed to form and to define the soul's personality. At the other end of existence, at the time of death, freed from its carnal attachments to the body, which then turned to matter, the soul returned to its celestial homeland.*[1072]

[1067] Schmidt (2014), p. 11.

[1068] SOURCE: https://www.encyclopedia.com/environment/encyclopedias-almanacs-transcripts-and-maps/soul-ancient-near-eastern-concepts retrieved on 25 March 2021.

[1069] Wilson (1946), p. 102.

[1070] Finkel (2021), pp. 14-16.

[1071] Finkel (2021), p. 16, p. 18, pp. 180-181.

[1072] Bottero (2004), p. 214.

Irving Finkel quotes the work of Ancient Middle East Art Historian Amy Gansell in support of his theory that ghosts/the souls of the dead were a common belief in ancient Mesopotamia. Gansell believes that the complex design and lavish accoutrements included in the graves of selected Mesopotamian queens are evidence that the Mesopotamians believed that the spirit of a dead queen could engage with the living, the dead, and that of the divine.[1073] Louise Pryke has explained how the Mesopotamian culture required ongoing care of the spirits of dead relatives:

> *Spirits were thought to rise and receive offerings and smell burning incense provided by loved ones.... There was an element of danger to the neglect of the dead; ghosts could easily turn into demons, which might return to terrify the living if disturbed or improperly buried.*[1074]

This Mesopotamian concept has some fascinating parallels with its adaptation into contemporary Jewish and Christian beliefs—the soul comes from and returns to heaven; the human body is formed from earth, to which it returns; and it is the soul that gives the body/human the divine right of passage. These are adaptations of the initial animistic mythological stories evolving over thousands of years until their emergence in a new form in Judaism and Christianity.

The initial totemic, shamanic, and animistic concept of having a soul was adapted by Plato (428 BCE to 348 BCE) from his experience with the Mesopotamians.[1075, 1076] This was then adapted by the Hebrew scribes into the Bible under the influence of Mesopotamian, Persian/Zoroastrian, and Hellenistic philosophy during their Babylonian exile (around 590 BCE to 530 BCE).[1077] It was then later modified by Catholic theologian Thomas Aquinas (1224 CE to 1274 CE) into a belief that all organisms have a soul but only humans have an immortal soul.[1078] The contemporary legacy of these beliefs is the continuing belief in Judaism and in some Christian denominations that all human beings have immortal souls.

The origin of the book of judgement

The Zoroastrians were the first to introduce the mythology that each person had a book of judgement that recorded their everyday acts and that they would each face judgement

---

[1073] Finkel (2021), pp. 37-38.

[1074] Pryke (2017), p. 51.

[1075] SOURCE: https://en.wikipedia.org/wiki/Plato%27s_theory_of_soul retrieved on 7 December 2020.

[1076] Crickmore (2009).

[1077] SOURCE: https://en.wikipedia.org/wiki/Soul_in_the_Bible retrieved on 2 February 2021.

[1078] SOURCE: https://cct.biola.edu/thomas-aquinas-human-nature-soul-afterlife/ retrieved on 7 December 2020.

and be resurrected to an earthly paradise.[1079] The Hebrew scribes copied this idea into the concept of the 'day of the Lord' (Isaiah 13:6-13) when, at some unknown time in the future, the Hebrew god would pass judgement on each person. The authors of the Book of Revelation (Christian New Testament, Revelations 13:8) repackaged this concept (in around 96 CE) into the Book of Life:

> And all that dwell upon the earth shall worship him, whose names are not written in the book of life of the Lamb slain from the foundation of the world.

Each year from 25 September to 27 September, it is the beginning of the Jewish New Year (Rosh Hashanah). It is believed that this is the date when the Jewish god created Adam and Eve. On this day, practising Jews wish each other '*Ketivah v'chatima tovah*'. This translates as a wish that their book of life has good inscriptions and sealing by their god.

The origin of the Adam story

Genomics has provided irrefutable evidence that:

> … *modern humans had their origins in Africa within the last hundred and fifty thousand years. At some point, about a hundred thousand years ago, modern humans began to spread out of Africa to begin eventual colonisation of the rest of the world. Incredible as it may seem, we can tell from genetic reconstructions that this settlement of the rest of the world involved only one of thirteen African clans.[1080]*

Like most of the HB/OT, the Adam story is a composite and recasting of ideas from previous mythologies from the times when the Bible was being written and rewritten.

For the Sumerians, the goddess of creation Nammu asks her son Enki, the god of wisdom and knowledge, to 'fashion servants of god'. He arranges for some 'womb-goddesses' to fashion the first humans from clay and water from the abyss.[1081]

Jean Bottero has outlined how the Hebrew scribes adapted the Mesopotamian version of humans being created by a mix of clay and the blood of a god. They wrote in the first chapters of Genesis that Yahweh created Adam from clay and, in the absence of another god's blood, simply breathed life into the clay (Genesis 2:7).[1082] The Hebrew word for man is *adam* and the Hebrew word for earth is a*damah*.[1083]

[1079]   SOURCE: Iran Chamber Society: Religion in Iran: The Secrets of Zoroastrianism retrieved on 1 March 2022.

[1080]   Sykes (2002), p. 277.

[1081]   SOURCE: https://faculty.gvsu.edu/websterm/SumerianMyth.htm retrieved on 1 May 2023.

[1082]   Bottero (2004), pp. 207-208.

[1083]   SOURCE: https://womeninthebible.net/bible-archaeology/farming-agriculture/ retrieved on 9 March 2023.

The name Adam is itself a play on words. The Bible claims that God said to Adam:

By the sweat of your brow, you will eat your food until you return to the ground, since from it you were taken; for dust you are and to dust you will return.[1084]

American philosopher J.B. Callicott has outlined how the Hebrew word *adamah* means 'earth' and that the name chosen by the Hebrew scribes may well be a triple wordplay. According to Callicott, 'earth', 'ground/red soil', and/or 'humankind' are all translations of the name Adam that have been suggested by different biblical scholars.[1085]

Graves and Pattai explain that the concept that god made the first man from dust was a widely held view across many of the cultures that predated its adaptation by the Hebrew scribes. They state that:

The myth of Man's creation from earth, clay or dust is (was) widely current. In Egypt, either the God Khnum or the God Ptah created man on a potter's wheel; in Babylonia, either the Goddess Aruru or the God Ea kneaded man from clay. According to a Phocian Greek myth, Prometheus used a certain red clay.[1086]

The origin of the Eve story

The Eve story is an adaptation of an ancient Mesopotamian myth and a Hindu myth. The Mesopotamian myth tells of the god Enki and the goddess Ninhursag. Enki has eight pains in eight different parts of his body. The mother goddess Ninhursag decides to give birth to eight different healing goddesses representing the eight different parts of Enki's body. Each goddess is given a name corresponding to the specific part of the body they represent.

Now the Sumerian word for 'rib' is *ti* (pronounced 'tee'). The goddess created for the healing of Enki's rib, therefore, was called, in Sumerian, Ninti—'the lady of the rib.' But the very same Sumerian word, *ti*, also means 'to make live.' The name Ninti may thus mean 'the lady who makes live,' as well as 'the lady of the rib.' In Sumerian literature, therefore, 'the lady of the rib' came to be identified with 'the lady who makes live' through what might be termed a play on words.[1087]

1084   Genesis 3:19.
1085   Callicott (1990), p 75-76.
1086   Graves and Pattai (1964), p. 63.
1087   SOURCE: https://faculty.gvsu.edu/websterm/SumerianMyth.htm retrieved on 1 May 2023.

Enki was saved from dying by the goddess Ninti, whose name literally translates as 'lady of the rib'. In Hebrew mythology (the Bible), Adam names the woman created from his rib Hawwah, which translates as 'life'—a clear reference to the Mesopotamian origin of the myth.

The link between a woman and a male rib is also found in ancient Hindu beliefs. The Hindu myth claims that the first man, Manu, created his wife from one of his own ribs, which marked the commencement of a new era of human creation.[1088]

Geoffrey Ashe believes that stories such as the one where a woman has caused the downfall of an otherwise 'golden era' are nostalgic folk stories symbolising the passing away and declining power of goddesses and the elevation of male humans and male gods–'demoted by masculine myth-making'.[1089]

The origin of the Garden of Eden

It was not until medieval times that people started looking for the Garden of Eden. Prior to this time, it was considered a paradisiacal realm created by God for the benefit of our first parents, Adam and Eve, who had lived in a state of perpetual bliss and happiness, not knowing death, pain, or hunger.[1090]

In the Bible, it is claimed that Eden is the garden of God, which is located on the holy mountain of God (Ezekiel 28:13-15). This mountain is not in the holy land (Israel), but somewhere in the north.[1091] Paul Kriwaczek and George Roux both believe that the original concept of a garden of Eden is based on the Sumerian term *edin*, which described the vast plains, great steppes, cultivated fields, and open land that stretched from the base of the Zagros Mountains to Arabia.[1092]

The ancient Persians had a myth that has the same underlying message as the Adam and Eve in the Garden of Eden story. To the Persians, the first mortal couple were Mashya and Mashyanag, who were given souls by Āhurā Mazdā through his breath. They lived harmoniously until the destructive spirit Angra Mainyu told them that he was their true creator.

[1088] Wilkinson (2009), p. 191.
[1089] Ashe (2018), p. 187.
[1090] Collins (2014), p. 226.
[1091] Ashe (2018), pp. 185-186.
[1092] Kriwaczek (2010), p. 86; Roux (1992), p. 104.

The couple believed this lie and fell from grace, afterwards left to live in a world of disorder and strife.[1093]

Mythologist Joseph Campbell sees the Garden concept as a metaphor for innocence that is not shaken, dominated or corrupted by fear, a place of nonduality of male and female, good and evil. If you eat the duality, you are on your way out of the garden. Eden is 'the kingdom of the Father (which) is spread upon the earth, and men do not see'.[1094]

The Sumerians had a myth involving a healthy willow tree standing by the banks of the Euphrates River. It is buffeted and blown by the wind and is under threat of a flood. The Sumerian fertility goddess Inanna, queen of heaven, saves the tree and brings it to her holy garden. The tree matures and grows but Inanna is unable to cut it because a snake 'who knows no charm' has built its nest around the base of the tree.[1095]

Joseph Campbell has summarised the ancient tradition of linking a tree and a snake to a woman and the resulting benefit for a man:

> *We have Sumerian seals from as early as 3500 BCE showing the serpent and the tree and the goddess, with the goddess giving the fruit of life to a visiting male.*[1096]

Eric Cline has reviewed a large number of suggestions of where the Garden of Eden might be and supports the concept that it is possibly a geographic reality—located perhaps, somewhere in Mesopotamia or the Fertile Crescent.[1097] Andrew Collins believes that it was in Armenia, modern-day eastern Türkiye.[1098]

The Sumerian myths do not appear to contain a parallel story to the biblical Adam and Eve story. However, they did have a concept that the east was the *land of the living* and the west was the *land of the dead*. According to the Sumerian myth *Enki and Ninhursag*, in the east on the island of Dilmun (modern-day Bahrain), there was a clean, pure, and bright country where old age, disease, and death were unknown and where humans and animals lived happy lives.[1099]

William Dever has explained the Adam and Eve and the Garden of Eden myth in the following way:

[1093]   Mark (2019).
[1094]   Campbell and Moyers (1991), p. 59; p. 113; p. 285.
[1095]   Kramer (2007), pp. 48-49.
[1096]   Campbell and Moyers (1991), pp. 54-55.
[1097]   Cline (2007), pp. 13-14.
[1098]   Collins (2014), p. 237.
[1099]   Roux (1992), pp. 104-105.

No archaeologist would go looking for the Garden of Eden. ... The story is really about Mankind (Heb. adam, 'man') and the Mother of all living things (Heb. hawwa, 'life-giver') in an earthly paradise (Heb. gan eden)—in short, an idyllic and profoundly 'true' story about the fact that when any man and any woman find each other, in love as it should be, there is Paradise. Eden is not a place on a map, but a state of mind.[1100]

The apple tree in ancient mythology

The wild apple, *Malus sieversii*, originated in central Asia, east of the Caspian Sea (modern Kazakhstan). It is the main progenitor of today's cultivated apples. It is believed that apple seeds were initially transported out of Kazakhstan by birds prior to humans cultivating them. They became a common food in Mesopotamia (circa 2500 BCE onwards).[1101]

The apple tree was regarded as mythologically interesting to the Mesopotamians. Semitic Akkadian Queen Puabi (ca. 2600 BCE), whose tomb has been thoroughly explored, was buried with several servants whose headgear was designed with necklaces of apple leaves and apple flowers.[1102] There is an ancient Mesopotamian poem about the goddess of love, Inanna, in which the apple tree plays a major role. In the poem entitled *Inanna and the God of Wisdom*, Inanna leans against an apple tree and:

> *... her vulva was wonderous to behold. Rejoicing at her wondrous vulva, the young woman Inanna celebrated herself. She decided to make a journey.*

According to the poem, Inanna was then able to journey to visit Enki, the Sumerian god of wisdom; they drank beer together and Enki bestowed on Inanna knowledge, wisdom, and many godly powers and controls.[1103]

The modern-day Zoroastrian/Persian spring festival celebration of Nowruz is also a fertility festival. The celebration includes seven symbolic items, one of which is an apple, which is regarded as a symbol of fertility.[1104]

[1100] Dever (2002), p. 98.

[1101] Source: https://www.sonneruplund.dk/eng/applesmesopotamien.html retrieved on 16 November 2022.

[1102] See: https://www.sonneruplund.dk/eng/applesmesopotamien.html retrieved on 16 November 2022.

[1103] SOURCE: https://inannadumuzi.wordpress.com/inanna-the-god-of-wisdom/ retrieved on 16 November 2022.

[1104] SOURCE: https://www.nationalgeographic.com/history/article/nowruz-ancient-festival-celebration-springtime-new-year retrieved on 28 November 2022.

Greek mythology has Zeus, the king of gods, marrying his beautiful sister Hera, the queen of gods. The wedding present is a golden apple tree, which she plants in her garden on Mount Atlas at the northern edge of the world. To prevent anyone from picking the apples, Hera places a dragon around the tree. Heracles the Greek god of strength and heroes, kills the dragon and steals the apples. However, because these apples belonged to the gods and were, therefore, a 'forbidden fruit', Heracles is forced to return them.[1105]

Whilst the commonly held belief is that the Hebrew Bible has Eve eating an apple, this is not technically correct. The fruit mentioned in the Bible is a forbidden fruit, the tree of which is described in the Bible as 'the tree of knowledge of good and evil' (Genesis 2:17). This is a link to wisdom and may well have also been influenced by the *Inanna and the God of Wisdom* myth.

Irrespective of this, the important role of apples and apple trees, a common theme in Mesopotamia, is continued through many sections of the HB/OT. Genesis 1:29 tells of God the creator giving 'every plant yielding seed that is on the face of all the Earth, and every tree with seed in its fruit. You shall have them for food'. There are biblical references to apples (apple of his/your eye) and/or apple trees in Proverbs (7:2, 25:11), Psalms (17:8), Song of Solomon (2:3, 2:5, 7:8), Joel (1:12), Deuteronomy (32:10), and Zechariah (2:8).

The snake in ancient mythology

The snake as a symbol of the underworld and/or death can be dated back some 12,000 years to shamanic times. Benz and Bauer have undertaken a wide-ranging analysis of the role of animals in historic and contemporary shamanism. They show how snakes were used to assist shamans in travelling to the underworld and that shamans could also have the skill to influence and direct snakes.[1106] Fabric snakes and snake-like creature motifs commonly adorned the clothes of the Siberian shamans. The snake was regarded in Siberia as a powerful spirit associated with the water spirits. The shamans wore the snake for protection and power.[1107]

The snake was also linked to the moon; prehistoric mythologies saw the power and the cycle of life reflected in the phases of the moon—immortal energy and an image of life, generation after generation, being born again. The moon shedding its shadow (moon phases)

[1105]   SOURCE: https://www.constellation-guide.com/constellation-list/draco-constellation/ and https://www.perseus.tufts.edu/Herakles/apples.html retrieved on 26 April 2023.

[1106]   Benz and Bauer (2015) pp. 6-8.

[1107]   SOURCE: http://www.3worlds.co.uk/Articles/Shaman-Snakes.pdf retrieved on 17 March 2021.

was believed to be like a snake shedding its skin. Snakes, even the most poisonous ones, were seen as symbolic of life and were often revered.[1108]

A link between snakes and women (also linked to the moon) was common in the mythologies surrounding the Hebrew scribes.[1109] Fertility goddesses were frequently shown with snakes around them or in their hands.[1110] Yulia Ustinova has described the reason why the snake and the female were linked across several mythologies in the Middle East during the Bronze Age prior to the emergence of the Israelites:

> *Snakes are complex symbols, in view of, for example, their ability to disappear below ground, their venom, skin-sloughing, fertility and sinuous movement. They evoke the nether world, death, renewal, fertility and more across a range of peoples. The union of snake and woman is to be understood as an enhancement of those evocations.*[1111]

The snake is commonly found in the mythologies of almost all prehistoric Indo-European cultures—specifically and usually in a battle ending with a hero or god slaying a serpent or dragon of some sort.[1112] For the Steppe nomadic warriors, the Scythian's creation story included a cave-dwelling Earth goddess/female monster ('mistress of the country') with the torso of a female and the body of a snake.

In the Sanskrit epic stories of ancient India (mostly written at the same time as the HB/OT), Indra, the ancient Vedic guardian deity of Buddhism, kills Vritra, the snake god who had kept the waters of the world captive.[1113] The prehistoric Bronze Age Minoan civilisation in Knossos on the island of Crete (1600 BCE) worshipped a snake goddess who symbolised the integration of the underworld and the upper world of the sky god. The Minoan snake goddess figurine stands holding a double-edged sword in one hand and a snake in the other.[1114]

The prehistoric Egyptian goddess Wadjet, who was the patroness of the Nile Delta and protector and patron of all of Egypt, was depicted as a snake-headed woman or as a snake—usually an Egyptian cobra, a venomous snake. The cobra snake image is commonly found on the masks of pharaoh mummies.

[1108] Campbell with Bill Moyers (1991), p. 53.

[1109] See: Hall (1980).

[1110] Munnich and רינומ יאיסמ (2005), p. 52.

[1111] Ustinova (2005), p. 68.

[1112] SOURCE: https://en.wikipedia.org/wiki/Proto-Indo-European_mythology retrieved on 3 February 2021.

[1113] Witzel (2012), p. 150, and also: https://en.wikipedia.org/wiki/Vritra retrieved on 17 March 2021.

[1114] Hall (1980), p. 9.

In Mesopotamian divination texts (in *Šumma Ālu ina Mēlê Šakin*), specific omens relate to ophiomancy—divination or misfortune by snakes. Duane Smith has shown how more than forty of the omens in the Mesopotamian divination texts show a man, a woman, the unexpected arrival of a snake and negative outcomes—a separation, divorce, dismantling of a household, or death. Smith outlines how the Mesopotamians believed that good or evil divine messages could be sent via a range of mechanisms, including animal omens. He believes there is a very high probability that the Hebrew scribes, in full knowledge of the Mesopotamian tradition, adapted it to their Adam and Eve story:

> Now the serpent was more crafty than any of the wild animals the Lord God had made. He said to the woman, 'Did God really say, 'You must not eat from any tree in the garden'?'
>
> The woman said to the serpent, 'We may eat fruit from the trees in the garden, but God did say, 'You must not eat fruit from the tree that is in the middle of the garden, and you must not touch it, or you will die.'
>
> 'You will not certainly die,' the serpent said to the woman. 'For God knows that when you eat from it your eyes will be opened, and you will be like God, knowing good and evil.'
>
> When the woman saw that the fruit of the tree was good for food and pleasing to the eye, and also desirable for gaining wisdom, she took some and ate it. She also gave some to her husband, who was with her, and he ate it. Then the eyes of both of them were opened, and they realized they were naked; so they sewed fig leaves together and made coverings for themselves.[1115]

Snake cults were well established in the prehistoric Canaanites. Prior to the emergence of YHWH, snakes and their association with wisdom, women, and fertility were venerated by the Hebrews as they continued this Canaanite tradition.[1116] Hebrew scribes reflected the Canaanite/Hebrew snake tradition and the broad prehistoric mythological association of snakes with women when they constructed the story of the temptation of Eve by a snake in the Garden of Eden.

It is a myth largely promoted by the Christian faith that the snake that tempts Eve in the Garden of Eden is the devil/Satan. Baptist authority on the Old Testament Marvin E Tate has shown how the HB/OT does not mention the snake being the devil or Satan. He shows how the snake is referred to in the Hebrew Bible/Old Testament as belonging to 'wild creatures'; that it belongs to a mortal domain and cursed is the snake above all cattle

---

[1115] Smith, D.E. (2015).
[1116] Munnich and רינוומ יאיסמ (2005), pp. 41-44.

and above all wild animals. Tate explains that the biblical reference to the snake talking to Eve merely continues the common practice of ancient mythologies at the time of having animals speaking divine messages to humans on behalf of their deities.[1117]

The origin of the Cain and Abel story

The worship and symbolism around pairs of concepts date back to prehistoric nature-based mythologies. There was a binary basis to many prehistoric mythologies. Two-headed spirits, paired characteristics, paired heroes, and divine couples protecting cities can be found in the prehistoric mythologies of the Middle East, Anatolia, Syria, and Jordan.[1118]

A range of myths about divine twin brothers is almost universally found across every prehistoric Indo-European mythology. These stories predate the Hebrew Bible by thousands of years. Their origin and mythological roles and lives vary somewhat depending on the specific prehistoric mythology. The divine twins are often differentiated from one another. One is seen as a young warrior, while the other is seen as a healer or concerned with domestic duties.

The Scythians, like many of the Indo-European mythologies of the time, saw the divine twins as companions of the mother goddess.[1119] The notion of two brothers, divine twins, one of whom sacrifices the other in order to create the world, is a common myth across many prehistoric mythologies.[1120]

The astrological sign of Gemini reflects this widely held view of spiritual twins—in Roman and Greek mythology, Gemini was the astrological embodiment of Castor and Pollux, the semi-divine twin sons of Zeus or Jupiter.

In the first century CE, the Jewish and Christian gnostic sect text Pistis Sophia was written at the same time as the Christian New Testament. It was widely supported in the Mediterranean Christian groups at the time before it was declared heresy. The Pistis Sophia tells of the birth of two Jesus children continuing the mythological tradition of the sacred twins.[1121]

[1117] Tate (1992), pp. 466-467.
[1118] Kornienko (2009), p. 93.
[1119] Cunliffe (2019) p. 282.
[1120] SOURCE: Proto-Indo-European mythology—https://en.wikipedia.org/wiki/Proto-Indo-European_mythology retrieved on 2 February 2021.
[1121] Black (2007), p. 211.

The biblical version of the Cain and Abel story

Depending on the source, the HB/OT proposes that God's creation of the universe and Adam and Eve occurred around either 3761 BCE or early to mid-5000 BCE.[1122, 1123] In the biblical Book of Genesis, Cain and Abel are the first two sons of Adam and Eve. The HB/OT states (Genesis 4:1-4):

> *Now the man knew his wife Eve, and she conceived and bore Cain, saying, 'I have produced a man with the help of the Lord.' Next, she bore his brother Abel. Now Abel was a keeper of sheep, and Cain a tiller of the ground. In the course of time Cain brought to the Lord an offering of the fruit of the ground, and Abel for his part brought of the firstlings of his flock, their fat portions.*

The myth of a pastoralist disagreeing with a farmer is a very common metaphor from Middle East cultures prior to the emergence of the Israelites. There are two Sumerian myths that involve fighting between a pastoral and an agricultural being or a god. The first involves the air god Enlil creating two cultural beings, Enten and Emesh, who have a violent struggle to determine who is the 'farmer of the gods'.

The second Sumerian myth involves two gods—Lahar, the cattle god (pastoral)—and his sister, Ashnan, the grain goddess (agricultural); they drink too much wine and quarrel. Sumerian authority Samuel Kramer believes that both Sumerian myths were influential on the Hebrew scribes in their writing of the Cain (agricultural) and Abel (pastoral) story.[1124]

According to the Bible, God accepted the offering from Abel (the shepherd) and rejected the offering from Cain (the farmer). Cain became angry and kills Abel. This may be another creative device used by the Hebrew scribes to show their god's preference for the foundational nomadic pastoral life of the early Israelites and the continuation of the metaphor of the Lord being their shepherd (Psalm 23:1-3).

The Bible does not provide the date for the birth of Cain or Abel, but biblical advocates have claimed that they were born not long after the biblical date of creation (either around 5000 BCE or 4000 BCE, depending on biblical authority).[1125] The fact

---

1122   SOURCE: https://www.jewishvirtuallibrary.org/timeline-for-the-history-of-judaism.
1123   SOURCE: https://en.wikipedia.org/wiki/Dating_creation.
1124   Kramer (2007), pp. 72-73, and p. 78.
1125   See: https://creation.com/cain-chronology (for 5000 BCE) or http://fellowshiproom.com/bible-his-tory-chart/ (for 4000 BCE) retrieved on 13 July 2021.

that the first biblical humans to be born could have spontaneously become a shepherd and a farmer is interesting in light of archaeological evidence. There is an enormous quantity of evidence in the Levant and in modern Israel highlighting the origin of farming and pastoralism. It shows how these two activities emerged in the Middle East very slowly over hundreds of thousands of years. These two economic activities—farming and pastoralism—were well and widely established prior to the biblical date of the birth of Cain and Abel.

The ancient origin of flood stories

The biblical flood story has several precedents. The Noah story is a hybridisation of flood stories from Sumerian, Babylonian, Egyptian, and Hindu mythologies. These earlier myths were linked to the frequent flooding of the Nile (Egypt), the Tigris and Euphrates River in Mesopotamia, and the Indus River in the Indus Valley.

Hindu mythology relates the story in the Shatapatha Brahmana ('Brahmana of one hundred paths'), which is dated from around 1000 BCE. It tells of the first king of India and archetypal man Manu Vaivaswata (3102 BCE), the son of the Hindu god Brahma and husband of the first woman created by Brahma Shatarupa.

Manu is warned by a fish of an impending flood in the Indus Valley—the location of the merging of five Indus River tributaries (Punjab = *panj-ab*, 'five rivers'). Manu is warned that the flood would sweep away the heavens and the Earth. He builds a wooden ark and invites seven wise sages to join him. They survive the flood and Manu becomes the first king of India. The seven sages become the seven stars of the Big Dipper.[1126]

Whilst the Indus Valley myth of the flood was influential, most researchers see the Noah story as being more closely linked to the much older Sumerian/ Mesopotamian Epics of Gilgamesh and Atrahasis (both written around 1,750 BCE to 2,500 BCE). These ancient Mesopotamian precedents told the story of how a god had sent a universal flood to destroy humanity.

The Epic of Gilgamesh was broadly popular across the Fertile Crescent. It was copied as part of cuneiform scribal education throughout the Middle East. Versions of the epic have been found in Ugarit (Iran), Nippur (Iraq), Emar (Northern Syria), and Megiddo (Northern Israel).[1127]

[1126] Bauer (2007), pp. 32-33; Leeming (1990), p. 55; Kriwaczek (2010), pp. 66-75.
[1127] Schniedewind (2019), p. 144.

All of these flood and ark stories are metaphors. In the words of Joseph Campbell:

Men mount expensive expeditions to locate the remains of Noah's ark on Mt Ararat but, of course, they never find it. They believe, however, that they have just missed out for the ark must literally have existed and its timbers must rest somewhere, still hidden from eyes. The ark, however, can be found easily and without travel by those who understand that it is a mythological vessel in an extraordinary story whose point is not historical documentation but spiritual enlightenment ....This stuttering inability to catch up with the mythological structures of the religious imagination has isolated fundamentalist believers in their fierce and often violent defenses of literalist, concrete beliefs.[1128]

Inconsistencies in the Abraham story

The biblical evidence of the existence of Abraham was finalised around 600 BCE, more than one thousand years after the date of Abraham's biblical date of birth (around 1996 BCE). There is substantial evidence that the Abraham story has strong links to Mesopotamian moon worship (see *Abraham, the Bible, and the moon*, page 118).

One of the most often cited pieces of evidence for the mythology of the Abraham story relates to the mention of camels in the Bible. Camels are mentioned more than forty times in the Bible, particularly around stories about the Jewish patriarchs—Abraham, Joseph, and Jacob. The biblical stories include descriptions of camels as domesticated animals. For example, Genesis 24:11 tells of how Abraham's servant took Abraham's fully loaded camels to drink at a well.

The domestication of camels occurred originally in Somalia, Southern Arabia, and east of the Zagros Mountains (around 3500 BCE to 3000 BCE). It is possible that domesticated camels may have made their first appearance in Mesopotamia in around 2500 BCE. Evangelical archaeologist Joseph P Free, who was an advocate and promoter of Bible-believing archaeological studies, did his utmost to seek out evidence of the existence of domesticated camels in Abraham's time. But his work was largely speculative, clearly biblically influenced, and inconclusive.[1129]

In fact, the earliest domesticated camel bones yet found in Israel or even outside the Arabian Peninsula, date to around 930 BCE. As Murdock has queried:

[1128]   Eugene Kennedy in Campbell (2001), p. xvi.
[1129]   Free (1944), pp. 192-193.

Since camels evidently were domesticated in Arabia by the twentieth century BCE … and if patriarchs had packs of these beasts of burden (Gen 24), it seems inexplicable that they were never used again after he (Abraham) allegedly arrived with them in Israel and that domesticated camel bones discovered there would date only from a thousand years later.[1130]

The anachronistic biblical mention of camels provides further strong evidence that the biblical stories of the use of camels by Abraham, Jacob, Esau, and Joseph were written well after the biblical times of these patriarchs. Edwin James, an anthropologist and authority on philosophy and religion, has openly declared that 'there is no archaeological confirmation of the alleged Abrahamic migration from Ur to Harran'.[1131]

Some Jewish authorities accept that the Abraham story is unlikely to be factual. Rabbi Jeremy Schneider states that:

As Jews, we do not look to the stories of Abraham for history; we look to these stories as the source of our religious and ethical values. We have long recognised that these stories are not historical narratives, but theological legends. The lessons that we derive from them are independent of their historicity.[1132]

Biblical Abraham may have been a black-headed Sumerian or Amorite

The origin of the Sumerians may still be open to question, but the people of Sumer referred to themselves as 'black-headed ones' or 'black-headed people'.[1133] Indeed, many scholars have concluded that the founders of the first Mesopotamian civilisation were Black Sumerians.

Mesopotamia was the biblical land of Shinar (Sumer), which sprung up around 3000 BCE. After deciphering the cuneiform script and researching ancient Mesopotamia for many years, Henry Rawlinson (1810-1895) speculated that the founders of the Sumerian civilisation were of Kushite (Cushite) origin (from the southern Egyptian Nile Valley).[1134] He made it clear that the Semitic speakers of Akkad and the non-Semitic speakers of Sumer were both black people who called themselves *sag-gig-ga* or 'black heads.'[1135]

[1130]   Murdock (2014), p. 28.
[1131]   James (1999), p. 35.
[1132]   Schneider (2018).
[1133]   SOURCE: https://en.wikipedia.org/wiki/Sumer.
[1134]   Kingdom of Kush was an ancient kingdom in Nubia at the Sudanese and southern Egyptian Nile Valley.
[1135]   SOURCE: https://atlantablackstar.com/2014/04/16/5-ancient-black-civilizations-africa/5/.

John Baldwin is quoted as stating that 'the early colonists of Babylonia were of the same race as the inhabitants of the Upper Nile.' Chandra Chakaberty, in his book, *A Study in Hindu Social Polity*, is quoted as stating that

> *based on the statuaries and steles of Babylonia, the Sumerians were of dark complexion (choc-olate colour), short stature, but of sturdy frame, oval face, stout nose, straight hair, full head; they typically resembled the Dravidians (from the Indian subcontinent), not only in cranium, but almost in all the details.*[1136]

According to the HB/OT, Abraham was a descendant of Arpachshad (a grandson of Noah). Some ancient Jewish sources, particularly the Jewish Book of Jubilees (extensive fragments of which were found in the Dead Sea Scrolls), suggest erroneously that Arpach-shad was the founder of Ur of the Chaldeans.[1137]

As with most ancient biblical figures, little if any direct archeological evidence exists concerning Abraham. Based solely on the biblical text, some scholars link Abraham and, indeed, Israel to the semi-nomadic Amorites who invaded Sumer in around 2000 BCE most likely originally coming from Arabia.[1138] The Amorites are regarded by some schol-ars as the pre-Israelite inhabitants of Canaan. These scholars believe that the patriarchs of Israel, as outlined in the Bible, would have been descended from the Amorites and that the Hebrew scribes then went to great lengths to separate their own identity from their actual ancestors, the Amorites. In the Book of Deuteronomy, the Amorites are described as the last remnants of the giants who once lived on Earth, and in the Book of Joshua, they are the enemies of the Israelites who are destroyed by General Joshua.[1139]

This raises an interesting question—if the biblical stories are true, was Abraham an Arabian Amorite or a Sumerian 'black-headed one'? Being born around one thousand years before the Chaldeans came to Sumer, he could not have been a Chaldean. Gert Muller (2019) has undertaken a lengthy analysis of this issue. He has found that the Semitic speakers, such as the Canaanites, Amorites, and Akkadians are usually shown as of African complexion, and the Assyrians are usually shown as of pale or fair complexion. Muller suggests that according to biblical evidence, Abraham was an Amorite—who are descen-dants of the Aramaeans. According to the Bible, Abraham married a Midianite woman.

[1136] SOURCE: https://atlantablackstar.com/2014/04/16/5-ancient-black-civilizations-africa/.

[1137] SOURCE: https://en.wikipedia.org/wiki/Book_of_Jubilees.

[1138] SOURCE: https://www.britannica.com/topic/Amorite.

[1139] Mark (2011B), pp. 1-2.

All these semi-nomadic groups—Aramaeans, Amorites, and Midianites—were of African complexion.[1140]

Moses birth myth

The modern scholarly consensus is that Moses is a mythical figure.[1141] There is no Egyptian source that mentions Moses or the events of Exodus, nor has any archaeological evidence been discovered in Egypt or in the Sinai Desert of the Israelites' wilderness wanderings (see *The Exodus Myth*, page 406).

It is well-established that a single author did not write the first five books of the Bible. So, it is worth pursuing the most likely origins of the Hebrew scribes' character of Moses. It is generally accepted that the story of the birth of Moses (with a biblically calculated date of around 1390 BCE) was adapted from regional mythologies and, specifically, from the birth myth of Sargon of Akkad.

A god-child being surreptitiously born and placed in a basket or hidden in the reeds or marshes had many precedents across the mythologies of India, the Middle East, and Egypt. The Hindu god Krisha (3200 BCE) was carried in a basket across a river to hide him from potential danger.[1142] The Ancient Egyptian myth of the birth of Horus (the god of kingship and the sky) has his mother Isis (goddess of kingship and protection of the kingdom) giving birth to Horus in the Nile Delta marshes.[1143] The Moses story continues this theme and appropriates the much earlier birth story of Sargon of Akkad.

Sargon of Akkad was born, according to legend, in the city of Saffron on the banks of the Euphrates, probably around 2340 BCE. His father was a nomad, his mother a temple votary or priestess who set him afloat in a basket. He was found by a peasant who adopted him and brought him up.

There are many royal inscriptions written by the Babylonian scribes in Sumerian and Akkadian attributing many great achievements to Sargon. In the words of Assyriologist and Mesopotamian authority, Gwendolyn Leick, 'Sargon's inscriptions were assiduously collected and copied, and tales of his birth and conquests circulated in oral as well as literary form.'[1144]

1140   Muller (2019), pp. 26-45.
1141   SOURCE: https://en.wikipedia.org/wiki/Moses.
1142   https://www.britannica.com/topic/Krishna-Hindu-deity retrieved on 3 September 2022.
1143   Shaw (2014), pp. 84-85.
1144   Leick (2002), p. 96.

Sargon's birth story was written 1,500 years before the Hebrew scribes wrote the Bible and some 1,000 years before the biblical birth of Moses (calculated as being around 1390 BCE). The Hebrew scribes would have been aware of the general myth and of the Sargon story when they were in exile in Babylonia (from around 590 BCE to 530 BCE). According to the legend, Sargon was the illegitimate son of a priestess. The Neo-Assyrian account of Sargon's birth and his early childhood is thus:

> *My mother was a high priestess, my father I knew not. The brothers of my father loved the hills. My city is Azupiranu, which is situated on the banks of the Euphrates. My high priestess mother conceived me, in secret she bore me. She set me in a basket of rushes, with bitumen she sealed my lid. She cast me into the river, which rose over me. The river bore me up and carried me to Akki, the drawer of water. Akki, the drawer of water, took me as his son and reared me.[1145]*

The Sargon of Akkad birth story was appropriated by the Hebrew scribes in the development of the Moses biblical story. Probably the most comprehensive analysis of the Moses story was published in 2014 by Dorothy Milne Murdock (also known by the pen name of Acharya S). She concludes:

> *The figure of Moses constitutes a mythical compilation of characters, the significant portion of which are solar heroes or sun gods, along with fertility, serpent, storm and wine deities and attributes.*

The Exodus Myth

The Exodus story and the escape from Egypt in the HB/OT is a key foundational story of the people in Israel. According to the HB/OT, the 'exodus' from Egypt involved the Israelites wandering in the wilderness for forty years, eating quail and manna and visiting forty-two different locations as they wandered. Based on the biblical evidence, if the Exodus happened, it would have happened around the mid-1300s BCE.[1146] Ron Hendel, the Professor of HB/OT and Jewish Studies at the University of California, Berkeley has described the significance of the Exodus story in the following way:

[1145]   SOURCE: https://www.ancient.eu/article/746/the-legend-of-sargon-of-akkad/.
[1146]   Cline (2014), p. 90.

The exodus from Egypt is a focal point of ancient Israelite religion. Virtually every kind of religious literature in the Hebrew Bible—prose narrative, liturgical poetry, didactic prose, and prophecy—celebrates the exodus as a foundational event. Israelite ritual, law, and ethics are often grounded in the precedent and memory of the exodus.[1147]

Despite this, there are no Egyptian texts found to date that contain any reference to the existence of large numbers of 'Hebrews' or 'Israelites' in Egypt and none contain any reference to the exodus.[1148] In the words of Kenton Sparks:

The trouble with this story, historically speaking, is that the Egyptians seem to have known nothing of these great events in which thousands of Israelite slaves were released from Egypt because of a series of natural (or supernatural) catastrophes—supposedly including even the death of every first-born Egyptian man and beast.[1149]

Nadav Na'aman has described the variety of opinions about the Exodus story in the following way:

The range of opinions stretches from those who suggest that the nucleus of the story is basically authentic and [it] reflects an important event in the early history of Israel ... on the one hand ... [to] those who entirely dismiss the historicity of the episode, emphasise that the story was written at a later time and suggest it mainly reflects the time of its composition. According to the latter view, the Exodus story is essentially a myth that was formulated in late time and does not reflect the reality of the early history of Israel. Between these two extremes lie scholars who accept the historicity of a few details in the story and suggest that the story includes a nucleus—albeit small—of historical events that took place on Egyptian soil.[1150]

Some scholars believe that the four most likely scenarios or influences that the Exodus story was based on are:

- several Israelite prisoners of war in the lost battle with the Pharaoh Merenptah (mentioned in the Merenpath Stele) who were taken to Egypt and they or their descendants were, at some later date, allowed to return to the Levant[1151]

[1147] Hendel (2001), p. 601.
[1148] Dever (2003), p. 13.
[1149] Sparks (2007), p. 588.
[1150] Na'aman (2011), pp. 39-40.
[1151] Grabbe (2018B), pp. 181-182.

- the expulsion of the Hyksos as 'invaders' by Ahmose I, King of Egypt. The Hyksos were most likely a Canaanite (Syria/Palestine), Semitic-speaking, and possibly Hebrew community occupying Northern Egypt from around 1670 BCE until their expulsion in 1523 BCE[1152]

- a myth constructed by the Hebrew scribes to build a believable story of origins based on adopting many Egyptian influences learnt through cultural interactions whilst they were a subservient, enslaved, and vassal group to the occupying Egyptians in the first millennium BCE (from around 1500 BCE to 1000 BCE) or during Egyptian cultural and ideological influence in the Levant during the writing of the HB/OT (900 BCE to 300 BCE)[1153]

- a merging of the historical memory of the collective relief and celebration of the end of the oppressive Egyptian occupation of the Southern Levant (as above), coinciding with the broader cultural collapses attributed to the sea peoples (adopting this as a story of the Israelites invading and conquering the Canaanites), moulding a sense of liberation of the emerging Israelite nation and repackaging this with the Assyrian birth myth of Sargon of Akkad (appropriating the birth story and replacing Sargon with the Egyptian name of Moses).[1154]

It is most likely that the Exodus story is a creative combination of parts of these four—an adaptation of a cultural memory instigated to put Egypt in its place and to generate a story of emerging nationhood and a unique relationship of struggle with their god.

Schmid and Schroter drew the following conclusion about the Exodus story:

It is certain that no such event ever took place precisely as it is described in the Bible. That kind of mass departure would have left behind traces that would subsequently have been found by archaeologists. But more importantly, the Israelite people had not as yet become the kind of large-scale cohesive group that could have staged a mass exodus from Egypt. Such a population only emerged gradually in the land of Canaan. The absence of any cultural differences and upheavals of civilisation in the late Bronze Age indicate that Israel essentially evolved out of Canaan through a gradual process of internal differentiation.[1155]

1152   Matyszak (2020), pp. 47-53; Van De Mieroop (2007), p. 123.
1153   See: Hendel (2001) and Ben-Dor Evian (2018).
1154   Na'aman (2011).
1155   Schmid and Schroter (2021), p. 76.

Israel Finkelstein, citing the work of David Clines and Yair Hoffman, suggests that there are metaphoric parallels between the Exodus story and the exile and post-exile stories of the Hebrew scribes:

> *Both stories tell us how the Israelites left their land for a foreign country; how after a rough period in exile the Hebrew/Judahites came back to their homeland; how on the way back the returnees had to cross a dangerous desert; how the return to the homeland evoked conflicts with the local population; how the returnees managed to settle only parts of their promised land; and how measures were taken by the leaders of the returnees to avoid assimilation between the Israelites and the population of the land.*[1156]

This recurring metaphor of ethnic struggle against circumstance and rebuilding of a new culture and a new religion harks back to the observation of Jonathan Lipnick of the Israel Institute of Biblical Studies. Lipnick sees the Israelites' emerging religion as being defined as an 'active relationship of struggle, confrontation and dialogue'.[1157] The word 'Israel' is a metaphor for the essence and nature of this relationship with God. The Exodus and Exilic stories were metaphors for this struggle.

Reimagining and repackaging of the Exodus story

Most researchers regard the Exodus story as a 'foundation myth'—a myth constructed to build a believable story of origins. When the Hebrew scribes wrote the Bible, they were largely either adapting or borrowing versions of previous mythologies or using the biblical text to convey certain values, beliefs, and behaviours. The forty-two locations identified in the exodus story fall largely into the latter category—using a mythological story to convey and reinforce the values, beliefs, and behaviours they wished to propagate and promote.

It is possible that there is a small historical fact behind the story that was elaborated by successive Hebrew scribes into an elaborate biblical tradition. Many scholars, including Jewish Archaeologist Nadav Na'aman, believe the Exodus story was written primarily to play a major role in shaping the self-portrait, emerging consciousness, and beliefs of early Israelite society.[1158]

In his investigation into the possible origin of the Israelites, Dever has suggested that, because the biblical Exodus story was written down by the Hebrew scribes at least

---

[1156] Finkelstein (2007B), pp. 52-53.
[1157] SOURCE: https://www.youtube.com/watch?v=VxxhgzDOd58 retrieved on 18 February 2021.
[1158] Na'aman (2011), p. 39.

500 years after the Exodus is supposed to have happened, its trustworthiness should be seriously questioned.[1159] Ron Hendel has a much more interesting explanation of the likely origins of the Exodus story. Accepting that it was written hundreds of years after the supposed event, he believes that it may be a metaphoric story.

Hendel believes that the Exodus story links the memories of historical oppression of the Israelites during the Egyptian occupation of the Levant, previous Levantine plagues, traces of other historical events, and persons (imagined and real) together with mythic motifs, themes, and structures. It is a conflation of history and memory to make the past truly memorable—a conjectured past, perceived, mingled, coloured, and merged with subjective concepts, hopes, and fears.[1160]

The origin of the Exodus plagues

The biblical Exodus story was most probably written while the Hebrew scribes were in exile Babylonia (from around 590 BCE to 530 BCE). The story revolves around a presumption that the Hebrews were enslaved in Egypt and that their god sent ten plagues down on their oppressors. The Exodus plagues included turning the waters of the Nile into blood, the death of fish, plagues of frogs, lice, flies, gnats, locusts, boils, and livestock (Exodus 7:17 to 11:7).

The notion that the gods could send plagues down on enemies or perpetrators of evil was a common mythological concept in Mesopotamia. For example, in the Sumerian mythological story of Inanna and Su-kale-tuda (1800 BCE), Inanna, the goddess of love, sex, and war sends three plagues of water turned to blood in the wells, storm winds, floods, and the blocking off the trade highways in her search for her rapist.[1161]

In discussing the Sumerian legacy and the significant impact of many Sumerian religious beliefs on the Hebrew scribes, Samuel Kramer describes the similarities between the Inanna story and the Exodus plague story in the following way: 'In both cases, a deity angered by the misdeeds and obduracy of an individual sends a series of plagues against an entire land and its people.'[1162]

[1159] Dever (2003), p. 8.
[1160] Hendel (2001), pp. 620-622.
[1161] Mark (2022D).
[1162] Kramer (1971), p. 296.

Origin of the forty-two exodus encampments

For centuries, archaeologists and biblical scholars have been trying to identify the forty-two locations mentioned in the Exodus story without success.[1163] Despite many archaeological expeditions, biblical scholars are still unable to find or to agree on the locations or towns mentioned in the biblical list of the 42 encampments of the wandering Israelites. The early locations, such as Pithom, have been clearly identified, but the 'Reed Sea', which others have translated as the 'Red Sea' might be the Bitter Lakes, or the shallow string of saltwater lakes on the Mediterranean coast. Similarly, Mt Sinai has potential candidates in either the Arabian Peninsula or across the Gulf of Aqaba in Midian or is a poetic reference to the Sumerian moon god Sin.

It is not surprising that the majority of the 42 Exodus stations have not been found despite many years of enthusiastic and well-funded archeologic expeditions by biblical advocates. The HB/OT is an allegorical journey and not an historical document. Its main role was to promote the values and beliefs of an emerging Judaism. The HB/OT's authors have used a variety of creative, allegorical, and often poetic literary mechanisms to convey and reinforce their religious beliefs, values, and origin. The Exodus story is full of metaphors for the emerging belief system being promoted by the Hebrew scribes.

Appendix A explains the Hebrew translations and the metaphorical meanings for the names chosen by the Hebrew scribes for the 42 exodus stations, and it further summarises the extent of knowledge of where these locations might have been. It clearly shows that a vast majority have not and probably will never be found.

It is very difficult to imagine the cultural and mythological environment in the Levant, Babylonia, and Egypt in and around 900 BCE to 300 BCE—when most of the biblical text was written and finalised. So, the Hebrew language messages conveyed through the sequence of names of the 42 stations and the logic of the sequence of messages (right-hand column of Appendix A) can only be surmised.

David Lewis-Williams has explained the key problem with this search for the 42 stations of the exodus myth:

> *Some writers naively imply that if they can establish the general historical accuracy of biblical narratives (there really was a man named Moses, the Israelites really did wander in the Sinai desert….) they will have, in some measure, vindicated the general spiritual truths of the Bible.*

[1163]   SOURCE: https://en.wikipedia.org/wiki/Stations_of_the_Exodus retrieved on 8 March 2021, and also https://www.wikiwand.com/en/Stations_of_the_Exodus retrieved on 8 March 2021.

Not so. The possible historical status of places, people and events in the Bible does not tell us anything about the spiritual implications of the narratives or of the book as a whole. Archaeological success (has) no bearing on the spiritual, or moral, meaning of the story.[1164]

JF Bierlein has described the meaning of the Exodus story in the following way:

The Exodus in Egypt is projected mythically from something that happened at a particular time into something that is continually happening, and it thus comes to exemplify the situation and experience of all men everywhere—their emergence from the bondage of obscurantism, their individual revelations … their trek through a figurative wilderness, even their death in it so that their children or children's children may eventually reach the figurative 'promised land'.[1165]

Manna and the quails

According to the HB/OT, when the Israelites wandered in the desert, they complained about their lack of food, despite the availability of milk and meat from the livestock with which they travelled and the references in the biblical text to provisions of fine flour, oil, and meat in parts of the journey's narrative.[1166] In response, God sent in flocks of quail and rained down 'manna from heaven'.[1167] It is a reasonable question to ask, 'Why manna and why quail?'

Here there is a simple metaphorical explanation. The meaning of the Hebrew word *mān* has been variously debated. Prior to the HB/OT delivering a more contemporary meaning of 'miraculous food' or 'an edible substance provided by God', the word *mān* had the meaning in Hebrew of 'a portion, dose or ration'.[1168] So the subliminal message is one of 'take only your share and stop complaining'—a key theme in this section of the biblical text.

Quail were common in the Mediterranean at the time (*Coturnix dactylisonans*). They were a frequent source of protein in ancient Egypt (they had their own hieroglyph). They are migratory birds, and this alone carried significant symbolism for the Hebrew scribes

---

[1164] Lewis-Williams (2010), p. 177.
[1165] Bierlein (1994), p. 306.
[1166] SOURCE: https://en.wikipedia.org/wiki/Manna#Origin.
[1167] SOURCE: https://www.biblegateway.com/passage/?search=Exodus+16&version=NLT.
[1168] SOURCE: https://www.hebrewversity.com/word-mannamean-hebrew/.

and the Exodus story. But the quail was recognised regionally as a symbol of a contrite spirit, communal love, and higher consciousness.[1169]

So, the manna from heaven and the flocks of quail were not actuality. They were a mechanism for the Hebrew scribes to convey and consolidate a set of values and beliefs appropriate to the religion they were promoting within their community.

The pomegranate

The tradition of glorifying or deifying natural phenomena is still reflected in some of the practices and beliefs that continue to be reflected in the HB/OT and contemporary Jewish practices and beliefs. The most significant yearly Jewish festivals have been located so that they align with the sun and moon and seasonal lambing and cropping patterns. Symptoms of this legacy can be seen in the role of the pomegranate in the Jewish canon.

The pomegranate is widely considered to have originated in the region from Iran to northern India. Over time, it made its way to the Levant, Europe, and Asia. The pomegranate's healing properties were widely recognised and symbolised in antiquity. The Zoroastrians, whose mythology was adapted by the Hebrew scribes into their biblical stories, would create a sacred ritual drink from a mixture of pomegranate, *haoma* (also regarded by the Zoroastrians as a divine plant), ephedra twigs (a Chinese herbal plant), concentrated water and goat's milk for use by their priests in a ritual involving the reciting of holy Zoroastrian texts.[1170]

Owing to its aesthetic shape, this delicious fruit features in various symbolic representations, having diverse cultural-religious significance. It has been regarded as a symbol of life, fertility, and abundance owing to its many seeds but also as a symbol of power (imperial orb), blood, and death. For instance, pomegranates symbolised fertility, beauty, and eternal life in Greek and Persian mythology.

The pomegranate was ubiquitous in emerging Judaism. A small ivory pomegranate made from the canine tooth of a hippopotamus and believed to have originally been part of a wand or sceptre has been the subject of much speculation. There appears to be no doubt that it originated from around 800 BCE and was probably from the staff of priests serving in the Temple of Jerusalem, at the time.[1171]

[1169] SOURCE: https://greekmythology.wikia.org/wiki/Quail.
[1170] Stausberg (2012), p. 607.
[1171] Cline (2009), pp. 116-118.

The pomegranate is described in the Bible as one of the seven most important agricultural products enumerated in the Torah as special to the Land of Israel, 'a land with wheat and barley, vines and fig trees, pomegranates, olive oil and honey'. (Deuteronomy 8:8)[1172] As illustrated throughout this discussion, the Hebrew scribes chose these seven products for their deeper cultural significance. In Hebrew, each corresponds to one of the seven *sefirot* (divine emotive attributes) and they are currently eaten on Jewish holy days followed by a special blessing being recited after eating them:

- wheat = kindness
- barley = severity
- grapes = harmony
- figs = perseverance
- pomegranates = humility
- olives = foundation
- dates = royalty.[1173]

One of the 42 stations that the HB/OT identifies as a waystation for the wandering Israelites during the Exodus was Rimmon-Perez. In Hebrew, this means 'pomegranate of the breach'. Jewish tradition teaches that the pomegranate symbolises righteousness and abundance.[1174] This is because it contains 613 seeds, which they claim corresponds with the 613 *mitzvot* (commandments) in the Torah (the first five books/Pentateuch/five books of Moses). This is a myth. Research has shown that the number of seeds in a pomegranate can vary from 200 to 1,400.[1175]

The HB/OT often mentions pomegranates. Today, the hems of Jewish high priest's sacred outer garments which are heavily influenced by the biblical Exodus myth are decorated with a stylised form of this fruit. In many ways, the elevation of the pomegranate to this high level of religious symbolism simply reflects the prehistoric glorification and deification of nature that pre-existed the emergence of the Hebrew scribes. It is sustained in a metaphoric sense in much of their biblical writings.

[1172]   SOURCE: https://www.alimentarium.org/en/knowledge/pomegranate-miracle-fruit.

[1173]   SOURCE: https://www.chabad.org/library/article_cdo/aid/3567733/jewish/What-Is-So-Special-About-the-7-Species-of-Fruit-With-Which-Israel-Was-Blessed.htm.

[1174]   SOURCE: https://jewishaction.com/religion/jewish-law/whats_the_truth_about_pomegranate_seeds / retrieved on 15 March 2021.

[1175]   https://www.aquaphoenix.com/misc/pomegranate/ retrieved on 15 March 2021.

Biblical advocates' defence of the Exodus story

Archaeology by biblical advocates has tended to focus on archaeological excavations and discoveries in modern Israel, Jordan, Lebanon, Syria and Egypt—locations related to selected stories in the HB/OT. Archaeology owes a great debt to biblical archaeologists. Despite their biblical motivation and their preoccupation with investigating locations mentioned in the Bible, they have been at the forefront of innovations in the methods, techniques, and operations of archaeology.[1176]

Vetus Testamentum is a quarterly journal focusing entirely on all aspects of Old Testament study. It includes articles on history, literature, religion and theology, text, versions, language, and the influence of the Old Testament on archaeology and the study of the Ancient Middle East. Not surprisingly, the articles published often focus entirely on the content of the HB/OT and differences of opinion on what happened according to the biblical account. This often occurs without reference to sources outside of the Bible itself.

For example, there have been many articles debating the actual number of Israelites who, according to the Bible, escaped from Egypt during the Exodus story.[1177] These are scholarly papers largely preoccupied with differences of opinion about the meaning of the words used by the Hebrew scribes and how these should be interpreted numerically. Opinions vary from a total number in excess of 600,000 to fewer than 20,000 Israelites participating in the Exodus. In very few of these articles is the issue of the veracity of the event itself questioned—despite most independent scholars confirming that the Exodus story is largely a cultural foundation myth!

Journals such as *Vetus Testamentum* are well-meaning within the context of Bible-only scholarship. In the worst cases, biblical archaeology reflects the 'blind faith' movement—Bible-only research by biblical believers. There is a taken-for-granted belief in the veracity of the Bible. Work by biblical archaeologist James K Hoffmeier from Trinity Evangelical Divinity School and amateur biblical advocate Larry D Bruce from the Baptist College of Florida exemplify this group of biblical advocates. Both Hoffmeier and Bruce offer circumstantial and biblically influenced support for the veracity of the Exodus.

Hoffmeier has published a comprehensive defence of the veracity of the biblical Exodus story in his book *Israel in Egypt*: *The Evidence for the Authenticity of the Exodus Tradition*.[1178] Both Hoffmeier and Bruce start with the assumption that the biblical Exodus

---

[1176]   See: Cline (2009) for an excellent summary of the history of Biblical Archaeology.
[1177]   See for example: Humphreys (1998); Waite (2010); Kislev (2013).
[1178]   Hoffmeier (1996).

story is an historical fact. Hoffmeier relies on indirect and circumstantial evidence including the frequency of Egyptian 'loan words' in the Bible to justify that the Israelites must have been in Egypt. Otherwise, how could they have this many Egyptian loan words in the Bible or demonstrate such a knowledge of Egyptian culture as illustrated in the Exodus story?

Advocates undervaluing the interdependence of the Levant and Egypt

Hoffmeier appears to undervalue three significant objective historical facts. Firstly, the Levant was occupied, and the Canaanites (including the emerging Israelites) were vassal states of Egypt from around 1500 BCE to 1000 BCE. They had at least four hundred years to adopt parts of Egyptian terminology and learn Egyptian cultural attributes. Contrary to Hoffmeier's view, biblical expert Thomas Staubli has presented extensive evidence of the complex interdependence of the Levant and Northern Egypt from the fourth millennium BCE onwards. Staubli outlines evidence of the impact of the long-lasting migration and cross-cultural travel during the first millennium BCE when the Bible was being written. He documents many examples where the Hebrew scribes borrowed their stories from pre-existing ancient Egyptian myths and/or the key characteristics of Canaanite-Egypt relations.[1179] By way of example, he outlines how the biblical story of Abraham travelling to Egypt contains many of the characteristics of the hundreds of years of Levant and Egypt relations, including:

> … refuge in hard times, human trafficking, trade, Egyptian border control, diplomatic relations between Canaanites and Egyptians, and stock breeding of the Canaanites in the eastern delta.[1180]

The Hyksos (also called the 'shepherd kings') who were most likely Canaanites (Syria/Palestine) invaded and occupied parts of Egypt from 1670 BCE until their expulsion back to the Levant by the Egyptian King Kamose in 1523 BCE.[1181] The Egyptians returned to occupy the Southern Levant between 612 BCE and 604 BCE after the Babylonians and the Medians defeated the Assyrians. The Egyptians were then removed from the Southern Levant when defeated by the Babylonians in 604 BCE.[1182]

[1179]   Staubli (2016).
[1180]   Staubli (2016), p. 63.
[1181]   Matyszak (2020), pp. 47-53; Van De Mieroop (2007), p. 123.
[1182]   Fiaccavento (2014), p. 235.

The significant relationship between the Levant and Egypt is reflected in the extent to which the Hebrew scribes wrote Egypt into their stories. Many of the Old Testament and New Testament stories involve Egypt—the Exodus, pharaohs being punished by God for keeping the Hebrews in bondage, Abraham's journey to Egypt, Joseph being enslaved in Egypt and rising to become second in charge to the pharaoh, and as an escape location for Jesus, Mary, and Joseph. The historically long relationship was integral to understanding how Egypt was embedded into the HB/OT.

The Egyptian influence was not only in the Levant. There is substantial evidence of Egyptian influence on the Persian Achaemenid Empire during the time that the Persians conquered and occupied the Levant and Egypt (525 BCE to 332 BCE).[1183] This corresponds with the time that most of the biblical text of today was written and finalised.

Advocates undervaluing the common use of 'loan words' in the Bible

The second fact that Hoffmeier undervalues is the fact that the Hebrew scribes spent time under the control of several different empires (either as a vassal state or in exile). This included being under the influence and control of Assyrians, Egyptians, Babylonians, Persians, and Greeks. The Hebrew scribes were significantly influenced by the culture, mythologies, and language of neighbouring regions (Sumer, Mesopotamia, Iranian Plateau, Indus Valley). As a result, the HB/OT contains loan words from many other cultures. This includes loan words in the Bible from different ancient Hebrew Semitic dialects (Canaanite, Phoenician, Aramaic, Akkadian) and from non-Semitic dialects (Egyptian, Greek, Hittite/Luvian, Hurrian, Old Iranian, Persian, Sumerian via Akkadian).

Advocates undervaluing the extent of 'migratory words' in the Bible

The third oversight in Hoffmeier's work relates to the common occurrence of 'migratory words' across the cultures of the ancient Middle East. These are words that travel together with the technological, mythological, or cultural innovations to which they relate. The Hebrew scribes were writing at a time of extensive trade networks and great economic, cultural, mythological, and social innovation. It was a time of frequent territorial advancement and decline and increasing interchange through trade and technological innovation. Assyriologist Gonzalo Rubio cites the word for wine as an example of a typical

---

[1183]   Algarvio (2021).

migratory word in the ancient Middle East at the time—*wayn* in Semitic and Arabic; *yayin* in Hebrew; *wns* in Egyptian; *(w)oinos* in Greek; *wiyana* in Hittite; *ywino* in ancient Georgian.[1184]

The evidence suggests that specific loan and migratory words in the Bible tended to follow the patterns of the Hebrew's original location, their role in a vassal state under Egyptian control (1500 BCE to 1000 BCE), their exile locations, the political history, their influences during the times that the Levant was a major trading partner of the Egyptians (1100 BCE to 300 BCE), and when and where the specific biblical texts were written and the locations being promoted in the biblical text.[1185] Hoffmeier omits discussion of the extensive evidence of the influence of 'loan' words from the Zoroastrian, Sumerian, Babylonian, Hindu, Persian, and Canaanite mythologies (as well as Egyptian) on the various stories adapted into the HB/OT. For instance, Llewellyn-Jones cites the frequency of use of the Persian word *data*, which meant 'divine commandment', in the biblical Books of Esther, Daniel, and Ezra as confirmation that those biblical Books were written during the Jewish exile in the Persian period.[1186]

The extent of Hoffmeier's belief in the singularity of the HB/OT can be best understood in a 2020 podcast of an interview Hoffmeier gave with fellow biblical advocate Dr Dru Johnson. Hoffmeier is asked why the Bible is written in the language of the Hebrews escaping Egypt, which contains a mixture of Egyptian and Hebrew phrases, rather than only in the Hebrew language of God's chosen people. Hoffmeier explains that this is because God communicates with his people in the language of their culture. An alternative and more objective view would be that the text attributed to God was actually written in this language by the Egyptian-influenced Hebrew scribes themselves.[1187]

Other biblical advocates' defence of the Exodus and the Bible

Biblical researcher Larry D. Bruce is more open about his belief in the historical accuracy of the Bible and, specifically, the Exodus story. He argues that the Bible's accounts of the Exodus, the wanderings in the desert, and the conquest of Canaan are historically accurate, largely because they are in the Bible. Bruce advocates that archaeologists who

---

[1184]   Rubio (1999), p. 8.
[1185]   Ben-Dor Evian (2017).
[1186]   Llewellyn-Jones (2022), p. 127.
[1187]   Listen, for instance to https://hebraicthought.org/podcast/historical-exodus-egyptology-james-hoffmeier/ (29:00 to 31:42) retrieved on 14 December 2021.

are outside of the evangelical community are mistaken for not including 'the qualifying testimony of the biblical narrative' in their accumulation of evidence.[1188]

Like Hoffmeier and Bruce, biblical advocate Gerard Gertoux is a prolific writer and staunch advocate of the historical veracity of the Bible. Gertoux can be quite extreme in his attacks on scientists who are less inclined to treat the Bible as an accurate historical document, exemplified by the following:

> One must be aware that some scholarly attacks to discredit the authenticity of the Old Testament, made by some academics (for most Egyptologists) as a means to eradicate religious obscurantism, are in fact the result of an ideological propaganda initiated by the Nazi Party in 1933 to impose a vision of a world governed solely by eugenics (The Brave New World).[1189]

Biblical archaeologists tend to have an advocacy agenda in promoting and proving the authenticity and historical accuracy of the Bible and the Exodus as the Israelite foundation myth. Where biblical archaeologists rely on or reference the Bible, they are most often choosing archaeology that is interpreted within their own personal investment and beliefs.

Shirly Ben-Dor Evian, archaeologist at the Israel Museum in Jerusalem, describes the approach by biblical advocates as 'biblical Egyptology'. She describes biblical Egyptology as a field of study where the scholarship is based on a preconceived quest to prove the authenticity of the HB/OT.[1190]

Other biblical advocates appear to be more objective and systematic in their support of a belief in the historical uniqueness of the Bible. Evangelical biblical researcher Marc Madrigal, for instance, undertakes an extensive analysis of the two thousand years of similar but prior mythological stories to those found in the HB/OT. His focus, however, is on demonstrating the subtle differences rather than the obvious similarities between earlier Hittite, Mesopotamian, and Sumerian mythologies and those retold in slightly different forms in the HB/OT.[1191]

Other biblical advocates simply take the Bible's stories for granted. By way of example, renowned Jewish art historian Ernst Gombrich, who later converted to Protestantism, in

---

[1188] Bruce (2019), pp. 463-465, and p. 493.
[1189] Gerard Gertoux (undated), *Dating the Birth of Israel: ca 1500 or 1200 BCE?,* https://www.academia. edu/3807111/Dating_the_Birth_of_Israel_ca_1500_or_1200_BCE_ retrieved on 1 June 2022.
[1190] Ben-Dor Evian (2018), p. 1.
[1191] See The Bible in the Istanbul Archaeology Museum / İstanbul Arkeoloji Müzesinde Kitab-ı Mukaddes | Marc Madrigal—Academia.edu retrieved on 7 June 2022.

his otherwise exceptionally good book, *A Little History of the World* retells unquestionably the biblical stories in a chapter entitled 'The One and Only God'.[1192]

Lester Grabbe, a leading scholar of the HB/OT and early Judaism, describes efforts by conservative evangelicals and believers to promote the veracity of the Bible as 'special pleading'![1193] Mythologist Joseph Campbell has described the efforts of advocates of the factual or historical veracity of the Bible as 'misinterpreting spiritual metaphors as historical facts'.[1194]

The four main functions of the Exodus story

Excluding the biblical myth of the escape from Egypt, the Exodus story is most probably a mixture of four concepts explicitly or implicitly embedded in the story through multiple revisions over hundreds of years by the Hebrew scribes. These are:

- the birth of a nation
- a reimagining and repackaging of a significant past event
- a metaphor for the liberation from being a vassal state under the domination of Egypt in the Levant
- an historical metaphor for a spiritual journey of discovery fundamental to the emerging character and beliefs of Judaism.

The mountain as a symbol of access to the divine

The idea that the world was an island with a holy mountain in the middle where the gods lived above is a common theme across many cultures.[1195]

In shamanism, the top of a mountain is regarded as the place for easiest access to the 'otherworld'—what contemporary believers call 'heaven'. The early creation stories from the Eastern Steppe (Mongolia/Siberia) and from Buddhism involve the creator sitting on top of a golden mountain in the middle of the sky prior to creating the cosmos. In Buddhism, this mountain, central to creation, is called Sumeru; in Mongolian, it is referred to as either Sumer or Sumeru.[1196] Bellah explains how a shamanic pattern of communing

---

[1192]   Gombrich (2008), pp. 24-28.
[1193]   Grabbe (2018B), p. 182.
[1194]   Eugene Kennedy in Campbell (2001), p. xvi.
[1195]   Jacquet (2021), p. 200.
[1196]   Ashe (2018), p. 48.

with a powerful spiritual being often involved a shamanic person undergoing 'austerities in some remote spot, often a mountain top, in an effort to find … a guardian spirit … though in other instances the spirit take the initiative in "calling" the individual.'[1197]

The Canaanite/Ugaritic/Semitic king of the gods and universal god of life and fertility, Baal, lived on Mount Zaphon. According to Canaanite mythology, Baal's throne at the top of the mountain was challenged by the astral god identified with the planet Venus, Athtar.[1198]

The Amorites, who were in control of Babylon under their King Hammurabi (1792 BCE to 1750 BCE), believed in two supreme deities—Amurru, who was regarded as the Lord of the Mountains, and his wife, Belit-Seri, who was regarded as the Lady of the Desert.[1199]

In Egyptian mythology, prior to creation, there was a primordial hill, known as the *ben-ben*, upon which stood the great god Atum/Ptah who became bored and so created the world. It is highly likely that the first Egyptian pyramid (the Step Pyramid of Djoser, constructed 2630 BCE–2611 BCE) was designed to symbolise the belief that god the creator stood on this high mound of earth while creating the world.[1200] In the words of Othmar Keel:

> *Almost all the great Egyptian sanctuaries claimed to house within their courts the primeval hill, the 'glorious hill of the primordial beginnings' which had first emerged from the floods of Chaos.[1201]*

The word *pyramid* was a Greek term. The Egyptian word for their pyramids was *mer*, which translates as the 'site of ascension'. The pyramids were regarded by the Egyptians as a stairway to heaven.[1202] To the ancient Greeks, the twelve gods of Olympus, led by the god of the sky and their chief god, Zeus, lived on top of Mount Olympus.

The Hebrew scribes continued the ancient link between God and mountains in the story of Moses receiving the Commandments from their God atop Mt Sinai (Exodus 19-24). The scribes also carried this link of mountains to the divine in Psalm 2:4–6 where they claim that:

[1197] Bellah (2011), p. 164.
[1198] Tate (1992), p. 469.
[1199] Mark (2011B).
[1200] Holland (2010), p. 5.
[1201] Keel (1997), p. 113.
[1202] Luberto (2007), p. 106.

The One enthroned in heaven laughs; the Lord scoffs at them. He rebukes them in his anger and terrifies them in his wrath, saying 'I have installed my king on Zion, my holy mountain.

Psalm 48:1–2 states:

Great is the Lord, and most worthy of praise, in the city of our God, his holy mountain. Beautiful in its loftiness, the joy of the whole earth, like the heights of Zaphon is Mount Zion, the city of the Great King.

These Psalms (and other biblical mentions in 2 Samuel 5:7, 1 Chronicles 11:5; 1 Kings 8:1, 2 Chronicles 5:2) established the significance of Mount Zion, an otherwise nondescript hill. Biblically, it is described as being in three different locations in Jerusalem. It has become a holy mountain metaphor for the entire land of Israel.

As Michael Moore has pointed out, 'the association of height with the sacred has also motivated generation after generation of worshippers to imitate nature by raising very high structures'.[1203]

Although largely associated exclusively with Egypt, the pyramid shape was first used in ancient Mesopotamia in the mud-brick structures known as ziggurats, and continued to be used by the Greeks and Romans. Pyramids are also found south of Egypt in the Nubian kingdom of Meroe, in the cities of the Maya throughout Central and South America, and, in a variation on the form, in China.[1204]

The belief that a mountain brought believers closer to God literally or metaphorically lies behind the fact that the majority of Christian churches have been built on high ground.[1205]

Samuel's appropriation of the Sumerian and Babylonian 'ways of the king'

Scholars accept that the biblical Books of Samuel were written by the Hebrew scribes while they were in exile in Babylon around 550 BCE.[1206] In fact, the explanation of the 'ways of the king' in First Samuel (1 Samuel 8) is almost a word-for-word appropriation of the ways of the Mesopotamian, Sumerian, and Babylonian kings commencing from around

---

[1203]   Moore (1982), p. 45.
[1204]   Mark (2009B).
[1205]   SOURCE: https://aleteia.org/2017/08/07/why-are-so-many-churches-built-on-mountains/ retrieved on 16 April 2023.
[1206]   SOURCE: https://www.britannica.com/topic/Books-of-Samuel retrieved on 14 December 2020.

5000 BCE.[1207] This was some four and a half thousand years prior to the Hebrew scribes being in Babylon and seeing and experiencing this form of governance in action.[1208]

The Hebrew scribes were essentially taking traditional Babylonian governance practices and adapting them into their own material, to serve their theological perspective.

The origin of the last rites

Both Judaism and Christianity have a religious process accorded to the dead. In both cases, this is believed to prepare the person for their life after death. It is commonly referred to as the *last rites*. In the Jewish case, it involves the reciting of the Psalms from the HB/OT. In the Christian case, the following prayer is read by a priest: 'Through this holy anointing may the Lord in his love and mercy help you with the grace of the Holy Spirit. May the Lord who frees you from sin save you and raise you up.'

This is a practice that has been adapted from the Egyptians, the Egyptian Book of the Dead (circa 1550 BCE), and the ancient Egyptian personalised shamanic prayer for each of the deceased (often written as a spell by Egyptian scribes). Egyptologist EA Wallis Budge has documented several examples of this practice each of which has an uncanny likeness to that adopted much later by the Jewish and Christian scribes. For the Egyptian deceased to receive the full benefits of their text or spell, it had to be read by a person who was ceremonially pure and who had not eaten fish or meat and had not consorted with women.[1209] The texts were meant to convey the deceased person to the great and supreme power that the Egyptians believed had created the Earth, the heavens, the sea, the sky, all humans, animals, birds, and everything that has and will ever be. Prehistoric Egyptian funerary text examples include:

- He weigheth words, and, behold, God hearkeneth unto the words
- God hath called Teta in his name
- Thou hast received the form of God, thou hast become great herewith before the gods.[1210]

The origin of tithing

In the ancient Middle East lie the origins of a sacral offering, or payment of a tenth part of stated goods or property to honour a king or a deity. Often given to the king or to the

---

[1207] Holy Bible English Standard Version (2002), p. 278.
[1208] Pollock (1999).
[1209] Wallis Budge (2010), pp. 13 and
[1210] Wallis Budge (1967), pp. lxxxiii to lxxxiv.

royal temple, the 'tenth' was usually approximate, not exact. The practice is known from Mesopotamia, Syria-Palestine, Greece, and as far to the west as the Phoenician city of Carthage. Tithing also continued in Christian Europe as a church tithe and as a tax upon Jewish landholdings formerly owned by Christians (or claimed to have been so).[1211]

A tributary economy is characterised by a political elite extracting goods and labour from primary producers. The elite were urban and depended on the primary producers of the hinterland to grow food and make craft products (who had their own means of doing so), with some of the surplus being collected as tribute.[1212]

This practice of rendering tithes of property for sacral purposes was common all over the ancient Middle East well prior to the emergence of the Hebrew scribes. There is well-documented and firsthand evidence concerning tithes coming mainly from Mesopotamia, although there is no doubt that the practice is much older. The tithe was a royal tax on one hand and a sacred donation on the other.

The oldest examples of Ancient Mesopotamia writings are documents concerned with goods and trade and include records of taxes, tithes, and tributes. The earliest tax records known were from the ancient Mesopotamian city-state of Lagash, where tax rates were typically low, but in times of crisis or wars, the rate would be 10% of all goods. The taxes were often paid with a portion of the crop yield or some other food. These taxes were used to supply the defence of the city-state and for trade with other city-states.[1213]

Tithing is mentioned as a sanctioned and sacred practice several times in the HB/OT. In Genesis 14:20, Abraham gives a tithe to Melchizedek, the king-priest of Shalem, and in Genesis 28:22, Jacob vows to pay a tithe at Beth-El, the 'royal chapel' of the Northern Kingdom.[1214]

The notion that all good things come from the divine and that a proportion should be offered back has been incorporated into the practices and beliefs of many religions.

The ancient Greek Thargelia festival, one of the primary rites dedicated to Apollo at Athens, was a vegetation ritual named after the first bread baked from the newly harvested wheat. Similarly, in modern Sri Lanka at harvest time, the Buddha is ceremonially

---

[1211] https://www.encyclopedia.com/environment/encyclopedias-almanacs-transcripts-and-maps/tithes retrieved on 10 December 2020.

[1212] Source: https://database.ours.foundation/LQ2FFQ5/ retrieved on 21 July 2023.

[1213] SOURCE: https://taxfitness.com.au/Blog/earliest-taxes-ancient-mesopotamia-6000-bc retrieved on 10 December 2020.

[1214] SOURCE: https://www.encyclopedia.com/philosophy-and-religion/bible/bible-general/tithes retrieved on 10 December 2020.

offered a large bowl of milk and rice, while in Shintō, the first rice sheaves of the harvest are presented as offerings (*shinsen*) to the *kami* (god or sacred power) during agricultural and other festivals.

In Judaism, the first-fruits ceremony is known as Shavuot. The belief is that fruit trees live their own life and are to remain untrimmed for three years after they are planted. But even then, their fruits cannot be enjoyed until God is given his share.[1215]

The notion of tithing that the Hebrew scribes adapted into the HB/OT has now become a major source of income for Christian churches and, specifically and overwhelmingly, the 'prosperity theology' churches. In the words of Shayne Lee, sociologist and expert in contemporary American religion and culture:

> *Prosperity theology emphasises that God will open the windows of heaven and pour out blessings to the faithful Christian who consistently gives money to his local church. This pervasive ideology helps churches secure more resources while allowing pastors to enjoy large salaries and unprecedented wealth.*[1216]

The origin of salvation faiths

Prehistoric mythologies transitioned from totemism, shamanism, and animism through a deification of natural and planetary phenomena to a belief in an anthropomorphic male god, an afterlife, the netherworld, and a battle between good and evil. Jewish biblical mythology tends not to be about a passive relationship of blind obedience to a god but about an 'active relationship of struggle, confrontation, and dialogue'.[1217]

Judaism and Christianity both promote the idea of salvation, redemption, and a better experience in the afterlife, provided a person lives a holy life and honours God's commands. This idea of salvation or redemption in the afterlife is a concept borrowed from mythologies that predated the Jewish Bible.

The Sumerians, some three thousand years before the Israelites, saw the afterlife as largely a dismal, wretched reflection of life on Earth. They saw private devotion and personal piety as important but, they strongly believed that ceremony, rite, and ritual played the most important role in securing a better afterlife.[1218]

[1215] https://www.britannica.com/topic/first-fruits-ceremony retrieved on 22 June 2021.
[1216] Lee (2007), p. 231.
[1217] SOURCE: https://www.youtube.com/watch?v=VxxhgzDOd58 retrieved on 18 February 2021.
[1218] Kramer (1971), p. 135.

The ancient Egyptians, who predate the Hebrew scribes by some two thousand years and whose mythology significantly influenced the Hebrew scribes, had a concept of salvation. The Ancient Egyptians' concept of salvation, however, was salvation from death and a resultant journey to immortality that would fulfil all their dreams of eternal life in the company of their gods.[1219]

It was the Zoroastrians who introduced the notion of salvation most closely related to the HB/OT. The Zoroastrians saw salvation as a key component of the netherworld and of a potentially blissful afterlife. Mary Boyce, a leading authority on Zoroastrianism, has proposed that the concept of salvation first began with the Zoroastrians. It most likely originated with peaceful prehistoric Iranian Steppe communities wanting confidence that there would be relief from the marauding mercenary Steppe warriors of their time—most likely the warrior Scythians. Here was:

> ... *the birth of salvation faiths, with hopes of peace and justice shifting from this world to the next. And Zoroastrianism is in fact the oldest of such faiths, and has been the prototype for many others.*[1220]

It is not a coincidence that the translation into the English word 'salvation' in modern English versions of the Hebrew Bible/Old Testament is often an approximation to more a meaningful Hebrew word that better reflects the Zoroastrian origin of the idea. For example, the Ancient Hebrew word for 'save' in Deuteronomy 20:4 means 'to rescue' and the Ancient Hebrew verb *y-sh-ah* (in Judges 3:9) means 'relief' in the sense of being rescued from an enemy, a trouble, or an illness.[1221]

Boyce summarises the significant influence of Zoroastrianism's prophet Zoroaster on the shaping of Hebrew and Christian beliefs in salvation in the following way:

> *Zoroaster was thus the first to teach the doctrines of an individual judgement, Heaven and Hell, the future resurrection of the body, the general last judgement and life everlasting for the reunited soul and body.*[1222]

[1219] Assmann (2005), p. 389.
[1220] Boyce (2001), pp. xiv-xv.
[1221] SOURCE: https://www.ancient-hebrew.org/definition/salvation retrieved on 24 March 2021.
[1222] Boyce (2001), p. 29.

Zoroastrianism was the first mythology to explain that this salvation will come from a miraculous virgin birth/conception of a righteous messianic male saviour born from the seed of the prophet but to human parents.[1223]

The origin of prosperity theology

The word 'prosperity' can have a variety of meanings depending on the context. In the current context, it is best defined as 'the pursuit of growth, success, wellbeing, abundance, or benefits'.[1224] Contemporary prosperity theology emerged initially from the Pentecostal Church and is currently booming in many parts of the developed world. For prosperity theologians, it is basically a belief that poverty is the curse of the devil and that financial blessings, health, and wellbeing, are the will of God. According to prosperity theology, faith and donations to religious causes will increase one's health, wealth, and prosperity.[1225]

Prosperity theology is a relatively recent phenomenon, having emerged in the USA in the 1960s.[1226] Despite its relative recency, it is built on traditions of religious practice that go back literally thousands of years. The notion that God would reward the devout with prosperity and good health can be traced back to the Sumerians from around 3500 BCE. In an ancient Sumerian religious poem, *Ludlul*, the person liberated from his misfortunes by god (Marduk) travels on a pious and devout journey through many temple gates, after each of which he receives favours from god. He travels through:

- the Gate of Prosperity—'prosperity was given to me'
- the Gate of the Guardian Spirit—'a guardian spirit drew nigh to me'
- the Gate of Wellbeing—'I found wellbeing'
- the Gate of Life—'I was granted life.'[1227]

The Sumerians had two major motivations in life—a love of life and material prosperity and wellbeing:

The Sumerians prized highly wealth and possessions, rich harvests, well-stocked granaries, folds and stalls filled with cattle large and small, successful hunting on the plains and good

---

[1223]   Boyce (2001), p. 42.
[1224]   SOURCE: https://www.thesaurus.com/browse/prosperity retrieved on 22 June 2021.
[1225]   Lee (2007), p. 230.
[1226]   Lee (2007), p. 227-228.
[1227]   Bottero (2004), pp. 118-119.

fishing in the sea ... and Sumerian proverbs contain many a jibe at the weakness, ineffectualness, and wretchedness of the poor.[1228]

The Babylonian Akitu festival, which was held at the Northern Hemisphere spring equinox (predating the Jewish Passover and the Christian Easter celebrations by hundreds of years), was a celebration of the gods getting together in a Chamber of Destinies and considering the fate of society and deliver abundance and prosperity.[1229]

The Mahābhārata, which is the ancient Sanskrit philosophical and devotional poem written around the same time as the HB/OT, also has one of the four goals of life as 'Artha'. This translates as 'prosperity and economic values'. The Egyptian wisdom literature (2300 BCE onwards) includes an ethical principle referred to as 'Maat'. Maat was the Egyptian goddess who personified truth and justice. The ancient Egyptians believed that a person who reflects Maat in their behaviours and actions would reach prosperity.[1230]

The modern prosperity evangelist reflects this tradition that goes back as far as the first spiritual mediators of the Stone Age, the Siberian shamans. The modern prosperity theologian's practice reflects:

- a belief that a deity or deities control everything, which originated with totemism
- the notion of god-granted prosperity comes from the Sumerians
- prosperity religion's reliance on hymns and singing accompanied by music from a wide range of instruments originated with the Sumerians (who played lyres, harps, flutes, horns, trumpets, drums, tambourines, bells and rattles)[1231]
- affirmations about praise to the gods, personal healing, personal destinies, and avoidance of hell originated with the Mesopotamians (from around 3500 BCE).[1232]

French archaeologist and recognised authority on the prehistory of the Levant and Middle East Jaques Cauvin believes that the human search for prosperity is a fundamental human desire. He believes that the somewhat unnecessary prehistoric transition from the 'economy of abundance' attributable to the hunter-gatherer lifestyle to the overproduction

---

[1228]   Kramer (1971), p. 263.
[1229]   James (1999), p. 144.
[1230]   Adams (2020), pp. 313-314.
[1231]   Bottero (2004), p. 131 and pp. 139-145.
[1232]   Sandars (1971), pp. 23-24.

created through agriculture was, in part, driven by this human desire for prosperity. To Cauvin, the desire for prosperity was a prerequisite cultural condition and a symbol of a 'collective readiness' behind the transformation and preparation for sedentarism and agriculture. He states that:

> *The importance of social norms of prosperity, where collective psychology is closely involved and which can vary in space and time for reasons that are not ecological, seems very much under-valued by current theories of the origins of agriculture.*[1233]

This transformation occurred in or around the tenth millennium BCE. It was not based on a dynamic impulse for change, but a collective cultural belief about a 'new way of life'. Cauvin's hypothesis is supported by evidence that the emergence of the first hut compounds and the formation of villages in the Middle East from around 9000 BCE had already occurred well before the emergence of agriculture.[1234]

The innate human desire for prosperity is the fundamental premise of contemporary prosperity theologians. They have contemporised ancient mythological practices and human desires through the building of megachurches, creating a collectively celebrated but dated mythology, leveraging the contemporary music industry and harnessing notions of celebrity to create (in the words of Kate Bowler and Wen Reagan):

> *a theological outlook (overlapping) with the music industry ... a blessed life ... well-marketed, outcome oriented with active participation and requiring the constant hard work of self-promotion before audiences (that are) both worldly and divine.*[1235]

Although clearly and simply a modern adaptation of ancient mythological ceremonies:

> *It is ironic that Pentecostalism, the branch of Christendom that once harboured ardent anti-secular sentiment, [has] transformed into a new Pentecostal movement with the strongest embrace of technology, secularism, capitalism and popular culture.*[1236]

[1233] Cauvin (2003), pp. 65-66.
[1234] Flannery (1973), p. 274 and p. 307.
[1235] Bowler and Reagan (2014), p. 211.
[1236] Lee (2007), p. 235.

The origin of a religious creed

Zoroastrianism's Avesta predates Christianity as an exemplar of the very first creedal religion—a religion whose basic beliefs are defined in a set statement of faith.[1237] An excerpt from the Zoroastrian creed states:

> I declare myself a Mazda-worshipper, a supporter of Zarathustra, hostile to the Daevas, fond of Ahura's teaching, a praiser of the Amesha Spentas, a worshipper of the Amesha Spentas. I ascribe all good to Ahuramazda, 'and all the best,' Asha-endowed, splendid, xwarena-endowed, whose is the cow, whose is Asha, whose is the light, 'may whose blissful areas be filled with light'.

The first Christian creed was the Nicene Creed (325 CE—some two thousand years after Zoroastrianism). The Nicene Creed is the basis of the contemporary Catholic religion's creed/prayer:

> I believe in one Lord Jesus Christ, the Only Begotten Son of God, I believe in the Holy Spirit, the Lord, the giver of life, who proceeds from the Father and the Son, I believe in one, holy, catholic and apostolic Church. I confess one Baptism for the forgiveness of sins.

The Nicene Creed and the Catholic prayer the 'Our Father' was heavily influenced by, if not adapted from, the Zoroastrian creed.[1238]

The origin of religious vestments

The very first individuals to have claimed an ability to mediate on behalf of humans with the divine were the shamans who practiced in many prehistoric communities across the Middle East, Central Asia, and the Eurasian Steppe.

Benz and Bauer have highlighted the fact that a shaman who performed shamanic rituals for a wider public in prehistoric times would usually wear special dresses and special paraphernalia.[1239] Here, in the costume and in the belief in a costumed mediating role with the higher spirits, was the prototype and embryonic form of biblical prophets and today's Hindu monastic or holy men, modern-day clergy, clerics, popes, priests, pastors, rabbis, imams, and gurus. Shamanic clothing was the origin of the special clothing that

---

[1237]   Bauer (2007), p. 765.

[1238]   https://www.livius.org/sources/content/avesta/avesta-the-zoroastrian-creed/ retrieved on 17 February 2022.

[1239]   Benz and Bauer (2015).

the spiritual intermediary needed to wear to differentiate themselves from the general populous (see Figure 44).

The Eurasian Steppe Scythians had many priests and soothsayers who used a variety of techniques for prophesying and foretelling the future. They continued the shamanic practice of dressing differently as a symbol of their powers. Barry Cunliffe described how the Scythian mystics presented themselves in this way:

> It was in the interests of all priesthoods that they should present themselves as different from ordinary mortals. This was done through dress, behaviour, and secret ritual. The Scythian priests paraphernalia included effeminate behaviour, bark and bundles of sticks, headdresses, drums, ornate poles, ornate rattles and bells.[1240]

As religious beliefs evolved and the influential Sumerian population emerged to create a more anthropomorphic (gods with the shape of humans) and centralised ideology, the divine symbolism of special clothing strengthened. The divine powers of the human-like Sumerian gods, who were superior to human beings, were reflected in their garments, personal adornments, and armaments. The Sumerians believed that stripping the gods of their clothing and associated paraphernalia would strip them of the divine powers these garments represented. The power of a god's divine garments and the related supernatural strength could be transferred to other gods and to mortal heroes by the wearing of the god's garments.[1241]

The HB/OT contains the Hebrew god's specific instructions on the vestments that must be worn. This occurs in Exodus 28, Exodus 39, and Leviticus 8. According to Exodus 28, God's sacred garments must include:

> A breastpiece, an ephod, a robe, a woven tunic, a turban, and a sash. They are to make these sacred garments for your brother Aaron and his sons, so they may serve me as priests. Have them use gold, and blue, purple, and scarlet yarn, and fine linen.

The Hebrew god's message about sacred clothing included the important role of the pomegranate (Exodus 39):

> They made the robe of the ephod entirely of blue cloth—the work of a weaver—with an opening in the centre of the robe like the opening of a collar, and a band around this opening, so that it would not tear. They made pomegranates of blue, purple and scarlet yarn and finely

---

1240   Cunliffe (2019), pp. 273-274.
1241   Holland (2010), p. 112.

Siberian Shaman	Jewish Rabbi	Christian Pope	Turkish Imam

Figure 44: *The emergence of religious vestments for mediators with the divine* [c]

---

[c] Adapted from (Shaman vestments) https://www.pinterest.com.au/pin/682154674785093188/; (Rabbi vestments) https://www.thetorah.com/article/garments-of-the-high-priest-anthropomorphism-in-the-worship-of-god; (Pope's vestments) https://www.pinterest.com.au/pin/214695107216111691/ ; (Turkish Imam) https://commons.wikimedia.org/wiki/File:Weigel-Turkish_imam.jpg.

twisted linen around the hem of the robe. And they made bells of pure gold and attached them around the hem between the pomegranates. The bells and pomegranates alternated around the hem of the robe to be worn for ministering, as the Lord commanded Moses.

The symbolic use of clothing, jewellery and various adornments on priest's clothing continues today across many religions to symbolise the belief that a specific individual so uniquely dressed (priest, pope, pastor, rabbi, imam) can in some way mediate with a religion's chosen divine being/s (Figure 44).

Chapter 22

How the Hebrew Bible/Christian Old Testament was Constructed

The leading French anthropologist and ethnologist Claude Levi-Strauss, in 1955, introduced a new approach to the study of myth by applying the French word *mytheme* to his analysis. Mythemes are shared stories with fundamentally the same substance, structure, relationships, and the same or closely related messages. These can be repetitive substantive myths within one culture or similar myths across different cultures. They are fundamentally the same or similar myths repeated and reassembled in various new ways to essentially convey the same thematic religious, ethical, or philosophical message. Levi-Strauss' innovation was to suggest that a singular preferred myth should not be studied alone. It is necessary to study all occurrences of fundamentally the same myth—'repetition has as its function to make the structure of the myth apparent' and 'a myth consists of all of its versions'.[1242]

It is now generally accepted that the HB/OT emerged as a pastiche of myths and metaphors derived from ancient Middle East oral traditions edited and adapted over hundreds of years. The primary objective of this process was to use the emergence of the alphabet and written communication to create a cultural identity and cohesiveness through a fully articulated worldview.

The HB/OT is an anecdotal and folklorist codification of a specific culture. This was achieved by purposeful articulation, elaboration, and repetition of selected key mythological, historical, cultural, and ideological 'markers' of differentiation. It was written, changed, adapted, and orchestrated by hundreds of scribes over hundreds of years. These scribes were well-meaning advocates and promoters who borrowed and modified previous prehistoric cultures' legends and myths. In the process, they embellished them through, in part, their fascination with the newly available alphabet and the creative opportunities of communicating and unifying through writing.

[1242] Levi-Strauss C. (1955), pp. 436-443.

The HB/OT makes sense in the context of the prehistoric and subsequent influencing and exiling of the early Israelites to and from parts of Egypt, Canaan, Assyria, and Babylon and their early history of living under imperialistic control. In the absence of a consolidated, long-term locational culture and history, the challenge was to create a belief in a common historical and biological descent, primacy, a shared past, a common ideology, and a unifying belief in an ultimate God-given 'homeland'.

The Hebrew scribes were, in Lord Raglan's words, 'ritualists':

> [The] idea of history is meaningless to the ritualist. History is what happens once, but things that happen once only are nothing to the ritualist, who is concerned only with things that are done again and again.[1243]

The major techniques used by the Hebrew scribes

Archaeologist Kit Wesler has described the Hebrew Bible in this way: 'the Bible is not a complete (historical) record but a very selective, focused message'.[1244]

The selectively focused message was achieved using a variety of literary techniques, including:

- **Appropriation/ Religious Syncretism**—gleaning stories from surrounding cultures/ mythologies and shaping them into their own mythological narrative. Religious syncretism involved the harmonious blending together of different religious ideologies, beliefs, rituals, customs, and practices into a unified religion. It was commonly accepted practice from around 300 BCE to 300 CE[1245]. This practice, common to the Hebrew scribes, was regularly and consistently used in the transition from Jewish to Christian mythology. Most of the Christian feast days are appropriated and re-badged from the Jewish religion or from previous cultures' mythologies.[1246] Throughout history, there are multiple examples of Christian leaders appropriating 'pagan' or other mythologies' celebrations and re-badging them as Christian Feast or Saint's days. *For example*:
  - the early Christian philosopher Origen (184 CE to 253 CE) was based in Alexandria in Egypt and was heavily influenced by the Greek philosopher

---

[1243]   Raglan (1956), pp. 146-147.

[1244]   Wesler (2014), p. 183.

[1245]   See: https://www.britannica.com/topic/religious-syncretism retrieved on 27 May 2024

[1246]   SOURCE: https://www.youtube.com/watch?v=ptlsXtTf6n0&ab_channel=BruceAvilla retrieved on 21 December 2020.

Plato's concept of the soul. He advised Christian intellectuals of the benefits of combining Jewish, pagan, and prior Christian reflections through his own scriptural writing and oratory[1247]

- ○ Bishop Eusebius, a great fan of Origen's, is accredited with influencing the conversion to Christianity of Constantine the Great (307 CE to 337 CE). He influenced Constantine, who became the first Roman Emperor to make Catholicism the official religion of the Roman Empire. Eusebius was a prolific writer about early Christian doctrine who has gone to great lengths to confirm the alignment of the Christian Easter celebrations with the Jewish Passover[1248]

- ○ Bishop Cyril of Alexandria (376 CE to 444 CE) appropriated the Ancient Egyptian mythology around the healing goddess Isis by leading a solemn procession along the fabled Isis processional way to the Isis temple in Menouthi (now Abu Qir) to install a temple, shrines, and ceremonies filled with mythological stories of Christian healing saints in and around the Isis temple[1249]

- ○ Pope Gregory the Great, in 601 CE, instructed missionaries in England to appropriate existing pagan celebrations[1250]

- ○ A typical example relates to the Irish Catholics' patron saint, St Brigid. St Brigid is a Christianisation of the goddess of the pre-existing Irish Celtic goddess (of the same name and same sacred day) associated with the spring season, fertility, healing, poetry, and smithing. The Christian Saint Brigid has appropriated most of the mythological skills of the original Celtic goddess.[1251]

- **Mytho-history**: the HB/OT is not a chronological or historical sequence of events but rather episodes selectively woven together in a way that was meaningful to the scribes' view of their world and the hybridisation of a religion from existing mythologies. In their writings, men and gods, geography, communities, history, and myth intertwine and become indistinguishable from facts or evidence. Their task was to organically and creatively evolve a single canon of scripture over several hundred years of selective hybridisations of existing mythologies and beliefs.

- **Ahistorical**—whether by default, design, or a simple fixated belief in their task of documenting and unifying the beliefs of their emerging mythology, the Hebrew

---

[1247]   McGuckin (2020A), p. 7.
[1248]   Eusebius (2011) pp. 229-230.
[1249]   McGuckin (2020B), p. 15.
[1250]   Spiegel (2007), p. 2.
[1251]   Cathain (1992), pp. 14-15.

scribes demonstrated a lack of concern for history, factual evidence, and cultural precedent.

- **Folkloric devices**—folklore is codified oral traditions involving multiple similar stories with the same underlying message, moral lesson, or mythological reflection. 'In folklore there is no one correct version; there are only alternative versions.'[1252]
  - Folklore is the traditional beliefs, customs, and stories of a community or, in this case, a region, passed through the generations by word of mouth or once writing was invented through allegorical stories or a body of popular myths or beliefs relating to a particular place, activity, or group of people. Stories, customs, and beliefs that are passed from one generation to the next to provide historical information regarding the origins of a group of people *'one ought to be extremely cautious when one seeks to interpret a myth, for myths are protean. They have no single constant meaning; they change their spots. All is in flux according to place and time'.*[1253]
- **Myth appropriation**—where the Hebrew scribes have taken and subverted a dominant culture's narrative and integrated it into their own cultural framework and beliefs to assign it new mythological meaning.[1254]
- **Poetic and allegorical appropriation** (i.e., place names)—Sacred places, spiritual landscapes, cultural geographic appropriation, cognitive geography, sociospatial schema, behavioural geography—explaining how people make decisions and act in geographic space.
- **Mesopotamian Naru Literature**/fictitious autobiographies—good stories with an important message, but which are largely legendary and usually fictitious. They usually present a famous historical figure in a fictional tale about a relationship with the gods. They are shaped to communicate to and convince a contemporary audience of events that may have never happened, preserving the past and relating vital cultural values through the creation of entertaining and memorable tales.
- **Symbolism**. A preoccupation with the imagined divine. Lynn White has elaborated on the role that symbolism has played from prehistoric times up until the Middle Ages. He described the approach as 'extreme anthropocentrism', reflected in how early writers lived not in the world of visible facts but rather in a world

---

[1252]   Dundes (1999), p. 28 and p. 117.
[1253]   Jacobsen (1981), p. 529.
[1254]   Hendel (2005) pp. 25-32.

of symbols … Behind every object and event lay and idea, a spiritual entity or meaning of which the immediate experience was merely the imperfect reflection or allegory. The world had been created by God for the spiritual edification of man, and served no other purpose … The effect upon science of such a view of nature was of course disastrous.[1255]

Dead Sea Scrolls scholar Russell Gmirkin, who sees very strong parallels between Greek philosopher Plato's Laws and those of the HB/OT, states that:

The Hebrew Bible as a whole can best be understood as a literature intended for the education of the soul, utilising all the tools in the Platonic psychagogic arsenal: poetry, myth and song, theology and prayers, pageant and spectacle, theatre, drink and dance and persuasive rhetoric that appealed to the patriotic, praised the noble and exalted and condemned the wicked and disobedient, who were threatened with punishments in this life and terrors in the next.[1256]

The codification of culture

The Hebrew Bible and the Christian Old and New Testaments are demonstrably cultural, ideological fairy tales. They fulfil and have fulfilled a cultural differentiation and strengthening role over many hundreds of years.

Rebecca Denova has described the imaginative writing styles of the ancient scribes in the following way:

The methods by which ancient philosophers often described the universe, as well as traditional myths, was through allegory and metaphor. Allegory is a literary device that posits hidden meanings through symbolic figures, actions, images, and events, usually to provide a spiritual, or moral interpretation. Allegory offers a way in which a text can be open to more interpretations than traditionally understood. A metaphor is a figure of speech in which a word or phrase is substituted, for example: 'The Universe is a sea of troubles'.[1257]

The HB/OT has been a codification of culture, a cultural manifesto brought together over many hundreds of years in many hundreds of iterations by many hundreds of writers. It defines, elaborates, and reinforces a claim and a specification for being an identifiably different ethnic identity historically and contemporarily. It has done this through a variety of devices—by promoting a unique, but largely embellished heritage, creating historically

---

[1255] White (1978), p. 27.
[1256] Gmirkin (2019), p. 267.
[1257] Denova (2022).

retrospective cultural primacy (been here since God created the universe), articulating a composite mythology of God-given values, behaviours, beliefs, claiming religious exclusivity ('the chosen people') and ultimately a geographic/territorial righteousness ('the promised land'). It is essentially a repackaged, exaggerated historical recollections interwoven with myth, legend and regionally accepted concepts of life, death and the hereafter.

The codification of culture occurs in all cultures across multiple dimensions—expressed through common language, family and community structure and strictures, codes of behaviour and values, and beliefs about morality, marriage, lifestyle, religion, ritual, and burial practices. It is a self-reinforcing package that can be quite comprehensive, repetitive, and well-integrated.

Insights into the Christian New Testament

Although this research has been primarily focused on the Hebrew Bible/Christian Old Testament, several ancient mythological traditions have been found that have an uncanny similarity to stories in the Christian New Testament.

Common underlying themes in the Buddha and Jesus stories

Buddhism emerged in around 563 BCE, some five hundred years before the Jesus, son of God story. German Lutheran theologian, philosopher, and comparative religionist Rudolf Otto has documented the common thematic structure that underlies both the Buddha and the Jesus stories.

According to Rudolf Otto, Buddha and Jesus both had the same 'three modes of existence'—a bodily human or corporeal one involving all of the usual human needs (food, drink, shelter); contact with and knowledge of the spiritual world (as did their shamanic and god- king predecessors); and they eventually abandon their corporeal body and emerge as an eternal essence who existed before time began.

This common underlying thematic structure pervaded Middle Eastern mythological stories about gods and god-kings at the time (from Mesopotamian city-kings to Egyptian pharaohs). It was ubiquitous in regional mythologies when the Hebrew scribes and, much later, the Christian gospel writers were developing their stories.

Buddha and Jesus are both believed to have been responsible for each religion's canonical scriptures. The oldest Buddhist scriptures discovered so far, date from around 100 BCE (the Sutras); the oldest examples of the Christian scriptures (the four gospels/ New Testament) discovered so far date from around the second century CE. The Hebrew Bible,

Christian Old Testament, the Buddhist Sutras, and the Christian New Testament all reflect a similar ancient writing and mythology communication style. They can be easily communicated from a teacher to student, easily memorised for discussion or self- study or used as self- reinforcing religious reference texts. This ancient practice has continued as the identifiable, ubiquitous, and recommended modus operandi of modern-day Christian biblical advocates, pastors, proselytisers, and believers.

Multiple examples of ancient stories linked to the Jesus story

In summary, the following patterns have emerged that cause reflection on the potential origin of parts of the New Testament Jesus story:

- the Zoroastrians and Hindus, whose mythology predates Christianity by thousands of years, each believed that their god had a son who was sent to Earth to assist or save humans
- close similarities between the Buddha and the Jesus stories (above)
- hundreds of years before the Jesus story, the Zoroastrians, the Hindus, the Persians, and the Egyptians all had a form of divine worship based on eating bread or a bread substitute and drinking wine or a similar intoxicating drink. As happens in Christianity, this practice allowed these believers to enter communion with a divine being the celebration of the birth of Jesus occurs at Christmas, which is the same time as many ancient Northern Hemisphere celebrations of the winter solstice
- the celebration of Jesus's death and resurrection occurs on the same dates as the many ancient Northern Hemisphere spring equinox and fertility celebrations
- the ancient lunisolar dates for celebration are carried over in other aspects relating to the story of Jesus. John the Baptist is born to a virgin after an announcement from the archangel Gabriel. John the Baptist's saint's day is Midsummer's Day. Midsummer's Day is the Northern Hemisphere date of the June solstice (24 June)
- the celebration of the annunciation by the archangel Gabriel to the Virgin Mary is celebrated on 25 March, which is also the time of the death and resurrection of Jesus. This conforms to an ancient Mesopotamian mythological belief that a person dies on the same date as their conception
- there are multiple examples of mythologies that predate the Jesus story by thousands of years wherein a god or god- king is born of a virgin, dies, and is resurrected (Zoroastrian, Mesopotamian/Babylonian, Phoenician, Egyptian, Anatolian, Hindu, Greek, Persian, Nepalese). This was a popular idea well before the writing of the New Testament. These similarities are either coincidental or

they highlight the likely ancient mythological origin of many of the Jesus stories in the New Testament.

- In line with the ancient Middle Eastern tradition, Both Buddha and Jesus are described as commencing their religious journey at 30 years of age
- Both the Buddha and Christian scriptures contain varying biographical narratives and life scenarios written retrospectively by subsequent followers who were not present during their lifetimes. Each of these narratives eventually became two new distinctive faiths.

These similarities are either coincidental or they highlight the likely ancient mythological origin of many of the Jesus stories in the New Testament.

Chapter 23

Conclusion

The serendipitous human species

The human species has experienced some rather fortuitous, historically circumstantial events that have facilitated its long-term emergence and development over millions of years. Geologist and geochemist Marc Defant has explained how the emergence of hominins was largely the result of rare, statistically improbable events in galactic time.[1258] The unique evolution of human life on Earth was the result of an unusual coincidence of favourable events and circumstances.

Sixty-six million years ago, a large asteroid slammed into the sea just off Mexico's Yucatan Peninsula, wiping out the dinosaurs. The placental mammals survived.[1259] Over geological time and through a complex chain of events, the human species emerged from this ancient accident as a sub-set of this placental mammal species.[1260]

A significant factor in the success of the human species was the unique brain-to-body mass ratio, unique DNA attributes, frontal and temporal brain capabilities that emerged over millions of years. These created evolutionary biological advantages including extraordinary abilities to think in the abstract, imagine, invent, make tools, share information, cooperate, communicate, and organise collectively. It was not these individual capabilities that, by themselves, distinguished the human species. It was the related ability to work flexibly and collectively in large numbers through sophisticated networks of cooperation. Neurophysiological capability and the ability to cooperate on a mass scale are directly linked to the emergence of love, fear, mystical awe, spiritual consciousness, religious symbolism, and ritual.

[1258] See: Why We are Alone in the Galaxy | Marc Defant | TEDxUSF—YouTube retrieved on 2 February 2023.

[1259] SOURCE: https://www.nationalgeographic.com/science/article/last-day-dinosaurs-reign-captured-stunning-detail?loggedin=true&rnd=1683506214780 retrieved on 8 May 2023.

[1260] Lloyd (2012), pp. 70-82.

These unique abilities—combined with significant geodynamic, geomorphic, and natural environmental conditions—were the necessary ingredient for the formation of several 'cradles of civilisation' in several locations in ancient times. The natural environment played a significant part:

> *Of the roughly 200,000 plant species in the natural world, only a couple of thousand are suitable for human consumption, and just a few hundred of these offer potential for domestication and cultivation.*[1261]

One of these potential 'cradles of civilisation' was in a unique geographic position and was the location of a range of edible plants and animals that were capable of being domesticated. Archaeobotanical researchers have identified eight plant species whose wild ancestors were instrumental in the progression from forager to farmer to crop domestication in the Levant, Anatolia, and the Fertile Crescent. These are referred to as 'founder crops' and include:

- flax (or linseed)
- emmer wheat
- einkorn wheat
- barley
- lentil
- pea
- chickpea
- bitter vetch.[1262]

These edible crops were in the same region where the ancient Asian mouflon (ancestor of domesticated sheep), the wild bezoar ibex (ancestor of domesticated goats) and the Middle Eastern wild ox (ancestor of today's cattle) wandered. Just to the north (in Anatolia and the Eurasian Steppe) were the wild *Equus caballus* (the ancestor of today's domesticated horses). These fortunate circumstances combined with the emerging sedentary habits of the human species in the Middle East to lay the groundwork for the emergence of early civilisation.

The Middle East and, specifically, Mesopotamia, was on a magnificent river system cradled to the north and east by arcing mountain ranges, with a lengthy Mediterranean shoreline and the only land bridge out of Africa. This region, 'the Fertile Crescent', included the Levant and Israel. It became one of the oldest places external to Africa where archaeological evidence of the ancient human species has been found. Over time, largely kinship-based

---

[1261] Dartnell (2018), p. 87.
[1262] SOURCE: https://www.worldatlas.com/articles/the-8-crops-to-be-first-domesticated-by-humans-the-neolithic-founder-crops.html retrieved on 2 March 2022.

tribal groups of hunter-gatherers and fishers settled down into ever increasingly larger sedentary agricultural, pastoral, and mining communities that required external unification. Not surprisingly, organised religion initially and eventually emerged in this Middle East region as one of several systems of unification, cultural differentiation, and control.

The one-dimensional view of the emergence of 'civilisation'

The Hebrew Bible and most historical books emerging from Western civilisation do a disservice to the complexity and the multi-dimensionality of human emergence and human existence. Globally, five separate locations emerged as potential 'cradles of civilisation'. These were in the Middle East, China, Egypt, Mesoamerica, and the Andes in South America. Some may well have influenced each other, but others appear to have emerged independently due to the creativity of the human species and to the availability of locally favourable environments, geography, animal species, and edible plants.

Even in the Middle East, there were multiple diverse communities, cultures, and mythologies operating at the same time as the Hebrew Bible began to emerge. The Greeks, who are erroneously regarded as the founders of modern philosophy and democracy, are known to have based many of their ideas on the earlier developments and discoveries of the Mesopotamians.

Israeli archaeologists Ayelet Gilboa and Ilan Sharon have discussed the three competing narratives that inform a more accurate understanding of ancient history:

- Archaeological – based on artefactual evidence and the dating of this material largely using radiocarbon dating;
- Historical – based on available textual material, cuneiform, hieroglyphic and other writings from the wide range of cultural group artefacts across the ancient Middle East
- Biblical – accepting the chronology and the evidence presented in the HB/OT.

Based on their extensive study and dating of pottery artefacts from the ancient Middle East and specifically the Levant, they suggest that the least reliable chronological source for our understanding of the past is the Biblical chronology. They conclude that when looking for the most reliable chronology of the times when the HB/OT was being written (Iron Age – around 1200 BCE to 600 BCE)

It is our conviction that the solution must be realised archaeologically, through the construction of high-resolution relative sequences nailed to an absolute time scale by 14C dating (i.e. carbon dating).[1263]

[1263] Gilbao and Sharon, (2003), p. 72

The misconceptions about the history of the human species and of the complexity of how and what happened historically are widespread and unfortunate. Classical archaeologist and ancient historian Naoíse Mac Sweeney has expressed her concern about the one-dimensionality of the contemporary Western historical narrative in this way:

> *Put simply, the real history of the West is much richer and much more complex than the traditional grand narrative of Western Civilisation acknowledges. It is not a golden thread but a golden tapestry—in which strands of diverse peoples, cultures, and ideas have been woven together over the centuries.*[1264]

This observation applies particularly to the ancient Middle East, Egypt, the Indus Valley, and the Eurasian Steppe cultures. There has been an historical disregard for the existence, complexity, and influence of these many ancient cultures on the emergence of civilisation and on the writing of the HB/OT. Schmid and Schroter have explained it in this way:

> *The pre-eminence of these older civilisations was largely overlooked in the theological and historical research of the nineteenth and early twentieth centuries. Thanks to the powerful historical influence of the Bible, the ancient Near East was viewed chiefly as the backdrop to the Bible. Its designation as the Holy Land in writing in this period perfectly expresses this viewpoint. Egypt and Mesopotamia were regarded as the periphery, while Israel and Judah occupied centre stage. Biblical scholarship concerned itself primarily with the literature of revelation, while Egyptology and Assyriology were cast in the role of ancillary disciplines. But in the twentieth century, scholars researching the history of the Bible and the ancient Near East showed that the historical significance of these two regions was the exact opposite. Israel and Judah did not become politically and culturally relevant until after the great civilisations of the region had long been established and were already setting the agenda for the cultural and historical development of the region.*[1265]

The ubiquity of religion

Organised religion is ubiquitous. There are currently more than four thousand religions globally, most of which differ in their stories, narratives, beliefs, imagery, and explanations of life. Underneath all religions, there appear to be four common underlying influences:

- a series of myths built around complex symbolic metaphorical thinking[1266]

[1264] Mac Sweeney (2023).
[1265] Schmid and Schroter (2021), pp. 53-54.
[1266] Witzel (2012), pp. 252-253.

- a uniquely human, largely neurologically driven, intentional pursuit of different levels of feeling, consciousness, imagination, fantasy, and wonder[1267]
- the human species' collective desire to belong and to participate in shared stories, whether factual or mythological
- governing bodies' desire to unify and control a specific cultural mosaic, the belief systems, morality, economics, manageability, and expectations of large groups of people (whether geographically co-located or scattered globally).

Religion is like language, dress, and social and political structures. It is part of the overall chemistry of cultural identity, differentiation, and belonging. It is a codification of culture, cultural identification, and cultural differentiation.

Most contemporary religions started as prehistoric lunisolar-related mythologies. A globally shared lunisolar rationale is the main underlying structure of most contemporary religions, albeit obfuscated by imagination, fantasy, and faux tradition. From the lunisolar tradition, each religion became a theatrical orchestration of rules and rituals around a mythological god or groups of gods. All religions are fascinating, but they are not about existing supreme beings or spirits. They largely fulfil and reflect a range of cultural and human desires.

The content of all religions

All religions are manifestations of the human imaginative and creative search for meaning. Most religions have all or most of the following contents:

- **myths**—stories about the early history and achievements of a specific people and culture, often involving cultural heroes and supernatural beings
- **allegory**—apparently truthful stories or creative writing (poems, drawings, pictures) that have a metaphoric or hidden moral, ethical, cultural, or political message
- **beliefs**—sacred laws, ethical, and moral codes, often attributed to a deity or divine source
- **symbolism**—a range of images, mystical messages, ideas, and objects (statues, diagrammatic or geometric symbols), deified emblems, and paraphernalia representing or reinforcing the religious message
- **rites**—social customs, ceremonies, or practices that most often descend from, reflect, and strengthen the myths and allegories

---

[1267] Lewis-Williams (2010) pp. 154-158.

- **rituals**—formal, customarily repeated and endorsed practices, oaths, observances, social norms, behaviours (kneeling, facing cardinal directions, hand gestures), and spoken or sung prayers and/or hymns in honour of a specific deity or deities.

From religion to science

There is a generally held view that, in the Middle Ages, science emerged from religion. This view is strengthened by the religious background of several of the founding fathers of modern-day science:

- Leonardo da Vinci (1452 CE to 1519 CE) was a religious man who believed in the ultimate truth of the Bible
- Copernicus (1473 CE to 1543CE) was a priest
- Giordano Bruno (1548 CE to 1600 CE) was a priest
- Galileo Galilei (1564 CE to 1642 CE) was a priest
- Johannes Kepler (1571 CE to 1630 CE) was a seminarian
- Isaac Newton (1643 CE to 1727 CE) was a Protestant theologian.

Scientific thinking predates these highly respected founders of modern scientific thought by thousands of years. Scientific thinking and the pursuit of objective knowledge can be traced back to Mesopotamia, the Sumerians, and the Ancient Egyptians. These ancient peoples are the original source of mathematics, technology, astronomy, and medicine and were very influential on Greek philosophy. AC Grayling has elucidated how, in prehistoric times, religion emerged from the scientific curiosity of humankind. Prehistoric attempts at understanding and explaining the mechanisms and phenomena of nature involved building a framework of explanation. This was early scientific thinking. It was an attempt to disentangle enquiry into principles of nature.

Over time, this transitioned into mythologies, superstitions, and rituals to appease imagined deities. In prehistory, the nascent scientific impulse detoured into religion. From da Vinci and Copernicus onwards, science—the natural human desire to pursue knowledge and meaning—transitioned back from religion to scientific enquiry.[1268] Fundamentally, they are the same human pursuit of understanding, knowledge, and meaning.

Grayling could be right that science and religion are both examples of humankind's natural curiosity and innate desire to understand and explain the world by establishing meaningful explanatory frameworks. However, scientists and religious believers appear to use two totally different neurocognitive mechanisms in coming to their explanatory frameworks. Scientists

---

[1268] Adapted from Grayling (2021), pp. 59-60.

tend to use a 'top-down approach' while religious believers tend to use a 'bottom-up approach'. These different neurocognitive processes can be explained in the following way:

- Scientists tend to use a top-down approach. This is a strategy for processing information where a problem is defined and the whole system is firstly conceptualised and is then analysed into sub-systems and component parts. The thinking moves from the general to the specific.
- Religious believers tend to use a bottom-up approach. This moves from the specific to the general. It is largely influenced and driven by sensory and perceptual observation of patterns. These are then intuitively transformed into explicit, usually religious, beliefs about how this has happened.[1269]

How fictional stories through a repetitive medium become beliefs

The impact of fiction (through all forms of media) on the human species' beliefs about the factual world is now a major academic study. It is referred to as 'cultivation theory'. Cultivation theory describes the academic study of the effect of long-term exposure to a specific medium (in contemporary studies largely television; in the current case the HB/OT) and the impact this has on the belief systems of those exposed to this medium.

Although ostensibly and largely a contemporary TV-focused phenomenon, cultivation theory suggests that *media effects are massive, long term, and cumulative, influencing a large and heterogeneous public by exposing the public to recurrent patterns of stories, images, and messages.*[1270]

Psychologist, media, and communications academic Markus Appel cites examples of profound persuasive effects of fictional texts on people's under and overestimations of the extent of meanness, scariness, morality, or justice in the real world. Appel believes that fictional narratives are a powerful means of changing beliefs. He has coined the term 'persuasion through fiction' to describe this effect.[1271]

Philosopher and expert in comparative literature, Kai Mikkonen suggests that "It is only human to mistake the make-believe for the factual or to believe a lie". Mikkonen is but one of the growing group of experts attempting to better understand the human species' propensity to interweave and confuse concepts of fictionality, myth, narrativity, and literary texts with facts. Key concepts for converting fiction or myth to fact and thence to a belief appear to be (1) the extent of relevance of the fictional story to a person's life, (2) strong emotional content, (3) anomalous situations and (4) the text losing its literary and fictional merit.[1272]

[1269] Adapted from Weinberger et al. (2020).
[1270] Adapted from: https://www.sciencedirect.com/topics/social-sciences/cultivation-theory retrieved on 29 August 2023.
[1271] Appel (2008), pp. 3-4.
[1272] Adapted from Mikkonen (2006), pp. 293-302.

Leiden University Centre for the Study of Religion academic Markus Altena Davidsen has been specialising in the study of the textual features that facilitate a fictional story being used as a religious narrative and inspiring supernatural belief. His work focusses on contemporary fiction such as *Harry Potter, Star Wars, and Lord of the Rings*.[1273] The work discussed by Davidsen originated in a 2014 International Symposium on the persuasive power of religious narratives and supernatural fiction. The symposium discussions suggested that, in the contemporary world, fiction can be relatively easily distinguished from religion because publishing convention distinguishes them and categorises them accordingly. However, for ancient texts, when the difference between religious texts, fiction and fact was not a convention, the differentiation is far more difficult.

For fictional texts to be believed as religious and to inspire a belief in the supernatural, the 2014 symposiums suggested that the texts would require these five characteristics:

- supernatural beings and supernatural powers are present in the real/story world
- evidence is presented to demonstrate how the supernatural occurs in and is experienced in the real world
- the text contains models of religious practice and rituals
- the mode of narration invites the reader to see their own lives as a continuation of the narrative
- elements of the story are anchored in and can be easily mapped into the real world.

Although all this research is relatively recent, it does provide insights into understanding the wide acceptance of the HB/OT. The five characteristics identified by Davidsen taken together with Mikkonen's four concepts provide a model for how fictional narrative can transition from myth to fact to belief. It creates an interesting framework for a better understanding of how the codification of culture embedded in the HB/OT has been considered as factual history:

- supernatural beings and powers are woven into the story
- there is a real world context
- the stories have strong emotional content
- the stories are embedded in the real world and are relevant to everyday life
- there are anomalous events throughout
- the text contains models of religious practice and rituals
- the literary and fictional merit of the narrative is replaced by a perception of factual reality.

[1273] See: Davidsen (2016).

The unique human species linking beliefs to behaviours

There is a growing body of research that demonstrates that belief-based expectations in the human species impact not only perception and behaviours but also personal health, performance, and objectivity. Whether through religion, mysticism, mythology, witch doctors, shamans, sports psychologists, therapists, placebos, medical specialists, or altered states of consciousness, for centuries there has been an acknowledged transformative power in belief.[1274]

Transcendental beliefs can create a range of positive emotional effects. This can occur whether the transcendental experience is religious-based (Judaism, Christianity, Islam, Buddhism, Hinduism) or not (meditation, yoga, being in nature, shamanic trances, using psychoactive drugs, making, or listening to music, falling in love, underwater diving, sustained experience of awe).[1275] The emotional and psychological comfort of continuous and ongoing transcendental experiences can actively reduce stress and anxiety, induce peace, tranquillity, comfort, happiness, general health, and resistance to infection.[1276] Religion is but one of those comforting experiences.

The international tennis, football, boxing, or chess player who blesses themselves and looks to the heavens after a big win are confirming the lunisolar origins of gods and the afterlife being "up there somewhere". They are also acknowledging a belief in the impact their transcendent belief has had on their performance.

The transition from the totemic beliefs of the hunter-gatherers to the institutionalised religions of the contemporary world reflect a move from a horizontal "unifying energy" (spiritual explanations across the landscape) to a vertical "unifying ideology" (the divine is anthropomorphic and located above and below).

Here is direct and recurring evidence of the intellectual/cognitive capacity of the human species' unique ability to create explanations of the world through the interaction of imagination, ideas, images, and fantasies.[1277] This recurring pattern of behaviour (across millennia) is symptomatic of the unique human brain-to-body mass ratio, unique DNA attributes, frontal and temporal brain capabilities delivering extraordinary abilities to imagine, invent, make tools, share information, cooperate, communicate, and organise collectively. The emotive religious component of these gestures and these outcomes is largely attributable to the physical and psychological influence of powerful spiritual, emotional, mystical awe, and religious symbolism capabilities of the unique temporal and frontal lobes in the human brain.[1278]

[1274]   See: Unlocking the Healing Power of You (nationalgeographic.com) retrieved on 26 March 2022.
[1275]   Allen (2018).
[1276]   See: Koenig, 2020.
[1277]   Harari (2015), p. 42.
[1278]   Joseph (2011).

The Bible as a unique example of ancient mythological writing

The Jewish scribes were writing between 900 BCE and 300 BCE. They were writing in detail about events that they claim occurred several thousand or more years before the time in which they were writing. They retrospectively commenced their biblical creation story at around 4000 BCE. These were times from which there were no supporting documentary records, no alphabet, and no writing or simple forms of communication. There is no evidence of the existence of the Israelites or any records of their unique beliefs prior to 1205 BCE. The Hebrew scribes had no tangible evidence to draw on except perhaps oral histories passed down for thousands of years. Their observations of and borrowing from other mythologies were supplemented by their own imagination.

Biblical scholar Marc Brettler writing in the Cambridge Guide to Jewish History, Religion, and culture states about the bible:

> *The Bible cannot be used as a straightforward historical source. Many biblical texts were written down centuries after the events they purport to describe. More significantly, our notion of history, which involves reproducing the past as accurately as possible, is modern. In earlier times, stories about the past were written for a variety of reasons such as to provide entertainment, to forge group identity, to justify hatred of enemies, and to bolster the authority of powerful elites. These (biblical) stories may contain a historical kernel, but it is often difficult to determine its extent.*[1279]

The network of prehistoric gene pathways and land routes in and around the Eurasian Steppe, Mesopotamia, and Egypt worked in parallel with an extensive network of regional trade routes to create significant overlaps in culture and beliefs. The HB/OT is an example of ancient Middle Eastern mythological writing. The multiple authors have produced a narrative written in the Middle Eastern Bronze Age literature style containing elaborated, often allegorical versions of oral history interwoven with epic tales, legends, contrived genealogies, laws, moral codes, ethnic markers, and ethnic differentiations.[1280] The extensive non-biblical evidence shows that the HB/OT is not a unique collection of the words of a god. It is a continuing tradition of prehistoric mythological beliefs embellished, expanded, and modernised over time.

The Bible emerged from this amazingly diverse cultural and mythological landscape, beginning in the Stone Age and morphing towards an anthropomorphic monotheism in prehistoric times to eventually become the mythological textbook for Judaism and Christi-

---

[1279] Brettler (2010), p.16.
[1280] Adapted in part from Moye (1990).

anity. Theologian and Old Testament Scholar Daniel Pioske has undertaken a wide-ranging analysis of Biblical writing. He sees the Bible as a genre-specific Bronze and Iron Age piece of historicising. It combines legendary oral story-telling, textual allusions, poetry, ancient beliefs, texts that were often written independently of each other, reflecting ancient modes of thought and knowledge, having some semblance with the past but largely a typical example of stories that communicate about the past to build a sense of identity.[1281]

The Hebrew Bible/Christian Old Testament is a singular example of ancient mythological writing. It should be accepted as such and be lauded and respected for that. It is one of the few surviving examples of the creative mythological writing of the ancient Middle East.

Hebrew Bible and Christian Old Testament as mythologised history

Myths, legends, and beliefs are cultural inventions that were originally developed to explain the unknown. They may have been with humans from earliest times, not because they are obviously useful, but because there was little or nothing to expose their falsity and thus hinder their spread.[1282]

The HB/OT is 'mythologised history'. It is largely a creative pastiche of many reinterpreted previous mythological and largely fanciful stories drafted over hundreds of years. On the evidence discovered and presented here, the HB/OT's lack of credibility or believability as 'the word of God' is not in question, but it is intriguing how these believable and entertaining stories have survived for so long?

There appear to be at least eight main reasons for the survival of the HB/OT:

1. An apparent human need for a sense of belonging, a sense of continuity, and a sense of certainty
2. The existence of a tangible written code, widely endorsed, widely distributed, and repetitively quoted/asserted
3. The written code confirming that the world, humanity, and an individual's future is fundamentally predictable and foreseeable if certain values and behaviours are followed
4. A (claimed) long historical link of the specific religion to a sense of belonging, cultural integrity, righteous government, and national identity

---

[1281] Pioske, D. (2022).
[1282] Brown, D.E. (2004), p. 50.

5. A contemporary priestly hierarchy and/or historical gurus/prophets who claim to have insider knowledge of the universe—its origins, its direction, its future, and the human implications

6. The adoption of Christianity as the official religion of the Roman Empire by Constantine the Great in 313 CE. This included bankrolling church-building projects, commissioning new copies of the Bible, fighting in the name of God, and summoning councils of theologians to hammer out the religion's doctrinal kinks.[1283] What followed was often ruthless enforcement of the biblical canon over hundreds of years

7. Centralised control over information, destruction of books, and the enforcement of guilt and religious adherence[1284]

8. Over time, the Christian Church undertook the systematic removal of individuals, alternative theories, or evidence that was contrary to the biblical code.

Historically, within the major religions, there has been an active advocacy against any alternative views. This needs to be acknowledged. It is a major reason behind the growth of these religions and the suppression of the general public's access to a wider historical and cultural context within which these religions developed.

The way forward

The evidence in this book has not been hard to find and collate. The ancient Middle East, Egypt, and the Indus Valley have a complex, dynamic, and multi-faceted history dating back thousands of years. Culturally, mythologically, economically, and technologically, these regions have laid the foundation for the modern world. The Hebrew Bible/Christian Old Testament has had a role to play as a specific cultural and religious statement. However, its predominance and the collectively held belief that it is a history book has, over time, obscured the complex and foundational history of these many ancient cultures.

There are currently around two hundred thousand Torah students in Bnei Brak in Israel, more than two thousand Jewish Rabbis globally, more than eight hundred religious Roman Catholic leaders in the Vatican, more than four hundred thousand Roman Catholic priests, around one hundred and fifty thousand protestant ministers and hundreds

1283 SOURCE https://www.britannica.com/biography/Constantine-I-Roman-emperor retrieved on 3 May 2023.
1284 SOURCE: https://www.worldhistory.org/article/2018/index-of-prohibited-books/ retrieved on 3 May 2023.

of Evangelical Pastors in the United States. It is a reasonable question to ask—why have these leaders and Biblical experts not undertaken, published, and promoted research into the origin of the Bible, its prehistoric context, and the previous mythologies from which it borrowed its stories. They tend largely to be advocates of one major source ("the Book") in which they have and hold undying faith.

They are perhaps, in part, motivated by the common underlying and continuously recurring myth across the Hebrew Bible, Old Testament and New Testament that a belief in the divine will deliver a bountiful return. This occurs not only in the Exodus myth but in many other similar Biblical metaphoric stories. For example:

- the Widow of Zarephath story (1 Kings 17:8-16) where Elijah magically turns a small piece of bread and a small jug of oil into a bountiful supply of both, or
- the myth of Jesus feeding five thousand people from just five loaves of bread and two fishes (Mathew14: 13-21).

The unique human species' storyline that a belief in a divine being will lead to bountiful rewards is presented in many varied and creative ways throughout the Bible. It is the underlying principle in the foundational belief that a wonderful afterlife awaits those who believe in a god. It is also the basic myth that has seen the incredible financial bounty harvested by contemporary prosperity evangelists.

A focused, objective, historical analysis of the repetitive story lines, their origins and the underlying metaphors in ancient Biblical texts is absent in the work and writings of most Biblical researchers, Biblical literalist, and Evangelical advocates. They are theologians not historians.

It is, no doubt, hard for them to deny a certain set of beliefs that they have heard consistently and exclusively from childhood, at home, in school, in church, in the media, in language, in familiar clichés and amongst their friends. They believe that the information in front of them and in 'the Book' is historical, factual, or a truthful account of the past. Religious believers will always find it difficult to look objectively at the information brought together in the current book.

However, it is long overdue and well past the time for an open discussion about the various forms and the historical origin of biblical texts. Many still see the HB/OT as a factual, historical document, yet there is an extraordinary amount of evidence external to the Bible highlighting the complex environment from which the Hebrews and their ideas emerged. This rich tapestry of sources and influences is only allegorically referenced or alluded to in the biblical text.

There is a massive amount of literature about the Ancient Middle East, Ancient Iraq, the Sumerians, the Mesopotamians, Babylon, and the Cradle of Civilisation, but nothing or very little on the Hebrews/Israelites prior to 1205 BCE. The only surviving information from the Hebrews is the retrospectively written HB/OT. It tells much more about the Hebrew scribes' hybridisation of the mythologies of the Ancient Middle East at the time of their writing than about themselves. They have left no artefactual or tangible evidence prior to 1205 BCE.

The contrast is with the extensive evidence of the vibrant and diverse cultures, mythologies, discoveries, innovations, and alliances that preceded and were occurring at the time of the emergence of the HB/OT. They confirm the singularly mythological, allegorical, and historical inaccuracies of the stories in the HB/OT (Figure 45).

The path to enlightenment is painful and arduous, says Plato. This requires a move from the mythical to the rational which, in Plato's view, requires four stages of development:

1. Freedom from imprisonment and from being chained in the cave of ignorance (the imaginary world of the HB/OT)
2. Release from these chains (abandoning the perceived, mythical, sensual world, the world of shadows and deception)
3. Ascent out of the cave (moving up and out towards the world of ideas, evidence-based, scientific world, demonstrable truth, and objective reality)
4. The way back to help our fellows (belief in humanity, the innate fairness, generosity, empathy and wonder of humanity without the cave of ignorance, mythological stories, and dictates).[1285]

The belief in unseen intentional forces and judgements from an imagined divine being; the view of the world in terms of agency, purpose, and design belongs in the prescientific, prehistoric mythological fantasies of five thousand years ago. A time when the masses believed that the Earth was flat, that God lived on top of a large dome above the sky, and that an evil god lived in the underground. The fact that so many still believe this mythology is to the everlasting discredit of rational, inquisitive, capable, and intelligent human beings.

[1285]   SOURCE: https://www.thoughtco.com/the-allegory-of-the-cave-120330 retrieved on 3 May 2023.

Unique regional opportunities

- Geological/ geographical/ geomorphological and climatic opportunities

- Significant growth in human abilities to imagine, invent the unknown, think symbolically in the abstract and communicate collectively

- Regional availability of a complex mix of edible plants/crops and domesticable animals

- Slowly emerging shared agriculture/ farming/ animal husbandry practices & patterns

- Regional availability of metals, lapis lazuli, gold, bronze, turquoise, carnelian, and amber - many with imagined spiritual or healing powers

- Technological, cultural, mythological and community developments in the Eurasian Steppe and Fertile Crescent ecoregions

- Emerging Anatolian/ Sumerian/ Babylonian/ Mesopotamian, Fertile Crescent, Egyptian and Indus Valley cultures

- Formation of complex, hierarchical, sedentary, centralised communities/empires generating economic surpluses across the region

- Growth in complex, multi-directional prehistoric trade, economic and cultural exchange routes

How the Bible was invented in the Middle East *(dates shown are historically accepted best estimates)*

Anatomically modern humans leave Africa via the Levant - many different waves settle there

100000 BCE to 10000 BCE

↓

Natufians/Amorites/Canaanite/Habiru/ Hyksos/ Shasu - early low status tent dwelling nomadic pastoralists move around the Levant and the Canaan hills

10000 BCE to 1500 BCE

↓

The emergence regionally of writing systems, unique poetic writing styles and the interpretative and creative role of Scribes

1500 BCE to 300 BCE

↓

The Bronze Age major kingdoms' collapse and a coalition of a differentiated Israelite/ Hebrew pastoralist groups forms in the Canaanite hills

1200 BCE to 300 BCE

↓

Blending of stories and storylines from multiple other mythologies into a foundational mythological document by hundreds of Hebrew Scribes

900 BCE to 300 BCE

↓

Multiple books, chapters, writings/versions of potential texts available for the Hebrew Bible

300 BCE to 100 CE

↓

The contemporary Hebrew Bible and the Christian Old Testament canon finalised, enforced and promoted

Mythological influences

- Hunter gatherer shamanic beliefs and practices

- Ancient astronomical beliefs

- Zoroastrian/ Indo -Iranian/ Persian mythologies

- Regional trend for centralised divine legitimisation of the elite, and of power, control and beliefs

- Sumerian/ Babylonian/ Mesopotamian god-king mythologies

- Akkadian mythological stories

- Assyrian mythological stories

- Egyptian mythological stories

- Indus Valley mythological stories

- Canaanite mythological stories

Figure 45: *How the Human Species Invented the Bible*

Appendix A: Hebrew translations of the 42 Exodus Stations

Names of the 42 Exodus locations A1:A1:E31	Biblical reference	Description	Possible modern location/ encampment/ town	Hebrew translation or metaphorical meaning of the key word/s* (where applicable)
Raamses	Ex. 12:37; Nu. 33:3,5	The Raamses district was of the highest quality land in Egypt (Ge. 47:11)	uncertain but it has been suggested that it was East of the Nile Delta and possibly either Pi-Ramesses or Pithom	Could be an obtuse reference to the Pharaoh Ramesses II (1279 BCE to 1213 BCE) but there is nothing in the Egyptian records linking Ramesses to the Exodus, and indeed nothing at all in the Egytpian records of that time about the Israelites and their slavery
Sukkot (Succoth)	Ex. 12:37, 13:20; Nu. 33:5-6	An Egyptian city near the border	uncertain but is has been suggested that it was East of the Nile Delta and was possibly Pithom/Tjeku (Zuko)	Sukkot = a booth or hut roofed with branches, built against or near a house or synagogue
Etham	Ex. 13:20; Nu. 33:6-8	"On the edge of the wilderness"	Etham is another Hebrew word for Khetam (*fortress*). It is possibel, but not proven, that it might be close to Ismailia.	Etham = solid or enduring or fortress
Pi-Hahiroth	Ex. 14:2-3; Nu. 33:7-8	Lit. *Mouth of the Gorges*, "between Migdol and the sea, opposite Ba'al-Zephon" (possibly "the Bay of Hiroth")	Probably a channel opening into one of the Bitter Lakes or the Mediterranean. Pi-Hahiroth was located near the Red Sea.	Pi-Hahiroth = mouth of the gorges or where desert tracks begin

457

Appendix A (cont'd)

Names of the 42 Exodus locations A1:A1:E31	Biblical reference	Description	Possible modern location/ encampment/ town	Hebrew translation or metaphorical meaning of the key word/s* (where applicable)
Marah/ the Wilderness of Shur	Ex. 15:23; Nu. 33:8-9	Book of Numbers and Exodus disagree here. Numbers omits *Marah* and replaces it with the *Wilderness of Shur*	location unknown despite some speculation	Marah = bitterness; The word Shur comes from the verb to be raised, but can also mean bull, wall or line of fortresses
Elim	Ex. 15:27, 16:1; Nu. 33:9-10	Had 12 wells and 70 palm trees	location unknown despite some speculation	Elim = protruders or big trees. It could also be derived from the Semetic root (El) meaning gods
By the Red Sea	Nu. 33:10-11	Book of Numbers and Exodus disagree here. Exodus omits any mention of the Red Sea station	unverified location could possibly be near the Gulf of Suez	not applicable
Sin Wilderness	Ex. 16:1, 17:1; Nu. 33:11-12	God supplies quail and manna, "Between Elim and Sinai"		biblical scholars suspect that the name Sin refers to the semitic moon-deity Sin, who was worshipped widely around the entire periphery of prehistoric Arabia, the Levant and Mesopotamia.
Dophkah	Nu. 33:12-13		location unknown despite some speculation	Dophkah = to thrust; drive; knock; drive hard, i.e., to overdrive a herd of cattle
A'lush	Nu. 33:13-14		location unknown	A'lush = a crowd of men

458

Appendix A (cont'd)

Names of the 42 Exodus locations A1:A1:E31	Biblical reference	Description	Possible modern location/ encampment/ town	Hebrew translation or metaphorical meaning of the key word/s* (where applicable)
Rephidim	Ex. 17:1, 19:2; Nu. 33:14-15	God commands Moses to strike a "Rock of Horeb", water gushes forth to alleviate thirst.	location unknown	Rephidim = most probably means supports; Horeb = to dry up or lay waste; dryness or desolation
Sinai Wilderness	Ex. 19:1-2; Nu. 10:12, 33:15-16	Near Mount Sinai	exact location of Mount Sinai is unknown despite much speculation	not applicable
Kibroth-Hattaavah	Nu. 11:35, 33:16-17	Lit. *Graves of Longing or Graves of Lust*	location unknown	Kibroth-Hattaavah = graves of craving or lust. This is the location where the Bible claims that the Israelites were complaining about constantly eating only Manna
Hazeroth	Nu. 11:35, 12:16, 33:17-18		location unknown	Hazeroth = villages or courts
Rithmah	Nu. 33:18-19		location unknown	Rithmah = wild broom, the broom valley, or valley of broombushes
Rimmon-Perez	Nu. 33:19-20		location unknown	Rimmon-Perez = pomegranate of the breach. Rimmon = pomegranate (Hebrew); the thunderer (Akkadian); the chief god (Aramean); the Lord par excellence (Syria).
Libnah	Nu. 33:20-21		possibly in the Sinai Desert but exact location unknown	Libnah = whiteness
Rissah	Nu. 33:21-22		location unknown	Rissah = dew or fall of dew; watering; distillation; also a ruin or dripping to pieces

459

Appendix A (cont'd)

Names of the 42 Exodus loca-tions A1:A1:E31	Biblical reference	Description	Possible modern location/ encampment/ town	Hebrew translation or metaphorical meaning of the key word/s* (where applicable)
Kehelathah	Nu. 33:22-23		location unknown	Kehelathah = assembly or convocation; also a place for gathering antimony (a chemical element use as medicine and cosmetics, known by the Arabic name kohl)
Mount Shapher	Nu. 33:23-24		location unknown	Shapher = brightness
Haradah	Nu. 33:24-25		location unknown	Haradah = fright or fearful
Makheloth	Nu. 33:25-26		location unknown	Makheloth = assemblies
Tahath	Nu. 33:26-27		location unknown	Tahath = below
Tarah	Nu. 33:27-28		location unknown	Tarah = ibex, wild goat or wanderer; loiterer; can also mean a hair, a wretch or one banished. Tarah (Thara) can also be an alternative spelling for Terah the father of the Hebrew patriarch Abraham
Mithcah	Nu. 33:28-29		location unknown	Mithcah = sweetness
Hashmonah	Nu. 33:29-30		location unknown	Hashmonah = fertile or fatness
Moseroth	Nu. 33:30-31		location unknown	Moseroth = band, bond, bind or tied up
Bene-Jaakan	Nu. 33:31-32		location unknown	Bene-Jaakan = the wells of the children of Jaakan. Jaakan = he twists; Jaakan was also a Biblical person claimed to be one of the sons of Ezer (Ezer = to store or to help)
Hor Haggidgad	Nu. 33:32-33		location unknown	Hor Haggidgad = cavern of felicity/good fortune or happiness, cavern of thunder, the central light of little fortunes

ADAPTED FROM ORIGINAL SOURCE: https://en.wikipedia.org/wiki/Stations_of_the_Exodus   * = edited from multiple sources

Appendix A (cont'd)

Names of the 42 Exodus locations	Biblical reference	Description	Possible modern location/ encampment/ town	Hebrew translation or metaphorical meaning of the key word/s* (where applicable)
Jotbathah	Nu. 33:33-34		location unknown	Jotbathah = natural and moral goodness
Abronah	Nu. 33:34-35		location unknown	Abronah = passage or pass
Ezion-Geber	Nu. 33:35-36		Near northern tip of Gulf of Aqaba	Ezion-Geber = backbone of a man, foundation of human essence
Kadesh	Nu. 20:1,22, 33:36-37	Located in the Wilderness of Zin; Miriam's burial place	Probably Ain el Qadeis	Kadesh = holy or sacred
Mount Hor	Nu. 20:22, 21:4, 33:37-41	On the Edomite border; Aaron's burial place	location unknown	Hor = mountain. Literally Mount Hor means Mount Mountain!
Zalmonah	Nu. 33:41-42		location unknown	Zalmonah = the shade, shady
Punon	Nu. 33:42-43		location unknown	Punon = darkness; can also mean precious stones
Oboth	Nu. 21:10-11, 33:43-44		location unknown	Oboth = holes dug for water, water bottles made of skins
Abarim Ruins	Nu. 21:11, 33:44-45		location unknown	Abarim = to passover, by or through; regions beyond or crossings; those on the other side
Dibon Gad	Nu. 33:45-46		location unknown	Dibon Gad = great understanding, abundance of sons. Dibon = abundance of knowledge. Gad = fortune or luck
Almon Diblathaim	Nu. 33:46-47		location unknown	Almon Diblathaim = hidden towards two (fig) cakes (meaning is ambiguous and uncertain)

461

Appendix A (cont'd)

Names of the 42 Exodus locations	Biblical reference	Description	Possible modern location/ encampment/ town	Hebrew translation or metaphorical meaning of the key word/s* (where applicable)
Abarim Mountains	Nu. 33:47-48	Israelites encamped beneath Mount Nebo	location unknown	Abarim = to passover, by or through; regions beyond or crossings; those on the other side
Moab Plains	Nu. 22:1, 33:48-50	Israelites encamped on the Jordan River from Beith Hayishimoth to Aveil Hashittim	Occupied most of the Trans-Jordan region	not applicable - now west-central Jordan
ADAPTED FROM ORIGINAL SOURCE: https://en.wikipedia.org/wiki/Stations_of_the_Exodus				* = edited from multiple sources

Bibliography

Abulafia, D., (2012), *The Great Sea: A Human History of the Mediterranean*, Penguin Books, London.

Adams, S.L., (2020), *Wisdom Literature in Egypt*, in Adams, S.L. and Goff, M. (eds), The Wiley Blackwell Companion to Wisdom Literature, John Wiley and Sons, West Sussex, pp. 310-327.

Adjepong, A., (2020), *What is History: The Science of the Past in Perspective*, International Journal of Trend in Scientific Research and Development (IJTSRD), Vol. 4, Issue 3, March-April, pp. 13-41.

Adler, Y. (2022), *The Origins of Judaism: An Archaeological-Historical Reappraisal*, Yale University Press, USA.

Agranat-Tamir et al., (2020) *The Genomic History of the Bronze Age Southern Levant*, Cell 181, pp. 1146–1157, May 28. https://doi.org/10.1016/j.cell.2020.04.024.

Algarvio, C. (2021), *Egyptian Acculturation in Achaemenid Persia: The Iconographic Evidence*, Academia Letters, Article 397, March, https://doi.org/10.20935/AL397, retrieved on 27 July 2022.

Allen, S., (2018), *The Science of Awe*, A white paper prepared for the John Templeton Foundation by the Greater Good Science Center at UC Berkeley, September.

Ancient History Encyclopedia, (2020), *Alexander the Great and Hellenization in the 4th Century BCE,* 20 July, accessed 5 August 2020.

Annus, A. (ed), (2012), *Divination and Interpretation of Signs in the Ancient World,* The Oriental Institute of the University of Chicago, Oriental Institute Seminars, Seminar 6, Chicago, Illinois.

Anthony, D.W., (2007), *The Horse, the Wheel and Language: How Bronze-age Riders from the Eurasian Steppes shaped the Modern World*, Princeton University Press, New Jersey.

Appel, M., (2008), *Fictional Narratives Cultivate Just-World Beliefs*, Journal of Communication, 58 (1), pp. 62-83.

Armstrong, K., (1993), *A History of God: The 4,000-year Quest of Judaism, Christianity and Islam*, Ballantine Books, New York.

Armstrong, K., (2005), *A Short History of Myth*, Canongate, Edinburgh.

Armstrong, K., (2006), *The Great Transformation: The Beginning of Our Religious Traditions*, Anchor Books, New York.

Armstrong, K., (2007), *The Bible; A Biography*, The Books that Changed the World, Grove Press, New York.

Armstrong, K., (2022), *Sacred Nature: How we can recover our bond with the natural world*, The Bodley Head, London.

Arnold, B.T., (2015), *Was Ancient Israel Just Like Its Neighbours? A Singular Israel in a Pluralistic World*, The Seedbed Daily Text, June 30.

Arranz-Otaegui, A., Carretero, L.A., Roe, J., Richter, T., (2018*), Founder crops v wild plants: Assessing the plant-based diet of the last hunter-gatherers in southwest Asia*, Quaternary Science Reviews, 186, pp. 263-283.

Ashe, G., (2018), *Eden in the Altai: The Prehistoric Golden Age and the Mythic Origins of Humanity*, Bear and Company, Rochester, Vermont.

Asimov, I., (1981), *Asimov's Guide to the Bible: Two Volumes in One*, Wings Books, New Jersey.

Askarov, A. Shirinov, T. (1994), *The 'Palace', Temple and Necropolis of Jurkutan*, Bulletin of the Asia Institute, New Series, Vol 8, The Archaeology and Art of Central Asia Studies from the former Soviet Union, pp. 13-25.

Assmann, J. translated by David Lorton, (2005), *Death and Salvation in Ancient Egypt*, Cornell University Press, Ithaca and London.

Atzmon, G. et al., (2010), *Abraham's Children in the Genome Era: Major Jewish Diaspora Populations Comprise Genetic Clusters with Shared Middle Eastern Ancestry*, The American Journal of Human Genetics, 86, June 11, pp. 850-859.

Badger, L.F., (1886), *The Assyrian Eponym Canon and the Chronology of the Bible*, The Old Testament Student, June, Vol. 5, No. 10, pp. 388-394.

Baldwin, J.D., (1869), *PreHistoric Nations*, Harper & Brothers, New York, p192, cited in https://atlantablackstar.com/2014/04/16/5-ancient-black-civilizations-africa/5/.

Bandura, A., (2006), *Toward a Psychology of Human Agency*, Perspectives on Psychological Science, June, Vol. 1, No. 2, pp. 164-180.

Banner, J.M., (2022), *All History Is Revisionist History*, Humanities, Vol. 43, Issue 3, Summer, Summer 2022 | The National Endowment for the Humanities (neh.gov) retrieved on 12 July 2022.

Bar-Yosef, O., Goern-Inbar, N. (1993), *The Lithic Assemblages of 'Ubeidiya: a Lower Palae-olithic Site in the Jordan Valley*, Qedem, Vol. 34, pp. I-XIV, 1-266. Published by: Institute of Archaeology, Hebrew University of Jerusalem.

Barako, T.J., (2007), *Coexistence and Impermeability: Egyptians and Philistines in Southern Canaan During the Twelfth Century BCE*, in Bietak, M., Czerny, E., (2007), *The Synchronisation of Civilisations in the Eastern Mediterranean in the Second Millenium B.C. III*, OAW, Wien, Austria, pp. 509-516.

Barker, R.G., Wright, H., (1949), *Psychological Ecology and the Problem of Psychosocial Development*, Child Development, September, Vol. 20, No. 3, pp. 131-143.

Barker, R.G., Wright, H., (1955), *Midwest and its Children*, Harper and Row, New York.

Barker, R.G., Gump, P., (1964), *Big School, Small School*, Stanford University Press, Stanford.

Barnikel, F., Vetter, M. (2012), *Earthquakes in History—Ways to Find out About the Seismic Past of a Region* in Sebastiano D'Amico (ed) (2012), *Earthquake Research and Analysis: Seismology, Seismotectonic and Earthquake Geology*, Intech Open, Croatia, February, pp 1-21.

Barr, J., (1985), *The Question of Religious Influence: The Case of Zoroastrianism, Judaism and Christianity*, Journal of the American Academy of Religion, June, Vol. 53, No. 2, pp. 201-235.

Barth, F., (2007), *Overview: Sixty Years in Anthropology*, Annual Review of Anthropology, Vol. 36, 21 October, pp. 1-16.

Bauer, S.W., (2007), *The History of the Ancient World, From the earliest accounts to the fall of Rome*, W W Norton, New York USA.

Baumer, C., (2016), *The History of Central Asia: The Age of the Steppe Warriors*, Vol 1, I.B. Taurus, London.

Bellah, R.N., (2011), *Religion in Human Evolution: From Paleolithic to the Axial Age*, Belknap Press of Harvard University, Cambridge, Massachusetts.

Ben-Dor Evian, S., (2017), *Egypt and Israel: The Never-Ending Story*, Near Eastern Archaeology, Vol. 80, No. 1, March, pp. 30-39.

Ben-Dor Evian, S., (2018), *The Past and Future of 'Biblical Archaeology'*, Journal of Ancient Egyptian Interconnections, Vol. 18, June, pp. 1-11.

Bennett, M.R. et al., (2021), *Evidence of humans in North America during the Last Glacial Maximum*, SCIENCE, 24 September, Vol 373, Issue 6562, pp. 1528-1531.

Benz, M., Bauer, J., (2015), *On Scorpions, Birds and Snakes—Evidence for Shamanism in Northern Mesopotamia during the Early Holocene*, Journal of Ritual Studies, Vol. 29, No. 2, pp. 1-23.

Beyl, T, (2013), *Phoenicia: Identity, and Geopolitics in the Iron I-IIA Period: An Examination of the Textual, Archaeological, and Biblical Evidence*, Doctor of Philosophy Dissertation In Bible and Ancient Near East, The School of Graduate Studies of the Hebrew Union College-Jewish Institute of Religion, Cincinnati, Ohio.

Bharatiya Vidya Bhavan, (2018), *The History and Culture of the Indian People, The Vedic Age*, Vol. 01, Bhavan's Book University. https://dokumen.pub/qdownload/the-history-and-culture-of-the-indian-people-11-vol-set-1-11.html retrieved on 27 April 2023.

Bharucha, Z., Pretty, J., (2010), *The roles and values of wild foods in agricultural systems*, Philosophical Transactions of the Royal Society, 365, pp. 2913-2926.

Bible 2002, *Holy Bible,* Harper Collins USA.

Bierlein, J.F., (1994), *Parallel Myths*, Ballantine Books, The Random House Publishing Group, New York.

Bietak, M., (2018), *The Antagonism between Animosity and Peace-making in Ancient Egypt: Between Ideology and Practical Foreign Policy. An Extended Synopsis*, in Lanfranchi, G.B., Ponchia, S., Rollinger, R., (eds), Melamuu Workshops and Monographs 5: *Making Peace in the Ancient World*, Proceedings of the 7th Melammu Workshop, Padova, 5-7 November, pp. 63-106.

Birney, K.J., (2007), *Sea Peoples or Syrian Peddlers? The Late Bronze Age—Iron Age Presence in Syria and Cilicia*, Dissertation presented in partial fulfilment of the requirements of Doctor of Philosophy in the subject of Archaeology of the Levant, May, Harvard University, Cambridge Massachusetts.

Black, J., (2007), *The Secret History of the World*, Quercus, London.

Blenkinsopp, J. (2011), *Creation, Un-Creation, Re-Creation: A Discursive Commentary on Genesis 1-11*, T & T International, London.

Bloch-Smith, E., (2003), *Israelitete ethnicity in Iron I: Archaeology preserves what is remembered and what is forgotten in Israel's history*, Journal of Biblical Literature; Atlanta, Vol. 122, Issue 3, (Fall), pp. 401-425.

Boaretto, E. et al., (2021), *The absolute chronology of Boker Tachtit (Israel) and implications for the Middle to Upper Paleolithic transition in the Levant*, Proceedings of the National Academy of Sciences, Vol. 118, No.25, pp. 1-9.

Bohstrom, P., (2021), *Were Hebrews Ever Slaves in Ancient Egypt? Yes*, Haaretz, March 25, https://www.haaretz.com/israel-news/2021-03-25/ty-article/were-hebrews-ever-slaves-in-ancient-egypt-yes/0000017f-f6ea-d47e-a37f-fffeebef0000 retrieved on 7 March 2023.

Boivin, N., Crowther, A., (2021), *Mobilizing the past to shape a better future*, Nature Ecology and Evolution, Vol. 5, March, pp. 273-285.

Bottero, J., (1995) translated by Zainab Bahrani and Marc Van De Mieroop , *Mesopotamia: Writing, Reasoning and the Gods*, The University of Chicago Press, USA.

Bottero, J., (2001) translated by Antonia Nevill, *Everyday Life in Ancient Mesopotamia*, The John Hopkins University Press, Maryland.

Bottero, J., (2004) translated by Teresa Lavender Fagan, *Religion in Ancient Mesopotamia*, The University of Chicago Press, Chicago.

Bowler, K., Reagan, W., (2014), *Bigger, Better, Louder: The Prosperity Gospel's Impact on Contemporary Christian Worship*, Religion and American Culture: A Journal of Interpretation, Vol. 24, No. 2, Summer, pp. 186-230.

Boyce, M., (1984), *On the Antiquity of Zoroastrian Apocalyptic*, Bulletin of the School of Oriental and African Studies, University of London, Vol. 47, No. 1, pp. 57-75.

Boyce, M., (2001), *Zoroastrians: Their religious Beliefs and Practices*, Routledge Taylor & Francis Group, London.

Brettler, M.Z., (2010) *The Hebrew Bible and the Early History of Israel*, in Baskin, J.R., Seeskin, K. (eds) (2010), *The Cambridge Guide to Jewish History, Religion and Culture*, Cambridge University Press, pp. 6-33.

Broshi, M., Gophna, R. (1986), *Middle Bronze Age II Palestine: Its Settlements and Population*, Bulletin of the American Schools of Oriental Research, No. 261, February, pp. 73-90.

Broshi, M., Finkelstein, I., (1992), The Population of Palestine in Iron Age II, Bulletin of the American Schools of Oriental Research, No. 287, August, pp. 47-60.

Brown, C.S., (2012), *Big History: From the Big Bang to the Present*, New Press, New York.

Brown, D.E., (2004), *Human Universals, Human Nature & Human Culture*, Daedalus, Fall, Vol. 133, No. 4, On Human Nature, pp. 47-54.

Brown, D., (2006), *Astral Divination in the Context of Mesopotamian Divination, Medicine, Religion, Magic, Society and Scholarship*, East Asian Science, Technology and Medicine, Vol. 25, Issue 1, June, pp. 69-120.

Bruce, L.D., (2019), *The Merenptah Stele and the Biblical Origins of Israel*, Journal of the Evangelical Theological Society, 62.3, September, pp. 463-493.

Bryce, T., Birkett-Rees, J. (2016), *Atlas of the Ancient Near East: from prehistoric times to the Roman imperial period*, Routledge, New York.

Burmeister, S., (2017), *Early Wagons in Eurasia: Disentangling and Enigmatic Innovation*, in Stockhammer P.W., Maran J. (eds) (2017), *Appropriating Innovations: Entangled Knowledge in Eurasia 5000—1500 BCE*, Oxbow Books, Oxford.

Bycroft, P., Judd, B., (1989), *Evaluating Housing Standards and Performance*, Housing Issues 4; Royal Australian Institute of Architects Education Division, Canberra, Australia.

Callaway, E., (2019), *Siberia's ancient ghost clan starts to surrender its secrets*, Nature, Vol. 566, 28 February, pp. 445-446.

Callicott, J.B., (1990), *Genesis Revisited: Murian Musings on Lynn Whit Jr. Debate*, Environmental History Review, Spring-Summer, Vol. 14, No. 1/2, pp. 65-90.

Calvino, I., (1979), *Invisible Cities*, Pan Books, London.

Campbell, J. with Bill Moyers (1991), *The Power of Myth*, 1st Anchor Books, USA, July.

Campbell, J., (2001), *Thou Art That: Transforming Religious Metaphor*, New World Library, Novato, California.

Campbell, J., (2004), *Pathways to Bliss: Mythology and Personal Transformation*, New World Library, California.

Captivating History, (2019A), *Ancient Anatolia; A Captivating Guide to Ancient Civilisations of Asia Minor, Including the Hittite Empire, Arameans, Luwians, Neo-Assyrian Empire, Scythians, Persians, Romans and More*, Captivating History.

Captivating History, (2019B), *The Phoenicians: A Captivating Guide to the History of Phoenicia and the Impact made by one of the Greatest Trading Civilisations of the Ancient World*, Captivating History.

Captivating History, (2022), *The Akkadian Empire: A Captivating Guide to the First Ancient Empire of Mesopotamia and How Sargon the Great of Akkad Conquered Sumerian City-States*, Captivating History.

Carroll, J. (2011), *Jerusalem, Jerusalem: How the Ancient City Ignited Our Modern World*, Scribe Publications Ltd, Melbourne, Australia.

Cartwright, M. (2016), *Castor and Pollux*, World History Encyclopedia, 10 June, https://worldhistory.org/Castor_and_Pollux/ retrieved on 25 October 2021.

Cartwright, M. (2021), *A Gallery of Historical Maps*, World History Encyclopedia, May, https://www.worldhistory.org/collection/122/a-gallery-of-historical-maps retrieved on 2 June 2021.

Castellano, N. (2019), *The Book of the Dead helped Egyptians prepare for the afterlife where Osiris, god of the underworld, would judge them*, National Geographic Magazine,

February 9, https://www.nationalgeographic.com/history/history-magazine/article/egypt-book-of-the-dead retrieved on 15 April 2021.

Catalano, R., Bruckner, T., (2008), *Ambient temperature predicts sex ratios and male longevity*, Proceedings of the National Academy of Sciences, 105 (6), March, pp. 2244-2247.

Cathain, S., (1992), *Hearth Prayers and Other Traditions of Brigit: Celtic Goddess and Holy Woman*, The Journal of the Royal Society of Antiquaries of Ireland, Vol. 122, pp. 12-34.

Cauvin, J., Hodder, I., Rollefson, G.O., Bar-Yosef, O., Watkins, T., (2001), *Review of The Birth of the Gods and the Origin of Agriculture by Jacques Cauvin, Translated by Trevor Watkins,* (New Studies in Archaeology) Cambridge Archaeological Journal, 11, No. 1, pp. 105-121.

Cauvin, J. (2003), *The Birth of the Gods and the Origins of Agriculture*, Cambridge University Press, UK.

Chakaberty, C., (1987), *A Study in Hindu Social Polity*, Mittal Publications, Delhi, p33, cited in https://atlantablackstar.com/2014/04/16/5-ancient-black-civilizations -africa/5/.

Charles River Editors (undated), *Eridu: The History and Legacy of the Oldest City in Ancient Mesopotamia*, USA.

Chen, S.X., (2014), *The Creation of Female Origin Myth: A Critical Analysis of Gender in the Archaeology of Neolithic China*, Totem: The University of Western Ontario Journal of Anthropology, Vol. 22, Issue 1, Article 4, pp. 23-30.

Chessa, B. et al., (2009), *Revealing the History of Sheep Domestication Using Retrovirus Integrations*, Science, April 24; 324(5926): 532–536, doi: 10.1126/science.1170587.

Christian, D., (1991), *The Case for 'Big History'*, Journal of World History, Fall, Vol. 2, No. 2, pp. 223-238.

Clarke J. et al., (2016), *Climatic changes and social transformations in the Near East and North Africa during the 'long' 4th millennium BC: comparative study of environmental and archaeological evidence*, Quaternary Science Reviews, Vol. 136, 15 March, pp. 96-121.

Clarke, L.W., (1962), *Greek Astronomy and Its Debt to the Babylonians*, The British Journal for History of Science, June, Vol 1, No. 1, pp. 65-77.

Cline, E.H. (2007), *From Eden to Exile, Unravelling Mysteries of The Bible,* National Geographic, USA.

Cline, E.H., O'Connor, D., (2007), *The Mystery of the 'Sea People'*, in O'Connor, D. and Quirke, S. (eds), Mysterious Lands, UCL Press, Institute of Archaeology, February, pp. 107-135.

Cline, E., (2009), *Biblical Archaeology: A Very Short Introduction*, Oxford University Press, Oxford.

Cline E.H. (2014), *1177 B.C: The Year Civilisation Collapsed*, Princeton University Press, Oxfordshire, UK.

Cohen, S., Adams, M.J., (2019*), Introduction: Movement and Mobility Between Egypt and the Southern Levant in the Second Millennium BCE*, Journal of Ancient Egyptian Interconnections, Vol. 21, March, pp. 1-4.

Cohen, S.B; Kliot, N., (1992), *Place-Names in Israel's Ideological Struggle over the Administered Territories*, Annals of the Association of American Geographers, Dec., Vol 82, No 4, pp. 653-680.

Cohen-Sherbok, L., (1999), *A Concise Encyclopaedia of Judaism*; One World Publications, Oxford.

Collins, A., (2014), *Göbekli Tepe: Genesis of the Gods: The Temple of the Watchers and the Discovery of Eden,* Bear & Company, Vermont.

Collins, J.J., (2011), *King and Messiah as Son of God*, in Pongratz-Leisten, B. (ed), (2011), *Reconsidering the Concept of Revolutionary Monotheism*, Eisenbrauns, Winona Lake, Indiana.

Collins, P., (2008), *From Egypt to Babylon: The International Age 1550-500BC*, The British Museum Press, London.

Collins, R. (2004), Princeton University Press, Princeton New Jersey.

Cooley, J.L., (2011) *Astral Religion in Ugarit and Ancient Israel*, Journal of Near Eastern Studies, Vol. 70, No, 2, October, pp. 281-287.

Cornell, S., Costanza, R., Sörlin, S., & Van Der Leeuw, S. (2010). *Developing a systematic ' science of the past' to create our future.* Global Environmental Change, 20(3), 426-427. https://doi.org/10.1016/j.gloenvcha.2010.01.005.

Coss, R.G., (2017), *Drawings of Representational Images by Upper Palaeolithic Humans and their Absence in Neanderthals Reflect Historical Differences in Hunting Wary Game*, Evolutionary Studies in Imaginative Culture, Vol. 1, No. 2, Fall, pp. 15-38.

Costanza, R. et al., (2012), *Developing an Integrated History and future of People on Earth (IHOPE)*, Current Opinion in Environmental Sustainability, Volume 4, Issue 1, February, Pages 106-114

Cox, G., Morris, J., (2012), *Why Circumcision: From Prehistory to the Twenty-First Century*, in D.A. Bolnick et al., (eds), *Surgical Guide to Circumcision*, Springer-Verlag, London, pp. 243-259.

Crickmore, L., (2009), *A possible Mesopotamian origin for Plato's World Soul*, Hermathena, Summer, No. 186, pp. 5-23.

Cunliffe, B., (2011), *Europe between the Oceans: 9000BC-AD1000*, Yale University Press, New Haven.

Cunliffe, B., (2017), *By Steppe, Desert, and Ocean; The Birth of Eurasia*, Oxford University Press, Oxford, UK.

Cunliffe, B., (2019), *The Scythians Nomad Warriors of the Steppe*, Oxford University Press, New York.

Curry, A., (2008), *Göbeklitepe: The World's First Temple? Predating Stonehenge by 6,000 years, Türkiye's stunning Göbeklitepe upends the conventional view of the rise of civilization*, Smithsonian Magazine, November, https://www.smithsonianmag.com/history/Göbeklitepe-the-worlds-first-temple-83613665/ retrieved on 7 March 2021.

Dalrymple, W., (2024), *The Golden Road: How Ancient India Transformed the World*, Bloomsbury Publishing, Great Brittain.

Dartnell, L., (2018), *Origins: How the earth made us*, The Bodley Head, London.

Davidsen, M.A., (2016), *Fiction and religion: how narratives about the supernatural inspire religious belief – introducing the thematic issue*, Religion, Vol. 46, No. 4, pp. 489-499.

de Barros Damgaard, P. et al., (2018), *The First Horse Herders and the Impact of Early Bronze Age Steppe Expansion into Asia*, Science, 360 (6396), June 29.

Delisle, R.G., (2012), *The Disciplinary and Epistemological Structure of Palaeoanthropology: One Hundred and Fifty Years of Development*, History and Philosophy of the Life Sciences, Vol. 34, No. 1/2, Human Evolution Across Disciplines: Through the Looking Glass of History and Epistemology, pp. 283-329.

Dell, K.J., Millar, S.R., Keefer, A.J., (2022), *The Cambridge Companion to Biblical Wisdom Literature*, Cambridge University Press, Cambridge, UK.

Denning-Bolle, S.J., (1987), *Wisdom and Dialogue in the Ancient Near East*, Numen, December, Vol. 34, Fasc. 2, pp. 214-234.

Denova, R., (2021A), *The Origin of Satan*, World History Encyclopedia, 18 February, https://member.worldhistory.org/article/1685/the-origin-of-satan/, retrieved on 24 February 2021

Denova, R., (2021B)). *The Gospels*. World History Encyclopedia, February 26, https://www.ancient.eu/The_Gospels/ retrieved on 3 March 2021.

Denova, R., (2021C), *Constantine's Conversion to Christianity*, World History Encyclopedia, 10 May, https://worldhistory.org/article/1737/constantines-conversion-to-christianity/ retrieved on 12 May 2021.

Denova, R., (2021D), *Ten Commandments*, World History Encyclopedia, 13 July, https://member.worldhistory.org/Ten_Commandments/ retrieved on 7 June 2021.

Denova, R., (2022), *Gospel of John*, World History Encyclopedia, 14 June, Gospel of John—World History Encyclopedia, retrieved on 28 June 2022.

Dever, W.G., (2002), *What Did the Biblical Writers Know & When Did They Know It?*, William B. Eerdmans Publishing Company, Grand Rapids, Michigan.

Dever, W.G., (2003), *Who Were the Early Israelites and Where Did They Come From?* William B. Eerdmans Publishing Company, Grand Rapids, Michigan.

Diamond, J., (2005), *guns, germs and steel: a short history of everybody for the last 13,000 years*, Vintage Books, London.

Douglas, M., (1966), *Purity and Danger: An analysis of conceptions of pollution and taboo*, Routledge and Kegan Paul, United Kingdom.

Draper, S., (2014), *Effervescence and Solidarity in Religious Organizations*, Journal for the Scientific Study of Religion, June, Vol. 53, No. 2, pp. 229-248.

Dundes, A., (1999), *Holy Writ as Oral Writ: The Bible as Folklore*, Rowman and Littlefield, Maryland, USA.

Eitam D, Kislev M, Karty A, Bar-Yosef O, (2015), *Experimental Barley Flour Production in 12,500-Year-Old Rock-Cut Mortars in Southwestern Asia*. PLoS ONE 10(7): e0133306. https://doi.org/10.1371/journal.pone.0133306 retrieved on 2 March 2022.

Elkins, D.N., (1998), *Beyond Religion: 8 Alternative Paths to the Sacred: A Personal Program for Building a Spiritual Life Outside the Walls of Traditional Religion*, Quest Books, Wheaton, Illinois.

Ellwood, C.A., (1913), *The Social Function of Religion*, American Journal of Sociology, November, Vol. 19, No. 3, pp. 289-307.

Ellwood, C.A., (1918), *Religion and Social Control*, The Scientific Monthly, October, Vol. 7, No. 8, pp. 335-348.

Emanuel, J.P., (2016), *Maritime Worlds Collide: Agents of Transference and the Metastasis of Seaborne Threats at the End of the Bronze Age*, Palestine Exploration Quarterly, 148:4, pp. 265-280.

Erdos, L., Ambarli, D., Anenkhonov, O., Batori, Z., Cserhalmi, D., Kiss, M., Kroel-Dulay, G., Liu, H., Magnes, M., Molnar, Z., (2018), *The edge of two worlds: A new review and synthesis on Eurasian forest-steppes*, Applied Vegetation Science, Vol 21, Issue 3, 20 April, pp. 1-48.

Eshed, V., Gopher, A., (2018), *Agriculture and life style: A Paleodemography of Pottery Neolithic (8500-6500 cal. BP) Farming Populations in the Southern Levant*, Paleorient, Vol. 44, No. 2, pp. 93-112.

Esparza, D., (2016), *When the Earth was flat: a map of the universe, according to the Old Testament, Art & Culture*, July; https://aleteia.org/2016/07/07/when-the-earth-was-flat-a-map-of-the-universe-according-to-the-old-testament/ accessed on 28 July 2020.

Eusebius, (2011), *The History of the Church*, translated by G.A. Williamson, The Folio Society, London.

Fairbridge R.W., (2009), *History of Paleoclimatology*. In: Gornitz V. (eds) *Encyclopedia of Paleoclimatology and Ancient Environments*. Encyclopedia of Earth Sciences Series. Springer, Dordrecht. https://doi.org/10.1007/978-1-4020-4411-3_104.

Faust, A., (2015), *The Bible, Archaeology, and the Practice of Circumcision in Israelitete and Philistine Societies*, Journal of Biblical Literature, 134, No. 2, pp. 273-290.

Faust, A., (2018), *Pigs in Space (and Time): Pork Consumption and Identity Negotiations in the Late Bronze Age and Iron Age of Ancient Israel*, Near Eastern Archaeology, 81.4, pp. 276-299.

Faust, A., Katz, H., (2011), *Philistines, Israelites and Canaanites in the Southern Trough Valley during the Iron Age I*, Egypt and the Levant 21, pp. 231-247.

Feldman, M. et al., (2019), *Ancient DNA sheds light on the genetic origins of early Iron Age Philistines*, Science Advances, Research Article, 5, 3 July, pp. 1-10.

Feuerstein, G., Kak, S., Frawley, D., (2001), *In Search of the Cradle of Civilisation: New Light on Ancient India*, Quest Books, Wheaton, Illinois.

Fiaccavento, C., (2014), *Destructions as historical markers towards the end of the 2ⁿᵈ and during the 1ˢᵗ millennium BC in Southern Levant*, in Nigro, l. (ed), (2014), *Overcoming Catastrophes. Essays on disastrous agents characterizations and resilience strategies in pre-classical Southern Levant* (ROSAPAT 11—PRN 2009—The Seven Plagues) Roma, pp. 205-259.

Fincke, J.C., (2013) *The Solar Eclipse Omen Texts from enuma anu enlil*, Bibliotheca Orientalis (BiOr), 70.5-6, pp. 582-608.

Finnchuill's Mast, (2018), *Origin of the World's Mythologies: Book Review*, August 24, https://finnchuillsmast.wordpress.com/2018/08/ retrieved on 29 November 2021.

Finkel, I., (2014), *The Ark Before Noah: Decoding the Story of the Flood*, Hodder & Stoughton, London.

Finkel, I., (2021), *The First Ghosts: Most Ancient of Legacies,* Hodder & Stoughton, London.

Finkelstein, I., (1990), *Early Arad—Urbanism of the Nomads*, Zeitschrift des Deutschen Palastina-Vereins (1953-), Bd. 106, pp. 34-50.

Finkelstein, I., Silberman, N.A., (2002), *The Bible Unearthed, Archaeology's New Vision of Ancient Israel and The Origin of its Sacred Texts*, Touchstone, New York.

Finkelstein, I., Mazar, A., Schmidt, B. (ed), (2007A), *The Quest for Historical Israel*, The Society of Biblical Literature, Atlanta.

Finkelstein, I., (2007B), *Patriarchs, Exodus, Conquest: Fact or Fiction*, in Finkelstein, I.; Mazar, A., Schmidt, B. (ed), (2007), *The Quest for Historical Israel*, The Society of Biblical Literature, Atlanta, pp. 41-55.

Finkelstein, I., (2007C), *King Solomon's Golden Age: History or Myth*, in Finkelstein, I.; Mazar, A., Schmidt, B. (ed), (2007), *The Quest for Historical Israel*, The Society of Biblical Literature, Atlanta, pp. 107-116.

Finkelstein, I., (2010), *A Great United Monarchy? Archaeological and Historical Perspectives, One God—One Cult—One Nation: Archaeological and Biblical Perspectives* edited by Reinhard G. Kratz, Herman Spieckermann, Bjorn Corzilius and Tanja Pilger, Berlin, New York: De Gruyter, pp. 1-28. https://doi.org/10.1515/97831102235831.1.

Finkelstein, J.J., (1963), *Mesopotamian Historiography*, Proceedings of the American Philosophical Society, December, Vol. 107, No. 6, pp. 461-472.

Finlayson, B. et al., (2011), *Architecture, sedentism, and social complexity at Pre-Pottery Neolithic A WF16, Southern Jordan*, Proceedings of the National Academy of Sciences May, 108 (20) 8183-8188; DOI: 10.1073/pnas.1017642108.

Flannery, K.V., (1972), *The Cultural Evolution of Civilisations*, Annual Review of Ecology and Systematics, Vol. 3, pp. 399-426.

Flannery, K.V., (1973), *The Origins of Agriculture*, Annual Review of Anthropology, Vol. 2, pp. 187-193.

Foster, B.R., Foster, K.P., (2009), *Civilizations of Ancient Iraq*, Princeton University Press, USA.

Fox, M.V., (1974), *The Sign of the Covenant: Circumcision in the Light of the Priestly 'ot Etiologies'*, Revue Biblique, Vol. 81, No. 4, October, pp. 557-596.

François, A., (2008), *Semantic maps and the typology of colexification: Intertwining polysemous networks across languages*, in Vanhove, M. (ed), (2008), *From Polysemy to Semantic Change: Towards a typology of lexical semantic associations*, John Benjamins Publishing Company, Amsterdam, Netherlands, pp. 163-215.

Frankopan, P., (2016), *The Silk Roads: A New History of the World*, Bloomsbury, London.

Free, J.P., (1944), *Abraham's Camels*, Journal of Near Eastern Studies, July, Vol 3, No 3, pp. 187-193.

Friederici, A.D., (2011), *The Brain Basis of Language Processing: From Structure to Function*, Physiological Reviews, American Physiological Society,91, pp. 1357-1392, 1 October, https://doi.org/10.1152/physrev.00006.2011 retrieved on 23 August 2023.

Friedman, R.E., (1997), *Who Wrote the Bible*, HarperSanFrancisco, USA.

Friedmann, J.L., (2020), *The Fall of Jericho as Earthquake Myth*, Jewish Bible Quarterly, Vol. 48, No. 3, pp. 171-178.

Gamble, C., (2015), *The anthropology of deep history*, The Journal of the Royal Anthropological Institute, Vol. 21, No. 1, March, pp. 147-164.

Gamble, C., (2016), *The Death of Prehistory*, Quaderni storici, NUOVA SERIE, Vol. 51, No. 151 (1), April, pp. 284-289.

Gardiner, A.H., (1920), *The Ancient Military Road between Egypt and Palestine*, The Journal of Egyptian Archaeology, April, No. 2, Vol. 6., pp. 99-116.

Gearhart, R., (2015), *Prehistoric Religion*, https://www.academia.edu/12113493/Prehistoric_Religion, 25 April.

Geers, F.W., (1926), *A Babylonian Omen Text*, The American Journal of Semitic Languages and Literature, October, Vol. 43, No. 1, pp. 22-41.

George, A., (2021), *Mammoth ivory pendant is oldest decorated jewellery found in Eurasia*, New Scientist Humans, 25 November, https://www.newscientist.com/article/2299071-mammoth-ivory-pendant-is-oldest-decorated-jewellery-found-in-eurasia/ retrieved on 29 November 2021.

Gibbons, A., (2020), *These 120,000-year-old footprints offer early evidence for humans in Arabia*, Science, September 17, https://www.sciencemag.org/news/2020/09/these-120000-year-old-footprints-offer-early-evidence-humans-arabia retrieved on 31 May 2021.

Gilad, E., (2020), *The Pagan Gods That Still Exist in the Holy Land's City Names*, Haaretz, 16 June, retrieved on 5 August 2021.

Gilad, E., (2021), *The Surprising Ancient Origins of Passover*, Haaretz, 31 March, retrieved on 15 September 2021.

Gilboa, A., (2005), *Sea Peoples and Phoenicians along the Southern Phoenician Coast—A Reconciliation: An interpretation of Sikila (SKL) Material Culture*, Bulletin of the American Schools of Oriental Research, Vol. 337, February, pp. 47-78.

Gilboa, A., (2014), *The Southern Levant (CISJORDAN) During the Iron Age I Period*, in Killebrew, A.E., Steiner, M. (eds), *Oxford Handbook of the Archaeology of the Levant (ca. 8000-332 BCE)*, Oxford University Press, Oxford, UK, January, pp. 624-648.

Gilboa, A., Sharon,I., 2003, *An Archaeological Contribution to the Early Iron Age Chronological Debate: Alternative Chronologies for Phoenicia and Their Effects on the Levant, Cyprus, and Greece*, Bulletin of the American Schools of Oriental Research, No.332. (Nov., 2003), pp. 7-80.

Giuffra, E. et al., (2000), *The Origin of the Domestic Pig: Independent Domestication and Subsequent Introgression*, Genetics, 154, April, pp. 1785-1791.

Glassman, R.M., (2017), *The Origin of Democracy in Tribes, City-States and Nation-States*, Springer International Publishing, Cham, Switzerland.

Glassner, Jean-Jacques, (2004), *Mesopotamian Chronicles: Writings from the Ancient World*, Society of Biblical Literature, Atlanta.

Gmirkin, R.E., (2019), *Plato and the Creation of the Hebrew Bible*, Routledge, London.

Gnuse, R., (2014), *Misunderstood Stories: Theological Commentary on Genesis 1-11*, Cascade Books, Eugene, Oregon.

Goldberg, A., Gunther, T., Rosenberg, N.A., Jakobsson, M., (2017), *Ancient X chromosomes reveal contrasting sex bias in Neolithic and Bronze Age Eurasian migrations*, Proc Natl Acad Sci U S A, Mar 7; 114(10), pp. 2657–2662.

Golden, P.B., (2011), Central Asia in World History, Oxford University Press, New York.

Gombrich, E.H., (2008), A Little History of the World; Yale University Press, New Haven.

Gong, Y., Yan, H., Ge Y., (2009), *The Accounts of the Origin of Writing from Sumer, Egypt, and China—A Comparative Perspective*, Wiener Zeitschrift fur die Kunde des Morgenlandes, Vol. 99, pp. 137-158.

Goodman, M., (2008*), Rome and Jerusalem: The Clash of Ancient Civilisations*, Penguin Books, London.

Goring-Morris, A.N., Belfer-Cohen, A., (2011), *Neolithization Processes in the Levant: The Outer Envelope*, Current Anthropology, Vol. 52, No. 4, The origins of Agriculture: Ne Data, Ne Ideas, October, pp. S195-S208.

Grabbe, L.L., (2018A), *Late Bronze Age Palestine: If we had only the Bible…*, in Grabbe, L.L.(ed), (2018C) *The Land of Canaan in the Late Bronze Age*, Bloomsbury T&T Clark, London, pp. 11-56.

Grabbe, L.L., (2018B), *Reflections on the Discussion…*, in Grabbe, L.L.(ed), *The Land of Canaan in the Late Bronze Age*, Bloomsbury T&T Clark, London, pp. 179-187.

Grabbe, L.L.(ed), (2018C), *The Land of Canaan in the Late Bronze Age*, Bloomsbury T&T Clark, London.

Graves, R., Patai, R. (1964); *Hebrew Myths: The Book of Genesis*; Doubleday and Company, New York.

Graves, R (1961), *The White Goddess*, Faber and Faber, London.

Gray, R.D., Atkinson, Q.D., Greenhill, S.J., (2011), *Language evolution and human history: what a difference a date makes*, Philos Trans R Soc Lond B Biol Sci. Apr 12; 366(1567): 1090–1100.

Grayling, A.C., (2021), *The Frontiers of Knowledge: What We Now Know about Science, History and the Mind*, Viking an Imprint of Penguins Random House Books, UK.

Greenberg, G., (2008), *The Moses Mystery: The Egyptian Origins of the Jewish People*, Pereset Press, New York.

Greenberg, G., (2019), *Genesis Chronology and Egyptian King-Lists: The Egyptian Origins of Genesis History*, Pereset Press, New York.

Gregory, B.S., (2017), *Disembedding Christianity. The Reformation Era and the Secularisation of Western Society*, in Dalferth, I.U. (ed), *Reformation Und Sakularisierung*, Mohr Siebeck GmbH and Co. KG.

Guillaume, P., (2018), *Debunking the Latest Scenario on the Rise of the Pork Taboo*, Etudes et Travaux, Vol. 31, pp. 145-166.

Gump, P., (1971), *The Behavior Setting: A Promising Unit for Environmental Designers*, Landscape Architecture Magazine, January, Vol. 61, No. 2, pp. 130-134.

Gzella, H., (2014), *Peoples and Languages of the Levant during the Bronze and Iron Ages*, in Killebrew, A.E., Steiner, M., *The Oxford Handbook of the Archaeology of the Levant: c. 8000-332 BCE*, Oxford University Press, Oxford, UK, pp. 24-34.

Haldon, J. et al., (2018), *History meets palaeoscience: Consilience and collaboration in studying past societal responses to environmental change*, Proceedings of the National Academy of Sciences, March, pp. 1-9.

Hall, N., (1980), *The Moon and The Virgin,* The Women's Press Limited, London.

Hallock, R.T., (1969), *Persepolis Fortification Tablets*, University of Chicago Oriental Institute Publications, Volume XCII, University of Chicago Press, Illinois.

Halpern, B., (2006-2007), *The Sea-Peoples and Identity*, Scripta Mediterranea, Vol. XXVII-XXVIII, pp. 15-32.

Hancock, J., (2022), *Dynamics of the Neolithic Revolution*, World History Encyclopedia 7 February, Dynamics of the Neolithic Revolution—World History Encyclopedia retrieved on 9 February 2022.

Harari, Y.N., (2015), *Sapiens: A Brief History of Humankind*, Vintage, London.

Haring, B., (2015), *Halaham on an Ostracon of the Early New Kingdom*, Journal of Near Eastern Studies, Vol. 74, No. 2, October, pp. 189-196.

Harmatta, J., Puri, B.N., Lelekov, L., Humayun, S., Sircar D.C., *Religions in the Kushan Empire*, UNESCO, Religious Life in Bactria, ISBN 978-92-3-102846-5 retrieved on 1 May 2023.

Harper, W.R., (1894), *The Sons of God and the Daughters of Men. Genesis VI*, The Biblical World, June, Vol. 3, No. 6, pp. 440-448.

Harris, S., (2015), Waking Up: *Searching for spirituality without religion*, Transworld Publishers Black Swan, London.

Hasel, M.G., (1994), *Israel in the Merneptah Stela*, Bulletin of the American Schools of Oriental Research, Nov., No. 296, pp. 45-61.

Hayes, W.C., (1965), *Most Ancient Egypt*, edited by Keith C. Selee, The University of Chicago Press, Chicago and London.

Helle, S., Helama, S., Jokela, J., (2007), *Temperature-related birth sex ratio bias in historical Sami: warm years bring more sons*, Royal Society Publishing: Biology Letters, Vol. 4, Issue 1, 27 November.

Hendel, R., (2001), *The Exodus in Biblical Memory*, Journal of Biblical Literature, Winter, Vol. 120, No. 4, pp. 601-622.

Hendel, R., (2005), *Genesis 1-11 and its Mesopotamian Problem*, in Gruen, E.S. (ed), *Cultural Borrowings and Ethnic Appropriations in Antiquity*, Franz Steiner Verlag, Stuttgart, pp. 23-36.

Henrich, J., (2021), *The Weirdest People in the World: How the West Became Psychologically Peculiar and Particularly Prosperous*, Penguin's Random House, UK.

Hesketh, I., (2014), *The Story of Big History(s),* History of the Present, Vol. 4, No. 2, Fall, pp. 171-202.

Hiebert, T., (2007), *The Tower of Babel and the Origin of the World's Cultures*, Journal of Biblical Literature, Spring, Vol. 126, No. 1, pp. 29-58.

Highcock, Nancy, (2017), *The Old Assyrian Period (ca. 2000–1600 B.C.).* In Heilbrunn Timeline of Art History. New York: The Metropolitan Museum of Art, 2000. http://www.metmuseum.org/toah/hd/assy_2/hd_assy_2.htm (December 2017).

Hilliard, A.G., Williams, L.,Damali, N (eds), (1987), *The Teachings of Ptahhotep: The Oldest Book in the World*, Blackwood Press, Atlanta, Georgia, USA.

Hodges, F.M., (2001), *The Ideal Prepuce in Ancient Greece and Rome: Male Genital Aesthetics and Their Relation to 'Lipodermos', Circumcision, Foreskin Restoration and the 'Kynodesme'*, Bulletin of the History of Medicine, Vol. 75, No. 3, Fall, pp. 375-405.

Hoffman, J.M., (2004), *In the Beginning: A Short History of the Hebrew Language*, New York University Press, New York.

Hoffmeier, J.K., (1996), *Israel in Egypt: The Evidence for the Authenticity of the Exodus Tradition*, Oxford University Press, Oxford.

Hoffner Jr., H.A., (1969), *Some Contributions of Hittitology to Old Testament Study*, The Tyndale Biblical Archaeology Lecture 1968, Tyndale Bulletin, 20, pp. 27-55.

Holland, G., (2010), *Gods in the Desert: Religions of the Ancient Near East*, Rowman & Littlefield Publishers Inc, Plymouth, UK.

Hooke, S.H., (1955), *Omens. Ancient and Modern*, Folklore, September, Vol. 66, No. 3, pp. 330-339.

Hope, M., (1996), *The Sirius Connection, Unlocking the Secrets of Ancient Egypt*, Element Books, London.

Hornung, E., (1992), *The Rediscovery of Akhenaten and His Place in Religion*, Journal of the American Research Center in Egypt, Vol. 29, pp. 43-49.

Horwitz, L. et al., (2017), *A Contribution to the Iron Age Pig Debate*, in Lev-Tov, J., Hesse, P., Gilbert, A. (eds), *The Wide Lens in Archaeology: Honoring Brian Hesse's Contributions to Anthropological Archaeology*, Lockwood Press, Atlanta, USA, pp. 93-116.

Huizinga, J., (1936), *A Definition of the Concept of History*, in *Philosophy and History, Essays presented to Ernst Cassirer*, eds R. Klibansky & H.J. Paton (Oxford), pp. 1-10.

Hummell, E., (2014), *Standing the Test of Time—Barth and Ethnicity*, Coolabah, February, No.13, ISSN 1988-5946, The Australian and Transnational Studies Centre at the Universitat de Barcelona, pp. 46-60.

Humphreys, C.J., (1998), *The Number of People in the Exodus from Egypt: Decoding Mathematically the Very Large Numbers in Numbers I and XXVI*, Vetus Testamentum, April, Vol. 48, Fasc. 2, pp. 196-213.

Husain, S., (1997), *The Goddess, Creation, Fertility, Female Essence the Sovereignty of Woman Worship, Love Abundance*, Duncan Baird Publishers, London.

Irwin, W.A., (1946), *The Hebrews: God*, in Frankfort H and H.A. et al., (1946) *The Intellectual Adventure of Ancient Man: An Essay on Speculative Thought in the Ancient Near East*, The University of Chicago Press, Chicago, pp. 223-254.

Issa, J., (2017), *Book of Amos*, 18 May, Book of Amos—World History Encyclopedia, retrieved on 27 July 2022.

Izdebski, A. et al., (2016), *Realising consilience: How better communication between archaeologists, historians and natural scientists can transform the study of past climate change in the Mediterranean*, Quaternary Sciences Reviews, 136, pp. 5-22.

Jack. J. (2016) *Akhenaten's Monotheism and its Relationship with Ancient Hebrew Religion,* University of New England, https://www.academia.edu/33957139/Akhenatens_Monotheism_and_its_Relationship_with_Ancient_Hebrew_Religion retrieved on 14 May 2024.

Jacobs, S., (2011), *Expendable Signs: The Covenant of the Rainbow and Circumcision at Qumran*, in Lange, A. et al. (2011), *The Dead Sea Scrolls in Context: Integrating the Dead Sea Scrolls in the Study of Ancient Texts, Languages, and Cultures, Volume 2*, Brill Publishers, Leiden, Boston, pp. 563-575.

Jacobsen, T., (1946A), *Mesopotamia: The Cosmos as State*, in Frankfort H and H.A. et al, (1946) *The Intellectual Adventure of Ancient Man: An Essay on Speculative Thought in the Ancient Near East*, The University of Chicago Press, Chicago, pp. 125-184.

Jacobsen, T., (1946B), *Mesopotamia: The Function of the State*, in Frankfort H and H.A. et al, (1946) *The Intellectual Adventure of Ancient Man: An Essay on Speculative Thought in the Ancient Near East*, The University of Chicago Press, Chicago, pp. 185-201.

Jacobsen, T., (1976), *The Treasures of Darkness: A History of Mesopotamian Religion,* Yale University Press, New Haven and London.

Jacobsen, T., (1981), *The Eridu Genesis*, Journal of Biblical Literature, Dec., Vol. 100, No. 4, pp. 513-529.

Jacobson, D.M., (1999), *Palestine and Israel*, Bulletin of the American Schools of Oriental Research, No. 313, February, pp. 65-74.

Jacquet, R., (2021), *In Search of the Sacred Tetragrammaton Name of God: The Quest to rediscover the Sacred Name and the Origin of the Universe*, 22 August, USA https://www.academia.edu/50988090/Myths_Legends_and_Chronological_Narratives_on_the_Origin_of_the_Universe retrieved on 20 December 2022.

James, E.O., (1999), *The Ancient Gods,* Phoenix, London.

James, W., (1948), *Psychology*, The World Publishing Company, Cleveland and New York.

Jarve, M. et al., (2019), *Shifts in the Genetic Landscape of the Western Eurasian Steppe Associated with the Beginning and End of Scythian Dominance*, Current Biology, 29, July 22, pp. 2430-2441.

Jeong, C. et al., (2019), *The genetic history of admixture across inner Eurasia*, Ecology & Evolution, Vol. 3, June, pp. 966–976.

Jeremias, A.,(1902), *The Babylonian Conception of Heaven and Hell*, HardPress, Miami, Florida.

Joffe, A.H., (2002), *The Rise of Secondary States in the Iron Age Levant*, Journal of the Economic and Social History of the Orient, Vol. 45, No. 4.

Jeske, A., (2019), *Mid-to-Late 18th Dynasty Egyptian Functionaries Serving in the Southern Levant: Can We Trace the Individuals*, Journal of Ancient Egyptian Interconnections, Vol. 21, March, pp. 31-47.

Joseph, R., (2011), *Evolution of Palaeolithic Cosmology and Spiritual Consciousness and the Temporal and Frontal Lobes*, Journal of Cosmology, April-June, Vol. 14, pp. 4400-4440.

Karmin M, et al., (2015), *A recent bottleneck of Y chromosome diversity coincides with a global change in culture.* Genome Res., Apr; 25(4), pp. 459-66. doi: 10.1101/gr.186684.114. Epub 2015 Mar 13. PMID: 25770088; PMCID: PMC4381518.

Kaufman, W.R.P., (2013), *Review: The Origins of the World's Mythologies by E.J. Michael Witzel*, Vol. 8, No. 3, September, pp. 518-523.

Keane, W., (2008), *The Evidence of the Senses and the Materiality of Religion*, The Journal of the Royal Anthropological Institute, Vol. 14, pp. S110-S127.

Keel, O., translated by T.J. Hallett, (1997), *The Symbolism of the Biblical World; Ancient Near Eastern Iconography and the Book of Psalms*, EISENBRAUNS, Winona Lake, Indianna.

Kehoe, A.B., (1991), *The Invention of Prehistory*, Current Anthropology, Aug-Oct, Vol. 32, No. 4, pp. 467-476.

Kelly, L., (2024), *The Knowledge Gene*, Allen & Unwin, NSW, Australia

Kennedy, E., (1979), *Earthrise*, New York Times, April 15, https://www.nytimes.com/1979/04/15/archives/earthrise-the-dawning-of-a-new-spiritual-awareness.html?auth=login-google1tap&login=google1tap retrieved on 30 September 2022.

Key, A.F., (1965), *Traces of the Worship of the Moon God Sin among the Early Israelites*, Journal of Biblical Literature, Vol. 84, No. 1, March, pp. 20-26.

Kislev, I., (2013), *The Census of the Israelites on the Plains of Moab (Numbers 26): Sources and Redaction*, Vetus Testamentum, Vol 63, Fasc. 2, pp. 236-260.

Kenyon, K.M., (1978), *the Bible and Recent Archaeology*, John Knox Press, Atlanta.

Kislev, M.E., (1984), *Emergence of Wheat Agriculture*, Paleorient, Vol. 10, No. 2, pp. 61-70.

Kitchen, K.A., (2003), *On the Reliability of the Old Testament*, William B. Eerdmans Publishing Company, Grand Rapids, Michigan.

Kitchen A, Ehret C, Assefa S, Mulligan CJ., (2009), *Bayesian phylogenetic analysis of Semitic languages identifies an Early Bronze Age origin of Semitic in the Near East.* Proc Biol Sci., Aug 7; 276(1668):2703-10. doi: 10.1098/rspb.2009.0408. Epub 2009 Apr 29. PMID: 19403539; PMCID: PMC2839953.

Klein, C. (2018), *DNA Study Finds Aboriginal Australians World's Oldest Civilization*, History.com, 22 August retrieved on 8 January 2021.

Kneale, M., (2013), *An Atheist's History of Belief: Understanding our most extraordinary invention*, The Bodley Head, London.

Koenig, H.G., (2020), *Maintaining Health and Well-Being by Putting Faith into Action During the COVID-19 Pandemic*, Journal of Religious Health, 59 (5), pp. 2205-2214.

Koestler, A., (1956), *The Sleepwalkers*, Penguin Books, Middlesex, England.

Koffka, K., (1935), *Principles of Gestalt Psychology*, Harcourt, Brace and Company Inc, USA.

Kohl, P.L., (2008), *The Making of Bronze Eurasia*, Cambridge University Press, Cambridge, UK.

Kornienko, T.V., (2009), *Notes on the Cult Buildings of Northern Mesopotamia in the Aceramic Neolithic Period*, Journal of Near Eastern Studies, Vol 68, No. 2, April, pp. 81-102.

Kozuh, M., (2010), *Lamb, Mutton and Goat in the Babylonian Temple Economy*, Journal of Economic and Social History of the Orient, Vol. 53, No. 4, pp. 531-578.

Kramer, S.N., (1956) 3rd revised edition (1981), *History Begins at Sumer: Thirty-nine Firsts in Recorded History*; University of Pennsylvania Press, Philadelphia.

Kramer, S.N., (1968), *Cradle of Civilisation*, Great Ages of Man, Time Life Books, Netherland, N.V.

Kramer, S.N., (1971), *The Sumerians: Their History, Culture and Character*, The University of Chicago press, London.

Kramer, S.N., (2007), *Sumerian Mythology: A Study of Spiritual and Literary Achievement in the Third Millennium B.C.*; Forgotten Books.

Kramer, K.L., Schacht, R., Bell, A., (2017), *Adult sex ratios and partners scarcity among hunter-gatherers: implications for dispersal patterns and the evolution of human sociality*, Phil. Trans. R. Soc. B 372: 20160316. http://dx.doi.org/10.1098/rstb.2016.0316.

Krause, J., Trappe, T., (2021), *A Short History of Humanity: How Migration Made Us Who We Are*, WH Allen, London.

Kriwaczek, P., (2010), *Babylon: Mesopotamia and the Birth of Civilization*, Atlantic Books, London.

Kuhrt, A., (2009A), *The Ancient Near East, c 3000-330 BC, Volume 1*, Routledge, New York.

Kuhrt, A., (2009B), *The Ancient Near East, c 3000-330 BC, Volume 11,* Routledge, New York.

Kurtkaya, M., (2020), *Sumerian Turks: Civilisation's Journey from Siberia to Mesopotamia*, San Bernardino, California, May.

Lawler, A., (2013), *The Everlasting City*, Archaeology, Vol. 66, No. 5, September/October, pp. 26-32.

Lawler, A., (2021), *These archaeological findings unlocked the stories of our ancestors*, National Geographic, 21 October, https://www.nationalgeographic.com/magazine/article/these-archaeological-findings-unlocked-the-stories-of-our-ancestors-feature, retrieved on 29 October 2021.

Le Dosseur, (2003), *Bone Objects in the Southern Levant from the Thirteenth to the Fourth Millennia*, Bulletin du Centre de recherche français à Jérusalem, No. 12, pp. 111-125, https://journals.openedition.org/bcrfj/552#tocto2n5 retrieved on 11 April 2023.

Lee, S., (2007), *Prosperity Theology: T.D. Jakes and the Gospel of the Almighty Dollar*, Cross-Currents, Vol. 57, No. 2, Summer, pp. 227-236.

Leemans, W.F., (1960), *Foreign Trade in the Old Babylonian Period: as revealed by Texts from Southern Mesopotamia*, E.J Brill, Leiden, Netherlands.

Leeming, D.A., (1990), *The World of Myth: An Anthology*, Oxford University Press, New York.

Leick, G. (2002), *Mesopotamia: The Invention of the City*, Penguin Books, England.

Levine, B.A., (2005), *Assyrian Ideology and Israelite Monotheism*, Iraq, Spring, Vol. 67, No. 1, Nineveh. Papers of the 49th Rencontre Assyriologique Internationale, Part Two, pp. 411-427.

Levi-Strauss C., (1955), *The Structural study of myth*, Journal of American Folklore. 68 (270): 428–444. https://doi.org/10.2307/536768 retrieved from 101.187.146.33 on Sunday, 07 Mar 2021 23:33:09 UTC.

Levy, T.E., Adams, R.B., Muniz, A., (2004), *Archaeology and the Shasu Nomads: Recent Excavations in the Jabal Hamrat Fidan, Jordan*, in Friedman, R.E. and Propp, W.H.C., (eds), *Le-David maskil: A Birthday Tribute for David Noel Freedman*, Penn State University Press, University Park, USA, pp. 63-89.

Lewin, K., (1951), *Field Theory in Social Science*, Harper & Brothers Publishers, New York.

Lewis-Williams, D., (2010), *Conceiving God: The Cognitive Origin and Evolution of Religion*, Thames and Hudson, London.

Lincoln, B., (2013), *Review of: E.J. Michael Witzel, 'The Origins of the World's Mythologies'*, Asian Ethnology, November, pp. 443-449.

Littleton, J., Allen, H., (2007), *Hunter-gatherer burials and the creation of persistent places in southeastern Australia*, Journal of Anthropological Archaeology, 26, June, pp. 283-298.

Llewellyn-Jones, L., (2022), *Persians: The Age of the Great Kings*, Wildfire/ Headline Publishing Group, London.

Lloyd, C., (2012), *What on Earth Happened: The Complete Story of the Planet, Life & People from the Big Bang to the Present Day*, Bloomsbury Publishing, London.

Lopez-Ruiz, C., (2016), *Greek Literature and the Lost Legacy of Canaan*, in Aruz, J., Seymour, M. (eds), *Assyria to Iberia: Art and Culture in the Iron Age,* The Metropolitan Museum of Art, New York, distributed by Yale University Press, New Haven and London, pp. 316-321.

Losey, R.J. et al. (2011), *Canids as persons: Early Neolithic dog and wolf burials, Cis-Baikal, Siberia*, Journal of Anthropological Archaeology, 30, pp. 174-189.

Loy, T.H., Spriggs, M., Wickler, S., (1992), *Direct evidence for human use of plants 28,000 years ago: starch residues on stone artefacts from the northern Solomon Islands*, Antiquity, Vol. 66, No. 253, December, pp. 898-912.

Luberto, M., (2007), *The Pyramids—the great mysteries of archaeology*, David and Charles, Cincinnati.

Luckenbill, D.D., (1918), *On Israel's Origins*, The American Journal of Theology, Jan., Vol 22, No. 1, pp. 24-53.

Macquire, K., (2022), *The History of Astronomy in the Ancient World*, World History Encyclopedia, 17 May, The History of Astronomy in the Ancient World - World History Encyclopedia retrieved on 26 May 2022.

Mac Sweeney, N., (2023), *Why the Idea of Western Civilization is More Myth Than History*, Literary Hub, May 23, https://lithub.com/why-the-idea-of-western-civilization-is-more-myth-than-history/ retrieved on 24 May 2023.

Maeda, O., Lucas, L., Silva, F., Tanno, K., Fuller, D.Q., (2016), *Narrowing the harvest: Increasing sickle investment and the rise of domesticated cereal agriculture in the Fertile Crescent*, Quaternary Science Reviews, Volume 145, pp. 226-237.

Maiocchi, M., (2019), *Writing in Early Mesopotamia: The Historical Interplay of Technology, Cognition, and Environment*, in Love, A.C., Wimsatt, W.C., (eds), (2019), *Beyond the Meme: Development and Structure in Cultural Evolution*, University of Minnesota Press, USA, pp. 395-424.

Makarewicz, C.A., (2016), *Caprine Husbandry and Initial Pig Management East of the Jordan Valley: Animal Exploitation at Neolithic Wadi Shu'eib, Jordan*, Paleorient, Vol. 42, No. 1, pp. 151-168.

Malandra, W. (1983). *An Introduction to Ancient Iranian Religion: Readings from the Avesta and Achaemenid Inscriptions,* University of Minnesota Press.

Manco, J., (2015), *Ancestral Journeys: The Peopling of Europe from the First Venturers to the Vikings*, Thames and Hudson, London.

Manning, J.G., Ludlow, F., Stine, A.R. et al., (2017), *Volcanic suppression of Nile summer flooding triggers revolt and constrains interstate conflict in ancient Egypt.* Nature Communications, 8, 900. https://doi.org/10.1038/s41467-017-00957-y.

Mansfield, D.F., Wildberger, N.J., (2017), *Plimpton 322 is Babylonian exact sexagesimal trigonometry*, Historia Mathematica, Vol. 44, Issue 4, pp. 395-419.

Mark, J. J., (2009A), *Ancient Egypt,* World History Encyclopedia, 2 September, retrieved from https://member.worldhistory.org/egypt/ on 24 April 2023.

Mark, J. J., (2009B), *Pyramid.* Ancient History Encyclopedia, 2 September, retrieved from https://www.ancient.eu/pyramid/ on 17 February 2021.

Mark, J. J., (2011A), *Akkad.* World History Encyclopedia, 28 April, retrieved from https://member.worldhistory.org/akkad/ on 8 March 2023.

Mark, J.J., (2011B), *Amorite.* Ancient History Encyclopedia, 28 April, retrieved from https://www.ancient.eu/amorite/ on 10 August 2020.

Mark, J.J., (2014), *Mesopotamian Naru Literature*, World History Encyclopedia, 15 August, https://member.worldhistory.org/Mesopotamian_Naru_Literature/ retrieved on 11 October 2022.

Mark, J.J., (2016), *The Marduk Prophecy*, Ancient History Encyclopedia. 14 December, retrieved from https://ancient.eu/article/990/the-marduk-prophecy/ on 10 August 2020.

Mark, J.J., (2018A), *Yahweh*, Ancient History Encyclopedia. Retrieved from https://www.ancient.eu/Yahweh/ accessed on 16 July 2020.

Mark, J.J., (2018B), *Canaan*, Ancient History Encyclopedia. Retrieved from https://www.ancient.eu/Canaan/ accessed on 5 March 2021.

Mark, J.J., (2018C), *Enuma Elish—The Babylonian Epic of Creation—Full Text*, World History Encyclopedia, 4 May, https://worldhistory.org/article/225/enuma-elish---the-babylonian-epic-of-creation---fu/ retrieved on 8 June 2022.

Mark, J.J., (2019), *Ancient Persian Religion*, 11 December, https://member.worldhistory.org/Ancient_Persian_Religion/ retrieved on 20 March 2023.

Mark, J.J., (2020A), *The Dates of the Buddha*, Ancient History Encyclopedia, 20 September, retrieved from https://member.worldhistory.org/article/493/the-dates-of-the-buddha/ on 21 September 2021.

Mark, J.J., (2020B), *Pre-Socratic Philosophers*. World History Encyclopedia. Retrieved from https://www.ancient.eu/Pre-Socratic_Philosophers/ on 21 October 2020

Mark, J.J., (2020C), *Indus Valley Civilisation*. World History Encyclopedia. Retrieved from https://member.worldhistory.org/Indus_Valley_Civilization/ on 1 May 2023.

Mark, J.J., (2021A), *Code of Hammurabi*, Ancient History Encyclopedia. Retrieved from https://www.ancient.eu/Code_of_Hammurabi/ on 30 June 2021.

Mark, J.J., (2021B), *Tara*, Ancient History Encyclopedia. Retrieved from https://member.worldhistory.org/Tara_(Goddess) on 11 August 2021.

Mark, J.J., (2022A), *Greek Astronomy*, Ancient History Encyclopedia. Retrieved from https://member.worldhistory.org/Greek_Astronomy on 18 February 2022.

Mark, J.J., (2022B), *Ten Great Mesopotamian Women*, World History Encyclopedia, 12 October, Ten Great Ancient Mesopotamian Women—World History Encyclopedia retrieved on 2 November 2022.

Mark, J.J., (2022C), *Trade in Ancient Mesopotamia*, World History Encyclopedia, 22 November, Trade in Ancient Mesopotamia—World History Encyclopedia retrieved on 23 November 2022.

Mark, J.J., (2022D), *Inanna and Su-kale-tuda*, World History Encyclopedia, 9 December, Inanna and Su-kale-tuda—World History Encyclopedia retrieved on 14 December 2022.

Mark, J.J., (2022E) Babylon, World History Encyclopedia, 14 October, https://member.worldhistory.org/babylon/ retrieved on 15 March 2023.

Mark, J.J., (2023A), *Medicine in Ancient Mesopotamia*, World History Encyclopedia, 25 January, https://member.worldhistory.org/article/687/medicine-in-ancient-mesopotamia/ retrieved on 2 February 2023.

Mark, J.J., (2023B), *Kesh Temple Hymn*, World History Encyclopedia, 13 March, Kesh Temple Hymn—World History Encyclopedia retrieved on 15 March 2023.

Mark, J.J., (2023C), *Fashion & Dress in Ancient Mesopotamia*, World History Encyclopedia, 16 March, Fashion & Dress in Ancient Mesopotamia—World History Encyclopedia retrieved on 22 March 2023.

Mark, J.J., (2023D), *Schooldays: Sumerian Satire & the Scribal Life*, Schooldays: Sumerian Satire & the Scribal Life—World History Encyclopedia, 13 January, retrieved on 20 April 2023.

Mark, J.J., (2023E), *The Shabti: The Workforce in the Afterlife*, World History Insider, June, pp. 18-23.

Martinon-Torres, M. et al., (2021), *Earliest known human burial in Africa*, Nature, Vol. 593, 6 May, pp. 95-100.

Masalha, N., (2018), *Palestine: A Four Thousand Year History*, Zed Books Ltd, London.

Massa, M. Palmisano, A., (2017), *Change and continuity in the long-distance exchange networks between western/central Anatolia, northern Levant and northern Mesopotamia*, Journal of Anthropological Archaeology, 49, December, pp. 65-87.

Masson, V.M., (1996), *The Decline of the Bronze Age Civilization and Movements of the Tribes*, UNESCO Silk Roads Program, pp. 326-345; https://en.unesco.org/silkroad/knowledge-bank/decline-bronze-age-civilization-and-movements-tribes, retrieved on 7 April 2021.

Mathews, V.H., (1981), *Pastoralists and Patriarchs*, The Biblical Archaeologist, Autumn, Vol. 44, No. 4, pp. 215-218.

Matyszak, P., (2020), *Forgotten Peoples of the Ancient World*, Thames and Hudson, USA.

Maynes, M.J., Waltner, A., (2012*), Temporalities and Periodization in Deep History: Technology, Gender, and Benchmarks of 'Human Development'*, Social Science History, Spring, Vol. 36, No. 1, pp. 59-83.

Mazar, A., (2007), *The Patriarchs, Exodus, and Conquest Narratives in Light of Archaeology*, in Finkelstein, I.; Mazar, A., Schmidt, B. (ed), (2007), *The Quest for Historical Israel*, The Society of Biblical Literature, Atlanta, pp. 57-65.

McGovern, P. et al., (2017), *Early Neolithic wine of Georgia in the South Caucasus*, Proceedings of the National Academy of Sciences of the United States of America, Vol. 114, No. 48 (November), pp. E10309-E10318.

McGuckin, J. A., (2020A), *Cyril of Alexandria: The 'Christian Pharaoh': An Introductory Context*, ANTIQVVS, December, pp. 65-87.

McGuckin, J. A., (2020B), *Cyril of Alexandria*, ANTIQVVS, December, pp. 15-24.

McLuhan, M., (2010), *The Gutenberg Galaxy: The Making of Typographic Man*, University of Toronto Press, Toronto.

Megahed, M., Vymazalova, H., (2011), *Ancient Egyptian Royal Circumcision from the Pyramid Complex of Djedkare*, Anthropologie, Vol. 49, No. 2, pp. 155-164.

Memmott, P., (2007), *Gunyah, Goondie + Wurley: The Aboriginal Architecture of Australia*, First Edition, University of Queensland Press, St Lucia, Queensland, Australia.

Memmott, P., (2022), *Gunyah, Goondie + Wurley: The Aboriginal Architecture of Australia*, Second Edition, Thames and Hudson, Port Melbourne Victoria, Australia.

Mercader, J., *Mozambican grass sed consumption during the Middle Stone Age*, Science, 326 (5960), pp. 1680-1683.

Michel, C., (2008), *The Old Assyrian Trade in the light of Recent Kultepe Archives*, Journal of the Canadian Society for Mesopotamian Studies, pp. 71-82.

Mikkonen, K., (2006), *Can Fiction Become Fact? The Fiction-to-Fact Transition in recent theories of Fiction*, Style, Vol. 40, No. 4, General Issue (Winter), pp. 291-312.

Miles, R., (2011), *Ancient Worlds: The Search for the Origins of Western Civilization*, Penguin Books, London.

Millard, A., (1994), *The Eponyms of the Assyrian Empire 910-612 BCE*, State Archives of Assyria Studies, The Neo-Assyrian Text Corpus Project.

Miller II, R.D., (2011), *Shamanism in Early Israel*, Wiener Zeitschrift fur die Kunde des Morgenlandes, published by the Department of Oriental Studies, University of Vienna, Vol. 101, pp. 309-341.

Miyagawa, S., Lesure, C., Nobrega, V.A., (2018), *Cross-Modality Information Transfer: A Hypothesis about Relationship among Prehistoric Cave Paintings, Symbolic Thinking, and the Emergence of Language*, Frontiers in Psychology, Vol. 9, 20 February, https://www.frontiersin.org/articles/10.3389/fpsyg.2018.00115/full retrieved on 16 December 2021.

Moore, M., (1982), *On the Significance of Mountains, Towers and Other High Places*, Leonardo, Vol. 15, No. 1, pp. 45-48.

Morris, E.F., (2005), *The Architecture of Imperialism: Military Bases and the Evolution of Foreign Policy in Egypt's New Kingdom*, Brill Leiden, Boston.

Moye, R.H., (1990), *In the Beginning: Myth and History in Genesis and Exodus*, Journal of Biblical Studies, Winter, Vol. 109, No. 4, pp. 577-598.

Muller, G., (2019), *The Ancient Black Hebrews: Abraham and His Family*, Pomegranate Publishing, London.

Mumford, G.D., (2014), *Chapter 5: Egypt and the Levant*, in M. Steiner & A. E. Killebrew (eds.), *The Oxford Handbook of the Archaeology of the Levant c. 8000-332 BCE*, Oxford University Press, Oxford UK, pp. 69-89.

Munnich, M. and רינומ יאיסמ, (2005), *The Cult of Bronze Serpents in Ancient Canaan and Israel*, Iggud: Selected Essays in Jewish Studies, Vol 1: The Bible and Its World, Rabbinic Literature and Jewish Law, and Jewish Thought, Published by the World Union of Jewish Studies, pp. 39-56.

Munoz, O. et al., (2020), *Marking the sacral landscape of a north Arabian oasis: a sixth-millennium BC monumental stone platform and surrounding burials*, Antiquity Journal, Volume 94, Issue 375, June, pp. 601-621.

Murdock, D.M., (2014), *Did Moses Exist: The Myth of the Israelitete Lawgiver*, Stellar House Publishing, Seattle, Washington.

Muroi, K., (2014), *The Origin of the Mystical Number Seven in Mesopotamian Culture; Division by Seven in the Sexagesimal Number System*, https://arxiv.org/ftp/arxiv/papers/1407/1407.6246.pdf accessed on 17 July 2020.

Na'aman, N., (2011), *The Exodus Story: Between Historical Memory and Historiographical Composition*, Journal of Ancient Near Eastern Religions, 11.1, pp. 39-69.

Narasimhan V.M. et al, (2019), *The formation of human populations in South and Central Asia*, Science Vol.365, Issue 6457, September.

National Library of Australia, (2013), *Mapping Our World: Terra Incognita to Australia*, National Library of Australia, Canberra.

Nickerson, R., (1998), *Confirmation Bias: A Ubiquitous Phenomenon in Many Guises*, Review of General Psychology, Vol. 2, No. 2, pp. 175-230.

Nicol, T., (1899), *Recent Archaeology and the Bible*, HARDPRESS Classic Series, Miami, Florida, 2007.

Niesiolowski-Spano, L., (2015), *Food or Drink? Pork or Wine? The Philistines and their 'Ethnic' Markers*, Scandinavian Journal of the Old Testament, Vol. 29, No. 1, pp. 110-116.

Nijssen, D., (2018), *Cyrus the Great*, https://www.worldhistory.org/Cyrus_the_Great/, 21 February, retrieved on 31 March 2023.

Nissen, H.J., (1985), *The Emergence of Writing in the Ancient Near East*, Interdisciplinary Science Reviews 10, No.4, pp. 349-361.

Nur, A., Cline, E.H., (2000), *Poseidon's Horses: Plate Tectonics and Earthquake Storms in the Late Bronze Age Aegean and Eastern Mediterranean*, Journal of Archaeological Science, 27, pp. 43-73.

Nuzzolo, M., Krejei, J., (2017), *Heliopolis and the Solar Cult in the Third Millenium BC*, Egypt and the Levant, Vol, 27, pp. 357-380.

O'Connell, J. F. et al., (2018), *When did the human species first reach Southeast Asia and Sahul* (Australia, Tasmania, New Guinea, Seram/Indonesia, and neighbouring islands)? PNAS Perspective, Vol. 115, No. 34, August 21, pp. 8482-8490.

O'Grady, C., (2015), *Neolithic culture may have kept most men from mating: Y chromosome diversity suggests male reproductive bottleneck 8,000 years ago*, https://arstechnica.com/science/2015/03/neolithic-culture-may-have-kept-most-men-from-mating/ retrieved on 12 August 2022.

Olalde I. et al., (2019), *The genomic history of the Iberian Peninsula over the past 8000 years*, Science, Vol. 363, Issue 6432, 15 March, pp. 1230-1234.

Ono, M., (1996), *Collective effervescence and symbolism*, Durkheimian Studies / Etudes Durkheimiennes, New Series, Vol. 2, pp. 79-98.

Otto, R., Almond, P.C., (1984), *Buddhism and Christianity: Compared and Contrasted*, Buddhist-Christian Studies, Vol. 84, pp. 87-101.

Ozdogan, M., (2014), *Anatolia: From the Pre-Pottery Neolithic to the End of the Early Bronze Age (10,500-2000 BCE),* in Renfree, C., Bahn, P., (eds), *The Cambridge World History*, Cambridge Histories Online, pp. 1508-1544 retrieved on 28 November 2022.

Panitz-Cohen, N., (2013) *The Southern Levant (CISJORDAN) during the Late Bronze Age*, in Killebrew, A.E. and Steiner, M., (eds), The Oxford Handbook of Archaeology of the Levant (c8000—332 BCE), November, pp. 541-560, ISBN, 9780199212972, Published online: March 2014, DOI, 10.1093/oxfordhb/9780199212972.001.0001.

Parker, S.B., (2000), *Ugaritic Literature and the Bible*, Near Eastern Archaeology, December, Vol. 63, No. 4, pp. 228-231.

Pasztor, E., (2011), *Prehistoric astronomers? Ancient knowledge created by modern myth*, Journal of Cosmology, Vol. 14, https://thejournalofcosmology.com/Consciousness159.html retrieved on 19 January 2023.

Patai, R., (1998), *The Children of Noah: Jewish Seafaring in Ancient Times*, Princeton University Press, New Jersey.

Penglase, C., (1994), *Greek Myths and Mesopotamia: Parallels and Influence in the Homeric Hymn and Hesiod*, Routledge, Abingdon, Oxfordshire, England.

Person Jr. R.F., (1998), *The Ancient Israelite Scribe as a Performer*, Journal of Biblical Literature, Vol. 117, No. 4, Winter, pp. 601-609.

Pettitt, P.B., White, M.J., (2011), *Cave Men: Stone Tools, Victorian Science, and the 'Primitive Mind' of Deep Time*, Notes and Records of the Royal Society of London, Vol. 65, No. 1, 20 March, pp. 25-42.

Pioske, D. (2022), *An Archaeology of Ancient Thought: On the Hebrew Bible and the History of Ancient Israel*, Harvard Theological Review, Vol. 115, Issue 2, April, pp. 171-196.

Platt, D. E. et al., *Mapping Post-Glacial expansions: The Peopling of Southwest Asia*. Scientific Reports, 7, 40338; doi: 10.1038/srep40338 (2017).

Pollock, S. (1999), *Making a living: tributary economies of the fifth and fourth millennia*, in Pollock, S. (1999), *Ancient Mesopotamia: the eden that never was*, Cambridge University Press, UK.

Pongratz-Leisten, B. (ed), (2011), *Reconsidering the Concept of Revolutionary Monotheism*, Eisenbrauns, Winona Lake, Indiana.

Pongratz-Leisten, B., (2023), *Emotions and religion: Ritual Performance in Mesopotamia*, in Sonik, K. and Steinert, U. (eds), 2023, *The Routledge Handbook of Emotions in the Ancient Near East*, Routledge, New York, pp 425-439.

Porten, B., Zadok, R. Pearce, L., (2016), *Akkadian Names in Aramaic Documents from Ancient Egypt*, Bulletin of the American Schools of oriental Research, No. 375, May, pp. 1-12.

Potts, D.T., (2004), *The Archaeology of Elam: Formation and Transformation of an Ancient State*, Cambridge University Press, UK.

Pringle, H. (2010), *Ancient Sorcerer's 'Wake' Was First Feast for the Dead*, National Geographic Magazine, September 1, https://www.nationalgeographic.com/culture/article/100830-first-feast-science-proceedings-israel-shaman-sorcerer-tortoise retrieved on 15 April, 2021.

Pryke, L.M., (2017), *Ishtar*, Routledge, Taylor & Francis Group, London.

Puhvel, J., (1989), *Comparative Mythology*, The John Hopkins University Press, Baltimore and London.

Radau, H., (1902), *The Cosmology of the Sumerians*, The Monist, Vol. 13, No. 1, October, pp. 103-113.

Raglan, F.R.S., (1956), *The Hero; A Study in Tradition, Myth and Drama*, Unabridged Dover (2003) republication of the 1956 Vintage Books (New York).

Ramos, A., (2016), *Early Jericho*, World History Encyclopedia, 19 September, https://worldhistory.org/article/951/early-jericho/.

Rawlinson, H., (1862), *Assyrian History*, Athenaeum: Journal of Literature, Science, and the Arts, No. 1805, January to June, pp. 724-725, Hathi Trust Digital Library, retrieved on 22 November 2022.

Redford, D.B., (1980), *The Sun-Disc in Akhenaten's Program: Its Worship and Antecedents, II*, Journal of the American Research Center in Egypt, Vol. 17, pp. 21-38.

Redford, D.B., (1992), *Egypt, Canaan and Israel in Ancient Times*, Princeton University Press, Princeton, New Jersey.

Reich, D., (2019), *Who We are and How We Got Here*, Oxford University Press, Oxford, UK.

Rendsburg, G.A., (2003), *Semitic Languages (with Special Reference to the Levant)*, in Richard. S., *Near Eastern Archaeology: A Reader*, Penn State University Press, University Park, Pennsylvania, pp. 71-73.

Rettner, R., (2014), *Climate Change Could Alter the Human Male-Female Ratio*, LiveScience, 1 October, https://www.livescience.com/48070-male-fetus-climate-change.html retrieved on 12 August 2022.

Rindos, D. et al., (1980), *Symbiosis, Instability, and the Origins and Spread of Agriculture: A New Model*, Current Anthropology, Vol. 21, No. 6, December, pp. 751-772.

Roberts, J.R., (2020), *The Biblical Cosmos is Three-Tiered—No Question.* Academia Letters, Article 44. https://doi.org/10.20935/AL44 .

Rochberg, F., (1999), *Empiricism in Babylonian Omen Texts and the Classification of Mesopotamian Divination as Science*, Journal of the American Oriental Society, October-December, Vol. 119, No. 4, pp. 559-569.

Rollefson, G.O., Kohler-Rollefson, I., *PPNC Adaptations in the First Half of the 6ᵗʰ Millennium B.C.*, Paleorient, Vol. 19, No. 1, pp. 33-42.

Roothaan, A., (2015), *The 'Shamanic' Travels of Jesus and Muhammad: Cross-cultural and Transcultural Understandings of Religious Experience*, American Journal of Theology & Philosophy, Vol. 36, No. 2, May, pp. 140-153.

Roux, G., (1992), *Ancient Iraq*, 3ʳᵈ Edition, Penguin Books, London.

Rowan, Y.M., Ilan, D., (2012), *The Subterranean Landscape of the Southern Levant during the Chalcolithic Period,* in Moyes, H. (ed) Sacred Darkness: A Global Perspective on the Ritual Use of Caves, University of Colorado Press, Boulder, Colorado, pp. 87-107.

Rowland, I.D., (2008), *Giordano Bruno: Philosopher/Heretic*, University of Chicago Press, Chicago.

Rowley-Conway, P., (2014), *Foragers and farmers in Mesolithic/Neolithic Europe, 5500-3900 cal BC: beyond the anthropological comfort zone*, in Wild Things: recent advances in Palaeolithic and Mesolithic research, Oxford: Oxbow Books, pp. 185-201.

Roy, A., (2015), *The Virus of Faith*, Free Enquiry, secularhumanist.org, April/May, pp 59-62.

Rozwadowski, A., (2019), *Sacred Holes: Portals to the World of Spirits in Siberian Shamanism*, in Pasztor, E. (ed), (2019), *Shamanism and Nature Worship: Past and Present*, Baja: Türr István Museum, pp. 174-203.

Rubio, G., (1999), *On the Alleged 'Pre-Sumerian Substratum'*, Journal of Cuneiform Studies, Vol. 51, pp. 1-16.

Russell, N., During, B.S., (2006), *Worthy is the Lamb: a Double Burial at Neolithic Catalhoyuk (Türkiye)*, Paleorient, Vol 32/1, pp. 73-84.

Rutz, M.T., (2006), *Textual Transmission between Babylonia and Susa: A New Solar Omen Compendium*, Journal of Cuneiform Studies, Vol. 58, pp. 63-96.

Sandars, N.K., (1971), *Poems of Heaven and Hell from Ancient Mesopotamia*, Penguin Books, England.

Sapir-Hen, L., Bar-Oz, G., Gadot, Y., Finkelstein, I., (2013), *Pig Husbandry in Iron Age Israel and Judah: New Insights Regarding the Origin of the 'Taboo'*, Zeitschrift des Deutschen Palastina-Vereins (Journal of the German Palestinian Society), No.129 (1), pp. 1-20.

Sasson, J.M., (1966), *Circumcision in the Ancient Near East*, Journal of Biblical Literature, Vol. 85, No. 4, December, pp. 473-476.

Sauer, K. (2017), *From Counting to Writing: The Innovative Potential of Bookkeeping in Uruk Period Mesopotamia*, in Stockhammer P.W., Maran J. (eds) (2017), *Appropriating Innovations: Entangled Knowledge in Eurasia 5000—1500 BCE*, Oxbow Books, Oxford, pp. 12-28.

Schmidt, W. translated by H.J. Rose, (2014), *The Origin and Growth of Religion: Facts and Theories,* Wythe-North Publishing, USA.

Schmandt-Besserat, D., (1998), *A Stone Metaphor of Creation*, Near Eastern Archaeology, June, Vol. 61, No. 2, pp. 109-117.

Schmid, K., Schroter, J., (2021), *The Making of the Bible: From the First Fragments to Sacred Scripture*, The Belknap Press of Harvard University Press, London, England.

Schneider, T., (2018), *A Double Abecedary? Halaham and Abgad on the TT99 Ostracon*, Bulletin of the American Schools of Oriental Research, No. 379, May, pp. 103-112.

Schneider, J. Rabbi, (2018), *Did Abram exist? Does it matter?* Jewish News, October. http://www.jewishaz.com/religiouslife/did-abram-exist-does-it-matter/article_ed3eb05c-d232-11e8-aebb-c32f329659db.html accessed on 27 July 2020.

Schniedewind, W.M., (2019), *The Finger of the Scribe: How Scribes Learned to Write the Bible*, Oxford University Press, New York.

Schomp, V., (2005), *Ancient India*, People of the Ancient World, Scholastic Inc, New York.

Schuler, D., (2007), *Greece and Mesopotamia: Origins of Greek Thought*, http://theglitteringeye.com/greece-and-mesopotamia-origins-of-greek-thought/, accessed on 5 August 2020.

Schwartz, H., (2007), *Tree of Souls: The Mythology of Judaism*, Oxford University Press, New York.

Scott, J.C., (2017), *Against the Grain: A Deep History of the Earliest States*, Yale University Press, New Haven and London.

Scott Smith, P., (2021), *Scythian Religion*, 3 December, https://worldhistory.org/Scythian_Religion/ retrieved on 20 July 2022.

Scutti, S., (2019), *Climate Change will affect gender ratio among newborns, scientists say*, CNNhealth, January, https://edition.cnn.com/2019/01/23/health/climate-change-infant-sex-ratio-intl/index.html retrieved on 12 August 2022.

Shane, O.C., Kucuk, M., (1998), *The World's First City*, Archaeology, Vol. 51, No. 2, March/April, pp. 43-47.

Shea, J.T., (1998), *Neanderthal and Early Modern Human Behavioral Variability: A Regional Scale Approach to Lithic Evidence for Hunting in the Levantine Mousterian*, Current Anthropology, Vol. 39, No. S1, June, pp. S45-S78.

Sheldrake, R., (2020), *The Science Delusion*, Coronet, Hodder and Stoughton, London.

Sherry, P., (2003), *The Religious Roots of Natural Theology*, New Blackfriars, June, Vol. 84, No. 988, pp. 301-307.

Shilov, Y., (2015), *Ancient History of Aratta-Ukraine 20,000 BCE—1,000 BCE*, Trishula Translations, 29 January.

Shimelmitz, R., Kuhn, S.L., Weinstein-Evron, M., (2020), *The evolution of raw material procurement strategies: A view from the deep sequence of Tabun Cave, Israel*, Journal of Human Evolution, Vol. 143, June, 102787.

Silberman, N. A., (1992), *Who were the Israelites ?*, Archaeology, March/April, Vol 45, No. 2, pp. 22-30.

Skipwith, G.H., (1904), *The Origin of the Religion of Israel—The Cretan Zeus; Babel and Bible*, The Jewish Quarterly Review, Vol 17, No.1, Oct., pp. 57-64.

Skutsch, C., (2013), *Encyclopedia of the World's Minorities*. Routledge. p. 149. ISBN 978-1-135-19388-1.

Shaw, G.J., (2014), *The Egyptian Myths: A Guide to the Ancient Gods and Legends*, Thames and Hudson, London.

Shreeve, J., (2005), *This Face Changes the Human Story. But How?* National Geographic, 10 September, https://www.nationalgeographic.com/history/article/150910-human-evolution-change retrieved on 6 May 2021.

Smith, D.E., (2015), *The Divining Snake: Reading Genesis 3 in the Context of Mesopotamian Ophiomancy*, Journal of Biblical Literature, Vol. 134, No. 1, pp. 31-49.

Smith, F.M., (2013), *Review Essays: The Palaeolithic Turn: Michael Witzel's Theory of Laurasian Mythology*, Religious Studies Review, Vol. 39, No. 3, September, pp. 133-142.

Smith, G., (1875), *The Assyrian Eponym Canon*, Samuel Bagster and Sons, London.

Smith, M.S., (2002), *The Early History of God: Yahweh and the Other Deities in Ancient Israel (2nd Edition)*, William B. Eerdmans Publishing Company, Cambridge, UK.

Smith, M.S., (2010), *God in Translation: Cross0cultural Recognition of Divinity in Ancient Israel*, William B. Eerdmans Publishing Company, Grand Rapids, Michigan.

Smith, M.S., (2011), *God in Translation: Deities in Cross-Cultural Discourse in the Biblical World*, in Pongratz-Leisten, B. (ed), (2011), *Reconsidering the Concept of Revolutionary Monotheism*, Eisenbrauns, Winona Lake, Indiana, pp. 241-270.

Smith, R., (2022), *Britain's Stone Age Building Boom, Stonehenge was just one triumph in a surprising prehistoric building boom (nationalgeographic.com),* retrieved on 20 July 2022.

Snir A, Nadel D, Groman-Yaroslavski I, Melamed Y, Sternberg M, Bar-Yosef O, et al. (2015) *The Origin of Cultivation and Proto-Weeds, Long Before Neolithic Farming.* PLoS ONE 10(7): e0131422. doi:10.1371/journal.pone.0131422.

Soffer, O., Adovasio, J. M. Adovasio, Hyland , D. C., (2000), *The 'Venus' Figurines: Textiles, Basketry, Gender, and Status in the Upper Palaeolithic*, Current Anthropology Vol. 41, No. 4, August–October, pp. 511-537.

Sohn, S., Wolpoff, M.H., (1993), *Zuttiyeh Face: A View from the East*, American Journal of Physical Anthropology, 91, pp. 325-347.

Sparavigna, A. C., (2016). *The Temple Complex of Ggantija and the Major Lunar Standstill as Given by the Photographer's Ephemeris.* SSRN Electronic Journal, 10.2139/ssrn.2828614.

Sparavigna, A. C., Dastru, L., (2018), *Some Churches Dedicated to the Holy Wisdom and their Sunrise Orientation*, HAL open science, hal-01761340 retrieved on 8 December 2021.

Sparks, K.L., (2007), *Religion, Identity and the Origins of Ancient Israel*, Religion Compass, 1/6, pp. 587-614.

Spiegel, F., (2007), *The 'tabernacula' of Gregory the Great and the conversion of Anglo-Saxon England*, Anglo-Saxon England, Vol. 36, pp. 1-13.

Spielmann, K.A., Eder, J.F., (1994), *Hunters and Farmers: Then and Now*, Annual Review of Anthropology, Vol. 23, pp. 303-323.

Stanford Encyclopedia of Philosophy, (2017), *Religion and Science*, January 2017, https://plato.stanford.edu/entries/religion-science/#BrieHistFielScieReli retrieved on 13 June 2022.

State Library of New South Wales, (2006), *First Sight: The Dutch Mapping of Australia 1606-1697*, State Library of New South Wales, 6 March 2006.

Staubli, T., (2016), *Cultural and Religious Impacts of Long-Term Cross-Cultural Migration Between Egypt and the Levant*, Journal of Ancient Egyptian Interconnections, Vol. 12, December, pp. 50-88.

Stausberg, M., (2012), *Hinduism and Zoroastrianism*, Brill's encyclopedia of Hinduism, Volume 4, pp. 605-615.

Steele, F.R., (1948), *The Code of Lipit-Ishtar*, American Journal of Archaeology, July-September, Vol. 52, No. 3, pp. 425-450.

Stewart, J.R., Stringer, C.B. (2012), *Human Evolution Out of Africa: The Role of Refugia and Climate Change*, Science, Vol. 335, Issue 6074, 16 March, pp. 1317-1321.

Stieglitz, R.R., (1990), *The Geopolitics of the Phoenician Littoral in the Early Iron Age*, Bulletin of the American Schools of Oriental Research, No. 279, August, pp. 9-12.

Stockhammer P.W., Maran J. (eds) (2017), *Appropriating Innovations: Entangled Knowledge in Eurasia 5000—1500 BCE*, Oxbow Books, Oxford.

Susman, R. L., (1991), *Who Made the Oldowan Tools? Fossil Evidence for Tool Behavior in Plio-Pleistocene Hominids*, Journal of Anthropological Research, Vol. 47, No. 2, Summer, pp. 129-151.

Svizzero, S., (2014), *Pre-Neolithic Economy*, History of Economic Ideas, Vol. 22, No. 2, pp. 25-40.

Sweatman, M.B., Tsikritsis, D., (2017), *Comment on 'More Than a Vulture: A Response to Sweatman and Tsikritsis*, Mediterranean Archaeology and Archaeometry, Vol 17, No. 2, pp. 63-70.

Swinburne, R., (2007) *The Revival of Natural Theology*, Archivio di Filosofia, Vol. 75, No. 1/ 2, pp. 303-322.

Sykes, B., (2002), *The Seven Daughters of Eve*, Norton and Company, New York.

Tantuğ A.C., Adalı E. (2018) *Machine Translation Between Turkic Languages*. In: Oflazer K., Saraçlar M. (eds) *Turkish Natural Language Processing. Theory and Applications of Natural Language Processing*. Springer, Cham. https://doi.org/10.1007/978-3-319-90165-7_11.

Tate, M.E., (1992), *Satan in the Old Testament,* Review & Expositor, Vol 89, No. 4, December, pp. 461-474.

Tedlock, B., (2005), *The Woman in the Shaman's Body: Reclaiming the Feminine in Religion and Medicine*, Bantam Books, New York.

Tejero, J. et al., (2021), *Personal ornaments from Hayonim and Manot caves (Israel) hint at symbolic ties between the Levantine and the European Aurignacian*, Journal of Human Evolution, Volume 160, November, 102870.

The Metropolitan Museum of Art, (2000), *Egypt, 8000–2000 B.C.*, In Heilbrunn Timeline of Art History, New York, October, http://www.metmuseum.org/toah/ht/?period=02&region=afe retrieved on 23 April 2023.

Theodorides, K., (2022), *Revisiting the tradition of Palamedes as inventor of the alphabet*, Academia Letters, Article 5305, May, retrieved on 18 April 2023.

Thompson, T.L., (1999), *The Mythic Past: Biblical Archaeology and the Myth of Israel*, Basic Books, New York.

Thompson, T., (2013), *Review of The Origins of the World's Mythologies*, Journal of Folklore Research, https://jfr.sitehost.iu.edu/review.php?id=1613 retrieved on 27 November 2021.

Throop, C.J., Laughlin, C.D., (2002), *Ritual, Collective Effervescence and Categories: Toward a Neo-Durkheimian Model of the Nature of Human Consciousness, Feelings and Understanding*, Journal of Ritual Studies, Vol. 16, No. 1, pp. 40-63.

Tobolczyk, M., (2016), *The World's Oldest Temples in Göbekli Tepe and Nevali Cori, Türkiye in the Light of Studies in Ontogenesis of Architecture*, Procedia Engineering, 161, pp. 1398-1404.

Togaev, J.E., Usarov, U.A. (2017), *Characteristics of Architecture of Ancient Bactria (in example Sapallitepa and Jarkutan)*, International Scientific Journal Theoretical & Applied Science, 10, Vol 54, pp. 28-31.

Togaev, J., (2020), *Historical Reconstruction of Social Relations of the Bronze and Early Iron Age*, International Journal of Scientific & Technology Research, Vol. 9, Issue 2, February, pp. 1579-1584.

Tomasello M, Melis AP, Tennie C, Wyman E, Herrmann E., (2012), *Two key steps in the evolution of cooperation: The interdependence hypothesis,* Current Anthropology, 53(6), pp. 673–692.

Tomasello, M., (2014) *The ultra-social animal*, European Journal of Social Psychology, April, 44(3), pp. 187–194.

Tonelli, G., (2021) translated by Erica Segre and Simon Carnell, *Genesis: The Story of How Everything Began*, Profile Books, London.

Torrance, T.F., (1970), *The Problem of Natural Theology in the Thought of Karl Barth*, Religious Studies, June, Vol. 6, No. 2, pp. 121-135.

Torres, H.R., Groman-Yaroslavski, I., Weinstein-Evron, M., Yeshurun, R., (2020), *A micro-wear analysis of Natufian gazelle phalanx beads from el-Wad Terrace, Mount Carmel, Israel*, Journal of Archaeological Science: Reports, Vol. 31, 30 June.

Trickett, P., (2007), *Beyond Capricorn: How Portuguese Adventurers Secretly Discovered and Mapped Australia 250 Years Before Captain Cook*, East Street Publications, Illustrated edition, South Australia.

Trinkaus, E., (1995), *Near Eastern Late Archaic Humans*, Paléorient, Vol. 21, No. 2, L'Anthropologie du Moyen-Orient. Apports Récents, pp. 9-24.

Tubb, J.N., (1998), *People of the Past; Canaanites*, University of Oklahoma Press, London.

Unterlander, M., Palstra, F. et al., (2017), *Ancestry and demography and descendants of Iron Age nomads of the Eurasian Steppe* Nature Communications, Vol 8, 3 March, pp. 1-10.

Ustinova, Y. (2005), *6 Snake-Limbed and Tendril-Limbed Goddesses in the Art and Mythology of the Mediterranean and Black Sea*, in Braund, D., (ed), *Scythians and Greeks*.

Cultural Interactions in Scythia, Athens and the Early Roman Empire, Exeter University Press, Exeter, pp. 64-78.

Vahdati, A.A. et al., (2019), *Preliminary report on the first season of excavations at Tepe Chalow,* in Meyer, Jan-Waalke (ed.) et al. The Iranian Plateau during the Bronze Age: Development of urbanisation, production and trade. New edition [online]. Lyon: MOM Éditions,pp. 179-200; https://books.openedition.org/momeditions/8086?lang=en retrieved on 7 April 2021.

Van Der Crabben, J., (2020), *Map of Mesopotamia and the Ancient Near East, c. 1300 BCE,* World History Encyclopedia, 1 February, retrieved on 24 September 2021 from https://member.worldhistory.org/image/11823/map-of-mesopotamia-and-the-ancient-near-east-c-130/.

Van Der Crabben, J., (2021), *Agriculture in the Fertile Crescent & Mesopotamia,* World History Encyclopedia, 4 June. Retrieved on 9 June 2021 from https://www.worldhistory.org/article/9/agriculture-in-theferetile-crescent--mesopotamia.

Van De Mieroop, M., (2007), *A History of the Ancient Near East ca 3000-323BC,* Blackwell Publishing, Oxford, UK.

Van De Mieroop, M., (2017), *Philosophy before the Greeks: The Pursuit of Truth in Ancient Babylonia,* Princeton University Press, New Jersey.

Van Der Toorn, K., (2007), *Scribal Vulture and the Making of the Hebrew Bible,* Harvard University Press, Cambridge, Massachusetts.

Van Oudheusden, L., (2019), *Death in Sumerian Literary Texts: Establishing the existence of a Literary Tradition on How to Describe Death in the Ur III and Old Babylonian Periods,* Research Masters Thesis, Classics and Ancient Civilisations—Assyriology, Leiden University, Netherlands, Faculty of Humanities, 1 July.

Ventegodt S, Kordova P., (2017), *The Thousand-Year-Old Shamanistic Tradition of Healing Touch in the Northeast Australian Rain Forrest.* International Journal of Complementary and Alternative Medicine 8(3): 00259. DOI: 10.15406/ijcam.2017.08.00259.

Verhoeven, M., (2011), *The Birth of a Concept and the Origins of the Neolithic: A History of Prehistoric Farmers in the Near East,* Paleorient, Vol. 37, No. 1, pp. 75-87.

Vermes, G., (1965), *The Dead Sea Scrolls in English,* Penguin, England.

Violatti, C., (2013), *Hipparchus of Nicea,* Ancient History Encyclopedia, 2 April, accessed 10 August 2020.

Wade, N., (2007), *Before the Dawn: Recovering the Lost History of Our Ancestors,* Penguin Books, New York.

Wade, N., (2010), *The Faith Instinct: How Religion Evolved and Why it Endures,* Penguin Books, New York.

Wade, N., (2012), *Family Tree of Languages Has Roots in Anatolia, Biologists Say*, The New York Times, 23 August.

Waite, J., (2010), *The Census of Israelite Men after their Exodus from Egypt*, Vetus Testamentum, Vol. 60, Fasc. 3, pp. 487-492.

Walker, B., (2010), *Man Made God*, Stellar House Publishing, Seattle WA.

Wallis Budge, E.A., (1967), *The Egyptian Book of the Dead: (The Papyrus of Ani) Egyptian Text Transliteration and Translation*, Dover Publications Inc, New York.

Wallis Budge, E.A., (1971), *Egyptian Magic*, Dover Publications Inc, New York.

Wallis Budge, E.A., (1995), *Egyptian Ideas of the Afterlife*, Dover Publications Inc, New York.

Wallis Budge, E.A., (2010), *The Book of the Dead*, Benediction Classics, USA.

Wallis Budge, E.A., (2016), *The Egyptian Heaven and Hell*, Lushena Books Inc, Bensenville, Illinois.

Wang, C-C, Reinhold, S., Haak, W., (2019), *Ancient human genome-wide data from a 3000-year interval in the Caucuses corresponds with eco-geographic regions*, Nature Communications, 10, p. 590.

Warren, M., (2018), *Mum's a Neanderthal, Dad's a Denisovan: First discovery of an ancient-human hybrid: Genetic analysis uncovers a direct descendant of two different groups of early humans*, Nature 560, pp. 417-418.

Watson, J., Crick, F., (1953) *Molecular Structure of Nucleic Acids: A Structure for Deoxyribose Nucleic Acid.* Nature Vol.171, pp. 737–738.

Watson, J.D., with Andrew Berry, (2006), *DNA: The Secret of Life*, Alfred A. Knopf, New York.

Watts, F., (2020), *The evolution of religious cognition*, Archive for the Psychology of Religion, Vol. 42 (1), pp. 89-100.

Weinberger, A.B., Gallagher, N.M., Warren, Z.J. et al., (2020), *Implicit pattern learning predicts individual differences in belief in God in the United States and Afghanistan.* Nature Communications, 11, No. 4503, 9 September, https://doi.org/10.1038/s41467-020-18362-3.

Wiener, M.H., (2007), *Times Change: The Current State of the Debate in Old World Chronology,* in Bietak, M., Czerny, E. (eds), (2007), *The Synchronisation of Civilisations in the Eastern Mediterranean in the Second Millennium B.C. III*, Proceedings of the SCIEM 2000—2nd EuroConference, Vienna, 28thof May—1st of June 2003, Österreichische Akademie der Wissenschaften, Wien.

Weninger, S.(ed), (2011), *The Semitic Languages: An International Handbook*, in collaboration with Khan, G., Streck, M.P., Watson C.E., Handbooks of Linguistics and Communication Science HSK36, Walter de Gruyter GmbH & Co. KG, Berlin/Boston.

Wesler, K.W., (2014), *An Archaeology of Religion*, University Press of America, Lanham, USA.

Westenholz, J.G., (1983), *Heroes of Akkad*, Journal of the American Oriental Society, Vol. 103, No.1, Jan-Mar, pp. 327-336.

White, L., (1967), *The Historical Roots of Our Ecological Crisis*, Science, New Series, Vol. 155, No. 3767 (Mar. 10) pp. 1203-1207.

White, L., (1978), *Medieval Religion and Technology: Collected Essays*, University of California Press, Berkeley.

White, M., (2007), *Galileo, Antichrist: A Biography*, Weidenfeld & Nicolson, London.

Wilkinson, P., (2009), *Myths and Legends: An Illustrated Guide to Their Origins and Meanings*, Dorling Kindersley Ltd, London.

Williams Jackson, A.V., (1896), *On the Date of Zoroaster*, Journal of the American Oriental Society, Vol. 17, pp. 1-22.

Williams, Jennifer, (2014), *From Aset to Jesus: The History of the Goddess Aset in Ancient Kemet from Circa 3000 BCE Until the Removal of Feminine Salvation Circa 400 CE*, Journal of Black Studies, March, Vol. 45, No. 2, pp. 102-124.

Williams, Raymond, (1961), *The Long Revolution*, Penguin Books, England.

Witzel, E.J.M., (2012), *The Origins of the World's Mythologies*, Oxford University Press, New York.

Zangani,F., (2018), *Foreign-Indigenous Interactions in the Late Bronze Age Levant: Tuthmosid Imperialism and the Origin of the Amarna Diplomatic System*, in Mynarova, J.; Kilani, M.; Alivernini (eds) Stranger in the House—the Crossroads lll, Proceedings of an International Conference on Foreigners in Ancient Egyptian and near Eastern Societies of the Bronze Age, Prague, September 10-13, pp. 405-424.

Zeder, M.A., (2011), *The origins of Agriculture in the Near East*, Current Anthropology, Vol. 52, No. S4, October, pp. S221-S235.

Zevit, Z., (2001), *The Religions of Ancient Israel: A Synthesis of Parallactic Approaches,* Continuum, London.

Zonshine, I., (2021), *Humans, Neanderthals coexisted in the Negev desert 50,000 years ago*, Jerusalem Post, June 15.

Acknowledgements

Personal Acknowledgements

I will be forever grateful to Sue, my family, my colleagues, friends, and my legal advisers, Denise Maxwell at Hensen Maxwell Solicitors, Gary Rogers at Blueprint Law, and publisher Clark & Mackay for their patience and support. I am not sure that they were convinced that this book would ever eventuate! But here it is! My heartfelt thanks go out to everyone who has watched from the sidelines, supported me, edited and advised on specific text and waited patiently for it to arrive. I dedicate the book to the growth of knowledge and to all those who gave me the strength and encouragement to carry on. Thank you.

Acknowledgement of sources

There are more than eight hundred and fifty references cited in this work. There are around five hundred and sixty Bibliographical footnotes, one thousand three hundred footnotes, including more than three hundred and forty cited separately to those referenced in the Bibliography. I could not have researched this topic so thoroughly without the availability of many trustworthy and comprehensive resources. This has included information from sources such as National Geographic, World History Encyclopedia, Encyclopedia Britannica, the JSTOR digital library, Academia.edu, ScienceDirect, multiple University-based publishing houses, the ResearchGate networking site, multiple online journals, and scientific papers, online postgraduate Masters and PhD documents, online and local specialist bookstores. I am grateful for these sources and the excellent research, scientific analysis, and documentation available therein.

www.ingramcontent.com/pod-product-compliance
Lightning Source LLC
Chambersburg PA
CBHW080414030426
42335CB00020B/2447